LAURA BATTIFERRA AND HER LITERARY CIRCLE

THE
OTHER VOICE
IN
EARLY MODERN
EUROPE

A Series Edited by Margaret L. King and Albert Rabil Jr.

RECENT BOOKS IN THE SERIES

MARIA GAETANA AGNESI ET ALIA
The Contest for Knowledge: Debates over Women's Learning in Eighteenth-Century Italy
Edited and Translated by Rebecca Messbarger and Paula Findlen
Introduction by Rebecca Messbarger

FRANCISCA DE LOS APÓSTOLES
The Inquisition of Francisca: A Sixteenth-Century Visionary on Trial
Edited and Translated by Gillian T. W. Ahlgren

GIULIA BIGOLINA
Urania: A Romance
Edited and Translated by Valeria Finucci

GABRIELLE DE COIGNARD
Spiritual Sonnets: A Bilingual Edition
Translated and Edited by Melanie E. Gregg

VITTORIA COLONNA
Sonnets for Michelangelo: A Bilingual Edition
Edited and Translated by Abigail Brundin

MARIE DENTIÈRE
Epistle to Marguerite de Navarre and Preface to a Sermon by John Calvin
Edited and Translated by Mary B. McKinley

MADAME DE MAINTENON
Dialogues and Addresses
Edited and Translated by John J. Conley, S.J.

ISOTTA NOGAROLA
Complete Writings: Letterbook, Dialogue on Adam and Eve, Orations
Edited and Translated by Margaret L. King and Diana Robin

JOHANNA ELEONORA PETERSEN
The Life of Lady Johanna Eleonora Petersen, Written by Herself: Pietism and Women's Autobiography
Edited and Translated by Barbara Becker-Cantarino

MADELEINE DE SCUDÉRY
Selected Letters, Orations, and Rhetorical Dialogues
Edited and Translated by Jane Donawerth and Julie Strongson

ELISABETTA CAMINER TURRA
Selected Writings of an Eighteenth-Century Venetian Woman of Letters
Edited and Translated by Catherine M. Sama

MADAME DE VILLEDIEU (MARIE-CATHERINE DESJARDINS)
Memoirs of the Life of Henriette-Sylvie de Molière: A Novel
Edited and Translated by Donna Kuizenga

Laura Battiferra degli Ammannati

LAURA BATTIFERRA AND HER LITERARY CIRCLE: AN ANTHOLOGY

Edited and Translated by Victoria Kirkham

THE UNIVERSITY OF CHICAGO PRESS
Chicago & London

Laura Battiferra degli Ammannati, 1523–89

Victoria Kirkham is professor of Romance languages at the University of Pennsylvania. She is the author of three books, most recently of *Fabulous Vernacular: Boccaccio's Filocolo and the Art of Medieval Fiction,* winner of the Scaglione Prize for a manuscript in Italian studies of the Modern Language Association.

The University of Chicago Press, Chicago 60637
The University of Chicago Press, Ltd., London

Printed in the United States of America

15 14 13 12 11 10 09 08 07 06 1 2 3 4 5

ISBN: 0-226-03922-6 (cloth)
ISBN: 0-226-03923-4 (paper)

The University of Chicago Press gratefully acknowledges the generous support of James E. Rabil, in memory of Scottie W. Rabil, toward the publication of this book.

Library of Congress Cataloging-in-Publication Data

Battiferri degli Ammannati, Laura, 1523–1589.
[Selections. English]
Laura Battiferra and her literary circle : an anthology / Laura Battiferra degli Ammannati ; edited and translated by Victoria Kirkham.
p. cm. — (The other voice in early modern Europe)
Includes bibliographical references and index.
ISBN 0-226-03922-6 (cloth : alk. paper) — ISBN 0-226-03923-4 (pbk. : alk. paper)
1. Italian poetry—16th century—History and criticism. I. Kirkham, Victoria.
II. Title. III. Series
PQ4607 . B6A24 2006
851′ .5—dc22

2005024004

♾ The paper used in this publication meets the minimum requirements of the American National Standard for Information Sciences—Permanence of Paper for Printed Library Materials, ANSI Z39.48-1992.

CONTENTS

Appendixes

ILLUSTRATIONS

ACKNOWLEDGMENTS

The opportunity to explore aggressively archives and libraries in Italy for information about Laura Battiferra degli Ammannati was made possible by a fellowship from the National Endowment for the Humanities (1996–97), supplemented by sabbatical salary from the University of Pennsylvania. Both contributed to a concurrent semester of residence as a Visiting Professor at Villa I Tatti, the Harvard Center for Renaissance Studies in Florence. As director, Walter Kaiser gave vigorous and gracious academic hospitality. Fiorella Superbi of the I Tatti Fototeca, everyone on the library staff, and several longtime scholarly affiliates, among them Alan Grieco and Eve Borsook, were always helpful interlocutors. My research continued during the academic year 2000–2001, thanks to a Rockefeller Foundation Fellowship in Gender Studies in Medieval and Early Modern Europe at the Newberry Library in Chicago, again aided by a sabbatical from the University of Pennsylvania. I am grateful to the other fellows in my cohort and to all the staff there for providing a setting so ideally conducive to learning about Battiferra's intellectual environment from sixteenth-century Italian books, especially the director, James Grossman; his associate, Sara Austen; and Carla Zecher, Director of the Center for Renaissance Studies. To guide my many hours in the Rare Book Room, Paul Gehl shared collegial expertise on site as well as over pleasant scholarly lunch breaks in the Newberry neighborhood. Summer support, which paid for an important trip to Urbino, came from the Henry Salvatori Research Fund, administered through the Center for Italian Studies at the University of Pennsylvania. In the later stages of this book, much appreciated aid to encourage its completion came from my portion of a National Endowment for the Humanities Collaborative Research Grant, "A Tradition Discovered: Women Writers in Italy, France, and Germany, 1400–1750" (2002–2003). Finally, I have a happy debt, both symbolically and financially, to the Henry Salvatori Fund and the University of Pennsylvania Center for Italian Studies for providing the subvention requested by the University of Chicago Press, critical for publishing this book.

A project ongoing for fifteen years has allowed countless peaceful retreats into many library reading rooms. Some of my first and most satisfying expeditions were to Washington, D.C., where Georgianna Ziegler hosted me both in the Folger Shakespeare Library and in her home as houseguest. In Italy, many of her colleagues assisted me in travels from city to city—in Florence, at the Biblioteca Medicea Laurenziana, at the Biblioteca Riccardiana, and especially at the Biblioteca Nazionale; in Urbino, at the Biblioteca Universitaria; in Venice at the Marciana; in Foligno at the Biblioteca del Seminario Iacovilli; in Parma at the Biblioteca Palatina; in Padova at the Biblioteca del Seminario; and in Rome at the Biblioteca Angelica. During repeated visits to Rome to study the last unpublished manuscript of Battiferra's *Rime* at the Biblioteca Casanatense, I was kindly assisted by Isabella Ceccopieri and Alessandro Pelle.

To help me launch core documentary research in the Archivio di Stato Fiorentino, Gino Corti was an invaluable finder, reader, and transcriber. Lodovico Branca expedited my photographic orders, and he considerately arranged useful introductions. In Rome the Archivum Romanum Societatis Iesu received me politely and helped with my inquiries into relations between the Ammannati and the Jesuits. At the Archivio di Stato in Urbino, Leonardo Moretti and Giuseppina Paolucci offered practical advice and pleasant companionship during many hours of pouring through notarial *filze* in search of biographical data on the Battiferri family. Through the intermediary of Sabina Eiche, I was privileged to meet in the Urbino archive Don Franco Negroni, a scholar steeped in local history, who helped me sort out the Battiferra family tree. Enrico Maria Guidi, my Urbino counterpart in Battiferra studies, has been an essential correspondent, sending me as a gift his new edition of her *Primo libro* of 1560, mailing his offprints, and sharing prized photocopies and notes from manuscript material in Perugia new to me and now anthologized in this volume.

Fabio Finotti gave a patient, close reading to chapter 1 and its commentary. Many other colleagues in an international community have contributed, knowingly or not, to filling in parts of my introduction, translation, and commentary—a giant jigsaw puzzle with thousands of pieces. Among them are Pamela Benson, the late Vittore Branca, Giulia Calvi, Philippe Canguilhem, Matteo Casini, Alessandro Cecchi, Janet Cox-Rearick, Sabina Eiche, Joseph Farrell, P. Giovanni Ferrara, Valeria Finucci, Pier Massimo Forni, Sara Matthews Grieco, Julia Hairston, Irma B. Jaffe, Stephen Lehmann, Ellen

Liebman, Armando Maggi, Millicent Marcus, Ronald Martinez, Ann Matter, Phil Miraglia, Francesco Sberlati, Deanna Shemek, Janet Smarr, Carlo Vecce, Elissa Weaver, Rebecca West, and Gabriella Zarri.

A powerfully supportive, eagle-eye outside reading of the manuscript for the Press—the kind of collegial support that renews faith in our profession—came from William J. Kennedy. More than any other single individual, Al Rabil must have the credit for making possible a book called *Laura Battiferra and Her Literary Circle: An Anthology.* I thank him thrice over, once for changing his mind, after at first informing me flatly that my work was unsuitable for the Other Voice series, second, for all the time he has invested in this manuscript since his conversion, indefatigably bringing under preliminary editorial control a long manuscript with formatting challenges that have tried patience, and third, for giving it a title that would fit on the cover. Randolph Petilos, my good-humored editor at the University of Chicago Press, has steered the manuscript into production, cracking a reassuring whip.

Mary Elizabeth Erwin Kirkham, my mother, courageously buttressed this project with her enthusiasm for the feminist subject and her faith in my abilities, even through the months of her last illness, when she insisted I not come visit her in Iowa, but stay in Italy and continue uninterrupted my research. My sister, Mary Beth Kirkham, a professor of soil science at Kansas State University, has carried on the family tradition of staunch moral support, helping me survive my own medical adventure and coming back to pick up the threads of life and the scholarship I love.

Victoria Kirkham

THE OTHER VOICE IN EARLY MODERN EUROPE: INTRODUCTION TO THE SERIES

Margaret L. King and Albert Rabil Jr.

THE OLD VOICE AND THE OTHER VOICE

In western Europe and the United States, women are nearing equality in the professions, in business, and in politics. Most enjoy access to education, reproductive rights, and autonomy in financial affairs. Issues vital to women are on the public agenda: equal pay, child care, domestic abuse, breast cancer research, and curricular revision with an eye to the inclusion of women.

These recent achievements have their origins in things women (and some male supporters) said for the first time about six hundred years ago. Theirs is the "other voice," in contradistinction to the "first voice," the voice of the educated men who created Western culture. Coincident with a general reshaping of European culture in the period 1300–1700 (called the Renaissance or early modern period), questions of female equality and opportunity were raised that still resound and are still unresolved.

The other voice emerged against the backdrop of a three-thousand-year history of the derogation of women rooted in the civilizations related to Western culture: Hebrew, Greek, Roman, and Christian. Negative attitudes toward women inherited from these traditions pervaded the intellectual, medical, legal, religious, and social systems that developed during the European Middle Ages.

The following pages describe the traditional, overwhelmingly male views of women's nature inherited by early modern Europeans and the new tradition that the "other voice" called into being to begin to challenge reigning assumptions. This review should serve as a framework for understanding the texts published in the series the Other Voice in Early Modern Europe. Introductions specific to each text and author follow this essay in all the volumes of the series.

TRADITIONAL VIEWS OF WOMEN, 500 B.C.E.–1500 C.E.

Embedded in the philosophical and medical theories of the ancient Greeks were perceptions of the female as inferior to the male in both mind and body. Similarly, the structure of civil legislation inherited from the ancient Romans was biased against women, and the views on women developed by Christian thinkers out of the Hebrew Bible and the Christian New Testament were negative and disabling. Literary works composed in the vernacular of ordinary people, and widely recited or read, conveyed these negative assumptions. The social networks within which most women lived—those of the family and the institutions of the Roman Catholic Church—were shaped by this negative tradition and sharply limited the areas in which women might act in and upon the world.

GREEK PHILOSOPHY AND FEMALE NATURE. Greek biology assumed that women were inferior to men and defined them as merely childbearers and housekeepers. This view was authoritatively expressed in the works of the philosopher Aristotle.

Aristotle thought in dualities. He considered action superior to inaction, form (the inner design or structure of any object) superior to matter, completion to incompletion, possession to deprivation. In each of these dualities, he associated the male principle with the superior quality and the female with the inferior. "The male principle in nature," he argued, "is associated with active, formative and perfected characteristics, while the female is passive, material and deprived, desiring the male in order to become complete."[1] Men are always identified with virile qualities, such as judgment, courage, and stamina, and women with their opposites—irrationality, cowardice, and weakness.

The masculine principle was considered superior even in the womb. The man's semen, Aristotle believed, created the form of a new human creature, while the female body contributed only matter. (The existence of the ovum, and with it the other facts of human embryology, was not established until the seventeenth century.) Although the later Greek physician Galen believed there was a female component in generation, contributed by "female semen," the followers of both Aristotle and Galen saw the male role in human generation as more active and more important.

In the Aristotelian view, the male principle sought always to reproduce

1. Aristotle, *Physics* 1.9.192a20–24, in *The Complete Works of Aristotle,* ed. Jonathan Barnes, rev. Oxford trans., 2 vols. (Princeton, 1984), 1:328.

itself. The creation of a female was always a mistake, therefore, resulting from an imperfect act of generation. Every female born was considered a "defective" or "mutilated" male (as Aristotle's terminology has variously been translated), a "monstrosity" of nature.[2]

For Greek theorists, the biology of males and females was the key to their psychology. The female was softer and more docile, more apt to be despondent, querulous, and deceitful. Being incomplete, moreover, she craved sexual fulfillment in intercourse with a male. The male was intellectual, active, and in control of his passions.

These psychological polarities derived from the theory that the universe consisted of four elements (earth, fire, air, and water), expressed in human bodies as four "humors" (black bile, yellow bile, blood, and phlegm) considered, respectively, dry, hot, damp, and cold and corresponding to mental states ("melancholic," "choleric," "sanguine," "phlegmatic"). In this scheme the male, sharing the principles of earth and fire, was dry and hot; the female, sharing the principles of air and water, was cold and damp.

Female psychology was further affected by her dominant organ, the uterus (womb), *hystera* in Greek. The passions generated by the womb made women lustful, deceitful, talkative, irrational, indeed—when these affects were in excess—"hysterical."

Aristotle's biology also had social and political consequences. If the male principle was superior and the female inferior, then in the household, as in the state, men should rule and women must be subordinate. That hierarchy did not rule out the companionship of husband and wife, whose cooperation was necessary for the welfare of children and the preservation of property. Such mutuality supported male preeminence.

Aristotle's teacher Plato suggested a different possibility: that men and women might possess the same virtues. The setting for this proposal is the imaginary and ideal Republic that Plato sketches in a dialogue of that name. Here, for a privileged elite capable of leading wisely, all distinctions of class and wealth dissolve, as, consequently, do those of gender. Without households or property, as Plato constructs his ideal society, there is no need for the subordination of women. Women may therefore be educated to the same level as men to assume leadership. Plato's Republic remained imaginary, however. In real societies, the subordination of women remained the norm and the prescription.

The views of women inherited from the Greek philosophical tradition became the basis for medieval thought. In the thirteenth century, the su-

2. Aristotle, *Generation of Animals* 2.3.737a27–28, in *The Complete Works,* 1:1144.

preme Scholastic philosopher Thomas Aquinas, among others, still echoed Aristotle's views of human reproduction, of male and female personalities, and of the preeminent male role in the social hierarchy.

ROMAN LAW AND THE FEMALE CONDITION. Roman law, like Greek philosophy, underlay medieval thought and shaped medieval society. The ancient belief that adult property-owning men should administer households and make decisions affecting the community at large is the very fulcrum of Roman law.

About 450 B.C.E., during Rome's republican era, the community's customary law was recorded (legendarily) on twelve tablets erected in the city's central forum. It was later elaborated by professional jurists whose activity increased in the imperial era, when much new legislation was passed, especially on issues affecting family and inheritance. This growing, changing body of laws was eventually codified in the *Corpus of Civil Law* under the direction of the emperor Justinian, generations after the empire ceased to be ruled from Rome. That *Corpus,* read and commented on by medieval scholars from the eleventh century on, inspired the legal systems of most of the cities and kingdoms of Europe.

Laws regarding dowries, divorce, and inheritance pertain primarily to women. Since those laws aimed to maintain and preserve property, the women concerned were those from the property-owning minority. Their subordination to male family members points to the even greater subordination of lower-class and slave women, about whom the laws speak little.

In the early republic, the *paterfamilias,* or "father of the family," possessed *patria potestas,* "paternal power." The term *pater,* "father," in both these cases does not necessarily mean biological father but denotes the head of a household. The father was the person who owned the household's property and, indeed, its human members. The *paterfamilias* had absolute power—including the power, rarely exercised, of life or death—over his wife, his children, and his slaves, as much as his cattle.

Male children could be "emancipated," an act that granted legal autonomy and the right to own property. Those over fourteen could be emancipated by a special grant from the father or automatically by their father's death. But females could never be emancipated; instead, they passed from the authority of their father to that of a husband or, if widowed or orphaned while still unmarried, to a guardian or tutor.

Marriage in its traditional form placed the woman under her husband's authority, or *manus.* He could divorce her on grounds of adultery, drinking wine, or stealing from the household, but she could not divorce him. She could neither possess property in her own right nor bequeath any to her children upon her death. When her husband died, the household property passed not to her but to his male heirs. And when her father died, she had no claim to any family inheritance, which was directed to her brothers or more remote male relatives. The effect of these laws was to exclude women from civil society, itself based on property ownership.

In the later republican and imperial periods, these rules were significantly modified. Women rarely married according to the traditional form. The practice of "free" marriage allowed a woman to remain under her father's authority, to possess property given her by her father (most frequently the "dowry," recoverable from the husband's household on his death), and to inherit from her father. She could also bequeath property to her own children and divorce her husband, just as he could divorce her.

Despite this greater freedom, women still suffered enormous disability under Roman law. Heirs could belong only to the father's side, never the mother's. Moreover, although she could bequeath her property to her children, she could not establish a line of succession in doing so. A woman was "the beginning and end of her own family," said the jurist Ulpian. Moreover, women could play no public role. They could not hold public office, represent anyone in a legal case, or even witness a will. Women had only a private existence and no public personality.

The dowry system, the guardian, women's limited ability to transmit wealth, and total political disability are all features of Roman law adopted by the medieval communities of western Europe, although modified according to local customary laws..

CHRISTIAN DOCTRINE AND WOMEN'S PLACE. The Hebrew Bible and the Christian New Testament authorized later writers to limit women to the realm of the family and to burden them with the guilt of original sin. The passages most fruitful for this purpose were the creation narratives in Genesis and sentences from the Epistles defining women's role within the Christian family and community.

Each of the first two chapters of Genesis contains a creation narrative. In the first "God created man in his own image, in the image of God he created him; male and female he created them" (Gn 1:27). In the second, God created Eve from Adam's rib (2:21–23). Christian theologians relied principally on Genesis 2 for their understanding of the relation between man and woman, interpreting the creation of Eve from Adam as proof of her subordination to him.

The creation story in Genesis 2 leads to that of the temptations in Genesis 3: of Eve by the wily serpent and of Adam by Eve. As read by Christian theologians from Tertullian to Thomas Aquinas, the narrative made Eve responsible for the Fall and its consequences. She instigated the act; she deceived her husband; she suffered the greater punishment. Her disobedience made it necessary for Jesus to be incarnated and to die on the cross. From the pulpit, moralists and preachers for centuries conveyed to women the guilt that they bore for original sin.

The Epistles offered advice to early Christians on building communities of the faithful. Among the matters to be regulated was the place of women. Paul offered views favorable to women in Galatians 3:28: "There is neither Jew nor Greek, there is neither slave nor free, there is neither male nor female; for you are all one in Christ Jesus." Paul also referred to women as his coworkers and placed them on a par with himself and his male coworkers (Phlm 4:2–3; Rom 16:1–3; 1 Cor 16:19). Elsewhere, Paul limited women's possibilities: "But I want you to understand that the head of every man is Christ, the head of a woman is her husband, and the head of Christ is God" (1 Cor 11:3).

Biblical passages by later writers (although attributed to Paul) enjoined women to forgo jewels, expensive clothes, and elaborate coiffures; and they forbade women to "teach or have authority over men," telling them to "learn in silence with all submissiveness" as is proper for one responsible for sin, consoling them, however, with the thought that they will be saved through childbearing (1 Tm 2:9–15). Other texts among the later Epistles defined women as the weaker sex and emphasized their subordination to their husbands (1 Pt 3:7; Col 3:18; Eph 5:22–23).

These passages from the New Testament became the arsenal employed by theologians of the early church to transmit negative attitudes toward women to medieval Christian culture—above all, Tertullian (*On the Apparel of Women*), Jerome (*Against Jovinian*), and Augustine (*The Literal Meaning of Genesis*).

THE IMAGE OF WOMEN IN MEDIEVAL LITERATURE. The philosophical, legal, and religious traditions born in antiquity formed the basis of the medieval intellectual synthesis wrought by trained thinkers, mostly clerics, writing in Latin and based largely in universities. The vernacular literary tradition that developed alongside the learned tradition also spoke about female nature and women's roles. Medieval stories, poems, and epics also portrayed women negatively—as lustful and deceitful—while praising good housekeepers and loyal wives as replicas of the Virgin Mary or the female saints and martyrs.

There is an exception in the movement of "courtly love" that evolved in southern France from the twelfth century. Courtly love was the erotic love between a nobleman and noblewoman, the latter usually superior in social rank. It was always adulterous. From the conventions of courtly love derive modern Western notions of romantic love. The tradition has had an impact disproportionate to its size, for it affected only a tiny elite, and very few women. The exaltation of the female lover probably does not reflect a higher evaluation of women or a step toward their sexual liberation. More likely it gives expression to the social and sexual tensions besetting the knightly class at a specific historical juncture.

The literary fashion of courtly love was on the wane by the thirteenth century, when the widely read *Romance of the Rose* was composed in French by two authors of significantly different dispositions. Guillaume de Lorris composed the initial four thousand verses about 1235, and Jean de Meun added about seventeen thousand verses—more than four times the original—about 1265.

The fragment composed by Guillaume de Lorris stands squarely in the tradition of courtly love. Here the poet, in a dream, is admitted into a walled garden where he finds a magic fountain in which a rosebush is reflected. He longs to pick one rose, but the thorns prevent his doing so, even as he is wounded by arrows from the god of love, whose commands he agrees to obey. The rest of this part of the poem recounts the poet's unsuccessful efforts to pluck the rose.

The longer part of the *Romance* by Jean de Meun also describes a dream. But here allegorical characters give long didactic speeches, providing a social satire on a variety of themes, some pertaining to women. Love is an anxious and tormented state, the poem explains: women are greedy and manipulative, marriage is miserable, beautiful women are lustful, ugly ones cease to please, and a chaste woman is as rare as a black swan.

Shortly after Jean de Meun completed *The Romance of the Rose,* Mathéolus penned his *Lamentations,* a long Latin diatribe against marriage translated into French about a century later. The *Lamentations* sum up medieval attitudes toward women and provoked the important response by Christine de Pizan in her *Book of the City of Ladies.*

In 1355, Giovanni Boccaccio wrote *Il Corbaccio,* another antifeminist manifesto, although ironically by an author whose other works pioneered new directions in Renaissance thought. The former husband of his lover appears to Boccaccio, condemning his unmoderated lust and detailing the defects of women. Boccaccio concedes at the end "how much men naturally surpass women in nobility" and is cured of his desires.[3]

3. Giovanni Boccaccio, *The Corbaccio, or The Labyrinth of Love,* trans. and ed. Anthony K. Cassell, rev. ed. (Binghamton, NY, 1993), 71.

WOMEN'S ROLES: THE FAMILY. The negative perceptions of women expressed in the intellectual tradition are also implicit in the actual roles that women played in European society. Assigned to subordinate positions in the household and the church, they were barred from significant participation in public life.

Medieval European households, like those in antiquity and in non-Western civilizations, were headed by males. It was the male serf (or peasant), feudal lord, town merchant, or citizen who was polled or taxed or succeeded to an inheritance or had any acknowledged public role, although his wife or widow could stand as a temporary surrogate. From about 1100, the position of property-holding males was further enhanced: inheritance was confined to the male, or agnate, line—with depressing consequences for women.

A wife never fully belonged to her husband's family, nor was she a daughter to her father's family. She left her father's house young to marry whomever her parents chose. Her dowry was managed by her husband, and at her death it normally passed to her children by him.

A married woman's life was occupied nearly constantly with cycles of pregnancy, childbearing, and lactation. Women bore children through all the years of their fertility, and many died in childbirth. They were also responsible for raising young children up to six or seven. In the propertied classes that responsibility was shared, since it was common for a wet nurse to take over breast-feeding and for servants to perform other chores.

Women trained their daughters in the household duties appropriate to their status, nearly always tasks associated with textiles: spinning, weaving, sewing, embroidering. Their sons were sent out of the house as apprentices or students, or their training was assumed by fathers in later childhood and adolescence. On the death of her husband, a woman's children became the responsibility of his family. She generally did not take "his" children with her to a new marriage or back to her father's house, except sometimes in the artisan classes.

Women also worked. Rural peasants performed farm chores, merchant wives often practiced their husbands' trades, the unmarried daughters of the urban poor worked as servants or prostitutes. All wives produced or embellished textiles and did the housekeeping, while wealthy ones managed servants. These labors were unpaid or poorly paid but often contributed substantially to family wealth.

WOMEN'S ROLES: THE CHURCH. Membership in a household, whether a father's or a husband's, meant for women a lifelong subordination to others. In western Europe, the Roman Catholic Church offered an alternative to the career of wife and mother. A woman could enter a convent, parallel in function to the monasteries for men that evolved in the early Christian centuries.

In the convent, a woman pledged herself to a celibate life, lived according to strict community rules, and worshiped daily. Often the convent offered training in Latin, allowing some women to become considerable scholars and authors as well as scribes, artists, and musicians. For women who chose the conventual life, the benefits could be enormous, but for numerous others placed in convents by paternal choice, the life could be restrictive and burdensome.

The conventual life declined as an alternative for women as the modern age approached. Reformed monastic institutions resisted responsibility for related female orders. The church increasingly restricted female institutional life by insisting on closer male supervision.

Women often sought other options. Some joined the communities of laywomen that sprang up spontaneously in the thirteenth century in the urban zones of western Europe, especially in Flanders and Italy. Some joined the heretical movements that flourished in late medieval Christendom, whose anticlerical and often antifamily positions particularly appealed to women. In these communities, some women were acclaimed as "holy women" or "saints," whereas others often were condemned as frauds or heretics.

In all, although the options offered to women by the church were sometimes less than satisfactory, they were sometimes richly rewarding. After 1520, the convent remained an option only in Roman Catholic territories. Protestantism engendered an ideal of marriage as a heroic endeavor and appeared to place husband and wife on a more equal footing. Sermons and treatises, however, still called for female subordination and obedience.

THE OTHER VOICE, 1300–1700

When the modern era opened, European culture was so firmly structured by a framework of negative attitudes toward women that to dismantle it was a monumental labor. The process began as part of a larger cultural movement that entailed the critical reexamination of ideas inherited from the ancient and medieval past. The humanists launched that critical reexamination.

THE HUMANIST FOUNDATION. Originating in Italy in the fourteenth century, humanism quickly became the dominant intellectual movement in Europe. Spreading in the sixteenth century from Italy to the rest of Europe, it fueled the literary, scientific, and philosophical movements of the era and laid the basis for the eighteenth-century Enlightenment.

Humanists regarded the Scholastic philosophy of medieval universities as out of touch with the realities of urban life. They found in the rhetorical discourse of classical Rome a language adapted to civic life and public speech. They learned to read, speak, and write classical Latin and, eventually, classical Greek. They founded schools to teach others to do so, establishing the pattern for elementary and secondary education for the next three hundred years.

In the service of complex government bureaucracies, humanists employed their skills to write eloquent letters, deliver public orations, and formulate public policy. They developed new scripts for copying manuscripts and used the new printing press to disseminate texts, for which they created methods of critical editing.

Humanism was a movement led by males who accepted the evaluation of women in ancient texts and generally shared the misogynist perceptions of their culture. (Female humanists, as we will see, did not.) Yet humanism also opened the door to a reevaluation of the nature and capacity of women. By calling authors, texts, and ideas into question, it made possible the fundamental rereading of the whole intellectual tradition that was required in order to free women from cultural prejudice and social subordination.

A DIFFERENT CITY. The other voice first appeared when, after so many centuries, the accumulation of misogynist concepts evoked a response from a capable female defender: Christine de Pizan (1365–1431). Introducing her Book of the City of Ladies (1405), she described how she was affected by reading Mathéolus's Lamentations: "Just the sight of this book . . . made me wonder how it happened that so many different men . . . are so inclined to express both in speaking and in their treatises and writings so many wicked insults about women and their behavior."[4] These statements impelled her to detest herself "and the entire feminine sex, as though we were monstrosities in nature."[5]

The rest of *The Book of the City of Ladies* presents a justification of the female sex and a vision of an ideal community of women. A pioneer, she has received the message of female inferiority and rejected it. From the fourteenth to the seventeenth century, a huge body of literature accumulated that responded to the dominant tradition.

4. Christine de Pizan, *The Book of the City of Ladies,* trans. Earl Jeffrey Richards, foreword by Marina Warner (New York, 1982), 1.1.1, pp. 3–4.

5. Ibid., 1.1.1–2, p. 5.

The result was a literary explosion consisting of works by both men and women, in Latin and in the vernaculars: works enumerating the achievements of notable women; works rebutting the main accusations made against women; works arguing for the equal education of men and women; works defining and redefining women's proper role in the family, at court, in public; works describing women's lives and experiences. Recent monographs and articles have begun to hint at the great range of this movement, involving probably several thousand titles. The protofeminism of these "other voices" constitutes a significant fraction of the literary product of the early modern era.

THE CATALOGS. About 1365, the same Boccaccio whose Corbaccio rehearses the usual charges against female nature wrote another work, Concerning Famous Women. A humanist treatise drawing on classical texts, it praised 106 notable women: ninety-eight of them from pagan Greek and Roman antiquity, one (Eve) from the Bible, and seven from the medieval religious and cultural tradition; his book helped make all readers aware of a sex normally condemned or forgotten. Boccaccio's outlook nevertheless was unfriendly to women, for it singled out for praise those women who possessed the traditional virtues of chastity, silence, and obedience. Women who were active in the public realm—for example, rulers and warriors—were depicted as usually being lascivious and as suffering terrible punishments for entering the masculine sphere. Women were his subject, but Boccaccio's standard remained male.

Christine de Pizan's *Book of the City of Ladies* contains a second catalog, one responding specifically to Boccaccio's. Whereas Boccaccio portrays female virtue as exceptional, she depicts it as universal. Many women in history were leaders, or remained chaste despite the lascivious approaches of men, or were visionaries and brave martyrs.

The work of Boccaccio inspired a series of catalogs of illustrious women of the biblical, classical, Christian, and local pasts, among them Filippo da Bergamo's *Of Illustrious Women*, Pierre de Brantôme's *Lives of Illustrious Women*, Pierre Le Moyne's *Gallerie of Heroic Women*, and Pietro Paolo de Ribera's *Immortal Triumphs and Heroic Enterprises of 845 Women*. Whatever their embedded prejudices, these works drove home to the public the possibility of female excellence.

THE DEBATE. At the same time, many questions remained: Could a woman be virtuous? Could she perform noteworthy deeds? Was she even, strictly speaking, of the same human species as men? These questions were debated over four centuries, in French, German, Italian, Spanish, and English, by authors male and female, among Catholics, Protestants, and Jews, in ponderous volumes and breezy pamphlets. The whole literary genre has been called the querelle des femmes, the "woman question."

The opening volley of this battle occurred in the first years of the fifteenth century, in a literary debate sparked by Christine de Pizan. She exchanged letters critical of Jean de Meun's contribution to *The Romance of the Rose* with two French royal secretaries, Jean de Montreuil and Gontier Col. When the matter became public, Jean Gerson, one of Europe's leading theologians, supported de Pizan's arguments against de Meun, for the moment silencing the opposition.

The debate resurfaced repeatedly over the next two hundred years. *The Triumph of Women* (1438) by Juan Rodríguez de la Camara (or Juan Rodríguez del Padron) struck a new note by presenting arguments for the superiority of women to men. *The Champion of Women* (1440–42) by Martin Le Franc addresses once again the negative views of women presented in *The Romance of the Rose* and offers counterevidence of female virtue and achievement.

A cameo of the debate on women is included in *The Courtier,* one of the most widely read books of the era, published by the Italian Baldassare Castiglione in 1528 and immediately translated into other European vernaculars. *The Courtier* depicts a series of evenings at the court of the Duke of Urbino in which many men and some women of the highest social stratum amuse themselves by discussing a range of literary and social issues. The "woman question" is a pervasive theme throughout, and the third of its four books is devoted entirely to that issue.

In a verbal duel, Gasparo Pallavicino and Giuliano de' Medici present the main claims of the two traditions. Gasparo argues the innate inferiority of women and their inclination to vice. Only in bearing children do they profit the world. Giuliano counters that women share the same spiritual and mental capacities as men and may excel in wisdom and action. Men and women are of the same essence: just as no stone can be more perfectly a stone than another, so no human being can be more perfectly human than others, whether male or female. It was an astonishing assertion, boldly made to an audience as large as all Europe.

THE TREATISES. Humanism provided the materials for a positive counterconcept to the misogyny embedded in Scholastic philosophy and law and inherited from the Greek, Roman, and Christian pasts. A series of humanist treatises on marriage and family, on education and deportment, and on the nature of women helped construct these new perspectives.

The works by Francesco Barbaro and Leon Battista Alberti—*On Mar-*

riage (1415) and *On the Family* (1434–37)—far from defending female equality, reasserted women's responsibility for rearing children and managing the housekeeping while being obedient, chaste, and silent. Nevertheless, they served the cause of reexamining the issue of women's nature by placing domestic issues at the center of scholarly concern and reopening the pertinent classical texts. In addition, Barbaro emphasized the companionate nature of marriage and the importance of a wife's spiritual and mental qualities for the well-being of the family.

These themes reappear in later humanist works on marriage and the education of women by Juan Luis Vives and Erasmus. Both were moderately sympathetic to the condition of women without reaching beyond the usual masculine prescriptions for female behavior.

An outlook more favorable to women characterizes the nearly unknown work *In Praise of Women* (ca. 1487) by the Italian humanist Bartolommeo Goggio. In addition to providing a catalog of illustrious women, Goggio argued that male and female are the same in essence, but that women (reworking the Adam and Eve narrative from quite a new angle) are actually superior. In the same vein, the Italian humanist Mario Equicola asserted the spiritual equality of men and women in *On Women* (1501). In 1525, Galeazzo Flavio Capra (or Capella) published his work *On the Excellence and Dignity of Women.* This humanist tradition of treatises defending the worthiness of women culminates in the work of Henricus Cornelius Agrippa *On the Nobility and Preeminence of the Female Sex.* No work by a male humanist more succinctly or explicitly presents the case for female dignity.

THE WITCH BOOKS. While humanists grappled with the issues pertaining to women and family, other learned men turned their attention to what they perceived as a very great problem: witches. Witch-hunting manuals, explorations of the witch phenomenon, and even defenses of witches are not at first glance pertinent to the tradition of the other voice. But they do relate in this way: most accused witches were women. The hostility aroused by supposed witch activity is comparable to the hostility aroused by women. The evil deeds the victims of the hunt were charged with were exaggerations of the vices to which, many believed, all women were prone.

The connection between the witch accusation and the hatred of women is explicit in the notorious witch-hunting manual *The Hammer of Witches* (1486) by two Dominican inquisitors, Heinrich Krämer and Jacob Sprenger. Here the inconstancy, deceitfulness, and lustfulness traditionally associated with women are depicted in exaggerated form as the core features of witch behavior. These traits inclined women to make a bargain with the devil—

sealed by sexual intercourse—by which they acquired unholy powers. Such bizarre claims, far from being rejected by rational men, were broadcast by intellectuals. The German Ulrich Molitur, the Frenchman Nicolas Rémy, and the Italian Stefano Guazzo all coolly informed the public of sinister orgies and midnight pacts with the devil. The celebrated French jurist, historian, and political philosopher Jean Bodin argued that because women were especially prone to diabolism, regular legal procedures could properly be suspended in order to try those accused of this "exceptional crime."

A few experts such as the physician Johann Weyer, a student of Agrippa's, raised their voices in protest. In 1563, he explained the witch phenomenon thus, without discarding belief in diabolism: the devil deluded foolish old women afflicted by melancholia, causing them to believe they had magical powers. Weyer's rational skepticism, which had good credibility in the community of the learned, worked to revise the conventional views of women and witchcraft.

WOMEN'S WORKS. To the many categories of works produced on the question of women's worth must be added nearly all works written by women. A woman writing was in herself a statement of women's claim to dignity.

Only a few women wrote anything before the dawn of the modern era, for three reasons. First, they rarely received the education that would enable them to write. Second, they were not admitted to the public roles—as administrator, bureaucrat, lawyer or notary, or university professor—in which they might gain knowledge of the kinds of things the literate public thought worth writing about. Third, the culture imposed silence on women, considering speaking out a form of unchastity. Given these conditions, it is remarkable that any women wrote. Those who did before the fourteenth century were almost always nuns or religious women whose isolation made their pronouncements more acceptable.

From the fourteenth century on, the volume of women's writings rose. Women continued to write devotional literature, although not always as cloistered nuns. They also wrote diaries, often intended as keepsakes for their children; books of advice to their sons and daughters; letters to family members and friends; and family memoirs, in a few cases elaborate enough to be considered histories.

A few women wrote works directly concerning the "woman question," and some of these, such as the humanists Isotta Nogarola, Cassandra Fedele, Laura Cereta, and Olympia Morata, were highly trained. A few were professional writers, living by the income of their pens; the very first among them was Christine de Pizan, noteworthy in this context as in so many others. In addition to *The Book of the City of Ladies* and her critiques of *The Romance of the Rose,* she wrote *The Treasure of the City of Ladies* (a guide to social decorum for women), an advice book for her son, much courtly verse, and a full-scale history of the reign of King Charles V of France.

WOMEN PATRONS. Women who did not themselves write but encouraged others to do so boosted the development of an alternative tradition. Highly placed women patrons supported authors, artists, musicians, poets, and learned men. Such patrons, drawn mostly from the Italian elites and the courts of northern Europe, figure disproportionately as the dedicatees of the important works of early feminism.

For a start, it might be noted that the catalogs of Boccaccio and Alvaro de Luna were dedicated to the Florentine noblewoman Andrea Acciaiuoli and to Doña María, first wife of King Juan II of Castile, while the French translation of Boccaccio's work was commissioned by Anne of Brittany, wife of King Charles VIII of France. The humanist treatises of Goggio, Equicola, Vives, and Agrippa were dedicated, respectively, to Eleanora of Aragon, wife of Ercole I d'Este, Duke of Ferrara; to Margherita Cantelma of Mantua; to Catherine of Aragon, wife of King Henry VIII of England; and to Margaret, Duchess of Austria and regent of the Netherlands. As late as 1696, Mary Astell's *Serious Proposal to the Ladies, for the Advancement of Their True and Greatest Interest* was dedicated to Princess Anne of Denmark.

These authors presumed that their efforts would be welcome to female patrons, or they may have written at the bidding of those patrons. Silent themselves, perhaps even unresponsive, these loftily placed women helped shape the tradition of the other voice.

THE ISSUES. The literary forms and patterns in which the tradition of the other voice presented itself have now been sketched. It remains to highlight the major issues around which this tradition crystallizes. In brief, there are four problems to which our authors return again and again, in plays and catalogs, in verse and letters, in treatises and dialogues, in every language: the problem of chastity, the problem of power, the problem of speech, and the problem of knowledge. Of these the greatest, preconditioning the others, is the problem of chastity.

THE PROBLEM OF CHASTITY. In traditional European culture, as in those of antiquity and others around the globe, chastity was perceived as woman's quintessential virtue—in contrast to courage, or generosity, or leadership, or rationality, seen as virtues characteristic of men. Opponents of women charged them with insatiable lust. Women themselves and their defenders—

without disputing the validity of the standard—responded that women were capable of chastity.

The requirement of chastity kept women at home, silenced them, isolated them, left them in ignorance. It was the source of all other impediments. Why was it so important to the society of men, of whom chastity was not required, and who more often than not considered it their right to violate the chastity of any woman they encountered?

Female chastity ensured the continuity of the male-headed household. If a man's wife was not chaste, he could not be sure of the legitimacy of his offspring. If they were not his and they acquired his property, it was not his household, but some other man's, that had endured. If his daughter was not chaste, she could not be transferred to another man's household as his wife, and he was dishonored.

The whole system of the integrity of the household and the transmission of property was bound up in female chastity. Such a requirement pertained only to property-owning classes, of course. Poor women could not expect to maintain their chastity, least of all if they were in contact with high-status men to whom all women but those of their own household were prey.

In Catholic Europe, the requirement of chastity was further buttressed by moral and religious imperatives. Original sin was inextricably linked with the sexual act. Virginity was seen as heroic virtue, far more impressive than, say, the avoidance of idleness or greed. Monasticism, the cultural institution that dominated medieval Europe for centuries, was grounded in the renunciation of the flesh. The Catholic reform of the eleventh century imposed a similar standard on all the clergy and a heightened awareness of sexual requirements on all the laity. Although men were asked to be chaste, female unchastity was much worse: it led to the devil, as Eve had led mankind to sin.

To such requirements, women and their defenders protested their innocence. Furthermore, following the example of holy women who had escaped the requirements of family and sought the religious life, some women began to conceive of female communities as alternatives both to family and to the cloister. Christine de Pizan's city of ladies was such a community. Moderata Fonte and Mary Astell envisioned others. The luxurious salons of the French *précieuses* of the seventeenth century, or the comfortable English drawing rooms of the next, may have been born of the same impulse. Here women not only might escape, if briefly, the subordinate position that life in the family entailed but might also make claims to power, exercise their capacity for speech, and display their knowledge.

THE PROBLEM OF POWER. Women were excluded from power: the whole cultural tradition insisted on it. Only men were citizens, only men bore arms, only men could be chiefs or lords or kings. There were exceptions that did not disprove the rule, when wives or widows or mothers took the place of men, awaiting their return or the maturation of a male heir. A woman who attempted to rule in her own right was perceived as an anomaly, a monster, at once a deformed woman and an insufficient male, sexually confused and consequently unsafe.

The association of such images with women who held or sought power explains some otherwise odd features of early modern culture. Queen Elizabeth I of England, one of the few women to hold full regal authority in European history, played with such male/female images—positive ones, of course—in representing herself to her subjects. She was a prince, and manly, even though she was female. She was also (she claimed) virginal, a condition absolutely essential if she was to avoid the attacks of her opponents. Catherine de' Medici, who ruled France as widow and regent for her sons, also adopted such imagery in defining her position. She chose as one symbol the figure of Artemisia, an androgynous ancient warrior-heroine who combined a female persona with masculine powers.

Power in a woman, without such sexual imagery, seems to have been indigestible by the culture. A rare note was struck by the Englishman Sir Thomas Elyot in his *Defence of Good Women* (1540), justifying both women's participation in civic life and their prowess in arms. The old tune was sung by the Scots reformer John Knox in his *First Blast of the Trumpet against the Monstrous Regiment of Women* (1558); for him rule by women, defects in nature, was a hideous contradiction in terms.

The confused sexuality of the imagery of female potency was not reserved for rulers. Any woman who excelled was likely to be called an Amazon, recalling the self-mutilated warrior women of antiquity who repudiated all men, gave up their sons, and raised only their daughters. She was often said to have "exceeded her sex" or to have possessed "masculine virtue"—as the very fact of conspicuous excellence conferred masculinity even on the female subject. The catalogs of notable women often showed those female heroes dressed in armor, armed to the teeth, like men. Amazonian heroines romp through the epics of the age—Ariosto's *Orlando Furioso* (1532) and Spenser's *Faerie Queene* (1590–1609). Excellence in a woman was perceived as a claim for power, and power was reserved for the masculine realm. A woman who possessed either one was masculinized and lost title to her own female identity.

THE PROBLEM OF SPEECH. Just as power had a sexual dimension when it was claimed by women, so did speech. A good woman spoke little. Excessive speech was an indication of unchastity. By speech, women seduced men. Eve had lured Adam into sin by her speech. Accused witches were commonly accused of having spoken abusively, or irrationally, or simply too much. As enlightened a figure as Francesco Barbaro insisted on silence in a woman, which he linked to her perfect unanimity with her husband's will and her unblemished virtue (her chastity). Another Italian humanist, Leonardo Bruni, in advising a noblewoman on her studies, barred her not from speech but from public speaking. That was reserved for men.

Related to the problem of speech was that of costume—another, if silent, form of self-expression. Assigned the task of pleasing men as their primary occupation, elite women often tended toward elaborate costume, hairdressing, and the use of cosmetics. Clergy and secular moralists alike condemned these practices. The appropriate function of costume and adornment was to announce the status of a woman's husband or father. Any further indulgence in adornment was akin to unchastity.

THE PROBLEM OF KNOWLEDGE. When the Italian noblewoman Isotta Nogarola had begun to attain a reputation as a humanist, she was accused of incest—a telling instance of the association of learning in women with unchastity. That chilling association inclined any woman who was educated to deny that she was or to make exaggerated claims of heroic chastity.

If educated women were pursued with suspicions of sexual misconduct, women seeking an education faced an even more daunting obstacle: the assumption that women were by nature incapable of learning, that reasoning was a particularly masculine ability. Just as they proclaimed their chastity, women and their defenders insisted on their capacity for learning. The major work by a male writer on female education—that by Juan Luis Vives, *On the Education of a Christian Woman* (1523)—granted female capacity for intellection but still argued that a woman's whole education was to be shaped around the requirement of chastity and a future within the household. Female writers of the following generations—Marie de Gournay in France, Anna Maria van Schurman in Holland, and Mary Astell in England—began to envision other possibilities.

The pioneers of female education were the Italian women humanists who managed to attain a literacy in Latin and a knowledge of classical and Christian literature equivalent to that of prominent men. Their works implicitly and explicitly raise questions about women's social roles, defining problems that beset women attempting to break out of the cultural limits that had bound them. Like Christine de Pizan, who achieved an advanced education through her father's tutoring and her own devices, their bold questioning makes clear the importance of training. Only when women were educated to the same standard as male leaders would they be able to raise that other voice and insist on their dignity as human beings morally, intellectually, and legally equal to men.

THE OTHER VOICE. The other voice, a voice of protest, was mostly female, but it was also male. It spoke in the vernaculars and in Latin, in treatises and dialogues, in plays and poetry, in letters and diaries, and in pamphlets. It battered at the wall of prejudice that encircled women and raised a banner announcing its claims. The female was equal (or even superior) to the male in essential nature—moral, spiritual, and intellectual. Women were capable of higher education, of holding positions of power and influence in the public realm, and of speaking and writing persuasively. The last bastion of masculine supremacy, centered on the notions of a woman's primary domestic responsibility and the requirement of female chastity, was not as yet assaulted—although visions of productive female communities as alternatives to the family indicated an awareness of the problem.

During the period 1300–1700, the other voice remained only a voice, and one only dimly heard. It did not result—yet—in an alteration of social patterns. Indeed, to this day they have not entirely been altered. Yet the call for justice issued as long as six centuries ago by those writing in the tradition of the other voice must be recognized as the source and origin of the mature feminist tradition and of the realignment of social institutions accomplished in the modern age.

We thank the volume editors in this series, who responded with many suggestions to an earlier draft of this introduction, making it a collaborative enterprise. Many of their suggestions and criticisms have resulted in revisions of this introduction, although we remain responsible for the final product.

PROJECTED TITLES IN THE SERIES

Isabella Andreini, *Mirtilla,* edited and translated by Laura Stortoni

Tullia d'Aragona, *Complete Poems and Letters,* edited and translated by Julia Hairston

Tullia d'Aragona, *The Wretch, Otherwise Known as Guerrino,* edited and translated by Julia Hairston and John McLucas

Francesco Barbaro et al., *On Marriage and the Family,* edited and translated by Margaret L. King

Francesco Buoninsegni and Arcangela Tarabotti, *Menippean Satire: "Against Feminine Extravagance" and "Antisatire,"* edited and translated by Elissa Weaver

Rosalba Carriera, *Letters, Diaries, and Art,* edited and translated by Catherine M. Sama

Madame du Chatelet, *Selected Works,* edited by Judith Zinsser

Vittoria Colonna, Chiara Matraini, and Lucrezia Marinella, *Marian Writings,* edited and translated by Susan Haskins

Princess Elizabeth of Bohemia, *Correspondence with Descartes,* edited and translated by Lisa Shapiro

Isabella d'Este, *Selected Letters,* edited and translated by Deanna Shemek

Fairy Tales by Seventeenth-Century French Women Writers, edited and translated by Lewis Seifert and Domna C. Stanton

Moderata Fonte, *Floridoro,* edited and translated by Valeria Finucci

Moderata Fonte and Lucrezia Marinella, *Religious Narratives,* edited and translated by Virginia Cox

Catharina Regina von Greiffenberg, *Meditations on the Life of Christ,* edited and translated by Lynne Tatlock

In Praise of Women: Italian Fifteenth-Century Defenses of Women, edited and translated by Daniel Bornstein

Lucrezia Marinella, *L'Enrico, or Byzantium Conquered,* edited and translated by Virginia Cox

Lucrezia Marinella, *Happy Arcadia,* edited and translated by Susan Haskins and Letizia Panizza

Chiara Matraini, *Selected Poetry and Prose,* edited and translated by Elaine MacLachlan

Alessandro Piccolomini, *Rethinking Marriage in Sixteenth-Century Italy,* edited and translated by Letizia Panizza

Christine de Pizan, *Debate over the "Romance of the Rose,"* edited and translated by David F. Hult

Christine de Pizan, *Life of Charles V,* edited and translated by Nadia Margolis

Christine de Pizan, *The Long Road of Learning,* edited and translated by Andrea Tarnowski

Madeleine and Catherine des Roches, *Selected Letters, Dialogues, and Poems,* edited and translated by Anne Larsen

Oliva Sabuco, *The New Philosophy: True Medicine,* edited and translated by Gianna Pomata

Margherita Sarrocchi, *La Scanderbeide,* edited and translated by Rinaldina Russell

Gabrielle Suchon, *"On Philosophy" and "On Morality,"* edited and translated by Domna Stanton with Rebecca Wilkin

Sara Copio Sullam, *Sara Copio Sullam: Jewish Poet and Intellectual in Early Seventeenth-Century Venice,* edited and translated by Don Harrán

Arcangela Tarabotti, *Convent Life as Inferno: A Report,* introduction and notes by Francesca Medioli, translated by Letizia Panizza

Laura Terracina, *Works,* edited and translated by Michael Sherberg

Katharina Schütz Zell, *Selected Writings,* edited and translated by Elsie McKee

VOLUME EDITOR'S INTRODUCTION

THE OTHER VOICE: "THIS NEW SAPPHO OF OUR TIMES"

Celebrated by her contemporaries, Laura Battiferra degli Ammannati flourished as a poet at the crossroads of Renaissance and Catholic Reformation culture. An arresting profile by Agnolo Bronzino, court painter to the Medici, depicts her as a Petrarchist at the height of her glory, around 1560 (figs. 1, 2).[1] Battiferra in old age, a devoutly religious matron, appears with her husband Bartolomeo Ammannati witnessing a Gospel miracle in Alessandro Allori's panel for the couple's funeral chapel in the Florentine Jesuit church of San Giovannino (figs. 3, 4).[2] Fellow writers praised her as a phenomenon, remarkable among women for talent, intellect, and moral character. They canonized her among celebrated moderns, compared her with Plato, and avowed her superiority to Sappho, legendary ancestress of all female writers. Beginning in the decade of the 1550s, prominent male peers embraced her in their intellectual communities, from prestigious Italian academies to more informal groups that met like salons to engage in the latest literary debates. Of a spiritual bent fiercely loyal to the Roman Catholic Church, these coteries gravitated to the venerable monastery of Santa

1. The portrait hangs today in Florence at the Palazzo Vecchio. Battiferra's open book displays Petrarch's sonnets 64 and 240. For a catalog description, see Janet Cox-Rearick, "Agnolo Bronzino, *Laura Battiferra degli Ammannati*," in *The Medici, Michelangelo, and the Art of Late Renaissance Florence* (New Haven: Yale University Press, 2002), 149–50 (with an excellent color reproduction); for further discussion, see Victoria Kirkham, "Dante's Fantom, Petrarch's Specter: Bronzino's Portrait of the Poet Laura Battiferra," in Deborah Parker, ed., *"Visibile parlare": Dante and the Art of the Italian Renaissance*, *Lectura Dantis* 22–23 (1998): 63–139; and Carol Plazzotta, "Bronzino's Laura," *Burlington Magazine* 140.1142 (April 1998): 251–63.

2. See Simona Lecchini-Giovannoni, *Alessandro Allori* (Turin: Umberto Allemandi and Co., 1991) for the panel (ca. 1590) in the Ammannati funeral chapel, 272–73, fig. 281 and no. 113. Battiferra kneels at far right, holding a small book; her bearded husband stands in the guise of Saint Bartholomew leaning on a crook behind the Canaanite woman.

1. Agnolo Bronzino, *Laura Battiferra,* oil on wood, ca. 1561. Florence, Palazzo Vecchio. Photograph: Soprintendenza per i Beni Artistici e Storici, Gabinetto Fotografico, Florence.

Maria degli Angeli in the heart of Florence beside Brunelleschi's Rotunda, to patrician villas in the surrounding countryside, and sometimes to the warmth of Battiferra's own fireside. Their circles, in ever shifting combinatory activity, produced fashionable, multivoiced lyric anthologies, preserved in print and manuscript, that measure the parabola of Battiferra's fame.

Battiferra's portrait by Bronzino, of undocumented date, probably coincides with her publishing debut in 1560, *Il primo libro delle opere toscane di Madonna Laura Battiferra degli Ammannati* (The First Book of Tuscan Works by Madonna Laura Battiferra degli Ammannati [Florence: Giunti, 1560]) (figs. 5, 6). An impressive project in its final form, this carefully shaped lyric anthology collects 187 poems, 146 by the author and forty-one by distinguished male correspondents, among them Benedetto Varchi, il Lasca, Agnolo Bronzino, and Benvenuto Cellini. Her "second book," forecast in the title of the first, appeared at the same press in 1564, *I sette salmi penitentiali del santissimo profeta*

2. Agnolo Bronzino, *Laura Battiferra*, ca. 1561. Detail of book open to two sonnets by Petrarch. Photograph: Soprintendenza per i Beni Artistici e Storici, Gabinetto Fotografico, Florence.

Davit. Tradotti in lingua Toscana da Madonna Laura Battiferra Degli Ammannati. Con gli argomenti sopra ciascuno di essi, composti dalla medesima: insieme con alcuni suoi sonetti spirituali (Seven Penitential Psalms of the Prophet David, Translated into the Tuscan Language by Laura Battiferra degli Ammannati, with Considerations on Their Subject by the Same Lady, Together with Some of Her Spiritual Sonnets). Its subject matter reflects the new, more somber religious climate of the Catholic Reformation, which had drawn churchmen from all Europe to discuss, draft, and publish stringent guidelines for the community of the faithful at the Council of Trent (1545–63). Had she lived to see it through, Battiferra would have published a third book. Entitled simply *Rime*, it survives in a late-sixteenth-century manuscript left incomplete at her death and recently rediscovered at the Casanatense Library in Rome (figs. 7, 8).[3] Conceived as a compendium of her life's work, the *Rime* was intended to reprint everything from her first two books and all she had written after (chap. 1)—except for some of her poetry as preserved in collections published by

3. Rome, Biblioteca Casanatense, MS 3229, Laura Battiferra degli Ammannati, *Rime*. I announced my discovery of this manuscript in "Laura Battiferra's 'First Book' of Poetry: A Renaissance Holograph Comes out of Hiding," *Rinascimento* 35 (1996): 351–91. See below for its history.

3. Alessandro Allori, *Christ and the Canaanite Woman,* oil on canvas glued to wood, ca. 1590. Florence, San Giovannino degli Scolopi, Ammannati funeral chapel. Photo: Soprintendenza per i Beni Artistici e Storici, Gabinetto Fotografico, Florence.

others (chap. 2). The *Rime* includes a hidden trove of close to one hundred pieces that express her intensifying religious sentiments during the 1570s and 1580s, when both Ammannati became generous patrons of the Jesuits. To the same late period belongs her one known prose composition, the "Orison on the Nativity of Our Lord," an impassioned meditation on the Christmas manger scene inspired by the *Spiritual Exercises* of Saint Ignatius Loyola (chap. 3). The few extant letters by Battiferra (only eighteen) and a surviving handful sent to her are sad remnants of what must have been a voluminous correspondence with the same eminent personalities who figure as recipients and dedicatees of her poetry (chap. 4; figs. 9, 10). In all, Laura Battiferra degli Ammannati can be credited with a corpus of nearly five hun-

4. Alessandro Allori, *Christ and the Canaanite Woman,* ca. 1590. Detail with portraits of Bartolomeo Ammannati as Saint Bartholomew (standing with crook) and Laura Battiferra (kneeling with book at right). Florence, San Giovannino degli Scolopi. Photo: Soprintendenza per i Beni Artistici e Storici, Gabinetto Fotografico, Florence.

dred fifty Italian poems, including more than one hundred from correspondents in sonnet exchanges.

Although samples of Battiferra's elegant, fluid prose survive in her letters and her "Orison on the Nativity of Our Lord," her forte is lyric poetry, above all the sonnet. An anecdote recorded by Lodovico Domenichi in 1564 memorializes her authority in that quintessential Petrarchan form:

> Madonna Laura Battiferra, a lady most virtuous and of most excellent intellect and endowed with judiciousness, whom I always refer to everywhere with protestations of honor and reverence, when once

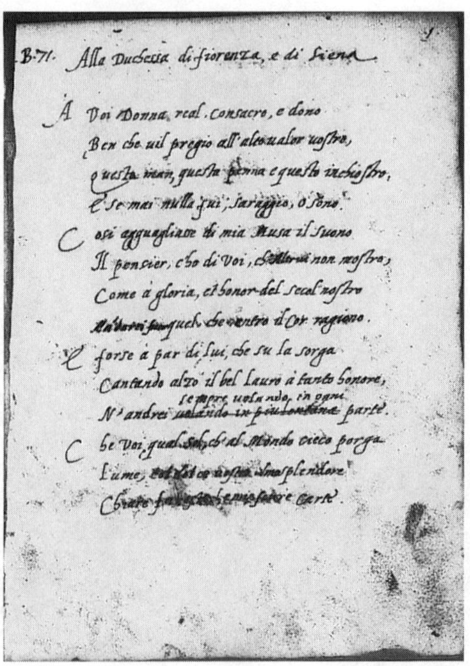

B.71. Alla Duchessa di Fiorenza, e di Siena

A Voi Donna real consacro, e dono
Ben che uil pregio all'alto ualor uostro,
Questa man, questa penna e questo inchiostro,
E se mai nulla fui, saraggio, o sono.
Cosi agguagliasse di mia Musa il suono
Il pensier, che di Voi, [illegible] non mostro,
Come a gloria, et honor del secol nostro
[illegible] quel che dentro il Cor ragiono.
E forse a par di lui, che su la Sorga
Cantando alzo il bel Lauro a tanto honore,
N'andrei sempre uolando, in ogni parte.
Se Voi, qual Sol, ch'al Mondo cieco porga
Lume, [illegible] splendore
Chiare [illegible] carte.

5. Laura Battiferra degli Ammannati, *Primo libro dell'opere toscane,* autograph. Florence, Biblioteca Nazionale, MS Magl. 7.778, fol. 1r, sonnet to Eleonora de Toledo, Duchess of Florence and Siena (1.1), retouched with erasures (where words are smudged) and strike-through corrections. Photo: Biblioteca Nazionale, Florence.

asked her opinion concerning certain sonnets, which were thoroughly clumsy and full of swollen words, answered that they were like lovely, tall cypress trees, but what she did not say was that there was no fruit in them, just as in those sonnets there was no substance.[4]

In formal terms, the two parts of the Italian sonnet (an octave consisting of two quatrains and a sestet consisting of two tercets) can be compared to a syllogism. Typically the octave lays out the premises, the sestet, the conclusion. Its ideal syntax is a single sentence, a taut and difficult standard that Battiferra is well capable of reaching in her mature poetry. Sonnets attributable with certainty to her youth, such as those on the death of her first husband, tend to be choppier, more fragmented, separating into their four parts (1.106). Her best work establishes a momentum in the dictum that over-

4. Lodovico, Domenichi, *Historia varia di M. Lodovico Domenichi* (Venice: Gabriel Giolito de' Ferrari, 1564), 829.

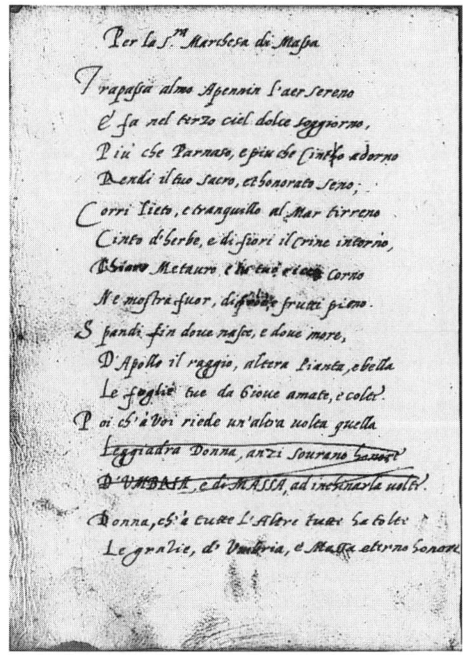

Per la S.ra Marchesa di Massa

Trapassa almo Apennin l'aer sereno
E fa nel terzo ciel dolce soggiorno,
Più che Parnaso, e più che Cintho adorno
Rendi il tuo sacro, et honorato seno;
Corri lieto, e tranquillo al Mar tirreno
Cinto d'herbe, e di fiori il crine intorno,
[illegible] Metauro [illegible] Corno
Ne mostra fuor, di [illegible] frutti pieno.
Spandi fin doue nasce, e doue more,
D'Apollo il raggio, altera Pianta, e bella
Le foglie tue da Gioue amate, e colte.
Poi ch'à Voi riede un'altra uolta quella
~~Leggiadra Donna, anzi Sourano honore~~
~~D'VMBRIA~~, e di MASSA, ad inchinarla uolte.
Donna, ch'à tutte l'Altre tutte ha tolte
Le gratie, d'Vmbria, e Massa eterno honore

6. Laura Battiferra degli Ammannati, *Primo libro dell'opere toscane,* Autograph. Florence, Biblioteca Nazionale, MS Magl. 7.778, fol. 33v, sonnet to the marquise of Massa, Elisabetta Della Rovere (1.37), retouched with erasures and strike-through corrections. Photo: Biblioteca Nazionale, Florence.

comes formal divisions and drives the thought to its logical end, as if all in a single breath. Often the end reserves a surprise, a witty punch line. It may, for example, reveal an unexpected speaker—an angel from heaven (1.6), the Tiber River (1.13), Jove (1.18), all the best poets (1.27). It may rise to a rhetorical climax, as does her sonnet to Vincenzo Grotti about the Duchess of Camerino's country gatherings, a syntactic tour de force topped with a pun on the name of the woman Cibo ("food") who inspires her circle with spiritual nourishment (1.45). The same unified rising dynamic structures her finest madrigals (1.61), a variant form she often uses to mark closure in a microsequence of sonnets (1.32).

Battiferra proves herself in other Petrarchan forms as well. She composed a number of madrigals, one *sestina* (1.48), and two *canzoni* (2.20).[5] *Terza rima,* powerfully authorized by Dante's *Comedy* and Petrarch's *Triumphs,* provides her a vehicle for "Orazione di Geremia profeta" (Jeremiah's Lament) in

5. She seems not to have written in the ballad form.

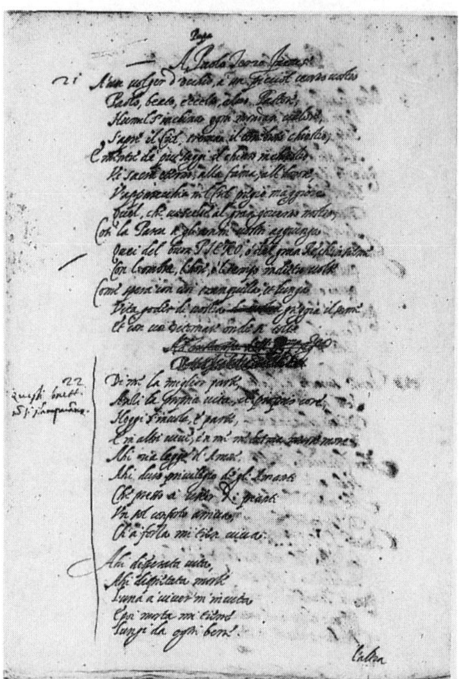

7. Rome, Biblioteca Casanatense, MS 3229, *Rime di Madonna Laura Battiferra degli Ammannati,* fol. 8v: Sonnet to Pope Paul III at top (1.20) and below, obliterated rubric to Isabella de' Medici, with autograph marginal note from Laura to typographer, "These sonnets are not to be printed" (1.21). Photo: Biblioteca Casanatense, Rome.

her *Primo libro* and the "Letter from Lentulus" in her *Rime* (1, pt. 2.24). Significantly, the *Primo libro,* which also includes an eclogue, allows no unpetrarchan forms, and neither does her second, since Petrarch had also composed a version of the seven Penitential Psalms. Her third and final anthology admits of more variety, however, attesting to her mature assertion of independence and her interest in metrical experimentation. She chooses *ottava rima* [the octave] for her "Stanzas on the Faith and Obedience of Abraham" (1.25) and for her untitled fragmentary epic on the biblical story of Samuel (1.26). The lighter lyric form of the *canzonetta* (1, pt. 2.25, 1, pt. 2.26) clearly also appealed to her, perhaps from Bernardo Tasso, a favored poet of hers who had used it in his *Amori* of 1555 (1.21, 40). Tasso, the most talented exponent of a tradition that sought to recover classical Latin forms and adapt them to *Petrarchismo,* was an important model for "verso sciolto" (free verse) as well, a medium that had been practiced and theorized by Gian Giorgio Trissino earlier in the sixteenth century. Ideal for narrative, lacking the constraints of rhyme and metrical stanzas, it lent itself to translation (Battiferra

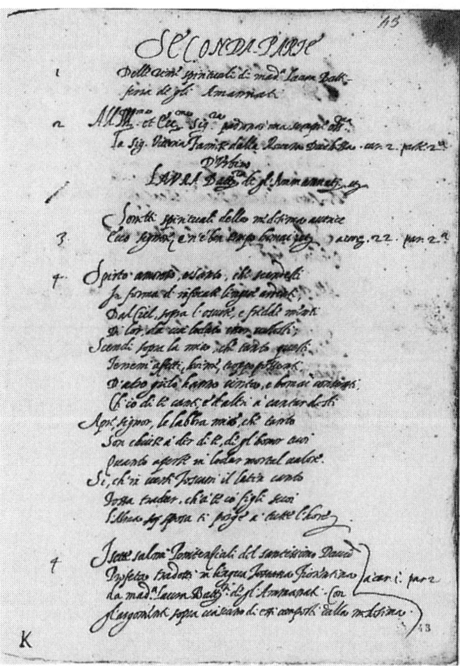

8. Rome, Biblioteca Casanatense, MS 3229, *Rime di Madonna Laura Battiferra degli Ammannati,* fol. 43r: Beginning of the K signature and "Seconda parte delle *Rime spirituali* di Madonna Laura Battiferra degli Ammannati" (1, pt. 2.2). Photo: Biblioteca Casanatense, Rome.

used it in *I sette salmi penitentiali*) and forms in dialogue like the eclogue (1.120). Comparable to Latin hexameter in its capacity for unimpeded narrative flow, free verse appealed to sixteenth-century poets as a "classical" form, like the *canzonetta,* which after the fashion of the Horatian ode mixed long and short verses, rhyme and blank verse. Battiferra's metrical departures from Petrarch are eclecticism that reflects her classicism.[6]

Her work falls into two periods. Petrarchism as an expression of mannerism, steeped in Renaissance classicism, characterizes her earlier years, from the late 1540s to 1560, when she published her *Primo libro.* Personified river gods take the place of city names; her dukes Cosimo and Guidobaldo are new Joves; Cosimo's Roman son-in-law Paolo Giordano Orsini is a new "Quirinus" (Romulus); Chiappino Vitelli is Hercules, Hector, Ulysses, and Scipio, whose praises even Homer and Virgil would have been hard put to sing. The poet's *I sette salmi penitentiali* of 1564 exemplifies a spiritualized *Pe-*

6. Francesco Bausi and Mario Martelli, *La metrica italiana: Teoria e storia* (Florence: Le Lettere, 1993), 147–58, discusses the evolution of Italian metrical forms in the sixteenth century.

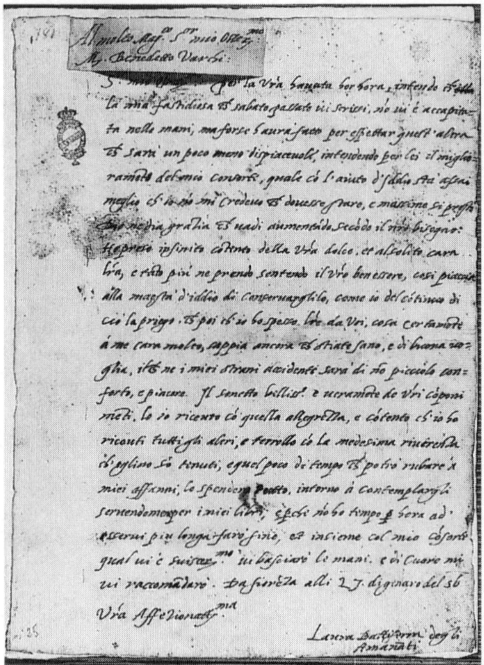

9. Autograph letter from Laura Battiferra degli Ammannati to Benedetto Varchi of January 27, 1556 [=1557 modern style]. Florence, Biblioteca Nazionale, Fondo Autografi Palatini 1, 18 (4.1). Photo: Biblioteca Nazionale, Florence.

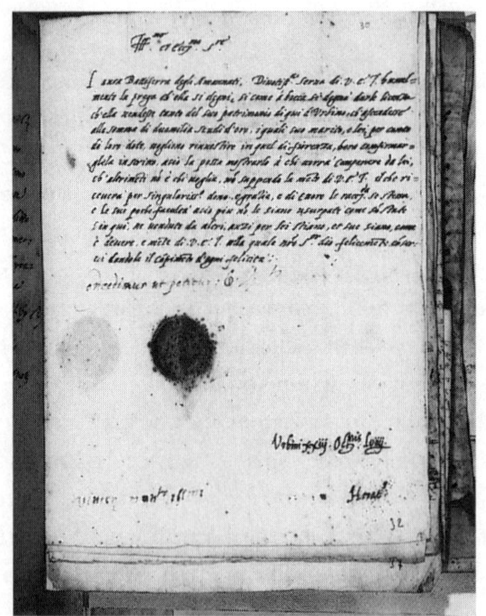

10. Autograph letter from Laura Battiferra to Duke Guidobaldo II Della Rovere with acknowledgment dated Urbino, October 23, 1559. Photo: Archivio di Stato, Florence.

trarchismo that leads as a transition into her later period, roughly the last two decades of her life, when her emphasis shifts from profane to sacred under new post-Tridentine esthetic ideals. The elevated Petrarchan lexicon descends to a more humble Gospel register. The Society of Jesus labors in Christ's "vineyard"; their Father General Claudio Acquaviva flows as a font of "living waters." Now she puts her hand to narrative verse in *ottava rima,* telling the story of Abraham and Isaac (1, pt. 2.25). Now she sets out to compose a religious epic (1, pt. 2.26). Going by the structure of her final anthology, that heroic poem based on the biblical account of Samuel was her last project.[7] Laura Battiferra's two periods define her evolution as an artist—from Medici partisan to Jesuit patron, from a young woman in quest of public celebrity to an older matron who wrapped herself in the quietude of prayer, from a student of the classics and follower of Petrarch, to biblical scholar and a mirror of the Catholic Reformation.

HER LIFE: "HONOR OF URBINO"

Laura Battiferra was the younger of two illegitimate children, and the only daughter, born to Giovan'Antonio Battiferri, an upper-crust prelate from Urbino whose talents propelled him to the Papal court. Her mother, his concubine Maddalena Coccapani of Carpi, bears a surname that signals blood origins in a family of privilege and culture. The day and month of Battiferra's birth lie hidden in an introspective sonnet that she composed on her twenty-ninth birthday (1, pt. 2.17). Perhaps while praying before a religious image of him, Laura invokes the martyred apostle Andrew, who passed through heaven's gates on the same day that she entered the world. If we can take her lyric literally, as Petrarchism in the service of an autobiographical moment, she was born on Saint Andrew's Day, November 30. Since the widower Ammannati made arrangements for her funeral in early November 1589, and she was then sixty-six according to their tomb inscription, she had been born in the year 1523 and was just short of sixty-seven at her passing.[8]

7. Whether because illness stopped her or, as seems more likely, because her Jesuit scribe was called away from Florence to preach a Lenten cycle of sermons elsewhere, the manuscript that was to have served the printer for Madonna Laura's *Rime* breaks off in midpage, after only the first eighteen stanzas of the untitled epic. See Pietro Pirri, S.J., "L'architetto Bartolomeo Ammannati e i Gesuiti," *Archivum Historicum Societatis Iesu* 12 (1943): 5–57, for Ammannati's correspondence with Claudio Acquaviva and his plea for a Jesuit to complete the manuscript of Madonna Laura's *Rime.*

8. See below in this introduction and Victoria Kirkham, "Laura Battiferra degli Ammannati benefattrice dei Gesuiti fiorentini," in Sara F. Matthews Grieco and Gabriella Zarri, eds., *Committenza artistica femminile, Quaderni storici* 104(2) (2000): 331–54, for the epitaph and the Ammannati funeral chapel. Guido Zaccagnini first recognized that the sonnet "Servo fedel, che in alta

11. Urbino, Via Maia, no. 6, Home of Laura's great-grandfather, the physician Jacopo Battiferro. Photograph by the author.

By all accounts, Urbino was her native city. With ancestral origins in the small town of Mercatello on the Metauro River, Laura's great-grandfather Jacopo Battiferro (see app. B for the family genealogy) joined a fifteenth-century demographic shift to larger population centers when he purchased a home there in 1462. Still standing at the heart of the city, among tall medieval dwellings tightly clustered on the narrow Via Maia, that gray stone domicile bears an identifying inscription over the portal, DOMUS LAURAE BATTIFERRI (fig. 11). Jacopo had been able to buy this stately townhouse with "ample riches" accumulated during his career as a teacher and practitioner of medicine in Venice, Ragusa (on the Dalmatian coast), Crete, Corfu, and Rome. So eminent did he become that his list of patients counted Duke Federico da Montefeltro, who spoke of his doctor as "an able man whom I hold in great affection."[9]

croce affisso" holds the clue to Battiferra's birthday (Zaccagnini, "Lirici urbinati del secolo XVI," *Le Marche* 3 [1903]: 87–114).

9. The inscription that identifies the house may have been carved in the eighteenth century at the initiative of a local antiquarian, perhaps Father Vernaccia. Battiferra probably lived as a girl in the house her father owned in the nearby Via del Pozzo Nuovo (see below, notes 13 and 18, 19). Filippo Ugolini, *Storia dei conti e duchi d'Urbino* (Florence: Grazzini e Giannini, 1859), 308–10, reports the letter from Federigo da Montefeltro to "maestro Battiferro." See also June Osborne, *Urbino: The Story of a Renaissance City* (Chicago: University of Chicago Press, 2003), 64, which tells how this physician saved the duke's sight and was paid the handsome sum of 150 ducats for that. The classic scholarly English history of Urbino, its territories, rulers, and culture remains James Dennistoun, *Memoirs of the Dukes of Urbino* (London: Longman, Brown,

Henceforth the Battiferri would be close to the Urbino court. Social status in the city's intellectual aristocracy allowed them to possess a coat of arms, a hand on a blue field among red flames, the heraldic equivalent of their name "iron pounder," from a more humble ancestor's toils.[10] Jacopo's elder son Matteo Battiferro emulated his father, becoming a doctor of liberal arts and a physician. In 1488 he published a milestone in the history of medicine, the first edition of Albertus Magnus's commentary on Aristotle's *Physics*, dedicated to his father. A versatile individual, Laura's great-uncle also put his hand to poetry, writing in a mode consonant with his Catholicism. He appears, posthumously anthologized, among the contributors to *Tesauro spirituale vulgare in rima* (A Spiritual Treasury of Vernacular Verse), published at Venice in 1524.[11]

Matteo had a younger sibling, Francesco, through whom the family line continued, prominent in Urbino's professional class. Francesco's son Marcantonio served Duke Guidobaldo II as a secretary and administrative judge; when entertainments were called for, he could perform in the gentlemanly capacity of amateur actor in court plays.[12] One daughter married the physician Girolamo Virgili, a brother of the famous scholar Polydoro Virgili, and another was the wife of "the most celebrated" Guido Maschi, a doctor of civil and canon law. Alongside these legitimate children, Francesco raised in

---

Green, and Longmans, 1851). Cecil H. Clough, *The Duchy of Urbino in the Renaissance* (London: Variorum Reprints, 1981), has contributed much additional information, especially on the period of Federigo da Montefeltro. A document of June 8, 1462, in the Urbino archives attests to the fair value of the house Jacopo purchased as determined by witnesses whom both the sellers and buyer had chosen when it was transferred for 110 Bolognese florins to "*Magister* Battiferro, distinguished doctor in arts and medicine" (SASU, Fondo Notarile, Not. Simone d'Antonio Vanni, fol. 53r). Two of Jacopo's wills survive in the Urbino archives, both drafted by the notary Simone di Antonio. The first was dictated on November 1, 1465. The second, dated March 13, 1468, contains a notation that he died three days later.

10. For the coat of arms, see *Indice biografico italiano*, fiche 121, col. 240. The family is now extinct.

11. *Tesauro spirituale vulgare in rima* (Venice: Niccolò Zoppino and Vincenzio Compagno, 1524). On Matteo's life, see Paola Zambelli, "Battiferri, Matteo," in *Dizionario biografico degli Italiani* (Rome: Istituto dell'Enciclopedia Italiana, 1960–), 7: 245–46 (but see my app. B for his place in the family tree—he seems to have been Laura's great-uncle, not her grandfather); also Lazzari in Giuseppe Colucci, *Delle Antichità picene dell'Abate Giuseppe Colucci Patrizio camerinese ed ascolano*, 30 vols. (Fermo: dai torchi dell'autore per G. A. Paccaroni, 1786–96), 26: 137. In the copy of his edition of Albertus Magnus on Aristotle's *Physics* owned by the Philadelphia College of Physicians, the colophon reads, "Explicit commentum Doctoris excellentissimi Alberti Magni ordinis praedicatorum in libros physicorum. Impressum Venetiis per Joannem de Forlivio et Gregorii fratres. Anno domini mccccIxxxviij die viij Januarij."

12. Franco Piperno, *L'immagine del duca: Musica e spettacolo alla corte di Guidubaldo II duca d'Urbino* (Florence: Leo S. Olschki, 2001), 32, 48, and 266, mentions Marcantonio's activity as a gentleman of Guidobaldo's court.

his household Cassandra Battiferra, "claiming her as his daughter."[13] Possibly his natural child, she lived out her adult life as a nun at Santa Lucia. Laura must have been fond of this woman, her aunt, to whom she dedicated one of her penitential psalms and whom she remembers with a bequest in all of her wills (app. A). On visits back to Urbino, perhaps she walked up to the northwest end of the city to visit Cassandra at her convent, society's repository for so many girls of good families who grew old and died within its walls. Their ghosts linger at the Santa Lucia gate, whose name preserves memory of the cloister, long since gone.

Giovan'Antonio Battiferro, Laura's father, left a more restless, complicated trail than either Matteo or Francesco. Plausibly the illegitimate son of Jacopo's natural daughter Antonia, he would himself produce three illegitimate children—two by Maddalena Coccapani and a third named Giulio, born of a different unwed woman (app. B).[14] Like his uncle Matteo, Giovan'Antonio became a cleric at Rome. There he lived on multiple income-rich preferments and ecclesiastical benefices as a scriptor of briefs in the *Camera Apostolica,* the nerve center that handled Vatican finances and foreign affairs. Biographers remember him for his impressive education—perhaps a university background in canon law, but certainly knowledge of both Greek and Latin.[15] Patronized by the Medici cardinal who later became Pope Clement VII (1523–34) and a "familiar" of Paul III (1534–49), sometime before 1520 Giovan'Antonio Battiferro built a house in the nearby neighborhood of the Borgo. It must have been an eye-catching structure, to judge from the tantalizing glimpse in Vasari's 1568 *Lives of the Artists.* As was the custom of the day for well-to-do homeowners, he had its facade decorated with paintings.

13. Francesco's will of August 30, 1536, contains crucial information for the reconstruction of the family tree. See the copy in Urbino, Biblioteca Universitaria, busta 4, fasc. 4, "Posizione dell'Eredità di Francesco Battiferri." Cf. Luigi Moranti, *Urbino,* in *Inventari dei manoscritti delle Biblioteche d'Italia,* vol. 80 (Florence: Olschki, 1954), 69. A partial genealogical chart and the biographical sketches compiled in the eighteenth century by father Pier Girolamo Vernaccia, *Elogio degli uomini illustri d'Urbino,* Fondo Comune, vol. 59 (Urbino: Biblioteca Universitaria, 1720), a local prelate steeped in archival lore on Urbino's leading families, are also important though not entirely reliable sources.

14. Information that can be deduced from family wills leaves some of the relationships unclear. Vernaccia's family tree makes Giovan'Antonio the son of Matteo. I thank Don Franco Negroni for suggesting that this is an error and that the Antonia mentioned in Francesco's will was the mother of Giovan'Antonio by an unknown father.

15. Antonio Lazzari, *Dizionario storico degli uomini illustri di Urbino,* in Colucci, *Delle Antichità picene,* 26: 159–60: "He was a Count Palatine and Apostolic Protonotary. From Archpriest of Barberano in the Diocese of Viterbo, where he stayed for seven years, he passed to the dignity of Provost of Fossombrone. He lived in the Roman court, where he was held in high esteem for his great learning. Cardinal Giulio de' Medici, who was extremely fond of him, accorded him the broadest privileges for creating honorary Apostolic Protonotaries, bestowing doctorates, and legitimizing bastards." Lazzari draws closely on Vernaccia's *Elogio* 59: fol. 229v.

For their design he turned to a personal friend, his compatriot Raphael. Executed by Raphael's follower, Vincenzo da San Gimignano, they display dynastic power with a mythological program allusive to the surname Battiferri:

> Because of [Giovan'Antonio's] close friendship with Raphael, he got from him the design for that facade, and he got through his mediation at the Vatican Court many benefices and a huge income ("grosse entrate"). Now in this design, which was then carried out by Vincenzo, Raphael, by way of allusion to the Battiferri lineage, put the Cyclops, who are forging lightning bolts for Jove; and in another part, Vulcan, who is turning out arrows for Cupid; along with some very beautiful nudes and other stories and very beautiful statues.[16]

Later, probably after the 1527 Sack of Rome, Giovan'Antonio would acquire a dwelling "at the Portuguese Arch" in the city's Campo Marzio district, held on emphyteutic (long-term) lease from his confreres, the Chaplains in the Chapel of Innocent VIII at Saint Peter's Cathedral.[17] An inventory of real estate assets at his death, which come to the imposing sum of 8,650 scudi, itemizes income-bearing farm properties near Rome as well as Urbino, and in the latter city, his single most valuable holding, "a large house with two little houses adjacent, one with the stable and the other with the oven," worth 1,800 scudi.[18]

Laura Battiferra's mother emerges from anonymity in notarial papers

16. Giorgio Vasari, *Le vite dei più eccellenti pittori, scultori e architetti,* ed. Licia Ragghianti and Carlo L. Ragghianti, 4 vols. (Milan: Rizzoli, 1971–78), 3: 12.

17. The Portuguese Arch, which no longer exists, was built in the time of the emperor Hadrian on ruins of the *Ara Pacis Augustae.* In the Renaissance it acquired the name "Portuguese" from Cardinal George of Portugal, who purchased a Quattrocento palace beside it known today as Palazzo Fiano. A commemorative marker at its former site, on the northeast corner of the Corso at the intersection with Via della Vita, announces that it was destroyed by Pope Alexander VII in 1665 to straighten the street so carriages could pass more quickly. At the time of that urge to urban renewal, some of the surrounding houses were also razed, perhaps including the Battiferri residence. Its exact location remains unknown. For Cinquecento illustrations of what the Portuguese Arch looked like, see Phyllis Pray Bober and Ruth Rubinstein, *Renaissance Artists and Antique Sculpture: A Handbook of Sources* (London: H. Miller; Oxford: Oxford University Press, 1986), frontispiece and 228.

18. ASF, Comp. Soppr. da Leopoldo, *filza* 238, fol. 61r: "una casa grande e con doi casette aderentj dove in una è la stalla, nell'altra è il forno." See Victoria Kirkham, "Laura Battiferra degli Ammannati benefattrice dei Gesuiti fiorentini," 332–37, and "Creative Partners: The Marriage of Laura Battiferra and Bartolomeo Ammannati," *Renaissance Quarterly,* 55 (2002): 498–502, for further information and documentation on Giovan'Antonio Battiferro. This may have been the house in Via del Pozzo Nuovo ("Contrata Putej Novj") mentioned in documents describing Giovan'Antonio's business transactions in Urbino. See, e.g., SASU, Fondo Notarile, not. Felice Guiducci, vol. 773 (1538–43), fol. 556r.

associated with this valuable Urbino townhouse, which Giovan'Antonio had rented from the local bishop and intended to pass on to his children. Rental renewal agreements of 1533 and 1540 name them, Ascanio and Laura, identifying their mother as "Maddalena Coccapani of Carpi."[19] A family of intellectuals like the Battiferri, the Coccapani had settled by the Quattrocento in Carpi, a satellite town near Modena in territory controlled by the Este dukes of Ferrara. Brief biographies of several who would have been Laura's contemporaries survive in the encyclopedia by Modena's eighteenth-century polymath Girolamo Tiraboschi. Giulio Cesare Coccapani composed sonnets, translated the Penitential Psalms, and served as *podestà* toward 1560 in the Tuscan town of Lucca, where he was close to the widowed poet Chiara Matraini. Another contemporary, Camillo, nicknamed "Poetino" for his commentaries on Aristotle's *Poetics* and Horace's *Poetic Art,* became a professor at Modena, corresponded with Torquato Tasso, and taught the poetess Tarquinia Molza.[20] How Maddalena fit into the Coccapani family tree is not known. She floats unanchored to any blood relatives except the two children that she bore in concubinage to the cleric Giovan'Antonio Battiferri.

Laura's older brother Ascanio is repeatedly cited in family documents, first with all the privileges of a beloved son and then, in bitterness, as the family outcast. Giovan'Antonio would eventually disown this black sheep, transferring all his worldly goods to Laura, whose inheritance made her a wealthy woman. Accused in the father's will of "notorious machinations," Ascanio had become entangled with a fallen woman ("una donna poco honesta") in Rome and secretly tried to sell the house at the Arco di Portogallo, causing a legal nightmare that dogged Laura and Bartolomeo Ammannati well into old age, as late as the 1580s. From Urbino, Ascanio pursued his sister for years with legal maneuvering in an effort to claim control of family property and extricate himself from debts with Jewish money lenders.[21] Al-

19. ASF, Comp. Soppr. da Leopoldo, *filza* 238, fols. 155r–156r and 170r on the rental renewals of 1533 and 1540 with Maddalena Coccapani's name and references to Giovan'Antonio as the children's tutor (*preceptor*). This seems to be a different property from the house purchased by Jacopo Battiferri in 1462 in the Via Maia.

20. For the Coccapani family of Carpi, see Girolamo Tiraboschi, *Biblioteca Modenese,* 6 vols. (Modena: Società Tipografica, 1781–86), 1: 40–53. A note on their ancient origins appears in the *Indice biografico,* s.v. "Coccapani."

21. Giovan'Antonio Battiferro's will, dictated on his deathbed in the house at the Portuguese Arch, survives in the ASF, Comp. Soppr. da Leopoldo, *filza* 238, fols. 48r–49v. See Kirkham, "Laura Battiferra degli Ammannati benefattrice dei Gesuiti fiorentini," 334–38, for a reconstruction of Ascanio's "machinations." Documentation in Ammannati-Battiferri papers at the Florentine archives records their struggle over decades to assert a rightful claim after Ascanio clandestinely sold the family house to pay off the father of a shady lady with whom he had be-

though Laura's poems express great sorrow at the death of her husband in a brief first marriage (1.106–14), love for her Florentine husband of nearly forty years (1.39, 46–47, 90–91, 120), and grief at her father's death in 1561 (2.7–8), never once in all her writings does she refer to Ascanio, her brother-german, or to her mother, Maddalena. Neither does she leave any public hint of her younger half-sibling, Giulio, known only from his fleeting mention in the document of all three children's legitimation, a papal brief from Paul III of February 9, 1543.[22]

The education for which contemporaries admired Battiferra came initially from her father, a humanist secretary at the Vatican court. Her beautiful Italian chancery script reflects his influence, and he probably set her to learning such classics as Virgil and Ovid, who left visible traces in her vernacular poetry. Whatever the precise outlines of Laura's lessons from her father, he must have passed on to her more generally a Battiferri tradition of learning in the liberal arts, philosophy, and science. As for her Coccapani relatives, lawyers and literati who distinguished themselves in careers both secular and ecclesiastical and who collectively authored a good many books, some of which made their way out into the world in the perambulatory form of print, whether or not she had contact with them, they obviously contributed by heredity to Laura's gift for poetry.

Her earliest small body of verse are nine sonnets, never published, to the departed soul of "Vittorio," who has left her after a short marriage to grieve in widow's weeds (1.106–14). The husband she mourns, now happily sheltered in the "blessed life," was the organist Vittorio Sereni of Bologna, "musician and familiar" of Guidobaldo II Della Rovere.[23] This marriage must have taken place sometime after February 9, 1543, when the document of

---

came entangled. See ASF, Comp. Soppr. da Leopoldo, *filza* 238, fols. 293r and 314r. Laura, who inherited the house from her father, continued to maintain it and pay out rent of 35 scudi annually for it until her death. Over the years, Ammannati seems to have stayed there when he was in Rome on business. Various documents in the Urbino archives record Ascanio's involvements with Jewish moneylenders, e.g., SASU, Fondo Notarile, Not. Sebastiano Vannucci, vol. 1141 (1561–78), fol. 16v, for the year 1561; and vol. 1129 (1560–66), fols. 55r–54v, for the year 1562.

22. The brief is preserved in ASF, Comp. Soppr. da Leopoldo, *filza* 238, fols. 7r–8r. Curiously, among the miscellaneous manuscripts with poetry by Battiferra, in the Biblioteca Nazionale in Florence there is one (MS Magl. 7.380) with an inscription that names as successive owners Giulio and Ascanio: "Contuis Ascanius possidet nunc quippe libellum; possedit quem olim Iulius ipse diu" [(?)'Ascanio owns this book—now anyway—which Julius himself once owned for a long time']. Perhaps it was once in the family library.

23. Guidobaldo's enthusiasm for keyboard music motivated much of his patronage, documented in the rich study by Franco Piperno, *L'immagine del duca,* which does not mention Vittorio Sereni degli Organi.

her legitimation still refers to Laura by maiden name. Battiferra's sonnets of sorrow and Sereni's will, dictated on his deathbed on January 25, 1549, concur in their picture of a loving union, too soon cut short. The testator splits a modest estate of 300 scudi equally between his wife and brother, Altobello degli Organi, further specifying that she is to have several pieces of gold jewelry he has acquired and as much of the dowry as his father-in-law has thus far paid on account:

> Since he knows that he owes a great deal to his wife who was always—and still is—docile, obedient, benevolent, dear, faithful, and loving toward him, recognizing her faithfulness and servitude, he leaves, gives, and bequeaths to her this gold jewelry, provided she be still living, which jewelry he does not wish to be counted in any way as part of his wife's dowry. . . Similarly, by the law of restitution, he leaves to said lady Laura, his wife, 900–1,000 gold scudi . . . which he had in the computation of her dowry from lord Giovan'Antonio Battiferri of Urbino, and as part of the 1,500 scudi promised him by the same Giovan'Antonio for the dowry of his lady.[24]

Unfortunately, Altobello refused to relinquish the dowry money that should have reverted to Laura for her second marriage, precipitating legal problems that dragged on for years. Notarial documents, a sonnet (1.10), and autograph letters by Battiferra (4.2–3) chronicle the long battle for restitution.[25]

The lives of Battiferra and Bartolomeo Ammannati, her second husband, may have first intersected in Urbino in the late 1530s or early 1540s, before her marriage to Sereni. The Tuscan sculptor was then employed by Duke Guidobaldo II Della Rovere for work at the Villa Imperiale in nearby Pesaro and in Urbino to assist on a tombstone for Guidobaldo's father.[26]

24. For Vittorio Sereni's will of January 25, 1549, see ASF, Comp. Soppr. da Leopoldo, *filza* 238, fol. 10r. A legal document of May 1561, prepared in Bologna in connection with the money still owing Battiferra from Altobello for her dowry (ASF, Comp. Soppr. da Leopoldo, *filza* 238, fol. 42r) refers to the bequest of her former husband "Victorii de Sirenis alias de Organis eius primi mariti" and names also his brother, Altobello degli Organi.

25. The dowry had initially been set at 1,000 scudi and was to have become 2,000 scudi, at the suggestion of the Duke of Urbino. Evidently, Giovan'Antonio had wanted a compromise of 1,500. ASF, Comp. Soppr. da Leopoldo, *filza* 238, fol. 13r: "pro eius [Laurae] dote dederit et soluerit [Ioannes Antonius] dicto domino Victorio scuta noningenta seu mille auri et ulterius intuitum illustrissimi domini ducis Urbini ultra dicta scuta mille."

26. Ammannati, like his wife, still awaits a comprehensive modern biography. As an older man, around 1580, he left an autograph note with some personal *ricordi* (ASF, Comp. soppr. da Leo-

12. Urbino, Via Maia, no. 14, Portal of the Confraternity of the Dead ("Oratorio della Morte"), attributed to Bartolomeo Ammannati. Just steps away from the Battiferri house, this is the place according to local legend where the poet fell in love with her second husband while he was building the doorway. Photograph by the author.

Local legend has it that their romance began on the Via Maia house doorstep, when around 1538 he was said to have been working on a portal for the Confraternity of the Dead, just around the corner (fig. 12). During the period between the end of her first marriage and the beginning of her second, the twenty-five-year-old widow was for a time placed in a convent for her own protection by the Duke of Urbino. Eventually, her father must have gone to fetch her from Urbino and taken her back to Rome, probably to live in the Campo Marzio house at the Portuguese Arch.[27] As it chanced, Laura's

poldo, *filza* 242, fols. 16r–17r). His contemporaries Vasari and Borghini make mention of him, but the first *vita* of substance did not appear until about a century after his death, in Baldinucci's lives of the artists. In modern times, Fossi has contributed usefully to the subject. See also Belli Barsali and Venturi (but neither is fully reliable). Welcome new information appears in the commemorative anthology by Niccolò Rosselli del Turco and Federica Salvi, eds., *Bartolomeo Ammannati: Scultore e architetto 1511–1592* (Florence: Alinea, 1995). Michael Kiene, *Bartolomeo Ammannati* (Milan: Electa, 1995), also has a helpful overview. On his early activity, the most richly documented studies are those by Charles Davis, "Ammannati, Michelangelo, and the Tomb of Francesco del Nero," *Burlington Magazine,* 118.880 (July 1976): 472–84, and "Four Documents for the Villa Giulia," *Römisches Jahrbuch für Kunstgeschichte* 16 (1978): 219–23. For Urbino, Peter Kinney, *The Early Sculpture of Bartolomeo Ammannati* (New York: Garland, 1976), chap. 6, is also helpful.

27. Laura Battiferra, *Il primo libro delle opere toscane,* ed. Enrico Maria Guidi (Urbino: Accademia Raffaello, 2000), 10, n. 13. Laura, however, presumably had lived in the Via del Pozzo Nuovo

widowhood coincided with the period of Ammannati's professional debut in Rome. There, whether as old friends or recent acquaintances, they came together through mutual connections in Vatican circles.

By April 1550, the twenty-six-year-old Laura was already remarried to Bartolomeo, a match that seems to have been made in heaven but was surely brokered by her worldly father. By a small miracle of history, there survives an eyewitness account of the ceremony, which took place at one of the most venerated pilgrimage shrines in all Christendom, the *Casa Santa* in Loreto.[28] Laura's interest in the "Holy House" of Mary's Annunciation is quite in keeping with her paternal heritage and her pious personality. From childhood she was steeped in the culture of Catholic Rome, a background that was to prepare her for translating into Italian the Penitential Psalms (1, pt. 2.3), for composing dozens of spiritual sonnets (1, pt. 2), and for her charities late in life as a Jesuit patron. The intensity of her religious emotions vibrates most stunningly in her "Orison on the Nativity of Our Lord," a meditation on the Christmas crèche inspired by the *Spiritual Exercises* of Ignatius Loyola (chap. 3). Alessandro Allori's portrait of her in old age, in a panel commissioned by Ammannati for their funeral chapel, depicts a woman who clasps what looks like a small prayer book and kneels devoutly before Christ in the dramatic moment of a Gospel miracle (figs. 3, 4 above).[29] In 1550, approaching her twenty-seventh birthday, she may have had a more private reason for visiting this Marian shrine, where she and Bartolomeo exchanged wed-

---

(see above, notes 9, 18) house before her marriage. After being widowed, she was apparently left without a suitable guardian in Urbino, or even money to eat. See Duke Guidobaldo's letter of concern, written to his mother from Venice on July 20, 1549 (ASF, Ducato di Urbino, *filza* 108, fol. 712). I thank Sabine Eiche for this reference.

28. The marriage took place on April 17, 1550. For an eyewitness account of Battiferra's marriage, signed by the sculptor Girolamo Lombardo, see ASF, Comp. Soppr. da Leopoldo, *filza* 238, fols. 15r–15v; and Kirkham, "Creative Partners," 506–7. This "Holy House" of the Annunciation to Mary was said to have been transported by angels from the Holy Land to an Italian hill of laurels ("Loreto"). On that site, a great sanctuary was built in the fifteenth century to house the small one-room structure (actually carried back to Italy by Crusaders, brick by brick), and in the sixteenth century, many Italian sculptors worked over decades to provide the *Casa* with a richly carved marble encasement. Cloth fragments of the red crosses the Crusaders wore, laid between the bricks in reassembly of the *Casa Santa,* have been rediscovered in recent archeological exploration. On the history of the shrine, see Giuseppe Santarelli, *Loreto Its History and Art* (Bologna: La Fotometalgrafica, 1987), 4–12; *Le Marche,* 4th ed. (Milan: Touring Club Italiano, 1979), 414; and for the artists who worked there, Kathleen Weil-Garris, *The Santa Casa di Loreto: Problems in Cinquecento Sculpture,* 2 vols. (New York: Garland, 1977).

29. See Lecchini-Giovannoni, *Alessandro Allori,* for the panel in the Ammannati funeral chapel, fig. 281 and 272–73, entry no. 113.

ding vows at the altar before the marble casing around the *Santa Casa*, just beneath Andrea Sansovino's masterful scene of *The Annunciation*. Her first marriage, which could have lasted as long as five or six years, had been barren. Perhaps she now prayed to the Madonna for a child. If so, her hopes went unanswered.

During their first five years of married life, the Ammannati resided in Rome. Bartolomeo, who won Michelangelo's admiration and the patronage of Julius III (1550–55), solidified his professional status, while Laura took root in the cosmopolitan surroundings she loved. Some of her most beautiful sonnets express her abiding attachment to the Tiber city, its seven hills so richly layered with ancient monuments and Christian history (1.57). Her earliest datable Roman poem, which predates her marriage by a few months, is a get-well sonnet to the aging Pope Paul III (fig. 7 above), for whom she displays her learned familiarity with the Bible (1.20). Judging by other highly placed personages associated with the verse of her Roman period,[30] Battiferra moved in elite circles, thanks to her wealthy father's connections and her husband's growing patronage network, animated by cardinals with ample means to sponsor art. For her professional ambitions, the most important friendship she developed from this period was with Annibal Caro (1.66–68), a personage whom no other papal courtier could rival for wide-reaching contacts in the world of letters. No wonder that when the death of Julius forced Ammannati to seek a new patron in Cosimo de' Medici, Battiferra's poetry expresses consternation at her forced departure from Rome (1.51).

In the summer of 1555, the Ammannati moved to Florence.[31] Laura's sonnets bespeak her wrenching loneliness at the separation from Rome, even after she has begun to connect with a new literary community whose "learned minds" she respects (1.35). Benedetto Varchi (fig. 13), an acquaintance probably made through their mutual friend Annibal Caro, was instrumental in helping establish her in these new surroundings. Letters from her correspondence with Varchi date from February of 1556. In November of 1557, she writes him that Leonora Cibo de' Vitelli (herself a poet) had invited Laura to compose a sonnet in honor of her husband Chiappino (1.28). In December of 1557, enclosing a madrigal by Giovan Battista Strozzi, she

30. See, e.g., Ersilia Cortese de' Monti (1.33); Livia and Ortensia Colonna (1.34–35); Cardinal Francesco Soderini (1.36); and Madonna Eufemia, a Neapolitan lady so excellent in music and song "that she drew in her train all Rome" (1.42).

31. Pope Julius III, Ammannati's patron, died on March 23, 1555. Mazzino Fossi and E. Kasten, *Künstler-Lexikon*, s.v. "Ammannati, Bartolomeo di Antonio," 3: 253–58, place the trip from Rome to Florence in early May.

13. Titian (Tiziano Vecellio), *Benedetto Varchi*. Kunsthistorische Museen, Vienna. Photo: Museum.

happily reports having been informed that a sonnet of hers has been a hit at court, a coup for which she gives Varchi the credit: "I had letters from Signor Chiappino and from Messer Sforza, who say that my sonnet much pleased the court, and I wanted to be sure and write this because it's all thanks to you."[32]

During this same period, Benvenuto Cellini sends Varchi a sonnet that refers approvingly to the latter's protégé. Punning on her first name in good Petrarchan style, he imagines that this new arrival on the scene is a laurel tree, young but with much promise, a "rich plant, although somewhat unripe . . . even now the bark thickens and the trunk strengthens, glory of the fair Arno" (2.24).[33] During the next five years, her comet shone over Italy at its brightest, with sightings reported as far distant as Prague and Madrid. The

32. Which sonnet it was is unclear (1.17). Carlo Gargiolli ed., *Lettere di Laura Battiferri Ammannati a Benedetto Varchi,* Scelta di curiosità letterarie inedite o rare dal secolo XIII al XIX, dispensa 166, 1879. Reprint, Bologna: Commissione per i testi di lingua, 1968, 15–17, no. 2; 40, no. 9.

33. Benvenuto Cellini, *Opere,* ed. Giuseppe Guido Ferrero (Turin: Unione Tipografico-Editrice Torinese, 1971), 905–906.

newly published poetess begins to make cameo appearances in books by others too.[34] By 1560, she had assembled enough poems—and people—to fill her *Primo libro,* an anthology of generous proportions and a stunning social act.

Although Battiferra's poetry had been circulating in manuscript for almost a decade before she published the *Primo libro,* its release dramatically heightened her visibility. Not coincidentally, the year 1560 saw her induction into the prestigious Accademia degli Intronati of Siena, where she took the humorous academic name "la Sgraziata" (the Graceless Woman).[35] Bronzino's *Portrait of Laura Battiferra,* an arresting profile that implies her likeness to the Trecento poets Dante and Petrarch, probably dates from soon after her *Primo libro* and celebrates its publication (figs. 1–2 above).[36] For the first time, she appears anthologized in a volume compiled by another editor, Giovanni Offredi.[37] Her entry, a sonnet addressed to Sleep, pays homage to Giovanni Della Casa, whose exquisitely crafted model she emulates to orient her poetry in elegant precincts (2.1). In 1564, to accompany a reprint of Della Casa's *Rime* prepared by her friend Gherardo Spini, the publisher Filippo Giunti offers Battiferra "a Rhyming Dictionary, drawn from the poems of Monsignor Della Casa, which all judicious intellects so praise and hold in esteem that they should be nothing if not most welcome to you, who in that

34. Linked with Varchi's, her name inaugurates Pietro Calzolari's *Historia monastica* (Florence: Lorenzo Torrentino, 1561); their pair of complimentary sonnets hails his pious initiative (1.63). She participates in the same fashionable ritual of prefatory congratulations to Bernardo Gamucci for his *Le antichità della città di Roma raccolte sotto brevità da diversi antichi et moderni Scrittori* (Venice: Gioliti, 1565), this time as one of a trio with Varchi and Gherardo Spini (2.21). Gamucci's dedicatory letter flatters Cosimo's son Francesco de' Medici, noting how the family's remodeled Pitti Palace in Florence resembles the classic structures of Rome, imitated by the Pitti architect Bartolomeo Ammanati. The architect's wife, in turn, credits Gamucci in her sonnet for descriptions and drawings of the city that make it rise from the ruins more beautiful than before. Gamucci's book enjoyed considerable success, with reprints in 1569, 1580, 1585, and 1588. Battiferra will shape her own last book, *Rime,* so that it begins with just this kind of ceremonial inauguration. She borrows sonnets already sent her by Spini and Don Silvano Razzi for her penitential psalms (where they are the caboose), and she reuses them, together with another by Francesco de' Medici's personal theologian, in order to lend her final anthology at the outset a spiritual imprint of masculine authority (1.I–III).

35. Guido Zaccagnini, "Lirici urbinati," reports Battiferra's academic pseudonym. See also Adolfo Venturi, "Bartolomeo Ammannati," in *Storia dell'arte italiana* (Milan: Hoepli, 1936), vol. 10, pt. 2, "La scultura del Cinquecento," 348–49, which cites a letter from Ammannati in Siena of November 3, 1559, to Cosimo's secretary Bartolomeo Concini, in which he describes his decorations for Cosimo's triumphal entry and his wife's invitation to join the Accademia degli Intronati.

36. See above, introduction note 1.

37. Giovanni Offredi, ed., *Rime di diversi autori eccellentissimi* (Cremona: Vincenzo Conti, 1560).

profession are not only unique among the women of our age, but are held in esteem among the rare men."[38]

Sonnets of congratulation for her *Primo libro* fly to Florence from poets in other cities, who see what luster she sheds not only on her Arno "nest" but on her ancestral city in the Apennines.[39] From the pen of Bernardo Tasso (fig. 14), a worthy poet who would be better remembered today were it not for the brighter light of his son Torquato, comes her euphonious epithet "honor of Urbino." Bernardo, patronized by Duke Guidobaldo II Della Rovere of Urbino, bows to her in his chivalric epic *Amadigi*, a gigantic project published the same year as Laura's *Primo libro* (1560). Its final and one-hundredth canto unfolds as a pageant of famous personages, many of them illustrious ladies. The procession, inspired by Ariosto's homage to women of the day in his *Orlando furioso* (1532),[40] leads off with Catherine de' Medici, queen of France; close behind her parade Isabella of Spain and Marguerite of Savoy. As the line advances, monarchs yield to poets. The divine Vittoria Colonna, just thirteen years deceased, naturally has a place. Tasso's gaze then turns to a troop of male writers, pausing on Annibal Caro, Benedetto Varchi, Lelio Capilupi, and Dionigi Atanagi. With these men, Battiferra's admirers and correspondents, she herself marches, "Laura Battiferra, onor d'Urbino."[41]

Bernardo Tasso's imaginary assembly has its counterpart in real-life col-

38. Cf. 1.58 (from Battiferra's *Rime*) and 2.1 (its variant in Offredi's anthology).

39. Among those who wrote Battiferra from afar was Ludovico Beccadelli of Bologna, the archbishop of Ragusa (Dubrovnik), who participated over many years at the Council of Trent. His copy of the poem he sent survives side by side in a manuscript with a sonnet for Christopher Columbus, among verse he had addressed to such other notables as Della Casa, Titian, and Michelangelo (2.15). From Adriatic shores Malatesta Fiordiano of Rimini (d. ca. 1576) sends accolades to Battiferra in a poem appended to his *La bellezza della donna* (Beauty of Woman). With "divine accents" that "amaze learned minds," he declares, she "illuminates" both herself and her "nest" ("con stup[o]r delle più dotte genti, / hoggi illustri te stessa, e il tuo bel nido"). Fiordiano, who authored a treatise on the nature and quality of fish, published *La bellezza della donna* in Rimini in *ottava rima* in 1562. I thank Allan Grieco and Francesco Sberlati for references to Fiordiano and the latter for his transcription of the poem to Battiferra. Laura Terracina of Naples plies a well-inked quill from her abundant supply—it furnished the world with eight printed volumes of her verse—to salute the lady whose "fame and proud laurel" everywhere spread her name. As was fitting, Battiferra answers from Florence with a *risposta* of modest demurral (2.37–38). Sadness grates upon her heart, she writes, since heaven has hidden "her who was once my prize and worth" (Battiferra's patron, the duchess Eleonora de Toledo, who died of sudden illness in December of 1562). The young poet Curzio Gonzaga of Mantua respectfully invites her to compose a sonnet eulogy on his distinguished kinsman Cardinal Ercole Gonzaga (d. 1563), an admired theologian who had passed away while performing in the stressful role of presiding legate at the Council of Trent (2.17).

40. See cantos 4–5, 27–29, and especially 42–43.

41. *Amadigi*, 100.37. Bernardo Tasso (1493–1569) was well known for his lyric poetry, the *Amadigi*, and his letters, which were considered models of the epistolary genre.

14. *Bernardo Tasso,* frontispiece of *L'Amadigi del S. Bernardo Tasso.* Venice: Gabriel Giolito de' Ferrari, 1560. Photo: Newberry Library, Chicago.

lective projects, whose male organizers marveled at Battiferra as a phenomenal woman and welcomed her as a collaborator.[42] Dionigi Atanagi, a native of Cagli in the Duchy of Urbino who marches with Laura in *Amadigi* and had been lately resident in Venice, invites her to write for his *Rime di diversi nobilissimi et eccellentissimi autori in morte della signora Irene delle signore di Spilimbergo* (Rhymes by Diverse Most Noble and Most Excellent Authors on the Death of Signora Irene of Spilimbergo), culled from across Italy to eulogize a young female prodigy who had studied painting under Titian.[43] After the death of

42. See Victoria Kirkham, "Sappho on the Arno: The Brief Fame of Laura Battiferra," in Pamela Benson and Victoria Kirkham, eds., *Strong Voices, Weak History: Early Women Writers and Canons in England, France, and Italy* (Ann Arbor: University of Michigan Press, 2005), 174–96.

43. By Corsaro's count, Atanagi's tribute to Irene contains 381 poems by 143 named authors, including 102 in Latin. See Antonio Corsaro, "Dionigi Atanagi e la silloge per Irene di Spilimbergo (Intorno alla formazione del giovane Tasso)," *Italica* 75.1 (1998): 45. For a witty (if somewhat withering) description of the anthology, see Anne Jacobson Schutte, "Irene di Spilimbergo: The Image of a Creative Woman in Late Renaissance Italy," *Renaissance Quarterly* 44

Luca Martini (1561), Cosimo's cultured administrator in nearby Pisa, she is one of the fifty-six friends who answer Varchi's call for sonnets of mourning. All but Laura send or receive only one poem, but she stands apart, being the author of three sonnets and recipient of four from Varchi, a measure of her favored status (2.2–6).[44] Unlike much verse in this genre, composed more to join ritualistically the group than to confess true sentiments of personal loss, her sonnet and finely wrought *canzone* on the death in 1564 of Michelangelo, a friend to both Ammannati, resonate movingly with grief. First displayed in the church of San Lorenzo at his funeral, attached to his catafalque as was the custom, they win a permanent place among twenty-two selected verse tributes and epitaphs published to preserve memory of that majestic Florentine ceremony (2.19–20). Varchi's death late in 1565 was another painful blow for Battiferra (1.96), who not only composed sonnets for the commemorative volume of 1566 (the first sonnets in the book are hers), but worked behind the scenes to collect poetry from other contributors, including Annibal Caro and Bernardo Tasso.[45]

Contemporaries canonized her as the new Sappho, beginning with Pietro Calzolari, whose fat *Historia monastica* displays her sonnet of greeting. Calzolari stages the five-day dialogue of a group in Padua gathered to create conversationally a gallery of pious notables. From popes to saints, their survey progresses on day three to "Empresses, Queens, and Other Illustrious and Holy Ladies who have been Nuns." One interlocutor asks rhetorically, remembering the colossal *Hercules* that Bartolomeo Ammannati had sculpted for the Paduan jurist, Marco Mantua Benavides:

(1991): 42–61. Battiferra's connections both to Bernardo Tasso and Dionigi Atanagi run through Urbino. The latter had assisted Tasso in bringing his *Amadigi* to press. Since Battiferra's sonnet for Irene di Spilimbergo was a late addition to the *Primo libro,* published only at the end of 1560 (Victoria Kirkham, "Laura Battiferra's 'First Book' of Poetry," 367–72), Battiferra may have composed it for Atanagi while keeping a copy for last-minute insertion in her own anthology. Corsaro notes the case of another poet, Luca Contile (a marcher with Battiferra in *Amadigi*), whose sonnet appeared first in his own canzoniere, *Le rime di messer Luca Contile,* printed in 1560, before it came out in the funerary anthology for Madonna Irene of 1561.

44. On Luca Martini, see Victoria Kirkham, "Cosimo and Eleonora in Shepherdland: A Lost Eclogue by Laura Battiferra degli Ammannati," in Konrad Eisenbichler, ed., *The Cultural Politics of Duke Cosimo I de' Medici* (Burlington, Vt.: Ashgate, 2001), 149–75. Her sonnets of grief for the loss of Giovanni, Garzia, and Eleonora de Toledo appear in two choral anthologies of 1563 (2.11–14).

45. Cimegotto prints two replies from Bernardo Tasso to Battiferra's letters on Varchi's death, both from Mantua. On January 30, 1566, he shares her grief and promises a poem of mourning; on March 14 he praises and thanks her for her "diligent" efforts to keep Varchi's name alive. Caro writes her from Rome on January 12, 1566, with a sonnet on the death of Varchi (*Lettere* 3: 263, no. 783).

> Has this age of ours any cause to envy the ancient and learned Sappho, since we have had our Vittoria Colonnas, Veronica Gambaras, and many others, famous indeed for their poetry in Italy and beyond Italy? And we had them not only in past years, but there lives today, to the infinite glory of women, the most learned and never adequately celebrated Madonna Laura Battifferra de gl'Amannati, wife of that Most excellent Messer Bartolomeo, who made, not many years ago, the very beautiful and big statue we see today in Padua . . .[46]

When Dionigi Atanagi, after publishing his tribute to Madonna Irene di Spilimbergo, collected poetry for another anthology by "noble Tuscan poets," he noted on a sonnet by Annibal Caro that it "answers one by Madonna Laura Battiferra of Urbino, whom he [Caro] praises highly for her intellect and her worth as a Tuscan poet, just as this new Sappho of our times truly deserves." The great humanist and Hellenist Piero Vettori, describing the unfairness of her isolation in a matroneum at Varchi's funeral in early 1566, compares favorably his friend Laura to Socrates for her intellect, and he judges her even superior to Sappho, whom she rivals as a poet but surpasses in morality (1, Intro. letter).[47] Giorgio Vasari, in the second edition of his *Lives of the Artists* (1568), pays Battiferra tribute in his account of Properzia de' Rossi, the only woman to whom he devotes an entire *vita.* His universal canon of women begins with twelve Amazons; next follow ten ancient poets, beginning with Corinna and Sappho; then eleven more ancients who excelled in various fields—philosophy, oratory, grammar, and prophecy (Cassandra and Manto); and finally, "women of our age who have acquired great fame": Vittoria Colonna, Veronica Gambara, Caterina Anguissola, la Schioppa, la Nogarola, Laura Battiferra, "and others."[48]

Yet just when her star was at its brightest, almost as suddenly as she flashed into prominence, Laura Battiferra's light faded from public view.

46. *Historia monastica,* day 3, p. 4. For his genteel gathering, Calzolari borrows eclectically from both the structure of Boccaccio's *Decameron* and the conversational model of Castiglione's *Book of the Courtier.*

47. Strangely, Atanagi does not publish the sonnet from Battiferra to which Caro replies. His note appears in the index, under the first line of Caro's sonnet.

48. I can find no references to the Caterina Anguissola Vasari names. Perhaps Vasari was thinking of Sofonisba Anguissola (1532–1625), whom he praises highly at the end of his life of Properzia de' Rossi. The first woman to gain international fame as a painter, she was especially renowned for her portraits, whose subjects range from her family members (she had five sisters) to Philip II of Spain. See, e.g., Ilya Sandra Perlingieri, *Sofonisba Anguissola: The First Great Woman Artist of the Renaissance* (Milan: Rizzoli, 1992). I am unable to identify "Schioppa." Vasari had published the first edition of his *Vite* in 1550.

15. Agnolo Bronzino, *Eleonora of Toledo,* ca. 1560. Washington, D.C., National Gallery of Art. Photo: Museum.

She herself seems to have withdrawn from the scene, called by converging events to a more meditative existence. Death levied heavy claims in the years of her greatest celebrity. She lost her father in August of 1561 (2.7–10). Public anchoring figures disappeared as well—Luca Martini that January (2.2–6); in 1562, her patron Eleonora de Toledo (fig. 15) and the boys Giovanni and Garzia de' Medici (2.11–14); in 1564, Michelangelo (2.19–20); in 1565, Benedetto Varchi (1.96); and in 1566, Annibal Caro (1.97). The political scene, like the landscape of her private life, changed. In the wake of his wife and sons' deaths Duke Cosimo de' Medici (fig. 16) ceded power to his son Francesco (1564). Battiferra attempted to flatter Francesco by writing adulatory verse for Bianca Cappello, the scandalous mistress who became his wife (1.65) after the death of his official consort, Giovanna of Austria (1.104–5). Whether her bid for renewed patronage failed, or because of shifting interests that led her to withdraw into devotional pursuits, Battiferra does not seem to have been as close to Florentine court circles as during the years that Eleonora de Toledo was alive. Once in a while, at least, she did break her self-imposed isolation and continue to compose poetry as a member of the local community who could be called on to serve civic entertainments. Her

16. Agnolo Bronzino, *Cosimo I de' Medici.* Oil on wood panel, 1546 or after. Toledo, Toledo Museum of Art. Photo: Museum.

celebrity status lasted into the decade of her death, the 1580s, when the German painter Hans von Aachen visited Florence and made a portrait of her to carry across the Alps so that compatriots could view this remarkable woman.[49]

Always a devout Catholic, Battiferra embraces a new militant Christianity in the religious climate created by reforms emerging from the Council of Trent, which held its final session in December of 1563. Even before, with her *Primo libro,* she had asserted her stance against the Turks (1.9), and she had contributed to Benedetto Varchi's *Sonetti contro gl'Ugonotti* (Sonnets against the Huguenots), a collection of sonnet dialogues that express frightened outrage at the rebellion of Protestants in Avignon around 1562 (2.40). Poets who share her pious bent greet her in print and imitate her choices.[50]

49. Hans von Aachen (1552–1615) was in Italy between 1574 and 1587/88 and in Florence in 1582/83. His lost portrait of Battiferra was last documented in 1618 by van Mander in *Het Schilder Boeck.* See Kirkham, "Dante's Fantom, Petrarch's Specter," 66 and 116, n. 8.

50. Pietro Massolo, who murdered his wife, retreated into monasticism, and collected eight hundred *Rime morali* that ran to four editions between 1564 and 1583, names Battiferra among a gallery of exalted sonnet recipients—the emperor Charles V, the king of France, Pope Paul III,

In 1586, three years before her death, Battiferra gains a place in an encyclopedia by Tomaso Garzoni, a learned canon at the Lateran in Rome: *Le vite delle donne illustri della scrittura sacra. Con l'aggionta delle vite delle donne oscure e laide dell'uno e l'altro Testamento. E un Discorso in fine sopra la nobiltà delle donne* (Lives of Illustrious Women of Sacred Scripture. With the Addition of the Lives of the Obscure and Ugly Women of Both Testaments. And a Discourse at the End on the Nobility of Women). His peroration, citing Plato's *Republic,* argues that men and women are equals in their capacity for learning and literary achievement. As ancient examples, he names such figures as Corinna and Aspasia; among the moderns, he names some from the fifteenth century (Isotta Nogarola is one); and then he continues, "Should I be silent on those who are the lights of our era: Vittoria Colonna, Laura Terracina, Laura Battiferra, Tarquinia Molza, and a thousand others who with their fame fill the whole universe?"[51]

In their last years, Laura Battiferra and Bartolomeo Ammannati aligned themselves staunchly with the Jesuits. Laura's first testament, dictated as heiress to her father's estate in 1563, names Ammannati as her chief beneficiary, but the second and third (1581 and 1587) designate the Jesuits as universal heirs (app. A). How passionately Laura embraced Loyola's teachings is evident from her recently rediscovered "Orison on the Nativity of Our Lord" (chap. 3), a meditation anchored to prayers on the life of Christ in the *Spiritual Exercises* (1548). The most visible monument to their generous joint patronage of the Society of Jesus is the Florentine church and attached *collegium* of San Giovannino, built with his services as architect and monies jointly contributed. Long lost in the forgotten late manuscript of her *Rime* are the poems she wrote during this period. While most are intensely spiritual sonnets on such favored Catholic Reformation subjects as the Cruci-

---

Andrea Doria, the Duke of Florence, the Duchess of Urbino, Cardinal Pole, and so forth. His collection first appeared as *Primo, et secondo volume delle rime morali di M. Pietro Massolo, gentil'huomo vinitiano, hora Don Lorenzo Monaco Cassinese* (Florence: Nella Stamperia Ducale, Appresso i figliuoli di M. Lorenzo Torrentino, et Bernardo Fabroni compagni, 1564). Francesco Sansovino, a childhood friend, enhanced it with a rich commentary in the edition published as *Rime morali di M. Pietro Massolo . . . hora Don Lorenzo monaco cassinese* (Venice: Gio. Antonio Rampazetto, 1583). A sonnet from her *Primo libro* crops up in "spiritual" poetry by the Venetian priest Faustino Tasso (1573), important in her literary fortunes as her imitator. Compare the title of the first part of Faustino's rhymes, *Il primo libro delle rime toscane,* with Battiferra's title *Primo libro dell'opere toscane.* According to his editor's introductory remarks to the second, spiritual part of the anthology, Faustino, like Battiferra, composed an "Oration by Jeremiah in *terza rima*" as well as penitential psalms.

51. Tomaso Garzoni, *Le vite delle donne illustri della scrittura sacra,* ed. Beatrice Collina (Ravenna: Longo, 1994), 245. The ladies of Scripture, thirty-five in all, run from Eve to Mary; the nine "unattractive" ones include Delilah, Jezebel, and Herodias.

fixion (1, pt. 2.14), Mary Magdalene (1, pt. 2.16), and the Massacre of the Innocents (1, pt. 2.18), others specifically address the Jesuits (1, pt. 2.15). Attributable to the general period from 1572 until her death in 1589, these include two that have precise occasions, the appointment of Claudio Acquaviva as General of the Society of Jesus on February 19, 1581 (1.62), and the death of Pope Gregory XIII in 1585 (1.119), her last datable poem.[52]

The little we know of Laura's own death, which fell just six months short of her fortieth wedding anniversary, survives in Messer Bartolomeo's handwritten notes of what he paid "to bury Madonna Laura his wife." On November 2, 1589, he rented from the druggist four large white candles, perhaps to be placed at the four corners of the body for the viewing; an unspecified number of smaller yellow candles in a quantity indicated by how much the wax in them weighed, and eight new yellow torches. The total, subtracting a refund for the partially burned candles, again based on weight of the wax, came to 230.16 lire. On November 4, he itemized further costs for "black mourning clothing for Madonna Laura's death": four black hats for people in the household, black veiling "to cover his hat," a complete mourning outfit for himself (black robe, cloak, jacket, and trimmings), tailor's charges (not listed), charitable offerings to several religious orders, and four grave diggers. His total recorded expenditures came to nearly 400 lire. By comparison, a bound copy of Battiferra's *Primo libro* cost 1 lira, and her *Salmi penitentiali* only about two-thirds that much (13.4 soldi).[53]

The architect himself built their funeral chapel in San Giovannino, a Florentine Gothic church remodeled for Jesuit use largely thanks to the Ammannati and fully complete by 1584. He commissioned a panel in oil by Alessandro Allori, Bronzino's adoptive son and follower (figs. 3–4 above). Representing *Christ and the Canaanite Woman,* it depicts Laura and her husband as they appeared in old age. He stands in the guise of Saint Bartholomew at the center of the panel, behind Christ, a bearded old man leaning on a crook whose downward gaze embraces two female figures, the suppliant Canaanite mother (Mt 15; Mk 7) and a kneeling woman at the far right. She is Laura as an elderly matron, her face now drawn and wrinkled, but still recognizable when compared with Bronzino's more famous likeness of her as a younger

52. On Battiferra's patronage of the Jesuits, see Kirkham, "Laura Battiferra degli Ammannati benefattrice dei Gesuiti fiorentini," 331–54.

53. For the funeral expenses see ASF, Comp. Soppr. da Leopoldo, *filza* 241, fol. 180r; for the price of Battiferra's books, ASF, Comp. Soppr. da Leopoldo, *filza* 241, fol. 28r. Figuring 7.5 lire in a scudo, the cost of Battiferra's funeral would have been about the same as that of her father's burial expenses, which are listed as 50 scudi in an inventory of debts against his estate (ASF, Comp. Soppr. da Leopoldo, fol. 59v).

poet. In the earlier pose, she held a manuscript open to a pair of sonnets by Petrarch; in this more somber context, perhaps a posthumous portrait, she clasps a small devotional volume. Grateful Jesuits inscribed a tombstone and laid it over their graves in the pavement at the foot of the chapel, adorned on its rear wall with their images in Allori's Gospel miracle:

> TO GOD SUPREME AND GREATEST. FOR BARTOLOMEO AMMANNATI AND HIS WIFE LAURA BATTIFERRA, THE COLLEGE OF THE SOCIETY OF JESUS, AUGMENTED BY THEIR GREAT BENEFICENCES, OF ITS OWN WILL AND WITH GRATEFUL SPIRIT, LAID THIS MONUMENT BEFORE THE VERY DEVOUT MARRIED COUPLE. THEY DIED, HE IN THE YEAR OF SALVATION 1592 AT THE AGE OF 82, AND SHE IN THE YEAR OF SALVATION 1589 AT THE AGE OF 66.[54]

WORKS: "BESIDE THE FIRE, SPEAKING OF POETRY"

The fall of 1564 brought a long chatty letter to Laura Battiferra in Florence from her friend and fellow poet, Gherardo Spini, a witty cosmopolitan who had been visiting Prague. Invited for court festivities, he and his Italian party had managed to reach that imperial outpost "intact," surviving murderous bands of brigands in the cold, muddy northern forests and an outbreak of plague that was making people around them drop dead daily. Now, as he collects his courage for a return journey through the Austrian provinces, his thoughts turn to the city on the Arno, where he good-humoredly imagines Laura, her husband Messer Bartolomeo, and a select group of others gathered at the warmth of her living room hearth. He looks forward to rejoining their circle, a "rarefied" literary salon:

> We shall return to Vienna free of plague, if nothing more happens, and if we can manage to scamper through the Hircinian Forest, then we shall be safe for a piece. We shall stay in Vienna for about ten days to

54. The painting still hangs in the Ammannati chapel, second on the left. Baldinucci 4: 27, records the original epitaph: D[EO] O[PTIMO] M[AXIMO]. / BARTOLOMMEO AMMANNATI / EIUSQUE UXORI / LAURAE BATTIFERRAE / COLLEGIUM SOCIETATIS / IESU / MAGNIS EORUM BENEFICIIS / AUCTUM SUAE ERGA / RELIGIOSISSIMOS CONIUGES / VOLUNTATIS ET GRATI / ANIMI MONUMENTUM / POS. / OBIERUNT ALTER A. SAL. / MDLXXXXII AET. LXXXII. / ALTERA A. SAL. MDLXXXIX. / AET. LXVI. This marker has disappeared and been replaced by a modern stone that fails to credit Battiferra's patronage and gives her age at death incorrectly (64 instead of 66): CINERES ET OSSA / BARTHOLOMMAEI AMMANNATI / HVIVS ECCLESIAE ARCHITECTI / O. AN. MDXCII AET. LXXXII / ET. LAURAE BATTIFERRAE UXORIS S / O. AN. MDLXXXIX AET. LXIV [= LXVI] [ASHES AND BONES OF BARTOLOMEO AMMANNATI, / ARCHITECT OF THIS CHURCH, / DIED IN THE YEAR 1592 AGED 82 / AND LAURA BATTIFERRA HIS WIFE / DIED IN THE YEAR 1589 AGED 64].

> take our leave of the Emperor and the other gentlemen. Then we shall set out for Italy, not returning through the Tyrol or Trent, but passing through Styria, Carinthia, and down into Friuli, and then Venice. Meanwhile, Your Ladyship will be beside the fire, speaking of Poetry and other clever subjects with a few rarefied minds. Do deign to mention me especially, I who frozen stiff shall keep pondering how I can protect myself from all the ice, mud, and snow to be able to come and be a participant. May Your Ladyship, together with Messer Bartolomeo, take care to stay healthy, and do please commend me to all my friends, and above all to Bronzino.

Earlier in this same lively letter, the traveler had described for Laura's benefit the strapping and aggressive women of Prague, reputedly descended from Amazons of yore (4.8), and he smilingly tantalizes her with a partial report of the evening he has spent with the emperor's personal physician, Pierandrea Mattioli. The Tuscan Mattioli, renowned throughout Europe as a scientist, had as a young man also displayed his poetic vein with charming stanzas on "the great palace" of his patron, the Cardinal of Trent. He won his eminent position in Prague by translating Ptolemy's book on geography and, more important, the classic Greek herbal by Dioscorides, which in his annotated version became a standard medical book of reference.

> We had a conversation about Your Ladyship, but I don't want to tell you what it was, so that, if for nothing else, you will have reason to wish for my return to hear what particularly interested him.[55]

One topic that must surely have engaged that eminent gentleman's curiosity was Battiferra's poetry, brought to print four years earlier in her *Primo libro dell'opere toscane* at the Florentine presses of Giunti (figs. 5, 6 above) and

55. Spini may have traveled to Prague for celebrations surrounding the coronation of Maximilian II, who had succeeded his father Ferdinand as emperor on July 25, 1564, the same occasion that had sent Mario Colonna (chap. 1, Letter from Vettori; 2.35) as an ambassador from Duke Cosimo. Pierandrea Mattioli (1500–1577) was born in Siena and trained in Padua, Perugia, and Rome. For mention of his poem *Magno palazzo del Cardinale di Trento* in *ottava rima* (Venice, 1539), see Carlo Dionisotti, "La letteratura italiana nell'età del concilio di Trento," in *Geografia e storia della letteratura italiana,* 183–204 (Turin: Einaudi, 1967), 196. Before joining the emperor's court, he served as physician to the cardinal of Trent, Bernardo Cles, a militant anti-Lutheran and one of the early advocates of the Council of Trent. See below, chap. 1.I, for a biographical sketch of Gherardo Spini, and further, Zygmunt Waźbiński, *L'accademia medicea del disegno a Firenze nel Cinquecento,* 2 vols. (Florence: Olschki, 1987), 1: 215–34. Spini says in his letter to Battiferra that he visited "the most excellent Matthioli, His Highness's doctor, who is the man who has made so many such beautiful additions to Dioscurides and to Ptolemy" (Pe 161v–162r). For more of Spini's letter and a note on Mattioli, see 4.8.

celebrated with a stunning portrait by the Medici court painter Bronzino (figs. 1, 2 above).[56] As Spini and Mattioli chatted, they could compare that Petrarchan anthology with her new publication, *I sette salmi penitentiali,* issued not long before, in March of 1564. Her translation of the Psalms into Tuscan verse, with summaries and explanations of all seven for the nuns to whom she sent them, would have appealed to Mattioli in his twin identity as a scholar and poet, all the more so since he undoubtedly sympathized with its Catholic Reformation spirit. Spini himself knew her Psalms well. He had participated in that book with a closing sonnet (1.I), praising Laura as a "living sun who adorns and brightens the Arno." When safely back home from the Bohemian capital, making his first reappearance among the regulars at her fireside, he must have set off ripples of excitement, as all eagerly heard gossip of the emperor and his court, the adventures of a harrowing journey, and how their "Arno sun" had broken the gloom of a northern autumn.

Spini's remarkable letter, carried across the Alps from the Hapsburg domain of Maximilian II to Medici Florence, is not the only record of Laura Battiferra's spreading fame, which reached well beyond Tuscany and even to countries beyond Italy. By 1557, three years before she had ventured into print with her *Primo libro,* verse by Battiferra had arrived at another royal court, the Madrid of Philip II. On December 11, she wrote this exciting news to Benedetto Varchi, the literary lion king of Florence (fig. 13 above). Informing him that she has drafted a pair of sonnets as requested, one for Philip and a mate for his wife "Maria" (the Catholic daughter of Henry VIII, known among English speakers as Bloody Mary), she now submits them to him, as was her custom, for a bit of editorial polishing:

> This week I had a letter from Messer Bernardino Bazino from the court of King Philip, and he informs me about certain sonnets of mine, which made their way to that land, I know not how; and he says that they have been praised, and he begs me to write something in praise of that king or queen. I, who doubt whether I am able or know how to loosen my tongue for such a high subject, much less sing, answer him with this sonnet that I now send you, and afterwards, I know not how, I wrote these two, as you can see.[57]

56. See above, note 1.

57. Gargiolli, ed., *Lettere di Laura Battiferri Ammannati,* 39. Her sonnet for Philip II, whether by her choice or Varchi's suggestion, takes its opening cue from his sonnet to Henry VIII (1.5). Friends within literary circles sent each other handwritten copies of their sonnets or sonnets by others they admired. In these exchanges, younger or less visible poets often asked prominent literati for their advice. Battiferra, for example, consulted both Annibal Caro (see, e.g., Kirkham,

17. Agnolo Bronzino, *Duke Guidobaldo II Della Rovere*. Florence, Pitti Palace. Photo: Art Resource.

Tongue-tied or not, she must have found words that met with Messer Benedetto's approval. Sonnets to King Philip and Queen Maria appear among the opening sequence of her *Primo libro,* a space reserved for recipients highest on her social ladder. Topmost is the Medici Duchess Eleonora de Toledo (fig. 15 above), then Duke Cosimo I de' Medici (fig. 16 above), and their son, the prince Francesco; next come the Florentine ruling family's counterparts in Urbino, Duke Guidobaldo II Della Rovere (fig. 17), Duchess Vittoria Farnese Della Rovere, and their dynastic heirs (1.1–10). Varchi himself holds a privileged position in the book, as befitted Duke Cosimo's official historian, elder statesman of the *Accademia Fiorentina,* a most prolific sonneteer, and Laura's respected friend (1.69, fig. 13 above). Together with Annibal Caro, he leads off a procession of distinguished writers whose names grace Batti-

"Laura Battiferra's 'First Book' of Poetry") and Benedetto Varchi on different occasions (4.5). It was not just women who submitted their work to older male poets. Men did so too, as is evident in correspondence from Caro to Piero Bonaventura, a soldier poet of Urbino who answered a sonnet from Laura in an exchange she anthologized in her *Primo libro* (1.70–71).

ferra's pages, not just to receive poems, but to participate in its literary space as partners with her in sonnet exchanges.

Battiferra's publishing debut, *Il primo libro dell'opere toscane* is a polyvocal anthology, its pages a virtual salon. As editorial mistress, she assembled a total of 187 poems. They are largely hers, but in the fashion of the day, forty-one are by other contributors who enter into dialogue with Laura, their "Daphne." In paired sonnet exchanges, they continue a tradition inherited from the medieval *tenzone,* revived in the mid-sixteenth century on a cue from Pietro Bembo, and favored by the female Petrarchists.[58] In this ritual, as enacted in the Cinquecento, one poet addresses another with a sonnet "*proposta*" (proposal); the second replies in a "*risposta*" (response). To follow strictly the rules of the game, the reply must be *per rime,* that is, match the rhyme scheme and rhyme sounds set out in the first poem. Although the medieval poets liked to pose questions of love casuistry for debate, their Renaissance descendants use this codified verse more freely, to strike up polite conversation and epistolary exchanges on all sorts of timely topics.[59]

The anthology shaped by a single author can be compared to an album, of the sort that young people used to make, in which friends inscribed and signed poems, drawings, a favorite saying, or sentiment. Battiferra and her contemporaries, through sonnet *proposta* and *risposta,* trade compliments in an "autograph" exchange couched as a rivalry of flattery. Originality within

58. Both Dante in the *Vita nuova* and Petrarch in his *Rime sparse* (Scattered Rhymes) included sonnets addressed to other poets, but they excluded the replies. Pietro Bembo (1470–1547) departed from those influential models when he anthologized poems by five of his correspondents in sonnet exchanges at the end of the second (1535) and third (1548) editions of his *Rime.* Among the first—male or female poets—to embed the replies in the body of a personal anthology, paired on a page, were Tullia d'Aragona (1547) and Laura Terracina (1548). The technique allowed women to connect with the community of male authors.

59. When Laura was inducted into the prestigious *Accademia degli Intronati* (Academy of the Dazed) in Siena, she received and answered congratulatory sonnets (1.82–85). Her *Primo libro* incorporates replies she sent to a quartet of sonnets praising the art of her husband, Bartolomeo Ammannati, from Lelio Bonsi, a Florentine Academy member friendly with Varchi, Bronzino, and Benvenuto Cellini (1.90–91). Bronzino's lyric poems preserve a round of sonnets that he initiated to condole with Battiferra, Benedetto Varchi, and their cohort Piero della Stufa on the passing of Laura's father, Giovan'Antonio Battiferri (2.10). Varchi shaped an entire volume of one hundred sonnets, uniting a large community of mourners, including Battiferra, for the death of Luca Martini, Cosimo's cultured ducal administrator in Pisa (2.2–6). After the Medici duchess and two of her sons suddenly died of malarial fever in 1562, funeral anthologies gather the bereaved to express their grief in shifting pairs, like guests at a wake who move through the room and pause to visit. Gherardo Spini, ever the gentleman, addresses Battiferra's husband Bartolomeo Ammannati, architect-in-chief of the "nest" (Palazzo Pitti) that the Medici duchess, Eleonora de Toledo, had purchased to remodel as a princely new family home (2.11); Battiferra joins in to express her own dismay at the loss of their Medici patron (2.13).

the confines of a highly constrained system is the point, hence the fun consists in outdoing each other with clever variation through hyperbole, amusing false modesty, and the classical arsenal of rhetoric. Criticism that dismisses *Petrarchismo* as unoriginal, superficial, or adulatory may fail to appreciate its witty sophistication and learned allusions, a fortiori if memory has been lost of a sonnet's link to a specific occurrence. Public events remain in history—a princely marriage (1.11–14), birth (2.22), death (1.102–12; 117–19), battle victory (1.38–39)—but the doings of daily life are more ephemeral, and so too the poems written about them—a visit from a friend (1.54), a gift of wine and apples (1.64), a petition (1.7), recovery from an illness (1.47).

Sometimes where printed books are silent, a search behind the scenes in handwritten originals can explain the poem's occasion. Ludovico Beccadelli, a conservative Bolognese prelate of prominent status, strong in his literary bent, declares that upon Laura's entry into Parnassus—that is, when she published her *Primo libro*—the muse Euterpe spoke, pronouncing her "the glory" of Urbino and Florence (2.15). Three years later, Laura writes that the Arno river is now "abundant in honor, in glory" since its shores have been gladdened by the "foot" of Beccadelli, archbishop of Ragusa (modern day Dubrovnik)—that is, he has come to Florence for a visit (2.16). Neither sonnet, in accordance with the conventions of a genre á clef, reveals its triggering circumstance, but this can be deduced from jottings that lie outside the texts elsewhere in their manuscripts. For Beccadelli's sonnet, the year "1560" clings to a rough draft predating the scribe's fair copy, from which dates have been banished. For Battiferra's sonnet, bound among Beccadelli's collected papers with the creases of the folds still evident that made the folio into a letter she sent him, a notation on the reverse reads "For Monsignor's coming to Tuscany 1563."[60]

In Laura's *Primo libro*, first among the corresponding poets is Annibal

60. Both sonnets survive only in manuscript, at the Palatine Library in Parma among the papers of Beccadelli, who for his own album collected them like letters from a host of admirers. At the Council of Trent, Beccadelli expressed firm support for the Index of Prohibited Books, adding "there's no need at all for [printed] books . . . better a thousand books be forbidden without deserving it than one permitted that deserves prohibition" (Sarpi, 2:757, my trans.). His sonnet to Battiferra is preserved in Parma, Biblioteca Palatina, MS 972, which is in three volumes. The first is the fair copy, and the second is the draft from which the scribe copied out the first. In both, the sonnet to Battiferra occupies fol. 7v, opposite the sonnet to Columbus, on fol. 8r. In the second volume, however, the poem to Laura is dated "1560" beside the dedicatory title, "A Madonna Laura Battiferra." The notation on the reverse of Battiferra's sonnet to Beccadelli runs vertically, a tight cursive in the upper left margin: "1563 Sonetti per la venuta di Monsignore in Toscana."

Caro (1.66–67), Varchi's predecessor as her literary advisor when she and Bartolomeo Ammannati lived in Rome, during the early years of their marriage. Caro basked in the patronage of Cardinal Alessandro Farnese, the grandson of Pope Paul III. As a humanist secretary, he wrote volumes of letters and completed an Italian translation of Virgil's *Aeneid.* During the late 1550s, he was much in view for his vociferous lampoons of the purist Girolamo Castelvetro, a commentator of the Italian classics whom Laura and her set mocked for advocating a particularly slavish brand of *Petrarchismo* (4.6). Of the men whom Caro and Varchi draw in their train—and men they all are—only a few bear names that still resonate today. There is Agnolo Bronzino, whom Gherardo Spini singles out for a greeting from chilly Prague. A versatile genius who wielded the pen as readily as the brush, he was Laura's frequent foil in Petrarchist sonnet exchanges (1.76–77; 1.88–89), where she plays the elusive "Dafne" and the aloof "iron lady"—a pun on her surname "Battiferri," or "iron pounder," "smith" (2.30). Time has smiled too on Benvenuto Cellini, if not for his Petrarchist sonnets (1.80–81), then for his craft as master goldsmith and for self-proclaimed heroism in his *Vita* as the caster of *Perseus Holding the Head of Medusa,* which already stood watch under the Loggia de' Lanzi over Piazza della Signoria as Laura was gathering the material for her book. Sonnets also arrive from Anton Francesco Grazzini, "il Lasca" (1.86–87), by then a senior member of the *Accademia Fiorentina,* noted for the *novelle* he authored in imitation of Boccaccio's *Decameron,* as well as for popular comic plays and humorous verse.

Others, although of more ephemeral fame, measure Laura's esteemed status in the community of Italian poets. Always a pious woman, Battiferra embraces the Venetian preacher Don Gabriello Fiamma (1.72–73), a marvel of eloquence, whose dazzling sonnet for her book is rhetorically true to his reputation. Girolamo Razzi (1.II; 1.63; 1.78–79), a friend who will appear in all three of Battiferra's books, here makes his first appearance. A playwright in youth, after taking the tonsure at about the time Laura's *Primo libro* appeared, he changed his name to Don Silvano and turned to moralistic writing. His monastery, the medieval Camaldolite house of Santa Maria degli Angeli, had been enhanced by Filippo Brunelleschi in the Quattrocento with a rotunda, a distinctive landmark at the heart of Florence. That rotunda came to define an important *cenacolo,* or cultural circle, over which Razzi and Varchi presided. In her sonnet exchange with Razzi, Laura punningly honors this center of creative activity, "there where your Parnassus is Rotund" (1.79).

Professional as well as amateur, arrayed by rank and station, the literati who exchange sonnets with Laura are not the only personages called to

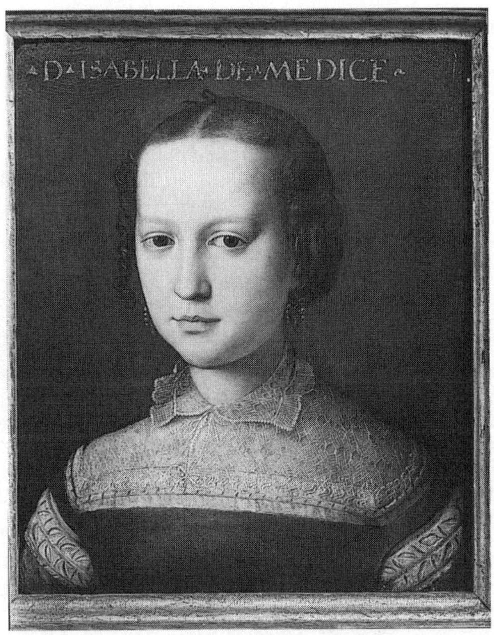

18. Agnolo Bronzino, *Isabella de' Medici*. Stockholm, National Museum. Photo: Museum.

her virtual salon. Many others appear in the *Primo libro,* not as corresponding writers, but more passively, as recipients of her occasional poetry. Representing some of Italy's most illustrious families, their names float across the pages in dedicatory titles: "To Signor Paolo Giordano Orsino" (1.4), "On the Nuptials of Signor Federigo Buonromeo and Signora Donna Virginia Della Rovere" (1.11–14); "To Pope Paul III Farnese" (1.20), "To Messer Luca Martini" (1.59), "To Father Claudio Acquaviva, General of the Society of Jesus" (1.62), "To Messer Giovan Battista Cini on the Death of his Consort, Madonna Maria Berardi" (1.102). Some of the social elite here honored are poets and literati themselves, true of Martini, Cini, and several ladies for whom Laura composes sonnets: Isabella de' Medici, daughter of Cosimo and Eleonora (1.21–26, fig. 18); Leonora Cibo de' Vitelli (app. C), a great-granddaughter of Pope Innocent VIII and wife of Duke Cosimo's military commander Chiappino Vitelli (1.30–32); Ersilia Cortese de' Monti, who had married into the family of Pope Julius III and rode the crest of a wave as the most powerful matron in Rome (1.33).[61] Counting sonnet correspon-

61. None of the women reply, a silence that is somewhat surprising. A sonnet exchange survives between Battiferra and the Neapolitan poet Laura Terracina (2.37–38), initiated by the

19. Bartolomeo Ammannati, *Neptune Fountain*. Marble and bronze, 1560–80. Florence, Piazza della Signoria. Photograph by Elizabeth Kirkham.

dents and recipients together swells the number of personalities in Battiferra's choral anthology to nearly one hundred. *Il primo libro delle opere toscane* reads like a *Who's Who* of mid-sixteenth-century Italy, from Cosimo de' Medici and his key ally King Philip of Spain (1.5), to his most trusted architect and sculptor, the author's own husband Bartolomeo Ammannati, winner of a coveted ducal commission for the *Neptune Fountain* in Piazza della Signoria (1.39 and fig. 19; 1.46; 1.90; 2.11).

Like most of the verse it contains, Battiferra's publishing debut is an occasional piece, crafted in the fashionable language of *Petrarchismo* to celebrate the Medici at an apogee of their power. She anchors her *canzoniere* to Cosimo's conquest of Siena, the result of a brutal siege and war (1553–55) in which his *condottiero* Chiappino Vitelli played a leading role. The duke offi-

---

latter and preserved in Terracina's last volume of collected poetry, which was never published. Laura did not anthologize either this exchange or another sonnet (unknown) that she sent to Lucia Bertana of Modena (4.6). The sole female voice in both of her published books is Battiferra's. In her unpublished third book, only one sonnet exchange includes the lady's reply (1.94–95).

cially received that Tuscan city as a fief from Philip II in 1557, a trophy that doubtless helped Laura find her voice and sing in words worthy of the Spanish sovereign.[62] Cosimo and Eleonora made their ceremonial entry into Siena on October 28, 1560, just as Laura was completing her *Primo libro,* which closes with sonnets inviting the ducal couple formally to take possession of their new territorial acquisition (1.16–17). Within a frame structure that features the Medici at the beginning and end, her book announces its political allegiance in other ways. Near the front she inserts sonnets to Cosimo's new son-in-law, the Roman noble Paolo Giordano Orsini (1.4), to his court secretary Bernardino Grazzini, and to Chiappino Vitelli and his wife Leonora Cibo (1.28–32). Near the end, she addresses the Medici *provveditore* in Pisa, Luca Martini, and she celebrates Cosimo's son Giovanni, fast-tracked for a papal tiara with his new cardinalate at sixteen (1.15).

Public and political in its outward appearance, the *Primo libro* has a more private side that discloses autobiographical moments. Here Battiferra confesses her deep attachment to Rome, as awesome to her for its ancient past as for its papal history (1.116). On the death of her husband's patron, Julius III, she confides her reluctance to leave that city (1.51), where she and her husband orbited the Vatican in high social circles (1.33–34). Florence, their new home, seems a lonely, unwelcoming "wilderness" in comparison (1.57); she misses her Roman friends (1.35), but soon through her professional energies and her husband's contacts she makes a network of new ones, emblazoned for all the world to see in her *Primo libro.* A devoted wife, she writes affectionately of her husband and his accomplishments—an illness of his (1.47), his restoration of an Arno bridge after the terrible flood of 1557 (1.46), his monumental sculpture (1.93). Other sonnets give glimpses of her strolls in the hills around the hamlet of Maiano (1.53), northeast of Florence, where the Ammannati had a country house. Three times she marks her birthday in the introspective tones of her literary model, Petrarch's anniversary poems (1, pt. 2.6, 2.7, 2.17).

Battiferra, like Petrarch, is torn between conflicting desires. Like him, she wishes for fame, and she feels her restless aspirations as a poet incompatible with her Christian need for inner peace, comforted by a sense of proximity to God. An undated sonnet among her late unpublished poetry admits to this struggle (1, pt. 2.13). In spite of her guilt, she keeps going

62. For an overview of this *canzoniere* and its making, see Kirkham, "Laura Battiferra's 'First Book' of Poetry." I use the word *canzoniere,* literally "song book," not in the strict sense of an imitation of Petrarch's model, with a narrative that tells a love story, but in the wider sense of "collection of poems," a poetic anthology.

back to the "glad troop (*schiera*), honor of Parnassus," that is, the friends in her Florentine literary circles: "Although conscience pricks and rasps my heart, and reason dictates truth to me, yet I follow habit, and I feel it to be errant and vain." Her religion becomes stronger as she grows older, reaching fundamentalist fervor, but well before, the *Primo libro* includes many selections of a meditative, prayerful stamp. These poems, as well as some of the company toward which she gravitated, suggest that Battiferra, like the more famous Vittoria Colonna a generation before, had leanings that put her in sympathy with the Italian Reformist movement.[63] Her sonnet for Vincenzo Grotti (1.45), otherwise unidentified, tells how she longs to join his "troop," presided over by a "great lady" she loves, who "with sweet Food (*Cibo*), nay with true manna, nourishes the soul and guides and sends it heavenward." This inspirational noblewoman is the Duchess of Camerino, Caterina Cibo. Esteemed for her knowledge of Latin, Greek, and Hebrew, she was the aunt and guardian who educated Laura's friend Eleonora Cibo de' Vitelli (app. C). Under the elder Cibo's wing, beside a loggia in "winsome countryside and green meadows," Laura can find wise and eloquent words of Christ "disencumbering my heart of vain frozen thoughts and replenishing my breast with warm love and faith."

Battiferra's own hearth in Florence, to which Gherardo Spini's thoughts fly as he thinks ahead from Prague, was the meeting place for a coterie whose members moved in other interlocking circles. Some who frequented her fireside must have been drawn in fair weather to those "green meadows" where Cibo dispensed manna for the spirit. Perhaps the loggia Laura mentions in her sonnet to Grotti flanked La Topaia, a villa in Fiesole given by Cosimo de' Medici to Varchi. Don Silvano Razzi recalls that she was among the "very noble and very virtuous women" who walked up there with like-minded men including Bronzino, Lucio Oradini, and Lelio Bonsi, to join in discussions about how to lead a good Christian life. Laura's city circle, overlapping with the country goers, closely intersected with Bronzino's "troop" (*schiera*), judging from her importance in his *canzoniere*, polyvocal like hers but never published.[64] She speaks too in her poetry of Santa Maria degli

63. Guidi, in his edition of Battiferra's *Il primo libro* and in "Salmi penitenziali di David," 83–92, argues for Battiferra's Reformist sympathies.

64. Bronzino's *Rime* was not published until the early nineteenth century by Domenico Moreni, an edition philologically unreliable. A small modern anthology can be found in Andrea Emiliani, *Il Bronzino* (Busto Arsizio: Bramante Editrice, 1960). For a recent discussion of his *canzoniere*, see Deborah Parker, *Bronzino: Renaissance Painter as Poet* (Cambridge: Cambridge University Press, 2000), chap. 2. Don Silvano Razzi names Battiferra and others who went to visit Varchi at La Topaia in his book *Della economia christiana* (1568), 8. In a spiritual counterpart to the *Decameron*, he imagines discussion among the members of a *brigata* whose interest turns on the relative merits of the active and contemplative life.

Angeli, where Varchi and Razzi attracted participants to their "rotund" Parnassus. Deeply resonant in the Italian literary tradition, the word *schiera* often appears in Battiferra's poetry to signal a literary circle. It can be translated "band," "group," "company," or as here, "troop." Dante gives it archetypical contexts in his *Divine Comedy,* first when Virgil tells how Beatrice came to the aid of the poet "who because of her left the vulgar troop" (*Inf.* 2.105); then in the Limbus, where it refers to the "school" of Homer, Horace, Ovid, Lucan, and Virgil that Dante so proudly joins: "e' sì mi fecer de la loro schiera, / sì ch'io fui sesto tra cotanto senno" (they made me one of their troop, so that I was sixth amid so much wisdom) (*Inf.* 4.94, 4.101–2); and in the following canto, applied to airborne ghosts damned for illicit love in "Dido's troop" (*Inf.* 5.85: "la schiera ov'è Dido"). Recalling Dante's classic canon, Petrarch turns back affectionately in thought to the "dolce amica schiera" (sweet troop of friends) that he leaves behind on a journey to Avignon (*RS* 139.2). The word recurs, colored with its amorous associations, in his sonnet of mourning for Sennuccio del Bene, a fellow poet whom Petrarch imagines has gone to the third heaven, ruled by Venus, to join other departed love poets—Guittone d'Arezzo, Cino da Pistoia, Dante, Franceschino degli Albizi, "et tutta quella schiera" (and all that troop, *RS* 287.11). Petrarch's vision of Sennuccio's afterlife circle, influenced by Dante's passage through Venus in the *Paradiso* (where he encounters the troubadour Folquet de Marseille) becomes a *locus classicus.* Boccaccio has it in mind when he addresses Petrarch, but lately deceased, "Or sei salito, caro signor mio" ('Now you have risen, my dear lord'), imagining him with Senuccio, Cino, and Dante. Bronzino, likewise imitating Petrarch, takes consolation in bereavement from his "friendly troop" (2.2). Another friend, Mario Colonna, urges Laura to rejoin their "candida schiera"—the "white troop" of "unsullied swans" (poets) who inhabit the Arno's banks. In good Petrarchist form Battiferra echoes members of the "schiera Intronata" when responding to their congratulations on her induction into yet another circle, the Academy of the Dazed, a troop both "learned" and "honored" (1.82, 1.84–85).[65]

Her letters to Varchi record names in contexts that put Battiferra at the mainstream of Florentine culture and connect her to wider networks of poets in other Italian cities during the 1550s and 1560s: she awaits a moral sonnet from "Messer Benvenuto," presumably Cellini (1.80–81; 2.24); "il Vivaldo" (the poet Michelangelo Vivaldi) has come to see her; she passes on to Varchi a new madrigal by the master of that miniature genre, Giovan Battista

65. I have preferred "troop" to the more semantically neutral "group" because of the particular connotations of *schiera* in the Italian literary tradition. Parker translates it as "company"; *Bronzino,* 45–70.

Strozzi (1.43); she informs Varchi that Giovan'Andrea Anguillara, who had survived the 1527 Sack of Rome to stage comic drama and translate Ovid's *Metamorphoses*, is in town and would like to see him; she has done her best with a sonnet for the poetess Lucia Bertana of Modena (4.6); the great Hellenist Piero Vettori and a "humanist from Pisa" honored her with a visit on July 20, 1561; she has received and answered a sonnet from the Neapolitan lady Laura Terracina (2.37–38).[66]

More than once she mentions fondly "a Soderini woman," either the Lucrezia in that magnate clan, to whom she dedicated wedding poems (1.36) or her mother, Fiammetta Soderini, sister of Cardinal Francesco Soderini. Herself a poet, Fiammetta was the lady for whom Mario Colonna turned out many a Tuscan ditty (2.35–36). Laura's friendship with this Fiammetta finds its way into a book of anecdotes compiled by their contemporary Lodovico Domenichi, better remembered today as the editor of the first anthology of all-female verse published in Europe (Lucca, 1559).

> One day, when the most noble and beautiful Madonna Fiammetta de' Soderini had as company in her carriage the most virtuous and gracious Madonna Laura Battiferra, it befell that while this couple of singular ladies was enjoying a ride around the city, as the coach was stopped, a number of gentlemen passed close by it, among whom there was one who, wanting to play the know-it-all ("fare il saccente"), after gazing on them a good bit, turned to his companions and said, "Signori, don't be scandalized by me since you must know those words of Scripture, 'Delectasti me Domine in fattura tua.'" So after hearing him, Madonna Laura said pleasantly to la Soderina, such that it was heard by all, "That gallant man must not have read what came next, because he would know that it's also written there, 'Averte oculos tuos ne videant vanitatem.'"[67]

Domenichi's collected pearls of wit, originally published in 1548, are gossipy snippets about the rich and famous, packaged for popular enter-

66. She refers to Cellini in a letter of June 9, 1557; to Vivaldi on August 6, 1557; to Strozzi on December 11, 1557; to Anguillara, Bertana, Vettori, and "l'umanista di Pisa" on July 21, 1561; to Terracina on March 1, 1562 (=1563 modern style). See Gargiolli, 27, 33, 41, 44, 45.

67. Guidi, ed. *Il primo libro*, 53, identifies Lucrezia as Fiammetta Soderini's daughter. The timing of Domenichi's published anecdote (*Facetie, motti, et burle, di diversi signori et persone private* [Venice: Giorgio de' Cavalli, 1565], 475–76) reflects the success of Battiferra's second book. Although the gentleman's Latin sally ("Lord, you delighted me in your creation") does not correspond verbatim to any scriptural verse, Battiferra's retort ("Turn away your eyes, lest they see vanity") wittily adapts Ps 119:37 "Averte oculos meos, ne videant vanitatem" (Turn away my eyes, lest they see vanity). I thank Ann Matter for confirming the biblical source of the anecdote.

tainment and a Venetian publisher's profit. This vignette featuring Battiferra, along with a companion piece for her husband Ammannati, appears among updates appended to an expanded edition of 1565. It situates Laura in high society, a wealthy leisured class that enjoys the luxury of a carriage for relaxational outings.[68] It pairs her with a sister poet of a patrician family. It announces her learning, her fluency in Latin, and her familiarity with the Bible. The verse she quotes comes from the Psalms, on which she had just published a new book. Domenichi, in short, has captured Battiferra in a characterizing moment.

I sette salmi penitentiali appeared at the presses of Giunti in 1564. Laura offers her *Psalms* to the duchess of her native Urbino, Vittoria Farnese Della Rovere (1519–1602), wife of Duke Guidobaldo II and a granddaughter of the Farnese pope who had convened the Council, Paul III. Addressing the duchess, she boldly identifies herself as a successor to King David in poetry, to Saint Jerome in translating the Bible, and to Saint Paul in her militant Christianity. After this general dedication, where the poet claims her place in a tradition reaching back to biblical times, every Psalm has an individual preface. These take the form of dedicatory letters from Laura, who speaks as a scriptural commentator to well-born women in nunneries of Florence and Urbino, explaining why each text is appropriate for its recipient (1, pt. 2.3). Nine of Laura's "spiritual sonnets" round off the book (1, pt. 2.1, 2.4–5). They begin with a poem that cites verbatim in its final verse the final line of Petrarch's first sonnet, his retrospective *pentimento:* "quanto piace al mondo è breve sogno" ('whatever pleases in the world is a brief dream'). To cap her own sequence, Laura publishes a pair of sonnets from Don Silvano Razzi and Gherardo Spini, who congratulate her on the success of her endeavor (1.II, 1.I).

Although a marriage of Psalms and sonnets might seem to violate modern notions of unity, Battiferra could have been thinking about this arrangement for several years, as a letter of April 5, 1561, from her husband to Michelangelo hints. With apologies for not yet having given the venerated older sculptor a copy of Laura's *Primo libro,* Ammannati writes, "I didn't send the book of my wife's poems before, as I promised Your Lordship, because

68. Ammannati kept a carriage, too. Among their surviving account records is a bill payment for the repair of a carriage wheel (ASF, Comp. Soppr. da Leopoldo, *filza* 241, fol. 75r: "per una ruota del suo cocio"). The accompanying anecdote about Laura's husband tells of a dinner guest familiar enough with Ammannati's household to go out into the kitchen, where he found the cook making a recipe for "uova maritate" (married eggs—perhaps an omelet or soufflé). "And because the poor woman had married a daughter of hers to a man who was wayward ("sviato"), he took occasion from those eggs to tease her, saying this, 'Monna Fabiana (for that was the servant's name), you know how to marry eggs better than daughters.' Whereupon she turned to him in anger and answered like this, 'You could say that if she had been given to you.'"

I was waiting for her to write some spiritual rhymes, as she has done. I thought Your Lordship would appreciate them more than the others, and so I have put them at the end of the book." Tucked in as loose folios at the back of that gift copy, the sonnets become integral to the printed format of her next book, taking their place at the end.[69]

Battiferra's "second book of Tuscan works" once again gathers poets and friends, chosen to suit the new occasion. Razzi the Camaldolite and Spini, who had declared Hebrew poetry the most ancient, dignified, and divinely authoritative of any on earth,[70] enjoy the privilege of final position. Both must have been particularly close to Laura, who would have shared her *Sette salmi penitentiali* with them privately, while the work was still in manuscript. Their compliments give Laura's biblical translation a sendoff, in the old medieval tradition of the *congedo,* a farewell to the work that grants it leave to travel forth in the world.

While Battiferra makes a point of bringing masculine expressions of approval to her project, she creates primarily a gathering of women in her dedicatees. Two of the Urbino nuns to whom she writes, Suor'Angela Virgili and Suora Violante de' Maschi, represent distinguished local families that married into the Battiferri (app. B). Another, Cassandra de' Battiferri, was the poet's aunt. Faustina Vitelli, who receives the first penitential Psalm, was a natural daughter of Chiappino, married to Leonora Cibo and owner of the home where until 1564 Ammannati had his workshop. The Vitelli are understandably a couple prominent among the dedicatees of Laura's poetry (1.28–32; 39). While still reaching out for patronage (surely a motive for directing the volume as a whole to Guidobaldo Della Rovere's duchess),[71]

69. The letter, from Ammannati in Florence to Michelangelo in Rome, is preserved autograph on microfilm in the Archivio Buonarroti, Florence, Biblioteca Medicea-Laurenziana, vol. 6, fol. 14r. (The original is in the Casa Buonarroti in Florence.) For a facsimile reproduction and translation, see Kirkham, "Creative Partners," fig. 3. The text can be found in the modern edition of Michelangelo's correspondence by Paolo Barocchi and Renzo Ristori, *Il carteggio di Michelangelo,* 5 vols. (Florence: Sansoni- S.P.E.S., 1968–83), 5: 250. In the 1564 *editio princeps* of Battiferra's *Salmi penitentiali,* the sonnet pages at the end have no pagination, only the signature numbers of gathering F, which suggests that whether they were planned or not to appear with the biblical translations, they were consigned separately from the Psalms to the printer.

70. The same year that Laura published her *Salmi penitentiali* and with the same press, Gherardo Spini brought out an edition of poetry by Giovanni Della Casa, to which the publisher Giunti appended a *Rimario* [rhyming dictionary] for Laura Battiferra (1.58). In his dedicatory letter to Mario Colonna, Spini writes that every nation on earth with respect for wisdom has honored the poetic art. Among those, the Hebrews produced the literature that is "first in time, in dignity, and divine witness." See Giovanni Della Casa, *Rime, et prose di M. Giovanni della Casa,* ed. Gherardo Spini (Florence: Giunti, 1564), 3–11.

71. A few months after the death of Laura's first husband, who had been a musician at the court of Guidobaldo II Della Rovere, the Duke of Urbino indicated his wish to contribute to her support. Piperno, *L'immagine del duca,* 61–62, quotes from a document of July, 1549, in which the

Laura in this book is less concerned about making a splash at court than with the more solitary search for a spiritual path. Her dedication of the Psalms to named nuns, like sonnets she wrote for others left in anonymity (1, pt. 2.11), must reflect her habit of visiting their religious houses. This dialogue with ladies under the veil certainly bespeaks great admiration for the contemplative life, into which she herself gradually withdrew during her later years. From the isolation of their cloisters—the Murate, the Chiarito, and Santa Marta of Florence; Santa Chiara and Santa Lucia at Urbino—they come together in an ideal community as readers of the Psalms in Battiferra's translation, a tribute to their quiet lives that affirms the power of their prayers.[72]

With her third book, the *Rime,* the poet's intention was clearly to reprint all that she herself had already published—her *Primo libro dell'opere toscane* (Florence, 1560) and *I setti salmi penitentiali* with their trailer of spiritual sonnets (Florence, 1564)—plus as much of her unpublished verse as she still possessed.[73] Like her first two books, this final anthology convokes the men and women who animated her world, now in wider circles that proclaim important new attachments, notably the Jesuits. Diverse personalities, they populate the places of her life—from Urbino, to which she belonged from birth until her first marriage and widowhood (1523–49); to Rome, where she spent five years happily remarried, close to her father in his Vatican circles (1550–55); and Medici Florence, her home with Bartolomeo Ammannati from the age of thirty-two until she died (1555–89).

HER ACHIEVEMENT: "WHEN DID OUR TENTH SISTER COME INTO THE WORLD?"

Laura Battiferra is unique in her literary identity, as much mythical icon as historical woman. Her first name makes her the perfect Petrarchan subject, a Laura who is metaphorically a laurel. She herself seems to have constructed

---

duke assumes "the protection of Laura Battiferra . . . since it seems to me that the wife of my servant should be so defended." Battiferra's poetry also thanks the Vitelli, whose house near Ponte alla Carraia provided both living quarters and Ammannati's workshop. See Hildegard Utz, "A Note on the Chronology of Ammannati's Fountain of Juno," *Burlington Magazine* 114.831 (June 1972): 394–95; also Charles Davis, "Four Documents for the Villa Giulia," *Römisches Jahrbuch für Kunstgeschichte* 16 (1978): 219–23.

72. See Elissa Weaver's excellent study of convent life and literature, both within the cloister and in relation to the world outside, *Convent Theater in Early Modern Italy* (Cambridge: Cambridge University Press, 2002).

73. Some of her poetry that correspondents published in their *canzonieri* does not appear in the Casanatense manuscript, but some does. For example, her sonnet to Sleep, modeled on the famous antecedent by Della Casa, appears in the anthology by Offredi published at Cremona in 1560 (2.1), but *Rime* reproduces a close variant from the *Primo libro* (1.58).

this persona, which allows her to be an androgynous composite, at once successor to the Tuscan master sonneteer and namesake of his lady. In her earliest datable sonnets, the verse of mourning for Vittorio Sereni, she imagines herself a modern-day descendent of Ovid's nymph Daphne, reincarnated in Petrarch's Laura. (1.113). Peers in the community of poets readily pick up her cues, as they shower her with compliments that reinforce that mythology. For her Urbino compatriot Antonio Gallo, she is an inspirational "gentle aura breathing sweet" (1.74). For Bronzino who mourns the death of a friend she consoles him as a "healing plant" (2.2); when he plays the part of her Platonic lover, she is "the bough that now beholds the Arno and Isauran wave" (2.29). Bronzino seems to be the only one who capitalizes as well on her family name, Battiferri ("iron beater," "smith"). True to the old medieval dictum that "Names are the consequence of things," his mannerist conceit recalls Dante's "Stony Rhymes," virtuoso pieces on a hard-hearted lady impervious to the poet's love. Pursuing his laurel as Apollo did Daphne, Bronzino despairs of reaching her "fair branches" for "the ice that surrounds her and the iron in which she has her roots" (2.30).

Laura-aura-Laurel-Daphne, like Ovid and Petrarch's ladies before her, is a nymph known from her aquatic haunts—Urbino, city of the Metauro River and its tributary the Isauro; Rome, on Tiber's banks; and Florence, jewel of the Arno. After Laura and Bartolomeo Ammannati move from Rome to Florence in 1555, il Lasca, prominent in the Florentine Academy, imagines Arno gloating over Tiber for his new prize, "first honor of the Muses and Phoebus" (1.86). Bernardo Tasso's "honor of Urbino" becomes for the Florentine Benvenuto Cellini "glory of the Arno" (2.24). Girolamo Razzi, referring to her birth city, versifies approvingly of Arno's pride in the chaste woman who has come to his city from Metauro (1.78). Some, like Ludovico Beccadelli (speaking through the Muse Euterpe), salute her dual citizenship, "Behold the sure glory of the fair Metauro and Tuscan rhymes" (2.15), or they sing, like Gabriele Fiamma, of the luster she brings her sex, "lady honor of ladies" (1.73). Still others lift her to realms beyond earthly geography or mortal gender. Sebastiano Sanleolino, who counts Laura among the lights of Cosimo's court, imagines that she has joined the Muses as a tenth sibling. Like Beccadelli, Sanleolino pretends to overhear one of the nine sisters as she exclaims in a distich over Battiferra's verse (2.23):

> CLIO Ammannatae audisset cum Carmina Laurae,
> "Quando", inquit, "nobis est decima orta soror"?[74]

74. Sebastiano Sanleolino assembled all the heroic events and enviable people of the Grand Duke's marvelous reign after that ruler had died in 1574 in his *Serenissimi Cosmi Medycis primi Hetruriae Magniducis Actiones* (Florence: Georgii Marescoti, 1578).

(When Clio heard the poems of Laura Ammannati, she asked, "When was a tenth sister born to us?")

Contrary to these witty images of Laura as a flighty nymph or recalcitrant iron lady, she was in reality a person who loved society, especially in her younger years, when she composed poetry by invitation—love songs for Isabella de' Medici (1.21–26); for Leonora Vitelli, who ordered a tribute to her husband (1.28); for Ortensia Colonna (1.35). Even in her later more religious period, she confesses to still feeling the pull of her coteries (1, pt. 2.13). Ever a reliable voice of the political regime, however, she continues to produce verse for public occasions: signs identifying the Wise and Foolish Virgins, evidently for a public procession (2.32); similar placards for rivers personified, again in a Medici entertainment (2.34); a madrigal sung on the feast of San Giovanni in 1577 for the birth of a Medici heir (2.22).

While Battiferra planned her books to honor topmost her patrons and their familiars, the poets in her circle are most important by number. Women not surprisingly hold a special place in her world, as Domenichi's anecdote of her coach ride with Fiammetta Soderini implies. Scattered dedicatees in both her *canzonieri,* they line up in a programmatic sequence carried over from her *Primo libro* to her *Rime,* beginning with the trio for Leonora Cibo de' Vitelli (1.30–32). Ladies are the sole dedicatees of her Psalms. After poets and women, another group striking for its presence are the religious. Verse to popes brackets her corpus at the earliest and latest periods (Paul III, 1549; Gregory XIII, 1585); she has a sonnet exchange with Grand Duke Francesco de' Medici's personal theologian, Agostino de' Cupiti da Evoli (1.III); Girolamo Razzi, later the Camaldolite Don Silvano, is a good friend who appears in all three of her books (1.II; 1.63; 1.78–79).[75]

Closest to Battiferra is her partner in art, Bartolomeo Ammannati. As she is "Dafne," he is "Fidia," heroic for restoring a flood-damaged Arno bridge (1.46), but vulnerable to illness from which she prays he recover (1.47), and honored for his sculpture in her eight-part sonnet exchange with Lelio Bonsi (1.92–93). Often during their forty-year union they lent their skills to the same projects or goals—Cosimo's triumphal entry in 1560 to take possession of his new fief Siena (1.16), the occasion for the publication of Laura's *Primo libro;* Michelangelo's funeral (2.19–20); Jesuit advocacy (1.62; 1, pt. 2.8). In her distinctive iconography as poetess her voice is a literary counterpart to the sculptural hand of her husband. One of Battiferra's favorite devices,

75. Her verse also gravitates toward other special population groups—the artists (Ammannati 1.90–91, 93; Bronzino 1.76–77, 88–89; Cellini 1.80–81), doctors (Apollo 1.47; Francesco Montevarchi, a new "Aesculapius" 1.52; Bartolomeo Strada 1.61), and soldiers (Chiappino Vitelli 1.28–29, 39; Don García de Toledo 1.38; Pietro Bonaventura 1.70).

for example, is to imagine her rivers personified as ancient fluvial gods (1.12; 1.19, etc.). She stages Arno and all his aqueous relatives in a sonnet composed after the flood of 1557 (1.46) as bearded, laureled old men who recline propped on one elbow as if in a river bed, their attributes a vase from which they pour their waters and a cornucopia of fruit and flowers to symbolize the life their shores nourish. The conception, which has its literary source in Ovid's Acheloüs myth (*Met.* 9.1–88), would have also been familiar to her from the visual arts and in examples that could not have been closer to home, the many representations of rivers and watery spirits wrought by her own husband, a master in that mixed genre—part sculpture, part architecture, and part hydraulic magic—the Renaissance fountain.[76]

Places no less than people shape her distinguishing image in the community of *Petrarchisti*. Tiber, Metauro, and Arno, while unique to her as a trio, are synecdoches for cities that she has in common with many other poets. Before Battiferra, for example, the Metauro River had already figured in rhymes written by Pietro Bembo during his six-year residency at the Della Rovere court and in verse by Giovanni Guidiccioni, bishop of Fossombrone, who found balm for his soul in the city so picturesquely set on that river's banks. Laura's sonnets also sing of Arno's smaller relative, the Mensola (1.53–54). A stream made famous in the Italian pastoral tradition by Giovanni Boccaccio's *Nymphs of Fiesole,* it flows in the Fiesolan hills below Mount Cecero near the village of Maiano, where the Ammannati enjoyed a country house. There Battiferra communed with nature in solitary strolls. Describing them lyrically, she follows precedent set both by Petrarch and the more proximate Benedetto Varchi, her neighbor in those environs.[77] Maiano, Mensola, and Cecero, far from city and court, are characterizing landmarks in the more intimate, confessional, and contemplative aspects of her poetry.

If Maiano is her Vaucluse, the beautiful meditative poetry she wrote there transcends mere imitation. Speaking more colloquially, she tells of quiet walks through that countryside in her letters to Varchi. Likewise, sonnets from "Dafne" to "Damon" (Varchi), while conventionally coded in pastoral form, refer to wine she herself has casked and apples from her orchard. Living between Florence and Maiano, the Ammannati seem to have been

76. For more on the professional collaboration of Battiferra and Ammannati, see Kirkham, "Creative Partners." Other poets before had personified rivers (cf. Petrarch, *RS* 180, 208), but Battiferra develops the classical personification imagery much more insistently and with greater visual emphasis.

77. Discounting the name of Dante's contemporary Dante da Maiano, "Maiano" does not appear in the lexicon of any poet in Quondam's monumental *Archivio della tradizione lirica da Petrarca a Marino* (Rome: Lexis, 1997) except that of Benedetto Varchi.

part-time gentlemen farmers. Their library included Pietro Crescentio's influential early thirteenth-century manual on agriculture, translated into Tuscan in the Quattrocento, essential for anyone who wished to follow Cicero's advice and enjoy the pleasures of a villa.[78] This activity gives a real-life context for Laura's frequent echoes of Luigi Alamanni's verse treatise *La coltivatione,* in the tradition of Virgil's *Georgics,* which she also knew (1.60).

Battiferra's personal idiom reflects as much the literature in her mental library as the people and places of her life. Contemporaries always emphasize her learning. Her writing, with hints of scholasticism (1.10, 1.72), confirms a remarkably cultured mind. Without ever directly attributing, she is constantly citing. Her sources range from the Bible to Ignatius Loyola, from Virgil and Ovid to Vittoria Colonna. Petrarchan borrowings lie most thickly on her pages, but Dante resonates there as well, as do Italy's great vernacular poets of successive generations—Sannazzaro, Bembo, Della Casa. Beyond the Latin and Italian classics, she displays a selective preference for poets with Urbino ties—natives like Antonio Gallo and Pietro Bonaventura, or visitors like Bembo, Bernardo Cappello, and Bernardo Tasso who sojourned for patronage there and in Pesaro, the duchy's administrative capital. Playing on the name Della Rovere ("oak"), she joins their chorus under boughs of oak, variant to the laurel. Her Ovidian epithet for the oak is "Chaonian plant," attached metonymically to Duke Guidobaldo (1.7).[79] She targets her borrowings with astonishing precision, tailoring her verse to the occasion at hand. Widowed of her first husband, she mourns by connecting with the archetypical widow poet, Vittoria Colonna, doubly appropriate to a new Urbino voice since Vittoria was a granddaughter of Duke Federico da Montefeltro (1.106 and app. C). The seventh poem for her departed "Vittorio," whom Duke Guidobaldo II Della Rovere had patronized, imitates closely a sonnet by Bernardo Cappello lamenting the death of Virginia Varana (d. 1547), Guidobaldo's first wife (1.112).

Other sources that flowed into her work can be traced to her Roman period. Anton Francesco Raineri's *Cento sonetti* (1553), dedicated to Fabiano del Monte and Pope Julius III (Ammannati's Roman patron), echo frequently in Battiferra's lyrics. Celebrating Cosimo's son Giovanni de' Medici's auspicious promotion to the rank of cardinal, a step away from the papacy (1.15), she quotes programmatically from a poem written half a century before by Gio-

78. See Kirkham, "Creative Partners," app. 6, for a list of books purchased by Ammannati.

79. Piperno, *L'immagine del duca,* 67–70, discusses the poets at Guidobaldo's court during the 1550s and 1560s. Under the oak's "sheltering boughs," the court became a "fertile laboratory for Petrarchist lyric."

vanni Muzzarelli for another Giovanni de' Medici, better known as Pope Leo X. Annibal Caro could have encouraged her interest in poetry composed by his close friend Giovanni Guidiccioni of Lucca, whom she probably read in Lodovico Domenichi's anthologies of Tuscan authors. Guidiccioni, moreover, would have been appealing for his connections to the Duchy of Urbino. He was bishop of Fossombrone on the Metauro, where Laura's father held an ecclesiastical benefice as provost (*preposto*).[80]

During her Florentine period she becomes Varchi's disciple. Perhaps more than any other poet except Petrarch, he colors her oeuvre. Writing Duke Guidobaldo of Urbino (1.7, fig. 17 above), she borrows from a parallel sonnet by Varchi to Duke Cosimo (and before, from Bembo to Duke Ercole d'Este); her sonnet to the Spanish king Philip II draws on Varchi's to the English king, Henry VIII. Other favorites included the Neapolitan Luigi Tansillo, fashionable in Medici Florence for the political ties that connected Cosimo to Naples, where his father-in-law was the Spanish viceroy. Although generally in strong alignment with the Medici orbit, Battiferra did not shy away from poets less politically correct. Often imitated in the sonnets of her first *canzoniere* is the exiled (and deceased) republican Luigi Alamanni, who had published his much admired *Opere toscane* in Lyon in 1532–33 (1.60). She proudly imitates Giovan Battista Strozzi (1.43), whose madrigals everyone was reading in privately circulated manuscripts, even though he belonged to a magnate clan of Cosimo's enemies in the siege of Siena. To solve the problem of bringing Giovan Battista into the virtual salon of her *Primo libro*, she suppresses the dedicatory titles of the madrigals she composed in his manner, but in the late *Rime*, not bound by any political allegiance, the same poems reappear, this time complete with the dedicatee's name.

Battiferra took seriously the precedent set by women poets. The division of her late *canzoniere* into two parts, with a second under the rubric of "spiritual rhymes," follows the pattern in publications of Vittoria Colonna's verse (and before it, Bembo's 1501 watershed edition of Petrarch's *Rime, in vita*

80. Sonnets by Rainiero/Raineri (1510–60) had begun to appear scattered in anthologies before 1553. See, e.g., Lodovico Domenichi's *Rime diverse di molti eccellentiss. Auttori nuovamente raccolte. Libro primo* (Venice: Gabriel Giolito di Ferrarii, 1545; 2d ed. 1546; 3d ed. 1549). Aided by Bembo, the pro-Medici Giovanni Muzzarelli (1486–1516) became governor of the Rocca di Mondaino, not far from Urbino. See the brief biography at http://www.vignettopoli.net/poeta.html. His verse also appears in anthologies published by Lodovico Domenichi. Giovanni Guidiccioni of Lucca (d. 1541) was a churchman who had spent time in Rome in the service of Pope Paul III and a literary friend of men whom Battiferra knew—Bernardo Tasso, Annibal Caro, and Benedetto Varchi. See Giovanni Guidiccioni, *Opere*, ed. Carlo Minutoli, 2 vols. (Florence: G. Barbèra, 1867) for Guidiccioni's life and poetry.

and *Rime, in morte* of Madonna Laura). By offering her *Primo libro* of 1560 to the Medici duchess, Laura follows in the footsteps of Tullia d'Aragona, who had dedicated her *Rime* to Eleonora in 1547. Simultaneously, she pays homage to Varchi, since he had been Tullia's literary advisor during her Florentine years. Hints of Gaspara Stampa hover in Battiferra's poetry, and more obvious traces of familiarity with Chiara Matraini of Lucca are allusively present in a mix with Petrarchan word bites in the very first sonnet of the *Primo libro* (1.1).

Ironically, over the centuries after her death, literary kinship with these women immured Battiferra in a virtual matroneum, isolating her from the cultural mainstream where once she thrived. Unlike the accomplished Vittoria Colonna, whose exemplary widowhood and attachment to such male luminaries as Michelangelo and Pietro Bembo helped assure her momentum in history, Battiferra's fortunes have been linked above all to her husband, as famous in his day as she was, but overshadowed historically by Michelangelo in the generation before and Giambologna in the generation after. An affable man, he participated in team projects that swallowed up his name; owing to unlucky circumstances, some of his most important individually signed works never were installed, and others were lost. The mannerism that both Ammannati practiced in their respective art forms fell out of favor, as did Laura's *Petrarchismo*. Jesuits paid homage to the couple, but their order was suppressed in the eighteenth century, severing a tradition. Qualities that won praise from contemporaries have distanced Battiferra's writing from our postmodern world—classical learning, a mannerist style of wit, versatility as an occasional poet, and Catholic Reformation religious values.[81] For us, her poetry requires an apparatus with the keys of commentary to unlock meanings no longer public.

Had she succeeded in publishing her *Rime,* Laura Battiferra's afterlife might have been a happier one. As it was, almost all of her late production, entrusted to a single manuscript, lay unnoticed in the Casanatense library for over four hundred years. Counting those poems and other verse that circulated only in handwritten copies, nearly half of Battiferra's corpus never saw publication. She has managed to survive as a marginal presence, but the same is true of the fellow poets who buoyed her reputation in the first place: Annibal Caro, Benedetto Varchi, Bernardo Tasso, Lodovico Domenichi—even the very visible Bronzino and Cellini, famous as artists but little known as lyric writers. Whereas in her midyears Battiferra aggressively sought rec-

81. My profile "Sappho on the Arno" traces her declining fortunes, showing how by the late nineteenth century she had suffered near total eclipse in Italian literary history.

ognition for her art, in later life she withdrew from public view, passing her days in the private chapel that Bartolomeo had had built for her at a villa in Camerata, near one of the Florence city gates.[82] She may herself have diminished the fame that she so aggressively pursued when younger by retreating into that more secluded life as an older woman to meditate on the vanities of the world,[83] to pray for salvation, and to compose religious poetry that never crossed the threshold of print.

82. Filippo Baldinucci, *Notizie de' professori del disegno da Cimabue,* 6 vols. (Florence: S. Franchi, et al., 1681–1728), 4: 18. In 1576, Bartolomeo Ammannati rented a villa in Camerata from the Camaldolites and Battiferra "stayed there most of the time, delighting in a new chapel that he had built there."

83. A letter by Bartolomeo Ammannati of August 13, 1573, to a former patron in Padua, the jurist Marco Mantua Benavides, informs him that he and Battiferra "by God's grace" are well and "mortified in part by the smoke and ambitions and vainglories of the world, we pray the bounty of God to take away from us what remains of them so that we can at last truly serve the purpose for which we are put by God in the world." Cited in Victoria Kirkham, "La poetessa al presepio," *Filologia e critica* 27 (2) (2002): 258–76.

VOLUME EDITOR'S BIBLIOGRAPHY

GENERAL REFERENCE WORKS FOR INFORMATION ON BATTIFERRA AND HER CIRCLE

Allgemeines Künstler-Lexikon. Munich and Leipzig: K.G. Sauer, 1992.

Crescimbeni, Giovan Maria. *Dell'istoria della volgar poesia scritta da Giovan Maria Crescimbene*. 6 vols. Venice: Lorenzo Basegio, 1730.

Dizionario biografico degli Italiani. Rome: Istituto dell'Enciclopedia Italiana, 1960–.

Indice biografico italiano. Archivio biografico italiano. Edited by Tommaso Nappo. Munich: Sauer, 1987–90.

Mazzuchelli, Giovanni Maria. *Gli scrittori d'Italia. Cioè notizie storiche e critiche intorno alle vite e agli scritti dei letterati italiani*. 6 vols. Brescia: Bossini, 1753–63.

Quadrio, Francesco Saverio. *Della storia e della ragione d'ogni poesia*. 4 vols. Bologna: Ferdinando Pisarri, 1739.

Shamà, Davide, and Andrea Dominici Battelli, eds. *Genealogie delle dinastie italiane*. http://www.sardimpex.com/index.htm.

Tiraboschi, Girolamo, et al. *Biblioteca Modenese, o notizie della vita e delle opere degli scrittori natii degli stati del serenissimo signore Duca di Modena*. 6 vols. Modena: Società Tipografica, 1781–86.

———. *Storia della letteratura italiana*. Modena: Società Tipografica, 1787–94.

PRIMARY SOURCES

Alamanni, Luigi. *Opere toscane*. 2 vols. Lyon: Sebast. Gryphius, 1532–33.

———. *Opere toscane di Luigi Alamanni al Christianissimo Rè Francesco Primo*. Venice: Per Pietro di Nicolini da Sabio, 1533.

———. *Della coltivatione*. Florence: Appresso Bernardo Giunti, 1549.

———. *Versi e prose*. Edited by P. Raffaelli. Florence: LeMonnier, 1859. In *Archivio della tradizione lirica da Petrarca a Marino*, edited by Amadeo Quondam. Rome: Lexis, 1997. CD-ROM.

Ammannati, Bartolomeo. *Zibaldone*. Florence: Biblioteca Riccardiana, MS Ed. Rare, 120.

D'Aragona, Tullia. *Dialogo della signora Tullia d'Aragona della inifinità di amore*. Venice: Gabriel Giolito de' Ferrari, 1547.

———. *Rime della signora Tullia di Aragona et di diverse a lei.* Venice: Gabriel Giolito de Ferrari, 1547.

Atanagi, Dionigi, ed. *Rime di diversi nobilissimi et eccellentissimi autori in morte della signora Irene delle signore di Spilimbergo, alle quali si sono aggiunti versi latini di diversi egregij poeti in morte della medesima signora.* Venice: Domenico et Giovanni Battista Guerra, 1561.

———, ed. *De le rime di diversi nobili poeti toscani, raccolte da M. Dionigi Atanagi.* Venice: Lodovico Avanzo, 1565.

Baldinucci, Filippo. *Notizie de' professori del disegno da Cimabue in quà per le quali si dimostra come, e per chi le belle arti di pittura, scultura e architettura, lasciata la rozzezza della maniera greca e gotica, si siano in questi secoli ridotte all'antica loro perfezione.* 6 vols. Florence: S. Franchi, P. Matini, Tartini & Franchi, G. Manni, 1681–1728.

Bargagli, Girolamo [il Materiale Intronato]. *Dialogo de' giuochi che nelle veggbie sanesi si usano di fare.* Siena: Luca Bonetti, 1572.

———. *La Pellegrina Commedia.* Siena: Luca Bonetti, 1589.

Barocchi, Paolo, and Renzo Ristori, eds. *Il carteggio di Michelangelo.* Edizione postuma di Giovanni Poggi. 5 vols. Florence: Sansoni-S.P.E.S, 1965–83.

Battiferra degli Ammannati, Laura. *Il primo libro dell'opere toscane di M. Laura Battiferra degli Ammannati.* Florence: Giunti, 1560.

———. *I sette salmi penitentiali del santissimo profeta Davit. Tradotti in lingua Toscana da Madonna Laura Battiferra Degli Ammannati. Con gli argomenti sopra ciascuno di essi, composti dalla medesima: insieme con alcuni suoi sonetti spirituali.* Florence: Giunti, 1564.

———. *Rime della Sig. Laura Battiferra nuovamente date in luce da Antonio Bulifon.* Naples: Antonio Bulifon, 1694.

———. *Lettere di Laura Battiferri Ammannati a Benedetto Varchi.* Edited by Carlo Gargiolli. Scelta di curiosità letterarie inedite o rare dal secolo XIII al XIX, dispensa 166. 1879. Reprint, Bologna: Commissione per i testi di lingua, 1968.

———. *Il primo libro delle opere toscane.* Edited by Enrico Maria Guidi. Urbino: Accademia Rafaello, 2000.

———. *I sette salmi penitenziali di David con alcuni sonetti spirituali.* Edited by Enrico Maria Guidi. Urbino: Accademia Raffaello, 2005.

Battiferri, Matteo, ed. *Commentum Doctoris excellentissimi Alberti Magni ordinis praedicatorum in libros physicorum.* Venice: Per Joannem de Forlivio et Gregorii fratres, 1488.

Beccadelli, Ludovico. *Rime.* Parma, Biblioteca Palatina, MS 972.

Bembo, Pietro. *Prose della volgar lingua. Gli Asolani. Rime.* Edited by Carlo Dionisotti. Turin: Unione Tipografico-Editrice Torinese, 1966.

Biblia sacra vulgatae editionis. Rome: Editionis Paulinae, 1957.

Boccaccio, Giovanni. *Famous Women.* Translated by Virginia Brown. I Tatti Renaissance Library. Cambridge, Mass.: Harvard University Press, 2001.

———. *Rime.* Edited by Vittore Branca. In *Tutte le opere,* Giovanni Boccaccio, vol. 5, pt. 1. Milan: Mondadori, 1992.

Bronzino, Agnolo. *Delle rime del Bronzino pittore.* Florence: Biblioteca Nazionale, MS Magl. 2.9.10.

———. *Rime del Bronzino ed altre rime inedite di più insigni poeti.* Edited by Domenico Moreni. Florence: Magheri, 1823.

———. *Antologia poetica.* Edited by Giorgio Cerboni Baiardi. In Andrea Emiliani, *Il Bronzino.* Con un'antologia poetica, scelta e presentata da Giorgio Cerboni Baiardi. Busto Arsizio: Bramante Editrice, 1960.

Buonarroti, Michelangelo. *Rime.* Edited by E. N. Girardi. Bari: Laterza, 1960. In Quondam, *Archivio.*

Calzolari, Pietro. *Historia monastica di D. Pietro Calzolari, da Buggiano di Toscana, Monaco della Badia di Firenze, della congregatione di Monte Casino, Distinta in cinque giornate, nella quale, brevemente si raccontano tutti i Sommi Pontefici, e quelli, che hanno predicata la fede Christiana a i Gentili. Gl'imperadori, i Re, Duchi, Principi, e Conti. L'Imperatrici, e Reine, et altre Donne Illustri, e Sante. Huomini dotti, che hanno scritto qualche opera. E Santi, i quali sono stati dell'ordine Monastico.* Florence: Appresso Lorenzo Torrentino, 1561.

Capilupi, Lelio. *Rime del Signor Lelio e' fratelli de' Capilupi.* Mantua: Francesco Osana, 1585.

Cappello, Bernardo. *Rime.* Venice: Domenico et Gio. Battista Guerra Fratelli, 1560.

———. *Rime.* Tesi di laurea di E. Albini (rel. Cesare Bozzetti). Università di Pavia, 1969–70. In Quondam, *Archivio.*

Caro, Annibal. *Apologia de gli Academici di Banchi di Roma, contra M. Lodovico Castelvetro da Modena. In forma d'uno Spaccio di Maestro Pasquino. Con alcune operette del predella, del buratto, di ser Fedocco. In difesa de la seguente Canzone del Commendatore Annibal Caro. Appertenenti tutte a l'uso de la lingua toscana, et al vero modo di poetare:* Parma: In casa di Seth Viotto, 1558.

———. *Rime del commendator Annibal Caro.* Venice: Aldo Manuzio, 1569.

———, trans. *L'Eneide di Virgilio.* Venice: B. Giunti e Fratelli, 1581.

———. *Lettere.* Edited by Aulo Greco. 3 vols. Florence: Le Monnier, 1957–61.

Cellini, Benvenuto. *Opere.* Edited by Giuseppe Guido Ferrero. Turin: Unione Tipografico-Editrice Torinese, 1971. Also in Quondam, *Archivio.*

———. *The Autobiography of Benvenuto Cellini.* Translated by John Addington Symonds. New York: Modern Library, n.d.

Christiani, Francesco, ed. *Rime di diversi eccellenti autori, in vita, e in morte dell'illustrissima Livia Colonna.* Rome: Antonio Barrè for M. Francesco Christiani, 1555.

Cimegotto, Cesare. "Laura Battiferri e due lettere inedite di Bernardo Tasso." *Giornale Storico della Letteratura Italiana* 24 (1894): 388–98.

Cirni, Anton Francesco. *La reale entrata dell'ecc.mo signor duca et duchessa di Fiorenza, in Siena, con la significatione delle Latine inscrittioni, e con alcuni Sonetti, scritta per Anton Francesco Cirni Corso.* Rome: Antonio Blado Stampator Camerale, 1560.

———. *Comentarii d'Antonfrancesco Cirni corso, ne quali si descrive la guerra ultima di Francia, la celebratione del Concilio Tridentino, il soccorso d'Orano, l'impresa del Pignone, e l'Historia dell'assedio di Malta diligentissimamente raccolta insieme con altre cose notabili.* Rome: Giulio Accolto, 1567.

Colonna, Mario. *Poesie toscane dell'illustris. sign. Mario Colonna, et di M. Pietro Angelio con l'Edipo Tiranno Tragedia di Sofocle Tradotta dal medesimo Angelio.* Florence: Bartolomeo Sermartelli, 1589.

Colonna Vittoria. *Rime.* Edited by Alan Bullock. Bari: Laterza, 1982. In Quondam, *Archivio.*

Crescentio, Pietro. *Pietro Crescentio tradotto novamente per M. Francesco Sansovino. Nel quale si trattano le cose della villa . . .* Venice: Rampazetto, 1564.

Cupiti [Copeti] da Evoli, Agostino de'. *Rime spirituali del R. P. Agostino de' Cupiti da Evoli Min.Osser. Alla Sereniss. Sig.[a] L'Infante Donna Caterina d'Austria Duchessa di Savoia.* In Vico Equense: Appresso Gioseppe Cacchi, 1592.

Dante Alighieri. *La divina commedia secondo l'antica vulgata.* Edited by Giorgio Petrocchi. 4 vols. Florence: Le Lettere, 1966–67.

———. *The Divine Comedy.* Edited and translated by Charles S. Singleton. 6 vols. Princeton: Princeton University Press, 1970–75.

Della Casa, Giovanni. *Rime, et prose di M. Giovanni della Casa. Riscontrate con i migliori originali, et ricorrette con grandissima diligentia. Ove si sono poste piu rime del medesimo Auttore di nuovo ritrovate, et insieme una tavola di tutte le desinentie delle sue rime ridotte co i versi interi sotto le lettere vocali.* Edited by Gherardo Spini. Florence: Giunti, 1564.

———. *Rime.* Edited by Roberto Fedi. Rome: Salerno Editrice, 1978. In Quondam, *Archivio.*

———. *Rime.* Edited by Roberto Fedi. Milan: Biblioteca Universale Rizzoli, 2000.

Del Tempio alla Divina signora donna Giovanna d'Aragona. Edited by Girolamo Ruscelli. 1555.

Dolce, Lodovico, ed. *Rime di diversi signori napolitani e d'altri.* Venice: Gabriel Giolito de' Ferrari, 1556.

Domenichi, Lodovico, ed. *Rime diverse di molti eccellentiss. auttori nuovamente raccolte. Libro Primo.* Venice: Gabriel Giolito de' Ferrarii, 1545; 2d ed., 1546; 3d ed., 1549.

———, ed. *Rime diverse d'alcune nobilissime, et virtuosissime donne.* Lucca: Busdragho, 1559.

———, ed. *Poesie toscane, et latine di diversi eccel. ingegni, nella morte del S. D. Giovanni Cardinale, del sig. Don Grazia de Medici, et della S. Donna Leonora di Toledo de Medici Duchessa di Fiorenza et di Siena.* Florence: L. Torrentino, 1563.

———. *Historia varia di M. Lodovico Domenichi, nella quale si contengono molte cose argute, nobili, e degne di memoria, di diversi Principi et huomini illustri; divisa in XIIII libri: con due tavole, la prima de' nomi delle persone e delle cose notabili, et l'altra della proprietà delle cose.* Venice: Gabriel Giolito de' Ferrari, 1564.

_____ *Facetie, motti, et burle, di diversi signori et persone private raccolte per M. Lodovico Domenichi et da lui di nuovo del settimo libro ampliate. Con una nuova aggiunta di Motti raccolti da Thomaso Porcacchi.* Venice: Giorgio de' Cavalli, 1565.

Esequie del Divino Michelangelo Buonarroti Celebrate in Firenze dall'Accademia de' Pittori, Scultori, et Architettori Nella Chiesa di S. Lorenzo il dì 14 Luglio. Florence: Giunti, 1564.

Feliciangeli, B. *Notizie e documenti sulla vita di Caterina Cibo-Varano Duchessa di Camerino.* Camerino: Tipografia Savini, 1891.

Fiamma, Gabriello. *Rime spirituali del R. D. Gabriel Fiamma, Canonico Regolare Lateranense; esposte da lui medesimo. All'Illustr.mo et eccell.mo s.re il S. Marc'antonio Colonna, duca di Tagliacozzo, e gran Contestabile del Regno di Napoli.* Venice: Francesco de' Franceschi Senese, 1570.

Firenzuola, Agnolo. *Opere.* Edited by Adriano Seroni. Florence: Sansoni, 1958.

Gambara, Veronica. *Le rime.* Edited by Alan Bullock. Florence: Olschki, 1995.

Gamucci, Bernardino. *Le antichità della città di Roma raccolte sotto brevità da diversi antichi, et moderni Scrittori per M. Bernardino Gamucci da San Gimignano: Et con nuovo ordine fedelmente descritte, et rappresentate con bellissime figure, nel modo che a' tempi nostri si ritrovano, in quest editione emendate, et corrette da Tomaso Porcacchi.* Venice: Appresso li Gioliti, 1585.

Garzoni, Tomaso. *Le vite delle donne illustri della scrittura sacra. Con l'aggionta delle vite delle donne oscure e laide dell'uno e l'altro Testamento. E un Discorso in fine sopra la nobiltà delle donne.* Edited by Beatrice Collina. Ravenna: Longo, 1994.

Gilio, Giovanni Andrea. *Due dialogi di M. Giovanni Andrea Gilio da Fabriano. Nel primo de' quali si ragiona de le parti Morali, e Civili appertenenti a Letterati Cortigiani, et ad ogni gentil'Huomo, e l'utile, che i Prencipi cavano da i Letterari. Nel secondo si ragiona de gli errori de Pittori circa l'historie, con molte annotationi fatte sopra il Giuditio di Michelangelo, et altre figure, tanto de la vecchia, quanto de la nova Cappella: Et in che modo vogliono esser dipinte le sacre Imagini. Con un discorso sopra la parola Urbe, Città, Colonia, Municipio, Prefettura, Foro, Conciliabolo, Oppido, Terra, Castello, Villa, Pago, Borgo, e qual sia la vera Città.* Camerino: Antonio Gioioso, 1564.

Gonzaga, Curtio. *Rime dell'illustrissimo Curtio Gonzaga.* Vicenza: Nella Stamperia Nova, 1585.

Guidiccioni, Giovanni. *Opere.* Edited by Carlo Minutoli. 2 vols. Florence: G. Barbèra, 1867.

Guinizelli, Guido. *Rime.* In *Poeti del dolce stil nuovo,* edited by M. Marti. Florence: Le-Monnier, 1969. In Quondam, *Archivio.*

Ignatius of Loyola. *The Spiritual Exercises of St. Ignatius of Loyola.* Translated by Father Elder Mullan, S. J. http://www.ccel.org/i/ignatius/exercises/exercises.html.

I manoscritti della Biblioteca Moreniana. Vol. 3, fasc. 1–10. *Provincia di Firenze.* Florence: Tip. Nazionale, 1976–79.

Livy, *History of Rome,* Translated by B. O. Foster, et al. 14 vols. Loeb Classical Library. Cambridge, Mass.: Harvard University Press, 1919–59.

Magno, Celio. *Rime.* Testo provvisorio di Francesco Erspamer. In Quondam, *Archivio.*

Malipiero, Girolamo. *Petrarca spirituale.* In Quondam, *Archivio.*

Manfredi, Muzio. *Per donne romane.* 2 vols. Bologna: A. Benacci, 1575.

Martellini, Antonio. *La solenna entrata dello illustrissimo, et eccellentiss. sig. il sig. duca di Fiorenza et Siena.* Florence: Laurentius Torrentinus, 1560.

Massolo, Pietro. *Primo, et secondo volume delle rime morali di M. Pietro Massolo, gentil'huomo vinitiano, hora Don Lorenzo Monaco Cassinese.* Florence: Nella Stamperia Ducale, Appresso i figliuoli di M. Lorenzo Torrentino et Bernardo Fabbroni Compagni, 1564.

———. *Rime morali di M. Pietro Massolo . . . hora Don Lorenzo Monaco Cassinese.* Venice: Gio. Antonio Rampazetto, 1583.

Matraini, Chiara. *Rime et prose di Madonna Chiara Matraini.* Lucca: Busdraghi, 1555.

———. *Rime e lettere.* Edited by Giovanna Rabitti. Bologna: Commissione per i Testi di Lingua, 1989.

Mattioli, Pier Andrea. *I discorsi di M. Pietro Andrea Mattioli Medico Sanese, ne i sei libri della materia medicinale di Pedacio Dioscoride Anazarbeo con i veri ritratti delle piante & de gli animali, nuovamente aggiuntivi dal medismo.* Venice: V. Valgrisi, 1555.

Morra, Isabella. *Rime.* Edited by Maria Antonietta Grignani. Rome: Salerno Editrice, 2000.

Muzzarelli, Giovanni. *Rime.* Edited by G. Hannüss Palazzini. Mantua: Arcari Editore, 1983. In Quondam, *Archivio.*

New Catholic Edition of the Holy Bible. Translated from the Latin Vulgate. The Old Testament Douay Version; The New Testament Confraternity Edition. New York: Catholic Book Publishing Company, 1949–50.

Offredi, Giovanni, ed. *Rime di diversi autori eccellentissimi.* Cremona: Vincenzo Conti, 1560.

Oradini, Lucio. *Due Lezzioni lette publicamente nell'Accademia Fiorentina.* Florence: Lorenzo Torrentino, 1550.

Ovid, *Fasti.* Translated by Sir James George Frazer, 2d ed. rev. by G. P. Goold. Cambridge, Mass.: Harvard University Press, 1989.

———. *Heroides, Amores.* Translated by Grant Showerman, rev. G. P. Goold. Loeb Classical Library. Cambridge, Mass.: Harvard University Press, 1977.

———. *Metamorphoses.* Translated by Frank Justus Miller. 2 vols. Loeb Classical Library. Cambridge, Mass.: Harvard University Press, 1916. Reprint, 1966–68.

Petrarca, Francesco. *Petrarch's Lyric Poems.* Edited and translated by Robert M. Durling. Cambridge, Mass.: Harvard University Press, 1975.

———. *Triumphi.* Edited by Marco Ariani. Milan: Mursia, 1988.

Pigna, G. Battista. *Il ben divino.* In Quondam, *Archivio.*

Pliny. *Natural History.* Translated by H. Rackham, et al. 10 vols. Loeb Classical Library. Cambridge, Mass.: Harvard University Press, 1938–62.

Quondam, Amadeo, ed. *Archivio della tradizione lirica da Petrarca a Marino.* Rome: Lexis, 1997. CD-ROM.

Quinquaginta fere auctorum et praesertim academicorum Intronatorum Senensium carmina italica. Rome, Biblioteca Angelica, MS 1882.

Rainerio, Anton Francesco. *Cento sonetti.* Milan: G. A. Borgia, 1553.

——— (Raineri). *Cento sonetti.* Tesi di laurea di Guglielmo Gorni, Università di Pavia. In Quondam, *Archivio.*

Razzi, Girolamo. *Della Economica christiana, e civile di don Silvano Razzi. I due primi libri. Ne i quali da una nobile brigata di Donne, et Huomini si ragiona della cura, e governo famigliare: secondo la legge Christiana, e vita Civile.* Florence: Bartolomeo Sermartelli, 1568.

———. *Delle vite delle donne illustri per santità cavate da diversi cattolici et approvati autori dal Padre Abate Don Silvano Razzi Camaldolense.* 6 vols. Florence: Giunti, 1595–1602.

Rime di diversi eccellentissimi autori fatte nella morte dell'Illustrissima et Eccellentissima Duchessa di Fiorenza et Siena, et degli Illustrissimi Signori suoi figliuoli. Ferrara: Valente Panizza Mantovano, 1563.

Rime di diversi nobili huomini et eccellenti poeti nella lingua thoscana. Libro secondo. Venice: Gabriel Giolito de' Ferrarii, 1547.

Ruscelli, Girolamo, ed. *Del Tempio alla Divina signora donna Giovanna d'Aragona, fabricato da tutti i più gentili Spiriti, et in tutte le lingue principali del mondo,* Venice: Plinio Pietrasanta, 1555.

———. *Le imprese illustri del S.or Ieronimo Ruscelli.* Venice: Appresso F. da Franceschi. 1584.

Salviati, Leonardo. *Avvertimenti della lingua sopra 'l Decameron.* 2 vols. Venice: Domenico e Giovan Battista Guerra, 1584; Florence: Giunti, 1586.

Sanleolino, Sebastiano. *Serenissimi Cosmi Medycis primi Hetruriae Magniducis Actiones Sebastiano Sanleolino I. C. Florentino Auctore.* Florence: Typis Georgij Marescoti, 1578.

Sannazzaro, *Arcadia.* In *Opere volgari,* edited by A. Mauro. Bari: Laterza, 1961. In Quondam, *Archivio.*

Stampa, Gaspara, and Veronia Franco. *Rime.* Edited by A. Salza. Bari: Laterza, 1913. In Quondam, *Archivio.*

———. *Rime.* Introduction by Maria Bellonci. Commentary by Rodolfo Ceriello. 3d ed. Milan: Rizzoli, 1994.

Statius. *Silvae, Thebaid.* Edited by J. H. Mozley. 2 vols. Loeb Classical Library. Cambridge, Mass.: Harvard University Press. 1928. Reprint, 1967.

Strozzi, Giovan Battista (the Elder). *Madrigali.* Edited by L. Sorrento. Strassburg: Biblioteca Romanica, 1909. In Quondam, *Archivio.*

———. *Madrigali inediti.* Edited by Mariani. Urbino: Argalia, 1975. In Quondam, *Archivio.*

Strozzi, Giovan Battista (the Younger). In *Miscellanea di poesie italiane,* vol. 1 of the Strozzi Collection. Chicago, Newberry Library, MS Case 6A-11.

Strozziana Classi I–XL. 11 vols. Florence, 1789. See *Catalogo dei Codici della Libreria Strozziana.*

Stufa, Piero, ed. *Componimenti Latini, e Toscani da diversi suoi amici composti nella morte di M. Benedetto Varchi.* Florence: n. p., 1565 [= 1566 modern style].

Tansillo, Luigi. *Il canzoniere.* Edited by Erasmo Pèrcopo. 2 vols. N. p., 1926. Reprint, Naples, 1996. Also in Quondam, *Archivio.*

Tasso, Bernardo. *I tre libri de gli amori di M. Bernardo Tasso.* Venice: Gabriel Giolito de' Ferrari, et fratelli, 1555.

———. *Amori.* In *Rime,* edited by D. Chiodo and V. Martignone. Turin: RES, 1995. In Quondam, *Archivio.*

———. *L'Amadigi.* Venice: Gabriel Giolito de' Ferrari, 1560.

———. *Rime di Messer Bernardo Tasso. Divise in cinque libri nuovamente stampate.* Venice: Gabriel Giolito de' Ferrari, 1560.

———. *Salmi.* Venice: Gabriel Giolito de' Ferrari, 1560.

———. *Salmi.* In *Rime,* edited by D. Chiodo and V. Martignone. Turin: RES, 1995. In Quondam, *Archivio.*

Tasso, Faustino. *Il primo [e secondo] libro delle rime toscane.* Turin: Francesco Dolce e Compagni, 1573.

Il Tempio della divina signora donna Geronima Colonna D'Aragona. Edited by Ottavio Sammarco. Padua: Lorenzo Pasquati, 1568.

Terracina, Laura. *Rime spirituali, morte di Principj, et di signori titulati; et non titulatj, con altri sonetti a particulari gentil'homini et Donne. Composti per la signora Laura Terracina.* Libro Nono. Florence, Biblioteca Nazionale, MS Palat. 229.

Tesauro spirituale vulgare in rima. Venice: Niccolò Zoppino and Vincenzio Compagno, 1524.

Turchi, Francesco. *Salmi penitenziali, di diversi eccellenti autori con alcune rime spirituali di diversi illust. cardinali, di Reverendissimi vescovi, & d'altre persone Ecclesiastiche. Scelti dal reverendo P. Francesco da Trivigi Carmelitano [Francesco Turchi] nuovamente da lui corretti et ristampati* Venice: Gabriel Giolito de' Ferrari, 1568.

Valerius Maximus. *Memorable Doings and Sayings.* Edited and translated by D. R. Shackleton Bailey. 2 vols. Loeb Classical Library. Cambridge, Mass.: Harvard University Press, 2000.

Varchi, Benedetto. *De Sonetti di M. Benedetto Varchi: Parte prima and Parte seconda.* Florence: Lorenzo Torrentino, 1555–57.

———. *Sonetti spirituali di M. Benedetto Varchi: Con alcune risposte, et proposte di diversi eccellentissimi ingegni.* Florence: Stamperia de' Giunti, 1573.

———. *L'Hercolano. Dialogo di Messer Benedetto Varchi, nel qual si ragiona generalmente delle lingue, et in particolare della toscana, e fiorentina.* Venice: Filippo Giunti e Fratelli, 1570.

———. *Cento sonetti sopra la morte di Luca Martini.* Florence, Biblioteca Nazionale, MS 2.8.140.

———, ed. *Sonetti contro gl'Ugonotti.* Florence, Biblioteca Nazionale, MS Magl. 2.8.137.

———, ed. *Sopra il dolorosissimo e pericolosissimo accidente dell'Illustrissimo et eccellentissimo Duca.* Florence, Biblioteca Nazionale, MS Magl. 7.341.

———. *Opere di Benedetto Varchi.* 2 vols. Trieste: Lloyd Adriatico, 1858–59.

Vernaccia, Pier Girolamo. "Battiferri [famiglia] estinta." Urbino, Biblioteca Universitaria, Fondo Comune, busta 131, fasc. I, fol. 37.

———. *Elogio degli uomini illustri d'Urbino.* 1720. Urbino, Biblioteca Universitaria, Fondo Comune, vol. 59.

Vettori, Piero. *Petri Victorii epistolarum libri X. Orationes XIIII. et Liber de Ludibus Ioannae Austriacae.* Florence: Giunti, 1586.

Virgil, *Eclogues, Georgics, Aeneid.* Translated by H. Rushton Fairclough. 2 vols. Loeb Classical Library. Cambridge, Mass. Harvard University Press, 1974.

SECONDARY SOURCES

Adversi, Aldo. *Inventari dei manoscritti delle biblioteche d'Italia.* Vol. 100, pt. 1. Macerata. Florence: Olschki, 1981.

———, Dante Cecchi, Libero Paci, eds. *Storia di Macerata.* 5 vols. Macerata: Tipografia Romano Compagnucci, 1972.

Bausi, Francesco, and Mario Martelli. *La metrica italiana: teoria e storia.* Florence: Le Lettere, 1993.

Belli Barsali, Isa. "Ammannati, Bartolomeo." *Dizionario biografico degli Italiani.* Rome: Istituto dell' Enciclopedia Italiana, 1960, 1: 798–801.

Bertoni, Giulio. "Lucia Bertani e Laura Battiferra." *Gionale Storico della Letteratura Italiana* 85 (1925): 379–8.

Biagi, Luigi. "Di Bartolommeo Ammannati e di alcune sue opere." *L'Arte* 26 (1923): 49–66.

Blouet, Brian. *A Short History of Malta.* New York: Frederick A. Praeger, 1967.

Bober, Phyllis Pray, and Ruth Rubinstein. *Renaissance Artists and Antique Sculpture: A Handbook of Sources.* London: H. Miller; Oxford: Oxford University Press, 1986.

Borsook, Eve. "Art and Politics at the Medici Court II: The Baptism of Filippo de' Medici." *Mitteilungen des Kunsthistorischen Institutes in Florenz* 13(1–2) (December 1967): 95–114.

Brown, Judith C. "Everyday Life, Longevity, and Nuns in Early Modern Florence." In *Renaissance Culture and the Everyday,* edited by Patricia Fumerton and Simon Hunt. Philadelphia: University of Pennsylvania Press, 1998.

Butters, Susan. "Ammannati et la villa Médicis." In *La Villa Médicis,* edited by André Chastel and Philippe Morel, 2: 257–316. Rome: Académie de France à Rome, 1991.

Campbell, Malcolm. "Observations on Ammannati's *Neptune Fountain:* 1565 and 1575." In *Renaissance Studies in Honor of Craig Hugh Smyth,* edited by Andrew Morrogh, Fiorella Superbi Gioffredi, Piero Morselli, and Eve Borsook, 2: 113–36. Florence: Giunti Barbèra, 1985.

Castagnola, Raffaella. "Un oroscopo per Cosimo I." *Rinascimento* 29 (1989): 125–89.

Catalogo dei Codici della Libreria Strozziana comprati dopo la morte di Alessandro Strozzi da S. A. R. Pietro Leopoldo Granduca di Toscana, e passati alla Pubblica Libraria Magliabechiana . . . 1786 . . . Compilato dal Bibliotecario Properzio Ferdinando Fossi nel 1789 e trascritto da Antonio Montelatici secondo chiesto dei custodi di questa Libreria [photocopy in modern binding, Florence, Biblioteca Nazionale].

Charlton, H. B. *Castelvetro's Theory of Poetry.* Manchester: University Press, 1913.

Cipriani, Giovanni. *Il mito etrusco nel rinascimento fiorentino.* Florence: Olschki, 1980.

Clough, Cecil H. *The Duchy of Urbino in the Renaissance.* London: Variorum Reprints, 1981.

Clubb, Louise George, and William G. Clubb. "Building a Lyric Canon: Gabriel Giolito and the Rival Anthiologists, 1545–1590." *Italica* 68(3) (Autumn 1991): 332–44.

Cochrane, Eric. *Florence in the Forgotten Centuries 1527–1800.* Chicago: University of Chicago Press, 1973.

Coffin, David R. *Gardens and Gardening in Papal Rome.* Princeton: Princeton University Press, 1991.

Cole, Michael. *Cellini and the Principles of Sculpture.* Cambridge: Cambridge University Press, 2002.

Colucci, Giuseppe. *Delle Antichità picene dell'Abate Giuseppe Colucci Patrizio camerinese ed ascolano.* 30 vols. Fermo: dai torchi dell'autore per G. A. Paccaroni, 1786–96.

Corsaro, Antonio. "Dionigi Atanagi e la silloge per Irene di Spilimbergo. (Intorno alla formazione del giovane Tasso)." *Italica* 75(1) (1998): 41–61.

Cox-Rearick, Janet. *Bronzino's Chapel of Eleonora in the Palazzo Vecchio.* Berkeley: University of California Press, 1993.

———. "Agnolo Bronzino, *Laura Battiferra degli Ammannati.*" In *The Medici, Michelangelo, and the Art of Late Renaissance Florence,* 149–50. New Haven: Yale University Press with the Detroit Institute of Arts, 2002.

Davis, Charles. "Ammannati, Michelangelo, and the Tomb of Francesco del Nero." *Burlington Magazine* 118.880 (July 1976): 472–84.

———. "Four Documents for the Villa Giulia." *Römisches Jahrbuch für Kunstgeschichte* 16 (1978): 219–23.

De Caro, G. "Bianca Capello." In *Dizionario biografico degli Italiani.* Rome: Istituto dell'Enciclopedia Italiana, 1960–, 10: 15–16.

Dennistoun, James. *Memoirs of the Dukes of Urbino, Illustrating the Arts, Arms, and Literature of Italy from 1440 to 1630.* 3 vols. London: Longman, Brown, Green and Longmans, 1851.

Dersofi, Nancy. "Laura Terracina (1519–c. 1577)." In *Italian Women Writers: A Bio-Bibliographical Sourcebook,* edited by Rinaldina Russell, 423–30. Westport, Conn.: Greenwood Press, 1994.

Dionisotti, Carlo. "La letteratura italiana nell'età del concilio di Trento." In *Geografia e storia della letteratura italiana,* 183–204. Turin: Einaudi, 1967.

Durling, Robert M., and Ronald L. Martinez. *Time and the Crystal: Studies in Dante's Rime petrose.* Berkeley: University of California Press, 1990.

Eisenbichler, Konrad. "Bronzino's Portrait of Guidobaldo II delle Rovere." *Renaissance and Reformation/Renaissance et Réforme* 24(1) (1988): 21–33.

———. *The Boys of the Archangel Raphael: A Youth Confraternity in Florence, 1411–1785.* Toronto: University of Toronto Press, 1998.

Emiliani, Andrea. *Il Bronzino.* Con un'antologia poetica, scelta e presentata da Giorgio Cerboni Baiardi. Busto Arsizio: Bramante Editrice, 1960.

Farulli, Gregorio. *Istoria cronologica del nobile ed antico Monastero degli Angioli di Firenze, del Sacro Ordine camaldolese.* Lucca: Pellegrino Frediani, 1710.

Feo, Michel Angelo. "Giovan Battista Cini." *Dizionario biografico degli Italiani.* Rome: Istituto dell'Enciclopedia Italiana, 1960–, 25: 609–12.

Forster, Kurt W. "Metaphors of Rule: Political Ideology and History in the Portraits of Cosimo I de' Medici." *Mitteilungen des Kunsthistorischen Institutes in Florenz* 15 (1971): 65–104.

Fossi, Mazzino. *Bartolomeo Ammannati architetto.* Vol. 10. Pubblicazioni dell'Università degli Studi di Florence, Facoltà di Magistero. Cava dei Tirreni: Morano, 1967.

Fossi, Mazzino, and E. Kasten. "Ammannati, Bartolomeo di Antonio." In *Allgemeines Künstler-Lexikon,* 3: 253–58. Munich and Leipzig: K.G. Sauer, 1992.

Gallucci, Margaret. *Benvenuto Cellini: Sexuality, Masculinity, and Artistic Identity in Renaissance Italy.* New York: Palgrave Macmillan, 2003.

Gentile, Luigi. *I codici palatini della R. Biblioteca Nazionale Centrale di Firenze.* In *Cataloghi dei manoscritti della R. Biblioteca Nazionale Centrale di Firenze compilati sotto la direzione del Prof. Adolfo Bartoli.* Vol. 1, fasc. 1. Rome: Presso i Principali Librai, 1885.

Girardi, Enzo Noè. "Battiferri, Laura." *Dizionario biografico degli Italiani.* Rome: Istituto dell' Enciclopedia Italiana, 7: 242–44.

Guidi, Enrico Maria. "Un manoscritto del '500 per la tipografia dei Giunti." *Studi Urbinati.* B. Scienze Umane e Sociali 67 (1995–96): 345–64.

———. "Salmi penitenziali di David nella traduzione di Laura Battiferri." *Accademia Raffaello: Atti e Studi* 1 (2004): 83–92.

Heikamp, Detlef. "Ammannati's Fountain for the *Sala Grande* of the Palazzo Vecchio in Florence." In *Dunbarton Oaks Colloquium on the History of Landscape Architecture,* edited by Elisabeth B. Macdougall, 5: 115–74. Dunbarton Oaks: Washington, D.C., 1978.

Hibbert, Christopher. *The House of Medici: Its Rise and Fall.* New York: William Morrow and Co., 1975.

Hoppen, Alison. *The Fortification of Malta by the Order of St. John, 1530–1798.* Edinburgh: Scottish Academic Press, 1995.

Hurtubise, Pierre. *Une famille-témoin: Les Salviati.* Città del Vaticano: Biblioteca Apostolica Vaticana, 1985.

Kamen, Henry. *Philip of Spain.* New Haven: Yale Univeresity Press, 1997.

Kiene, Michael. *Bartolomeo Ammannati.* Milan: Electa, 1995.

Kinney, Peter. *The Early Sculpture of Bartolomeo Ammannati.* New York: Garland, 1976.

Kirkham, Victoria. "Laura Battiferra's 'First Book' of Poetry: A Renaissance Holograph Comes out of Hiding." *Rinascimento* 35 (1996): 351–91.

———. "Dante's Fantom, Petrarch's Specter: Bronzino's Portrait of the Poet Laura Battiferra." In *"Visibile parlare": Dante and the Art of the Italian Renaissance,* edited by Deborah Parker. *Lectura Dantis* 22–23 (1998): 63–139.

———. "Laura Battiferra degli Ammannati benefattrice dei Gesuiti fiorentini." In *Committenza artistica femminile,* edited by Sara F. Matthews Grieco and Gabriella Zarri. *Quaderni Storici* 104(2) (2000): 331–54.

———. "Cosimo and Eleonora in Shepherdland: A Lost Eclogue by Laura Battiferra degli Ammannati." In *The Cultural Politics of Duke Cosimo I de' Medici,* edited by Konrad Eisenbichler, 149–75. Burlington, Vt.: Ashgate, 2001.

———. "Creative Partners: The Marriage of Laura Battiferra and Bartolomeo Ammannati." *Renaissance Quarterly* 55 (2002): 498–558.

———. "La poetessa al presepio: Una meditazione inedita di Laura Battiferra degli Ammannati." *Filologia e Critica* 27(2) (2002): 258–76.

———. "The Tale of Guiglielmo Borsiere (I.8)." In *The Decameron: First Day in Perspective,* edited by Elissa Weaver, 179–206. Toronto: University of Toronto Press, 2004.

———. "Sappho on the Arno: The Brief Fame of Laura Battiferra." In *Strong Voices, Weak History: Early Women Writers and Canons in England, France, and Italy,* edited by Pamela Benson and Victoria Kirkham, 174–96. Ann Arbor: University of Michigan Press, 2005.

Kristeller, Paul Oskar. *Iter italicum. Accedunt alia itinera: A Finding List of Uncatalogued or Incompletely Catalogued Humanistic Manuscripts of the Renaissance in Italian and Other Libraries.* London: Warburg Institute, 1963–.

Lamberini, Daniela. *Il principe difeso: Vita e opere di Bernardo Puccini.* Florence: La Giuntina, 1990.

Lazzari, Antonio. *Dizionario storico degli uomini illustri di Urbino.* In Colucci, *Delle antichità picene.*

Lazzaro, Claudia. *The Italian Renaissance Garden: From the Conventions of Planting, Design, and Ornament to the Grand Gardens of Sixteenth-Century Central Italy.* New Haven: Yale University Press, 1990.

Lecchini-Giovanoni, Simona. *Alessandro Allori.* Turin: Umberto Allemandi & Co., 1991.

Le Marche. 4th ed. Milan: Touring Club Italiano, 1979.

Manacorda, Guido. *Benedetto Varchi: l'uomo, il poeta, il critico.* Pisa: Tipografia Succ. Fratelli Nistri, 1903.

Maylender, Michele. *Storia delle accademie d'Italia.* 5 vols. Bologna: Licinio Cappelli Editore, 1926–30.

Mazzatini, Giuseppe. *Inventari dei manoscritti delle biblioteche d'Italia.* Forlì: Luigi Bordandini, 1890–.

Mazzatini, Giuseppe, and Fortunato Pintor. *Florence.* In *Inventari dei manoscritti delle biblioteche d'Italia.* Vols. 10–13, 1900–1906.

The Medici, Michelangelo, and the Art of Late Renaissance Florence. New Haven: Yale University Press with the Detroit Institute of Arts, 2002.

Michelangeli, Raffaella. *I Bonaventura: Una famiglia del patriziato urbinate.* Urbino: Arti Grafiche Stibu, 1999.

Montella, Luigi. *Una poetessa del Rinascimento: Laura Terracina con le Le None Rime inedite.* Salerno: Edisud, 1993.

Moranti, Luigi. *Urbino.* In *Inventari dei manoscritti delle Biblioteche d'Italia,* vol. 80. Florence: Olschki, 1954.

Nardelli Petrucci, Franca. See Petrucci.

Nelson, Jonathan. "Creative Patronage: Luca Martini and the Renaissance Portrait." *Mitteilungen des Kunsthistorischen Institutes in Florenz* 39.2/3 (1995): 282–305.

Osborne, June. *Urbino: The Story of a Renaissance City.* Chicago: University of Chicago Press, 2003.

Palermo, Francesco. *I manoscritti palatini di Firenze.* Vol. 1. Florence: Biblioteca Palatina, 1853.

Parker, Deborah. *Bronzino: Renaissance Painter as Poet.* Cambridge: Cambridge University Press, 2000.

Perlingieri, Ilya Sandra. *Sofonisba Anguissola: The First Great Woman Artist of the Renaissance.* Milan: Rizzoli, 1992.

Petrie, Charles. *Philip II of Spain.* London: Eyre and Spottiswoode, 1963.

Petrucci, Franca. "Caterina Cibo." In *Dizionario biografico degli Italiani.* Rome: Istituto dell'Enciclopedia Italiana, 1960–, 25: 237–41.

Pettas, William A. *The Giunti of Florence: Merchant Publishers of the Sixteenth Century. With a Checklist of all the Books and Documents Published by the Giunti in Florence from 1497 to 1570, with the Texts of Twenty-Nine Documents from 1427 to the Eighteenth Century.* San Francisco: Bernard M. Rosenthal, 1980.

Pilliod, Elizabeth. *Pontormo, Bronzino, Allori: A Genealogy of Florentine Art.* New Haven: Yale University Press, 2001.

Piperno, Franco. *L'immagine del duca: Musica e spettacolo alla corte di Guidubaldo II duca d'Urbino.* Florence: Olschki, 2001.

Pirotti, Umberto. *Benedetto Varchi e la cultura del suo tempo.* Florence: Olschki, 1971.

Pirri, Pietro, S. J. "L'architetto Bartolomeo Ammannati e i Gesuiti." *Archivum Historicum Societatis Iesu* 12 (1943): 5–57.

Plazzotta, Carol. "Bronzino's Laura." *Burlington Magazine* 140.1141 (April 1998): 251–63.

Poligrafo Gargani. Notes at the Biblioteca Nazionale in Florence. s.v. "Ammannati," Pachetto, 89.

Ponchiroli, Daniele. *Lirici del cinquecento.* Turin: Unione Tipografico-Editrice Torinese, 1958.

Prodi, Paolo. "Silvio Antoniano." In *Dizionario biografico degli Italiani.* Rome: Istituto dell'Enciclopedia Italiana, 1960–, 3: 511–15.

Promis, Carlo. *Biografie di ingegneri militari italiani dal secolo XIV alla metà del XVIII.* In *Miscellanea di storia patria,* 14: 428–46. Turin: Fratelli Bocca Librai di S.M., 1874.

Quondam, Amadeo. *Petrarchismo mediato.* Rome: Bulzoni, 1974.

Quondam, Amadeo, and Marco Santagata, eds. *Il libro di poesia dal copista al tipografo.* Ferrara: Panini, 1989.

Robertson, Clare. *Il gran cardinale: Alessandro Farnese, Patron of the Arts.* New Haven: Yale University Press, 1992.

Rodini, Robert J. *Antonfrancesco Grazzini: Poet, Dramatist, and Novelliere, 1503–1584.* Madison: University of Wisconsin Press, 1970.

Rosselli Del Turco, Niccolò, and Federica Salvi, eds. *Bartolomeo Ammannati: Scultore e architetto 1511–1592.* Florence: Alinea, 1995.

Russell, Rinaldina, ed. *Italian Women Writers: A Bio-Bibliographical Sourcebook.* Westport, Conn., 1994.

Santarelli, Giuseppe. *Loreto Its History and Art.* Bologna: La Fotometalgrafica, 1987.

Sarpi, Paolo. *Istoria del Concilio Tridentino.* Edited by Corrado Vivanti. 2 vols. Turin: Einaudi, 1974.

Sbaragli, Luigi. "'I Tabelloni' degli Intronati." *Bollettino Senese di Storia Patria.* 3d series, 1 (1942): 177–87.

Schutte, Anne Jacobson. "Irene di Spilimbergo: The Image of a Creative Woman in Late Renaissance Italy." *Renaissance Quarterly* 44 (1991): 42–61.

Sorbelli, Albano. *Roma. R. Biblioteca Angelica.* In Mazzatinti, *Inventari dei manoscritti delle biblioteche d'Italia,* vol. 56. Florence: Olschki, 1934.

———. *Bologna, Biblioteca Comunale dell'Archiginnasio.* In *Inventari dei manoscritti delle biblioteche d'Italia,* vol. 69. Florence: Olschki, 1939.

Ugolini, Filippo. *Storia dei conti e duchi d'Urbino.* Florence: Grazzini e Giannini, 1859.

Utz, Hildegard. "A Note on the Chronology of Ammannati's Fountain of Juno." *Burlington Magazine* 114.831 (June 1972): 394–95.

Vasari, Giorgio. *Le vite dei più eccellenti pittori, scultori e architetti.* Edited by Licia Ragghianti and Carlo L. Ragghianti. 4 vols. Milan: Rizzoli, 1971–78.

Vecchietti, Filippo. *Biblioteca Picena o sia Notizie istoriche delle opere e degli scrittori piceni,* 5 vols. Osimo: Domenicantonio Quercetti, 1790–96.

Venturi, Adolfo. "Bartolomeo Ammannati." In *Storia dell'arte italiana,* vol. 10, pt. 2, 347–432. "La scultura del Cinquecento." Milan: Hoepli, 1936.

Vermiglioli, Giovan Battista. *Biografia degli scrittori perugini e notizie delle opere loro.* 2 vols. Perugia: Vincenzio Bartelli e Giovanni Costantini, 1829.

Waźbiński, Zygmunt. *L'accademia medicea del disegno a Firenze nel Cinquecento.* 2 vols. Florence: Olschki, 1987.

Weaver, Elissa B. *Convent Theater in Early Modern Italy: Spiritual Fun and Learning for Women.* Cambridge: Cambridge University Press, 2002.

Weil-Garris, Kathleen. *The Santa Casa di Loreto: Problems in Cinquecento Sculpture.* 2 vols. New York: Garland, 1977.

Wells, Maria Xenia. *Italian Post-1600 Manuscripts and Family Archives in North American Libraries.* Ravenna: Longo, 1992.

Winspear, Fabrizio. *Isabella Orsini e la corte medicea del suo tempo.* Florence: Olschki, 1961.

Wittkower, Rudolf, and Margot Wittkower. *The Divine Michelangelo: The Florentine Academy's Homage on His Death in 1564. A Facsimile Edition of Esequie del Divino Michelangnolo Buonarroti Firenze 1564.* London: Phaidon Press, 1964.

Zaccagnani, Guido. "Lirici urbinati del secolo XVI." *Le Marche* 3 (1903): 87–114.

Zambelli, Paola. "Battiferri, Matteo." *Dizionario biografico degli Italiani.* Rome: Istituto dell'Enciclopedia Italiana, 1960–, 7: 245–46.

NOTE ON TRANSLATION

RATIONALE FOR SELECTIONS INCLUDED IN THIS TRANSLATION

The selections in this anthology have been chosen to portray Laura Battiferra's unique identity and art as a writer, to represent the full chronological arc of her career, to illustrate her celebrity, to establish her historical context, to profile her literary genealogy, to publish insofar as realistically feasible material that has never before seen the light of print, and to include samples from all known sixteenth-century sources in which her work appeared. Her principal surviving writings are three collections of verse: *Il primo libro dell'opere toscane* (The First Book of Tuscan Works; Florence, 1560); *I sette salmi penitentiali . . . con alcuni suoi sonetti spirituali* (The Seven Penitential Psalms . . . with Some Spiritual Sonnets; Florence, 1564); and the *Rime* (R = Rome, Biblioteca Casanatense, MS 3229). Since the last subsumes the first two and preserves much additional verse never published, that manuscript provides the basis for my edition and translation of her poetry in chapter 1. My selected poems follow the ordering in *Rime*—sonnets to rulers first, a set of sonnets for women, a "Roman" period, exchanges with other poets, a long funeral cortege, and a "Second Part" devoted to "spiritual rhymes." Chapter 2 anthologizes Battiferra's verse scattered in manuscript miscellanies or sixteenth-century printed books by other editors and poets. Chapter 3 presents the full text, never before published in translation, of Battiferra's meditation on the Christmas manger scene (her only known art prose), the "Orison on the Nativity of Our Lord" (M = Macerata, Biblioteca Comunale Mozzi-Borgetti, MS 137). A sampling of her surviving epistolary correspondence appears in chapter 4.

Excepting the "Orison" and her letters, which range from chatty notes to formal humanistic petitions, her literary production is a poetic corpus running to nearly 550 pieces, mostly sonnets—371 by Laura, 117 sent to her by forty-seven correspondents, twelve addressed to her husband Bartolomeo Ammannati, and forty-three poems that are known to be lost. To redress older monographic editorial preferences and to reconstruct her cultural circles, many sonnet exchanges with her correspondents have been published intact, just as they appear in her *Primo libro* and *Rime*.[1] Where she exchanged more than one sonnet with someone, I have chosen a single pair to document the connection.

Battiferra intended her *Rime* for publication as a compendium of her life's work.[2] For those poems that were to be reprinted from *Il primo libro* and *I setti salmi penitentiali*, only the first line appears in the *Rime*. Marginal notes instruct the printer to take the complete texts from the published editions. From this system of abbreviating earlier poetry, we know that one manuscript of Battiferra's verse is lost, identified only by the Greek letter "Beta." With few ex-

1. By incorporating both sides of these exchanges in her anthologies, Battiferra follows other female poets (Tullia d'Aragona, Laura Terracina). Contrast this strategy with the more usual male procedure of grouping all the sonnet replies at the end (the second and third editions of Bembo's *Rime*, Bernardo Cappello's *Rime* of 1560, Varchi's funerary anthology for Luca Martini of 1561, etc.). Not all of Battiferra's correspondents appear in the present anthology. Omitted are Domenico Alamanni, Savino Bobali [Bobalio, Babalio = Sabo Bobaljevic Misetic of Ragusa], Baldello Baldelli, Francesco Baldelli, Fabio Benvoglienti, Abbot Casale, Paolo Casale, il Cavaletto, Malatesta Fiordiano da Rimini, Felice Gualtieri, Francesco Martelli, Guglielmo Martelli, Pietro Massolo, the Count of Monte d'Oglio ("lo Sdegnoso"), Carlo Passi, Lionardo Salviati, Fabio Segno, and Piero Stufa. Sometimes, in the interest of economy, I have anthologized only one side or the other of a sonnet exchange.

2. R, Rome, Biblioteca Casanatense, MS 3229, late sixteenth century, quarto, seventy-one folios, modern numeration. Paper, no watermarks, brown ink, bound in parchment, late sixteenth-century Jesuit hand. Enrico Guidi, who privileges the versions of Battiferra's poetry in print, designates the manuscript as "RBI" in his edition of *Il primo libro delle opere toscane* (Urbino: Accademia Raffaello, 2000), 28–29. A prefatory letter from Piero Vettori to Mario Colonna occupies three bifolios (= six folios, with the first bound in as a pastedown to the front cover). Signatures of four folios each are lettered as follows: A fols. 7r–10v; B fols. 11r–14v; C fols. 15r–18v; D fols. 19r–22v; E fols. 23r–26v; F fols. 27r–30v; G fols. 31r–34v; H fols. 35r–38v; I fols. 39r–42v; K [=Seconda Parte] fols. 43r–46v; L fols. 47r–50v; M fols. 51r–54v; N fols. 55r–58v; O fols. 59r–62v; P fols. 63r–67v [but fols. 65r–65v are a smaller piece of paper]; Q fols. 68r–71r, bound in to pastedown for back cover. The title page, fol. 1r, reads, "Rime di M. Laura Batti / ferra degli Ammannati"; then, in another hand, "Vari sonetti, epigrammi, et terze rime / in lode de' Principi, Pontefici, ed altri soggetti. / Parafrasi di qualche salmo, e del orazione di Geremia / Profeta (sono stati dati alle stampe dal Bulifon)." The subtitle was added sometime after the publication of *Rime della Sig. Laura Battiferra nuovamente date in luce da Antonio Bulifon* (Naples: Antonio Bulifon, 1694). The codex is divided into a "First Part" with 288 numbered poems (fols. 7r–42r) and a "Part Two of Spiritual Rhymes" with eighty-nine numbered poems (fols. 43r–70r). The numeration of the poems, original, is not entirely accurate. Foliation has been added in modern times. The lost Beta manuscript contained what were to have been poems numbered 217–59, according to a scribal insertion to the typographer on fol. 25v: "Nota che il libro segnato B è stato ataccato a quello stampato per esser tutti li seguenti sonetti scritti benissimo, et tutti per ordine dal num. 217 fino a 259 inclusive" (note that the book marked B has been attached to the printed book since all the following sonnets are written very well, and all in or-

ceptions, poems fully transcribed in the *Rime* are otherwise unknown.[3] Some predate the *Primo libro,* but most of what is new postdates *I sette salmi penitentiali.* Youthful poetry preserved by the *Rime* and excluded from those publications gives insight into the care with which she shaped her first two books. For example, the *Rime* is the sole source for sonnets she composed on her first husband's death (1549). Perhaps she chose not to include them in her *Primo libro* out of regard for Ammannati. Political and patronage concerns, on the other hand, explain the absence from her *Primo libro* of the sonnet she sent to Pope Paul III (d. 1549), an antagonist of both the Medici and Della Rovere rulers. From after 1564, the *Rime* is a repository for almost everything Battiferra wrote, a period when her literary activity was thought to have ceased.

The commentary in this anthology, placed at the end of the volume, is of two kinds. Preliminary historical notes give information on the dedicatees, authors, and topical content of the poetry. These notes also call attention to reordering, microsequences, and the shift in authorial emphasis from *Il primo libro* to the final *Rime,* more personal and religious in conception. Following these historical notes, a literary commentary keyed to the poetry by line numbers identifies sources and analogs. Such pointers are meant to be indicative, not exhaustive. They sketch a first profile of Battiferra's place in traditions that extend from Ovid and Virgil in antiquity, down through the Italian vernacular poets from Dante and Petrarch to her contemporaries.

For poetry, the Italian texts as I have edited them accompany their translated English counterparts, rendered in a prose version that attempts to reproduce as closely as possible the Petrarchan lexicon and the original sonnet structure in its four parts (two quatrains, two tercets). For prose (the "Orison" and the letters), only the translation is given. I have translated poetry cited in the notes, like the poems by Battiferra, into prose. Unless otherwise attributed, those translations are my own. For Petrarch I have cited

---

der from number 217 to 259 inclusive). A few marginal notes correct the transcription or give instructions to the typographer—e.g., fol. 5v, a pastedown, apparently in Battiferra's hand, instructs the printer to reverse the manuscript order of the first two sonnets of greeting from Don Silvano Razzi and Gherardo Spini: "Di grazia non si metta quello di Don Silvano cosi nel primo luogo, ma dopo" (Please do not put the one by Don Silvano first the way it is, but after); also for fol. 17v, the dedicatory title "Al Padre General della Compagnia di Giesù" has been changed, apparently by Ammannati, to "Al Padre Claudio Acquaviva General della Compagnia di Giesù" (1.62). The transcription breaks off midway through fol. 70r, after the eighteenth stanza of an untitled epic that begins, "Canto il valor de' primi antichi regi" (I sing the valor of the first ancient kings) and ends, "freddo marmo parea, non donna viva."

3. The *Rime* incorporates poems published separately in the funeral anthology for Benedetto Varchi of 1566 and in Mario Colonna's posthumous *canzoniere* of 1589.

throughout the translation by Robert M. Durling, sometimes with slight modification to tighten parallels with the Italian.

Dates, unless otherwise indicated, correspond to the modern calendar and assume the New Year to be January 1, as opposed to the old Florentine system of dating, with a New Year on March 25, the Feast of the Annunciation.

In adapting sixteenth-century Italian to modern editorial usage, I have left unchanged book titles, prose quotes, and proper names of dedicatees or historical personages referred to in the poetry. Some proper names have been Anglicized (Giesù > Jesus; Apelle > Apelles; Venere > Venus; Dafne > Daphne (Apollo's nymph); Fidia > Phidias—but "Dafne" and "Fidia" are retained when they refer to Laura and her sculptor husband. Where the name of a dedicatee has a different modern form, I have retained the former in the rubric (cf. 1.18 to "Madama Lucretia da Este") but used the latter in notes ("Lucrezia").

Abbreviations have been silently expanded. Punctuation has been modified to make the poetry more accessible for a reader today. Accents have been added (cosi > così; perche > perché) and removed (à as preposition > a). Embedded names in block capitals have been retained (but not capitalized first words of a poem). Original capitalization has also occasionally been retained when it contributes to visual punning on the page (Augelli-Angeli in 1.42) or underlines the virtuosity of the composition (Cielo-Terra in 1, pt. 2.22).

Spelling has been modernized in the poems as follows:

The Latin conjunction "et" has been changed to "e," except before a word beginning with "e," where it becomes "ed".

The etymological or paraetymological "h" has been eliminated: humile > umile; talhor > talor.

The letter "j" has been replaced with "i": chj > chi; miej > miei; testimonij > testimoni.

The palatal cluster "tio" has been assimilated to "zio": silentio > silenzio.

ABBREVIATIONS

For the key to manuscript abbreviations, see appendix F. The textual sources of the selections as well as variants known to me are given in appendix E. Where a poem appears in more than one source, the text cited has been marked in appendix E with an asterisk (*). In the volume editor's introduction and endnotes, I refer to selections in the anthology in parentheses by chapter and number—for example, (1.I) refers to chapter 1, the poem numbered I; (1, pt. 2.17) refers to chapter 1, "Second Part of the *Rime spirituali,*" the poem numbered 17; (4.8) refers to chapter 4, letter number 8. In chapter 1, poems have two numbers: the first is my sequential numeration; the second, in brackets, is the number assigned the poem in the Casanatense manuscript at Rome (R).

ABBREVIATIONS

Aen.	Virgil, *Aeneid*
App.	Appendix
ASF	Archivio di Stato di Firenze
Dec.	*Decameron*
Inf.	Dante, *Inferno*
Met.	Ovid, *Metamorphoses*
Not.	notaio (notary)
Par.	Dante, *Paradiso*
Purg.	Dante, *Purgatorio*
RS	Petrarch, *Rime Sparse*
SASU	Sezione Archivio di Stato Urbino

I

POEMS FROM *RIME DI MADONNA LAURA BATTIFERRA DEGLI AMMANNATI*

MEN WRITING TO BATTIFERRA

EPISTLE BY THE MOST ILLUSTRIOUS SIGNOR PIERO VETTORI[1] TO THE MOST ILLUSTRIOUS SIGNOR MARIO COLONNA

Together with Your Lordship, worthiest Signor Mario, truly a devotee of the good arts,[2] and with our bosom friend Messer Bartolomeo Valori,[3] I listened to Messer Lionardo Salviati[4] as he related Messer Benedetto Varchi's many gifts of mind and spirit in an elegant and copious oration at his funeral.[5] This office he performed most ably, and in the course of praising another, he won no small praise and glory for himself as well. I make so bold as to say this, speaking freely of him, because at the time I saw how much you praised him and how marvelously your celebratory words raised even higher, as it were, his manner of speaking and knowledge of many things. The truth is, of course, that he was lucky to have a very good subject, since Varchi was by nature endowed with a fine mind and he was born to pursue and practice that art which from the beginning of his life he had pursued constantly and never once abandoned in his graver years, that is, composing poetry, even though he had been taken from that study and assigned to other weightier duties far removed from it by a man[6] who could reasonably give orders to him and to all of us, as we should wish he always will. This man, who is certainly endowed with great and singular judgment and who has a keen understanding of people's minds, held him [Varchi] in the highest esteem, and he set no little store by his knowledge and memory of all things. Varchi, moreover, was adorned with other honest and honorable arts, and he had not encountered any discipline without wanting to progress in it and actually doing so in no little measure.

I recognize that it is not only unnecessary but beside the point for me to go on talking about such matters with you who already knew them perfectly well and who bore that man so much love and were often wont to take no little delight in his intellect, especially since Salviati, his close friend, so accurately reminded us of all these things, which he had most diligently assembled to praise him in that oration. I most certainly felt no little delight at that moment—even though the service was filled with sadness and mourning and in other respects increased my sadness and pain—when I saw such a good number of bright, noble young men assembled to celebrate Varchi and honor him with last rites, or rather, to hear praise for all the intellectual arts, which were being lauded at one with him to the heavens; and I frankly confess that I derived from it no little pleasure—strong and heartfelt it was too. Yet who, indeed, would not take delight and rejoice in his heart upon seeing his citizens kindled by zeal for the fairest and finest arts, especially when they turn to the art of poetry, verily an art celestial and divine? All the more since that study, which was once almost wholly extinct or merely left scattered in few and weak traces, has in our city[7] come back to life, and it has been not only resuscitated but has rightly grown fair and flowered, producing from the moment of birth fruits in abundance, in every part perfect and whole.

And then, my gladness waxed greater—this too it pleases me to remember now—when I saw that there was also a lady present at this oration, standing as close as she could get. Yet it did not move me to amazement, for why should a woman not want to visit that place where the talent and industry of poets are celebrated, one herself afire with that learning, one whom the Muses love above all other women and assist in writing comely, graceful verse? As a matter of fact, you must remember what I told you then, how we deplored, and rightly so, the rules of the place that excluded and segregated her, forcing her to watch from the rear, as if from behind a curtain. I reckoned that out of respect for her great intellect and her talent as an author of eminent verse she ought not to be counted as a woman but truly taken for a man, just as we read of Plato, who was judged not to be an Athenian citizen but rather a philosopher, when the most bitter hatred borne him by Dionysus the Tyrant caused him to be led into Aegina, a city in which the people had passed a law that the first Athenian to set foot on the island should be summarily sentenced to death. In the end, that most learned of men, the judges ruled, should be set free from such a cruel sentence.[8] Surely no one will reproach me if I compare a woman to Plato; on the contrary, I dare say it is my opinion that somehow a woman should be granted the same privilege as was allowed that wisest of men, the splendor of all Greece and the origin and font of all knowledge, when he was in capital danger. For I deem that we should not so much have regard merely for her species and sex as we should take into consideration her intellect and culture.

It is a point I can confirm with the example of an illustrious and weighty writer who with manifold studies and effort sought to dignify men by cleansing them of all filth and purging them of vice. Not wishing to be guilty himself of failing to be truthful, after assembling wide evidence to support his judgment, he boldly compared a woman of amazing nature to a man endowed with preeminent wisdom. I am referring to Maximus of Tyre,[9] a most polished and erudite writer, who demonstrated how the poetess Sappho was in her way of life and in her studies the equal of Socrates and how many things happened to each in their lives that were quite similar and hardly different at all, even though he knew that at first no one would lend an ear to that view but would think what he said false and silly. Nevertheless, he demonstrated that the truth stood otherwise and that no two things could possibly be more alike and similar than these two people, and he proved it with many valid reasons and arguments of substance.

Of course, I know very well that you know that this woman of ours—and would to God I were permitted to say truly ours, because she was not born here, rather she is an outlander and noble plant transported from other terrain into ours, where she has already put down roots together with her consort, he too an excellent artist, and as it were, a new Phidias—you know, I say, that Madonna Laura Battiferra (because I do not wish to hide her name) in her gifts of spirit and in her powers of composing is not a whit inferior to Sappho.[10] In fact, she has far and away outstripped and surpassed her in her life and in her morals, clear and obvious as it is to everyone that the Greek Sappho was also praised and always called divine by Plato. Still, it is not my intention now to go on in praise of Madonna Laura by celebrating and recalling every aspect of her character worthy of full honor and praise, for neither have I wanted to make it my task here to celebrate Varchi (though it seemed I was going to praise and commend him in these remarks), for I judge that he was sufficiently praised by that eloquent and erudite young man [Salviati] and because I likewise trust that our memories and the worthy, honorable writings he leaves behind will bring him praise enough and commendation, preserving his name to posterity for all centuries to come.

And now, noblest and illustrious Signor Mario, I have addressed these thoughts to you, a gentleman most honorable, because since for me that day was so joyful and instilled in my spirit pleasure pure and true, I wanted in this manner to prolong and bring increase to the experience. My end shall have been fully and firmly achieved, I judge, if I can know that this very long letter of mine has not caused you boredom or irritation. True enough, when I took pen in hand, I did not expect to be so long, but the very pleasure that I take in recalling these things to mind and the sweetness I feel every time it is my fortune to discourse familiarly with you have beguiled me and prevented me from keeping the letter to proper limits. Be well, therefore, and forgive me.

From Florence, the last day of January 1565
[January 31, 1566, modern style]

I[11] DI MESSER GHERARDO SPINI A MADONNA LAURA BATTIFERRA[12]

Mentre ch'in tosche rime apri e dichiari
quel che re saggio e lirico gentile
pianse, cantando al suon di cetra umile
con alti versi a Dio graditi e cari, 4
vivo sol, che 'l bell'Arno orni e rischiari,
or co' be' raggi ed or col vago stile,
ond'avvien ch'ogni cor più fero e vile 8
l'eterno sole a riverire impari,
l'antico Tebro mormorando dice,
"Lei, cui 'l ciel piacque già lontana farmi, 11
or di gloria il Giordan, me d'onor priva,
poiché del santo Ebreo gli eletti carmi
con L'AURA dolce del suo canto avviva,
e 'n sì vago idioma alto ridice." 14

II DEL REVERENDO SIGNOR DON SILVANO RAZZI, MONACO NEL MUNISTERO DEGLI ANGELI IN FIRENZE ALLA MEDESIMA[14]

Nuova fronde d'Apollo alta e gentile,
donna gloria e onor del secol nostro,
di bontà raro inusitato mostro,
vago di poesia fiorito aprile; 4
deh, seguit'or col chiaro ornato stile
dall'idioma ebreo nel dolce vostro
i voti e' prieghi por del re che mostro
n'ha quale esser dee cor contrito e umile; 8
che se fra mille di virtute essempi
raro al mondo vi fan quest'opre e quelle
ch'a voi dan somma gloria e lode altrui, 11
quanto sì degn'impresa alfin per vui
giunta, seggio immortal sopra le stelle
daravvi, e qui ghirlande, altari e tempi. 14

I FROM MESSER GHERARDO SPINI TO MADONNA LAURA BATTIFERRA

While in Tuscan rhymes you disclose and
declare what made a wise king and noble poet
weep, singing to the sound of a humble cithar with
lofty verses pleasing and dear to God, 4
living sun, who adorn and brighten the fair
Arno, now with your fair rays and now with your
winsome style, whence it befalls that every most
fierce and base heart must learn to revere the eternal sun; 8
the ancient Tiber says, murmuring, "She,
whom it pleased heaven to carry far from me, now
deprives Jordan of glory, me of honor, 11
for with the sweet AURA of her song she
brings life to the chosen poetry by the Hebrews'
holy man and loftily respeaks it in such winsome idiom."[13] 14

II FROM THE MOST REVEREND SIGNOR DON SILVANO RAZZI, MONK IN THE MONASTERY OF THE ANGELI IN FLORENCE, TO THE SAME LADY

New frond of Apollo lofty and noble, lady
the glory and honor of our century; rare, unwonted
marvel of goodness; fair flowering April of poetry; 4
pray, press on now with your bright ornate
style as you set into your sweet idiom from Hebrew
the vows and prayers of the king who showed us
what a contrite and humble heart must be; 8
for if these works and those that win you
consummate glory and people's praise make you a
rare example of virtue among a thousand, 11
all the more will an effort so worthy, once you have
at last finished, give you a seat immortal above the
stars, and here garlands, altars, and temples.[15] 14

III DEL PADRE FRATE AGOSTINO DE' COPETI ALLA MEDESIMA[16]

Or che l'alto stil vostro il ferro in oro
cangia, e poggiando ov'altri mai più salse,
i fiumi ferma, e chi fermarli valse
a calar move dal superno coro; 4
sacri a voi LAURA il più pregiato alloro
colui ch'al par d'Apollo n'arse ed alse,
e che 'n dolci onde ha sua cuna e tomba in salse
e del greco idioma il gran tesoro; 8
che le Muse i lor fonti e i cigni i fiumi
lascin per Arno, e per il vostro canto
le selve i Fauni e le Sirene il mare, 11
e di Parnaso Apollo scettro e manti
oggi vi doni, e di voi trasformare
non lasci Giove al fin nel ciel fra' Numi. 14

SELECTIONS FROM *LE OPERE TOSCANE,* PRIMA PARTE[18]

1 [1] ALLA DUCHESS DI FIORENZA E DI SIENA[19]

A voi, donna real, consacro e dono,
ben che vil pregio all'alto valor vostro,
questa man, questa penna e questo inchiostro
e se mai nulla fui, saraggio o sono, 4
così agguagliasse di mia Musa il suono
il pensier c'ho di voi, ch'altrui non mostro,
come a gloria ed onor del secol nostro,
mandarei fuor quel che entro il cor ragiono; 8
e forse a par di lui che su la Sorga
cantando alzò il bel lauro a tanto onore,
n'andrei sempre volando in ogni parte, 11
che voi qual sol, ch'al mondo cieco porga
lume, col dolce vostro almo splendore
chiare fareste le mie scure carte. 14

III FROM FRIAR AGOSTINO DE' COPETI TO THE SAME LADY

Now that your lofty style turns iron to gold
and, pressing upward where others before never
climbed, stops rivers and moves the one with power
to stop them to descend from the supernal choir, 4
may the man who flamed and froze like
Apollo consecrate to you LAURA the most prized laurel, he
who has a cradle in sweet waves, and a tomb in
salty, and the great treasure of the Greek language; 8
may the Muses leave their fonts, and swans
the rivers for Arno, and may Fauns leave the forests
and Sirens the seas because of your song; 11
and may Apollo give you scepter and mantle
today from Parnassus, and may Jove not forget to
translate you at last into the sky among the gods.[17] 14

SELECTIONS FROM *THE TUSCAN WORKS,* PART 1

1 [1] TO THE DUCHESS OF FLORENCE AND SIENA

To you, royal lady, I consecrate and give
this hand, this pen, and this ink, though base reward
for your lofty valor; and if ever I was or will be or am anything, 4
if only the sound of my Muse could match
my thought of you (which I show not to others),
then for the glory and honor of our age, I would
send forth that which I speak within my heart; 8
and perhaps a peer to him who raised the
fair laurel to such honor singing beside the Sorgue,
I should go winging always everywhere, 11
for you, like a sun that could bring light to
the blind world, with your sweet bountiful splendor
would brighten my dark pages.[20] 14

2 [2] AL DUCA DI FIORENZA E DI SIENA[21]

Quel largo cerchio che ricigne intorno
la nona spera, pien d'alto valore,
e quel che seco porta i giorni e l'ore,
di tante stelle e così chiare adorno,
stavan congiunti il fortunato giorno
ch'esser dovea del secol nostro onore;
ed ogni amico lume, ogni splendore,
lucea propizio nel più bel soggiorno.
Spargea dal ricco grembo arabi odori
l'aura soave, e 'n questa e 'n quella parte
rendea sereno il ciel, tranquille l'acque,
più dolce molto verdeggiar gli allori,
più fiero in vista folgorava Marte,
quando il buon Cosmo invitto al mondo nacque.

3 [3] AL PRENCIPE DI FIORENZA E DI SIENA[23]

O del primo e più saggio, o del migliore
duce, che vegga discorrendo intorno
il gran pianeta che n'apporta 'l giorno,
primo amor, prima speme e primo onore!
Quando si vide in sì giovenil core
sì canuti pensieri aver soggiorno?
Quando un bel volto d'ogni grazia adorno
tal fierezza mostrar? Tanto valore?
Or che fia poi, quando d'Italia il freno,
d'anni, di gloria e di trionfi carco,
reggerai col consiglio e colla mano?
Non vedrem noi tornar lieve e sereno
il secol grave e fosco? e te per varco
volar vivendo al ciel, diritto e piano?

2 [2] TO THE DUKE OF FLORENCE AND SIENA

That wide ring that circles round the ninth
sphere, full of lofty valor, and the one, adorned with
so many stars and so bright, that carries with it the
days and the hours, 4
stood conjoined on the fortunate day that
was to be the honor of our age; and every friendly
light, every splendor shone propitious in the fairest abode. 8
From her rich bosom the soft breeze spread
odors of Araby and rendered serene the sky
throughout, tranquil the waters; 11
still sweeter the laurels greened; more
fiercely Mars flashed in sight, when good Cosimo
unvanquished was born to the world.[22] 14

3 [3] TO THE PRINCE OF FLORENCE AND SIENA

O first love, first hope, and O, first honor
of the first and wisest, the best leader that the great
planet sees who carries us the day as round he
courses, 4
when do we behold such hoary thoughts
abiding in so youthful a heart? When such fierce
pride in a fair face adorned with every grace? Such
valor? 8
What then will it be when, weighty in years,
glory, and triumphs, you will hold the reins of Italy
with your counsel and your hand? 11
Shall we not see the burdened gloomy
century restored to levity and serenity? And you on
a straight smooth path take living flight to heaven?[24] 14

4 [4] AL SIGNOR PAOLO GIORDANO ORSINO[25]

Vero signor, ch'a quegli antichi eroi,
che del mondo gran tempo trionfaro,
di senno e di valor v'en gite al paro
per voi far divo e fortunati noi,
ecco che Roma a i cari figli suoi
rivolta dice, "Al mio novello e chiaro
Quirino, or qual memoria alta preparo
poi ch'ei fia sazio d'abitar fra voi?
Che poche aguglie e moli e mausolei,
ch'a Cesare, a Traiano e al grande Augusto
dier degni pregi a i chiari merti loro,
fieno a quei del mio forte e saggio e giusto
PAOLO, d'ogni mio danno ampio ristoro,
ch'io bramo tanto e più bramar devrei."

5 [5] AL RE FILIPPO[27]

Invitto rege, al cui valore immenso
quanto è dal nostro all'Antartico Polo
diede lassù chi tutto puote solo,
e qui de i saggi universal consenso,
e però dianzi eterno danno e intenso
dolor cadeo sovra 'l gallico stuolo,
che visto e vinto e morto attese solo
fuggir valor di giusto sdegno acceso.
E non pur noi, ma chi dell'oriente
nemico di Gesù l'imperio regge
vedrem chinarsi a' vostri piedi umile;
e l'altra a noi lontana, ignota gente,
nel nostro mondo non più scuro e vile,
solo uno scettro aver, solo una legge.

4 [4] TO SIGNOR PAOLO GIORDANO ORSINO

True lord, who walk as peer in wisdom and
valor to those ancient heroes who for a long time
triumphed over the world, to your godliness and our
good fortune, 4
behold how Rome speaks, addressing her
dear children, "Now what high memorial shall I
prepare for my new and illustrious Quirinus, since he
is sated with dwelling among you? 8
For obelisks and monuments and
mausoleums, which gave Caesar, Trajan, and the
great Augustus worthy rewards for their illustrious merits, 11
will be few for those of my strong and wise
and just PAOLO, healer of my every wound,
whom I so yearn for and should yearn for the more."[26] 14

5 [5] TO KING PHILIP

Unvanquished king, He who is alone all-
powerful above and the universal consensus of
wise men here below gave to your immense valor
everything that is from our pole to the Antarctic; 4
and hence ere now eternal harm and intense sorrow
befell the Gallic herd that, seen conquered and killed,
gave heed only to flee valor kindled with just disdain. 8
And we shall see not only ourselves,
but the enemy of Jesus who rules the empire of the orient,
bow humbly at your feet, 11
and the other distant, unknown people in our world,
no longer dark and base, shall have only one scepter,
only one law.[28] 14

6 [6] ALLA REINA MARIA[29]

"Sacra reina, a cui Natura e Dio
per far fede quaggiù d'ogni ben loro,
sangue, virtù, valor, stato, tesoro
e per isposo re, sì forte e pio, 4
dieder, doti conformi al bel disio
vostro di ritornar nell'antico oro
il ferro nostro, e dare alto ristoro
al secol, che fia buon, quant'ora è rio; 8
o più ch'altra ancor mai felice eletta
coppia, ov'è giunto in un potere e 'ngegno,
chi fia che 'n contra voi difesa faccia?" 11
Così dicea dal ciel pura angioletta,
e poi soggiunse, "E non fia vostro un regno,
ma quanto il sol riscalda e 'l mare abbraccia." 14

7 [7] AL DUCA D'URBINO[31]

Saggio signor, che con giustizia vera
e propria tua distribuendo vai
gli onori e i pregi a chi più merta, e dai
gastigo a qualunche opra indegna o fera, 4
perch'io la mente mia, che brama e spera
per te dar fine, e n'è ben tempo omai,
a i suoi sì lunghi e sì dolenti guai,
umile inchino a tua virtude altera; 8
e prego il ciel che 'n tuo favor rivolga
tutti i suoi corsi, e 'n fin sovra le stelle
erga la prisca tua caonia pianta; 11
e tal frutto di lei si veggia e colga,
che l'antich'opre e l'alme elette e belle
tornino al mondo, e già se 'ngloria e vanta. 14

6 [6] TO QUEEN MARIA

"Holy queen, to whom Nature and God bore
faith down here of their every good by giving
blood, virtue, valor, estate, treasure, and for spouse
a king so strong and pious, 4
gifts consonant with your fair desire to
restore our iron to ancient gold and bring a lofty
renewal to the age, which will be as good as it now
is evil; 8
O chosen couple, happier than ever any other
before, where power and intellect are joined as one,
who is there who could oppose you?" 11
Thus spoke from heaven a pure angel, and
then it added, "And yours will be not a kingdom,
but as much as the sun warms and the sea
embraces."[30] 14

7 [7] TO THE DUKE OF URBINO

Wise lord, you with your true and proper
justice go meting out honors and awards to those
who most deserve and give punishment to every
unworthy or cruel deed; 4
for which I humbly bow my mind to your
proud virtue, for it yearns and hopes through you to
put an end, and high time it is by now, to its so
long and so woeful sorrows; 8
and I pray Heaven to set all its courses in
your favor, and to raise above the stars your pristine
Chaonian plant, 11
and may we see and pick from it such fruit
that the deeds of the ancients and their fair chosen
souls return to our world, even now its pride and glory.[32] 14

8 [8] ALLA DUCHESSA D'URBINO[33]

Là verso l'Apennino, ove 'l Metauro
bagna le sue fiorite e vaghe sponde,
e dove con più chiare e rapid'onde
seco s'aduna il gentil fiume Isauro, 4
siede la donna, anzi 'l ricco tesauro
del cielo, a cui sì larghe grazie infonde
Giove, che alla sua antica amata fronde
promette onor via più ch'Apollo al lauro. 8
Così le rime al gran soggetto eguali
avess'io, che sonar farei il suo nome
fin dove nasce e si nasconde il sole; 11
ma poi ch'a sì gran volo ho corte l'ali,
co'l cor l'onoro e riverisco come
cosa bella immortal s'adora e cole. 14

9 [9] AL PRENCIPE D'URBINO[35]

Non è questo dell'alma pianta antica,
che non pur' il Metauro adombra e 'nfiora,
ma 'l mondo tutto, altero germe, ch'ora
cresce qual arbor verde in piaggia aprica? 4
Non è questo di quell'alta e pudica
palma, che tanto il sacro Tebro onora,
il trionfo e la gloria, e non è ancora
questi la speme della patria amica? 8
Non è questa la man, ch'ardire e forza
prende con gli anni, tal ch'adegua e passa
de' grandi avoli suoi le glorie prime? 11
Già il suo valore il fiero scita ammorza,
che tanto a terra la sua fronte abbassa,
quant'ei s'inalza alle più altere cime. 14

8 [8] TO THE DUCHESS OF URBINO

There toward the Apennines, where the
Metauro bathes its blossomed and winsome shores,
and where the noble river Isauro joins it with
clearer and more rapid waves, 4
resides the lady—nay, the rich treasure of
heaven, to whom Jove's largesse infuses such grace
that he promises his ancient, beloved boughs more
honor than Apollo to the laurel. 8
If only I had rhymes equal to the great
subject, I would make her name resound as far as
the sun's birth and hiding place; 11
but since my wings are short for so long a
flight, I honor and revere her with my heart, as one
adores and worships a beautiful, immortal thing.[34] 14

9 [9] TO THE PRINCE OF URBINO

Is this not from the bountiful ancient plant
that shades and brings to blossom not only the
Metauro, but the whole world, a seed that now
grows as green trees do on an open slope? 4
Is this not the triumph and glory of that lofty
and chaste palm tree that the sacred Tiber so
honors? And is it not again the hope of our friendly
fatherland? 8
Is this not the hand that grows with the years
in daring and strength, so much so that it equals and
surpasses the primal glories of his great forebears? 11
Already his valor stamps out the fierce
Scythian, who lowers his brow as far to
earth as he himself rises to the proudest peaks.[36] 14

10 [10] A DONNA VERGINIA VARANA DELLA ROVERE[37]

O di nome e d'effetti intatta e pura
vergine, che di senno e di beltade
trappassi lei che 'n mezzo a lance e spade
Roma e sé tolse a servitù sì dura, 4
per te, ma con diversa altra ventura,
l'alta tua Camerino in libertade
dolce, servendo a te per ogni etade,
lieta si mostrarà, non pur sicura. 8
Sì ristorare a pien vedremo i danni
di quell'alme beate che dal cielo
veggono in te di lor fiorir la speme, 11
e 'l tuo gran genitore, a cui t'affanni
farti simile, ancor nel mortal velo
goderà il frutto del suo chiaro seme. 14

11 [11] NELLE NOZZE DEL SIGNOR FEDERIGO BUONROMEO[39] E DELLA SIGNORA DONNA VIRGINIA DELLA ROVERE[40]

O d'ogni gloria, o d'ogni imperio degna,
coppia felice, a cui dal ciel fu dato
senno, bontà, vertù, ricchezza e stato,
cose ch'a gli altri dar rado s'ingegna; 4
se 'l gran vostro valor non si disdegna
che gli onor vostri e 'l vostro amico fato,
se ben degni di stil chiaro ed ornato,
la rozza musa mia cantando vegna, 8
forse anco un dì la sacra quercia antica
sì cara e conta a l'uno e a l'altro polo,
porria sentirsi in più sublime parte; 11
e l'alto fedeRICO e la pudica
VIRGINIA, ch'or tacendo ammiro e colo,
cantati andarne in mille e mille carte. 14

10 [10] TO DONNA VERGINIA VARANA DELLA ROVERE

O in name and deed intact and pure virgin,
who in wisdom and beauty surpass the lady who
amidst lances and swords snatched Rome from
herself and servitude, 4
because of you, but with other different
fortunes, your lofty Camerino will show herself
joyful in sweet liberty, not just secure, as she serves
you through the ages. 8
Truly, we shall see fully righted the wrongs
to those blessed souls who from heaven see their
hope flower in you, 11
and your great parent, whom you struggle to
emulate, still in mortal veil shall enjoy the fruit of
his bright seed.[38] 14

11 [11] ON THE NUPTIALS OF SIGNOR FEDERIGO BUONROMEO AND SIGNORA DONNA VIRGINIA DELLA ROVERE

O happy couple, worthy of all glory and
empire, to whom heaven gave wisdom, bounty,
virtue, riches, and rank, things that it rarely troubles
to give others, 4
if your great valor not disdain my coarse
muse, who comes to sing your honors and your
friendly destiny, deserving though they be of a
bright, ornate style, 8
perhaps yet one day the ancient sacred oak,
so dear and renowned from pole to pole, might be
heard of in a sublimer place; 11
and lofty FedeRICH and chaste VIRGINIA,
whom now in silence I admire and worship, could go
forth sung of in a thousand and thousand pages.[41] 14

12 [12] ALLA MEDESIMA[42]

"Prendete in mano il mio lucente corno,
di vaghi fior, di dolci frutti pieno,
leggiadre ninfe, che 'l mio fondo ameno
rendete tanto e sovra ogn'altro adorno,"
dicea il Metauro, "e dove fan soggiorno
valore e cortesia, dove il terreno
più d'altro è lieto, e l'aer più sereno,
itene in compagnia del nuovo giorno.
Ivi vedrete l'alma coppia eletta,
l'un nipote di lui, che 'n terra è dio,
l'altra del giusto mio gran duce figlia;
datele questo in dono, e dite ch'io
veggo di speme carco e meraviglia
il Tebro, che sol lor bramando aspetta."

13 [13] ALLA MEDESIMA[44]

"Ninfa gentil, ne' cui begli occhi Amore,
ch'altro non ha di lor più degno e vero
seggio e tesor, regge il suo grande impero,
onde versa onestà, senno e valore;
deh, per quel casto oggi novello ardore,
e per quell'amoroso alto pensiero,
che 'ncende e desta il vostro animo altero,
che si dormia sì freddo i giorni e l'ore,
non più del Metro le felici sponde
ornate; anch'io fresche acque e frutti e fiori
vi serbo e spargo nel mio bel soggiorno."
Così lieto il gran Tebro; ed ecco fuori
mille voci s'udir dal fondo, e l'onde
VIRGINIA rimbombar dentro e d'intorno.

12 [12] TO THE SAME LADY

"Take in hand my shining horn, filled with fair flowers and sweet fruits, blithe nymphs who make my bed so blissful and beauteous more than any other," 4

said the Metauro, "and where valor and courtesy make their abode, where the land is happier than any other, and the air more serene, go in company of the new day. 8

There you will see the blessed chosen couple, one a nephew of him who is God on earth; the other, daughter of my great just leader; 11

give them this as a gift, and say that I see the Tiber bursting with hope and marvel, who awaits yearning for them alone."[43] 14

13 [13] TO THE SAME LADY

"Noble nymph, in whose fair eyes Love, who has no other seat or treasure more worthy and true than they, rules his great empire, whence he bestows honesty, wisdom, and valor; 4

for that chaste new young ardor today, and for that lofty amorous thought that kindles and awakens your proud spirit, which was so coldly sleeping its days and hours, 8

pray, deck no longer the happy shores of the Metauro; I too keep and cast fresh waters and fruits and flowers for you in my fair abode." 11

Thus joyful the great Tiber; and behold, from out of the depth were heard a thousand voices, and the waves within and around echoing "VIRGINIA!" 14

14 ALLA MEDESIMA[45]

Scendi dal terzo cielo,
santa madre d'amor, Venere bella;
e tu, sposa e sorella
di lui che regge il tutto al caldo e al gelo,
dolce Imeneo, che fai
d'una medesma fiamma arder due cori;
e voi, leggiadri e pargoletti Amori
scendete in riva al grande Isauro omai,
lieti cantando intorno
al casto letto di quei chiari eroi
per cui vedrete poi
di lor feconda prole il mondo adorno.

15 [15] AL CARDINAL DE' MEDICI[47]

Terrestre Giove, a voi le chiavi e 'l freno
del ciel ne' più verdi anni e della terra,
serba l'alto motor che mai non erra,
per lo mondo allegrar d'angoscia pieno;
onde nel sacro vostro acerbo seno
maturo senno, ogn'or più largo serra,
e dolce pace dopo tanta guerra
mostra nel volto più del ciel sereno.
Vede egli il vostro giusto, invitto e chiaro
Saturno, a cui fedel sarete e pio,
quanto è 'l suo merto e 'l dever vostro ogn'ora,
e l'alma Berecinzia a paro a paro
agguagliar la speranza col disio,
di novello Leon vedervi ancora.

14 TO THE SAME LADY

Descend from the third heaven,
holy mother of Love, fair Venus;
and you, bride and sister of
him who rules all in warmth and frost,
sweet Hymen, who make
two hearts burn as one flame;
and you, blithe cherubic Amorini,
descend now to the shore of the great Isauro,
singing joyfully around
the chaste bed of those famed heroes,
whose fertile offspring
you will then see adorn the world.[46]

15 [15] TO THE MEDICI CARDINAL

Terrestrial Jove, for you in your budding
years the lofty mover who never errs reserves the
keys and reins of heaven and earth to gladden our
anguish-filled world;
hence in your sacred unripe bosom He locks
mature, ever wider wisdom, and after such long war
He shows sweet peace in your face,
serener than the sky.
He sees your just, unvanquished, and bright
Saturn, to whom you will be faithful and pious, as
much as are his deserts and your constant duty,
and bountiful Berecynthia measure for
measure matches hope with desire yet to see you a
new young Leo.[48]

16 [16] AL DUCA DI FIORENZA E DI SIENA[49]

Glorioso signor, cui teme ed ama
in un non pur la vostra Etruria bella,
ch'a ragion Duce e Padre suo v'appella,
ma Italia ancor, che d'obedirvi brama,
deh, se là dove alta virtù vi chiama,
che 'n voi fiorio fin dall'età novella,
vi scorga amica e graziosa stella
di gloria carco e d'onorata brama,
movete alla bell'Arbia vostra il piede,
ove statue, colossi, archi e trofei
vedrete eretti al vostro altero nome,
e mille cigni udrete, eterna fede
cantando fare al mondo tutto, come
loco vi serba il ciel fra gli altri dei.

17 [17] ALLA DUCHESS DI FIORENZA E DI SIENA[51]

Felicissima donna, a cui s'inchina
l'Arno superbo e la bell'Arbia ancora,
poscia ch'ad ambo ordine e legge ogn'ora
date sola di lor degna reina,
una, cui suo volere e 'l ciel destina
voi, che cotanto sovra ogn'altra onora,
riverir e cantar, ben ch'uopo fôra
a dire a pien di voi lingua divina,
queste del picciol suo sterile ingegno,
povero dono, incolte rime nuove,
sacra oggi e porge al vostro alto valore.
Non le sdegnate, prego, che 'l gran Giove,
che fece e muove il sol, non prende a sdegno
l'umili offerte d'un divoto core.

16 [16] TO THE DUKE OF FLORENCE AND SIENA

Glorious lord, feared and loved at once not
only by your fair Etruria, who rightly styles you her
leader and father, but Italy as well, who longs to
obey you, 4
pray, if a friendly and gracious star guide
you, weighty with glory and honorable longing,
there where you are called by lofty virtue, which
flowered in you from your vernal years, 8
move your steps to the fair Arbia, where you
will see statues, colossi, arches, and trophies raised
in your proud name 11
and you will hear a thousand singing swans bear
eternal witness to all the world how heaven reserves
you a place amongst the other gods.[50] 14

17 [17] TO THE DUCHESS OF FLORENCE AND SIENA

Happiest of ladies, to whom haughty Arno
and fair Arbia bow alike, for you ever give to both
order and law, alone their worthy queen, 4
a woman destined by heaven and her
desire to revere and sing of you, whom she honors
so far above every other lady, though it would take
a divine tongue fully to tell of you, 8
these uncultivated rhymes, a poor gift of
her small sterile intellect, she dedicates and offers
today to your lofty valor. 11
Disdain them not, I pray; for the great Jove,
who made and moves the sun, does not scorn the
humble offerings of a devoted heart.[52] 14

18 [19] PER MADAMA LUCRETIA DA ESTE PRINCIPESSA D'URBINO[53]

Oltra le nubi e 'nfin sovra le stelle,
vaga del ciel questa fenice aurata
sola se 'n gìa dalle sue proprie alzata
ali, più d'altre mai gradite e belle, 4
quando il gran Giove, rimirando in quelle
parti ch'adombra la sua fronde amata,
disse, "O felici voi, che 'n voi l'usata
antica gloria vien chi rinovelle." 8
Indi volto ver lei che 'n alto poggia,
"Qui t'annida, qui il moto e 'l volo affrena,
questo è degno oriente al tuo splendore. 11
Qui, come dal ciel cade amica pioggia,
per cui la terra è tutta d'amor piena,
cader di sovra te celeste onore." 14

19 [20] PER LA MEDESIMA[55]

Perché superbo e d'alta gloria adorno
sen vada il Tebro ancor del nome amico
di lei, ch'armata di pensier pudico
fece notte a se stessa a mezo 'l giorno; 4
non l'invidia il Metauro, né 'l suo corno
vede ei men colmo di valore antico,
né men di lui l'altero lido aprico
di trionfale onor cinge d'intorno; 8
poiché LUCRETIA, e casta e saggia e bella
con alto ciel via più benigno e chiaro,
raddoppia i pregi suoi famosi e tanti. 11
Questa simile a lor, prole novella,
che già dierono al mondo i primi vanti,
produr vedrassi, o tempo aurato e caro. 14

18 [19] FOR MADAMA LUCRETIA DA ESTE, PRINCESS OF URBINO

Beyond the clouds and even above the stars,
heaven her desire, this fair golden phoenix flew
alone, lofted by her own wings, lovelier and more
likesome than ever any others, 4
when great Jove, gazing down on those parts
shaded by his beloved branch, said, "Oh, happy
you are, for one comes to renew in you your wonted
glory of yore." 8
Then, facing her who presses loftily upward,
"Make here your nest, here check your flight and
motion; this is a worthy orient for your splendor. 11
Here as friendly rain falls from heaven,
filling all the earth with love, there falls over you
celestial honor."[54] 14

19 [20] TO THE SAME LADY

Although the Tiber still flows proud and
adorned with lofty glory for the amicable name of her
who, armed with chaste thought, made night for
herself at midday, 4
the Metauro envies him not, nor does he
see his own horn brim less with ancient valor, nor
does he cast a lesser circle than he of triumphal
honor around his proud sunlit shore, 8
since chaste and wise and fair LUCRETIA,
with lofty heaven ever more benevolent and bright,
redoubles his merits, famous and so many. 11
We shall see this lady produce new
offspring, like those who long ago first made the
world exult, O time engilded and dear.[56] 14

20 [21] A PAPA PAOLO TERZO FARNESE[57]

A un volger d'occhio, a un picciol cenno vostro,
Paolo, beato, eccelso, almo pastore,
umil s'inchina ogni mondan valore,
s'apre il ciel, trema il tenebroso chiostro; 4
e mentre de' più saggi il chiaro inchiostro
vi sacra eterno alla fama, all'onore,
v'apparecchia nel ciel pregio maggiore
Quel che vi scelse al gran governo nostro. 8
Così la Parca a gli anni vostri aggiunga
quei del buon PIERO, o del gran re, ch'insieme
con l'ombra, l'ore e 'l tempo indietro volse, 11
come spera con voi tranquilla e lunga
vita goder di vostra greggia il seme,
e con voi ritornare onde si tolse. 14

21 [22] AD INSTANZA DELL'ILLUSTRISSIMA SIGNORA DONNA ISABELLA DE' MEDICI[59]

Di me la miglior parte,
anzi la propria vita, il proprio core,
oggi s'invola e parte,
e in altri vive, e 'n me medesma more. 4
Ahi, ria legge d'Amore!
Ahi, duro privilegio degli amanti,
che presso a uscir di pianti
un sol conforto arriva,
ch'a forza mi tien viva! 9

Ahi, disperata vita!
Ahi, dispietata morte!
L'una a viver m'invita,
e poi morta mi tiene, 13
lungi da ogni bene.
L'altra a morir par che mi riconforte,
dandomi vita ogn'or gravosa e forte.
In così strane tempre
vivo morendo sempre. 18

20 [21] TO POPE PAUL III FARNESE

At a flick of your eye, at your slightest sign,
Paul, blessed, exalted, bountiful shepherd, every
worldly value humbly kneels, Heaven opens, the
tenebrous cloister trembles; 4
and while the lustrous ink of the wisest
consecrates you eternal to fame, to honor, He who
chose you for our great government readies for you
a finer prize in heaven. 8
Thus may the Fate add to your years those
of good PETER, or of the great king, who together
with the shadow turned back the hours and time, 11
just as the seed of your flock hopes to enjoy
long and tranquil life with you and return with you
whence it arose.[58] 14

21 [22] AT THE REQUEST OF THE MOST ILLUSTRIOUS SIGNORA DONNA ISABELLA DE' MEDICI

The better part of me,
rather my very life, my very heart,
flies away and departs today,
and he lives in others and dies within me myself. 4
Ah, cruel law of Love!
Ah, harsh privilege of lovers,
for near weeping's end
comes a lone comfort
that keeps me perforce alive! 9

Ah, hopeless life!
Ah, pitiless death!
One invites me to live
and then keeps me dead, 13
away from all well-being.
The other seems to coax me to die,
yet gives me life heavy and hard.
In such strange moods
I live, ever dying.[60] 18

22 [23] PER LA MEDESIMA[61]

Deh, quando il giorno, e deh, quando fia l'ora
che più benigno fato
renda a quest'alma il suo conforto usato?
Dolce pensier ch'ogn'ora
mi pasci di speranza e di desire,
deh, fa meco dimora,
sin ch'io veggia apparire
chi può solo acquetar lo mio martire.

Qual corpo suol da sua più nobil alma
misero abandonato
gelida rimaner, caduca salma,
tal'io, mia dolce ed alma
vita e sostegno amato,
al vostro dipartir lassa restai.
Santo Amor, tu che fai
quel ch'altri far non può, tornami in vita,
a mia bell'alma unita.

23 [24] PER LA MEDESIMA[63]

Lunga guerra e mortal, colpi aspri e feri,
sotto l'insegna tua, crudel tiranno,
voto di fe', di duol colmo e d'inganno,
fra mille e mille armati tuoi guerrieri,
donna sola ed inerme, or quale speri
di ciò vittoria? ogn'or più d'anno in anno
sostiene dolente; ed oh, pur l'aspro affanno
manchi faccia i suoi dì, torbidi e neri.
E questo premio a chi fedel commette
se stesso a servitude acerba e strana
rendon le leggi tue gravose e torte.
Dura condizion di nostra umana
vita, servir chi via più ardito e forte
per anciderti sol, par che s'affrette.

22 [23] FOR THE SAME LADY

Pray, when will the day, the hour come,
when a kindlier fate
restores to this soul its familiar comfort?
Sweet thought who ever
feed me on hope and desire,
pray, dwell with me
until I see him appear
who alone can calm my torment.

As a miserable body abandoned
by its more noble soul
is wont to remain a gelid short-lived corpse,
so I was left, alas, at your departure,
sweet strength of my
life and beloved support.
Holy Love, you who can do
what others cannot, bring me back to life,
joined with my fair soul.[62]

23 [24] FOR THE SAME LADY

Long and mortal warfare, blows bitter and
harsh beneath your ensign, cruel tyrant, empty of
faith, brimming with sorrow and deceit; from
among thousands upon thousands of your armed warriors,
a woman alone and defenseless, now what
victory do you hope for from that? Evermore
sorrowing, year after year she bears it; oh, may yet the
harsh suffering shorten her days, murky and black.
And this reward your heavy, twisted laws
render to whoever faithfully commits himself to
bitter and strange servitude.
A hard condition of our human life, to serve
him who hastens, by and by bolder and stronger,
only it seems to kill you.[64]

24 [25][65]

Per anciderti sol, par che s'affrette
l'empio signor che 'n mille vari modi,
or con finte lusinghe e vere frodi,
l'alme al suo duro imperio fa soggette.
Ivi la ragion serve, ivi neglette
son le virtuti, ed ivi ogn'or più annodi,
quanto scior tenti gl'intricati nodi
delle catene adamantine e strette
ch'al collo, a' piedi ed alle braccia intorno
t'avvinse crudeltà, ministra acerba
di lui, che 'l tuo languir gl'aggrada e piace.
E se morte, che sola disacerba
le nostre doglie, vien, fuggir la face
impietà, ch'appo lui fa suo soggiorno.

25 [26][67]

Impietà, ch'appo lei fa suo soggiorno,
è guida di martir, d'angoscie e stenti,
con quanti il re delle perdute genti
supplizi aduna ove non è mai giorno.
Voi che mirate d'un bel viso adorno
l'alte fattezze e i vaghi occhi lucenti,
chiudete i vostri, o pur non siate lenti
fuggir lontan tanto disonore e scorno;
e sentendo parlar cortese, umile,
d'alma saggia e gentil, fuggite, ahi lassi,
ch'ivi amor tende i suoi più occulti lacci,
onde preso e legato a morte vassi;
né ti potran levar da tanti impacci
favor celeste, o mortal lingua o stile.

24 [25]

Only to kill you, it seems the wicked lord
hastens, who in a thousand different ways, now
with false evil flattery and true trickery, makes
souls subject to his hard rule. 4

There reason serves, there the virtues are
neglected; and there, the more you try to loosen
them, the more intricately he knots the tight
adamantine chains 8

bound round your neck, feet, and arms by
cruelty, bitter minister of him to whose liking and
pleasure your languishing is. 11

And if death comes, who alone unsours
our sorrows, she is driven away by
pitilessness, who makes her abode at his side.[66] 14

25 [26]

Pitilessness, who makes her abode at her side,
is a guide to suffering, anguish, and privations,
with as many tortures as the king of the lost souls
musters where it is never day. 4

You who gaze upon the fine features and
bright lovesome eyes of a fair face,
close your own, or else be not slow
to flee far from such disgrace and shame; 8

and when you hear the courteous, humble
speech of a wise and gentle spirit, flee, ah alas, for
there love spreads his hiddenmost nets; 11

thus caught and bound folk go to death; nor
can you be freed from such entanglements by
heavenly favor or mortal tongue or style.[68] 14

26 [27][69]

Favor celeste, o mortal lingua o stile
non prezza Amor, ché deitate alcuna
non regna sopra 'l cerchio della luna
ch'ei non faccia cangiar sembianza e stile;
e qual fiero angue a suon dolce e sottile
si piega, e dritto è ben, poiché s'aduna
rabbia e veneno in lui fin dalla cuna,
ch'ei sia in natura a quel non dissimile.
Dunque miser colui che i giorni interi
ed intere le notti, e perde e spende
in sì ria servitù con tanti affanni;
chiaro esempio a chiunque e vede e 'ntende
sarà come m'han concio e petto e panni,
lunga guerra mortal, colpi aspri e fieri.

27 [28] PER LA SIGNORA DONNA HIERONIMA COLONNA[71]

Fra tante, che le chiare orme seguendo
vanno d'Apollo, e desiose e 'ntente
odono il suon della beata gente
che 'l sacro monte va di gioia empiendo,
ultima sono, e tal ch'a pena intendo
quanto con gran ragion brama la mente;
pur eccitando in me le forze spente,
me stessa affretto, e mia tardanza ammendo;
e saggia e bella ascolto di lontano
COLONNESE innalzar con nobil canto,
sì che 'l Tebro l'ammira e 'l Vaticano.
"Tacciasi or lei, che Roma accrebbe tanto
co'l suo morir," dice ogni stil sovrano,
"ché le dà questa in vita eterno vanto."

26 [27]

Heavenly favor, or mortal tongue or style—
Love prizes them not, for not one deity reigns over
the circle of the moon but that he does not
change their appearance and style; 4
and like a fierce asp, he bends to sweet and
subtle sound, and since rage and venom collect in
him from the cradle, he is quite rightly not
dissimilar to it in nature. 8
Hence miserable the man who wastes and
spends entire days and entire nights in such evil
servitude with so many cares; 11
how I have been battered, body and soul, by
long mortal warfare, harsh and fierce blows, will be
a plain example to whoever sees and understands.[70] 14

27 [28] FOR SIGNORA DONNA HIERONIMA COLONNA

Among so many ladies who go following
the famed footsteps of Apollo, and intent with
desire hear the sound of the blessed folk who go
filling the holy mount with joy, 4
I am last, and such that I scarcely apprehend
my mind's good reason for its great longing, yet
spurring my spent strength, I hasten on and remedy
my tardiness; 8
and from afar I listen to COLONNESE,
wise and beautiful, raised in noble song, for she is
the wonder of the Tiber and Vatican. 11
"Let her now be silent who so increased
Rome by dying," says every sovereign style, "for
this lady in life gives it vaunt eternal."[72] 14

28 [29] AL SIGNOR CHIAPPINO VITELLI[73]

Se gli antichi scrittori ornar le carte
de' nomi e d'opre di quei primi alteri
campioni e valorosi cavallieri
che l'insegne seguir del fiero Marte, 4
gìron cogliendo le lor glorie sparte
per molte etadi e per vari sentieri,
a' nostri tutti i fatti eterni e veri
in un soggetto solo il ciel comparte, 8
che 'l grande Alcide alle fatezze conte
rassembra, e 'l forte Ettorre e 'l saggio Ulisse,
d'anni e di valor l'alto Africano. 11
Chi più fedele al mondo o vive o visse?
chi più al volere ebbe le forze pronte
ch'al gran nostro VITEL non sia lontano? 14

29 [30] AL MEDESIMO[75]

Non l'alta penna e no 'l purgato inchiostro
del gran Virgilio e dell'antico Omero,
avrian, saggio signor, prode guerriero,
di senno, di valor, di bontà mostro, 4
descritto a pien del grande animo vostro,
le vere lodi e 'l raro pregio altero,
per cui malgrado dell'inerte e fero
secol si cangia in oro il ferro nostro. 8
Non marmi, non metalli e non colori,
di Fidia, di Pirgotele e d'Apelle,
sculpir, formare e colorir giamai 11
avrian potuto l'onorate e belle
imprese vostre e i trionfali onori,
a cui cedon gli antichi oggi d'assai. 14

28 [29] TO SIGNOR CHIAPPINO VITELLI

If the ancient writers adorned their pages
with the names and deeds of those first proud
champions and valorous knights who followed the
ensigns of fierce Mars, 4

they went about gathering their glories
scattered over many ages and diverse paths; for ours,
heaven apportions all eternal and true deeds in a
single subject, 8

who resembles great Alcides for his
renowned features, and strong Hector, and wise
Ulysses for his years, and the lofty African for
valor. 11

Who lives or lived truer to the world? Who
was so quick to summon his strength that our great
VITELLO does not far outstrip him?[74] 14

29 [30] TO THE SAME MAN

Not the lofty pen and not the refined ink of
the great Virgil and ancient Homer could have fully
described, wise lord, brave warrior, marvel of
wisdom, valor, and goodness, 4

the true praises and the rare proud
worth of your great spirit, through which our age,
although inert and wild, changes from iron to gold. 8

Not the marbles, not the metals, and not the
colors of Phidias, Pyrgoteles, and Apelles could
ever in sculpture, form, or color 11

have honored your fair deeds and your triumphal
honors, before which today the ancients deeply
bow.[76] 14

30 [32][77] ALLA SIGNORA LEONORA CIBO DE' VITELLI[78]

O di casta bellezza essempio vero,
e di rara virtude ardente raggio,
donna che 'n questo uman cieco viaggio
ne mostrate del ciel l'alto sentiero,
voi sola il nostro verno ingrato e nero
cangiate in chiaro e grazioso maggio;
voi sola col parlar cortese e saggio
rendete umile ogn'aspro ingegno e fero;
tal ch'io, che vaga son del vostro lume,
con l'ali del pensier tant'alto ascendo,
quanto in bianco augel basta a cangiarme,
indi fuor d'ogni mio vecchio costume,
da voi, dalla stagion novella, prendo
tanto vigor ch'io sento eterna farme.

31 [33] ALLA MEDESIMA[80]

Da l'alma dea ch'al terzo cielo impera
e i più leggiadri cor d'amore accende,
e da colei ch'eguale a Dio ne rende
scevri dall'ignorante e vile schiera;
il vero bel della sua vaga spera,
e 'l sommo buono, ond'ogni ben s'attende,
tolse Colui che sol se stesso intende,
per far l'alma di voi perfetta e 'intera,
donna più d'altra bella e più amorosa,
e più d'ogni altra saggia e più divina,
per cui di gire al ciel la via s'impara;
così—o che sper'io!—fosse pur'osa
l'alma mia d'appressar luce sì chiara,
come oggi da lontan v'adora e 'nchina.

30 [32] TO SIGNORA LEONORA CIBO DE' VITELLI

O true example of chaste beauty and ardent
ray of rare virtue, lady you who in this blind human
journey show us the lofty pathway to heaven, 4
you alone change our ungrateful and black
winter into a bright and gracious May; you alone
with your courteous and wise speech make humble
every harsh and fierce mind; 8
such that I, who long for your light, ascend
with the wings of thought as high as need be to turn
myself into a white bird, 11
then breaking from all my old habits, I take
from you, from the new season, vigor so great that I
feel myself made eternal.[79] 14

31 [33] TO THE SAME LADY

From the bountiful goddess who reigns in
the third heaven and kindles to love the most
winsome hearts, and from her who makes us the
equal of God, detached from the ignorant and base
herd; 4
He who alone understands Himself took the
true beauty of her lovesome sphere and the highest
good, whence we anticipate all good, to make your
soul perfect and whole, 8
lady, fairer and more amorous than any
other, and wiser than any other and more divine,
through whom we learn the way to go to heaven; 11
if only my own soul—oh, what do I hope!—
had as much daring to approach such bright light as
it adores and bows to you today from afar.[81] 14

32 [34] ALLA MEDESIMA[82]

Da Dio, alma gentile, il bello e 'l buono,
da gli spirti celesti
il puro cor prendesti,
dalle spere superne il canto e 'l suono,
dalla madre d'amore
virtù ch'encende ogni cortese core,
da Febo il lume e dalla sua sorella
mente d'ogni viltà sempre rubella,
alor che 'l tuo bel velo
per rivestir la terra, spogliò il cielo.

33 [36] ALLA SIGNORA HERSILIA CORTESI DE' MONTI[84]

Non siano oggi superbi Olimpo e Atlante,
perché di nubi l'un non copra il velo,
l'altro perché, cinto d'eterno gelo,
di sostener il ciel si glorii e vante,
ché 'l nostro Monte, in cui l'amate piante
pose Minerva, con sì caldo zelo
s'erge al primo, al secondo e al maggior cielo,
spargendo nettar dalle cime sante.
Parnaso, il lauro e le sorelle dive
cedano omai, poi che benigna stella
tutto il ben di lasù raccolto ha in una;
altre frondi, altro Monte ed altre rive
a noi discopre dea cortese e bella,
in cui tanto è valor quanto fortuna.

32 [34] TO THE SAME LADY

From God, noble soul, you took the fair and the good;
from the heavenly spirits,
your pure heart;
from the supernal spheres, your song and sound;
from the mother of Love,
your virtue, which kindles every courteous heart;
from Phoebus your light and from his sister
a mind always a rebel to all that is base,
while your fair veil
despoiled heaven to reclothe the earth.[83]

33 [36] TO SIGNORA HERSILIA CORTESI DE' MONTI

Let not Olympus and Atlas be proud today,
the one that no cloud veil covers it, the other that,
encircled with eternal ice, its glory and vaunt be to
support the sky,
for our Monte, on whom Minerva set her
beloved plants, so warmed by zeal
surges upward to the first, to the second, and to the greatest heaven,
sprinkling nectar from her holy peaks.
Now then, let Parnassus, the laurel,
and the divine sisters yield,
since a benign star has gathered
all the good from up there into one woman;
other boughs, another Mount, and other shores,
are revealed to us by a goddess Courteous and fair,
in whom valor is as great as good fortune.[85]

34 [37] PER LA SIGNORA LIVIA COLONNA[86]

Poscia che 'l sol d'alta virtute ardente,
che co' suoi raggi a Febo il lume adombra,
avrà fugata e dileguata l'ombra
c'ha tante luci e così chiare spente,
potrà l'avventurosa età presente
per l'alto lampo ch'ogni nebbia sgombra,
e di senno e valor le menti ingombra,
dar di sé invidia alla futura gente,
e quelle a gran ragion pregiate carte,
che sì dolce cantar per Laura e Bice,
saran men care assai di quel che foro,
e di Livia Colonna in ogni parte
s'udrà sonare il nome alto e felice
degno soggetto al più gradito alloro.

35 [41] ALLA SIGNORA HORTENSIA COLONNA[88]

Qui tanto, ahi lassa, a me negletta e schiva,
quanto pria me teneva ornata e cara,
mi trovo in vita più di morte amara,
di doglia colma e d'allegrezza priva;
né dell'Arno l'amata e fresca riva,
ch'ogni torbida mente orna e rischiara,
né i colti ingegni, ond'ogni onor s'impara,
né l'udir chi d'amor raconti o scriva,
ponno scemar l'ardente fiamma, ond'io
nodrisco il cor, che 'n più felice stato
creò talor concetti alti e diversi;
anzi lungi da voi di pianto un rio
verso per gli occhi, e 'l cor mesto e turbato
mi detta or bassi e dolorosi versi.

34 [37] FOR SIGNORA LIVIA COLONNA

After the sun aflame with lofty virtue, whose
rays overshadow the light of Phoebus, has driven
away and dissipated the shadow that has snuffed out
so many dear, so many bright lights,
the present fortunate age will be the envy of
future people for the lofty lightning flash that
dispels all fog and impels our minds to wisdom and valor;
and those pages, right well prized,
that sang so sweetly of Laura and Bice
will be far less dear than they were before;
and Livia Colonna's lofty happy name
will be heard resounding on all sides,
a worthy subject for the most pleasing laurel.[87]

35 [41] TO SIGNORA HORTENSIA COLONNA

Here, woe is me! I find myself neglected and
shunned as much as before I was graced and held
dear, in a life more bitter than death, brimming with
sorrow and bereft of joy;
neither the beloved cool bank of the Arno,
which graces and clears every clouded mind, nor the
cultured intellects from whom one learns all honor,
nor listening to whoever recounts or writes of love,
can diminish the burning flame
that nourishes my heart, which in a happier state
created betimes concepts lofty and diverse;
no, far from you I pour out a river of tears
from my eyes, and my downcast and troubled
heart now dictates to me low-lying sorrowful verses.[89]

36 [44] NELLE NOZZE DEL SIGNOR VESPASIANO PICCOLHUOMINI E DELLA SIGNORA LUCREZIA SODERINA[90]

Santissima Giunon, che 'n mille modi,
come a tua deità superna piace,
l'alme in ciel leghi con eterna pace,
e i corpi in terra castamente annodi;
santo Imeneo, che sol t'allegri e godi
arder due cori ad una stessa face;
e tu, dolce d'Amor madre verace,
che gli altrui giusti prieghi ascolte ed odi,
sovra 'l gran Tebro alla sinistra riva,
là ve l'antico mausoleo riserba
del grande Augusto le reliquie sante,
scendete, ch'ivi con umil sembiante
coppia v'attende sì leggiadra e diva,
che l'Arno altero va, l'Arbia superba.

37 [46] PER LA SIGNORA MARCHESA DI MASSA[92]

Trapassa, almo Appenin, l'aer sereno
e fa nel terzo ciel dolce soggiorno,
più che Parnaso e più che Cinto adorno
rendi il tuo sacro ed onorato seno;
corri lieto e tranquillo al Mar Tirreno,
cinto d'erbe e di fiori il crine intorno,
chiaro Metauro, e tu tuo ricco corno
ne mostra fuor, di frondi e frutti pieno;
spandi fin dove nasce e dove more
d'Apollo il raggio, altera pianta e bella,
le foglie tue da Giove amate e colte,
poi ch'a voi riede un'altra volta quella
donna ch'a tutte l'altre tutte ha tolte
le grazie, d'Umbria e Massa eterno onore.

36 [44] ON THE NUPTIALS OF SIGNOR VESPASIANO PICCOLHUOMINI AND SIGNORA LUCREZIA SODERINA

Most holy Juno, who in a thousand ways as
pleases your supernal godliness binds souls in
heaven with eternal peace and bodies on earth in
chastity;
holy Hymen, whose only delight and relish
is two hearts who burn from a single torch; and you,
sweet true mother of Love, who listen and harken to
all our just prayers,
descend to the great Tiber, on the left bank,
there where the ancient mausoleum preserves
the holy relics of great Augustus,
for there with humble appearance,
a couple awaits you, so graceful and divine
that the Arno goes proud and the Arbia haughty.[91]

37 [46] FOR SIGNORA THE MARQUISE OF MASSA

Pass beyond the serene air, bountiful
Apennine, and abide sweetly in the third heaven;
make fairer your sacred and honored breast than
Parnassus and Cynthus;
run blithe and tranquil to the Tyrrhenian Sea,
your locks encircled with greenery and flowers,
limpid Metauro, and show forth your rich horn,
filled with boughs and fruits.
Spread wide, out to where Apollo's ray is born
and where it dies, proud beauteous plant
whose leaves were loved and gathered by Jove,
for to you there returns once again that lady
who has taken all the graces from all others,
eternal honor of Umbria and Massa.[93]

38 [49] AL SIGNOR DON GRAZIA DI TOLEDO[94]

Voi che del sacro generoso fianco
fra 'l popol di Gesù divoto e quelle
tante squadre nemiche a Dio rubelle,
scudo faceste adamantino e franco;
prima verranno ad una ad una manco
dell'ampio ciel l'erranti e ferme stelle,
ch'all'opre vostre così chiare e belle
dar gloria il mondo e voi lodar sia stanco.
Guerriero invitto, or se ghirlande e pregi
si danno a quei che con possente mano
rende sicuro un uom d'alto periglio,
quai corone immortal, quai premi e fregi
si denno a voi, che da sì crudo artiglio
dianzi scampaste il buon nome Cristiano?

39 [50] AL SIGNOR CHIAPPINO VITELLI[96]

Or c'ha pur l'alto valor vostro invitto
vinta l'empia di Dio nemica gente,
ed al rio predator dell'oriente
d'acerbo telo il cor punto e trafitto,
di quei ch'ornaron già Roma e l'Egitto
alti colossi, a voi novellamente
erge, chiaro signor, l'età presente,
sì come fu nel ciel di voi prescritto;
ed or simile al suo Nettunno altero,
ch'a gli avversari di virtute ha tolto
le forze e 'nposto lor silenzio eterno,
opra del mio buon FIDIA e magistero,
un nuovo Alcide ch'aggia in fuga volto
gl'infidi mostri, a voi sacrar discerno.

38 [49] TO SIGNOR DON GRAZIA DI TOLEDO

You who with your sacred generous flank
made a shield, adamantine and true, between the
devout people of Jesus and those so many enemy
squadrons rebellious to God, 4
before the world tires of praising you and
glorifying your deeds, so bright and beautiful, the
wandering and firm stars of the wide heaven,
one by one, will disappear. 8
Invincible warrior, if now garlands and prizes
are given to him whose powerful hand
makes a man safe from high peril, 11
what crowns immortal, what rewards
and decorations are due you, who ere now
saved the good name Christian from such a cruel claw?[95] 14

39 [50] TO SIGNOR CHIAPPINO VITELLI

Now that your lofty valor invincible has
conquered even the wicked people, God's enemy,
and with a bitter lance stabbed and pierced the heart
of the evil predator from the east, 4
the present age, renowned lord, newly raises
to you noble colossi like those once adorning Rome
and Egypt, as it was forewritten of you in heaven; 8
and now similar to his proud Neptune, who
took away the adversaries' powers of strength and
imposed on them eternal silence, 11
I discern consecrated to you a new Alcides,
who has put to flight the infidel monsters, work and
clever art of my good PHIDIAS.[97] 14

40 [52] AL SIGNOR ALESSANDRO DE' MEDICI[98]

Nel regno almo e sovrano,
alla celeste mensa,
nettare non dispensa
della tua più vezzosa e dolce mano;
né in grembo scherza con più vago onore
della sua madre alcun pregiato Amore,
ch'appo te non sia vile,
fanciul chiaro e gentile.

"O pargoletto ramo,
o verde almo rampollo
del sacro arbor d'Apollo,
mentr'io," l'Arno dicea, "t'inchino ed amo,
mille palme per te, mille trofei
sperano i lidi miei;
cresci felice, cresci,
e le mie gioie e le mie spemi accresci."

Felice ramuscel pregiato e chiaro,
di quella pianta altera
che l'Arno adombra e sovra ogn'altra impera,
quel frutto dolce e caro
che 'n sua stagion perfetta
Flora tua bella ogn'or gustare aspetta,
già scorge nel tuo fiore,
soave e pien d'odore.

40 [52] TO SIGNOR ALESSANDRO DE' MEDICI

In the bountiful sovereign kingdom,
at the celestial board,
not one Cupid of worth
dispenses nectar sweeter than your pretty hand,
or plays with more winsome honor in his mother's lap,
but that he be poor compared to you,
bright and noble boy.

"O baby branch,
o bountiful green offshoot
of Apollo's sacred tree,
as I love and bow to you," Arno said,
"my shores hope
for a thousand palms from you, for a thousand trophies.
Grow happy, grow,
and increase my joys and my hopes."

Happy branchlet, prized and famed,
of that proud plant
that shades Arno and has dominion over every other,
in your flower, soft and full-scented,
your fair Flora already detects
that fruit sweet and dear
that in its perfect season
she ever looks forward to tasting.[99]

41 [55][100]

Del cattolico rege, o invitte schiere,
ch'oggi di Cristo e del suo vero armate
a sì gran passi seguitando andate
l'insegne sue, così pietose e fere,
deh, quel desio che v'empie di vedere
l'armi nimiche ogn'or rotte e spezzate,
scemi accorta e 'ngegnosa tarditate
delle prudenti vostre scorte altere,
sì che l'adverso stuol, per lungo affanno
ne' brevi giorni che tempesta adduce
fredd'Euro, rotto e sparso a terra caggia.
"Bella vittoria senza alcun suo danno,"
dirassi poi, "ebbe possente e saggia
gente per tutto ove il sol scalda e luce."

42 [56] ALLA SIGNORA EUFEMIA[102]

Del coro eterno e delle eterne genti
son queste voci angeliche e gioconde,
e 'l suon che tanta in noi dolcezza infonde,
donna, mercé de' tuoi celesti accenti;
e non pur noi, ma le tempeste e i venti
e le fere e gli Augelli e i pesci e l'onde
stanno, e gli Angeli stessi e i cerchi, donde
quaggiù scendesti, ad ascoltarti intenti.
Per te Sebeto, d'alta gloria adorno,
né 'l Tebro invidia, né 'l suo grande impero,
con quanti trionfar dall'Indo al Mauro;
e di frutti e di fiori empiendo il corno
va di te sola e del tuo nome altero,
d'edera cinto il petto e 'l crin di lauro.

41 [55]

O invincible troops of the Catholic king,
who armed today with Christ and his truth go
stoutly stepping behind His ensigns, so merciful and
fierce; 4
pray, may the desire that fills you to see the
enemy arms ever broken and splintered be
diminished by your prudent proud escorts' shrewd
and clever delay, 8
so that the adversary hoard, struggling long
in short days when cold Eurus comes stormy, may
fall to earth broken and scattered. 11
"A fair victory without self-hurt," they will
say then, "was had by people powerful and wise
wherever the sun warms and shines."[101] 14

42 [56] TO SIGNORA EUFEMIA

From an eternal chorus and those who live
eternally come these angelic smiling voices and the
sound that infuses us with such sweetness, lady,
thanks to your celestial tones; 4
and not only we, but tempests and winds and
beasts and birds and fish and waves pause, and the
very angels and the spheres, whence you descended
down here, to listen to you intently. 8
Sebeto, adorned by you with lofty glory,
envies neither Tiber nor his grand empire, with as
many as triumphed from Indian to Moorish seas; 11
and he goes filling his horn with fruits and
flowers for you alone and your proud name, his
breast circled with ivy, his locks with laurel.[103] 14

43 [60] A MESSER GIOVAN BATTISTA STROZZI[104]

Dolce, verde, fiorito e sacro monte,
che 'l tuo bel nome dalla pianta amica
di Minerva pudica
prendi, e superbo al cielo alzi la fronte, 4
così dal nostro all'ultimo orizonte,
e da questo a quel polo,
sopra Olimpo ed Atlante
s'ergano eterne le tue cime sante,
come io ammiro e colo
Cinthia tua saggia, e 'ndimion tuo solo. 10

44 [65] A MADONNA LAUDOMIA RUCELLAI[106]

O d'ogni laude e d'ogni' alto onor degna,
vergine pura e bella, ch'oggi tanto
delle figlie di Giove il sacro e santo
numero accresci, e per te vive e regna, 4
or che la voce tua non si disdegna,
con antico sermone e nuovo canto,
a me, che nulla imparo, ridir quanto
Febo nella sua scola ogn'or t'insegna, 8
e di quei fiori e di quei frutti eterni,
ch'or in Parnaso cogli, or lungo Eurota,
sì dolcemente mi comparti e doni, 11
non vo' più ch'altra Musa, e mi perdoni
qual oggi in Pindo è più famosa e nota,
questa man, questo stil regga e governi. 14

43 [60] TO MESSER GIOVAN BATTISTA STROZZI

Sweet, green, flowering, and sacred mount,
who take your fair name from the plant
friendly to chaste Minerva
and raise proud to heaven your brow,
so from ours to the last horizon
and from this to the far pole,
above Olympus and Atlas
may your holy peaks thrust eternal,
as I admire and worship
your wise Cynthia and Endymion, yours alone.[105]

44 [65] TO MADONNA LAUDOMIA RUCELLAI

O worthy of all laud and all lofty honor, pure
and fair virgin, who today so swell the sacred and
sainted number of Jove's daughters, he who through
you lives and reigns,
now that your voice, with old speech and
new song, disdains not once again to tell me, who
learn nothing, how much Phoebus in his school
keeps teaching you,
and that you so sweetly share with me and
give of those flowers and those eternal fruits you
gather, now in Parnassus, now along the Eurotas,
I no longer want any other muse—and may
whichsoever today is most famous and noted on
Pindus forgive me—to rule and govern this hand,
this style.[107]

45 [67] A MESSER VINCENTIO GROTTI[108]

GROTTI, né 'l temperato aer sereno,
né le vaghe campagne e i verdi prati,
né le fresch'erbe e i dolci colli amati,
né della loggia il ricco albergo ameno, 4
ma il parlar saggio e d'eloquenza pieno,
il dir di Cristo in stili alti e ornati,
sgombrare il cor de' van pensier gelati,
e d'amor caldo e fede empiere il seno, 8
son la cagion perch'io sospiro e bramo
esser dell'onorata vostra schiera,
ov'alberga onestate e cortesia, 11
e dove la gran donna, ch'io tant'amo,
di dolce Cibo, anzi di manna vera,
l'alma nodre e al ciel la scorge e 'nvia. 14

46 [70][110]

Così sempre, Arno, in te sian chiare l'onde
cui le ninfe e i pastor danzino intorno,
e verdeggin, o scemi o cresca il giorno,
di fior carche e di frutti ambe le sponde; 4
così ti sia dell'onorata fronde
l'umido crine eternamente adorno,
e d'Acheloo ti ceda il ricco corno,
e spirin l'aure al corso tuo seconde; 8
e 'l Nilo e l'Istro e l'Indo e gli altri fiumi
e 'l Mar Tirreno e 'l gran padre Oceano
con tutti i liti lor ti dian tributo; 11
come più chiaro tra cotanti numi
sarai, mercé dell'arte e della mano
del mio Fidia, novello oggi veduto. 14

45 [67] TO MESSER VINCENTIO GROTTI

GROTTI, neither the temperate air serene,
nor winsome countryside and green meadows, nor
fresh grasses and sweet beloved hills, nor the rich
delightful abode beside the loggia, 4
but wise conversing, filled with eloquence,
speaking of Christ in styles lofty and embellished,
disencumbering my heart of vain frozen thoughts, and
replenishing my breast with warm love and faith 8
are the reason why I sigh and long to be in
your honored troop, where abide honesty and
courtesy, 11
and where the great lady, whom I so love,
with sweet Food, nay with true manna, nourishes
the soul and guides and sends it heavenward.[109] 14

46 [70]

Thus always, Arno, may the waves in you be
clear, around which nymphs and shepherds dance,
and may both your shores green, whether day wax
or wane, under their weight of flowers and fruit; 4
thus may your moist locks be decked
eternally with the honored bough; and may the rich
horn of Acheloüs yield before you; and may
favorable breezes blow your currents; 8
and may the Nile and the Danube and the
Indus and the other rivers and the Tyrrhenean Sea
and the great father Oceanus with all their shores
pay tribute to you, 11
as more renowned among so many gods,
thanks to the art and hand of my Phidias, today you
will be seen renewed.[111] 14

47 [71][112]

Febo, per l'amoroso e caldo zelo
ch'al cor t'accese della ninfa il volto,
ch'or in arbor da te pregiato e colto
il mondo onora, non pur Cinto e Delo, 4
così tornando nel mortal suo velo,
stia dolcemente a te mai sempre volto,
e d'un laccio e d'un stral legato e colto
sia teco d'un ardor pari e d'un gelo; 8
pon man, ti priego, alla tua nobil arte,
a i succhi, a l'erbe, e la virtù smarrita
rendi a chi tien di me la miglior parte, 11
ché di frondi e di fior, l'alta e gradita
tua statua vedrai cinta, e 'n ogni parte
fia del miracol tuo la voce udita. 14

48 [73][114]

Qual per l'onde turbate e per gli scogli,
nel più gelato e tenebroso verno,
senza fido rettore e senza luce,
quando di lume è più spogliato il cielo,
sen' va dolente e travagliata nave,
cercando or questo ed or quell'altro mare; 6
tal per questo d'amor profondo mare,
pien di tempesta e di dubbiosi scogli,
passa la mia smarrita e debil nave,
cinta da nubiloso orrido verno,
errando sempre al caldo e al freddo cielo,
s'avvien che lungi stia dalla sua luce; 12
cara, dolce, alta e gloriosa luce,
che mi traesti già di cieco mare,
e mi mostrasti il temperato cielo,
ma che mi valse, oimè, se in fra gli scogli
sospinta fui da fiero algente verno,
come dall'onde disarmata nave? 18

47 [71]

Phoebus, for the amorous and warm zeal
kindled in your heart by the face of the nymph
whom now, prized and cultivated by you as a tree,
the world honors, not just Cynthus and Delos, 4
so, in a return to her mortal veil, may she
stand face toward you forever, and bound and
caught by noose and arrow, may she be as one with
you, equal in ardor and iciness; 8
set your hand, I pray, to your noble art, to the
potions, to the herbs, and restore the lost powers to
him who holds the better part of me, 11
for you will see your tall and likesome statue
circled with fronds and flowers, and in all parts
word will be heard of your miracle.[113] 14

48 [73]

As through turbulent waves and shoals,
in the most gelid and darkling winter,
without a trusty leader and without light,
when brightness most abandons the sky,
there goes a sorrowful and troubled ship,
seeking now this, now that other sea; 6
so on this deep sea of love,
swollen with storm and treacherous shoals,
there passes my lost and weak ship,
belted with cloudy and horrid winter,
wandering ever under hot and cold sky,
if it happen to stay far from its light. 12
Dear, sweet, high, and glorious light,
you pulled me before from a blind sea
and showed me a temperate sky;
but what, alas, did it avail me, if onto the shoals
I was pushed by fierce freezing winter
like a helpless wave-battered ship? 18

Volgi ora in porto la mia stanca nave,
o chiara, o desiata, alma mia luce,
e sgombra dal mio petto il gelo e 'l verno,
che l'han fatto un turbato ondoso mare;
che se questo m'avvien fra i duri scogli,
mai più m'intrica il variar del cielo.
So ben, che pria fia senza stelle il cielo,
ed andrà senza vele o remi nave,
e dura l'aura e molli fien gli scogli,
ch'a me si celi la mia altera luce,
ché tante arene non son dentro il mare
quant'ha di me pensier la state e 'l verno.
Ond'anzi che ne venga il freddo verno
e sparga il ghiaccio e le pruine il cielo,
altri lidi cercando ed altro mare,
forse in più salda e più felice nave,
fa' ch'io seguir ti possa, alma mia luce,
senza assalti temer di venti o scogli.
Lungi a gli scogli, e più lontan dal verno,
mi scorga la mia luce, e 'l vago cielo
non turbi il mare alla mia ardita nave.

49 [80][116]

Superbi e sacri colli,
sotto 'l cui glorioso e grande impero
tennero i figli vostri il mondo intero,
così fioriti e molli
vi serbi largo e temperato cielo,
né vi offenda giamai caldo né gelo;
e tu vago, corrente e chiaro fiume
che fai più adorna Roma,
così tua verde chioma,
del sol non secchi il troppo ardente lume.
Fate che mai non sia quel crudo giorno,
ch'io lasci 'l vostro dolce almo soggiorno.

Swing now into port my tired ship,
oh my bright, desired bountiful light,
and disencumber my breast of the frost and winter
that have made it a turbulent and heavy sea;
for if this happens to me amidst hard shoals,
never more will I be entangled by the variability of the sky.
I well know that there will be no stars in the sky,
and without sails and oars a ship will go,
and the air will be hard, and soft will be the shoals,
before I am denied my proud light;
for there are not so many sands inside the sea
as it has thoughts of me summer and winter.
Thus before we are met with cold winter,
and ice and hoarfrost are spread by the sky,
in search of other shores and another sea,
perhaps in a more solid and a happier ship,
let me follow you, my bountiful light,
without fearing assaults of winds or shoals.
Far from the shoals, and farther from winter,
may my light lead me; let not lovesome heaven
trouble the sea for my bold ship.[115]

49 [80]

Proud and sacred hills,
under whose glorious and great empire
your sons held the whole world,
may a generous and temperate sky
keep you like this in blossom and soft;
and may neither heat nor cold injure you ever;
and you, lovesome river flowing clear, who
make Rome more comely, so may your green tresses
not wither in the sun's too searing light. Let the
harsh day never come when I must leave your sweet,
bountiful abode.[117]

50 [81][118]

"O vago cielo, o dolce aer sereno,
che pria infondeste in me tranquilla vita,
quando fu alle terrene membra unita
quest'alma, a pie del sacro colle ameno,
mirate il pianto, che per gli occhi al seno
trova sì larga e sì continua uscita;
mirate il cor, ch'ognor vi chiede aita,
più di dolor che di speranza pieno.
Né consentite mai ch'aspro destino
nel poco dolce il molto amaro fele
meschi, o morte anzi tempo atra e funesta."
Così Dafne col volto umido e chino
in riva al Tebro, dolorosa e mesta,
dicea, spargendo al ciel giuste querele.

51 [82][120]

Ecco ch'io da voi, sacre alte ruine,
anzi da me medesma—ahi, crudel fato!
pur mi diparto. Or lassa, in quale stato
il mio grave dolor trovarà fine?
O, voi anime sante e pellegrine,
a cui sì largo don dal ciel fu dato,
che 'n pregio del valor vostro beato
siate or lasuso eterne cittadine,
fate, s'umil preghiera è in cielo udita,
mentre lontan su l'Arno in cieco orrore
starà vivo sepolto il mio mortale,
che 'l mio nome sul Tebro, il mio migliore,
ch'or con voi resta, scevro d'ogni male,
fra' vostri alti tesor rimanga in vita.

50 [81]

"O winsome sky, O sweet and serene air
that first infused in me tranquil life, when this soul
was united to its earthly members, at the foot of the
pleasant sacred hill; 4
behold the tears that from my eyes to my
breast trace so wide and so continuous a channel;
behold the heart that keeps asking you for help,
filled more with sorrow than with hope. 8
Never let harsh destiny mix with our small
sweetness its great bitter gall or death come before
its time, inky black and ill-fated." 11
Thus spoke Dafne, with damp and bowed
face on the shore of the Tiber, mournful and
downcast, scattering to the sky her just complaints.[119] 14

51 [82]

Here I am, sacred lofty ruins, taking leave of
you after all, nay of my very self—ah, cruel fate!
Now, alas, in what state will my heavy sorrow find
an end? 4
O you, holy and roving spirits, to whom so
fine a gift was given by heaven that you are up there
on high, eternal citizens, as a reward for your
blessed worth, 8
see to it, if a humble prayer is heard in
heaven, that while far away on the Arno, in blind
wilderness, my mortal part shall be buried alive, 11
my name—the better part of me that now
stays with you, severed from every ill—shall remain
alive on the Tiber among your lofty treasures.[121] 14

52 [86] A MESSER FRANCESCO MONTE VARCHI[122]

Nuovo Esculapio, che di Febo al paro
di virtute ven gite e di splendore,
poi che di lume e non men di valore
sete or, qual ei fu già, dotato e chiaro; 4
ben deve il ciel, ben dee tenervi caro
il mondo tutto, poi ch'a quel l'onore
spento rendete, a questo quel vigore
che torna dolce il viver nostro amaro; 8
ond'io, che dianzi infino a l'uscio corsi
di lei che l'erbe e i sughi vostri suole
temer, quanto altri i suoi spietati morsi, 11
almo FRANCESCO, mio terreno sole,
quando d'esser per voi viva m'accorsi,
vi sacrai l'alma, che v'ammira e cole. 14

53 [87][124]

Fra queste piagge apriche e chiusi orrori,
presso un bel rio che mormorando stilla,
lungi dal volgo in soletaria villa
compart'io il tempo e i giorni miei migliori; 4
e più m'aggrada udir ninfe e pastori,
quando Apollo da noi lontan sfavilla,
che desti al suon dell'amorosa squilla,
van palesando i lor graditi amori; 8
e Maiano veder con tanti intorno
folti boschi, alti monti e verdi campi,
e Mensola ch'al par dell'Arno corre; 11
che quante melodie, pallazzi ed ampi
tetti, rendon Fiorenza e 'l mondo adorno,
che 'nvidia e reo destin non mi puon torre. 14

52 [86] TO MESSER FRANCESCO MONTE VARCHI

New Aesculapius, who go about a peer of
Phoebus in virtue and splendor, since you are now,
as he once was, gifted and famed for your
enlightenment and no less for your worth, 4
well must heaven, well must the whole
world hold you dear, since you restore to the former
its snuffed-out honor and to the latter the vigor that
turns our living from bitter to sweet; 8
whence I, who ere now rushed up to the gate
of her who is wont to fear your herbs and potions as
much as others do her pitiless bites, 11
bountiful FRANCESCO, my earthly sun,
when I realized that I was alive because of you, to
you I devoted my soul, which worships you
in wonderment.[123] 14

53 [87]

Among these open slopes and secluded
wilds, by a beautiful stream that murmurs as it
trickles, far from the mob in a solitary villa I
apportion the time and my best days, 4
and it delights me more, when Apollo
sparkles far from us, to hear nymphs and shepherds,
awakened by the sound of the loving bell peal, who
go declaring their goodly loves, 8
and to see Maiano, so many thick groves
around it, tall mountains and green fields and
Mensola flowing as Arno's peer, 11
than all the melodies, palaces, and wide
roofs that give Florence and the world their beauty,
for envy and evil destiny cannot take them from me.[125] 14

54 [89][126]

Ergiti infin sovra le nubi in alto,
o sacro e bene avventuroso monte,
cingi di verde allor l'antica fronte,
e molle rendi il tuo sì duro smalto;
corri, Mensola, al mar con leggier salto,
raddoppia forza a l'onde chiare e pronte,
mai sempre a quelle del tuo sposo aggionte,
scorrendo il piano o giù cadendo d'alto;
rivesti, almo Maiano, i nudi campi
di verde spoglia, e di novelle fronde
orna le piante tue felici e liete;
non più venti contrarii, aure seconde,
spirate, sì ch'ogn'uom d'amore avampi,
poi che tanto al gran Varchi oggi piacete.

55 [91][128]

Temprato aer sereno,
che sì tranquilla infondi e lunga vita;
vago, dolce e soave colle ameno,
ov' Amor l'alme a poetare invita,
e tu, verde e fiorita
piaggia, che vedi ogn'ora
l'alto Pastor che i toschi lidi onora;
felici erbette, e voi
ch'ascoltate i leggiadri accenti suoi,
ahi, quante volte il giorno
a voi col pensier torno.

54 [89]

Hoist yourself up over the clouds on high,
O sacred and auspicious mountain, encircle with
green laurel your ancient brow, and render soft your
enamel so hard; 4
hurry, Mensola, to the sea, leaping lightly;
redouble the force of your clear and willing waves,
never joined ever to your groom's, crossing the plain
or cascading from on high; 8
reclothe, bountiful Maiano, the naked fields
with a coat of green, and grace with new little fronds
your glad and joyful plants; 11
blow no more contrary winds, favorable
breezes, so that every man may blaze with love,
since today you so please the great Varchi.[127] 14

55 [91]

Temperate serene air,
who infuse such tranquil and long life;
lovesome, sweet, and smooth hill of pleasure,
where Love invites souls to poetry; 4
and you, green and blossoming
slope, who ever see
the lofty shepherd who honors the Tuscan shores;
glad little grasses, and you
who listen to his delightful accents,
ah, how many times a day
do I turn to you in my thoughts.[129] 11

56 [92] [130]

Pria che la chioma che mi diè Natura,
e quel vigor ch'ancor riserbo intero,
si cangi e scemi al trapassar leggero
di lui, che 'l men ne lascia e 'l più ne fura,
spero quest'acqua, e sì chiara e sì pura,
e questa ombrosa valle e questo altero
monte tanto cantar, quanto il pensiero
per lor posto ha in non cale ogn'altra cura,
s'altrui volere e cruda invida stella,
usi a' giusti desii far danno e scorno,
non mi vietin fornire opra sì bella.
Apollo, tu ch'a queste piagge intorno
sai ch'ombreggia la fronde tua novella,
scendi talor nel dolce mio soggiorno.

57 [94] [132]

Alto monte, ima valle e dolce piano,
freschi antri, chiusi orrori e fiorite erbe,
e voi, frondi del sol verdi e superbe,
contra alle qual non può Cesar né Giano,
quante volte m'udiste, e sempre in vano,
nell'ore più mature e nelle acerbe,
chiamar lei, di cui sola par che serbe
memoria il cor, sia pur presso o lontano!
Siate voi testimonii a dir come io
tutta dentro e di fuor mi vo cangiando,
né però cangio il saldo pensier mio,
che quando i sette alteri colli e quando
le sacre valli e 'l bel terren natio
vado sotto altrui forme contemplando.

56 [92]

Before the tresses that Nature gave me, and the vigor that I still preserve entire, be changed and diminished at the light onward passing of him who leaves the lesser and steals the greater, 4

I hope to sing as much of this water, so clear and so pure, and this shaded valley and this proud mount, as I have thoughts of them, who have turned to nonchalance my every other care, 8

if another will and cruel envious star, wont to work harm and scorn against just desires, prevent me not from finishing such fine work. 11

Apollo, you who know that your branchlet casts its shade about these slopes, descend betimes to my sweet abode.[131] 14

57 [94]

Tall mountain, sunken valley, and sweet plain; cooling grottos, secluded wilds, and flowering grasses; and you, boughs of the sun green and stately, which neither Caesar nor Janus can harm; 4

how many times you have heard me, in the ripest hours and in the raw, and always in vain, call out to her, who seems to be my heart's only memory, whether nearby or far away! 8

May you be witnesses to tell how all of me goes on changing, inside and out; yet I do not for that change my steadfast thought, 11

except, as if in the form of another, when I go contemplating the seven proud hills and the sacred valleys and my fair native land.[133] 14

58 [96][134]

Sonno, che al dolor mio puoi sol dar pace,
sonno, onde attendo e spero ogni mio bene,
sonno, che dolce obblio d'amare pene
porti per gl'occhi al cor, quando a te piace,
al mio, ch'or senza te languendo giace,
omai, deh, porgi aïta, ch'altra spene
non ha se 'l tuo soccorso a lui non viene
altronde al martir suo duro e tenace.
Dalle Cimmerie valli e dall'antico
antro ti sveglia, o sonno; e in questi miei
occhi t'annida, o pur per poco torna;
ed io per Lete giuro, a te sì amico,
ogni luce odiar che 'l mondo adorna,
e drizzare al tuo nome archi e trofei.

59 [99] A MESSER LUCA MARTINI[136]

Deh, se quel vivo, chiaro sol che luce
sì, che non pur lo suo toscan paese
rischiara e desta a gloriose imprese,
ma 'l mondo tutto al primo oprar conduce,
a quella chiara vostra e viva luce
che mai non eclissò, largo e cortese
giunga sempre splendor che, senza offese
di nebbie o venti, altrui sia scorta e duce;
lasciate, prego, le pisane sponde,
LUCA gentile, e venite ove Flora
vostra vi chiama ogn'or tanti anni indarno.
Ella vi chiama, ma nessun risponde:
venite omai, ché qui sarete ancora
utile e caro al duce d'Arbia e d'Arno.

58 [96]

Sleep, who alone can give peace to my
sorrow, whence I await and hope for my every
good; sleep, who bear when it pleases you sweet
oblivion for bitter pains from the eyes to the heart, 4
to mine, which now lies languishing without
you, at last, pray, lend aid, for if your succor comes
not to it, it has no other hope otherwise for its hard
and tenacious suffering. 8
From the Cimmerian valleys and from your
ancient cave awaken, O sleep; and make your nest
in these eyes of mine, or else return for a little
while, 11
and I swear by Lethe, so friendly to you, to
hate every light that adorns the world and raise to
your name arches and trophies.[135] 14

59 [99] TO MESSER LUCA MARTINI

Pray, if that living, bright sun whose shining
not only brightens and awakens its own Tuscan
country to glorious deeds but leads the whole world
to pristine operation, 4
bring always, generous and courteous, to
that bright and living light of yours that it has never
eclipsed, splendor without offending fogs
or winds that be the people's escort and guide; 8
leave, I entreat you, the Pisan shores, noble
LUCA, and come where your Flora has been calling
you for so many years in vain; 11
she calls you, but no one responds; come,
now, for here you will still be useful and dear to
the Duke of Arbia and of Arno.[137] 14

60 [101] PER MESSER LUIGI ALAMANNI[138]

Arbor gentil, cui l'odor tanto crebbe,
cui l'ombra fu sì dolce, che empie ancora
d'immensa gioia non pur Cinthia e Flora,
ché l'una e l'altra a te cotanto debbe, 4
ma 'l mondo tutto, che per te riebbe
l'antico onor, di cui mendico fôra;
e 'l ciel più bello, ove sei traslato ora,
al qual lume maggior tua luce accrebbe; 8
quanto allegrar ti dei, ch'ambo i tuoi rami
raddoppian gli onor tuoi, di frutti adorni
pari e simili a sì gradito legno. 11
Deh, non sdegnar ch'io sì t'inchini ed ami
quantunque io sia arido tronco indegno,
e nelle frondi tue mi spechi ed orni. 14

61 [103] A MESSER BARTOLOMEO STRADA FISICO[140]

Egra giaceasi e 'n suon fioco ed umile,
lungo la riva d'Arno,
Febo chiamando al suo soccorso indarno
pastorella non vile, 4
ch'irato ancor, perch'ella serba il nome
di lei, che già verso il Peneo fuggendo
sentir gli feo dell'amorose some,
ond'ella al ciel volgendo
l'osure luci sue per grave duolo, 9
ecco venirne a volo
virtù celeste, per altra sovrana
STRADA, che la racqueta e la risana. 12

60 [101] FOR MESSER LUIGI ALAMANNI

Noble tree, whose fragrance so grew, whose
shadow was so sweet that it still fills with immense
joy not only Cynthia and Flora, for both owe
so much to you,
but all the world, which would be barren of
its ancient honor had you not brought that back, and
the fairest heaven, where you are translated now,
whose greatest brightness your light increased;
how gladdened you must be that both your
branches redouble your honors, adorned with fruit
equal in likeness to such goodly timber.
Pray, though I be an arid unworthy trunk,
disdain not that I bow so to you and love you
and in your boughs mirror and adorn myself.[139]

61 [103] TO MESSER BARTOLOMEO STRADA, PHYSICIAN

Infirm lay a little shepherdess, not lowly,
her sound weak and humble,
as she vainly called along the Arno shore
for aid from Phoebus,
still irate because she preserves the name
of her who made him feel all the weight of love
by fleeing toward Peneus,
hence as she was turning heavenward
her eyes, darkened by heavy aching,
behold there came flying
celestial virtue, by another supreme STRADA,
who restores her to peace and to health.[141]

62 [107] AL PADRE CLAUDIO ACQUAVIVA GENERALE DELLA COMPAGNIA DI GIESU[142]

Duce sovran di quella saggia e forte
milizia di Gesù, ch'armata in guerra
i tre nostri avversari vince e atterra,
che tanti han vinto e tanti han porto a morte, 4
già 'l vostro suon par che speranza apporte
che l'Indo e 'l Mauro ed ogni estrema terra
torni al Pastor di Cristo, ch'apre e serra
del suo sagrato ovile ambe le porte; 8
caro dono di Dio, fonte lucente
d'ACQUA VIVA, e tant'alta che salire
ne farà tutti in vita eterna e vera, 11
così potess'io in parte almen ridire
vostr'opre tante e vostra lode intera,
ch'infiammarei di Dio tutta la gente. 14

63 [108] A DON SILVANO RAZZI[144]

Silvan, che la più degna e miglior parte
che in eterno già mai non vi sie tolta,
uscendo fuor della mondana e stolta
schiera elegeste con ingegno ed arte, 4
quanto ammirar, quanto lodar le carte
devem di lui, che 'n voce chiara e colta,
i costumi e la vita in Dio raccolta
de' suoi fedeli a nostro esempio ha sparte? 8
e non pur noi, ma tutta l'alma e grande
religion de quei, che Benedetto
di nome fu, ma più coll'opre ancora; 11
PIERO divin, mentre per voi si spande
la fama altrui, voi stesso alzate ognora
dal mortal nostro all'eterno ricetto. 14

62 [107] TO FATHER CLAUDIO ACQUAVIVA, GENERAL OF THE SOCIETY OF JESUS

Supreme leader of that wise and strong militia
of Jesus that, armed in war, conquers and flattens
our three adversaries, who have conquered so many
and have carried so many to death, 4
your sound seems already to bring hope that
Indus and Maurus and every remote land may return
to Christ's Shepherd, who opens and closes both the
gates of his consecrated sheepfold; 8
dear gift of God, lucent font of LIVING
WATER, so lofty that you will make us all climb to
eternal and true life, 11
would that I could in part at least retell your
many deeds and your praise entire, for I would
inflame with God all the people.[143] 14

63 [108] TO DON SILVANO RAZZI

Silvan, who chose with wit and art to leave
the worldly and foolish troop so that your worthiest
and best part could never be taken from you
in eternity, 4
how much must we admire, how much
praise, the pages of him who, in voice lucent and
learned, has scattered among us as an example the
ways of those faithful gathered in their lives to God? 8
And not we alone, but all the bounteous and
great religious order of him who was Benedict by
name, but more yet with his deeds; 11
PIERO divine, by spreading the fame of
others, you ever raise yourself from our mortal to
the eternal refuge.[145] 14

64 [110][146]

Questo dolce di Bacco almo liquore,
che l'anno adietro con la propria mano
nell'antro suo da te poco lontano,
DAFNE imbottò con sì giocondo core,
a te, chiaro DAMON, d'Etruria onore,
manda, al cui dolce canto ogn'altro in vano
tenta agguagliarsi, ed ogni fero e strano
cor torni umil di ninfa e di pastore;
e questo pomo ancor di color d'oro,
ch'un picciolo arboscel dal vermo rio
con gran studio di lei serbato gli have;
e se 'l venir qua giù non ti fia grave,
una ghirlanda avrai, ch'ier lungo il rio
intrecciò del tuo verde amato alloro.

65 [112] ALLA SIGNORA BIANCA CAPPELLA[148]

Così caro tesoro e sì pregiata
gemma, che 'l mondo ricco far doveva,
che tanto in sè medesma risplendea,
tant'alta donna a tanti imperi nata,
quell'immensa bontà, mai sempre usata
a quanto in cielo, a quanto in terra crea,
se stessa palesar già non voleva,
ch'ella stesse fra noi così celata;
e però in sposa al più giusto e maggiore
duce d'Europa oggi vien data in sorte,
ambo d'onor, ambo di gloria degni,
ed ambo in ciel di pari amica sorte,
doppo aver vinto i più famosi regni,
avran corone d'immortal valore.

64 [110]

This sweet bountiful liquor of Bacchus,
which DAFNE last year with her own hand, in her
cave not far from you, casked with such smiling
heart, 4

she sends to you, renowned DAMON, honor
of Etruria, whose sweet song every other tries in
vain to match, and it humbles every nymph and
shepherd of stubborn and peevish heart; 8

and this apple, too, golden colored, that a
little sapling with her oversight has saved for him
from an evil worm, 11

and if you do not mind coming down here,
you shall have a garland, which yesterday along the
stream she wove of your green beloved laurel.[147] 14

65 [112] TO SIGNORA BIANCA CAPPELLA

So dear a treasure and a jewel so prized,
destined to make the world rich, this woman so
lofty, born to so many empires, who shone so
brightly within herself, 4

that immense bounty, forever accustomed to
whatever it creates in heaven, whatever on earth, did
not want to reveal itself, so that she might stay thus
hidden among us; 8

and thus it is her luck to be given today as a
bride to the most just and greatest leader in Europe,
both together worthy of honor, both of glory, 11

and both in heaven, favored equally by
fortune, after winning the most famous kingdoms,
will have crowns of immortal valor. 14

66 [116] A MESSER HANNIBAL CARO [149]

CARO, se 'l basso stile e 'l gran desio
fosser conformi, e la materia e l'arte,
le mie del vostro nome ornate carte
unqua non temerian di Lete il rio; 4
ma veggio ben che 'l frale ingegno mio,
cui Febo de' suoi don pochi comparte,
tanto più cade in odiosa parte,
quanto più verso il ciel l'ergo e l'invio; 8
e del figlio d'Apollo, audace e insano,
e d'Icaro sovviemmi; ond'ardo e tremo
sentendo a sì gran volo inferme l'ale; 11
pur voi seguendo, e forse non in vano,
salgo ov'io spero oltra 'l mio giorno estremo
viver solo per voi fatta immortale. 14

67 [117] RISPOSTA [151]

LAURA, sì voi mi sete e lauro e Clio,
pregio e valore, ond'io lieto e 'n disparte
andrei dal volgo; or chi da voi mi parte
s'amor, s'onor, se studio ambo ci unìo? 4
Deh, se giamai di vostre fronde anch'io
avrò come i pensier le chiome sparte,
forse sarò qual or vi sembro in parte,
ma ché! Febo anco indarno vi seguio; 8
e pur quanto vi scorge alto e lontano
il mio desir, non mai stanco né scemo,
col favor vostro a voi si spinge e sale; 11
o del ardire, o del sapere umano,
o voi stessa di voi pregio supremo,
CARO o vil ch'io mi sia per voi son tale. 14

66 [116] TO MESSER HANNIBAL CARO

CARO, if my lowly style and great desire
were in conformity, and my matter and art, my
pages adorned with your name would never fear the
stream of Lethe, 4
but I see well that my fragile mind, to which
Phoebus apportions but few of his gifts, falls the
more toward a hateful place, the more I hoist and
send it heavenward, 8
and I am reminded of Apollo's son, brazen
and insane, and of Icarus, whence I burn and
tremble, feeling my wings infirm for so great a
flight; 11
yet following you, and perhaps not in vain, I
climb to where I hope to live beyond my last day, by
you alone made immortal.[150] 14

67 [117] RESPONSE

LAURA, yes, you are to me both laurel and
Clio, prize and worth, hence I would go blithe and
aloof from the mob. Who now separates me from
you, if love, if honor, if study has united us both? 4
Pray, if ever my locks, like my thoughts, be
scattered with your boughs, perhaps I shall be what
now I seem to you in part. But nay! Phoebus too
followed you in vain; 8
and yet as much as my desire discerns you
on high and afar, never weak or worn, with your
favor it presses toward you and rises; 11
you, O prize supreme of daring, of human
wisdom, O of your very self, DEAR or base that I
be, I am what I am because of you.[152] 14

68 [118] AL MEDESIMO[153]

CARO, la verga gloriosa e santa
che 'l gran Tebro produsse e lieta voi,
gentile almo cultor, vedeste poi
divenire in su 'l Po, feconda pianta, 4
quale avreste nel cor letizia e quanta
s'oggi la rivedeste qui fra noi,
spander sopra 'l bell'Arno i rami suoi,
carchi di frutti di dolcezza tanta, 8
ove 'l gran duce delle tosche rive
nuovo e felice Augusto, ammira e gode
veder nuovo Maron surger per lui, 11
e 'l buon VARCHI, che tanto amate vui
quant'ei v'ammira, ch'or con vera lode
gli alti fatti di lui narrando scrive. 14

69 [120] A MESSER BENEDETTO VARCHI[155]

VARCHI, ch'al ciel le gloriose piume
qual bianco cigno eternamente alzate,
cinto le tempie delle vostre amate
frondi e sì care al gran rettor del lume; 4
se chi voi lodar vuole in van presume
rendervi conto alla futura etate,
se le glorie presenti e le passate
sono al vostro valor picciol volume, 8
io come mai potrò pur col pensiero
l'orme di voi seguir presso o lontano,
che 'n terra giaccio augel palustre e roco? 11
Ben ho provato sopra il corso umano
ergermi dietro il vostro raggio altero,
ma tosto Icaro fui tremante e fioco. 14

68 [118] TO THE SAME MAN

CARO, the glorious and holy shoot great
Tiber produced, and that you, noble bountiful
husbandman, then saw become happily
on the Po a fertile plant, 4
how deeply you would delight in your heart,
if today you saw it again here among us, spreading
upon the fair Arno its branches, laden with fruits of
such sweetness, 8
where the great duke of the Tuscan shores,
new and fortunate Augustus, admires and savors
seeing a new Maro rise for him, 11
and good VARCHI, whom you love as much
as he admires you, who now writes with true praise,
telling of his lofty deeds.[154] 14

69 [120] TO MESSER BENEDETTO VARCHI

VARCHI, who, like a white swan, eternally
lift your glorious plumes to heaven, temples circled
with your beloved boughs, dear indeed to the great
rector of light; 4
if whoever wants to praise you presumes in
vain to make you known to the future age, if
compared to your worth, present and past glories
are a small volume, 8
how can I, who lie down on earth a croaking
swamp bird, ever even in thought follow your
footsteps, near or far? 11
Well I have tried to raise myself above the
human course behind your proud ray, but quickly I
was Icarus, trembling and weak.[156] 14

70 [130] AL CAPITAN PIETRO BUONAVENTURA[157]

"Del mio novel Claudio Neron gli onori
di tante imprese note in ogni parte,
il furor che gli diede Apollo e Marte,
le ricche spoglie e i trionfali allori,
chi non ammira? e i tanti suoi favori
d'amiche stelle, di natura e d'arte,
che son già sparsi in più di mille carte
per man di dotti e sì rari scrittori?"
Così dicea, di vaghi fiori adorno
e di palma e di lauro il petto e 'l crine,
il bel Metauro in mezzo le sue sponde,
e s'udir' ad un tempo d'ogn'intorno
risonar le sue voci alte e divine,
e "PIETRO invitto," rinbombaron l'onde.

71 [131] RISPOSTA[159]

LAURA, che giunta al sacro fonte sei,
ed a quel colle faticoso ed erto,
ove fanno al tuo nome eguale il merto,
i lauri e l'acque che ne cogli e bei,
deh, perch'io teco, infra i tuo' semidei
m'accolga, all'ombra almen del tuo bel serto,
mostrami al venir suso il calle aperto,
se superbi non sono i prieghi miei;
ché, mal grado del tempo e della morte
vivronne, ove di Lete or m'ange e punge
l'oblio, ch'ancor vivendo al fin m'adduce.
Sian le vie pur sassose ed alte e torte,
ch'io salirovvi, sol che presso o lunge
te senta, o te per segno aggia o per duce.

70 [130] TO CAPTAIN PIETRO BUONAVENTURA

"My new young Claudius Nero's honors, for
so many deeds famous everywhere, the furor that
Apollo and Mars gave him, the rich spoils and
triumphal laurels, 4

who does not admire them? And his so
many favors from friendly stars, from nature and
art, which writerly hands so learned and so rare
have already scattered on more than a thousand
pages?" 8

Thus did speak, his breast and locks
bedecked with winsome flowers, with palm, and
with laurel, handsome Metauro betwixt his banks, 11

and all about voices together were heard,
resounding lofty and divine, and "PIETRO invictus"
the waves re-echoed.[158] 14

71 [131] RESPONSE

LAURA, who have reached the sacred font,
and that wearying and steep hill where the laurels
and waters that you gather and drink make your
merit equal your name; 4

that I be gathered to you among your
demigods, in the shadow at least of your fair
wreath, pray show me the open way to come up, if
my prayers are not proud; 8

for in spite of time and death, it shall make
me live, whereas now Lethe's oblivion crushes and
stings me, leading me to the end while yet I live. 11

Though the ways be stony and high and
twisted, I shall climb there, if only near or far I may
feel you or have you as sign or as guide.[160] 14

72 A DON GABRIELLO FIAMMA[161]

FIAMMA del ciel, che dal divino ardente
foco derivi, e qualitate prendi
dal valor suo, tal che rischiari e 'ncendi
ogni fosca alma, ogni gelata mente;
deh, se quel santo ardor, vivo e possente,
non pure in terra, ov'or sì lieta splendi,
ma lieve t'alzi al ciel, cui solo attendi
nota ad ogni'alta, ad ogni bassa genta,
resta con noi, che sì ne giova e piace,
chiara tromba di Dio, per la tua voce
udir del figliuol suo gli alti precetti,
ch'ancor fatti in oprar santi e perfetti,
teco, nuovo di Dio nunzio verace,
vivrem con lui che per noi morío in croce.

73 RISPOSTA[164]

Donna, onor delle donne, che d'ardente
virtute ornata ogni bell'alma prendi,
e del tuo onesto ardor l'infiammi e 'ncendi,
questo altri già, lo prova or la mia mente;
se fosse la mia fiamma almen possente
di pormi solo ove tu ascesa splendi,
direi ch'a ragion forse brami e attendi
di vedermi restar fra la tua gente,
ma s'all'alto Signor forse non piace
darvi sì indegno servo, e più alta voce
vuol che vi porti il suon de' suoi precetti,
adorate i giudizii suoi perfetti,
e tutti insieme con amor verace,
cerchiam di viver seco morti in croce.

72 TO DON GABRIELLO FIAMMA[162]

FLAME of heaven, who derive from divine,
ardent fire and take your quality from its worth, so
much that you brighten and burn every gloomy soul,
every icy mind; 4
pray, if that holy ardor, alive and mighty,
raise you up not only on earth, where now so joyful
you shine, known to all peoples high and low, but
lightly to heaven, your only heed, 8
stay with us, for it succors and pleases us to
hear, bright trumpet of God, through your voice His
son's high precepts, 11
for made holy and perfect in our works with
you, God's true new nuncio, yet we shall live with
Him who died for us on the cross.[163] 14

73 RESPONSE

Lady, honor of ladies, adorned with ardent
virtue, you capture and with your honest ardor,
inflame and enkindle every fair soul; this others
before, now my mind experiences; 4
if my flame were at least strong enough just
to set me where you shine, risen, I would say that
you rightly yearn and wait to see me become one of
your people, 8
but lest it perhaps not please the Lord on
high to give you such an unworthy servant, and He
wants a loftier voice to bear you the sound of His
precepts, 11
worship His perfect judgments, and let us
try all together with true love to live dead with Him
on the cross. 14

74 DI MESSER ANTONIO GALLO[165]

Mentre l'aura gentil dolce spirando
muove ne l'aria nuovi alti concenti,
verde è la terra e 'l mar tranquillo e i venti
quieti, e i tuoni e le tempeste in bando;
ma breve e gran diletto è però quando
ella si tace, ricoperti o spenti
del cielo i lumi, van folgori ardenti
a noi, quel che già a Flegra, minnacciando;
Eolo le nubi scinde e pioggia scende
qual al tempo di Pirra, Proteo adduce
suo gregge al monte, e l'aura anco non spira.
Aura, deh, spira, ché 'l tuo spirto rende
a gli elementi pace, al mondo luce,
e quanto è d'egro in lui per te respira.

75 RISPOSTA[167]

GALLO, che destro in su l'ali poggiando
ten vai vicino a i gran cerchi lucenti,
e con tuoi alti e sì graditi accenti
l'alme dal pigro sonno ogn'or destando,
ben fu ch'anco la mia, quasi obliando
se stessa, avendo in te suoi spirti intenti,
dietro la voce tua, ben che con lenti
passi, dolce d'Amore sen gìa cantando;
or da te lungi, sonnacchiosa attende
in van chi fida le sia scorta e duce,
e seco del suo mal piange e s'adira;
pur se mia indegnità non mi contende
il tuo cantar ch'al ciel dritto conduce,
spero d'alzarla un giorno ov'ella aspira.

74 FROM MESSER ANTONIO GALLO

While the gentle aura breathes sweet, it stirs
in the air lofty new harmonies; green is the earth
and the sea tranquil, and the winds quiet, and
thunderbolts and tempests banished; 4
but still, brief and great delight it is when
she falls silent, as heaven's lights, covered over or
spent, go threatening us with lightning bolts, as they
once did at Phlegra. 8
Aeolus rends the clouds and rain descends
as in the time of Pyrrha, Proteus leads his herd to
the mount, and neither does aura breathe. 11
Aura, pray, breathe, for your spirit restores
peace to the elements, light to the world, and
whatever in it is needful breathes because of you.[166] 14

75 RESPONSE

GALLO, who agile on your wings ascending
draw near the great lucent circles and with your
lofty and so welcome accents ever awaken our souls
from lazy slumber, 4
truly it was that mine, too, almost forgetting
itself, so intent were its spirits on you, went along
after your voice, albeit with slow steps, singing
sweet of love; 8
now far from you, it sleepily awaits in vain a
trusty escort and guide and weeps for its injury and
waxes angry; 11
yet if my unworthiness deny me not your
song, which leads straight to heaven, I hope to raise
it one day to meet its aspirations.[168] 14

76 DEL BRONZINO PITTORE[169]

Mentre sepolto e di me stesso in bando
mi sto com'uom che non più veggia e senta
che tenebre e martir, poi che m'ha spenta
morte ogni gioia, oimè, sì tosto, e quando,
sì dolce udire mi par l'Aura ir destando
le vive gemme, e sì bel raggio intenta
far la mia vista, che ridurmi tenta
l'alma u' si vive, i suoi danni obliando;
o vitale armonia, celeste lume,
s'al destin si potea tor l'arme, vostra
era la gloria, e ben temer si vide;
ma ch'io sol la sua voce oda e mi guide
lo buon pittor che fu dell'età nostra
specchio, è già fermo, e 'n doglia mi consume.

77 RISPOSTA[171]

Se fermo è nel destin che lacrimando,
l'alma vostra gentil viver consenta
per quella, ch'oggi in ciel lieta e contenta
gode, del vostro gir sì lamentando,
io, che fuor mal mio grado talor mando,
qual roco augel, voce imperfetta e lenta,
e se pur luce scopro, ella diventa
oscura nube, in cieca parte errando,
vi priego umil che l'onorate piume
seguiate e 'l dolce suon, che sì vi mostra
quel che dal volgo vil parte e divide;
ché forse un dì, se Morte non recide
anzi tempo il mio stame, all'alta chiostra
con voi sarò fuor d'ogni mio costume.

76 FROM BRONZINO THE PAINTER

While buried and banished from myself, I
stand like a man who no longer sees and feels
anything but shadows and suffering, since death has
snuffed out my every joy, alas, so soon; and when 4
I seem to hear Aura go so sweetly,
awakening the living gems, and a ray so beautiful
hold intent my sight, that it tries to restore my soul,
forgetting its troubles, to the realm of the living; 8
O vital harmony, celestial light, if destiny
could be disarmed, yours were the glory, and
awesome indeed we saw it, 11
but it is already decided that I merely hear her voice,
and be guided by the good painter who was a mirror of our age,
and I am consumed in sorrow.[170] 14

77 RESPONSE

If it is decided by destiny that your noble soul
consent to living in weeping for his who today,
blithe and happy, delights in heaven, lamenting the
way you go about, 4
I, who betimes in spite of myself send forth
like a croaking bird a voice imperfect and slow, and
even if I discover light, it becomes a dark cloud,
errant in a blind place, 8
I humbly pray you to pursue the honored
plumes and sweet sound that he shows you, who
parts and divides from the vulgar mob, 11
for perhaps one day, if Death not cut down
before its time my stem, I shall be with you in the
lofty cloister, outside my every custom.[172] 14

78 DI MESSER GIROLAMO RAZZI[173]

Ben puoi tu, Arno, omai girtene altero,
del Tebro al pari e del gran re de' fiumi,
poscia che 'n te fra' tuoi sì chiari lumi
splende non pur chi varca al primo vero, 4
ma casta donna, essempio sol di vero
pregio e valor, d'angelici costumi,
onde la gloria tua più s'alzi e allumi,
dal Metro vien nel tuo fiorito impero, 8
LAURA, che seco ogni virtute alberga,
e le penne miglior del secol nostro
adegua con antiche or prose or carmi; 11
te, delle donne raro e nuovo mostro,
col tuo Fidia gentil, ch'eterna i marmi,
tempo né morte mai tenebre asperga. 14

79 RISPOSTA[175]

RAZZI, io ben'ebbi, ed aggio ora in pensiero,
ed avrò sempre, que' miei quasi numi
seguir, ch'al volgo l'oscure ombre e i fumi
lasciando, il secol lor felice fero; 4
ma ch'io splenda appo lor, lungi è dal vero,
anzi tra sterpi e soletarii dumi,
u' non entran giamai d'Apollo i lumi,
picciol raggio vacillo infermo e nero; 8
ben se quel sol, ch'alteramente alberga
là v'è Ritondo il bel Parnaso vostro,
qualch'un de' raggi suoi vorrà prestarmi, 11
col mio Fidia, che 'n marmi e 'n bronzi ha mostro
quanto l'arte sua possa, ardirei alzarmi
chiara qual voi, ove rado è ch'uom s'erga. 14

78 FROM MESSER GIROLAMO RAZZI

By now, Arno, you well can go proudly your
way, a peer of Tiber and the great king of rivers, for
in you among your lights so bright shines not only
the one who crosses over to the first truth, 4
but a chaste lady, lone example of true merit
and worth, angelic in manners, the more to raise
and brighten your glory, from the Metauro comes to
your flowered empire, 8
LAURA, in whom every virtue dwells, and
who matches the best quills of our age, now with
ancient prose, now poetry; 11
rare and novel marvel among women,
with your noble Fidia, who makes marbles
eternal, let neither time nor death ever sprinkle you with
shadow.[174] 14

79 RESPONSE

RAZZI, I have indeed had, and now have,
and will have always, a mind to follow those
demigods of mine, who, leaving to the vulgar mob
dark shadows and smoke, made their age happy; 4
but that I shine beside them is far from true,
nay, among weeds and solitary thorns, where
Apollo's lights never enter, I flicker, a little ray
infirm and black; 8
but if that sun, who proudly dwells there
where your fair Parnassus is Rotondo, will agree
to lend me some of his rays, 11
with my Fidia, who in marbles and
bronzes has shown how much his art can do, I
would dare raise myself, bright like you, where man
rarely rises.[176] 14

80 DI MESSER BENVENUTO SCULTORE[177]

Con quel soave canto e dolce legno,
ne corse ardito Orfeo per la consorte,
Cerber chetossi e le tartaree porte
s'aperser, che Pluton ne lo fe' degno; 4
poi gli rendette il prezioso pegno,
ma d'accordo non fu seco la Morte.
Voi, gentil Laura, quanto miglior sorte
aveste al scendere al superno regno. 8
Lassù v'alzò il Petrarca, e dietro poi
ne venne a riverdervi in Paradiso,
sete scesi in un corpo ora ambidoi. 11
Felice Orfeo, s'avea tale avviso
cangiar la spoglia, aria fatto qual voi,
ch'Amor, vita e virtù non v'è diviso. 14

81 RISPOSTA[179]

Volesse pure il ciel, ch'all'alto segno,
ove giugneste voi per piane e corte
vie, che sono ad altrui sì lunghe e torte,
giugnesser l'ali del mio basso ingegno, 4
che come paurosa e debil vegno
a dir di voi; sicura alora e forte
verrei, né punto temeria di morte
l'ultimo assalto, ch'or temer convegno; 8
e direi come in un sceser fra noi
Pirgotele e Lisippo, onde conquiso
fu 'l vanto, prisca età, degli onor tuoi, 11
e perché 'l sacro Apollo mai diviso
da' più cari non v'ebbe amici suoi,
tal ch'io co' più perfetti in voi m'affiso. 14

80 FROM MESSER BENVENUTO THE SCULPTOR

With that suave song and sweet lyre,
Orpheus boldly rushed off for his consort, Cerberus
fell quiet, and the Tartarean Gates opened, for Pluto
made him worthy of them; 4
then he returned to him the precious pledge,
but Death did not go along with him. You, gentle
Laura, how much luckier you were to ascend to the
supernal kingdom; 8
Petrarch raised you up there and then came
after to see you again in Paradise. Now you both are
ascended in one body. 11
Happy Orpheus, had he thought to change
his body, he would have done as you, from whom
Love, life, and virtue are not parted.[178] 14

81 RESPONSE

If only heaven wished for the wings of my
lowly intelligence to reach the lofty sign that you
reached by the level and short paths that to others
are so long and twisted, 4
I, who come to speak of you as one fearful
and weak, would then come sure and strong, nor
would I fear a whit death's last assault, which I now
fearfully regard; 8
and I would say how Pyrgoteles and
Lysippus descended among us in one, whence the
vaunt, pristine age, of your honors was conquered, 11
and say why sacred Apollo never held you apart
from his dearest friends, such that I am with those most
perfect in my attachment to you.[180] 14

82 DI MESSER FEDERIGO LANTI[181]

Quello spirto divino ed immortale,
in cui tutto s'infonde Apollo, e inspira
il suo furor, che placa e tempra ogn'ira,
tal che par quel d'Apollo o almeno equale,
quella soave e lieve Aura, la quale
ne la schiera Intronata dolce spira,
sì ch'ivi è 'l sommo ben ov'ella gira,
o felice quel loco or ch'ella è tale!
Quell'Alma a cui drizz'Arbia altari, quella
a cui sparge Arbia incensi, quella ch'Arno,
Tebro e Metauro, non pur l'Arbia adora,
quella, spento carbon, lucente e bella
face m'accenda: io da me stesso indarno
a cotal fin le son d'intorno ogn'ora.

83 RISPOSTA[183]

Lanti, quanto più spiego ambedue l'ale
per volar alto ov'ogn'or l'alma aspira,
tanto nel maggior fondo più mi tira
questo terreno mio peso mortale,
e voi volete pur che bassa e frale
canna, a cui sì poca Aura entro respira,
suoni al par di sublime e forte lira,
piena del vostro fiato almo vitale,
e d'accendere altrui, spenta facella,
abbia possanza: io ben mi struggo e scarno,
ma 'ndarno tento di lodarvi ancora;
ma che poss'io contra mia scarsa stella,
da che sì poco ombreggio e meno incarno
quel che 'l vostro alto stil pinge e colora?

82 FROM MESSER FEDERIGO LANTI

That divine and immortal spirit, in whom
Apollo wholly instills himself and inspires her
furor, which so placates and tempers all ire such
that it seems to be Apollo's own or at least equal, 4
that suave and airy Aura, who in the troop
of the Dazed breathes sweet, so that the highest
good is there where she turns, oh happy that place
now that she is of it! 8
That soul to which Arbia raises altars, the
one to whom Arbia scatters incense, the one that
Arno, Tiber, and Metauro, not just Arbia, adore, 11
she lights from my spent charcoal a bright
and beautiful torch; to that end, useless by myself,
I am around her evermore.[182] 14

83 RESPONSE

Lanti, the more I spread both my wings to
fly high where my soul ever aspires, the more this
mortal earthly weight of mine pulls me into the
greatest depth, 4
and yet you want a lowly and fragile reed,
inside which so little Aura blows, to sound the same
as a sublime and strong lyre, filled with your
bountiful, vital breath 8
and that I, a spent torch, should have power
to kindle others: though I am indeed consumed and
grow thin, yet in vain I still attempt to praise you, 11
but what can I do against my stingy star,
since I cast so small a shadow and less do I incarnate
what your high-style paints and colors.[184] 14

84 DI MESSER GIROLAMO BARGAGLI MATERIAL INTRONATO[185]

Quella che già del divin capo armata
di Giove uscío la dotta Atene adore,
e la vezzosa dea, madre d'Amore,
defenda sempre pur Cipro odorata;
chè a più celeste diva oggi è sacrata
e da nume difesa assai maggiore,
questa, ch'adorna di sì nuovo onore,
l'altre avanza d'assai, schiera Intronata.
A costei come a' suoi Penati cari
sarà la Zucca un sacro tempio e santo,
e le rime leggiadre incensi sparsi,
e cinti poi di riverenza il manto,
de' nostri cori fien ne i puri altari
d'onorarla i desii sacrati ed arsi.

85 RISPOSTA[187]

Qual per bearmi amica stella e grata
girò tanto ver me del suo favore,
quel dì ch'a sì lucente almo splendore
fui da sì folte tenebre innalzata?
A qual più dotta schiera e più onorata
di questa, altrui vigilie e mio sudore,
perch'io non tema il trapassar de l'ore,
poteanmi aprir più gloriosa entrata?
Quanto dunque vi debbo, eletti e rari
spirti a me sì cortesi? oh almen quanto
odo ogn'or l'alma mia di voi lodarsi
dir potessi, ma chi potria mai tanto,
se sono a' vostri larghi doni e chiari,
non che 'l mio, tutti ingegni e scuri e scarsi?

84 FROM MESSER GIROLAMO BARGAGLI, MATERIAL INTRONATO

Let her who once came forth armed from the
divine head of Jove be adored by learned Athens,
and may the comely goddess, mother of love, ever
be defended too by scented Cyprus, 4
for consecrated to a more celestial divinity
today, and defended by a deity far greater, this troop
of the Dazed, adorned with so new an
honor, far surpasses the others; 8
to her as to her dear Penates, the Pumpkin
will be a sacred and holy temple, and graceful
rhymes will be scattered incense, 11
and girded then with a mantle of reverence,
to honor her let the desires of our hearts on pure
altars be consecrated and burned.[186] 14

85 RESPONSE

What friendly and welcome star blessed me
by turning toward me with so much of its favor that
day, when to such shining bountiful splendor I was
lifted from such thick shadows? 4
To what more learned and honored troop
than this one, that I not fear the passing of
the hours, could others' late-night vigils and my
sweat open to me a more glorious entry? 8
How much then do I owe you, elect and rare
spirits so courteous to me? Oh, if I could at least
speak the praises of you I hear in my soul, 11
but who could ever do so much, if, before
your generous and bright gifts, not only mine, but
all minds are dark and wanting?[188] 14

86 DEL LASCA[189]

Oggi, via più che mai beata e bella
si può dir con ragion la nobil Flora,
poi che 'ntro il suo bel sen colei dimora
cui par non vider mai né sol né stella. 4
Arno superbo il corso rinovella
e di se stesso vago s'innamora,
le rive, udendo, che'egli imperla e 'ndora,
"Laura" sonare in questa parte e 'n quella; 8
e del famoso Tebro ride seco,
poi che del suo più chiaro almo splendore
privo in tutto, rimaso è solo e cieco, 11
e dice, pien d'alta dolcezza il core,
"Mentre avrò sì gran donna, sarà meco
delle Muse e di Febo il primo onore." 14

87 RISPOSTA[191]

Sì come alor che rilucente e bella
nella nuova stagion ritorna Flora,
e che 'l sol fa con lei dolce dimora,
scaldando il Tauro od altra amica stella, 4
ride l'antica madre e rinovella
il vario parto, e 'l ciel di sé innamora,
e 'l superbo Oceano ingemma e 'ndora
l'alte sue sponde in questa parte e 'n quella, 8
così vidi allo stil che portò seco
un vago aprile, un subito splendore,
il mio destarsi adormentato e cieco. 11
Lasca gentil, da indi in qua il mio core
s'empie d'alti concetti, e saran meco
per farmi chiara, e vostro fia l'onore. 14

86 FROM IL LASCA

Today, noble Flora can rightly call herself
more blessed and beautiful than ever, since within
her fair bosom dwells a lady whose equal neither
sun nor star seems ever to have seen; 4

proud Arno renews his course, and yearning
for himself falls in love, as the banks that he
impearls and engilds hear "Laura" resound in parts
near and far, 8

and he laughs to himself at the famous
Tiber, for wholly deprived of his brightest most
bountiful splendor, he has been left alone and blind, 11

and Arno says, his heart filled with deep
sweetness, "As long as I have such a great lady,
will be with me the first honor of the Muses and Phoebus."[190] 14

87 RESPONSE

As when in the new season Flora returns
rebrightened and beautiful, and the sun makes with
her a sweet abode, warming Taurus or another
friendly star, 4

the ancient mother laughs and renews her
varied birthing, and heaven falls in love with itself,
and proud Ocean engems and engilds his high
shores in parts near and far, 8

so I saw in the style that brought with it a
winsome April, a sudden splendor awaken my own,
asleep and blind. 11

Noble Lasca, from now on my heart is filled
with lofty concepts, and they shall be with me to
make me famous, and yours shall be the honor.[192] 14

88 DEL BRONZINO PITTORE[193]

Io giuro a voi, per quella viva fronde
di cui voi fuste al sacro fonte pianta,
e per quella di lui, cortese e santa
fiamma, che regge il ciel, la terra e l'onde,
ch'alla sua felice ombra in sì gioconde
note ho veduto tal ch'onestà canta
ch'io tegno a vile omai qual più si vanta,
e dolcezza maggior non viemmai altronde;
ché se le fortunate Oretta e Bice
onora il mondo, all'altrui senno ed opra
si dee non men ch'a i lor merti dar vanto:
voi per proprio valor Laura e Beatrice
vincete e sete a i lor pregi di sopra,
e forse a i loro amanti in stile e canto.

89 RISPOSTA[195]

Sì come al fonte ebb'io larghe e seconde
le stelle a impormi il nome, avess'io tanta
grazia da lor pur' anco avuta quanta
a voi, novello Apelle, Apollo infonde,
ch'oggi le vostre altere rime, donde
verace amor di falso velo ammanta
il vero, a me con gran ragion cotanta
lode darian, ch'a lor sol corrisponde,
e forse delle due non men felice
sarei che stanno a tutte l'altre sopra,
co' lor casti amator per sempre a canto,
ma poi che 'n questa etate a voi sol lice
dar doppia vita altrui, perché non s'opra
per voi, sì ch'io con voi viva altrettanto?

88 FROM BRONZINO THE PAINTER

I swear to you by that living bough, whose
plant you were at the sacred font, and by that flame
courteous and holy, of him who rules the heaven,
earth, and waves, 4
that in its happy shadow I saw such a one
singing of purity in so joyous notes that I now hold
base whoever most vaunts himself, and nowhere
else does greater sweetness ever come to me; 8
for if the world honors the fortunate Oretta
and Bice, we should give vaunt to another's wisdom
and work no less than to the ladies' merit: 11
you, through your own valor, vanquish
Laura and Beatrice, and you are above them in
worth, and perhaps their lovers in style and song.[194] 14

89 RESPONSE

If only, just as I had at the font generous and
favorable stars to give me a name, I had had as
much favor again from them as Apollo infuses in
you, new Apelles, 4
so that today your proud rhymes, wherein
truthful love mantles with false veil the truth, would
give me most rightly as much praise as is due only
to them, 8
and perhaps I would be no less happy than
the two who stand above all other women, with
their chaste lovers beside them for always, 11
but since in this age you alone are allowed
to give people double life, why do you not arrange
for me to live with you as much?[196] 14

90 DE MESSER LUCIO ORADINI A MESSER BARTOLOMEO AMMANNATI[197]

Se chiaro ingegno avessi e perfetta arte,
e come voi, la man pronta e 'l colore,
da formar quel c'ho dentro al mondo fore
di vostre lodi alto modello in carte, 4
non s'erge in questa al cielo o in altra parte
opra, ond'eterno all'architetto onore
segua, ch'assai non fosse allor maggiore
la mia, ch'or giace in così bassa parte; 8
né 'n sasso fu sì saldo e di sì dura
pietra fin qui, né con tanto sottile,
da voi, né fia giamai degno lavoro, 11
né fermo oggi contesto ornato dura
ond'aggia il tempo in sempiterno a vile,
quanto il mio fôra allor nobil lavoro. 14

91 RISPOSTA[198]

LUCIO, a cui tanto oggi dal ciel comparte
Apollo del suo doppio, alto valore,
ch'eguale a lui di forza e di splendore,
sgombrate intorno l'atre nubi sparte, 4
tal ch'io, ch'oscura vivomi in disparte,
qual lume infermo ch'a poca aura muore,
con lui cui marital pudico amore
diede il mio cor, che mai dal suo non parte, 8
prendo tanto vigor dall'alma e pura
vostra luce gentil, che d'aspra e vile
pianta, divengo assai pregiato alloro, 11
ed ei che 'n marmi e 'n bronzi altri e sé fura
alla morte ed al tempo, in chiaro stile
per voi fia noto ancor dall'Indo al Moro. 14

90 FROM MESSER LUCIO ORADINI, TO MESSER BARTOLOMEO AMMANNATI

If I had a bright mind and perfect art, and like you, a ready hand and the color to form what I have inside for the world outside, a lofty model of your praises on paper, 4

then no work pushes heavenward in this or any other part, a source of eternal honor to its architect, but that mine, which now lies down in such a low place, would not be much the greater; 8

neither was there ever up to now a worthy labor in such solid stone and of such hard rock, nor will there ever be, so subtly wrought by you, 11

nor does an ornate structure endure firm today, such that it scorn time ever more, as much as would mine then be a noble labor. 14

91 RESPONSE

LUCIO, to whom Apollo from heaven today apportions so much of his double, lofty worth that you, his equal in force and splendor, carry away the spreading inky black clouds, 4

so that I, who live apart in obscurity, like a sickly light that dies out at a bit of breeze, with him to whom chaste marital love gave my heart, which never parts from his, 8

I take so much vigor from your bountiful and pure noble light, that from a coarse and base plant I become highly prized laurel, 11

and he, who in marbles and in bronzes steals himself and others from death and time, through you in bright style will yet be known from the Indian to the Moorish Seas.[199] 14

92 DI MESSER LELIO BONSI[200] A MESSER BARTOLOMEO AMMANNATI 4[201]

Non fosse in questa età si vile e ria
vostra onorata mano e 'ngegno altero,
che 'n chiari marmi e 'n vivi bronzi il vero
di natura coll'arte or finge, or cria, 4
non fossero i bei carmi e l'armonia
degna del ciel, ch'a lui n'apre il sentiero,
d'ella ch'a voi stelle benigne diero,
onesta e saggia e dolce compagnia, 8
chi con incude mai, né con martello
far più d'altra potria longeva e adorna
del gran Duce toscan l'altera reggia? 11
chi lui, che Flora e 'l secol nostro adorna,
rendere eterno a questo clima e a quello,
se voi coppia gentil nessun pareggia? 14

93 RISPOSTA 4[203]

Che del tuo gran valor minor non fia,
o dolce a i buon, quanto a i nemici fero,
degno che questo e quell'altro emispero,
a te soggetto in libertate stia, 4
ben mille scorge, non pure una via
l'alto tuo ingegno e 'l pronto occhio cervero,
ma per quanto a me par, s'io scerno il vero,
questa più breve e men segnata fia: 8
che potrà di costui l'alto scarpello
con la penna di lui, ch'oggi soggiorna
là 've Ritondo eguale a Pindo ombreggia, 11
far sì, che 'l mondo, che pregiato torna
per un Lisippo ed un Maron novello,
nuovo Alessandro e nuovo Augusto veggia. 14

92 FROM LELIO BONSI TO MESSER BARTOLOMEO AMANNATI 4

Were it not, in this age so base and evil, for
your honored hand and lofty mind, which in bright
marbles and in living bronzes now mimics, now
creates nature's truth with art, 4
were it not for the fair poems and the
harmony worthy of heaven, to which it opens our
pathway, of the woman whom kindly stars gave to
you, an honest and wise and sweet companion, 8
who could ever with anvil or with hammer
make the great Tuscan duke's proud kingdom the
most long-lived and adorned of all? 11
Who could make him, who adorns Flora and
our age, eternal in climes near and far if no one,
gentle couple, can equal you?[202] 14

93 RESPONSE 4

That not be less than your great worth, sweet
to good men as much as fierce to enemies,
deserving that this and the other hemisphere be
subject to you in liberty, 4
full a thousand ways, not just one, your lofty
mind and ready lynxlike eye discern, but as for
what I think, if I discern the truth, the shorter and
less marked way will be the one, 8
that this man's noble chisel can make, with
the pen of him who today dwells there where
Ritondo makes shade to match Pindus, 11
such that the world, whose esteem a new
Lysippus and Maro renew, may see a new
Alexander and a new Augustus.[204] 14

94 [208] A MADONNA ALESSANDRA DE' CORSI[205]

L'alte faville di quel puro ardente
foco, ch'entro 'l mio petto accese in pria
antico senno in nuova leggiadria,
e in singolar beltà pudica mente,
coperte furon sì, ma non già spente,
dal tempo che volando il tutto oblia,
ed or deste da man cortese e pia,
crescon l'incendio lor dolce e cocente;
così m'è CORSA nuovamente al core
ALESSANDRA gentil, la vostra luce,
che visto e vinto tutto inceso l'ave,
in tal guisa il tuo ardor caro e soave
provò chi fu del mio ministro e duce,
e sempre a' suoi desir proprio amore.

95 [209] RISPOSTA[207]

Né donna mai, qualor più dolcemente
casti pensieri al petto Amor l'envia,
di quell'alma virtute onde si cria
il foco che in due cori ardi sovente,
ebbe quant'io, né sì veracemente
legossi e strinse per sì dritta via,
a voi scorta m'avete e dalla ria
usanza sciolta dell'umana gente;
indi le penne al mio basso valore
spiegate all'AURA, il sol che 'n me riluce
seguo da lungi, benché tarda e grave;
così vostra virtù, donna, conduce
mio cor amando e con sì dolce chiave
l'apre, ch'io ne gradisco i giorni e l'ore.

94 [208] TO MADONNA ALESSANDRA DE' CORSI

The noble sparks of that pure ardent fire,
first kindled within my breast by aged wisdom in
youthful charm and a chaste mind in singular beauty, 4
were covered, yes, but not burnt out, by time
all-forgetting in his flight, and now, awakened by
a courteous and pious hand, they grow to a sweet and
searing blaze; 8
thus, gentle ALESSANDRA, your light has
newly COURSED to my heart, which, seen and
conquered, is all afire; 11
in such manner the one who was always my
minister and guide's own love felt your ardor, dear
and sweet.[206] 14

95 [209] RESPONSE

No woman, whenever Love most sweetly
sends chaste thoughts to her breast, ever had that
nurturing virtue, whence comes the fire that in two
hearts often burns, 4
as much as I, or was ever so truly bound and
pressed to such a straight way; you have led me to
you and untied me from the wicked habit of
humankind; 8
thence you spread to the AURA your
plumes before my lowly worth; the sun that shines
in me I, though slow and heavy, follow from afar; 11
thus your virtue, lady, leads my heart by
loving and opens it with such a sweet key that for it
I relish the days and hours.[208] 14

96 [263] IN MORTE DI MESSER BENEDETTO VARCHI[209]

VARCHI, io so ben che su nel terzo giro,
ove si rende all'opre eguale il merto,
come in lucido speglio vedi aperto
il mio qui senza te grave martiro,
onde meco di me talor m'adiro,
che troppo lungamente aggia sofferto
in preda al duol, quasi non sappia certo
ch'io morta son mentre qui parlo e spiro.
Non tu, che fuor del mondo empio e fallace
vivi beato, or che ti piango morto
turbando forse tua tranquilla pace,
ma che poss'io, se quel che più dispiace
e manco giova, uman giudizio torto,
dura condizion, seguir ne face?

97 [275] DI MESSER ANTONIO ALLEGRETTI[211]

Laura celeste al cui spirar s'avviva
pura fiamma d'amore in alti cori,
e teco porti tanti e tali odori
ch'Arno fai chiaro e verde ogni sua riva,
mentre che qui l'arbor Caro fioriva,
co' dolci frutti e coi soavi fiori,
delle Muse e del ciel grazie e favori,
di questa vita ogn'amaro addolciva;
e pur secco è 'l gran tronco e l'alte cime
a terra sparse, e quell'amate frondi
più non hanno il natio vago colore;
alla memoria sua e stile e rime
consacra omai, se no 'l vieta il dolore,
o le mie rozze almen leggi e rispondi.

96 ON THE DEATH OF MESSER BENEDETTO VARCHI

VARCHI, I well know how up in the third
circle, where merit is rendered equal to deeds,
in a lucid mirror you see openly my heavy
martyrdom here without you, 4
whence I betimes am angry with myself about myself,
for too long have I suffered, prey to
sorrow, as if I did not really know that I am dead
while here I speak and breathe. 8
Not you, who outside the impious and
fallacious world live blessed, now that I weep for
you dead, perhaps disturbing your tranquil peace, 11
but what can I do, if that which most
displeases and least avails, twisted human
judgment, makes us follow it as our harsh
condition?[210] 14

97 FROM ANTONIO ALLEGRETTI

Celestial Laura, at whose breath a pure
flame of love comes to life in lofty hearts and who
carry with you so much and such fragrance that you
make Arno bright and his every shore green, 4
while here the Caro tree bloomed, with its
sweet fruits and soft flowers, by the grace and
favors of the Muses and heaven, it sweetened this
life's every bitterness; 8
and yet the great trunk has gone dry, and the
tall peaks are scattered on earth, and those beloved
boughs no longer have the winsome color they were
born with; 11
now dedicate to his memory style and
rhymes, if sorrow not forbid it, or at least read and
answer my rough ones.[212] 14

98 [277] IN MORTE DI DONNA MARIA DE' MEDICI[213]

Non volle Dio che un'uom terreno e frale,
quantunque posto d'ogn'altezza in cima,
possedesse tesoro a cui mai prima
non fu nel mondo, e non fia poscia eguale; 4
e però dianzi il biondo crin fatale
svelse di lei, ch'era sua gloria prima
quaggiuso, e tanto in cielo or la sublima
quanto può salire alto alma mortale. 8
Vergine, che di stelle incoronata
presso a colei, da cui prendesti il nome,
e i costumi immitasti e l'opre sante, 11
lieta soggiorni, e noi tra quali e quante
lagrime lasci! Ed oh pur quando e come
rivedrem noi la luce tua beata? 14

99 IN MORTE DI MESSER LELIO CAPILUPI[215]

Poi ch'ebbe il mondo de' suoi onori ardenti
in mille guise alteramente ornato,
sazio il buon LELIO del mortale stato
s'en gìo con passi al terzo ciel non lenti; 4
quivi fra lor, che morte non ha spenti,
lieto s'assise al suo Virgilio allato,
lo cui leggiadro stil tanto onorato
fu da' suoi dolci e graziosi accenti; 8
talor con Dante e col Petrarca muove
soave il piede, ed or col Bembo intorno
va dolcemente compartendo l'ore; 11
or volto a questo basso umano orrore,
pietoso il ciglio, a quell'alto soggiorno
mi chiama e 'nvita ad opre elette e nuove. 14

119 [322] ON THE DEATH OF POPE GREGORY XIII

Leaving the mantle, both keys, and the
kingdom, which sent me bright among so many
heroes, today devoutly I come to your feet, Lord, as
a humble servant, as a sinner;
and if I failed in the lofty honor-worthy
office you entrusted me, I ask mercy, since in this
mortal condition of ours, actions go not apace with
good intentions.
I really did try to draw the Indian flock from
the world's remotest reaches into your Roman fold,
to make it ample and perfect;
send them now a Shepherd, who can with
greater wisdom and greater skill amend my fault,
and may all the earth be like the heaven.[254]

120 [327] THIRD ECLOGUE

Upon a flowering and delightful
hill that gazes adoringly on Arno and the
countryside roundabout, fertile and green,
that pours hope into weary farmers' hearts,
sits a proud edifice, so artfully made by such
an industrious hand that it is the envy not
only of all others there, resplendent with
craft and wealth, but of those in which Flora
measures her pride and worth. Nor truly was
any smaller or less welcome hostel
suited to such a noble and wise shepherd
than whom the Tuscan fields have no other
either so courteous or contented,
ALFEO, whose merit and destiny
made him long since their possessor, and with him his faithful
GALATEA, who seems to surpass
and outshine not only all other chaste ladies today,
but the holy goddesses of heaven, for her beauty,
for her worth famed and sublime,
to whom a kind and friendly heaven has
given an abundance of sweet and charming offspring,
in perfect keeping with their exalted fortune.

98 [277] ON THE DEATH OF DONNA MARIA DE' MEDICI

God did not wish that a man earthly and
frail, though placed at the peak of all heights, should
possess a treasure that never before was equaled in
the world and never after will be; 4
and so first He plucked out the fatal blond
lock of hair, hers who was his prime glory down
here, and now as high as mortal soul can climb, he
makes her that sublime in heaven. 8
Virgin, crowned with stars, beside her, from
whom you took your name and whose ways and
holy works you imitated, 11
gladly you dwell, but how many and what
tears do you leave behind with us? And oh, when
yet and how shall we see your blessed light?[214] 14

99 ON THE DEATH OF MESSER LELIO CAPILUPI

After he had with his glowing honors in a
thousand ways proudly adorned the world, when the
good LELIO was sated with his mortal state, unslow
of step he went off to the third heaven; 4
there among those whom death has not
snuffed out, gladly he sat down beside his Virgil,
whose sweet graceful accents so adorned his
delightful style; 8
sometimes with Dante and with Petrarch he
walks slowly along, and now with Bembo he
goes about sweetly marking the hours; 11
now facing this lowly human wilderness,
with a compassionate brow, to that lofty abode he
calls and invites me to deeds elect and new.[216] 14

100 IN MORTE DI MADONNA HIRENE[217]

Quanto ebbe dianzi il mondo e doglie e pianti,
alor che svelse ingorda morte acerba
al più bel fiore e 'l miglior frutto in erba,
tanto fu colmo il ciel di gioie e canti,
vergine eletta da i più alti e santi
chori, ove degno al tuo ben far si serba
pregio, a noi ti rivolgi e disacerba
con la tua vista i nostri dolor tanti;
sì risonare in ogni estrema parte
ne' secoli avvenire udrai 'l tuo nome,
ch'a' più chiari imporrà silenzio eterno,
e mille Atene e mille Flore e Rome
IRENE cantaran la state e 'l verno,
e fien piene di te tutte le carte.

101 [292] NELLA MALATTIA DEL CAVALLIER FRA PAOLO DEL ROSSO[219]

Se divoto pregar, fonte di vita,
eterno Febo, al tuo permesso santo
giunse già mai, giunga il nostro che tanto
porghiam divoti a tua bontà infinita.
Non sei tu quei che la mortal ferita
curasti al mondo, onde n'hai pregio e vanto?
Non ancidesti tu l'empio cotanto
Fiton, per dare alle nostr'alme aita?
Mira un de' figli tuoi più eletti e chiari,
un ch 'l tuo nome, la tua gloria e l'opre
cantar promette in vario e dolce stile,
che infermo langue; or tuo valor s'adopre
tanto in suo pro, che i foschi giorni amari
disgombri dolce e luminoso aprile.

100 ON THE DEATH OF MADONNA HIRENE

As much as the world had sorrow and tears
ere now, when greedy bitter death uprooted the
fairest flower and the meadow's best fruit, so much
was heaven filled with joys and songs, 4
maid, chosen by the highest and holiest
choirs, where fitting reward is reserved for your
good deeds, turn to us, and as you look remove the
sting of our so many sorrows; 8
so in every farthest reach, for centuries to
come, you will hear your name so resound that it
will impose on the brightest eternal silence, 11
and a thousand Athens and a thousand
Floras and Romes will sing "IRENE" summer and
winter, and you will fill all the poets' pages.[218] 14

101 [292] ON THE ILLNESS OF THE KNIGHT FRA PAOLO DEL ROSSO

If devout praying, font of life, eternal
Phoebus, ever attained your holy permission, may
ours that we offer so devoutly to your infinite
bounty attain it. 4
Are not you the one who cured the world's
mortal wound, whence your worth and vaunt? Did
you not slay Python so very wicked, in order to
succor our souls? 8
Behold one of your most chosen and
brightest sons, one who promises to sing your name, your
glory, and who works in varied and sweet
style, 11
who languishes infirm; now may your
power work on his behalf, that a sweet and
luminous April may carry away the gloom of bitter days.[220] 14

102 [297] A MESSER GIOVAN BATTISTA CINI, IN MORTE DI MADONNA MARIA BERARDI SUA CONSORTE[221]

Quanto amor casto in bella donna e saggia
e possa e vaglia, i santi effetti suoi,
CINI, per prova raccontare a noi
potete, ond'anco il mondo essempio n'aggia. 4
Qual parte, dunque, altrui chiusa e salvaggia,
lasso, non ricercate in van, da poi
che morte spense il bel lume ch'a voi
fu chiaro sol per quest'ombrosa piaggia? 8
Vedete come ancor arde e sfavilla
per voi, voi sol rimira e sol brama,
e 'n ciò fa il suo gioir beato appieno; 11
sentite quanta ognor dolcezza instilla
nell'alma vostra, ch'entro il suo bel seno
v'accoglie, vi trastulla e vi richiama. 14

103 [298] IN MORTE DEL GRAN DUCA DI TOSCANA[223]

1.
Quanto d'umani pregi illustre e adorno
il gran COSMO rendesti,
tanto e più de' celesti
rendil' or nel tuo santo almo soggiorno; 3
ché se per breve giorno
di vita, almo Signor, sì largo sei,
nel sempiterno poi quanto esser dei! 6
2.
Come all'aure vitali, al nostro mondo
alto chiamasti lui,
che sepolto giacea nel più profondo
centro de' regni bui; 10
così, Signor verace,
oggi ricevi in pace
l'alma del servo tuo, per cui devoti
t'offrian preghiere e voti. 14

102 [297] TO MESSER GIOVAN BATTISTA CINI ON THE DEATH OF HIS CONSORT, MADONNA MARIA BERARDI

How much chaste love in a fair and wise
woman can prevail and perform; its holy effects,
you can recount to us, CINI, so that the world may
also take it as an example; 4
what place then, wild and shut away from
others, do you not vainly seek, alas, since death
snuffed out the fair light who was for you a bright
sun on this shadowy shore? 8
See how she still burns and sparks for you,
beholds and longs for you alone, and in
that she fulfills her blessed joy; 11
feel how much sweetness she ever instills in
your soul, she who gathers you to her fair breast,
beguiles you, and calls you back.[222] 14

103 [298] ON THE DEATH OF THE GRAND DUKE OF TUSCANY

1.
As much as you rendered the great COSMO
bright and beautiful with human merits,
so much and more you make him now
in your bountiful abode with heavenly ones;
for if in a brief day of life, bountiful Lord, such is your largesse,
what must you be then in sempiternity! 6
2.
As you called to the living breezes,
to our high world, him
who was lying buried in the deepest
center of the dark kingdoms,
so true Lord,
today receive in peace
the soul of your servant, for whom devoutly
we offer you prayers and vows. 14

3.
Con la tua croce gloria,
e con gli scherni onore,
con la tua morte vita, almo Signore,
porgesti al mondo; e trionfo e vittoria
resurgendo da morte; 19
onde miracol tal par che n'apporte
speme di miglior vita;
o possanza infinita,
o vita vera, o spene alta e gioiosa,
ch'entro il sen del gran COSMO ognor riposa. 24
4.
Con l'alma del gran COSMO tuo, che dianzi
depose il mortal velo,
non entrar in giudizio alto del cielo,
Signor, che di pietà pietade avanzi, 28
perché chi fia che inanzi
al tuo cospetto merti aver perdono
se non se quanto è tuo cortese dono? 31

104 [303] IN MORTE DELLA SERENISSIMA GIOVANNA D'AUSTRIA GRAN DUCHESSA DI TOSCANA[225]

Spargete rose e fiori,
angeli santi, e voi, alme beate,
vaghe ghirlande e preziosi odori,
sopra le membra amate, 4
di lei, che sol giovar le piacque tanto,
come il suo nome segna;
ond'or che fatta è degna
del ciel col mezzo dell'oprar suo santo,
pregatela ch'ancora
giovar ne voglia ognora. 10

3.

With your cross, bountiful Lord,
you offered the world glory,
and with the mocking, honor;
with your death, life;
and with resurrection from the dead, triumph and victory;
whence such a miracle seems to bring us
hope of better life,
O infinite power,
O true life, O lofty and joyous hope,
ever resting within the great COSMO's breast.

4.

With the soul of your great COSMO, who has already
laid down his mortal veil,
enter not into high heaven's judgment,
Lord, who mercifully surpasses mercy,
because who shall merit
pardon in your presence
unless it be as much as is your courteous gift?[224]

104 [303] ON THE DEATH OF THE GRAND DUCHESS GIOVANNA D'AUSTRIA, GRAND DUCHESS OF TUSCANY

Scatter roses and flowers,
holy angels, and you, blessed souls,
winsome garlands and precious fragrance,
over the beloved limbs
of her whom it pleased so much only to avail,
as her name betokens,
whence now that she has been made worthy
of heaven by means of her holy works,
pray her that she still
wish ever to avail us.[226]

105 [304][227]

Coronata di gemme alte e lucenti,
l'alma reina nostra
fa di sé degna e gloriosa mostra
fra le beate genti;
ed ecco nuovo e candido angioletto
dir, "Madre mia, v'aspetto
a goder meco, e poich'io cagion solo
fui del vostro martir, del vostro duolo,
egli, che premia ogn'operar perfetto,
quest'aurata corona
per le mie man vi dona."

106 [305][228]

Non scrivo, alma mia stella, perch'io voglia
o pensi alla gran luce tua infinita
giunger punto di lume, ma m'invita
amore, mi sprona mia sfrenata voglia.
Ragion ognora a ragionar m'invoglia,
di te, ch'or godi in ciel beata vita,
dal vero oggetto tuo mai disunita,
u' morte o tempo non fia che ti rispoglia.
Così ponga omai fine al dolor mio
l'alta felicità, la tua memoria,
ch'ognor fa andar altier mio basso stile.
Non è d'acquistar lode il mio disio,
ma s'io parlo di te, alma gentile,
avrò di morte e dello oblio vittoria.

105 [304]

Crowned with gems noble and shining,
our bountiful queen
makes a worthy and glorious display of herself
among the blessed folk, 4
and behold, a new little pure white angel
says, "Mother of mine, I await you
to rejoice with me, and since I alone
was the cause of your martyrdom, of your sorrow,
He who rewards every perfect deed
gives you by my hands
this gilded crown." 11

106 [305]

I do not write, my bountiful star, because I
want to bring a bit of brightness to your infinite light,
or think I can, but love invites me,
my unbridled will spurs me. 4
Reason ever makes me want to speak with reason of
you, who now enjoy in heaven blessed life, never
disjoined from your true object, where death or time
will not be there to despoil you again. 8
Thus may lofty felicity, your memory,
which ever makes my lowly style go proud, now
put an end to my sorrow. 11
It is not my desire to acquire praise, but if I
speak of you, noble soul, I shall have victory over death
and oblivion.[229] 14

107 [306][230]

Se prego umano, amica suso in cielo
anima bella, piega il tuo fattore
che disacerbi il mio grave dolore,
o tronchi 'l debil stame o squarci il velo,
e mi conduchi u' mai caldo né gelo
si sente, né volar di tempo od ore,
ma gioia eterna ed infinito amore,
che nutron l'alme in amoroso zelo,
e se la sua bontà, se i prieghi tuoi,
non mi fan degna di quel santo loco,
in che poss'io sperar trovar pietade?
Pur mi conforto con piacer non poco,
sapendo che su in ciel gli eletti suoi
ardino come lui di caritade.

108 [307][232]

Alma mia bella, che le luci in pace
quel dì chiudesti lieta e senza affanno,
che le tue crudel Parche per mio danno
a troncar il bel fil forno sì audace,
vedi Imeneo con la già spenta face,
che accesa pur dovea tener qualch'anno;
le Grazie e le Virtù smarrite vanno,
e 'l cieco mondo si vergogna e tace,
ché ben sa ch'esso degno unqua non fue
che così largo e pietoso dono
gli desse il ciel di tante tue virtute;
or godi adunque inanzi al sommo trono,
e fa che per tuoi prieghi e grazie sue
gionger io possi al porto di salute.

107 [306]

If human prayer, friendly fair soul up in heaven, incline your creator to make less bitter my heavy sorrow, or cut the weak thread, or rend the veil, 4

and lead me where neither heat nor cold are ever felt, nor flight of time or hours, but eternal joy and infinite love, which nurture souls in amorous zeal, 8

and if His bounty, if your prayers, do not make me worthy of that holy place, where can I hope to find mercy? 11

Yet I take comfort with no little pleasure, knowing that up in heaven His elect ardently burn as He does with charity.[231] 14

108 [307]

Fair my soul, who smiling and without struggle closed your lights in peace the day that your cruel Fates, to my hurt, so brazenly severed the fair thread, 4

see Hymen with already spent torch, which yet he ought have kept a few years lit; the Graces and the Virtues go stricken, and the blind world is shamed and silent, 8

for well it knows that never was it worthy to be given by heaven such an ample and merciful gift of your so many virtues; 11

now, therefore, rejoice before the highest throne, and by your prayers and its graces, help me be able to reach the haven of salvation.[233] 14

109 [308][234]

Occhi miei lassi, rasciugate il pianto,
e mirate la gloria di quell'alma,
che in terra ha posto la terrena salma,
d'altra luce vestita e d'altro manto, 4
altro suono, altro riso ed altro canto
prova or di sue vittorie degna palma,
ch'essendo fatta in ciel gloriosa ed alma,
sol le dà noia il vostro pianger tanto; 8
e più dirò, che se doler si puote
anima santa in quel celeste regno,
essa sola si duol del vostro errore, 11
ché se d'averla il mondo non fu degno,
a che irrigar di pianto ambe le gote,
scemando forse sua pace e suo onore? 14

110 [309][236]

Discolorato è 'l viso in cui Natura
mostrò quanto poteva e ogni favore;
con sua falce seccato ha sì bel fiore
empia morte crudel, pallida e oscura, 4
qual, ben è ver che prima i miglior fura,
invida con l'acerbo suo furore,
e mostra a' rei più tardo il gran valore
dell'aspra spada sua tagliente e dura. 8
Pianga dunque ogni cor gentil la morte
di VITTORIO, che ben fu sì chiamato,
dalla cui chiara vista ogn'un vint'era, 11
e rallegrasi il ciel dov' è volato,
lasciando il mondo in così flebil sorte,
privato della sua virtude altiera. 14

109 [308]

Tired eyes of mine, dry your tears and
behold the glory of the soul that has laid on earth its
earthly remains, dressed in other light and another
mantle, 4
other sound, other laughter, other song,
its victories now win a worthy palm, for now that
it has been made glorious and bountiful in heaven,
only your weeping gives it distress; 8
and more I shall say, that if a holy soul can
be sorrowful in that celestial kingdom, it sorrows
only for your error, 11
for if the world was not worthy of having it,
why water with weeping both your cheeks, perhaps
shrinking its peace and honor?[235] 14

110 [309]

Drained of color is the face in which Nature
showed her power and every favor; wicked cruel
death, pale and dark, has slashed with her scythe
such a fair flower; 4
how true it is that she steals first the best,
envious with her raw furor,
and she shows the wicked later the great force
of her bitter sword, cutting and hard. 8
Let then every gentle heart weep
for VITTORIO, who well carried that name,
for everyone was conquered by the bright sight of him, 11
and let the heaven be gladdened where he has flown,
leaving in such tearful state the world,
deprived of his proud virtue.[237] 14

111 [310]

Fornito ha il corso il gran pianeta ardente
che ne rapporta in ogni parte il giorno,
e chiaro all'alma terra fa ritorno
per nudrir e crear l'umana gente;
sol me ritrova più che mai dolente,
che in triste noti faccio al tempo scorno,
e con l'amico mio pensier soggiorno,
che ogn'or travaglia la sbattuta mente;
con questi occhi di fuor il mio gran male
pianger mi face e mia doglia infinita
e chiamar morte, sol ch'avent'il strale;
con quelli interni miei scorger sua vita
più che mai lieta e in ciel fatta immortale,
e così a pianto e a gioia ogn'or m'invita.

112 [311][239]

Quella infelice son che negra vesta
mi cinge d'ogn'intorno e doglia 'l core,
poiché di questa vita uscito è fore
il mio conforto e me lasciata ha mesta.
Degna è la doglia mia e degna è questa
vesta, d'affetto piena e di dolore,
e degno ei sol ch'io sola porti onore
alla degna memoria ch'in me resta,
e degnissimo è ancor che gli occhi miei,
con calda pioggia mostran vero effetto,
quanto di lagrimar è il cor desio;
e degnissimo è ancor che dal mio petto
escon venti cocenti e caldi omei,
perduto avendo il dolce signor mio.

111 [310]

The great burning planet that brings us back
day in every part has run his course and brightly
makes his return to the bountiful earth to nourish
and create humankind;
me alone he finds more sorrowful than ever,
I who in sad notes make mockery of time and
abide with my friend thought, which ever troubles
my buffeted mind;
with these outer eyes my great hurt makes
me weep for my infinite sorrow and call upon
death, if only it loose its arrow;
with my inner ones, to perceive his life more
blissful than ever and made immortal in heaven,
thus ever it invites me to tears and to joy.[238]

112 [311]

Unhappy woman that I am, a black dress
encircles me all around and sorrow my heart, since
my comfort has departed this life and
has left me downcast.
Worthy is my mourning, and worthy this
dress, filled with affection and sorrow, and worthy
he alone that only I bear honor to the worthy
memory that remains in me,
and most worthy it is, too, that my eyes
with hot tears show true feeling,
as much as the heart desires to weep;
and most worthy it is, too, that from
my breast come forth searing winds and hot sighs
of woe, since I have lost my sweet lord.[240]

113 [312][241]

Quel primo lauro altier che, consacrato
per man del biondo Apollo, felice ogn'ora
è fatto e su nel ciel candida aurora,
seco vivendo in dolce e lieto stato,
quell'altro poi da Sorga al ciel alzato
per bocca del Toscan che 'l mondo onora,
ambi fatti immortai viveno ancora
nell'alto stil leggiadro et onorato.
Si sdegnan ch'una pianta al pianto avvezza
fra sterpi e spin che la circonda e serra
debbia mostrar già mai frutto né fiore;
e poi quei lumi ardenti della terra
non voglian ch'ella giunga a tanta altezza,
ma che gli ceda d'ombra, odore e onore.

114 [313][243]

Frate, che co 'l tuo stil non d'uom mortale
cercat'hai di onorar, di essaltar tanto
un lauro che non merta pregio o vanto
anzi da il primo molto è disuguale,
quel per sè fatto e per altr'immortale
degno è d'eterna lode in ogni canto;
quest'altro, che nudrito è sol di pianto,
nato è a sentir di morte il fiero strale;
ma perch'Amor t'inganna, ti fa dire
cose che fôran forse in dispiacere
a quelle frondi che ornan sacre chiome,
deh, guarda pur, ch'a te questo tuo ardire
non torni in danno, perché hai da sapere
che di quel non ritengo altro che il nome.

113 [312]

That first proud laurel, consecrated by
blond Apollo's hand, is forever made happy and a
bright dawn up in heaven, living with him in sweet
and glad state, 4
that other then raised from Sorgue to heaven
by the mouth of the Tuscan whom the world honors,
both made immortal live still in the lofty style,
delightful and honored. 8
They are indignant that a plant accustomed
to plaint amidst weeds and thorns that surround and
shut her in should ever show fruit or flower; 11
and then those ardent lights of the earth do
not want her to reach such a height, but for her to
yield to them in shadow, odor, and honor.[242] 14

114 [313]

Brother, who with your style not of mortal
man, have tried to honor, to exalt so much a laurel
that does not merit worth or vaunt, nay, it is very
unlike the first; 4
that one, made immortal on its own and by
another, is worthy of eternal praise in every song;
this other, who is nourished only on weeping, was
born to feel the fierce arrow of death; 8
but because Love deceives you, it makes
you say things that might perhaps displease those
boughs that adorn sacred tresses, 11
ah! beware yet, that this daring of yours
not turn out to harm, because you have to know that
I retain nothing of that one other than the name.[244] 14

115 [316][245]

Immortal uom, che con l'ingegno e l'arte,
co'l martel, co'l pennel, co'l grave inchiostro,
eterno fate ogn'ora il nome vostro
andar volando in questa e 'n quella parte,
degno voi sol che le più altiere carte
cantano il gran valor ch'a gli occhi è mostro,
ma 'l raro animo no, ch'altro che d'ostro
o di lauro corona in ciel comparte;
ed è ben giusto che cosa divina
non si possa capir da cori umani,
e sol s'ammirin l'opere al mondo sole,
quelle che 'l spirto han dall'accorte mani,
la fama vostra bella e pellegrina
alzano al cielo e fanvi eguale al sole.

116 [317][247]

Superbi monti, e voi, memorie antiche,
acquedotti, archi, tempi, opre alte e chiare,
trionfal pompe gloriose, care
a tante anime eccelse, fide amiche;
piramidi, colossi, alme fatiche,
trofei, teatri, terme altiere e rare,
colonne istoriate e singolare
spoglie e vittorie di gente inimiche,
voi pur, sagre reliquie, ancor tenete
Roma ne i primi onor, ne i primi seggi,
e bella e vaga la mostrate al mondo;
così benigno cielo e stelle liete
conservi in pace il bel stato giocondo,
come cosa non è che vi pareggi.

115 [316]

Immortal man, who with wit and art, with
hammer, with brush, with weighty ink, ever make
your name go flying eternal in parts near and far, 4
you alone are worthy to have the proudest
pages sing the great worth that is visible to our eyes,
but not your rare soul, to which heaven apportions
more than royal purple or a crown of laurel; 8
and it is just indeed that a divine thing not
be understood by human hearts and that we admire
uniquely works unique in the world; 11
those to which your wise hands have given a spirit
raise your fair and uncommon fame to heaven and make
you a match for the sun.[246] 14

116 [317]

Proud mounts, and you, memories of
antiquity, aqueducts, arches, temples, deeds lofty
and famous; triumphal glorious pomp, dear to so
many surpassing, trusty, kindred souls; 4
pyramids, colossi, bountiful labors, trophies,
theaters, baths proud and rare, singular historiated
columns, spoils and victories over enemy peoples; 8
you, too, sacred relics still sustain Rome in
her first honors, in the first ranks, and you show her
fair and winsome to the world. 11
Thus may kind heaven and happy stars
preserve in peace this fair smiling state, for nothing
there is that rivals it.[248] 14

117 [320] IN MORTE DI FRANCESCO BENNUCCI FIGLIO DOLCISSIMO[249]

Del tuo bel nome e dell'umil tuo manto,
glorioso Francesco, io venni adorno
tosto, che di quassù nel vil soggiorno
del mondo scesi a provar doglia e pianto;
ma quivi a pena dimorai per tanto
spazio che 'l sol corse due volte intorno
al suo bel cerchio, e poi lieto ritorno
qui fei, per viver teco in gioia e canto.
Se i genitori miei vedesser come
or qui mi godo, e come inanzi a Dio
preghi porgendo vo per la lor pace,
so che, deposte le gravose some
del dolor, che gli apporta il partir mio,
gioirebbon di quel ch'or sì gli spiace.

118 [320 = 321] IL MEDESIMO FRANCESCO ALLA MADRE[251]

Quando alla gran bontà del mio signore
piacque chiamarmi a sì beata sorte,
resi lieto il suo debito alla morte,
per qui nodrirmi del celeste amore;
or del carcer terreno uscito fuore,
e delle vie del mondo erranti e torte,
tema non ho che danno unqua m'apporte
il caldo, il gelo o 'l trapassar dell'ore.
Ben veggio il duol ch'ingombra e che possiede
voi, da cui presi la terrena vesta,
e veggio com'al pianto ogn'or v'invita.
Deh, se può in voi quanto l'amor, la fede,
non siate omai più lagrimosa e mesta,
ch'or ha principio in me l'eterna vita.

117 [320] ON THE DEATH OF FRANCESCO BENNUCCIO, SWEETEST SON

Your fair name, glorious Francis, and your
humble mantle early adorned me, who descended
from up here to experience grief and tears in the
world's base sojourn, 4
but there I dwelt barely for the span of the
sun coursing twice around its fair circle, and
then I made a happy return here to live with you
in joy and song. 8
If my parents saw how I now rejoice and
how I go before God offering prayers for their
peace, 11
I know that, setting down the heavy
burdens of sorrow my departure brings them,
they would rejoice for what now displeases them so.[250] 14

118 [320 = 321] THE SAME FRANCESCO TO HIS MOTHER

When it pleased the great bounty of my Lord
to call me to such blessed destiny, I rendered
blissful his debt to death to nourish myself here with
celestial love; 4
now that I have come forth from the earthly
prison, and from the pathways of the world, errant
and twisted, I have no fear of ever being harmed
by heat, cold, or the passing of the hours. 8
Well I see the sorrow that encumbers and
possesses you, from whom I took my earthly
vestment, and I see how it ever invites you to weep. 11
Pray, if faith can work as strongly in you as
love, be no longer tearful and downcast, for here begins
in me my eternal life.[252] 14

119 [322] IN MORTE DI PAPA GREGORIO XIII[253]

Lasciato il manto, ambe le chiavi e 'l regno,
ond'io sì chiaro andai fra tanti eroi,
oggi, Signor, divoto a' piedi tuoi,
qual servo umil, qual peccator io vegno;
e se mancai nel tuo d'alto onor degno
commesso offizio, mercè chieggio, poi
ch'alla mortal condizion di noi
non va co'l buon voler l'opra ad un segno.
Io ben cercai d'ogni più estrema parte
del mondo addurre al tuo romano ovile
Indiana greggia e farlo ampio e perfetto.
Mandagli or tu 'n Pastor che 'l mio difetto
con maggior senno adempia e maggior arte,
e sia la terra tutta al ciel simile.

120 [327] EGLOGA TERZA[255]

Sopra un fiorito e dilettoso colle
ch'Arno vagheggia, e le campagne intorno
fertili e verdi, che colmando vanno
di speme il petto a gli stanchi cultori,
siede altero edificio, e con tal'arte
fatto e da mano industriosa tanto,
ch'invidia face non pur ivi a quanti
risplendon per ingegno e per ricchezza,
ma a quei, per cui Flora si vanta e pregia.
Né minor già, né men gradito albergo
si conveniva a sì gentile e saggio
pastor, di cui non hanno i toschi campi
né più cortese già, né più felice,
ALFEO, che per suo merto e per destino
ne divenne ha gran tempo possessore;
e seco la sua fida GALATEA,
ch'ogn'altra oggi non par trapassa e vince
caste donne, ma dee celesti e sante,
di beltà, di valor chiaro e sublime;
a cui fatto ha benigno amico cielo
copia di dolce e graziosa prole,
conforme apunto all'alta lor fortuna.

Ivi il secondo dì del Re de' Mesi,
più de gli altri fiorito e più festoso,
in compagnia di molt'altri pastori—
chi sacrò all'alto e sempiterno Giove,
impetrando per noi venia e salute,
chi al guerreggiante e minaccioso Marte,
per dare al mondo poi tranquilla Pace;
quei di Pan, quei di Bacco sacerdoti
il viver ministrando a noi mortali—
si ritrovar due valorosi e saggi
pastor, l'un caro amico al biondo Apollo,
TIRSI gentil, che con sue dolci note
fa quando corre più veloce al mare
Arno arrestare ad ascoltarlo intento;
l'altro di marmo una persona viva
per far talor, talora in bronzo eterno,
mostrando quanto l'Arte la Natura
imitar possa, FIDIA vien nomato.
E loro in mezzo pastorella incolta
all'ultimo congiunta in stretto e santo
nodo d'ogn'altra libertà più caro;
che per sprezzar quant'ha[n] le donne in pregio
ogni cosa mortal tenendo a vile,
sol'è intenta a seguir d'Apollo l'orme,
forse quant'ei seguio qua giù per terra
l'amata sua, da cui prend ella il nome.
Quinci sopra fiorito e verde prato
assisi tutti, rimirando gìano
con vaghezza e stupor più che mai intenti,
chi i colti campi, chi l'ombrose e folte
selve, chi gl'alti magisteri eletti,
chi 'l pian, chi 'l monte, e chi l'altere piante
di lauri, d'elci, d'olmi e di ginepri,
ch'arditi inverso il ciel s'ergeano in alto;
altri l'aer dolcissimo e benigno
lodando gìa, benedicendo Febo,
ch'a quello inspira sì tranquilla vita;
altri in mirar l'alto e sacrato tempio,
che tant'alme in sè chiude elette e pure,
ch'in silenzio parole accorte e saggie
spiegano al sommo re dell'universo.

There on the second day of the King of Months,
more flowery and more festive than the others,
in the company of many other shepherds,
some who worshiped Jove high and sempiternal,
praying he pardon and save us,
some the warlike and menacing Mars
to give the world then tranquil peace,
as the priests of Pan and Bacchus
went about ministering to our mortal lives,
two worthy and wise shepherds met,
one a dear friend to blond Apollo,
noble TIRSI, who with his sweet notes
makes Arno stop, intent on listening to him
where he flows most swiftly to the sea;
the other called FIDIA for showing
how Art can imitate Nature,
sometimes by making a living person in marble,
sometimes in eternal bronze;
and between the two of them, an unlearned shepherdess,
conjoined to the latter in a tight and holy
knot dearer than any freedom,
who for disdaining as much as women prize,
holds all mortal things vile,
no less intent on following Apollo's footsteps,
perhaps, than he was to follow down here on earth
his beloved, from whom she takes her name.
There, upon a flowery and green meadow,
they all sat gazing about
with pleasure and amazement, never more intently,
some the cultivated fields, some the shady and thick forests,
some the privileged lofty peaks,
some the plane, some the mount, and some the proud plants
of laurel, ilex, oak, and juniper
that daringly thrust upward toward heaven;
others had praise for the air, sweet
and benevolent, blessing Phoebus
who inspires it to such tranquil life;
others admired the tall and consecrated temple
that encloses within so many souls, chosen and pure,
who in silence unfold words deep and wise
to the consummate king of the universe.

E 'n questa DAFNE, che d'ardente brama
d'alzar cantando tutta dentro ardea,
sì come meglio le dettasse Apollo,
con l'umil sua zampogna il bel paese
e 'l dolce loco che nell'alma ha impresso,
che sì come le rose ogn'altro fiore
vincono, questo di virtute avvanza
ogn'altro di bellezza e di bontate,
onde gl'antichi e memorandi vati
che dell'aria, dell'erbe e delle stelle
conosceano il valore insieme uniti,
e di comun consentimento tutti
volser che 'l nome suo fusse Le ROSE.
La Pastorella dunque incominciando
a dar principio all'umil canto suo,
sì come il cor avea colmo di gioia
così nel volto si mostrò gioconda:

"Perch'a mille famose altere fronti
s'intessino ghirlande, e a mille e mille,
spirti amorosi e conti,
si rinfreschin l'ardenti lor faville,
verdi piante novelle
ch'incendeste già tanto
lui ch'incende di sè le vaghe stelle,
spargete in queste e 'n quelle
parti i be' rami e l'odor sacro e santo.

E voi tranquille di Minerva insegna,
di pace annunzio e di gioconda vita,
frondi all'onesta e degna
coppia che ben' oprando al ciel n'invita,
infondete nel core
vostre gioie più elette,
sì che quai son quest'edre a tutte l'hore,
od in nodo maggiore,
stian sì bell'alme in un congiunte e strette.

Scendi, Venere bella, alla dolce ombra
del tuo sacro arbocel, deh, scendi omai;
e 'l terso oro ch'adombra
il sol, qual ora è più cinto di rai,

And then DAFNE, burning inside
with an ardent desire to stand
and, as Apollo best dictated to her,
to sing to her humble bagpipes, of the fair country
and the sweet place impressed in her soul,
that just as roses conquer every other flower,
so this spot surpasses all others in power,
beauty, and bounty, whence those ancient and
memorable bards of yore
who knew the combined properties
of the air, plants, and stars,
by common consensus all
wanted its name to be "The Roses."
The shepherdess thus began
to sing her humble song,
her heart brimming with joy
that shone in the jocundity of her face:
"O green young plants,
you who once inflamed him who
spreads his flame to the loving stars,
scatter in parts near and far
your fair boughs and your sacred, holy scent
so that we may weave garlands
for a thousand famous proud brows,
and bring cooling comfort for their sparks of ardor
to thousands upon thousands of amorous, luminous spirits.
And you, tranquil ensign of Minerva,
herald of peace and happy life,
branching over the honest and worthy couple
whose good deeds invite us to heaven,
infuse in our hearts
your most precious joys
so that, as the ivy ever twines here,
or in a greater knot,
close souls so fair may stay conjoined as one.
Descend, fair Venus, to the sweet shade
of your sacred sapling; pray, descend now;
and encircle with fresh roses
the pure gold that darkens

cingi di fresche rose,
or che tra l'erbe e i fiori
hanno i tuoi figli ardenti faci ascose
ch'alle celesti cose
infiammeranno i più leggiadri cori.
In queste ombrose valli e 'n queste selve,
gl'audaci veltri tuoi predando vanno
le timidette belve;
che 'n contra lor diffesa altra non hanno;
dunque, casta Diana,
muovi tua amica schiera,
quinci Ateon, quinci empia voglia insana
non è, ma saggia umana
gente e desir d'eterna gloria e vera.
Qui dove è l'aer più sereno e dove
l'ora più fresca, e son più chiare l'acque,
alme figlie di Giove,
a cui la terra un tempo abitar piaque,
or par che 'l ferro nostro
simil'è all'oro antico,
di virtute e d'onor tanto s'è mostro;
venite, e seggio vostro
fate il bel fonte e 'l dolce colle aprico.
Vago lume del ciel, se in variando
i tempi e l'ore, non variasti unquanco
il bel disio, ch'amando
ti fe in Tessaglia sì di correr stanco,
qui dove la tua fronde
gioia apporta e salute,
scendi e le piaghe tue sana profonde,
e con note gioconde
fa noto altrui l'immensa lor virtute.
I campi sicilian Cerere antica,
e 'l giovane Lico lasciar consente
sua bella NISA amica,
e 'n questo Monte dimorar sovente;
PAN vedesi e POMONA
gir spazziando intorno;
ogni piano, ogni colle s'abbandona
così secondo suona
l'aer ch'abbraccia questo bel soggiorno.

the sun to shadow, even when as now
it is most ringed with rays, now that your sons
have hidden amidst the grass and flowers,
burning torches that will inflame
the most comely hearts to matters celestial.
 In these shaded valleys and in these woods,
your daring hounds go preying
upon the timid little wild creatures
who have no other defense;
therefore, chaste Diana,
come with your friendly troop;
here there is no Actaeon, no wicked mad desire,
but wise human folk
and a desire for glory eternal and true.
 Here where the air is most serene
and the hour coolest and where the waters are clearest,
come, bountiful daughters of Jove,
whom once it pleased to inhabit the earth
now our iron
seems like the gold of yore,
so much virtue and honor has it shown;
come, and make the fair fountain
and the sweet open hillside your seat.
 Loving light of heaven, if you changed
the time and hours while never once changing
the fair desire that made you,
in love, so tire from running in Thessaly,
here where your branch
brings joy and strength,
descend and heal your deep wounds,
and make known to all
with happy notes the laurel's immense power.
 The Sicilian fields let ancient
Ceres leave and linger
often on this mount;
so, too, Lico lets his fair friend NISA come;
PAN and POMONA
can be seen roaming about;
plains and hills are everywhere emptied
when the air resounds
that embraces this fair dwelling.

Deh semplicetta mia, taci ch'io sento
nuovo et alto concento
apparecchiarsi; ond'io t'ascondo e 'nvolo."
Poscia il nobile ALFEO, tosto finito
ch'ell'ebbe, sciolse sì soavemente
la lingua al suon della sua altera cetra,
con cui fermato avea più volte il volo
de' vaghi augelli e delle fere il corso,
"All'acqua sagra del novello fonte
ch'a chi ne gusta infonde
rime liete e gioconde,
ascoltate, pastor del vago monte
che di rose ha la fronte,
gregge già mai né fera
non s'avvicini a turbar sua chiarezza;
che non Pallade pur con la sua schiera,
ma di venirci è avvezza
Diana casta spesso;
e chi le giugne appresso
mentre si bagna, o chi a quest'ombre dorme
cangiar fa in mille disusate forme."
Sì disse; e TIRSI, che sedea all'incontro,
già vedendol tacer lento non fue
quanto pensato avea cantando dire;
mostrando ben che lungamente avvezzo
fosse in Parnaso, e d'Helicona al fonte
fin dalle fasce poi beuto havesse.
"Fuor della pura e chiara
tranquilla Greve, uscite liete e pronte,
muschiose Ninfe, e su correndo a gara
questo salite vago altero monte,
ove tra l'erba e i fiori
in compagnia di mille almi pastori,
e mille accorte e belle
leggiadre pastorelle,
siede la lor reina, anzi lor dea
e bella e casta e saggia, GALATEA,
co'l suo via più d'ogni'altro avventuroso
felice sposo, Alfeo dotto e gentile;
e con sembiante umile

Pray, my simple little one, be still,
for I feel a new and lofty harmony
in the making, and so I hide you and put you away.
Then noble ALFEO, as soon as
she had finished, loosened his tongue
so sweetly to the sound of his proud lyre,
with which he had many a time halted
loving birds in flight and wild beasts on the run:
"At the sacred water of the fresh font
that infuses whoever tastes it
with rhymes glad and gay,
listen, shepherds of the lovesome mount
whose brow the roses cover,
let never herd nor beast
approach to disturb its purity;
for not only Pallas with her troop
is wont to come,
but often chaste Diana,
and whoever nears her
while she bathes, or whoever sleeps in these shadows,
she changes into a thousand unaccustomed forms."
Thus he spoke; and TIRSI, sitting opposite,
who already saw that he had fallen silent,
was not slow to say in song
what he had been thinking,
showing that he was indeed long accustomed to Parnassus
and had been drinking since infancy at Helicon's font.
"Come forth, glad and quick,
from the pure and clear and tranquil Greve,
musky nymphs, and race each other
up the slopes of this tall, lovesome mount,
where amidst grass and flowers,
accompanied by a thousand bountiful shepherds
and a thousand wise and fair
and blithe shepherdesses,
sits their queen, nay, their goddess
fair and chaste and wise, GALATEA,
with her happy spouse, far more fortunate than any other,
the learned and noble Alfeo.
And with humble mien,

mille e mille vezzose
cogliete ardenti rose,
e di mille colori,
mille fioretti di soavi odori;
e sopra lor con disusata foggia
fate arder spargendo lenta pioggia.
Poscia con riverenza
tiratevi da parte e rimirate
i balli e le sonate
che fatte sono all'alta lor presenza
da ninfe e da pastor soggetti loro
d'un faggio all'ombra, o d'un fronzuto alloro:
ma servando il decoro
come voi poi vedete
tacer ogn'un, cantando ardite e liete
mostrate il vostro immenso alto valore,
facendo a voi e a lor perpetuo onore;
onde vostra mercè gloria maggiore
arà la Greve e fregio un dì più bello
che non ha l'Arno o 'l Tebro suo fratello."
Poi perchè già dalla sinistra parte
Apollo si vedea scendere in fretta,
per tuffar la sua chiara fronte altera
nel profondo Ocean sdegnoso forse,
d'esser vinto quaggiù da mortal voce;
nel dolce albergo, in pie' rittosi ogn'uno,
movendo il passo dolcemente entraro.
Quel Sol che sol n'alluma e sol n'avviva
quando ver noi risplende,
or ch'altro clima di sé vago incende,
e di vita e del dì ne spoglia e priva.
Deh, chiara luce viva,
e deh, nostro vital chiaro splendore,
del tuo bell'Arno onore,
a noi riedi, a noi vieni, e da noi sgombra
quest'atra e mortal'ombra.

gather thousands upon thousands
of pretty flaming roses
and a thousand sweet-scented
blossoms of a thousand colors;
and with unaccustomed display,
make fire by scattering them in a shower.
Then reverently
step aside and behold
the dances and the music
played in their lofty presence
by the nymphs and shepherds who are their subjects,
under the shade of an oak or of a leafy laurel.
But in keeping with decorum,
when you see each one then
fall silent, show your immense lofty worth
by singing bold and blithe,
bringing yourselves and them honor perpetual.
For this, thanks to you, the Greve
will have greater glory and be one day more comely
than the Arno or Tiber, his brother."
    Then since they saw Apollo,
already fast descending on the left side,
dip his bright proud brow deep in the Ocean,
disdainful perhaps because
he had been bested down here by mortal voice,
each of them arose, heading back
with sweet step to their sweet dwelling place.
    That Sun that alone brings us
light and life when it shines our way,
now that it kindles another clime to love it,
despoils and deprives us of life and day.
Pray, bright living light,
and pray, bright vital splendor of ours,
the honor of your fair Arno,
make your way back to us, come to us, and dispel from us
this gloomy and mortal shadow.[256]

SELECTIONS FROM *RIME SPIRITUALI DI MADONNA LAURA BATTIFERRA DEGLI AMMANNATI*, PART 2

To the Most Illustrious and Most Excellent Signora, Ever My Most Revered Patron, Signora Vittoria Farnese della Rovere, Duchess of Urbino[257]

Laura Battiferra degli Ammannati

Perhaps I shall be reproached, Most Illustrious and Most Excellent Lady, by all those who may perchance know how I, who have always for the most part looked to human letters,[258] should now have dared to translate David's Penitential Psalms,[259] so divine and mysterious, without having expert knowledge of the Holy Scriptures, especially since he had the authority of the blessed Jerome,[260] and anyone is open to criticism who, after starting from such low and fragile studies might presume at present to treat of high and eternal ones. Yet why should I not be, if not praised, surely excused, for wanting to dwell no longer with the poets and with the philosophers (even though we find in their books no end of things that are useful and helpful for good living), because I wished with sincerity of heart to begin asking for grace from the Lord God with the same prayers as the most holy Hebrew poet?[261] I wanted him to press down upon me with his ardent spirit so that, through its mediation, I might be worthy of treating his divine sciences and speaking in his holy language. If people will be willing to judge me with a merciful eye and with reason, they cannot fail to commend my intention, which aims only to arm myself against my soul's enemies with those weapons that the powerful King David used for his protection. As we can see, neither Achilles in Homer[262] nor Aeneas in Virgil[263] has armor like that of this most prudent warrior, who with the helmet of salvation, with the shield of faith, and with the sword of the spirit, which is the word of God,[264] always accomplished his so many just and honored victories. For these reasons, therefore, I have set out to translate his penitential songs into Tuscan rhymes, with no other purpose than to pray that it please the Divine Bounty to support this hand and open these lips that have so greatly offended it, so that both may begin to accustom themselves to treating deeds suitable for celebrating His glory and exaltedness, and as Paul so well puts it, to give intelligence to the heart so that both accord in unison with the song and make it acceptable to Him. True enough, since this effort of mine is born of a pure and sincere desire, if the Lord God were to make me worthy for a soul so famous and stainless as Your Most Illustrious Excellency's to take some measure of consolation and happiness from it, that would double my happiness, and I should pay little heed to what others might think of it. And so with this hope, I have wanted to make a humble gift of it to Your Excellency, considering that you should also find it in some measure acceptable because a most devoted and most affectionate servant of yours gave birth to it. And if this is so, as I hope and certainly desire, it shall all be to the increase of Your Excellency's favor toward me, to whom with all reverence I humbly commend myself.

From Florence, on this day the 26th of March, 1564[265]

SONETTI SPIRITUALI DELLA MEDESIMA AUTRICE[266]

1 [3]

Ecco, Signore, e n'è ben tempo omai,
ch'a te rivolgo il mio cangiato stile;
non lo spregiar, s'a le tue orecchie umile
priego divoto e pio giunse giamai. 4
Quanto pur dianzi, ahi lassa, invan cercai
farmi a' miglior, ma sol di fuor simile,
quanto pregio stimai terreno e vile,
tanto il celeste e te, mio Dio, spregiai. 8
Ecc'or che tua pietà quest'alma ha desto,
alto Signore, al suo maggior bisogno,
onde 'l suo fallo apertamente vede, 11
ch'a te pentita ognor priega mercede,
perchè con lungo duol è manifesto
che quanto piace al mondo è breve sogno. 14

2 [4][268]

Spirto amoroso e santo, che scendesti
in forma d'infocate lingue ardenti
dal ciel, sopra l'oscure e fredde menti
di lor da cui lodata esser volesti, 4
scendi sopra la mia, che tanto questi
teneri affetti, oimè, troppo possenti,
d'atro gelo hanno cinta, e omai consenti
ch'io di te canti ed altri a cantar desti. 8
Apre, Signor, le labbra mie, che tanto
son chiuse, a dir di te, de gl'onor tuoi,
quanto aperte in lodar mortal valore, 11
sì ch'in versi toscani il latin canto
possa tradur, ch'a te co' figli suoi
l'alma sposa ti porge a tutte l'ore. 14

SPIRITUAL SONNETS BY THE SAME AUTHOR[266]

1 [3]

Behold, Lord—and high time it is by now—I
address to you my altered style; disdain it not, if
ever there reached your ears a humble prayer,
devout and pious. 4

How much before, alas, I sought in vain to
make myself like the best, but only with an outer
resemblance; as much as I esteemed earthly and
base reward, so much I disdained the heavenly and you, my God. 8

Behold, Lord above, now that your pity has
awakened this soul to its greater need, whence it
openly sees its fault, 11

repentant it prays ever for your mercy, since
with long sorrow it is manifest that whatever
pleases in the world is a brief dream.[267] 14

2 [4]

Loving and holy spirit, who descended in the
form of fiery burning tongues from heaven over the
dark and cold minds of those by whom you wished
to be praised, 4

descend over mine, which these tender
affections, too strong, have so long encircled, alas!
with black frost, and grant now that I sing of you
and awaken others to sing. 8

Open, Lord, my lips, which are as closed to
speaking of you, of your honors, as they are open in
praising mortal worth, 11

so that I may translate into Tuscan verses
the Latin song that your nurturing bride and her
children offer to you at all the hours.[269] 14

3 [5][270] THE SEVEN PENITENTIAL PSALMS BY THE MOST HOLY PROPHET DAVID, TRANSLATED INTO THE FLORENTINE LANGUAGE BY MADONNA LAURA BATTIFERRI DEGLI AMMANNATI, WITH A DISCUSSION OF EACH ONE COMPOSED BY THE SAME LADY

SUBJECT OF THE FIRST PENITENTIAL PSALM

To the Most Reverend and Illustrious Lady, Sister Faustina Vitelli, Most Worthy Nun in the Nunnery of the Murate in Florence: "*Domine ne in furore tuo arguas me.*"

This most devout and efficacious Psalm, which Church custom has instituted first of the Seven Penitentials, was made by the most holy prophet David when he was oppressed by grave infirmity, and since that brought him an awareness of his sins, fearing lest he might die, he begs almighty God not to judge him in his wrath and anger, but to want through His compassion to heal him and console his afflicted and troubled soul, letting him continue to live in order to make due penance for the errors he has committed in order not to be forced by dying to go to infernal sufferings, in a place where there is no one to praise Him and acknowledge His most glorious name. And to make his prayers more answerable, he showed the Lord his great repentance and his sorrow by means of infinite tears, and he continuously watered his downcast face and flooded his bed with them every night. In the end, when he saw that his humble orison had been answered and that he had recovered his lost health, he turned with great joy to the infinite number of his enemies, and to counter those who were expecting his death from one hour to the next, he said how his most merciful Lord had kindly received the most ardent affection in his prayers and because of that they should be ashamed now of the deceptions and the many iniquities they had committed against him and they should instantly flee him confounded and cease tormenting him. To these most holy words, most noble lady, I too had recourse, bound in so many infirmities of body and soul, and in imitation of David, wholly sorrowful and downcast, I have rendered them in our language, wanting to develop them into a weeping little songlet, as far as my small knowledge and my great contrition and humility have been able to dictate to me, hoping that divine mercy, by its own bounty, without any merit on my part, will forgive me for the errors I have committed and free me from such long afflictions, especially if through your most chaste mouth, so intent on praising and honoring his Majesty, it be carried into His most compassionate presence. This is the main reason that induces me to send it to you, and at the same time to beg you to remember me continuously in your orisons, in which I place the greatest hope. And I commend myself to Your Most Illustrious Reverence.

SALMO SESTO, E PRIMO DE' PENITENTIALI

Non voler con furore
riprendermi, Signore,
ne' miei commessi falli alfin punire
nell'ira tua con grave aspro martire.
Mercè, Signor, mercede,
il cor sempre ti chiede,
e perch'io sono infermo e frali ho l'ossa,
me sana e dona lor vigore e possa.
Afflitta è grandmente
quest'anima dolente,
ma tu, Signore, a por fine a' miei guai,
e all'ira tua fin quanto, ohimè, starai?
A me volgiti e togli
l'alma di tanti scogli,
almo Signore, e me per tua bontade
salva per grazia tua, per tua pietade.
Chi estinto e morto giace,
di te, Signor verace,
aver non può memoria, e nell'inferno
chi sia che ti confessi e chiami eterno?
Amaramente ho pianto,
e sospirar vo tanto
ciascuna notte, fin ch'un ampio rio
di tiepid'onde irrighi il letto mio.
Di lor virtù visiva
già 'l lungo pianto priva
quest'afflitt'occhi, e già di neve il crine
s'è fatto pur fra i miei nimici al fine.
Da me tutti partite,
voi ch'ogni iniqua lite
oprate contra me, poi che esaudito
ha 'l Signore il mio pianto e quel gradito.
I miei prieghi devoti
a Dio graditi e noti
pur sono stati, e ricevute sono
le prece mie dal suo celeste trono.
Omai tutta la schiera
empia, crudele e fera

SIXTH PSALM AND FIRST OF THE PENITENTIALS

Wish not, Lord, to reproach me with furor;
neither finally in your wrath
to punish me with harsh, heavy suffering
for errors I have committed.
Have mercy, Lord, mercy
my heart ever asks of you,
and because I am infirm and my bones
are frail, heal me and give them vigor and power.
Greatly afflicted is
this sorrowing soul,
but you, Lord, how long, alas, will you wait
to put an end to my woes and to your wrath?
Turn to me and take
my soul from so many shoals,
nurturing Lord, and by your bounty
save me, by your grace, by your pity.
He who lies snuffed out and dead
cannot have memory
of you, true Lord, and who is there in hell
to acknowledge and call you eternal?
Bitterly I have wept,
and every night I so sigh
until warm waves in a wide river
water my bed.
Long weeping has already deprived
these afflicted eyes of their visual strength,
and my hair has already turned to snow,
even finally among my enemies.
Depart from me,
all you who stir up iniquitous quarrels
against me, since the Lord has answered
my weeping and welcomed it.
My devout prayers
have been welcomed and known to God,
and my pleas received
upon his celestial throne.
Let now all the wicked troop
of my enemies, cruel and wild,

de' miei nemici di vergogna tinta
si mostri, e per gran duol turbata e vinta. 40

Sian di rossor conspersi
questi perversi, e pien d'invidia e scorno,
confusi indietro omai faccian ritorno. 43

4 [23][271]

Verace Apollo, a cui ben vero amore
impiagò 'l fianco di pietoso strale,
ed a prender fra noi forma mortale
già ti costrinse non mortale ardore; 4
ecco colei, lo cui gelato core
de l'onesto arder tuo non calse o cale,
l'errante Dafne, ch'ognor fugge quale
notturno augello il tuo divin splendore; 8
eccol'al fine in duro tronco volta,
e tu pur l'ami e segui, e cerchi ornare
tuo santo crin di sua negletta fronde. 11
O grand'amore, o pietà rara e molta
chi ti fugge seguir, chi t'odia amare,
amar chi tante frodi in sè nasconde. 14

5 [26][273]

Come chi di mortal certo periglio
si vede oppresso, sbigottito e smorto,
in tempestoso mar lungi dal porto,
alza divoto a Dio la mente e 'l ciglio, 4
e se ridotto mai dal grave esiglio
l'ha 'l ciel (poi che non fu da l'onde sorto)
al caro albergo, più che prima accorto,
cerca del viver suo nuovo consiglio; 8
sì nel fallace mar del mondo infido,
fra l'onde incerte de' pensier non saggi,
da Dio lontana, e con la morte appresso, 11
mi truovo, ahi lassa, e giorno e notte grido,
"Signor, deh, drizza i miei torti viaggi,"
ma 'l lito ancor veder non m'è permesso. 14

color with shame,
by great sorrow be troubled and vanquished. 40

May these perverse be immersed in red,
and let them go back whence they came,
confounded in envy and scorn. 43

4 [23]

Truthful Apollo, whose side true love
wounded with a compassionate arrow and whom
ardor not mortal once constrained to take among us
mortal form, 4
behold her, whose frozen heart did not
nor does care for your honest ardor, errant Dafne, who
keeps fleeing your divine splendor like a nocturnal
bird; 8
behold her finally turned into a hard trunk;
yet still you love and pursue her and seek to adorn
your holy locks with her neglected bough. 11
O great love, compassion rare and generous,
to pursue her who flees you, to love her who hates
you, to love one who hides in herself so many
deceits.[272] 14

5 [26]

As a man, dismayed and wan, who sees
himself oppressed by certain mortal danger, far
from port in a stormy sea, raises devout to God his
mind and brow, 4
and if heaven ever restored him (since the
waves did not yield him up) from that heavy exile to
his dear hostel, he seeks new counsel in his living,
more careful than before; 8
so in the fallacious sea of the faithless
world, amidst uncertain waves of unwise thoughts,
far from God and with death near, 11
I find myself, alas! and day and night I cry
out, "Lord, pray, straighten my twisted travels," but
I am not yet permitted to see the shore.[274] 14

6 [31][275]

Quando nell'ocean l'altera fronte
inchina il sole, e 'l nostro mondo imbruna,
e dal più basso ciel la fredda luna
sormonta e fa d'argento ogn'alto monte, 4
partesi il buon pastor dal chiaro fonte,
e la sua gregge alla sua mandra aduna,
e 'l stanco pellegrin raccoglie in una
le forze stanche al suo voler mal pronte; 8
ed io che veggio avvicinar la notte,
e volar l'ore e i giorni, gli anni e i lustri,
e già dal quinto indietro mi rivolgo, 11
il passo affretto, e prima che s'annotte,
lo stuol de' pensier miei sparsi raccolgo,
per fargli in cielo eternamente illustri. 14

7 [34][277]

Oggi Signor, che nel trentesimo anno
entro, del viver mio fallace e corto,
e ch'omai tempo è da ritrarsi in porto,
m'accorgo pur con mio gravoso danno; 4
onde le false duci, ch'ogn'or hanno
di cieco mare al peggior fondo scorto,
come del van disio ch'entro il cor porto,
ch'errar m'ha fatto d'uno in altro affanno, 8
se ben tardi, abbandono e sgombro il seno,
e te, Signor, te eterna requie e vita,
te fida scorta, e te mia gloria vera, 11
bramo, cerco, sospiro, e l'infinita
tua grazia cheggio, e pur perch'io non pera
ti miro in croce di clemenza pieno. 14

6 [31]

When into the ocean the sun bends his proud brow, and our world darkens, and from the lowest heaven the cold moon surmounts and silvers every lofty mountain, 4

the good shepherd departs from the clear fountain and gathers his herd into its flock and the tired pilgrim collects into one his tired powers, scarce able to answer his will; 8

and I, who see the night draw near and the hours and days fly, the years and the lustrums, and look back already from the fifth, 11

I hasten my step, and before night falls, collect the scattered multitude of my thoughts to make them eternally illustrious in heaven.[276] 14

7 [34]

Today, Lord, as I enter my thirtieth year, I realize, though hurtful weight to me, that my life is fallacious and short and that by now it is time to withdraw into port, 4

so I am abandoning the false guides that have only led over the blind sea to the worst depth, so too the vain desire I carry in my heart, which has made me stumble from one struggle to the next, 8

and albeit late, I unburden my breast, and you, Lord, you eternal rest and life, you trusted guide and you my true glory, 11

I yearn for, seek for, sigh for, and I ask your infinite grace; and that I yet not perish, I behold you on the cross in all your clemency.[278] 14

8 [37] DELLA COMPAGNIA DI GIESU[279]

Sotto l'invitta e militante insegna
del sangue di Gesù bagnata e tinta,
fra nobil gente ad alte imprese accinta,
loco non ave anima vile e 'ndegna, 4
chè quel Trionfator, che nel ciel regna,
ch'ebbe ogn' adversa forza e sparsa e vinta,
lasciando la sua vita in croce estinta,
guerra e morte soffrir sempre n'insegna; 8
onde seguaci vuol di fede armati,
voglie d'ardente caritade accese,
pensier rivolti a lui da speme alzati, 11
e che la guerra occulta e la palese
vinta, nel ciel di gloria incoronati
siano alla fin dalla sua man cortese. 14

9 [41]

Questo foco sì ardente e questa fiamma,
ch'esce del petto tuo, dolce Signore,
avvampa così il mio d'acceso ardore
ch'ognor via più m'infoca e più m'infiamma; 4
e questo ferro, che la destra mamma
tua aperse tutta ed indi passò al core,
trapassa tanto il mio dentro e di fuore
che per dolcezza manco a dramma a dramma; 8
m'impiagan tutta queste piaghe sante,
questa corona mi trafigge e punge,
e teco ogn'or m'inchiodan questi chiodi, 11
possente Amor, ch'al sempiterno Amante
l'anime lega con sì stretti nodi,
e mai per tempo alcun non le disgiunge. 14

8 [37] ON THE SOCIETY OF JESUS

Beneath the unvanquished and militant
ensign bathed and dyed in the blood of Jesus,
among noble people bent on high tasks, there is no
place for a base and unworthy soul; 4
for that Triumphant One, who reigns in
heaven and who scattered and conquered every
adverse force, leaving His life snuffed out on the
cross, teaches us always to suffer war and death; 8
whence followers He wants armed with
faith, wills kindled with ardent charity, thoughts
turned to Him lifted by hope; 11
and when the occult and open war is won,
may they be crowned in the end with glory in
heaven by His courteous hand.[280] 14

9 [41]

This fire so ardent and this flame that comes
forth from your breast, sweet Lord, so blazes in
mine with kindled ardor that it ever more and more
ignites and inflames me; 4
and this iron, which opened your right
breast, and thence passed into your heart, so
passes through mine within and without that it has
failed for sweetness dram by dram; 8
wholly I am wounded by these holy
wounds, this crown transfixes and pierces me, and
ever with you these nails nail me, 11
mighty Love, who bind souls to the
sempiternal Lover with such tight knots and
never at any time disjoin them.[281] 14

10 [42][282]

Questa è la requie mia, quest'è 'l riposo,
ov'io per sempre d'abitar m'eleggo;
qui tutti gli error miei purgo e correggo,
ed ogni mio pensier depongo e poso;
dolce del mio Signor petto amoroso,
in te sì come in chiaro specchio veggo
la mia salute, e per te a pien posseggo
quel che in parte bramar per me non oso;
e tu, profonda cicatrice aperta,
perchè sei tu così, se non perch'io
in te entri, in te alberghi e 'n te m'asconda?
O Paradiso mio, per cui sì certa
pace ritrovo! in te gl'angeli e Dio
contemplo, e per te il cor di gioia abonda.

11 [46][283]

Stringendo al petto la vermiglia e bella
croce di gloria e di trionfo segno,
ti consecrasti al Re del sommo Regno,
in fida sposa ed in umile ancella,
ove, quantunque chiusa in breve cella,
t'inalzi al ciel fuor d'ogn'uman ritegno,
ed ascolti in silenzio accorto e degno
celeste canto, angelica favella;
vergine saggia, che spregiando queste
fallaci pompe, le superne e vere
vagheggi ed ami, e di lor vaga sei.
Prega per me, che tante adre tempeste,
non mi vietino il porto al fin vedere,
dove tu più sicura arrivar dei.

10 [42]

This is my rest, this is the repose where I
choose forever to dwell; here all my errors I purge
and correct, and I depose and set down my every
worry; 4

sweet amorous breast of my Lord, in you as
in a clear mirror I see my salvation, and through
you I fully possess that which I dare not crave in
part by myself; 8

and you, deep open wound, why are you that
way, if not so that I might enter into you, shelter in
you, and hide in you? 11

O my paradise, through you I rediscover
such certain peace! In you I contemplate the angels
and God, and because of you my heart abounds in
joy. 14

11 [46]

Clasping to your breast the beautiful vermilion cross, sign
of glory and triumph, you consecrated yourself to
the King of the highest Kingdom, as trusted bride
and humble handmaiden, 4

where, though enclosed in a small cell, you
lift yourself to heaven, beyond all human restraint,
and listen in knowing and worthy silence to
celestial song, angelic speech; 8

wise virgin, who, scorning these fallacious
pomps, long for and love those supernal and true,
your heart's desire, 11

pray for me, that so many pitch black storms
not prevent me seeing in the end the port, where
you more assured must arrive.[284] 14

12 [47][285]

S'io gl'occhi inalzo a rimirar talora
il ciel, di tanti e sì bei lumi adorno,
e lui, che co'l partir, co'l far ritorno,
le stelle infiamma e le campagne infiora, 4
dico, "O quant'è più risplendente ogn'ora
d'altro del sommo sole alto soggiorno,
ch'immobil sempre il tutto muove intorno,
e di se stesso il tutto empie e innamora. 8
O come son di voi, stelle, più ardenti
gli spirti eletti e quell'anime care
che s'aggiran d'intorno al polo eterno! 11
O che felici influssi! O che possenti
effetti produr sanno!" E 'n questo alzare
sento me stesso al vero Ben superno. 14

13 [51][286]

In ermo loco e 'n solettario orrore,
piangendo le mie colpe ad una ad una,
devrei star sempre, e quando il sol s'inbruna,
e quando è più lucente il suo splendore, 4
e pur, misera me, dimostro fuore
qual dentro son, d'ogni dolor digiuna,
appressandomi in parte ove s'aduna
l'allegra schiera di Parnaso onore; 8
e se ben conscienza e punge e lima
il cor, e la ragion mi detta il vero,
seguo pur l'uso, e 'l sento errante e vano. 11
Alto Signor, quel ch'io mai far non spero,
faccialo, prego, il valor tuo soprano,
che 'l mio poter per sè nulla s'estima. 14

12 [47]

If I betimes raise my eyes to gaze upon the sky, adorned with so many lights and so fair, and him, who with his leaving, with making his return, inflames the stars and enflowers the meadows, 4

I say, "Oh how much more resplendent ever than any other is the soaring sun's lofty abode, which motionless ever moves all around it and fills and enamors all of itself! 8

O stars, how more ardent than you are the elect spirits and those dear souls that whirl around the eternal pole! 11

Oh what happy influences! Oh what powerful effects they know how to produce!" And as I do, I feel myself rising to the true supernal Good. 14

13 [51]

In a remote place and in solitary wilds, weeping over my faults one by one, I should stay always, both when the sun darkens and when its splendor shines the most, 4

and yet, miserable me, I show outside what I am inside, fasting from all sorrow, approaching a spot where the glad troop gathers, honor of Parnassus, 8

and although conscience pricks and rasps my heart, and reason dictates truth to me, yet I follow habit, and I feel it to be errant and vain. 11

Lord above, that which I never hope to do, let your sovereign valor do it, I pray, for by itself my power amounts to nothing. 14

14 [52][287]

Vorrei teco, Gesù, pendere in croce,
e soffrir teco i tuoi gravi tormenti,
l'acerbe piaghe aver, l'aspre e pungenti
spine sentir e ogni'altra pena atroce; 4
teco il fele gustar, teco la voce
alzar, porgendo a Dio gl'ultimi accenti,
l'alma essalar con gran sospiri ardenti,
e aver nel petto il ferro empio e feroce; 8
di croce tolta, entro 'l sepolcro ancora
star aspettando quel dolce ritorno,
per teco suscitar viva e immortale; 11
e teco alfin all'alto tuo soggiorno
salire: Oh, se mai grazia tanta e tale
avrò, quanto sarei beata alora! 14

15 [56] ALLA COMPAGNIA DI GIESU[289]

Nella mia tanto amata e tanto eletta
vigna, ch'io già piantai con tanto amore,
e poi co'l sangue mio, co'l mio sudore,
rigai, ingrassai, rendei sì pura e netta, 4
ite, o cari operai, ch'a voi s'aspetta
far l'ampia sì, che dove nasce e more
il sol, spanda i suoi rami, e 'l frutto e 'l fiore,
e torni al secol rio l'età perfetta; 8
nè temete per lei fatiche e stenti,
nè tormento nè morte aspra ed acerba,
della mia Compagnia guerrieri invitti; 11
tant'alto è 'l premio al fin che vi si serba,
qui dove sete eternamente ascritti,
che sol render vi può paghi e contenti. 14

14 [52]

I should like, Jesus, to hang on the cross and
suffer with you your harsh torments, to have the raw
wounds, to feel the sharp and stinging thorns and
every other atrocious pain; 4
to taste with you the bitter gall, to raise with
you my voice, offering God my last syllables, to
breathe out my soul with great burning sighs, and to
have in my breast the wicked and fierce iron; 8
taken from the cross, to lie yet waiting
inside the sepulcher for that sweet return, to
resuscitate with you alive and immortal; 11
and with you at last to rise to your lofty
abode. Oh, if ever I shall have such grace so great,
how blessed I would be then![288] 14

15 [56] TO THE SOCIETY OF JESUS

Into my so beloved and elect vineyard,
which I once planted with so much love, and then
with my own blood, with my sweat watered,
dressed, rendered so pure and clean, 4
go, oh dear workers, for it is up to you to
make it so widen that where the sun is born and dies
it will spread its branches, and fruit and flower, and
restore to our evil century the perfect age; 8
do not fear on her account toils and privations,
neither torment nor harsh and bitter death, invincible
warriors of my Society, 11
so high is the reward at the end reserved for
you, here where you are eternally inscribed, that it
can only render you well pleased and happy.[290] 14

16 [58][291]

Son questi i piedi, oh Signor mio, che tanto
in cercar me, furon fiaccati e lassi?
me, che con sì malvagi e torti passi
sì lungi andai dal sentier dritto e santo? 4
Son questi i pie' ch'io già bagnai co'l pianto
degl'occhi miei di luce or privi e cassi?
unsi, tersi, basciai perch'io impetrassi
grazia e perdon del mio fallir cotanto? 8
Ei sono, oimè, ben dessi; e chi macchiati
gl'ha sì di sangue? e chi con piaghe tali
gl'ha guasti? e dato morte acerba e ria? 11
Altro ch'amore, altro ch'alti e 'nfiammati
pensier di salvar noi egri mortali,
questo fatto non ha, nè far potria. 14

17 [64][292]

Servo fedel, che in alta croce affisso,
oggi simile al tuo Signor per morte,
salisti al ciel, fra le bell'alme accorte,
in Dio con dolci e maggior chiodi fisso; 4
a te del cielo, a me di questo abisso,
furo aperte in tal giorno ambe le porte,
tu lassù vivi, io quaggiù in doppia morte,
un'anno men del sesto lustro ho visso; 8
nè so ancor s'io son giunta al mezzo, o s'io
son presso al fin di mia giornata, ed anco
che più mi duol, s'entrarò in porto mai. 11
Almo Andrea, priega umil dunque oggi Dio,
che 'n tal tempesta e 'n sì continui guai,
sia l'alma pronta quanto il corpo è stanco. 14

16 [58]

Are these the feet, O my Lord, that were so
weakened and wearied in all your searching for me?
For me, who with steps so wicked and crooked went
so far from the straight and holy path? 4
Are these the feet that I once bathed with the
weeping of my eyes, now bereft and empty of light?
That I anointed, cleansed, kissed that I might beg
grace and pardon for my woeful failing? 8
They are, alas! Rightly I spoke. And who
has stained them so with blood? And who has
defiled them with such wounds? And given bitter,
evil death? 11
Nothing but love, nothing but lofty and
flaming thoughts of saving us needful mortals has
either done nor could do this. 14

17 [64]

Faithful servant, who affixed to a high cross
today, like your Lord in death,
you rose to heaven among fair wise souls
fixed to God with sweet and greater nails, 4
to you the gates of heaven, to me those of
this abyss were both on the same day opened; you
live up there, I down here in double death, one year
less than the sixth lustrum I have lived; 8
nor do I yet know if I have reached the midpoint
or if I am near the end of my day, and what
grieves me even more, whether I shall ever enter into port. 11
Nurturing Andrea, pray God then humbly
today that in such a storm, and in woes so continuous,
when the body is tired, my soul be ready.[293] 14

18 [70][294]

Per l'impietà d'un re che si credea
esser di tutto il mondo maggior donno,
fatto ha che gli occhi in sempiterno sonno
chiusi hanno mille fanciulli di morte rea;
ma quel Signor che in ciel nostr'alme crea,
essendo in terra aver già non lo ponno,
e quei che per suo amor uccisi sonno,
ne farà intorno al suo bel tron corea.
Itene adunque, o vaghi pargoletti,
insieme diportando a i Campi Elisi,
di bianchi fior tessendo ghirlandetti,
sinchè verrà il Signor che ai vostri risi
accrescerà la gioia e gli diletti,
nè sarete da lui già mai divisi.

19 [78]

Vergine bella, in cui tutta mia fede
e speme ho posta, doppo il grande Dio,
sol spero nel tuo aiuto, e credo, ond'io
avrò sotto i tuoi pie' leggiadra sede;
Vergine saggia, se la tua mercede
mi trarrà in tutto fuor del mondo rio,
dandomi al tuo figliuol, ch'el sangue pio
sparse per l'alme far del ciel erede,
dunque fa' che 'l tiran nemico tuo
non guasti, spezzi, con sue insidie ed arte,
ciò che salvato ha Dio, ciò che tu hai fatto;
anzi con l'ali della mente in parte
voli u' non gionga il crudel tosco suo,
restando ei vittoriosa, ed ei disfatto.

18 [70]

Because of an impious king, who believed
he was the greatest master of all the world, wicked
death made a thousand children close their eyes in
sempiternal sleep, 4
but that Lord who creates our souls in
heaven, although on earth they cannot have Him,
He will make a dancing ring of
those killed for His love around His fair throne. 8
Go forth then, O winsome babes, to the
Elysian Fields, playing together, weaving chaplets
of white flowers, 11
'til the Lord come to increase the joy and
delights of your laughter, and you will never again be
parted from Him.[295] 14

19 [78]

Beautiful Virgin, in whom I have put all my
faith and hope, after great God; in your help alone I
hope and I believe, whence at your feet I shall have
a blissful seat; 4
wise Virgin, if your mercy shall draw me
forth from the wicked world and give me to your
son, who shed his pious blood to make our souls
heaven's heirs, 8
then see that the tyrant your enemy not
spoil, break with his traps and art, that which God
has saved, that which you have wrought; 11
rather, fly on the wings of your mind to a
place beyond reach of his cruel poison, leaving one
in victory and one in defeat.[296] 14

20 [83][297]

Quella donna gentil che posto avea
sua speme in Dio, d'ogn'allegrezza porto,
morir s'elesse pria che veder morto
l'onor che in tanto pregio ella tenea.
Volta al suo Signor, così dicea,
"Padre, che i miei pensier segreti hai scorto,
mira or l'angustie mie, vedi 'l sconforto
in ch'io mi trovo per l'accusa rea."
Alora il pio Fattor, ch'alta pietade
congiunta tiene a giustizia infinita,
benigno accolse il priego di Susanna,
e con l'una a lei rende e fama e vita,
con l'altra i vecchi miseri condanna,
dando egual pena alla lor falsitade.

21 [88][299]

Chiaro, felice e glorioso giorno,
che 'l sol della giustizia, il Re del Cielo,
sotto terrestre velo
qua giù discese in questo uman soggiorno;
o sacro albergo e tant'alto ed adorno,
quanto pria basso e vile,
che quel che 'l ciel non osa
in sé capire in te si chiude e posa,
qui con sembiante umile,
adoriam Dio fatto oggi a noi simile.

20 [83]

That noble lady who had placed
her hope in God, harbor of all happiness,
chose to die rather than see dead
the honor that she held in such esteem. 4
Facing her Lord, she said this,
"Father, who have discerned my secret thoughts,
behold now my distress, see my sorry plight
because of the wicked accusation." 8
Then the pious Maker, who keeps lofty
compassion conjoined with infinite justice, kindly
received Susanna's prayer, 11
and with the one he restores her good name and
life, with the other he condemns the miserable old
men, dealing a punishment to match their deceit.[298] 14

21 [88]

Bright, happy, and glorious day,
when the sun of justice, the King of Heaven,
under terrestrial veil
descended here into this human sojourn;
O holy inn as lofty and fair
as it once was base and vile,
that what heaven dares not contain within itself
should be enclosed and rest in you,
here with humble mien
we adore God, made today in our likeness.[300] 10

22 [89][301]

Quel che la Terra feo di nulla e 'l Cielo,
e poi dal Ciel per noi discese in Terra,
la bassa Terra unendo all'alto Cielo,
con gran stupor del Cielo e della Terra;
per portar questa Terra insin' al Cielo
e gli onori del Ciel dare alla Terra,
morto e sepolto in Terra, al fine in Cielo
salendo aperse il Cielo a questa Terra.
Gl'indegni della Terra, e più del Cielo,
tu, gran Signor del Cielo e della Terra,
tolti da Terra avar riporti in Cielo;
stupisci meco, Ciel; stupisci, Terra,
poiche vedi la Terra ir sopra 'l Cielo,
e per me Terra il Ciel porto sotterra.

23 [92] SOPRA LA TAVOLA DELL'INVENTIONE DELLA CROCE[302]

Lascia del Tebro le famose sponde,
ogni cura real posto in oblio,
donna accesa d'ardente alto disio
di veder del Giordan l'incognite onde;
per trovar quel ch'empio Giudeo nasconde,
sacrato legno ove l'eterno Dio,
fatto uom mortal per salvar l'uom morio,
con strazi acerbi e piaghe aspre e profonde;
ed adorarlo in sì gentil sembiante
e così pio, qual'han di mostro espresso
del buon pittor la mano e l'intelletto.
Felice HELENA, or quante lodi e quante
grazie devemo al tuo pietoso affetto,
per tanto dono a tutti noi concesso?

22 [89]

He who made from nothing Earth and Heaven,
and then descended from Heaven for us to Earth,
uniting the lowly Earth to the high Heaven,
to the great astonishment of Heaven and Earth; 4
in order to carry this Earth as far as the Heaven
and give Heaven's honors to Earth,
dead and buried on Earth, rising in the end to Heaven,
He opened Heaven to this Earth. 8
Those unworthy of Earth and more, of Heaven,
you, great Lord of Heaven and Earth,
take from the miserly Earth, carrying them back to Heaven. 11
Be astonished with me, Heaven; be astonished, Earth;
for you see the Earth go above Heaven,
and for me who am Earth, I carry Heaven beneath the Earth. 14

23 [92] ON THE PAINTING OF THE DISCOVERY OF THE TRUE CROSS

She leaves the famous banks of the Tiber,
oblivious to every royal care,
a woman kindled with an ardent lofty desire
to see Jordan's mysterious waves; 4
to find what a wicked Jew is hiding,
sanctified wood where God eternal made mortal
man to save man did meet his death, with bitter
suffering and harsh and deep wounds, 8
and to adore Him, so gentle in mien and so
pious, just as the good painter's hand and intellect
have expressed the marvel. 11
Happy HELENA, how many praises now,
and how many thanks, we owe your pious affection
for so great a gift granted to us all. 14

24 [95] PISTOLA DI LENTULO RE, AL SENATO TRADOTTA IN VERSI[303]

Apparve a' giorni nostri ed è fra noi
un uom d'alta virtù, che Gesù Cristo
chiamano tutti gli seguaci suoi.
È verace profeta, al quale è misto
co'l divino il mortal, sì che già 'l nome
del gran figliuol di Dio s'ha fatto acquisto.
Ei, lei, che 'l mondo par che vinca e dome,
doma e vince ad ogn'or, tornando in vita
l'alme già scarche di lor grave some;
fianchi, stomachi, febbri e l'infinita
schiera al viver uman sì forte amara,
ha co'l proprio valor da noi sbandita.
La forma sua è d'una onesta e rara
statura, e 'l suo sembiante altero e umile,
in cui temere e amare in un s'impara.
Il piano e vago crin, lungo e sottile,
sino all'orecchie lucido si stende,
della nocciuola al bel color simile,
indi s'increspa, e più chiaro discende
a' begl'omeri sopra, ove talora
Zeffiro co'l spirar più vago il rende,
che 'n mezo il capo linea dritta ogn'ora
sparte egualmente quinci e quindi, e questo
de' Nazareni è propria usanza ancora.
La piana fronte sua chiara ed onesta,
la faccia senza ruga e macchia alcuna,
cui vago rossor pinge e fa modesta,
la bocca e 'l naso talche ne par una
amenda nova in lor colei che tanto
è di biasmare altrui sempre importuna;
la barba al mento è copiosa quanto
basta per non celar le gote e 'l volto,
a cui porge decoro onesto e santo,
dal biondo oro suo testo ha 'l color tolto,
nel mezo anch'ella in due parti è divisa,
crespa e gentil, nè pero lunga molto.

24 [95] EPISTLE FROM KING LENTULUS TO THE SENATE TRANSLATED INTO VERSE

There appeared in our days, and is among us,
a man of noble virtue,
whom all his followers call Jesus Christ.
He is a true prophet, in whom
the divine mingles with the mortal, and so it is that
he has already acquired the name Great Son of God.
She who seems to conquer and dominate the world he
dominates and ever conquers, bringing back to life souls
already unburdened of their heavy loads;
reins, stomachs, fevers, and the infinite horde
so bitter to human life
he has banished from us by his own power.
In appearance he is of honest and rare
stature, and his likeness, proud and humble,
teaches as one fear and love.
His straight and lovely locks, long and thin,
reach shiny to his ears,
similar to the hazelnut in their beautiful color;
then they grow curly and descend
with a lighter tint over his handsome shoulders,
where sometimes Zephyr's breath makes them lovelier;
in the middle of his head a straight line
keeps them parted evenly between each side,
and this is still the Nazarenes' local custom.
His smooth forehead, clear and honest,
his face without any wrinkle and blemish,
which a lovely blush tinges and makes modest;
the mouth and the nose are such
that they make amends for that part
that is always so importunate in criticizing people;
the beard on his chin is as copious
as need be not to conceal the cheeks and face,
to which it lends honest and holy decorum;
from blond gold it took its texture,
it too divided in two parts,
curly and noble, but not very long.

L'aspetto grave in disusata guisa,
è dolce insieme, e gl'occhi onesti e chiari,
ch'abbaglian più del sol chi in lor s'affisa.
Non fu chi mai vedesse a' dolci e cari
risi aprir le sue labbra, ma sì spesso
qual gl'occhi al pianto, a' sospir caldi e amari.
Che del corpo dirò? nel quale ha messo
Natura e 'l cielo ogni lor forza ed arte,
sì ch'ei sol puote assomigliar se stesso?
Che della bianca man, ben degna parte
di lui? che delle braccia svelte e preste
s'apena uman pensier v'arriva in parte?
Questi raro è nel suo parlar celeste;
è 'n somma alto del cielo angel novello,
fra noi disceso in nuove forme oneste,
e sopra ogn'altro grazioso e bello.

25 [76] STANZE DELLA FEDE, ET OBEDIENZA DI ABRAMO, ET AMORE VERSO DIO NELL'OFFERIRE IL SUO FIGLIUOLO[305]

1.

Mentre d'Abram nell'infiammato core
l'amor, la fede e la pietà s'annida,
disse, "Convien s'io voglio al mio Signore
oggi aggradir, che 'l mio figliuol ancida;
e no 'l facendo, in me doglia maggiore
nasce, che l'alma a crudel morte sfida.
Che farò dunque? io vuo' patir tal noia,
e spero nel mio duol ritrovar gioia.

2.

Mi diede egli costui nella mia vecchia
età per sua mercede, ed or me 'l toglie.
Ecco la destra man che s'apparecchia
fornir nel lume mio le giuste voglie.
Solo nel suo poter tutto si specchia
il guardo interno e d'ogni dubbio il scioglie,
perchè so' certo, egli è possente e forte
far che viva costui doppo la morte.

His somber aspect, such an unwonted manner,
is also sweet, and his eyes honest and bright
blind more than the sun whoever gazes upon them.
No one ever saw him open his lips
to sweet and dear laughter, to hot and bitter sighs,
as often as his eyes do to tears.
What shall I say of his body? Into it
Nature and heaven put their every strength and art,
and so it is that he can only resemble himself.
What of the white hand, worthy indeed
as part of him? What of the slim and quick arms,
if human thought barely reaches them in part?
This man is sparing in his celestial speech;
in sum, he is a new angel descended among us
from heaven above with rare honest looks,
more graceful and handsome than any other man.[304]

25 [76] STANZAS ON THE FAITH AND OBEDIENCE OF ABRAHAM, AND HIS LOVE FOR GOD IN OFFERING HIS LITTLE SON

1.

With love, faith, and piety nestled
in his flaming heart, Abraham said,
"So it must be, if I want to please my Lord
today, that I kill my son.
And if I do it not, a greater sorrow
is born in me that challenges my soul to cruel death.
What then shall I do? This pain I want to suffer,
and I hope in my sorrow again to find joy.

2.

"He gave this boy to me in my old age
by His mercy, and now He is taking him away.
Behold my right hand, which prepares
to carry out what I see as His righteous wishes.
In His power alone internal sight
is wholly mirrored and loosed of every doubt,
for I am sure He has the might and power
to make this boy live after death.

3.

Mancar ei non mi può, ch'egli è verace
d'ogni promessa e non inganna alcuno.
Secondo il detto suo, di qui gli piace
trar il Messia, che dee salvar ogn'uno,
dal qual lieta ne vien l'eterna pace,
che gioia fia per sempre di ciascuno
che dietro all'orma andrà de' suoi vestigi,
con viva fede nei suoi bei servigi.

4.

Dico che 'l mio Signor, chi tal offizio
vuol ch'esseguisca, di salvar la gente,
ritrar vuol di costui, come egli indizio
n'ha dato, e certo io so che non si pente;
ed or chiede da me ch'un sacrifizio
faccia di lui sovra la fiamma ardente;
voglio obedire però che modo a lui
non manca a suscitar poscia costui."

5.

E nel dir questo del fanciullo ei prende
la bella treccia ed alzagli la a Dio,
soggiongendo, "Signor, so che m'intende
la tua bontade e sa l'animo mio;
accetta il dono"; e ciò dicendo, estende
il ferro sopra il capo al figliuol pio
avendo co'l dolor la fede insieme,
che di lui nascea il già promesso seme.

6.

O viva, o vaga fede leggiadra e bella,
che sempre al sommo Dio fosti sì grata,
libera fai, anzi divota ancella,
al Re del Cielo ogn'anima beata.
Tu sei la scala, tu sostegno e quella
che d'andar a Gesù mostri l'entrata;
però ch'all'uom felice vita dai
in modo tal ch'egli non muor giamai.

3.

"Fail me, He cannot, since He is truthful
in every promise and does not deceive anyone.
According to His word, He is pleased
to bring forth from here the Messiah,
who is going to save everyone and from whom
glad peace eternal comes to us, joy for always to
everyone who will walk in his footsteps
with living faith in his fair service.

4.

"I say that my Lord, He wants to bring forth
the one He wants to execute this duty, of saving mankind,
from this boy, as He has shown
me by a sign, and I know for certain He does not repent,
and now He asks me to make a sacrifice
of him over the burning flame.
I want to obey so that after his death
He will not lack a way to resuscitate him."

5.

And saying this, he takes the little boy's
fair locks and raises them to God,
adding, "Lord, I know that your bounty understands me
and knows my soul;
accept the gift"; and saying that, he stretches
the iron above his pious little boy's head,
having with his sorrow faith too,
that the promised seed
was going to be born of him.

6.

O living, loving faith, comely and fair,
you who were always so welcome to God supreme,
you make free, nay, a devout servant
to the King of Heaven every blessed soul.
You are the ladder, you the support,
and you show us the entrance for going to Jesus,
because you give the happy man life
in such a way that he never dies.

7.

Buone son l'opre se tengono appresso
la fè, che sempre è lor fidata scorta,
e viva è lei se lei soggiorna spesso
con l'opre, e senza l'opre è vile e morta.
Ben gli è questo favor quivi concesso,
che lei d'entrar nel ciel primera porta,
io dico, chè qua giù la viva fede
tra le virtù sì tien la prima sede.

8.

Sirocchie sono, e senza l'altra l'una
mai l'uomo qui perfettamente tiene
s'avventuroso egli ne prende alcuna,
chè tutte l'altre egli abbia gli conviene.
Quivi signor ei fassi di ciascuno
s'ogn'or nel cor la vera fede ottiene,
qual bea l'uomo, e fuor di questa valle
colma di pianto, eterna vita dalle.

9.

Ecco la fè, ch'l buon vecchion ritenne
sempre nel cor, che poi gli rese il frutto,
chè lei co' volo altiero le sue penne
spiegò nel cielo al gran fattor del tutto.
Ne trasse un messaggier che 'n fretta venne,
l'aura solcando a terminar quel lutto,
e al braccio alzato diede allor di piglio;
gli tenne il colpo e non occise il figlio.

10.

Poi disse, "Ferma Abram, ferma la mano,
deh, ferma il braccio, e non seguir più inanzi,
che 'l sommo Re del Cielo alto e sovrano
non vuol quel che da te cercò pur dianzi;
nè men tal cosa egli ha richiesto in vano,
a veder se di fede ogn'altro avanzi,
ch'ei sapea il ver, ma qui nascoso stassi
l'effetto del Messia ne i stremi passi."

7.

People are good if they keep faith close;
it is always their trusted escort,
and faith is alive as long as it abides
with works, and without works it is mean and dead.
Down here it grants us this favor,
that it opens heaven to us firstly;
I say that here below living faith
holds the first seat among the virtues.

8.

Sisters they are, and without one
a man never has another perfectly
if he ventures to take one of them,
because he needs to have all the others.
Thus he masters each one
if in his heart he constantly keeps true faith,
that which blesses man and beyond this vale
filled with tears gives him eternal life.

9.

Behold the faith that the good elder always held
fast in his heart, which then bore fruit for him,
for faith with lofty flight spread her feathers
to the great maker of all in heaven.
Thence she summoned a messenger, who came in haste
plowing the air to end that grief
and firmly seized his upraised arm
and withheld his blow, and he did not kill his son.

10.

Then he said, "Stop, Abraham, stop your hand,
pray, stop your arm, and go no further,
for the supreme King of Heaven, noble and sovereign,
does not want what He asked of you just before,
but neither did He request that thing in vain,
to see if you surpass all others in faith,
for He knew the truth, but here
the Messiah's effect in his last steps stays hidden."

11.

Detto ch'ebbe tal cosa od altra tale,
disparve poi l'ambasciador celeste;
discese in ambidoi tal gioia quale
mai ebbe il mondo in altre parti o in queste; 84
si volse il vecchio e vidde l'animale
ch'avea tra spin le corna ivi conteste,
e sciolto Isache, con ardente zelo
offerse quello al gran Signor del cielo. 88

12.

Io taccio il pianto e 'l dire che Sarra fece,
quando ch'Abramo il fatto gli disciolse,
e com'al collo più di diece e diece
fiate del figliuol le braccia avvolse. 92
Mostrò che seco il duol rimase in vece
di lui, quando che lui da lei si tolse.
Gioisce al fin la donna al ciel gradita,
ch'a Dio sì piacque e lui restasse in vita. 96

13.

Aventurosa e fortunata prole!
quella ben fu ch'in Dio pose l'affetto;
quanto il ciel cuopre e quanto scalda il sole
unqua non ebbe amor così perfetto. 100
Beato quel che 'l suo Signor ben cole,
e fisso lo ritien dentro al suo petto,
perochè ei vive lieto, e poi giocondo
lui vola al ciel quando ch'ei lascia il mondo. 104

14.

Conchiudo dunque il mio parlare e dico,
"Felice quel che 'l buon sentier procaccia,
e con bel passo del gran Padre antico
segue mentre è qua giù la bella traccia; 108
con viva fede come fidele amico
ei volge al suo Signor l'interna faccia,
e crede e spera in lui, e tien per certo
solo gli sia da Cristo il ciel' aperto." 112

11.

When he had said this, or something else like it,
then the celestial ambassador disappeared;
joy descended into both such as
never the world had seen, in other parts or in these.
The old man turned, and he saw the animal
with its horns caught amidst the thorns,
and after he freed Isaac, with ardent zeal
he offered it to the Lord of heaven.

12.

I say nothing of Sara's weeping and her words
when Abraham loosed the truth to her
and how she threw her arms around her son's neck,
more than ten and ten times.
She showed that sorrow was left in his stead
when he was taken from her;
in the end she rejoices, the woman favored by heaven,
for it pleased God to keep him alive.

13.

Favored and fortunate offspring!
That woman was right to place her affection in God;
as much as heaven covers and as much as the sun warms
never knew such perfect love.
Blessed the man who worships his Lord
and keeps Him firm inside his breast,
because he lives happy and then he flies
joyous to heaven when he leaves the world.

14.

Thus I conclude my speech, and I say,
"Happy the man who pursues the good path
and follows with fair step while he is down here
the fair trail of the great Father of ancient days.
With living faith, as a faithful friend
he turns to his Lord his inner face,
and he believes and hopes in Him, and he believes for certain
that only by Christ will heaven be opened to him."

26 [FRAGMENT OF AN UNFINISHED EPIC ON THE EARLY HEBREW KINGS][306]

1.
Canto il valor de' primi antichi regi
scesi dall'alto e gran legnaggio ebreo,
alor che 'l ciel d'eterni privilegi
quel sopra ogn'altro memorabil feo,
le ricche spoglie e trionfanti pregi,
ch'or dell'Amalachita, or dell'Etheo,
o popol'altro più famoso e chiaro
invitti e gloriosi riportaro.

2.
Verace Apollo, che le nebbie oscure
sgombrando vai da' nostri freddi cori,
e gl'empi ognor d'ardenti e dolci cure
con la virtù de' vivi tuoi splendori,
odi le voci mie divote e pure,
ch'invocan liete i santi tuoi favori;
desta la musa mia, l'ingegno avviva,
sì ch'alti fatti e gloriosi scriva.

3.
Sacra Minerva, che del seno immenso
del sommo Giove eternamente uscisti,
sì che quando ci partiva il nero e 'l denso
dal bianco e raro inanzi a lui ne gisti;
sian le tue frondi a quanto io detto o penso
ampio ristoro e miei pregiati acquisti;
tu sii mia scorta in quest'alto viaggio,
e lume interno il tuo giudizio saggio.

4.
Al santo monte, ove le grazie eterne
stillano al mondo in gloriosa pioggia,
anela il cor, se ben vede e discerne
ch'ei sopra le sue forze indarno poggia;
l'acque felici, che le macchie insieme
purgando vanno in non più vista foggia
ama e ricerca, e ogn'altro fonte o colle
odiando fugge che già errante volle.

26 [FRAGMENT OF AN UNFINISHED EPIC ON THE EARLY HEBREW KINGS]

1.

I sing of the valor of the first ancient kings
descended from the noble and great Hebrew stock,
then when heaven with eternal privileges
made it memorable over every other,
the rich spoils and triumphant prizes
that they carried away, invincible and glorious,
now from the Amalekite, now from the Ethiopian,
or another people of more fame and renown.[307]

2.

Truthful Apollo, who dispel the dark
fogs from our cold hearts
and ever fill them with ardent and sweet cares
by the power of your living splendor,
hear thou my words, devout and pure,
as joyful they invoke your holy favors;
awaken my muse, quicken my mind,
so that I may write of high and glorious deeds.[308]

3.

Sacred Minerva, who came forth eternally
from supreme Jove's immense bosom,
so that when he divided the black and dense
from the white and thin, you went before him;
may your boughs, for whatever I dictate or think,
be ample succor and my prized acquisitions;
may you be my escort on this lofty journey
and may your your judicious wisdom be my internal light.[309]

4.

My heart, though it sees and discerns
that it is pressing vainly beyond its powers,
pants for the sacred mount, where eternal graces
bedew the world with a glorious rain;
it loves and seeks the happy waters
that together go purging stains in never before seen display,
and it flees in hate every other font or hill
that once errant it wanted.[310]

5.

Là dove il sol i primi albori usati
a poco a poco al mondo scuopre e rende,
e dove il ciel i suoi tesor più amati
sì largamente compartire intende,
giace una parte a cui gl'eterni fati,
come pioggia dal ciel che 'n terra scende,
sparsero grazie, tal che sempre poi
Palestina s'udio nomar fra noi.

6.

Un uom di nobiltade e di valore,
primo fra gl'altri in Palestina nacque,
non sol di LEVI alta progenie onore,
poi ch'all'eterno Dio cotanto piacque,
ma del gran sangue ebreo gloria e splendore,
in cui vera virtù sempre rinacque,
HELCANA detto, ch'a due vaghe accorte
donne del popol suo si feo consorte.

7.

ANNA che di bellezza i primi vanti
e di virtù fra l'altre donne avea,
piacque allo sposo sì che fra' suoi tanti
tesori ognor più in pregio la tenea,
sol gli dava cagion d'amari pianti
l'alvo infecondo suo, che ben vedea
esser di Cintia e di Lucina vano
l'oprar per cui s'accresce il seme umano.

8.

L'altra FENENNA, che d'amica salma
sempre gìa grave e di crescente prole,
onde superba ogn'or pungeva l'alma
d'ANNA, or con fatti acerbi, or con parole,
per fin ch'un giorno alla famosa ed alma
città di Silo, come ogn'anno suole
il giusto Helcana con la sua famiglia,
per adorar nel tempio il camin piglia.

5.

There where the sun its first wonted dawning
uncovers and renders little by little to the world,
and where heaven intends to apportion
so widely its most beloved treasures,
there lies a land upon which the eternal fates
scattered favor, like rain from heaven
that falls to earth, so that forever
after people here called it Palestine.

6.

A man of nobility and worth,
first over all others, was born in Palestine,
not only the high progeny and honor of LEVI
because he so much pleased eternal God,
but also the glory and splendor of the great Hebrew bloodline,
in which true virtue was always reborn;
ELKANAH he was called, who became the consort
of two women from his people, winsome and quick-witted.

7.

HANNAH, who among other women
had first vaunt for beauty and virtue,
so pleased the groom that among all his many
treasures he prized her ever more highly;
only her infertile womb gave him cause
for bitter weeping, for he could well see
Cynthia and Lucina working
in vain to increase human seed.[311]

8.

The other, PENINNAH, always went about
heavy with befriending weight and growing offspring,
and in her pride she pricked Hannah's soul,
now with the bitter deeds, now with words,
until one day, as everyone is wont to,
the just Elkanah with his family set out
on the road for the famous and fertile
city of Shiloh to worship in the temple.

9.

Indi co' figli e con le sue consorti,
s'accinge all'alto sagrifizio umile,
e 'l benigno animal, ch'a mille morti
straziato, tiene il lamentarsi a vile,
adducon tosto i fidi servi accorti,
e sparso il sangue suo puro e gentile,
da lui sopra il tremendo e santo altare,
sinchè vermiglio in ogni parte appare.

10.

Poichè con gl'occhi e con la mente al cielo
ebbe posto al gran Dio sospiri ardenti,
divoto HELCANA pien di santo zelo
parte in più parti le carni innocenti;
ma tosto fiede il cor pungente telo,
amareggiando i dolci suoi contenti,
quando rivolto ad ANNA una sol parte
della sacrata vittima comparte.

11.

L'altre tutte a FENENNA e a' figli porge,
perch'ella venne più superba in vista,
sì l'ira e l'odio in lei cresce e risorge
ver la compagna sua dolente e trista,
di che il consorte lor non pria s'accorge,
che con faccia di duol, di pietà mista,
come chi amor e sdegno nel cor porta,
l'una riprende e l'altra riconforta.

12.

ANNA senza gustar cibo o conforto
di nuovo al santo altar ritorna in fretta;
indi col viso sbigottito e smorto,
come chi teme e par salute aspetta,
dice, "Alto Dio, d'ogni tempesta porto,
ecco la serva tua vile e negletta,
che con la mente sol ti parla e mira,
e dal centro del cor piange e sospira.

9.

Thence with his children and with his consorts,
he humbly prepares for the solemn sacrifice
and his faithful quick servants
soon lead in the mild animal who,
strangled for a thousand deaths,
holds it cowardice to complain, and they sprinkled
its pure and gentle blood upon the awesome holy altar
until it ran red in every part.[312]

10.

With his eyes and with his mind heavenward,
after he had sent to the great God ardent sighs,
devout ELKANAH, taken by holy zeal,
parts in many parts the innocent flesh,
but a sharp spear soon pierces his heart,
embittering his sweet contentments
when, turning toward Hannah, he imparts
only one part of the sacrificial victim.

11.

All the others he proffers to PENINNAH and to her children,
which made her prouder to see,
so wrath and hatred wax within her and resurge
toward her sorrowful luckless companion;
no sooner does their consort notice it
then with a mixture of grief, of pity on his face,
like a man who carries love and scorn in his heart,
he reproaches one woman and consoles the other.

12.

HANNAH, without tasting food or comfort,
returns again in haste to the holy altar,
where stricken and wan of visage,
like one who fears and appears to hope for help,
she says, "God on high, port of every storm,
behold your lowly, forgotten servant,
who speaks to you with mind alone and eye
and who weeps and sighs from the center of her heart.[313]

13.

"Tu pur sei quel che con la sol parola
tanti spirti e sì chiari in ciel creasti,
perch'alla Maestà tua trina e sola
porgesser lode e prieghi umili e casti,
poscia in questa mortal terrestre mola
l'umana gente eguale a te formasti,
perch'ella del suo seme almo e fecondo
empiesse i larghi termini del mondo.

14.

A qualunque animal alberga in terra
doni virtù, benigno Padre eterno,
che l'un con l'altro con piacevol guerra,
cresca la spezie sua la state e 'l verno;
a quante piante in sen rinchiude e serra
l'antica madre, il tuo calor superno
comparti sì che gia mai non son parche
di mostrarsi di fior, di frutti carchi.

15.

Deh, Signor mio, s'alcun prego mortale
a pietade, a mercè già mai ti volse,
volgiti al mio, ch'in tanto estremo male
la bocca chiusa e 'l cor aperto sciolse.
Apri il mio ventre conturbato e frale,
ch'aspra sterilità già serrar volse,
e le viscere mie sana e ripurga,
sì che la morta speme omai risurga.

16.

Dammi un figlio, Signor, ch'io voglio e giuro
tosto renderlo a te, ch'ei vada o spiri,
sol perch'al tempio tuo sacrato e puro
sian sempre intenti i casti suoi desiri."
Intanto il mondo d'ogni'intorno scuro,
Febo lasciando i più superni giri,
si facea tutto, ed ANNA ancor dimora
nel santo albergo e non osa uscir fuora.

13.
"You indeed are the one who with word alone
created so many spirits so bright in heaven
that they might proffer to your single and triune Majesty
praises and prayers humble and chaste;
next, on this mortal terrestrial millwheel,
you formed humankind in your likeness,
that it might fill the wide limits of the world
with your nurturing, fertile seed.

14.
"To whatsoever animal dwells on earth
you give the virtue, benign Father eternal,
to increase its species summer and winter,
one with another with pleasurable warfare;
to as many plants as the ancient mother encloses and locks
in her breast, you apportion your supernal warmth
so that never are they loathe to show themselves
loaded with flowers and fruits.[314]

15.
"Pray, my Lord, if ever a mortal plea
moved you to pity, to mercy,
be moved by mine, which in such extreme pain
my closed mouth and open heart have raised.
Open thou my troubled and frail womb,
which harsh sterility long ago wished to lock,
and heal and recleanse my viscera,
that dead hope may at last resurge again.

16.
"Give me a child, Lord, for I wish and swear
quickly to render him unto you, as long as he
moves or breathes, just that his chaste desires may be devoted
always to your temple, consecrate and pure."
Meanwhile, the world was growing quite dark all about
as Phoebus left the supernal wheels,
and still HANNAH lingers
in the sacred dwelling and dares not come forth.

17.

HELI del tempio eletto sacerdote,
di lunga chioma e venerabil volto,
a cui candida neve ambe le gote
fioria d'intorno, il primo color tolto;
le bianche vesti fean palese e note
sue voglie sante, e 'l vestir schietto e sciolto
mostrava ch'ei, d'ogni terrena cura
libero e scarco, avea sol Dio cura.

18.

Assiso in alto ed onorata sede,
l'antico veglio in mezzo 'l tempio stava,
poi ch'a lui solo Iddio veder concede
gl'alti misterii ch'ad altrui velava;
gl'occhi gravi volgendo intorno vede
la mesta donna, ch'umilmente orava,
intenta sì che d'ogni senso priva,
freddo marmo parea, non donna viva.

17.

ELI, chosen priest of the temple,
with long hair and venerable face,
where white snow flowered around both cheeks,
the former color lost,
his white garments made evident and known
his holy wishes, and his plain loose robe
showed that, free and unburdened of every earthly care,
God alone was his concern.[315]

18.

Seated on a high chair of honor,
the aged elder sat in the middle of the temple,
since to him alone God grants
sight of the deep mysteries that he veiled to others;
turning his serious eyes about, he sees
the downcast woman who was humbly praying,
so absorbed that having lost all awareness,
she seemed cold marble, not a living woman.[316]

II
POEMS FROM OTHER COLLECTIONS

THE PERIOD 1560–77

1[1] DI MADONNA LAURA BATTIFERRO

O sonno, o de l'amena ombra fugace
condottier saggio, o di mia requie e bene
vera cagion, o dolce oblio di pene,
di Latona figliuol, dio de la pace, 4
deh, porgi aïta al cor, che langue e tace,
e le profonde sue più interne vene
ti scopre, intento a sua salute e spene,
sciolto d'ogni vil cura, empia e tenace; 8
da la Cimeria valle e da l'antiquo
antro risorgi, o sonno, e 'n questi mei,
anzi tuoi, divoti occhi omai ritorna, 11
ch'io per Lete ti giuro umido obliquo
odiar quanto di luce il mondo aggiorna,
e consacrarti ancor voti e trofei. 14

II
POEMS FROM OTHER COLLECTIONS

THE PERIOD 1560–77

1 BY MADONNA LAURA BATTIFERRO

O sleep, O wise bearer of blissful fleeting
shadow, O true source of my respite and well-
being, O sweet forgetfulness of pain, daughter of
Latona, god of peace, 4
pray, give help to my heart, which thinking
on its salvation and hope, silently languishes and
discovers to you its deep and innermost veins,
loosed from every base, wicked, clinging care. 8
From the Cimmerian Valley, and from your
ancient cavern arise, O sleep, and return now
to these devout eyes of mine, nay yours; 11
for I swear to you by Lethe, damp and
crooked, to hate whatever light the day brings, and
more, to consecrate to you vows and trophies.[2] 14

2 A MADONNA LAURA BATTIFERRA DELLI AMMANNATI[3]

[Bronzino]

Salutar pianta, il tuo cortese e saggio
cultor, che quasi nuovo sol t'onora,
languisce sì che dubbio è che 'n poc'ora
manchi, e si spenga un così chiaro raggio. 4
Movi l'aura soave, in cui speme aggio,
con sì dolce spirar, con sì dolce ora,
che l'ardente martir ch'entro 'l divora
lenti, e di morte il già corto viaggio. 8
Dilli, o Dafne gentil, che 'l buon Martino
non è morto, anzi vive, e 'n cielo è gito
a rallegrar la nostra amica schiera; 11
e gli affreni il dolor, ch'a lui vicino
tosto ed io seco fia, com'il gradito
suo merto accerta e la mia fede spera. 14

3 DI MADONNA LAURA IN RISPOSTA[5]

Sterile arbor son io, rozzo e salvaggio,
ch'al mio sì buon cultor, che tanto ognora
m'orna e m'abbella, non produssi ancora
frutti nell'autunno o fiori al maggio; 4
poca è l'aura, che dite, e fa passaggio
quasi in un punto, e quel che più m'accora,
a lui che più s'affligge d'ora in ora,
che può lauro giovare o quercia o faggio? 8
Dunque ditegli voi, caro Bronzino,
che 'l vostro e suo buon Luca, al ciel salito,
lieto si gode nella terza spera; 11
cessi il dolor, che l'ha curvato e chino,
e voi, ché cieco il mondo e sbigottito
non pianga addoppio ed io languendo pera. 14

2 TO MADONNA LAURA BATTIFERRA DELLI AMMANNATI

[Bronzino]

Healing plant, your courteous and wise
cultivator, who honors you as if a new sun, so
languishes that it is likely he will shortly fail and
such a bright ray will go out. 4
Bestir your soft breeze, which gives me
hope, with your breathing so sweet, with your aura
so sweet, that you may slacken the burning martyrdom
devouring him within and death's by now short journey. 8
Tell him, O kind Daphne, that the goodly Martini
is not dead, nay, he lives and has gone to heaven to cheer
our friendly troop; 11
and rein in his sorrow, for soon he and I
together shall be near him, as his pleasing merit
assures and my faith hopes.[4] 14

3 FROM MADONNA LAURA IN RESPONSE

A sterile tree am I, rough and wild, that have
not yet produced fruit in autumn or flowers in May
for my cultivator so true, who always much adorns
me and makes me fairer; 4
the aura, as you call it, is not much, and its flow
is almost down to a point, and what dispirits me most, how
can laurel or oak or beech avail him when he is more
afflicted by the hour? 8
Therefore tell him yourself, dear Bronzino,
that your Luca and his, risen to heaven, blithely
delights in the third sphere. 11
Let the sorrow cease that has curved and
bowed him down, and you, lest the blind and
stricken world weep twice over and I languishing perish.[6] 14

4 A MADONNA LAURA BATTIFERRA DEGL'AMMANNATI[7]

[Varchi]

Questa nostra caduca e fragil vita
come fiume sen va correndo al chino,
DONNA casta e cortese, ch'al mio bino
languir terza giugneste alma ferita. 4
Ecco che dianzi, o mia pena infinita,
più che pardo veloce o che delfino,
prese e portonne seco il buon MARTINO
lei, da cui spero, e non d'altronde, vita. 8
Quanto fora a quest'alma alta ventura
uscir del suo ricetto e d'esta invoglia
mortal, che già tanti anni il ciel le fura! 11
E se pur avverrà che non si scioglia
dal nodo in cui la strinse e tiene natura,
siate certa ch'uom mai non muor di doglia. 14

5 SONETTO DI MADONNA LAURA BATTIFERRA IN RISPOSTA DI QUELLO DI MESSER BENEDETTO VARCHI, CHE INCOMINCIA QUESTA NOSTRA CADUCA E FRAGIL VITA[9]

VARCHI, che farem noi s'ogn'or più ardita
lei, che parte il mortal dal suo divino,
tanto n'assale? e s'empio e reo destino
di nuovo a lagrimar, lassi, ne invita? 4
A pena fatto avea da noi partita
l'un, per cui Flora ha 'l volto umido e chino,
che l'altro, oimè, che 'n darno piange Urbino,
ha sua giornata anzi 'l suo dì fornita. 8
Chiaro MARTIN, GALLO gentile, oscura
ogni luce ne sembra, e sì n'addoglia
ogni cosa, ch'a gli altri il dolor fura; 11
privi di voi, che questa frale spoglia
squarciarem tosto, se celeste cura
da sì fermo voler non ci disvoglia. 14

4 TO MADONNA LAURA BATTIFERRA DEGLI AMMANNAT

[Varchi]

This fleeting and fragile life of ours goes by
like a downhill river, lady chaste and courteous,
who come a third wounded soul to my twin
despondency. 4
Behold how ere now, oh my infinite pain,
she and no one else, from whom I hope for life,
snatched and carried away with her the good
Martini, swifter than leopard or dolphin. 8
What good fortune it would be for this soul
to escape its container and this mortal wrapping,
which for so many years has already cheated it of heaven! 11
Yet if it should come to pass that it not be
loosed from the knot in which nature caught and
holds it, be certain that man never dies from grief.[8] 14

5 SONNET BY MADONNA LAURA BATTIFERRA IN RESPONSE TO THE ONE BY MESSER BENEDETTO VARCHI THAT BEGINS "THIS FLEETING AND FRAGILE LIFE OF OURS"

Varchi, what shall we do if she who parts
our mortal from the divine ever more boldly so
assaults us? And if wicked and evil destiny once
again, alas, invites us to weep? 4
Scarcely had one left us, for whom Flora's
face is damp and bowed, than the other, woe! for whom
Urbino weeps in vain, has finished out his day
before his time. 8
Goodly MARTIN, GALLO noble, every
light seems dark to us, and we are sorrowful for
everything that steals sorrow from others; 11
deprived of you, we may soon rend these
frail remains, if heaven's care not undo our wish to
be so firm of will.[10] 14

6 A MESSER BARTOLOMMEO AMMANNATI[11]

[Varchi]

In questa mia più d'altra amara sorte,
null'è che possa, che più debba atarme,
altro che i vivi bronzi e i vivi marmi
vostri, che danno vita e tolgon morte,
e la pudica vostra alta consorte
con sue pulite prose e tersi carmi
Ammannato gentil, cui veder parmi
tutto smarrito, ancor che saggio e forte.
Ma chi tal senno o fortezza ebbe od ave
moderno o prisco, che bastasse mai
a schernire o soffrir colpo sì grave?
Io per me tutto sbigottito e smorto
divenni, e sono ancor, quando ascoltai,
"Luca Martini, Luca Martini è morto."

7 DI MESSER GHERARDO SPINI NELLA MORTE DEL PADRE DI MADONNA LAURA BATTIFERRI[13]

Volete voi, gentil donna, formare
un vasto Egeo, un tempestoso Eussino,
di lacrime pietose che rigare
si veggion tante il volto almo e divino?
Non vi giovi per lor veder turbare
quanto cinge il Tirreno e l'Appennino;
possin le preci altrui, devote e care,
torvi quanto vi dà morte, destino;
né fate ingiuria all'onorata chioma,
ma cessi il duol e 'l pianto e 'l mondo scorga,
ch'ogn'effetto mortal v'incontra e cede:
dianzi cadde Cartago e fiorì Roma,
Arno fama ha per voi, già l'ebbe Sorga;
così tutto trapassa e mai non riede.

6 FROM BENEDETTO VARCHI TO MESSER BARTOLOMEO AMMANNATI

[Varchi]

In this my lot more bitter than any other,
there is nothing that can, that must any longer help
me other than your living bronzes and living
marbles, which give life and take away death, 4
and your pure-hearted, lofty consort, with her
polished prose and limpid verse, noble Ammannati,
who look wholly dismayed to me, albeit wise and
strong. 8
But who had or has such wisdom or
strength, modern or ancient, that he would be
sufficient to parry or suffer a blow so grave? 11
As for myself, I became all stricken and
ashen, and still am, when I heard, "Luca Martini,
Luca Martini is dead."[12] 14

7 FROM MESSER GHERARDO SPINI ON THE DEATH OF MADONNA LAURA BATTIFERRA'S FATHER

Do you wish, noble lady, to form a vast
Aegean, a tempestuous Euxine, of daughterly tears,
so many of which we see in streaks on your visage,
nurturing and divine? 4
Let not it avail you to see them roil as much
as the Tyrrhenian and Apennines gird; may others'
prayers, devout and dear, lift from you whatever
death, destiny bring to you. 8
Neither do hurt to your honored locks, but
cease your sorrow and weeping and look out at the
world, for every mortal effect meets you and yields. 11
Carthage fell aforetime, and Rome flowered;
Arno is famous because of you, so was Sorgue; thus
all passes away never to return.[14] 14

8 RISPOSTA DI MADONNA LAURA[15]

Altro che pianger sempre e sospirare
finché 'l giorno fatal mi sia vicino,
dolce refugio alle mie pene amare,
lassa me, più non bramo e non desiro, 4
or che l'altero tronco, che poggiare
faceami al ciel per sì dritto cammino,
e di cui ramo son, per tutto appare
secco l'antico umor, squallido e chino; 8
ben contra lui, che tutto vince e doma,
aggio uno schermo sol, ch'ancor risorga
la speme, ch'ei sotterra asconder crede. 11
Spina gentile, il vostro alto idioma
possent'è solo a far che chiaro sorga
qual nome oscuro più l'oblio possiede. 14

9 A MADONNA LAURA BATTIFERRA DEGL'AMMANNATI[17]

[Bronzino]

Quanto men del mortal più dell'eterno
avete, o donna, a cui non è simile,
men grave esser vi dee s'alma gentile
lieta sen vole ov'aggia il tempo a scherno; 4
e ch'altro è morir qui, che sempiterno
viver nel cielo? e 'n chiaro e dolce aprile,
sciolti dalla pregion terrena e vile,
cangiar quest'aspro, amaro e scuro verno? 8
Dunque al terrestre omai paterno velo,
chiaro per sé né men per voi, quel pianto
baste, ché tal fin qui dato gli avete, 11
e date all'alma, che beata in cielo
gode di gioia e di pace, altrettanto
tornando a voi donde partita sete. 14

8 MADONNA LAURA'S RESPONSE

Only to weep always and sigh until the
fateful day is near for me, sweet refuge from my
bitter pains, woe is me! I no longer yearn or wish
for anything else, 4
now that the proud trunk that set me
climbing to heaven on such a straight path, and of
which I am a branch, its aging sap dried, seems
withered all over and bent. 8
Indeed, against him who conquers and holds
all in his sway, I have only one shield, that there
resurge again the hope he thinks he can hide underground. 11
Noble Spini, your lofty speech alone has the
power to make even an obscure name closely
guarded by oblivion rise up in fame.[16] 14

9 TO MADONNA LAURA BATTIFERRA DEGLI AMMANNATI

[Bronzino]

The less you have of the mortal, the more you have of
the eternal, O lady, whom none other is like; it
should weigh less on you if a noble soul flies happy
to a place where it can disdain time; 4
and what else is it to die here, if not to live
eternally in heaven? And released from base and
earthly prison, to change this harsh, bitter, and dark
winter into a bright and sweet April? 8
Therefore enough now of that weeping for
the earthly paternal veil, famous in itself no less
than for you, for you have so far given him 11
and give his soul so much that, blessed in
heaven, he basks in joy and peace, returning as
much to you whence you departed.[18] 14

10 A MESSER BENEDETTO VARCHI[19]

[Bronzino]

Sacro Damon, s'alla tua fiamma terna,
ch'onestate e valor rendea sì chiara,
nuovo e subito schermo non ripara,
dall'umido Austro, onde s'oscura e alterna, 4
tosto fia spenta, ché per grave interna
doglia negli occhi, ov'ogni ben s'impara,
ch'Amor l'accese, appena tiensi, avara
fatta seguir nel ciel l'alma paterna. 8
Che fia di te? che fia di noi? del mondo
che fia, s'al ciel sen vola? e freddo e scuro
torna, né fia che più l'allume o scalde? 11
Opra, saggio Damon, tornar giocondo
sì fero assalto e 'l duolo acerbo e duro,
con dolci preghi e ragion vive e salde. 14

11 GHERARDO SPINI ALL'ECCELLENTE MESSER BARTOLOMEO AMANNATI, IN MATERIA DEL PALAZZO DE' PITTI, PER LA MORTE DELLA SIGNORA DUCHESSA[21]

Fidia, l'altero nido, emulo a quanti
già Menfi, Roma e Babilonia ornaro
de' marmi, onde son ricche e Luni e Paro,
più non fregiar, ma sol d'angoscie e pianti, 4
ché s'albergar non debbe i lumi santi,
che già vinser le stelle, ed or diparo
sen'van con Febo in cielo, senza il suo chiaro
sol, non più Delfo aver Flora si vanti. 8
Lascia pur d'illustrar tanto ricetto,
benché Scopa e Leon trapassi ognora,
ché solo il raggio suo le fea perfetto. 11
Ben ti lice sperar, saggio intelletto,
sì come fusti qui, d'essere ancora
suo celeste lassù degno architetto. 14

10 TO MESSER BENEDETTO VARCHI

[Bronzino]

Sacred Damon, if a new shield does not
quickly rescue your third flame, which honesty and
worth made so bright, damp Auster, who makes her
dim and waver, 4
will soon snuff her out, since she hardly
holds back the heavy inner sorrow in her eyes,
which teach all that is good, for Love lighted her,
and she wants selfishly to follow her father's soul into heaven. 8
What will become of you? What of us? If
she flies away to heaven, what will become of the
world? Will it go cold and dark, without anything
to bring back its light or warmth? 11
Work, wise Damon, to turn such a fierce
assault and the bitter, hard sorrow to joy, with sweet
prayers and reasons live and sound.[20] 14

11 FROM GHERARDO SPINI TO THE EXCELLENT MESSER BARTOLOMEO AMMANNATI ON THE MATTER OF THE PITTI PALACE, FOR THE DEATH OF SIGNORA THE DUCHESS

Fidia, adorn no more the lofty nest,
emulous of as many as once decorated Memphis,
Rome, and Babylonia, with those marbles that are
the wealth of Luni and Paros, but only with anguish
and weeping; 4
for if the holy eyes are no longer to dwell
there, they that once outshone the stars and now go
to heaven side by side with Phoebus, let Flora without its
bright sun no longer boast of having Delphi. 8
Leave off now making illustrious so great a
receptacle, even though you ever outstrip Scopas
and Leoni, for only her ray made them perfect. 11
You are entitled to hope, wise intellect, that
just as you were here, you will yet be up there her
worthy celestial architect.[22] 14

12 PER LA MORTE DEL CARDINAL DE' MEDICI,[23] LAURA BATTIFERRA

Com'apparir talor celeste e chiaro
lampo si vede, e balenar fuggendo,
tal apparve e sparío tuo lume, essendo
la terra indegna di splendor sì raro. 4
Così gustato appena il fele amaro,
che con breve dolcezza ir suol mescendo
questo mondo fallace, al ciel salendo
spregi quanto qui par dolce e caro. 8
Poiché nel sommo sol, da noi partito,
vivono intenti tuoi sereni lumi,
ch'han pochi eguali a te luci alme e vere, 11
mentre al mar correran veloci i fiumi,
e 'l ciel rivolgerà sue vaghe spere,
fia 'l tuo nome fra noi pianto e gradito. 14

13 IN MORTE DELLA DUCHESSA,[25] LAURA BATTIFERRA

Lassa, nel tuo partire, ahi lassa, in quante
lacrime io viva, in quante pene il core
fatt'albergo immortal d'alto dolore,
ben lo veggion dal ciel tue luci sante. 4
Indi d'amaro umor marmo stillante
il mio Fidia vedrai, ch'eterno onore
non chiede o spera, poiché 'l tuo splendore
sparìo, ch'illustri fea l'opre sue tante: 8
Ed io, che già lasciai l'ago e la gonna
per talor gir lunghesso Anfriso ed Ea
di te cantando, ancor ch'in basse rime, 11
che sperar deggio più, se musa e donna
qui non mi sei? se tu qual pria non stime
quest'umil serva tua, celeste dea? 14

12 FOR THE DEATH OF THE MEDICI CARDINAL BY LAURA BATTIFERRA

As a celestial and bright lightning burst is
sometimes seen and flashing flees, so your light
appeared and disappeared, since earth was unworthy
of a splendor so rare. 4
Thus, after barely tasting the bitter gall that
this deceitful world is wont to dilute with brief
sweetness, rising to heaven you disdain as
much as here seems sweet and dear. 8
Now that, departed from us, your serene
eyes live intent on the highest sun and few lights
there are the equal of yours, nurturing and true, 11
then as long as rivers will flow swiftly to sea and heaven
turns its loving spheres, your name is one we shall
weep for and welcome.[24] 14

13 ON THE DEATH OF THE DUCHESS BY LAURA BATTIFERRA

Alas, since your departure, alas, how many
the tears I live with! How many pains in my heart,
made a dwelling immortal for deep sorrow! Well
your holy eyes see it from heaven. 4
From there you will see my Fidia, who
sheds bitter marble teardrops, neither asking nor
hoping for everlasting honor since the loss of your
splendor, which made lustrous his so many works. 8
And I, who once set aside needle and skirt to
stroll betimes alongside Amphrysus and Aeas, as I
sing again of you, albeit in lowly rhymes, 11
what more can I hope if you are not here as
my muse and my mistress? If you do not esteem as
before this humble servant of yours, heavenly goddess?[26] 14

14 IN MORTE DI DON GRAZIA[27] LAURA BATTIFERRA

Ahi ciel, che giova 'l mar mostrar senz'onda
queto e nel lito ognor mille alcioni,
se in sul principio al bel Grazia t'opponi,
e spento lui ne dai piaga profonda? 4
D'appio lugubre, o di qual altra fronda
e più mesta, or si cinga e s'incoroni
Nettuno e Teti; or Noti ed Aquiloni
turbino 'l regno lor, battan la sponda. 8
Non però ti vantar ch'ei resti morto,
Parca crudel, che s'arrivare in Colchi
non può l'altero giovinetto accorto, 11
al Borea, all'Austro, all'occidente, all'orto,
ancor che vincitor l'Egeo non solchi,
la chiara fama sua troverà porto. 14

15 A MADONNA LAURA BATTIFERRA[29]

[Beccadelli]

D'edere e mirti e verdi lauri a schiera
ha Castalia una piaggia intorno cinta,
che dentro di fiorite erbe dipinta
spira soave e dolce primavera. 4
Quivi non falce, né pastor né fera
osa appressar, o man d'ingiuria tinta,
tale innocenza e purità non finta
guardia vi fanno da matino a sera; 8
ma ritrovano ben la strada aperta
pensier d'onore e voglie umili e caste,
che di virtute Amor nel cor imprime, 11
con le quai scorte quando LAURA entraste,
Euterpe disse, "Ecco la gloria certa
del bel Metauro e de le Tosche rime." 14

14 ON THE DEATH OF DON GRAZIA BY LAURA BATTIFERRA

Ah, heaven, what avails it for you to show
the sea at rest without waves and ever upon the shore a
thousand halcyons, if you are against fair Grazia from the start,
and after snuffing him out, you wound us deeply? 4
Let Neptune and Thetis gird and crown
themselves with lugubrious parsley or whatever
other bough is most mournful; let now Notus and
North Wind perturb their realm, let them beat upon the shore. 8
But do not boast that he will stay dead, cruel
Fate, for if the proud wise youth cannot arrive at
Colchis, 11
at Boreas, at Auster, at the occident, at the
rising sun, even though he not ply the Aegean as a
conqueror, his bright fame will find a port.[28] 14

15 TO MADONNA LAURA BATTIFERRA

[Beccadelli]

Ivies, myrtles, and green laurels in a troop
encircle Castalia on one of her slopes, upon whose
grasses painted with flowers springtime blows soft
and sweet. 4
There no scythe, no shepherd or beast,
dares approach, or a hand tinted with harm, for such
innocence and unfeigned purity stand guard there
from morning to evening, 8
but the way is indeed open to thoughts of
honor and humble and chaste desires, which
impress the heart with love of virtue, 11
when with those escorts you entered, LAURA,
Euterpe said, "Behold the sure glory of the fair
Metauro and of Tuscan rhymes."[30] 14

16 DI MADONNA LAURA BATTIFERRA[31]

Ben'ha il felice e nobil Arno donde,
di puro argento e luci d'ambre pieno,
il suo bel fonte colmi e 'l corno e 'l seno,
vie più sempre d'onor, di gloria abonde, 4
da poi che 'l vostro piè, che far può l'onde
eguali al gran Peneo del picciol Reno,
premendo intorno a lui l'erbe e 'l terreno,
gli veste di smeraldi ambe le sponde; 8
e debbe anco invidiar Felsina a Flora
con tutta Illiria, e non solo Epidauro,
a cui togliete voi sedia e dimora, 11
anzi quanta ebber mai gioia e tesauro
com'Etruria e 'l suo Re, ch'or sì v'onora,
speran de' danni lor per voi resaturo. 14

17[33]

Curzio, per cui l'antico secol d'auro
ritorna al suo primiero illustre vanto,
e 'n chiuso speco ricovrarsi in tanto
per te si vede lei che punse Aglauro, 4
or ch'io, tuo chiaro don, la chioma in lauro
veggio vicino a l'Olimpo, anzi altretanto,
alzarsi Catria mio ch'a la tua Manto
fu caro un tempo, e farsi oro il Metauro; 8
perch'io ben canterò come conquiso
dal sacro Ercole tuo fra noi si vede
altro Busiri, altr'Idra empia lernea, 11
in qual parte del cielo, in qual idea
ha il suo santo operar degna mercede:
nel tuo stil già penetro e 'n lui m'affiso. 14

16 BY LAURA BATTIFERRA DEGLI AMMANNATI

Glad and noble Arno has good reason, filled
with pure silver and lights of amber, to brim his fair
fountain and horn and breast, all the more that he
abound in honor, in glory, 4
since your foot, which can make the little
Reno's waves equal to great Peneus, pressing on the
grasses and terrain around him, dresses both his
shores in emerald; 8
and Felsina must also envy Flora, with all
Ilyria, and not just Epidaurus, from which you take
seat and dwelling, 11
nay, as much as they ever had joy and treasure,
like Etruria and her king, who now so honor you,
they hope by you to be restored of their hurts.[32] 14

17

Curzio, because of whom the ancient golden
age returns to its primal illustrious vaunt, and she
who pricked Aglauros is sighted, meanwhile taking
refuge because of you in a locked cave, 4
now that I, bright gift of yours, see near
Olympus, nay, rising as high, my laurel-tressed
Catria, who was at one time dear to your Manto, and
Metauro turning to gold, 8
for that I shall indeed sing of how we see
in our midst another Busirus, another wicked
Lernean Hydra, conquered by your sacred Ercole, 11
whatever part of heaven, whatever idea brings worthy
reward to his holy deeds; I pierce your style and
make myself fast to it.[34] 14

18[35] RISPOSTA DI MADONNA LAURA BATTIFERRA IN RISPOSTA DI QUELLO DEL VARCHI CHE INCOMINCIA PRIMA DOPO LA MIA PRIMIERA FRONDE

Sì come allor che oscura nube asconde
a' naviganti il lor gradito segno,
errando scorre il travagliato legno,
e par che d'ora in or rompa o s'affonde, 4
ma poi ch'amico ciel chiara diffonde
sua luce, o 'l doppio appar salubre segno,
la gente tolta all'aspro strazio indegno
empie l'aer di voci alte e gioconde. 8
Varchi, tal noi vedemmo in poco d'ora
chi libra Etruria con sì giusta lancia,
nostra fidata tramontana ognora, 11
di fero nembo aspersa e quasi allora
mostrarsi a noi, che 'n lagrimosa guancia
Dio ringraziam di tal periglio fuora. 14

19 NELLA MORTE DE MICHELAGNOLO BUONARROTI[37]

[Laura Battiferra degli Ammannati]

Ragione è ben ch'i freddi e duri sassi,
ch'ebber caldo da te molle spirare,
versin tutti ad ognor lagrime amare,
poi ch'oggi in terra gl'abbandoni e lassi; 4
ragion fia che i color caduchi e bassi,
di cui fingesti altere forme e rare
sì vere, che 'l ver finto in quelle appare,
d'onor sien privi e di vaghezza cassi. 8
Or convien ch'alti tempi e illustri tetti
cui sagro desti e sì real decoro,
giacciano oscuri, al lor fato vicino, 11
e che dolente d'Aganippe il coro
viva, poi che non più soli e perfetti
versi t'ode cantare, Angel divino. 14

18 MADONNA LAURA BATTIFERRA'S REPLY TO THE SONNET BY VARCHI THAT BEGINS "FIRST AFTER MY FIRST FROND"

As when dark cloud cover hides from
mariners the sign they welcome, and their troubled
vessel runs off course and from one moment to the
next seems ready to break up or sink, 4
but then, when a friendly sky diffuses its
bright light, or a double sign appears boding well,
the people snatched from that harsh, unwarranted
torment fill the air with voices loud and joyous, 8
Varchi, so we saw in a brief hour the man
who weighs Etruria with such just balance, ever our
trusted pole star, 11
aspersed with a fierce nimbus and almost
then appear to us, who with teary cheek thank
God that he is out of such peril.[36] 14

19 ON THE DEATH OF MICHELANGNOLO

[Laura Battiferra degli Ammannati]

Well right it is for the cold and hard stones,
warmed by your soft breath, all to pour forth
endlessly bitter tears, since today you abandon and
leave them on earth; 4
well right it will be for the fleeting and
lowly colors from which you feigned lofty forms
and rare, so true that the truth looks false in them, to
be deprived of honor and their delight shattered. 8
Now must lofty temples and illustrious
dwellings, to which you gave sacred and such regal
adornment, lie darkened as their fate approaches, 11
and Aganippe's chorus must live in grief,
since it no longer hears the perfect verses that only
you can sing, Angel divine.[38] 14

20 CANZONE NELLA MORTE DI MICHELAGNOLO BUONARROTI[39]

[Madonna Laura Battiferra degli Ammannati]

20.1

Quanti leggiadri fiori
nel ricco grembo accogli,
Flora, Flora gentil, deh, versa omai,
e sol d'aspri dolori
empi 'l bel seno e sciogli
voci interrotte e lagrimosi guai,
ché 'l tuo danno d'assai, 7
e sia quanto vuol grave,
vince ogn'altro, da poi
che con gl'acuti suoi
dardi lei, che mercè d'alcun non ave,
spense chi fea con sua mirabile arte
rivale in terra di Natura l'Arte. 13

20.2

Vint'ha l'empia ed ingorda
de' tuoi più chiari figli
lui, che l'invidia oppresse, ahi crudo fato,
ahi dispietata corda,
ahi fero stral, che pigli
oggi a turbar nostro felice stato;
oggi ben resta orbato 20
per lo tuo colpo fero
d'ogn'ornamento il mondo,
ch'ei dianzi alto e giocondo
rendè col suo celeste magistero,
e con profili e scorci, e lumi ed ombre
abbracciar ne feo marmi e stringer l'ombre. 26

20.3

Spirar sì dolce diede
ai color vaghi, ai sassi,
mentre fu in terra quest'Angel divino,

20 CANZONE ON THE DEATH OF MICHELAGNOLO BUONARROTI

[Madonna Laura Battiferra degli Ammannati]

20.1

As many lovely flowers
as you gather in your rich bosom,
Flora, noble Flora, oh, scatter now,
and fill your fair breast only
with harsh sorrows and send forth
halting words and tearful woes, 7
for your great loss,
as grave as can be,
conquers every other, now that
with her sharp darts,
she who spares no one
has snuffed out the man whose amazing art made
Art the rival of Nature on earth[40]. 13

20.2

She, wicked and greedy, has conquered
the brightest of your sons,
he whom envy oppressed, ah, cruel fate,
ah, the merciless bowstring,
ah, the fierce arrow that you snatch up
today to trouble our happy state;
today your fierce blow 20
has bereft of all
adornment the world
that he erstwhile rendered
lofty and joyful with his celestial mastery,
and with profiles and angles, lights and shadows,
he made us embrace marbles and clasp shadows.[41] 26

20.3

Breath so sweet
to winsome colors and to the stones
this Angel divine gave while he was on earth

che chi l'opre sue vede,
di stupor s'empie e fassi
quasi di pietra al bel lavor vicino.
O raro alto destino, 33
o forme uniche e nuove,
ch'in voi chiaro e distinto
sì 'l ver mostrate finto,
e finto il ver, ch'altri non sa ben dove
il ver oggetto mai ritrovar possa,
per ch'in voi scorge e spirto e carne ed ossa. 39

20.4

Già 'l coro d'Elicona
che lungi alle sagre onde,
dove ei talor cantò lodati carmi,
a lui cinge corona;
or di lugubri fronde
sé cinge, e dice in carte, in tele, in marmi,
"Di speme si disarmi 46
ogn'ingegno mortale
che tentasse onorare
con doti uniche e rare
questo spirto celeste ed immortale,
ché l'altere opre sue mostran fra noi,
ch'ogni gloria è minor de' pregi suoi." 52

20.5

Dunque sospir cocenti,
calde lagrime ognora,
faccian palese il nostro grave danno,
ché sue virtuti ardenti,
che 'l ciel loda ed onora,
di terren pregi altrui mestier non hanno. 58
Sol possa il nostro danno,
l'innumerabil pene,
non turbar le serene
eterne gioie sue negli'alti giri,
ov'è 'l BUON spirto, a' miglior spirti ARROTO
ma fargli in parte il grande affetto noto. 64

that whoever sees his works
is filled with stupor and nearly
turns to stone when approaching the fair workmanship.
O rare lofty destiny,
O unique and unseen forms of yours,
who show true things clear and distinct
as feigned and feigned things as true,
so that people do not know well where
they can ever find the true object,
because in yours they discern spirit, flesh, and bones.[42]

20.4

Already Helicon's chorus,
who along the sacred waves
where he betimes sang lauded verse,
circles him with a crown,
circles itself now with lugubrious boughs,
and says on paper, on canvases, in marbles,
"Be disarmed of hope
every mortal mind that
attempts to honor
with unique and rare gifts
this celestial and immortal spirit,
for among us his lofty works show
that all glory is lesser than his merits."[43]

20.5

Then let the searing sighs,
hot tears, ever
make public our grave loss,
for his ardent virtues,
which heaven praises and honors,
have no need for people's earthly prizes.
Only let our loss,
the countless pains,
not trouble his serene
eternal joys in the high circles,
where the GOOD spirit is, HONED to the better spirits,
but make him know in part our great affection.[44]

20.6

E tu mio caro e fido
dolce amato consorte,
ch'innanzi al nuovo Re de' lidi Toschi,
d'ogni virtute nido;
da sue parole accorte,
forse contra gli spirti ignari e loschi,
cui rende invidia foschi,
meritasti aver lode
non mendicata o finta;
ben giusto è se 'l duol vinta
ha la tua alma, e se di pianger gode
oggi dintorno all'alto suo feretro,
e s'io nel duol per lui teco m'impetro.

20.7

Canzon, vanne ancor tu mesta et dolente,
dove con esso Flora ognor esangue,
Dedalo, Apollo, Apelle, e Fidia langue.

21 DI MADONNA LAURA BATTIFERRA DE GLI AMMANNATI[47]

Cadde la gloriosa antica Roma
ne' tempi ingiusti, e sue vestigie sparte,
vero di maraviglia essempio e d'arte,
hanno or d'erbe neglette indegna soma;
ma nel tuo chiaro e candido idioma,
sol ne le tue moderne e dotte carte,
giovan'ANTICO, il buon popul di Marte
vede che l'opre sue tempo non doma;
ne' tuoi detti di fede e d'onor carchi,
d'altezza emuli al ciel, come pria scorge
e tempi e cerchi e terme e mole ed archi,
indi 'l famoso Tebro all'Elsa porge
eterne lodi, ed ambo in dir son parchi
ch'oggi Roma per te più bella sorge.

20.6

And you, my dear and faithful
sweet beloved consort,
who before the new king of the Tuscan shores,
nest of every virtue,
deserved from his wise words,
perhaps against ignorant or suspicious spirits,
whom envy renders dark, 71
to have praise
not beggared or feigned;
it is indeed just if sorrow has conquered
your soul, and if today it relishes weeping
around his noble bier,
and if in sorrow I bow down in prayer for him with you.[45] 77

20.7

Song, go you too downcast and sorrowful, where
Flora languishes, ever bloodless like him, with Daedalus,
Apollo, Apelles, and Phidias.[46] 80

21 FROM MADONNA LAURA BATTIFERRA DE GLI AMMANNATI

Glorious ancient Rome fell in unjust times,
and her scattered vestiges, true example of marvel
and of art, now have an unworthy burden of
neglected grasses, 4
but in your clear and pure idiom, only in
your modern and learned pages, young ANCIENT,
the good people of Mars see that time
does not prevail over their works; 8
in your words charged with faith and honor,
emulous of heaven in their height, no sooner does
famous Tiber discern the temples and circuses and
baths and buildings and arches 11
than he offers to Elsa eternal praises, and
both are frugal when they say that because of you
Rome today more beautiful rises.[48] 14

22[49]

Superna alma regina,
a cui la terra e 'l cielo
umile ognor s'inchina,
oggi colmi d'ardente e puro zelo, 4
ti preghian che 'l bel germe alto e gentile
cresca al gran tronco suo pari e simile,
sì che d'Etruria i tuoi devoti regi
abbino in terra e 'n ciel corone e fregi. 8

23[51] DE LAURA BATIFERRIA AMMANNATA

[Sanleolino]

CLIO Ammannatae audisset cum carmina Laurae,
"Quando", inquit, "nobis est decima orta soror"?

POEMS OF UNCERTAIN DATE

24[52]

[Cellini to Varchi]

La ricca pianta, ben ch'alquanto acerba,
che da voi surge a questo nuovo aprile,
laur che s'alza al ciel fresco e sottile,
frutti, ombre e fior già stende amplie all'erba, 4
mirate questo: a voi tal gloria serba
etterna, santa, sacra, alta e virile,
ch'ogni altra appo di lui fia bassa e vile,
pur or la scorza ingrossa e 'l fusto innerva, 8
gloria al bel Arno e gli ornamenti suoi,
rugiada infronda, infiora, infresca e dora
d'altre più nobil gemme rare e vaghe. 11
Se oggi a Maian, fra tante ninfe e maghe,
lei col canto i pastor vince e gli eroi,
questo 'l mondo di speme e d'opre onora. 14

22

Supernal, nurturing queen,
to whom earth and heaven
ever humbly bow,
today brimming with ardent and pure zeal, 4
we pray you that the fair seed grow tall and noble,
equal and like unto its great trunk,
so that your devoted kings of Etruria may
have crowns and adornments on earth and in heaven.[50] 8

23 ON LAURA BATTIFERRA AMMANNATI

[Sanleolino]

When Clio heard the poems of Laura Ammannati, she asked,
"When did our tenth sister come into the world?"

POEMS OF UNCERTAIN DATE

24

[Cellini to Varchi]

The rich plant, although somewhat unripe,
that surges where you are into this new April, a
laurel fresh and slim that rises to heaven, already
spreading fruits, flowers, and ample shade to the grass, 4
behold this: it promises such eternal, saintly,
holy, lofty, and virile glory to you, that every other
will be low and base by comparison; even now the
bark thickens and the trunk strengthens, 8
glory to the fair Arno and its ornaments, it
fronds, flowers, refreshes, and gilds with a dew
nobler than other rare, winsome gems. 11
If today at Maiano, among so many nymphs
and enchantresses, she with her song conquers
shepherds and heroes, this honors the world with hope and deeds.[53] 14

25 DEL LASCA SOPRA IL RITRATTO DI MADONNA LAURA BATTIFERRA AL BRONZINO[54]

Angelo esser devea, senon ch'invano
era ogni sua fatica, ogni opra, ogni arte;
non può cosa divina in nulla parte
esser ritratta mai da mortal mano;
dunque, voi spirito angelico e sovrano
potete sol pingendo a parte a parte
ritrar le grazie in lei diffuse e sparte,
ove ogni altro pennel sarebbe vano.
Come gl'occhi sereni e 'l santo viso
occhio terren saria stato possente
poter mai rimirare intento e fiso?
Beato voi, cui solo il ciel consente
il senno e la beltà di Paradiso
far conta e chiara alla futura gente!

26 RISPOSTA[56]

[Bronzino]

Lasca gentil, l'alto favor che 'n mano
lo stil mi pose, onde a vergar le carte
vi trae cortese e caldo affetto, e 'n parte
dal ver, per troppo amor, vi fa lontano;
non perch'io degno, o che forse altro umano
miglior di me ne fosse, a me comparte
dono intero di lui, non merto o d'arte,
ch'ha d'ogni grazia a pien l'arbitrio in mano.
Ei sol mi guida, e se da me diviso
non sia, ma regga e la mano e la mente
fin ch'io giunga felice al fin prefiso,
vi giuro, che per mio valor non sente
d'alzarsi l'alma a sì grand'opra assiso,
se non d'umil seguirla e reverente.

25 FROM IL LASCA ON THE PORTRAIT OF MADONNA LAURA BATTIFERRA

It must have been an angel, even though its
every effort, every act, and every art would have
been in vain; a divine thing cannot be portrayed in
any part by mortal hand; 4
thus, angelic and sovereign spirit, your
painting can only portray part by part the graces
diffused and scattered in her, where every other
brush would have tried in vain. 8
How ever could earthly eye have had the power
to gaze intent and fixed on her serene eyes, her
sainted face? 11
Blessed are you, you alone whom heaven
allows to make known and public to future people
the wisdom and beauty of Paradise![55] 14

26 RESPONSE

[Bronzino]

Kind Lasca, the favor from on high that put
the stylus in my hand, whence courteous and warm
affection impels you to set pen to paper and makes
you stray in part from the truth for too much love, 4
is apportioned to me not by merit or art, but
is a gift wholly from Him in whose hand lies fully
the power to choose all grace, not because I am
worthy, or because there might not be another
human better than I. 8
He alone guides me, and if He be not
separated from me, but sustain my hand and my
mind until I happily reach the preordained end, 11
I swear to you, seated before so great a
work, that by my power my soul feels incapable of arising,
but can only follow it humble and reverent.[57] 14

27 A MADONNA LAURA BATTIFERRA DELLI AMMANNATI[58]

[Bronzino]

Ben hai, Dafne, ragion se non per altro
che per essere stato a tali e tanti
pastori in pregio, se gl'estremi vanti
gli doni e 'l lodi sovra qualunque altro,
ma questi nodi, onde l'un lega l'altro?
che di' con sì bell'arte? e de' prestanti
intagli in treccie d'edere e d'acanti,
ond'io stupisco e più non penso ad altro?
Vedi in tre lingue appuntata e distinta
qual'è l'ornata gorbia, e di fin oro
la ghiera a stelle è smaltata e scolpita.
Tuo sia, che degna sol di tal tesoro
confesso, e baste a me questa dipinta
vetrice a darme, ove si cade, aita.

28 DI MADONNA LAURA BATTIFERRA A BRONZINO[60]

Così nel volto rilucente e vago
la pastorella tua, chiaro Crisero,
quanto brama il tuo cor casto e sincero
ti mostri aperto, e sii contento e pago;
come la propria mia novella imago
della tua dotta man lavoro altero,
ogni mio affetto scuopre ogni pensiero,
quantunque il cor sia di celarlo vago,
e così l'arbocel ch'amai cotanto,
degno rival d'Apollo in fino al cielo,
colto da te mai sempre verde s'erga,
com'io la tua mercé di doppio vanto
cingo il mio basso oscuro umile stelo
per ch'Austro od Aquilon non lo disperga.

27 TO MADONNA LAURA BATTIFERRA DELLI AMMANNATI

[Bronzino]

Truly, Daphne, you are right to give him the
highest honors and praise him over anyone
else, if for no other reason than that he is held
in esteem by so many and such great shepherds; 4
but these knots, whence are they bound one
to another? What are you saying with such fair art?
And about cunning carvings in tresses of ivy and of
acanthus, whence I marvel and no longer think of anything else? 8
You see how the ornate staff is pointed and
divided into three tongues, and the fine golden
circlet is enameled and sculpted with stars. 11
Let this treasure be yours, for I confess you
alone worthy of it, and for myself let suffice this
painted willow to give me help, should need befall.[59] 14

28 BY MADONNA LAURA BATTIFERRA TO BRONZINO

Just as your shepherdess, with face shining
and longing, openly shows you, bright Crisero, how
much she desires your chaste and sincere heart (be
you then content and satisfied), 4
so thus my own new image,
lofty work of your learned hand,
my every affection and every thought discloses ,
albeit my heart longs to keep them hidden. 8
And thus may the sapling that I so loved
soar always evergreen up to the sky, cultivated by
you, worthy rival of Apollo, 11
just as I, thanks to you, gird with double
honor my lowly, little-known, humble trunk, so that
Southwind or Northwind not blow it away.[61] 14

29[62]

[Bronzino]

Quindi u' l'aurora il ciel dipinge e 'naura,
e quinci ove più ferve il sole e splende,
move l'ardor, ch'addoppio il cor m'incende,
e quinci e quindi a rinfrescarmi l'aura; 4
e quella fronda, ch'Arno e l'onda Isaura,
felici rive, or mira e cotal rende
grato odor, che per tutto in pregio ascende,
di doppia speme il crin mi cinge e illaura. 8
L'alma ch'or questa, or quella luce accende,
cui parimente inchina, in lor restaura
virtù che l'alza ov'il suo ben conprende: 11
e s'Amor dice il ver, pria che quest'aura
passi all'eterna, ancor di farmi attende
tal che nol sdegne e l'una e l'altra LAURA. 14

30[64]

[Bronzino]

Vano è certo il desir e la speme, onde
si regge Amore? or le tue faci e i dardi
tue più calde, e più forti, e i più gagliardi
assalti, e quanto in te più forza abbonde 4
non hai già stanco? e non è questa all'onde
penee l'altera figlia, a cui fur tardi
del sole i passi? e già se ben riguardi
scopre il bel tronco e l'onorate fronde; 8
né so per quanto, ma tem'io che 'l ghiaccio,
che la circonda, e 'l ferro, ond'ha radice,
la faccia scarsa ancor de' suoi bei rami; 11
degg'io dunque seguir, vuoi tu ch'io brami
chi giungnere o piegar non puossi? o lice
stornar per preghi? o cinger divin braccio? 14

29

[Bronzino]

There where aurora paints and inaurates the
sky, and here where the sun shines most intensely
stirs the ardor that doubly burns my heart, and here
and there the aura that refreshes me; 4
and the bough that now beholds the Arno
and Isauran wave, happy shores! and renders such a
welcome odor that it everywhere rises in worth,
with double hope circles and enlaurels my tresses. 8
The soul now kindled by this light, now by that,
before both of whom it bows alike, restores in them
the strength that raises it up to comprehend its well-being, 11
and if Love tells the truth, before this aura
passes to the eternal, he still is waiting to make me
one that not be disdained by both one and the other LAURA.[63] 14

30

[Bronzino]

Are the desire and hope by which Love
rules surely vain? Your torches and darts, the hottest
and the strongest, and your most daring assaults,
and as much strength as abounds in you, by now 4
have they not tired you? And is this not the
Penean waves' proud daughter, with whom the sun
could not keep pace? And already, if you look well,
she reveals her fair trunk and the honored boughs; 8
for how long, I do not know, but I fear the ice
that surrounds her and the iron in which she has her
roots may yet make her hold back her fair branches; 11
must I thus follow? Do you want me to long
for someone I cannot reach or bend? Or who cannot be
persuaded with pleas? Or encircled by a divine arm?[65] 14

31 A MESSER BARTOLOMEO AMMANNATI SCULTORE[66]

[Anonymous]

I dolci vostri e quasi vivi marmi
che voi stesso ed altrui tolgono a morte,
caro Ammannato mio, chi fia che porte
cantando al ciel con prose degne o carmi? 4
Non io, ned altri ancor per quanto parmi,
ma sol l'al[ta] e gentil vostra consorte;
dunque ella sola a sì gran peso forte,
a la bell'opra e gloriosa s'armi; 8
e con quel vago suo leggiadro stile
per cui l'antica età la nuova invidia,
con altero sembiante in atto umile, 11
dica che 'l martel vostro non simile,
ma pari a Scopa a Prassitele a Fidia,
rende pregiato questo secol vile. 14

32 DI MADONNA LAURA BATTIFERRA[68]

1
Non per più chiaro farti ed immortale
men vengo a te, famoso inclito duce,
ché tua prudentia, ove per sé non sale
umano ingegno, in fin nel ciel traluce, 4
ma sol perché pregarti oggi mi cale
per questi servi tuoi che m'han per duce,
che imitando le vergini prudenti
sperano all'ombra tua viver contenti. 8

2
Mira le cinque verginette sagge,
le cinque stolte, alma città de' fiori;
non han queste dormendo ove sin ragge
spente lor faci di novelli ardori; 12
svegliansi l'altre e ciascuna umori tragge
nella sua lampa, onde 'l suo sposo onori.
Così tu, Flora, il re del ciel possente
attendi, acceso il cor di fede ardente. 16

31 TO MESSER BARTOLOMEO AMMANNATI SCULPTOR

[Anonymous]

Your sweet and almost living marbles,
which snatch you and others from death, my dear
Ammannati, who will bear them singing to heaven
with worthy prose or poetry? 4
Not I, nor anyone else besides as far as I can
see, but only your lofty and noble consort; then
since she alone has strength for such a load, let her
arm herself for the fair and glorious task, 8
and with that winsome, graceful style of
hers, for which the ancient age envies the new, with
proud semblance in humble mien, 11
let her say that your mallet, not similar but
as a peer to Scopas, Praxiteles, and Phidias, renders
stature to this base century.[67] 14

32 BY LAURA BATTIFERRA

1
Not to make you brighter and immortal do I
come before you, famous and glorious duke, for
your prudence, where human intelligence by itself
climbs not, shines as high as heaven; but only 4
because today it concerns me to pray you on behalf
of these servants of yours who have me as a leader
and who, by imitating the prudent virgins, hope to
live in your shadow content. 8

2
Behold the five little wise virgins,
the five foolish ones, nurturing city of flowers;
these while they sleep have nothing to kindle
the spent rays with new flames; 12
the others awaken and each one pours liquid
into her lamp so that her bridegroom will honor her.
Thus you, Flora, await the powerful king of heaven,
your heart kindled with ardent faith.[69] 16

33[70] DI MADONNA LAURA BATTIFERRA

Se dietro all'orme sante
di quest'immortal dea,
in sì verdi anni andrete,
spirti gentili, al fin lieti direte,
"Questa felici sol far ne potea;
questa dal vulgo errante
sola ne parte e con ardente zelo
ne 'nfiamma e scorge al cielo."

34[72] MADONNA LAURA BATTIFERRA

TIBER

Cinto l'umido crine e 'l petto intorno
d'antica quercia, pregio alto e sovrano
d'invitti eroi, con gli altri umile e piano
vegno in questo fiorito almo soggiorno,
o d'ogni gloria adorno,
o di tutti 'l maggiore,
duce, e 'l più giusto e saggio, a farvi onore,
sperando ancor da' sette colli miei
altri fregi apportarvi, altri trofei.

35 ALLA MEDESIMA

[A Madonna Laura Battiferra di Mario Colonna][74]

MUSA mortal, che mentre in dolci canti
spiri, gli sterpi fai verdi e immortali,
mira in quanti desii tu ponga e quali
noi della tua armonia devoti amanti;
indi i mirti lasciando e gli amaranti,
sì come premi al tuo merto inequali,
qui riedi, ove di Lauri trionfali
s'adorna il letto a i tuoi vestigi santi;
e se te, dea, l'umil pregar non muove
della candida schiera ad Arno fida,
che con l'onde de gli occhi il seno accresce,

33 BY MADONNA LAURA BATTIFERRA

If you go following in the footsteps
of this immortal goddess
while you are so youthful,
noble spirits, in the end you will say with delight, 4
"She alone can make us happy;
only she separates us from the errant mob
and with ardent zeal
inflames us and leads us to heaven."[71] 8

34 MADONNA LAURA BATTIFERRA

TIBER

With my damp locks and breast encircled
by ancient oak, lofty and sovereign prize
of invincible heroes, humbly and quietly with the others
I come to this blossoming, bountiful abode, 4
O duke adorned with all glory,
the greatest of them all
and the most just and wisest, to do you honor,
hoping yet from my seven hills
to carry you other decorations, other trophies.[73] 9

35 TO THE SAME LADY

[To Madonna Laura Battiferra from Mario Colonna]

Mortal MUSE, whose breath in sweet songs
makes brambles green and immortal, behold how
many desires and what kinds you arouse in us,
devoted lovers of your harmony; 4
so then, letting go of myrtles and amaranths,
as rewards unequal to your merit, come back here,
where the river bed puts on triumphal Laurels at
your holy footsteps; 8
and if you, goddess, are unmoved by the
humble prayer of the unsullied troop true to Arno,
who with waves from our eyes swells its breast, 11

cedi al forte valor del tuo gran Giove,
perch'io, ch'era tra cigni un muto pesce,
or chiamo te con desiose strida.

36 RISPOSTA DI MADONNA LAURA[76]

Spirto divin, che così dolce canti,
e con tai passi al sacro monte sali,
che quei che primi oggi vi spiegan l'ali
sorvoli e 'nvoli i lor più chiari vanti,
io, cui giusto disdegno asconde in quanti
antri a' Cimeri ogn'or più veggio eguali,
perché non fia chi bassi accenti e frali
oda fra cigni sì canori e tanti,
fuori esco alquanto, e le voci alte e nuove
tue queta ascolto, e se 'l disio m'affida
teco già mai cantar, vano riesce;
perch'io
ritorno alle mie antiche pruove,
e 'l pianto, che da gli occhi stillando esce,
mostra quant'è mia speme incerta e 'nfida.

37 ALLA SIGNORA LAURA BATTIFERRA DEGLI AMANNATI, LAURA TERRACINA[78]

L'altiera fama e l'onorato alloro
ch'il nome vostro in mille parti scrive
non sol de[l] lauro e di fiorite olive
v'adorna, ma di gemme e di fin'oro;
io mai sempre di sterpi e sassi infioro
di Mergellina mia l'amate rive,
di Muse scarse e di sirene prive,
perché poco ho de[l] loro alto tesoro.
Chi dunque canterà, chi m'assicura
che scorno al fin non abbia e disonore,
se per cantar di voi voglio esser prima?
Miracoli son questi di natura,
che già a voi sola diè tutto l'onore
di quanti scrisser mai prosa né rima.

yield to the strong worth of your great Jove,
because I, who among swans was a mute fish, now
call out to you with desiring cries.[75] 14

36 MADONNA LAURA'S RESPONSE

Divine spirit, who sing so sweetly and climb
the sacred mount with such steps that you outfly the
finest who today spread their wings there and
outstrip their brightest vaunts, 4
I, whom just disdain hides in as many
caves as now look to me most like Cimmeria's, lest
anyone among so many such canorous swans hear
lowly accents and feeble, 8
I sally forth a fair bit, and listen quietly to
your lofty new voice, and if desire ever encourages
me to sing with you, it is in vain, 11
so that I return to my old attempts, and the
tears that come forth in drops from my eyes show
how unsure and unsound is my hope.[77] 14

37 TO SIGNORA LAURA BATTIFERRA DEGLI AMANNATI FROM LAURA TERRACINA

The proud fame and honored laurel that
write your name in a thousand places, deck you not
only with laurel and blossoming olives, but with
gems and beaten gold; 4
I forever make weeds and stones bloom on
the beloved shores of my Mergellina, being short on
Muses and bereft of sirens, for I have little of their
lofty treasure. 8
Who, then, will sing, who will assure me that I will
not have disdain and dishonor in the end if by
singing of you I want to be first? 11
These are miracles of nature, which ere now gave to
you alone all the honor of as many as ever wrote in
prose or rhyme.[79] 14

38 ALLA SIGNORA LAURA TERRACINA DEGLI INCOGNITI LAURA BATTIFFERRA RISPOSTA[80]

Voi sì ch'in mezo al sacro Aonio coro,
a cui volger del ciel mai non prescrive
termine o legge, di vostre alme e vive
frondi tessete a voi degno lavoro;
io non ch'oscura vivomi con loro,
d'Apollo in ira e de le sante dive,
e s'a carte vergar vien mai ch'arrive
mia man, l'opra è sì vil ch'io mi scoloro,
e poich'avaro il ciel m'asconde e fura
lei che fu già di me pregio e valore,
ch'Arno tanto e Ibero onora e stima;
negletta e vil, di mia fera ventura
mi doglio e piango; il tormentoso core
occulta rode e dispietata lima.

39 SONETTO DI MADONNA LAURA BATTIFERRI DE GL'AMMANNATI[82]

Tu che esalando l'alma, e tombe e sassi
rompesti, questo cor di duro smalto
romperai quando? Venga omai dall'alto
virtù che spietri 'l mondo e i pensier bassi.
La tomba del suo petto aperta stassi
per tranghiottir il corpo, ed all'assalto
contr'a te pres'han già con l'armi 'l salto,
gl'empi nemici tuoi già mai non lassi.
Pallore, tremor, orror, sudor, e gelo
caggia sopra costor, scuoti la terra,
rompi l'antro, e di nuovo un mondo crea.
Quest'è fatto un inferno, quest' in cielo
insin le man distende a farti guerra;
tuona, fulmina, incendi ogn'alma rea.

38 TO SIGNORA LAURA TERRACINA OF THE INCOGNITI LAURA BATTIFFERRA'S RESPONSE

You, amidst the sacred Aonian chorus,
to whom heaven's turning never prescribed a limit or law,
do indeed weave of your nurturing and living boughs
work worthy of yourself;
I not only live in obscurity with those
in wrath of Apollo and the sacred goddesses,
but if my hand ever come to write on papers,
the work is so base that I pale,
and since miserly heaven hides from me and steals away
her who was once my prize and worth,
whom Arno and Iberus so honor and esteem,
neglected and lowly, I grieve and weep
over my cruel fortune; an occult and pitiless file
rasps my tormenting heart.[81]

39 SONNET BY MADONNA LAURA BATTIFERRA DEGLI AMMANNATI

You who breathing out your soul broke both
tombs and stones, when will you break this heart of
hard enamel? Let now power come from above to
destone the world and base thoughts.
The tomb of his breast stands open to
swallow up the body, and your impious enemies,
never yet wearied, have already taken up arms to
assault you.
Let pallor, trembling, horror, sweat, and ice
fall upon them; let the earth shake, the cave be
broken, and create again a world.
This one is made an inferno; this one even
reaches with its hands up to heaven to war with you;
strike down with thunder, lightning, and fire every wicked soul.[83]

40 RISPOSTA DI MADONNA LAURA BATTIFERRA AL SONNETTO [DI VARCHI] CHE INCOMINCIA QUANDO IO PENSO TRA ME, CHE 'L PENSO OGN'ORA[84]

La bella Donna, il cui amor trasse fuora
dell'alto albergo suo l'unico figlio
del Padre eterno in questo basso essiglio,
ove morte per lei sostenne ancora, 4
dianzi dal Tebro, ove ella fa dimora,
vide ed udio con mesto e lieto ciglio
l'aspra strage mortal, l'empio bisbiglio
del folle stuol, del cammin dritto fuora, 8
che sul Rodano feo con virtù tanta
il Signor vostro, quanto alcun già mai,
ch'alla Chiesa di Dio portasse amore. 11
VARCHI, il vano timor che 'l cor v'ammanta,
sgombrate fuor, ché di purpureo onore
cinto il vedrete e de' suoi propri mai. 14

40 RESPONSE BY MADONNA LAURA BATTIFERRA TO THE SONNET [BY VARCHI] THAT BEGINS, "WHEN I THINK TO MYSELF, AND I THINK IT ALL THE TIME"

The beautiful Woman, whose love drew
forth from His lofty abode the Eternal Father's only
begotten son into this low exile, where He even
sustained death for her, 4
upon the Tiber, where she makes her
dwelling, saw and heard with downcast and glad
brow the bitter mortal slaughter, the wicked
murmurings of the mad crowd, outside the straight path, 8
that on the Rhone your lord made with as
much strength as anyone ever who bore love for the
Church of God. 11
VARCHI, the vain fear that mantles your
heart, chase it away, for you shall see him girded
with royal purple honor and his own May branches.[85] 14

III
"ORISON ON THE NATIVITY OF OUR LORD[1]"

BY SIGNORA LAURA BATTIFERRA DEGLI AMMANNAT

That infinite and immense charity that moved you to create the world, Father infinite and immense, again moved you to send your only begotten son to earth to save it and redeem it, when you saw that the fullness

1. Surface simplicity, both in structure and language, belies Battiferra's magisterial control of her art as writer. The composition is at once an eternal circle of divine love and a ladder of spiritual ascent. Rising to mystical climax, she pauses in thought to focus on each member of the Holy Family. As she enters into dialogue with Jesus, Mary, and Joseph one by one, the female "I" speaks with a voice reminiscent of Augustine's *Confessions,* her words both penitential and prayerful. Her questions, exclamations, and commands (ten times she asks Christ to "come") directly engage each person and create the sense of a real conversation. Christ, babe-man and man-deity, miraculously closes the abyss between heaven and earth. To contain these polarities, which recall her tautly strung sonnet "He who made earth and heaven from / nothing" (1, pt. 2.22), Battiferra merges the *sermo humilis* of the Gospels with sophisticated tropes of Ciceronian rhetoric and puns proper to Petrarchist mannerism. Metaphor dematerializes Christ into "a true orient," "light," and "dawn," as her language in its general thrust dissolves the material world into metaphysical realities. Prose becomes poetry.

This passionate meditation on the Nativity belongs to a family of Christmas literature popular during the post-Tridentine period. Battiferra's only known work in prose beyond her letters, it has recently been credited to her biographical tradition (Battiferra, *Il primo libro,* ed. Guidi; Victoria Kirkham, "La Poetessa al Presepio: Una meditazione inedita di Laura Battiferra degli Ammannati," *Filologia e critica* 27.2 [2002]: 258–76). A single copy preserves the text at Macerata, a city in the region of Le Marche that was once an important center of Jesuit culture in the papal states. Transcribed in a Jesuit hand very similar to the script in the Casanatense manuscript, the "Orison" must date from after 1572, when documented collaboration between the Ammannati and the Jesuits begins. During that time of deepening religious devotion, Laura wrote many of her "Spiritual Rhymes," and Bartolomeo—probably with his wife's silent collaboration—composed his famous "Letter to the Academy of Design" admonishing fellow artists never to make "lascivious" nudes or anything that could arouse sinful thoughts.

Here the poet takes her inspiration from Ignatius Loyola's *Spiritual Exercises* (1548), a four-week itinerary for the mind's ascent to God. Her lyrical inner dialogue with the holy family finds its niche in the second week, on the life of Christ. She follows to the letter Loyola's three-point instructions for total sensory immersion in the scene of the Nativity:

> First Point. The first Point is to see the persons; that is, to see Our Lady and Joseph and the maid, and, after His Birth, the Child Jesus, I making myself a poor creature and a

of time had come, as it had been ordained in the eternal mind. He is born of a Virgin, made under the Law and in the likeness of sinful flesh, so that all those who were under that Law could be saved and freed. Great indeed is the first gift that you gave to men, making them be born, giving them being from the nothing that they were, and so noble a being for such a great thing that they are. But truly great, and more than words can ever say, is the second gift, redeeming their evil souls and saving their lost souls, as you found them. With such high price, with such worthy manner, and with such precious blood, the Lord looked upon our humility and baseness, and he who alone is powerful and strong worked great things in us. Our God showed us his mercy when his savior gave our salvation, the savior of the world, the

---

wretch of an unworthy slave, looking at them and serving them in their needs, with all possible respect and reverence, as if I found myself present; and then to reflect on myself in order to draw some profit.

Second Point. The second, to look, mark and contemplate what they are saying, and, reflecting on myself, to draw some profit.

Third Point. The third, to look and consider what they are doing, as going on a journey and laboring, that the Lord may be born in the greatest poverty; and as a termination of so many labors—of hunger, of thirst, of heat and of cold, of injuries and affronts—that He may die on the Cross; and all this for me: then reflecting, to draw some spiritual profit.

The Spiritual Exercises of St. Ignatius of Loyola, trans. Father Elder Mullan, S.J., available at http://www.ccel.org/i/ignatius/exercises/exercises.html.

The "Orison" unfolds as a tapestry of scriptural citation, its richly layered design drawn as well from many other sources, religious and secular, literary and visual. In "the fullness of time" God sends his "only begotten son" (Gal 4:4; Jn 1:14) as "savior of the world" (Jn 4:42). Pauline language, strong in Battiferra's dedicatory letter to the *I sette salmi penitentiali,* reverberates here in the exhortation to put off the old garment of Adam and reclothe oneself in Christ (Eph 4:24; Col 3:9–10). Summoning Christ into her heart, she connects typologically Old Testament prophecy (Is 7:14) with the Annunciation (Lk 1:26–33). In contrast to our mortal clay (Gn 1:7), Christ is the man in whom "all the tribes of the earth shall be blessed" (Gn 28:14), the bridegroom who proceeds from his glorious nuptial bed (Ps 19:7), and the "sun of justice" (Mal 4:2). In this last epithet, she also quotes her own earlier madrigal on Christmas (1, pt. 2.21). Recollection of the Exodus ("Pharaoh's harsh and ancient servitude") comes filtered through Dante's *Purgatorio,* and Dantesque as well is the "bread of the angels" (*Par.* 2.11; *Conv.* 1.1.7). Even Petrarch had authorized the crèche poetically with his sonnet on Madonna Laura's birth, in a "small village" like Bethlehem (*RS* 4). Equally important, surely, were the representations of the Nativity that Ammannati's wife would have seen in pictorial cycles, from the Byzantine mosaics of Rome (where Santa Maria Maggiore had a relic of the holy cradle) to brilliantly colored Tuscan Renaissance altarpieces with the shepherds and magi in adoration at the manger. Battiferra must have known, too, Federico Brandani's *Nativity,* an imposing stucco composition for the Urbino Oratory of San Giuseppe with life-sized figures in the round (1545–50). Her chronological dualism, which anticipates the Savior's martyrdom already in infancy, has its counterpart in the motif of the sepulchral newborn, frequent in painting from the late Quattrocento onward. For the original Italian text of this "Orison," see Kirkham, "La poetessa al Presepio."

omnipotent son, who came to us from his heavenly throne. In him shall be blessed all the tribes of the earth and all peoples shall serve him. Before him every knee bends and every tongue acknowledges him. Above him rests the spirit of the Lord, the spirit of wisdom. Around him stand thousands and thousands of celestial spirits who serve and bless him. Behind him go all the ranks of the blessed souls accompanying him and praising him. And he as the bridegroom comes forth from his glorious nuptial bed, most beautiful and most adorned, all replete with paternal beauty and abundant divine treasures.

Come, then, O King of all Peoples, so long awaited and desired by them. Come, O true orient of ours, splendor of light eternal, come and open to the world a bright and new day, more happy and blessed than any other ever imaginable. O lucent sun of justice, come, yea, come, and illumine all those who dwell in darkness and in the shadow of mortal night. Come, we all pray you, and save that man whom you formed of earth. Come now, since not only what the angel said to your glorious mother, ever virgin, is accomplished, but what was predicted of you and manifested of your salvific coming by the prophets and in the Psalms. Come, sweetest Lord, yea hasten to come. Come, and delay not; free your people from cruel and infernal Pharaoh's harsh and ancient servitude. Come, blessed and true hope of ours, for we are waiting for you to open the doors of heaven, locked by the first man, to save those damned by man. Let God become man so that man may be united with God; may the lord of the angels become man to give to men the bread of the angels.

Behold, my Lord, how I enter with the thought of your Advent into the deepest and most profound and most mysterious secret. Behold how the immense and incomprehensible event presents itself to my intellect, a secret and an event more to admire with silence than to express with the tongue; a mystery most great and most celebrated, yet not revealed to the angels themselves, but only known and understood to the most simple and individual Trinity. What shall I say then, Lord, what shall I think about, what shall I meditate on, on this so solemn night, in this season so glorious and happy? Night most bright and most splendid, season peaceful and more blessed than any other! Not the occult secrets, no; not the manner of this deep mystery, no; but the sum alone, your work as it has been revealed to the world. This I shall think about and on this alone I shall meditate. But still, even this is so high and great that my small and lowly intellect cannot comprehend it. Lift up, therefore, O my soul, unto high all your powers and strengths, and consider and behold the immense greatness of your King, who comes powerful to untie you from the knot that condemns you in bonds to perpetual imprisonment and comes a savior to save you and life to make you live again.

Behold how he descends from high heaven to fill all the earth with his brightness. Behold the one who loves you in perfect charity and has had compassion and mercy on you. Behold the one to whom is given every kingdom and honor, whose power is power eternal, which will never be taken away from him, and whose kingdom shall be without end. Behold the glorious King, who has the crown of the kingdom upon his head and the kingdom itself upon his shoulders. Be comforted, be comforted cowardly woman, do you not see that the dark night has already passed and that the brightest day is nearing? Take off, for it is high time, the old garment of Adam and reclothe yourself in the new Christ. Leave, pray leave, now the works of darkness and take up the arms of light that are readied for you. Do you not see how admirably he wants to reform the body of your humility and baseness in order to configure it to the body of his greatness and brightness? Behold the happy dew that descends to make fertile your servility. See how the clouds rain what is just and holy to justify you. Behold how the earth opens to germinate the Savior who will save and redeem you. Rejoice, rejoice wholly because your gladness is coming to us. Chase from yourself every fear, for your safety is near. Shake from yourself all your sorrows now that the Savior is come, he who will take away, will take away all your iniquities and throw them into the depth of the sea.

O highest and most merciful God, what things are these that you do to my soul, what works do I now see you working for me? If I do not understand them, at least in some small measure I shall be sufficient to thank you for them and to praise you for them. And if because of their infinite and immense greatness I cannot understand and grasp them, how shall I be able to place and store them in my innermost heart, that the immortal wish become mortal, that the incomprehensible be comprehended, that the creator become created, the lord servant, God man?

Speak for me yourself, only son. Say it yourself, most glorious child, you yourself express it for me, most great little boy. Pray, sweetest life of my soul, pray, if only I at least had speech able to amuse your tenderness, eyes to watch you in the manger and in the hay, ears to hear the pastoral and angelic voices, taste to taste the sweetnesses that your sweetest lips breathe forth, in which grace so very abundant is spread and diffused, nostrils to smell the fragrance and softness that come from your delicate and pleasing members, hands to do you, together with the Virgin Mary and pure Joseph, some service and honor. But since I do not see that I have any of these sentiments worthy of that, if only I had some pretty present, some delightful gift and some convenient offering, as is customary with little children, to be able to give and present you. I have nothing, my love, that is worthy of you. I have only myself, most unworthy and most obscure. But what conformity does purity have with impurity, simplicity with malice, and brightness with darkness, with the light that is celestial and divine light? And why do I want to offer myself, me, to you? Am I not already yours? Why am I now, if not because I am yours and because you made me? But you, delight of my soul and jubilation of my heart, are the one who gives yourself to me, and to me you present yourself, and you want to, and you are all mine, my flesh and my blood and my God, gift most precious, gift most great, and gift most excellent; gift and giver who give yourself to me as a gift to enrich me and to serve me. To serve me you came as a man, your divinity locked within yourself, and to be able to serve me you came as a God because with your humanity you carry upon yourself all my iniquities, and with your divinity you forgive me for all of them and blot them out. Fairest boy, you see well the gift and present that my wickedness makes to you, because no sooner did your tender humanity open its eyes than it saw before itself suffering, sins, horror, and death; and alongside, whips, thorns, lances and nails, cross and death, all of which things would make you suffer. These, alas, are the childish ornaments that I prepare for your head, your hands, your chest, and all your person. These are the games and these the sweet pastimes that you await because of me. Your delicate members tremble, your white face grows pale, your purest flesh takes fright at the presence of such a harsh and bitter spectacle, while I replete with jubilation rejoice and delight in my salvation. Pray, might it please your majesty at least for disdain against sin to be generated in me, considering that this all happens to you because of it, and to blot it out, such that I might chase it from myself and always abhor it and hate it. Humbly in the hut and in the hay of the manger your most noble body lies, beginning to suffer cold, poverty, tribulation, and deprivation, so that I might learn to expel pride and prideful excess, electing poverty and scorn for the world and fleeing comforts and conveniences in order to follow you. You obedient, you docile and merciful, teach me with your example obedience, docility, and mercy. You, replete with all the celestial and divine virtues, long for me to reclothe myself with them and strip myself of vices. Behold, sweetest Lord of mine, how to me you were given not only as a gift, but also as an example, and notwithstanding (and woe is me for that), I do not learn, I do not imitate you, and I do not depart from so much ignorance. O most lovable and delightful child, most beautiful over all the sons of men, font and origin of love! You are all sweet and delightful, and so you draw and move all creatures to love you. Draw me and conjoin me to you without ever letting me suffer. Woe, how much better it is for me always to stay with you in this hut and in this hay than it is for me to stay in the rich inns of the world, and where better can I live than close to the true life, and where be richer than beside the eternal treasure? And where be more blessed and happy than near perfect blessedness and happiness, and to whom better bond myself than to my God, to my most sacred love, who has bonded himself with me and like a true lover has transformed himself in me, becoming a man. And now do I not hear you weep for me and sigh and suffer all the penalties, tiny little babe? Do I not see hidden among these lowly wraps and among these swaddling clothes God glorious and immortal? Do I not behold brocade, the finest gold of the divinity concealed beneath mortal wraps and veils? Do I not consider, nay, do I not acknowledge through the eyes of faith that with Jesus, Mary, and Joseph dwell the Father, the Son, and the Holy Ghost in the purest and most simple union? O little Bethlehem, truly become greatest among cities, not only of Judea, but of all the world, and truly worthy of being named City of Bread because today there is descended unto you the true and living bread, the bread of the angels, the bread that nourishes and keeps our souls alive. O lowliest hut, O place chosen by the King of the Universe! And who ever would have thought, since you were assigned to lowly animals, that our redeemer wanted to be born and shelter in you? Ah, if only I could kiss the ground and the place touched by his most holy feet! And ah, my heavenly paradise, who enclose within yourself the holy angels, the blessed souls, Christ and God, why shall I not say, "This is my resting place, this is my little dwelling, which I elect for myself for always"?

And you, humble lady, far higher than any other ever born, to whom none was similar or second before, who in your virginal cloister bore our true sun, and now you bear and bring him back like a pure white dawn and manifest and discover him to us like a bright orient, tell me, I pray, what happiness, what sweetness never before felt were yours when, with such a divine mystery and so high a sacrament, you saw the little boy child born, beneath whose flesh you knew there was the true God? Tell me now how tender was your care for him, how reverent the zeal with which you adored and blessed him, how sweet and maternal your love as you pressed him to your breast and nursed him and kissed him! I well know that if God had not then concentrated within himself all his power and his ardor, that your breast could not have suffered it, or rather for excess of sweetness and love, it would have spread wide open and burned and set fire to your lips. What joy, what peace were yours as you nourished and served and watched over him! O, what sweet conversations you must have had with him, what wise discussion yours were, how with your holy words, full of prudent simplicity and simple prudence, you must have kept him at home and caressed him, knowing that even though the little baby could not speak, the great God understood it all and that clasped in your arms he freely governed the earth and ruled the heaven and struck fear into the abyss, there where he answered deep within your heart, and you duly kept it all, and you hid it in your heart.

But you, most fortunate groom, gladdest Joseph, what are you doing? What are you thinking? Guardian, tutor, and governor of so great a son and so great a mother, how solicitously, how diligently you must hasten to serve such a divine couple, Jesus and Mary! Oh, how many times while his mother was busy you must have stayed for the baby's needs at the manger, near its grotto, to gaze and contemplate God the child, God in human flesh, God covered with mortal accidents, and how many times when he cried you must have consoled him and amused him and when he was cold, warmed him and touched him! Oh what sweet exercise yours was, what infinite pleasure you felt! Breathe of it, pray, breathe strong of it into my heart, and see to it that through your prayers I deserve in some fashion to serve him. Teach me, pray, teach me to weary myself with you to caress him, to honor him, and to praise him.

O sweet Mary, I cannot not return to you, I cannot not melt for happiness with you, for your joy. O merciful mother, who bore in your womb mercy itself. Mother of mercy, who bore the merciful Christ. Mother of sinners, who gave us Jesus, who is savior. Loving mother, who nursed and nourished love, love and desire of our souls, love that nourishes and feeds of itself our minds, love that conjoins and bonds us to itself, love that burns and does not consume, love that vivifies and deifies us. O sweetest love, O purest and most holy love, sweetest Mary, who sweeten our bitternesses. Mary brightest star of this black and turbulent sea. Mary most trusted and safest haven of our salvation. In this night with your pure hands you wiped Eve's weeping eyes. In this hour with your strong foot you broke and shattered the ancient serpent's head. In this moment you opened paradise, so long locked, and you locked hell, so long left open. In this instant you repacified God with man, giving us the man-God. And now what soul can be so miserable and so unhappy that it depart from you without grace and gift? What hardened heart through your intercessions does not soften? What soul is so fierce and so prideful that by merit of your humility it does not humble itself and bend? Turn therefore, mother of grace, your clement eye and pray your sweet son for our common salvation. Let not us leave this place, this manger, this babe without renewal of life and reform of habit, so that, replete with spiritual grace, we can dwell always in this most holy meditation on our salvation and on your joy. May it please you, most beloved Jesus, returning to you whence I first departed with a sweet circle of love from Jesus to Mary, and from Mary to Joseph, that I return again from Joseph to Mary, and from Mary to Jesus, imitating in this God's most perfect love, which beginning in him and passing through his creatures returns to him and ends enduring eternally, perfect circle, loving circle, eternal circle of the loving God.

May it please you, loving child, that I never depart from you, at least, in my intention. And if it should happen that for a brief space I must depart, see that I make a speedy return and that I return to my greater profit. I shall search for my Lord where I expect to find him, and where shall I find him if not in you, Jesus, figure and substance of the very Father eternal? I shall invoke my God where he is nearest, and where is he nearest but in you, who are God himself? I shall therefore stay close to you, and I shall invoke you my God, my Jesus, most holy and purest word incarnate, I shall behold you with the eyes of my soul, and bending on the knees of my mind, I shall adore you on those of the body, saying, "Fortify yourselves, tender limbs, the better to expose yourselves to those torments that for me alone and for all the world await you. Fill yourselves, little veins, with precious blood in order to shed it all later for human salvation. Grow, pray, grow, immaculate and holy body, in order to give of yourself and grant yourself to harsh torture and atrocious death for the whole universe. Jesus, Jesus, Jesus, to you honor and power sempiternal in the perfect union of the Father and the Holy Ghost. Amen."

The end

IV
LETTERS[1]

LETTER 1

[To Benedetto Varchi][2]

My most honorable lord,

I gather from yours, just received, that an irksome letter of mine, which I wrote you last Saturday, has not come into your hands, but maybe it did

1. Only a handful of letters by Battiferra survive from what must have been a voluminous lifelong correspondence. They range from informal, chatty notes with news of health, thanks for a gift, and, most often, thoughts on the subject of poetry, to business communications on practical financial matters and formal literary dedications couched in elegant periodic prose. Extant are a bundle of sixteen letters to her Florentine mentor, Benedetto Varchi (1557–63); two petitions to the Duke of Urbino concerning the unreturned dowry money from her first marriage (1558, 1559); and dedicatory letters in her published books to the Duchess of Florence (recipient of her *Il primo libro dell'opere toscane,* 1560) and to the Duchess of Urbino (recipient of *I sette salmi penitentiali,* 1564), and to cloistered nuns in both cities, these last addressed individually in explanatory statements that precede each of the translated Psalms. We know about a few of the many other missives now lost from responses by three of her correspondents on issues involving poetry: one letter by Varchi (in response to Laura's letter of July 21, 1561), five by Annibal Caro (August 6, 1552, October 13, 1556, October 16, 1562, January 5, 1566, January 12, 1566) and two by Bernardo Tasso (January 30, 1566, March 14, 1566). The four letters of 1566 concern the death of Varchi and the anthology of mourning for him that Laura was helping to compile. Another cache of documents in Urbino at the Albani Library, known only through a general inventory, contained letters to her as well by Antonio Galli (1.74), Camillo Falconetti, and Carlo Casale. See Cecil H. Clough, "Sources for the History of the Duchy of Urbino," in *The Duchy of Urbino in the Renaissance* (London: Variorum Reprints, 1981).

In addition to conducting her own correspondence, Battiferra assisted her husband with his. Letters from him to personages of importance such as Duke Cosimo de' Medici and Michelangelo are in her hand, not Ammannati's. As his humanist secretary, she was following in the footsteps of her father, the cleric Giovan Antonio Battiferri, a scriptor of apostolic briefs in the Apostolic Chamber of the Vatican. In this capacity, it is quite likely that Battiferra not only transcribed some of her husband's more formal letters, but drafted the prose as well (Kirkham, "Creative Partners").

2. 4.1. This letter (fig. 13), the earliest to survive from Battiferra's correspondence with Varchi, gives insight into her personal life, her professional aspirations, and her religious faith. Typical

not in order to wait for this other one, which will be a bit less displeasing, as it will convey to you my husband's improvement, for with God's help he is much better than I thought he would be, especially so soon. May God give us grace that keeps increasing, according to our need.

I drew infinite happiness from your sweet and, as always, dear letter, all the more so from hearing that you fare well. May it please the majesty of God so to preserve you, as I continually pray that it will. For beyond often having letters from you—something I much care about, to be sure—I want to know that you are healthy and in good spirits, news of no little comfort and pleasure to me in my strange difficulties.

The sonnet is truly one of your most beautiful compositions. I received it with the joy and happiness that I felt when I received all the others, and I shall hold it in the very same reverence as I hold them, and what little time I can steal from my troubles I shall spend entirely in contemplating them, making use of them for my books.

And because I have no time for now to go on longer with you, I shall close, and together with my husband, who is most deeply fond of you, I shall kiss your hands and heartily commend myself to you.

From Florence, January 27, 1556 [1557 modern style]

LETTER 2

[To Duke Guidobaldo II Della Rovere, Duke of Urbino][3]

Lord Most Illustrious, Most Excellent, and Most Worthy of Reverence,

Messer Fabio Barignani has let me know that Your Illustrious Excellency would like to proceed now with the agreement reached in the year 1554 be-

in the concern and affection expressed for her husband, it reveals that by 1557 she was planning to write "books" incorporating sonnets from her correspondents. The composition she gratefully receives here is probably one of three Varchi sent her that she included in her *Primo libro*. Evidently, she had written him a few days before, expressing concern over Ammannati's health. Although this note gives no hint of what his illness was, we know that he suffered from chronic eye problems, perhaps a consequence of his work as a sculptor. The "strange difficulties" and "troubles" to which she refers must involve her long legal struggle to recover the dowry money from her first marriage.

3. 4.2. Battiferra appeals to Duke Guidobaldo for justice in the protracted litigious history of her efforts to recover the dowry from her first marriage to Vittorio Sereni of Bologna, an organist at the Urbino court. Sereni, who dictated his will on his deathbed (January 25, 1549), affectionately bequeathed Laura certain "gold jewelry" and 150 scudi; he named as heir to the rest of his small estate his brother, the musician Altobello degli Organi. Altobello failed to return the dowry, which should have passed to Bartolomeo Ammannati after he and Laura were

tween Messer Altobello, my former brother-in-law, and me in the lawsuit for the dowry that I was supposed to have from him nine years ago, which is why it seemed appropriate to me to appeal to Your Illustrious Excellency in this letter, thinking surely that I would receive no less understanding and help from you, thanks to your natural goodness, than he has, who has kept what is mine and caused litigation for so many years, against all reason and against the wishes of Messer Vittorio, God rest him, who not only wanted me to have it back, as we know, but to be his heir for all his portion, which I myself did not want to accept, but preferred freely to make a gift of it to his said brother; and that, and more due me, has been why I have for so many years gone without what is mine and been in litigation with him, to my great detriment and displeasure. Then, after I accepted the terms of said agreement at the commandment of Your Illustrious Lordship, he not only let pass the deadline we had agreed upon without giving me what was mine, but he let me resume the law suit, which Mr. Montino told me here in Florence I should pursue, since I was not bound because he had broken his word, sold all the estate, his mind bent on doing anything but satisfying me, who since 1550 until now have been married without having a penny of income and with nothing else in my name. And now that I was hoping to recover my dowry and the interest, he comes back to Your Illustrious Lordship again so that the agreement, which he did not let proceed then, should go ahead now. And because I do not believe that in order to help him you would wish to harm me, who am no less your most affectionate servant and subject, or harm my husband your servant too, or anyone else, I pray you that for the love of God, you let me have what is mine, for I do not see how I can go on like this. And from the sale of those things that, in accordance with the wishes of my aforesaid husband, were mine, let Messer Altobello have the profit, for he should be well content with that, having enjoyed them for so many years and forcing me to scrimp. And because I firmly hope in the goodness and clemency of Your Illustrious Excellency, who will not want me to be wronged, without saying more I shall here come to a stop,

---

married on April 17, 1550. Laura's father had initially promised Laura 1,000 scudi for her marriage to Sereni, but the sum was to have been raised to 2,000 scudi at the suggestion of the Duke of Urbino. For a commoner, this was a huge amount, enough to purchase several city houses. Frustration, indignation, exasperation, and anger all fuel the rapid sequence of concatenated clauses that remind the duke of how Laura has been cheated. Her outrage is all the greater because she had generously ceded to Altobello her portion of Sereni's bequest. Even after so much contention, she is willing to let Altobello keep the difference between the original and appreciated value of her dowry property. What she wants now is to recover the principal, leaving aside value accrued. This petition is implicit in her sonnet to the Duke of Urbino (1.7).

praying our Lord God to preserve you long in happiness. And kissing your hands with all humility, together with my husband I entrust these matters to you.

From Florence, July 9, 1558. Your Most Illustrious Excellency's most devoted servant, Laura Battiferra, degli Ammannati

LETTER 3

[To Guidobaldo II della Rovere, Duke of Urbino][4]

Most Illustrious and Most Excellent Lord,

Laura Battiferra degli Amannati, Your Excellency's most devoted servant, humbly prays you that, as you deigned by word of mouth to give her license to sell as much of her patrimony here in Urbino as will amount to the sum of 2,000 gold scudi, which she and her husband wish to invest as the money of their dowry in Florentine property, you deign now to confirm it for her in writing, so that she can show it to anyone who might want to buy it from her, because otherwise no one will want to, not knowing Your Illustrious Excellency's wishes. This she will take as a most singular gift and grace, and with all her heart she commends herself and her few properties to you so that they no longer be usurped, as they have been up to now, or sold by anyone else. Instead let them be for her and hers be, as they ought and as is Your Excellency's intention. May our Lord God felicitously protect you, bringing you fulfillment of all felicity.

[In another hand] *Let it be granted by us as petitioned. Urbino, October 23, 1559* [Seal of the Duke of Urbino]

4. 4.3. As of the following year, Altobello has still not returned the money, Laura now petitions the Duke to sell property in Urbino belonging to her father in order to obtain the cash equivalent for a purchase in Florence. From her phrasing, it is evident that she has already discussed the matter with Guidobaldo *viva voce*. Just as he gave her his word orally, so she now wants written confirmation for that agreement. Beside the Duke's seal at the bottom, his secretary adds a note with the date, October 23, 1559, and the outcome: her petition has been granted by Guidobaldo (fig. 17). Valuable as one of the rare surviving autograph letters by Laura, this one reveals her access to the ducal palace and her personal involvement in the administration of her Urbino property. Since she calls it her "patrimony," it is real estate she has received from her father, who at this date is still living. Yet even though it belongs to her, she cannot dispose of it on her own. Permission is required from an authoritative male, in this case the duke, to whom Laura is subject as a native of Urbino.

LETTER 4

[To Benedetto Varchi][5]

My Very Magnificent Most Honorable Messer Benedetto,

The Giunti have finished printing my book, and I thought that by now Messer Bartolomeo would have been back from Rome, as he had written me, and it hasn't turned out to be true, for I wanted to come up there to your Lordship's and talk with you about how we were going to do that dedicatory letter.[6] I had made a draft, but because I've never before made anything like it, it didn't come out right. It calls for only a few words (as I see it, not many are needed), so I would like them to be more fitting and beautiful than those I myself know how to say. Therefore I pray you with all my heart that since up to now you have done as much as you have, you gladly do still one last thing: shape for me those words that you think sound right. And to tell you in part what I had drafted, I didn't get into those deep waters[7] that so many have used and use every day of praising the duchess to whom the book is going, then excusing myself, because it would take me too much to get out of them. And anyway, the first and the last sonnet, if Your Lordship remembers well, are both done on this subject, and that's what they talk about. Rather I thanked well my good fortune, which had brought me this opportunity to show her Most Illustrious Excellency my loyalty and devotion with this little token, offering her these few efforts of mine. And I said I was greatly in debt to those who, wanting to have them printed against my will,

5. 4.4. Battiferra writes her mentor, asking for his help in composing the dedicatory letter and finalizing the title for her *Primo libro dell'opere toscane.* She had hoped to come see Varchi personally at his villa in Fiesole to discuss these professional matters, but her departure has been delayed because her husband is not yet back from a trip to Rome. Ammannati, who had been present in Siena for Cosimo's triumphal entry to claim the city as his fief (October 28, 1560), joined the duke's retinue for a continuation of the journey that took them to Rome, to visit Pope Pius IV. This letter makes it possible to date the completion of Battiferra's first book, timed to coincide with the occasion it celebrates, the expansion of the Medici territories resulting from Cosimo's conquest of Siena.

6. The Giunti were one of the most prominent publishing families in sixteenth-century Italy. Alongside Lorenzo Torrentino, Duke Cosimo's official publisher, they were the chief press in Florence. Battiferra's book was one of thirteen printed by Giunti in 1560, including Aristotle's *Ethics* and *Poetics* in editions by Piero Vettori, Della Casa's *Galatheo,* and the first book of Varchi's lectures to the Florentine Academy, *La prima parte delle lezzioni*. The Giunti imprint places Battiferra's publication in the cultural mainstream.

7. *deep waters* ("pelago"): cf. Dante, *Inf.* 1.23. Battiferra, who wants to avoid floundering in trite formulas of flattery, gives Varchi an idea of what was in her draft, which sounds very close to the final version.

were the reason why I had moved to send them forth myself, for fear they would be seen twisted and in worse form than they are. On my own I would never have done it; and I wanted this to serve as excuse for having had them printed. I wanted to signal my intention to you and entrust all of myself, all, to whatever you think best, because you know it much better sleeping than I do, or ever will, waking. It will also be of great value to me to know how you think the title stands better: *First Part of the Rhymes and Verses of Laura,* etc., or *First Part of the Tuscan Works,* or *Book,* however seems better to you, since there are rhymes and verses mixed.[8] Not needing anything else, I come to an end, commending myself to Your Lordship with all my heart that our Lord give you your every desire.

From Florence, on the 25th day of November of '60.

Do Your Lordship take your time, and don't pay attention to what I said about the book being ready because I'll make it wait as long as you want. And I commend myself again to you.

From Your Servant, Most Loving, Laura Battiferra degli Amannati

LETTER 5

To the Most Illustrious and Most Excellent Lady, the Lady Eleonora di Toledo, Duchess of Florence and Siena, Her Most Revered Lady and Patron[9]

It never occurred to me, Most Illustrious and Most Excellent Lady Duchess, that I would have to go into print with any of my compositions at

8. *rhymes and verses mixed* ("rime e versi mescolati"): Battiferra distinguishes between the sonnets and other lyric forms (madrigal, *canzone, sestina*) and the longer narrative poems at the end ("Hymn by Saint Augustine," "Oration of the Prophet Jeremiah"). In sixteenth-century usage, *versi* could also mean "prose."

9. 4.5. Writing woman to woman, Battiferra addresses her *Il primo libro dell'opere toscane* (1560) to Eleonora di Toledo, wife of Cosimo I de' Medici and Duchess of Florence. As the dedicatory letter makes clear, Laura honors this personage less for shared ties in sisterhood or for love of literature (Eleonora seems to have had little interest in intellectual matters), than in practical terms of court diplomacy, that is, for the duchess's power to bestow patronage. Hence the poet thanks her honorary recipient for what she has done to help the Ammannati in the past, and she expresses hope for continuing ducal protection. Whether Battiferra herself ever received payment or support for the poetry she composed in praise of the Medici is unknown; neither has any other communication between Laura and Eleonora so far surfaced from the Medici archives, still largely uncataloged. The fact that she includes her husband's name in this dedication reveals that she writes partly to help promote him at court. In this political and public wifely role, she is much more the woman beside the man than the woman behind the man. She is partner to her husband in the push for patronage, asserting their claims as a creative couple who form a team of Medici loyalists. It can hardly be coincidence that in the same year Batti-

this time, but since I have heard as most certain from trustworthy sources that some people have already assembled a good quantity of them and are trying even now to assemble some more, wanting to publish them not only without permission, but without my knowledge, I was not a little troubled;[10] and not knowing what else to do, I resolved for the least harm, with my husband's permission and the counsel of many friends, to go ahead and publish them myself and to address them to the glorious name of Your Most Illustrious Excellency, not because I thought them worthy of such highness, but to show you as best I could that if not entirely grateful, I am at least mindful in part of the many and very great benefices that you and the Most Illustrious Lord Duke have given and continue to give every day to me and to Messer Bartolomeo, my husband,[11] who desires nothing other, and I with him, than to be able to continue faithfully and worthily serving you. Taking account of his reverence and devotion and mine toward you, may Your Excellency deign, by your inborn bounty and infinite liberality, to accept these efforts of mine, taking them as they are, and keep us in your good graces and those of your Most Illustrious and Most Excellent consort. May the Lord

---

ferra brought out her *First Book,* dedicated to the Duchess Eleonora, Ammannati was appointed architect-in-chief for the renovation of the Pitti Palace, which Eleonora had purchased in 1549 for her rapidly growing family. In another sense, however, Battiferra's husband is still her lord, since she obtains his permission to publish the *Primo libro*. For the content, Battiferra asked Varchi's advice in her letter of November 25, 1560. This letter's counterpart, the dedicatory epistle of the *I sette salmi penitentiali,* heads "The Second Part" of the *Rime.* The letter to Eleonora, however, was not to be reprinted in Battiferra's final anthology, not just because the Medici duchess had long since died but because the *Rime* was more broadly conceived than the *Primo libro,* not as a tribute to the Medici but as a mirror of the poet's own writing career.

10. Who was threatening to pirate Battiferra's poetry? Perhaps it was Lodovico Domenichi, who edited many verse anthologies, including the first in Italy with all female authors (Lucca, 1559). Alternatively, Laura's claim that others are trying to preempt her may simply be the requisite disclaimer, a ceremonial nod to modesty.

11. The Ammannati had moved from Rome to Florence in 1555 when, after the death of his Roman patron Julius III, Bartolomeo entered Cosimo's service, commissioned to execute the *Fountain of Juno* for the Audience Hall in Palazzo della Signoria. Other important ducal commissions followed. In 1557, Cosimo assigned him the job of repairing the Arno bridges damaged in a devastating flood of that year, and in 1558 he sent Ammannati to Siena to supervise repairs for damage caused in his recent war of conquest and in an earthquake. In 1558–59, salaried by the duke, Ammannati built the great Laurentian Staircase to Michelangelo's model, and he was collaborating with Vasari on construction of the Uffizi. In 1560 he made repeated trips to Siena to oversee installation of the triumphal apparatus for Cosimo's formal entry into the city; he won the coveted commission for a Neptune fountain in Piazza della Signoria, beating in competition Benvenuto Cellini, Vincenzo Danti, and Giambologna; and he became the architect in charge of expanding the Pitti Palace, a project in which he would remain involved until 1577.

God preserve him together with you and with all your Most Excellent and Most Illustrious House healthy and happy for a very long time to come.

From the Most Humble and Most Devoted Servant of Your Most Illustrious Excellency, Laura Battiferra degli Amannati

LETTER 6

[To Benedetto Varchi] [12]

My Very Magnificent and Most Honorable Lord,

I'm sending Your Lordship a sonnet, something I did for that lady Sig-

12. 4.6. In spite of its brevity, this letter has much to tell about Battiferra's cultural activity and connections. It accompanies a lost sonnet she had written for the Bolognese poet Lucia Bertana dell'Oro (1521–67), known to her only by reputation. Gherardo Spini was evidently a catalyst in the connection, as the following letter from Bertana to Varchi helps explain:

> Very Magnificent Signor, as to a Most Honorable Older Brother,
>
> The long desire I have always had to visit and know Your Lordship with my letters, which I never fulfilled for various reasons, since it seemed to me almost mere presumption to accomplish such a thing without anyone's mediation, now I am granted the possibility of carrying out through the mediation of the most kind Messer Gherardo Spina, who comes to these parts for business of his. So I was determined not to miss such a convenient opportunity, rather I signified to him what pure affection I bear your virtue and valor, and in witness of such virtue I have given you one of my sonnets, such as it is, since the excuses I might adduce for it with Your Lordship didn't seem to me necessary—that I, a croaking bird, have made bold to present my songs to such a canorous swan, and this I should indeed excuse. But I have put my faith in your immense kindness, that you would accept all from me courteously, excusing my ignorance and accepting with pleasure my good and sincere disposition toward you. But by saying with more words what the aforementioned Messer Gherardo will explain better than I, I would bring boredom to Your Lordship and bother to myself, owing to my small adequacy, so I place myself in his hands; and to you in these parts or where I may, I offer myself in your every need, and I commend myself with my lord consort.
>
> From Modena, on the 20th of September, 1561
>
> From Your Magnificent and Virtuous Servant, as from a Loving Sister, Lucia Bertana (*Lettere di Laura Battiferri Ammannati a Benedetto Varchi,* Carlo Gargiolli, ed. [Bologna: Commissione per i testi di lingua, 1968], 59–60)

Little is known about Bertana, who "does not deserve to be removed from the discreet shadow that enfolds her," according to Giulio Bertoni ("Lucia Bertani e Laura Battiferra," *Giornale Storico della Letteratura Italiana* 85 [1925], 379–80). He remarked that these two women "were made to understand each other," both being hard-working wives who shunned worldly vanity. Bertana, however, sent sonnets to prominent poets and took a conspicuous position in the polemic that arose after Lodovico Castelvetro criticized Annibal Caro for his 1553 "*canzone* of the lilies," written in praise of the French royal house. Castelvetro attacked not on political grounds but because Caro had dared use language unauthorized by Petrarch, maintaining that only Petrarch's example could sanction contemporary practice. In an attempt to mediate, Bertana wrote two letters

nora Lucia Bertana, whom that man Spina[13] so praised to me. I'm waiting to hear your judgment on whether you think I should send it to her. And so too if I should give the other one to him, even though I sent it to you once before and didn't get it back, maybe because you didn't like it, so afterward I tinkered with it—I don't know whether it's become better or worse. Yesterday, which was Sunday, there came here to the house Messer Pier Vettorio and the humanist from Pisa, escorted by Messer Baccio Valori,[14] to whom I'm much obliged because he brought me the greatest pleasure. I had much desired to see those two great men whom I didn't know before.

May Your Lordship stay healthy and happy, and may God content you always. Messer Bartolomeo commends himself to you, and so do I heartily.

Bronzino[15] won't be convinced, no matter how often I've told him my opinion, where there is that *ella* [herself] in the last verse of the first quatrain of my sonnet to Casale on the death of the Marquise of Massa, which goes, as Your Lordship has seen,

> Casale, oimè! che dite voi di quella
> Che 'l mondo tutto in un momento attrista?
> Parve ei che quanto in molti anni s'acquista
> Repentina e crudel sgombri con ella![16]

---

to Caro, who published his own mock-savage *Apologia* in 1558. Laura and her friends snicker at those they consider Castelvetrists, that is, slavish imitators. Bertana's "consort" is her husband.

Battiferra's cover letter with the sonnet for Bertana allows us to hear a snatch of the kind of dialogue she and her friends carried on about their poetry, subjected to the most rigorous scrutiny. Here their debate centers on her use of a single preposition and pronoun in a sonnet of condolence on the death of the Marquise of Massa, Elisabetta Della Rovere Cibo (d. June 6, 1561), a sister of Duke Guidobaldo II of Urbino and a sister-in-law of Leonora Cibo de' Vitelli (see 1.30–32, and app. C). Laura hasn't been able to persuade Bronzino to accept her phrasing: Death, personified in female form ("la Morte"), has carried away so much "with herself." One deduces from Varchi's reply (below, 4.7) that Bronzino thought the words "with herself" superfluous. Both Bertana's and Battiferra's letters to Varchi give insight into the use of sonnetry as a courtesy form of praise, often sent from afar by an admirer rather like a modern fan letter.

13. Gherardo Spini was just about this time becoming a friend of the Ammannati (see 1.i; 2.7–8; and 4.8 below).

14. This letter to Varchi dates the beginning of Battiferra's acquaintance with the great classicist Piero Vettori, whose epistle recalling Varchi's funeral (with Baccio Valori in attendance and Laura exiled to the matroneum) she chose as the preface to her *Rime*. Pisa was the seat of the university fostered by Duke Cosimo. Vettori held a chair at that atheneum, later famous for Galileo's period on the faculty. The identity of Vettori's learned companion is unknown.

15. *Bronzino*: see 1.76.

16. I have not been able to locate the full text. Battiferra exchanges sonnets with two men of this Bolognese family in her *Primo libro*: Abbot Alessandro Casale (1533–82), a diplomat in the

[Casale, alas, what say you of her who in a single moment saddens the whole world? To him it seemed that as much as is acquired in many years, sudden and cruel, she carries away with herself.]

So it will be of value to me to hear Your Lordship's view, because I know they will believe you and be quiet. May God give you all you desire!

From Florence, on the 21st day of July of '61. From Your Servant, Most Affectionately, Laura Battiferra degli Amannati

LETTER 7

[From Benedetto Varchi to Signora Laura Battiferra Ammannati][17]
(undated, ca. 1561)

Very Magnificent and Most Virtuous Madonna Laura, my Most Honorable Signora,

I received and read this evening the letter from Your Ladyship in which there was your sonnet that begins

Casale, oimè, che dite voi di quella,
Che 'l mondo tutto in un momento attrista?

[Casale, alas, what say you of her who in a single moment saddens the whole world?]

---

service of Spain who was elevated to the purple in 1568 (Guidi, ed., *Il primo libro,* 131), and Captain Paolo Casale (d. 1575), who writes of Laura's friendship with Annibal Caro. Paolo Casale, the amateur author of a musical comedy performed for a court wedding at Urbino in 1565/66, was in correspondence with Caro (Piperno, *L'immagine del duca*).

17. 4.7. This undated letter reveals the way poetry circulated and was submitted to microscopic analysis among Battiferra and her coterie, all immersed in discussions concerning proper forms of the Italian language (the "questione della lingua"). Although it was not published until after his death, Varchi was working during the early 1560s on a compendious dialogue, *L'Ercolano* (1570), in which he takes sides with Caro in the Petrarchist polemic against Castelvetro and presents his views more generally on vernacular usage. Here Varchi offers a sprinkling of his expertise to his follower Battiferra, embroiled in minidisputes of her own for the sonnet she sent Casale on the death of the Marquise of Massa. Their exchange centers on the verb *sgombrare* (to disencumber, empty, carry away), which Battiferra had used in lamenting how much Death "carries away with herself." Discussing a range of meanings from literal to figurative and learned to colloquial for that verb, they further question whether the words "with herself" were superfluous ("useless and unnecessary") or not.

and attached to the sonnet are two riders,[18] the first of which says this: "These are the difficulties in the way the sonnet is phrased: first, to interpret SGOMBRI, i.e., 'carries away,' CON ELLA, i.e., 'with herself,' would be just fine, except that I don't anywhere find the verb SGOMBRARE [to carry away] for PORTARE [to carry]; second, to take SGOMBRI in its true meaning, *id est,* 'empties, chases away, sends away,' seems to me a hard way of speaking. Death, which here is agent, does that thing 'herself,' a word wholly useless and unnecessary." The second rider, which is of the same opinion as the first, but as far as I can judge, by another person who was asked his view, is this: "I say therefore that I believe that it is true that SGOMBRARE can't be found in any admired writer in the sense of 'carry,' and so I concur with the view of those who condemn it, interpreting it in the former sense. I don't think it can stand in the second sense, where it is used in its true meaning of 'to empty, to remove, or to send away,' for the same reason that is adduced in the first rider." And you write me that this dispute was born over the last two verses of the first quatrain of the sonnet quoted above:

> Parv'ei che quanto in molti anni s'acquista
> Repentina e crudel sgombri con ella.
>
> [To him it seemed that as much as is acquired in many years,
> sudden and cruel, she carries away with herself.]

And you add that after you had told some people there about the difference of opinion, and shown the two riders, you were advised either not to reply or to reply in jest, because in Florence even the porters know that people use SGOMBRARE for "carry" and that as far as they're concerned, that "useless and unnecessary" word is a Castelvetrism and the author of the second rider should know as much. And you come to me to ask my opinion, which although I am extremely busy in all kinds of other studies, I neither can nor must nor want not to give.

And first, I praise your sweet nature and prudence, which took a position before replying and then replied humanely, as it befits you and all noble spirits everywhere, and even though it seems to me, too, that the "useless and unnecessary" word sounds somehow a bit like Castelvetro, nevertheless, what does this add to the issue in dispute? I further confess that in Florence

18. These two "riders" ("polizze") must have been appended notes, written like commentary under the sonnet, which only filled the top part of the letter-sized folio that was then folded and addressed on the other side. Their authors are not identified. Perhaps one was Bronzino since Battiferra mentions his participation in the debate in her letter to Varchi above.

it is most obvious down to the porters—nay, to the porters more than to anyone else, since they are the ones who carry the things that are carried away—that *sgombrare* means *portare*. But you need to know that those who are not born into a language, or haven't learned it from those who were born into it, are bound to be uncertain about many things that are more than most obvious to those who have the language naturally. Indeed, I want to say to you moreover that even those who have the language naturally are quite often uncertain, though they be most learned, about things that to those who are uneducated are most manifest. Cicero, the most eloquent man who ever was and with the learning that we all know, erred in writing a letter to Pomponius Atticus, and he had to learn from an oarsman what *inhibere remos*[19] meant. But that's not all. When Marcus Agrippa, after building the temple that was then called the Pantheon and today Santa Maria Ritonda, wanted to make an inscription on the frontispiece, all the learned men of Rome gathered; and because he wanted to add to his name and surname how he had been consul three times, those most learned men couldn't ever come to agreement among themselves about whether in the Latin tongue one was supposed to say *tertio consul* or *tertium consul*; and as a last remedy they chose not to put it either way, but to have three I's, that is, three ones, so that whoever was reading could pronounce either *tertio* or *tertium*, however he thought better.

But to come to what you ask me, the author of the first rider, whoever he is, admits that if *sgombri* is interpreted as "carries" and *con ella* as "with herself," that such an expression would be just fine every time a person happened to be in a place where *sgombrare* meant *portare*; and the author of the second rider believes it is true that *sgombrare* is not found in any admired writer in the sense of *portare*, but that is as far from the truth, in my judgment, as those things that are farthest from it. Don't we say all the time in Florence, "I have moved (*io ho fatto sgombrare*) all my belongings," that is, "had them carried from one house to another"? How many times have the notices gone out ordering that all and sundry persons "carry" (*sgombrino*) all their food stuffs to fortified places, that is, that "they be carried"?[20] And if you said they won't want to believe how people speak in Florence, then you would be right to answer, for there is no doubt about this verb at all in Florence, and it's used indifferently as much by the learned as by lay people; and I would like to know what Petrarch meant when he said this, from which you took or imitated your concept:

19. *inhibere remos*: to pull in the oars, to stop rowing.

20. Such orders were issued when supplies were scarce, as under siege conditions or in famine.

Tolto ha colei che tutto 'l mondo sgombra[21]

[taken away by her who empties the whole world]?

And what else did he have in mind when he said

Ond'io perché pavento
Adunar sempre quel che un'ora sgombra[22]

[to gather always what one hour will carry away]?

that is, "take" and "carry away." Nor does what the first rider says and the second confirms seem true to me, that is, that the true meaning of *sgombrare* is *votare* [to empty], *scacciare* [chase away], *mandar via* [send away]; for if this were the true and proper meaning, one could say, "I have had the well sent away," that is "emptied it"; "you have chased away your barrels," that is "emptied them," and other such risible expressions. "The soldiers cleared out of [*sgomberarono di*] the piazza" doesn't mean "they emptied the piazza," but rather, "leaving the piazza, they left it empty of themselves." But if I were to say, "The soldiers emptied [*sgombrarono*] the piazza," whoever might say it meant "they left" would be exactly right. That *sgombrare* doesn't properly mean "chase and send away" is of itself clear. Suppose someone says, "so-and-so has cleared out the house," it doesn't mean "lifted and chased away," but "emptied" of furnishings, and he who "leaves" the country "goes with God," he isn't "chased away."

As for the "useless and unnecessary word," it doesn't seem so to me. On the contrary, it fits there gracefully, as when Petrarch said

Di me medesmo meco mi vergogno[23]

[I am ashamed of me myself within myself].

And with a more apposite example, he said elsewhere

E portarsene seco
La fonte e 'l loco, ecc.[24]

[and carry away with it the fountain and the place].

And everyday speech hardly ever has it any other way, and even if as far as meaning is concerned, it's the same to say "so-and-so is carrying away all I value" and "so-and-so is carrying away with himself all I value," nevertheless the elegant turns of language consist in such speech. "I'm coming with you" (*io vengo teco*), everyone knows what that means and that it's good speech

21. *RS* 327.4.

22. *RS* 264.70–71.

23. *RS* 1.11.

24. *RS* 323.46–47.

without adding anything else; and yet we often say, "I'm coming together with you" (*io vengo con teco*) against Latin usage. And it has seemed strange to me, to be perfectly frank, that someone, wanting to explain the meaning of the verb *sgombrare*, would say that it means *votare* [empty], *scacciare* [chase away], and *mandar via* [send away]. What the deuce does "empty" have to do with "chasing" or "sending away," properly speaking? You must know then, and this is where I think their error arises, that no verb can have more than one true and proper meaning, and all the others that are given to it are either metaphorical or associated. But here it would be necessary to enter into a long discussion, which I can't do now, both because I'm exhausted and because it's past the third hour[25] and I want to go eat a bit and get myself some rest.

I shall send this to you tomorrow with Nanni, who will bring the horse to Messer Bartolomeo. Remember me to him, and stay well both of you. May God make you always prosper. I don't want to forget to say that I don't like using *sgombri* [empties] in place of *si sgombri* [empties itself], and that Father,[26] who you say is so learned, seems to me to have understood that very well.

LETTER 8

To Laura Battiferra in Florence from Gherardo Spini in Prague[27]

As I wrote Your Ladyship, we left Vienna to go to metropolitan Prague in Bohemia for the concluding ceremonies with Archduke Ferdinand.[28] We

25. Probably the third hour of night, that is, three hours after sunset, which on an ideal day with twelve hours of daylight and darkness (at the equinox), would be about 9:00 P.M.

26. *Father* ("Padre"): an unidentified cleric.

27. 4.8. In the first part of this remarkable letter, Spini describes his journey from Vienna to Prague, fraught with brigands in the forests and an outbreak of plague. After an appreciative description of the city on the Moldau, he turns to matters of interest to his female reader—Prague's "Amazons," tidbits of court gossip, and religious heresies. Spini is struck both by these northern women's natural beauty and their aggressive role in public life. Implicit in his thought train is the overall sense of power that emanates from them, which must have reminded him of Laura. His description of their unusual height indicates that she herself was tall, a physical trait that would have enhanced her imposing stature as a poet and paragon of morality. What Spini writes also gives insight into the high level of Laura's intellectual life and the European reach of her fame. She figures in the conversation he has with the emperor's personal doctor, Pietro Andrea Mattioli of Siena. While traversing the cold, wet, muddy northern woods, Spini imagines Laura at her hearth, entertaining cultured guests in intellectual discussion. Spini, who wrote sonnets for Battiferra's book of Penitential Psalms, to console her when her father died, and to condole with Ammannati when Eleonora de Toledo's death threatened the future of the Pitti Palace project, must have been a welcome guest at those salon-like gatherings.

28. The Archduke Ferdinando (1529–95) was a younger brother of Maximilian II. The latter had inherited the throne in 1564 on the death of their father, Ferdinand I. Spini does not say what the court "ceremonies" were, but they must have related to Maximilian's accession.

arrived safely . . . This city was once ruled and governed by women, in the manner that the Amazons once did, and one can still see the traces of their palace, where their queen stayed. These women used men only to procreate, and when a boy child was born they cut off the index finger of his right hand so that he couldn't grasp a lance or pull a bow. And if it was a girl, like the Amazons, they burned off her right breast to make her more fit for combat. And thus they ruled for some time, warring with the neighboring peoples, and they expanded the borders of their kingdom. Still today the women of this city retain a certain I know not what of that haughtiness, for beyond being ordinarily very beautiful, and what's more, of a natural beauty not a bit aided by any artifice, all the affairs of any importance pass through their hands. They sell, buy, barter, and do everything else of the utmost importance that men are accustomed to doing. They all wear a pair of leather boots, without anything else on their legs, that is, without stockings. They encircle their head and throat with a kind of veil that makes them look like nuns, and these veils are dyed bright red in color, which reflects marvelously on their whitest faces, making them look quite pink, which makes them much more beautiful. For the most part they are tall, three fingers taller than Your Ladyship, which is saying a lot, I think, and none of them wears platform shoes. In sum, so as not to dwell longer either on their dress or their beauties, if they had Your Ladyship's beautiful and rare qualities of spirit, not only would they regain their lost dominion, but they would lord it over all of Germany, where such severe and rigid populations are the rule, or if they knew how great your virtues are, they certainly would make you their queen. Not from me, though, will they get the satisfaction of having you, first, because since we left Austria and entered Moravia, people don't speak German anymore, but Bohemian, so that the handful of words I had learned to speak in German aren't understood anymore in these lands, which means that I couldn't say a thing to them that they would understand; and second, because if our Italy were deprived of you, it would have lost one of its greatest adornments. But enough of this talk.

Day after tomorrow, we leave Prague and return posthaste to Vienna. All of us have been hosted affectionately by His Highness.[29] I shan't leave out saying either how I, too, personally kissed his hands, after the Grand Chancellor of Bohemia introduced me, and I was benevolently received. I visited the most excellent Mattioli, His Highness's doctor, who is the man who has made so many and such fine additions to Dioscorides and to Ptolemy.[30] We spoke of Your Ladyship, but I don't want to tell you about what,

29. The emperor, Maximilian II.

30. Pierandrea Mattioli (1500–1577), a native of Siena, studied medicine at Padua and went on to win celebrity in Europe for his scientific work, which included descriptions of some one hun-

so that, if for nothing else, you will have reason to wish for my return to hear about his particular interests.

Now, as I said, once tomorrow has passed, we shall return to Vienna free of plague, if nothing more happens; and if we can manage to scamper through the Hircinian Forest, then we shall be safe for a piece. We shall stay in Vienna for about ten days to take our leave of the emperor and the other gentlemen. Then we shall set out for Italy, not returning through the Tyrol or Trent, but passing through Styria, Carinthia, and down into Friuli, and then Venice. Meanwhile, Your Ladyship will be beside the fire, speaking of poetry and other clever subjects with a few rarified minds. Do deign to mention me especially, I who frozen stiff shall keep pondering how I can protect myself from all the ice, mud, and snow in order to be able to come and be a participant. May Your Ladyship, together with Messer Bartolomeo, take care to stay healthy, and do please commend me to all my friends, and above all to Bronzino.

I had forgotten to say how here in Prague one finds three different sorts of heresy, that is, the Anabaptist, Sacramentary, and Confessionary. The Anabaptist holds all goods and flesh in common, and what is yours is mine and what is mine is yours. The Sacramentary believes that Jesus Christ our redeemer doesn't come in the Host, and if anyone is against them, they assert it with arms. The Confessionary throw out confession [to a priest], each one confessing to God alone. May He be the one who remedies so many wicked and cruel disorders. From Prague, on the 12th day of October, 1564.

Of Your Most Virtuous Ladyship, Your Affectionate Servant Gherardo Spini

---

dred new plants. After publishing a treatise on syphilis in 1530, he translated into Italian the most famous herbal of antiquity, a treatise by Dioscorides written about 60 C.E. that remained a cornerstone of pharmaceutical practice in Europe for the next 1,500 years. Ten years later, Mattioli's Latin Dioscorides with commentary (1554) won him an invitation to serve in Prague as the Hapsburg emperor's personal physician. In 1558 he also translated into Italian Ptolemy's second-century *Geographia*.

APPENDIX A
BATTIFERRA'S WILLS

1. The 1563 Will

Three of Laura Battiferra's wills are known, each dictated in Latin on the same day, in the same place, with the same set of witnesses, and with the same notary public as a corresponding will made by her husband. She made the first after her father died (August 8, 1561) on August 17, 1563, naming her husband as heir; the second on February 16, 1580 [=1581]; and the third on March 25, 1587. In the latter two, after a clause assuring the surviving spouse income from their estate, both husband and wife designated the Jesuits as their universal heirs. This early will, which names Ammannati as universal heir, provides for only three other legatees. They are all women—a girl to be dowered and two cloistered nuns. Although such bequests were common in wills of both men and women, it is striking that here the testatrix privileges females for special legacies. The choice seems to reflect her special concern for family members excluded by the customary line of male inheritance—as she had been before her father's decision to disinherit his son.

In the name of our Lord Jesus Christ, Amen. In the year from His fruitful Incarnation 1563, Indiction VI, and the seventeenth day of the month of August.[1] Carried out in Florence in the palace of residence of the Magnificent Dominus the Podestà of the city of Florence[2] in the place of the dwelling and residence of the Magnificent Dominus Catelano Malatesta of Urbino, one of the six judges of the Florentine Rota, with all the witnesses named below present, in the words of the testatrix to all those named below . . . to wit:[3]

Magnificent Dominus Captain Malatesta, formerly in the service of Dominus

1. *Incarnation:* Florentines dated the New Year "from the Incarnation," March 25. Hence dates before March 25 in their annual calendar correspond to the following year in ours, reckoned from January 1. *Indiction:* in notarial language a cyclical period of fifteen years, dated from an arbitrarily determined starting point.

2. The Palace of the Podestà is the medieval Bargello, now the National Sculpture Museum.

3. The Florentine *Rota* was a court of law. The title "*Ser*" indicates a notary, one who bore official witness, composed, and transcribed legal documents, performing functions that today would be carried out by lawyers or solicitors. *Castiglione:* perhaps the central Tuscan village in Val d'Orcia; Marradi is in the Mugello, a region north of Florence.

Captain Meo Bacci of Castiglione; Giovan Battista, son of Dominus Girolamo Tizi, from the same place; Gherardo Bernardini de' Spini of Perugia; Ser Marco di Francesco Marco de' Guerrini of Marradi and Ser Polito, son of Ser Rosato de' Ricci of Urbino, both Notaries Public; Federigo di Girolamo of Mantua, in service of the Magnificent Dominus Pietro Lascisi of Verona, and Agostino, son of the late Giovanni de' Chiappardi of Genoa, in the service of Dominus Andrea Aliotti of Faenza, both judges of the Florentine Rota.

Since nothing is more certain than death and nothing more uncertain than its hour, and since a wise person should always be thinking about death, therefore the noble and venerable Domina Laura, daughter of the late Dominus Giovan'Antonio Battiferri of Urbino[4] and wife of Dominus Bartolomeo son of Antonio degli Ammannati, a noble Florentine sculptor, not wishing to die intestate but wishing to dispose of her goods as stated below, dictated the present testament orally, without writing it, in this form:

First, she commended her soul to omnipotent God and to his most glorious mother Mary, ever Virgin, and to all the heavenly court, humbly and most devoutly, and she elects and wishes that the burial of her body be in such church and grave as the aforesaid and below-named Bartolomeo Ammannati, her husband, shall designate and choose, and with whatever expenditure for her funeral that will please and seem fitting to said husband of hers.

Likewise, in accordance with the law of inheritance, she leaves and bequeaths to the Opera of Santa Maria de' Fiori three libri piccioli as required by ordinance.[5]

Likewise, in accordance with the law of inheritance, she leaves and bequeaths to one of the legitimate natural female children of Altobello, commonly known as Altobello degli Organi of Bologna, that is, to the eldest daughter, as part of her dowry when she marries, 100 gold scudi;[6] and if Altobello at the time of the death of this testatrix shall not have any daughters, she leaves and bequeaths the said 100 scudi to the eldest born of the masculine children of the said Altobello.

Likewise, in accordance with the aforesaid law, she leaves and bequeaths to the venerable nuns Sister Cassandra Battiferra and Sister Anna Vannuzia,[7] both nuns of

4. *Domina . . . Dominus:* I have retained these forms of address, which preserve the flavor of the original Latin legal document, and for which there exist various English equivalents ("Mistress," "Mr.," "Lady," "Lord").

5. All Florentines were required by city law to bequeath an established sum to the Cathedral of Santa Maria del Fiore, for improvements and maintenance.

6. Altobello degli Organi: the brother of Laura's deceased husband Vittorio Sereni and his heir, with whom she was in legal action for many years in the effort to recover her dowry. One hundred scudi was a standard testamentary bequest to people of the mercantile or artisan class. Contrast Laura's handsome dowry, which was initially set at 1,000 scudi, and at the suggestion of the Duke of Urbino, was to be raised to 2,000 scudi. At an opposite extreme, when the princess Lucrezia d'Este married Francesco Maria II Della Rovere in 1570, she brought 150,000 scudi in her dowry (1.18–19).

7. Cassandra Battiferra seems to have been a half-sister of Laura's father Giovan'Antonio, hence the poet's aunt (see app. B). A will dictated in 1536 by Giovan'Antonio's uncle Francesco left her 50 florins "so she can be counted among the nuns of Santa Lucia." Cassandra's name, again coupled with that of Anna Vannuzia, returns among the dedicatees of Battiferra's Penitential Psalms (1564). They are recipients of the seventh and last penitential psalm, "To the reverend

Urbino in the Urbino monastery of Santa Lucia,[8] in total 100 golden scudi, that is, 50 golden scudi for each of them, and if at the time of the death of this testatrix they shall not be living, or if either one of them shall not be living, she wishes the said 100 golden scudi or part thereof due whichever woman has already died to go to the said monastery in which the said nuns live; and thus in said case, she leaves to the monastery the said 100 scudi or part thereof due whichever woman has already died.

For all her goods movable and immovable, movable in and of themselves, in law, in name, in legal action, including emphyteutic property,[9] present and future . . . , she declares, makes, and wishes said Dominus Bartolomeo, son of the late Antonio degli Ammannati, her husband, as her universal heir. And this the said testatrix stated and wishes to be her last will and testament, which she wants to supersede any other last wills made heretofore. And if it be not valid by testamentary law, she wishes it to be valid according to the law of codicils, and if by the law of codicils it be not valid, she wishes it to be valid and to prevail by the law of deathbed donations or by whatsoever else governs last wills . . . The said lady, testatrix, hereby canceling, voiding, and annulling any other testament and any other last will up to now made in her hand and by any public notary whatsoever, . . .

I, Giovan Battista, son of the late Lorenzo de' Giordani, Notary Public and Florentine . . .[10]

2. The 1587 Will[11]

The only two special bequests in the will of 1582 are to Lodovico degli Organi, son of Altobello, for 100 scudi, and to Cassandra de' Battiferri and Anna de' Vannuzzi for 50 scudi each. This last will subsumes those gifts and adds several others. It was dictated in the home of Contessa degli Alessandri in Via de' Martelli in the presence of the following witnesses: Giovanni Maria, son of Filippo de' Biscioni of Figline; Benedetto, son of Pietro of Montacuto; Leone, son of Nicolai de' Medici; Raffaello, son of Carlo de' Federighi; Alessandro di Marco di Uzzano; Andrea Martini de' Pieri; Taddeo di Lodovido del Lavacchio.

In the name of God, Amen. In the year 1587 from His salvational Incarnation, Indiction XV, and the twenty-fifth day of March, during the felicitous rule of Pope Gregory XIII and the Most Serene Francesco de' Medici, great leader of Etruria.

---

sisters Sister Cassandra de' Battiferra and Sister Anna Vannuzia, most worthy nuns in the Monastery of Santa Lucia in Urbino." Both women were still alive in the 1580s, since Laura again remembers them in her two later wills. Beyond these references, I have not been able to identify Anna.

8. The medieval church and convent of Santa Lucia once stood at the northern end of Urbino, just inside the Santa Lucia gate, opposite the modern church of Santo Spirito.

9. Laura had inherited from her father Church-owned property that he held by emphyteusis (a lease valid for three generations, what we would call a "ninety-nine year lease"). This included the family house in the Campo Marzio district of Rome, at the Portuguese Arch.

10. ASF Panciatichi 174, 50. My thanks to Giulia Calvi, who happened upon this original transcription of the will in a box of miscellaneous items among the Panciatichi family papers. Its puzzling presence there may be due to Anton Maria Biscioni, who was the Panciatichi family archivist in the eighteenth century and who had been in possession of the printer's manuscript of Battiferra's *Primo libro dell' opere toscane.* See Victoria Kirkham, "Laura Battiferra's 'First Book' of Poetry."

11. ASF Notarile moderno, 4588, fols. 54r–57v.

Since nothing is more certain than death and no hour more uncertain than that, and since the duty of the wise person is to prepare for its coming, therefore the prudent woman Domina Laura, daughter of the late magnificent Dominus Giovan'Antonio Battiferri of Urbino and wife of Dominus Bartolomeo di Antonio degli Ammannati, sculptor and Florentine citizen, healthy by the grace of God in mind, in sense, in sight, in intellect, and in body, wishing while she has a sound mind in a sound body to dispose maturely of the temporal goods granted her by God, as it befits a wise person, in order that after her death there arise no quarrels . . . Through this oral testament, which she dictated without writing it, she acted, disposed, and ordered in the manner and form that follow, to wit:

[The first two clauses are much the same as in the wills of 1563 and 1582.]

Likewise, by the law of inheritance, for the love of God and the salvation of her soul, she left and bequeathed to Vittoria, daughter of the late Dominus Nicolai de' Spelli of Urbino, the sum and quantity of 100 golden scudi in the value of 7 libbre per scudo, to be given and paid out to her after the death of said Domina Laura and said Dominus Bartolomeo, her husband. And if this Vittoria shall no longer be among the living, she still wishes that sum to be paid out freely by her below-named heirs to the heirs of Domina Vittoria, which sum of 100 scudi this testatrix left and bequeathed by the law of inheritance to said Vittoria or to her heirs.[12]

Likewise, by the same law, for the love of God and for the salvation of her soul, she left and bequeathed to Carlo, Dominus Alessandro the priest, and Camilla, siblings and children of the late Girolamo de' Spelli of Urbino, 300 of the same scudi, that is, 100 scudi apiece, to be given and paid out to each and every one of them by her below-named heirs after the demise of said testatrix and of said Dominus Bartolomeo, her husband. And if Carlo, Dominus Alessandro, and Camilla shall no longer survive among the living, said testatrix wishes the said sum to be paid freely by the law of inheritance to the Spelli family, and she leaves and bequeaths it to their heirs.

Likewise, by the same law, for the love of God, and for the salvation of her soul, she left and bequeathed to Elisabetta, daughter of Dominus Girolamo de' Virgilii of Urbino, the sum of 100 of the same scudi, promised by this testatrix to Elisabetta in letters she sent to Dominus Polidoro, her brother, to be given and paid to her after the death of the said testatrix and of said Dominus Bartolomeo, her husband. And if this Elisabetta shall no longer be among the living, she wishes them to be paid out and freely given to the heirs of this Elisabetta, which 100 scudi by the law of inheritance she leaves and bequeaths to the said Elisabetta or to her heirs.

Similarly, by the same law, for the love of God, and for the salvation of her soul, she left and bequeathed to Dominus Camillo, son of Dominus Guido de' Maschi, 100 of the same scudi, to be given and paid out to him after the death of said testatrix and of said Dominus Bartolomeo, her husband. And if this Dominus Camillo shall not be living at that time, she wishes them to be paid out to the heirs of Dominus Camillo, which 100 scudi she leaves and bequeaths by the law of inheritance.[13]

12. Various members of the Spelli family appear in the Battiferri family papers in the Florentine archives. Laura's father promised money to dower two daughters of Girolamo Spelli, Emilia and Lodovica. Alessandro Spelli, a priest, served as a business agent in Urbino for Laura and her husband in 1583 (ASF Comp. soppr. Leopoldo 238, fols 59v, 101v, 254r).

13. Elisabetta, Polidoro, and Camillo were cousins of Laura's. For the Virgilii and Maschi families, into whom the Battiferri married, see app. B.

Likewise, by the same law, for the love of God, and for the salvation of her soul, she left and bequeathed after the death of said testatrix and of said Dominus Bartolomeo, her husband, to Dominus Lodovico di Altobello degli Organi of Bologna, the sum of 100 of the same scudi, to be given and paid out to him by her below-named heirs. And if this Dominus Lodovico shall not be in existence among the living, she wishes them to be paid out to the heirs of said Dominus Lodovico, which sum she leaves and bequeaths to him by the law of inheritance.

Likewise, by the same law, for the love of God, and for the salvation of her soul, she left and bequeathed to the sisters Cassandra Battiferra and Anna de' Vannucci, nuns in the monastery of Santa Lucia of Urbino, 100 of the same scudi, that is, 50 scudi to each of them, to be paid out by the below-named heirs of this testatrix and of said Dominus Bartolomeo, her husband. And if these nuns shall not be among the living, she wishes the money to be paid out freely and given to the nuns of said monastery of Santa Lucia of Urbino, which 100 scudi said testatrix leaves and bequeaths to those nuns for the love of God.

Likewise, the said testatrix said and affirmed that she had paid and given to Lodovica and Emilia, sisters and daughters of Dominus Girolamo de' Spelli, 200 of the same scudi, that is, 100 scudi to each of them, as part of each one's dowry. And this she declared lest in any way they might claim that nothing had been left to them by said testatrix.

Likewise, by the same law, she left and bequeathed to Dominus degli Ammannati, her husband, while he shall live, full, integral, and free use and usufruct of all the goods of the said testatrix . . . For all her other goods, present and future, she declares, makes, and wishes her universal heirs to be her sons and the masculine descendants, legitimate, natural, and still to be born of this testatrix and of said Dominus Bartolomeo; and if there be none surviving, her female children and descendants, legitimate and natural, in equal portions. And should she have no sons or daughters and legitimate masculine descendants, then in that case she declares her universal heirs the venerable School [*collegium*] of the Society of the Jesuit priests in the church of San Giovanni, who dwell next to the Medici Palace in the city of Florence, so that they may more easily repair and serve the needs of said School, which beyond doubt is of the greatest suitability and edification to be found and also an adornment in doctrine and decorum, as much to the practice of religion as to the city of Florence. She prohibits and expressly forbids the aforesaid declared heirs from selling, giving, and renting for a long term in all or in part any of the goods of said testatrix, because she wishes the aforesaid goods to stay always and remain and be preserved in the said school and among its priests, and from alienating in any way to another school or member of the said society of this order outside Florence in any preexisting place whatsoever. And if they should act or move against the aforesaid prohibition of alienation, she declared the aforesaid alienations null . . . and deprives them . . . And in said case, she declared or substituted as her universal heirs for the things and goods thus alienated the abbess and the nuns of the monastery of Santa Maria degli Angeli, in Borgo San Frediano of Florence,[14] with the same prohibition of alienating them as above.

14. *Santa Maria degli Angeli*: not to be confused with the Camaldolite monastery of the same name in central Florence, this was a Carmelite nunnery. It became famous for the visionary mystic Saint Maria Maddalena de' Pazzi (1566-1607).

[Abbreviated closing legal formulas].

Carried out in the home of said Mistress Laura, situated in the neighborhood of San Lorenzo, and in the street called della Stufa, in the presence of the witnesses named below, personally summoned . . . by the testatrix named below . . . , to wit:

1. Dominus Niccolò di Giovanni de' Brunetti, cleric
2. Dominus Bartolomeo di Giovanni di Montacuto, Florentine
3. Giovanni di Francesco de' Benci
4. Giovanni Francesco di Roberto de' Lippi
5. Jacopo di Donato de' Bonsignori, Florentine citizen
6. Andrea di Martino de' Ricci, Florentine citizen
7. Girolamo di Francesco de' Morelli, Florentine citizen

APPENDIX B
GENEALOGICAL CHART OF THE BATTIFERRI FAMILY OF URBINO

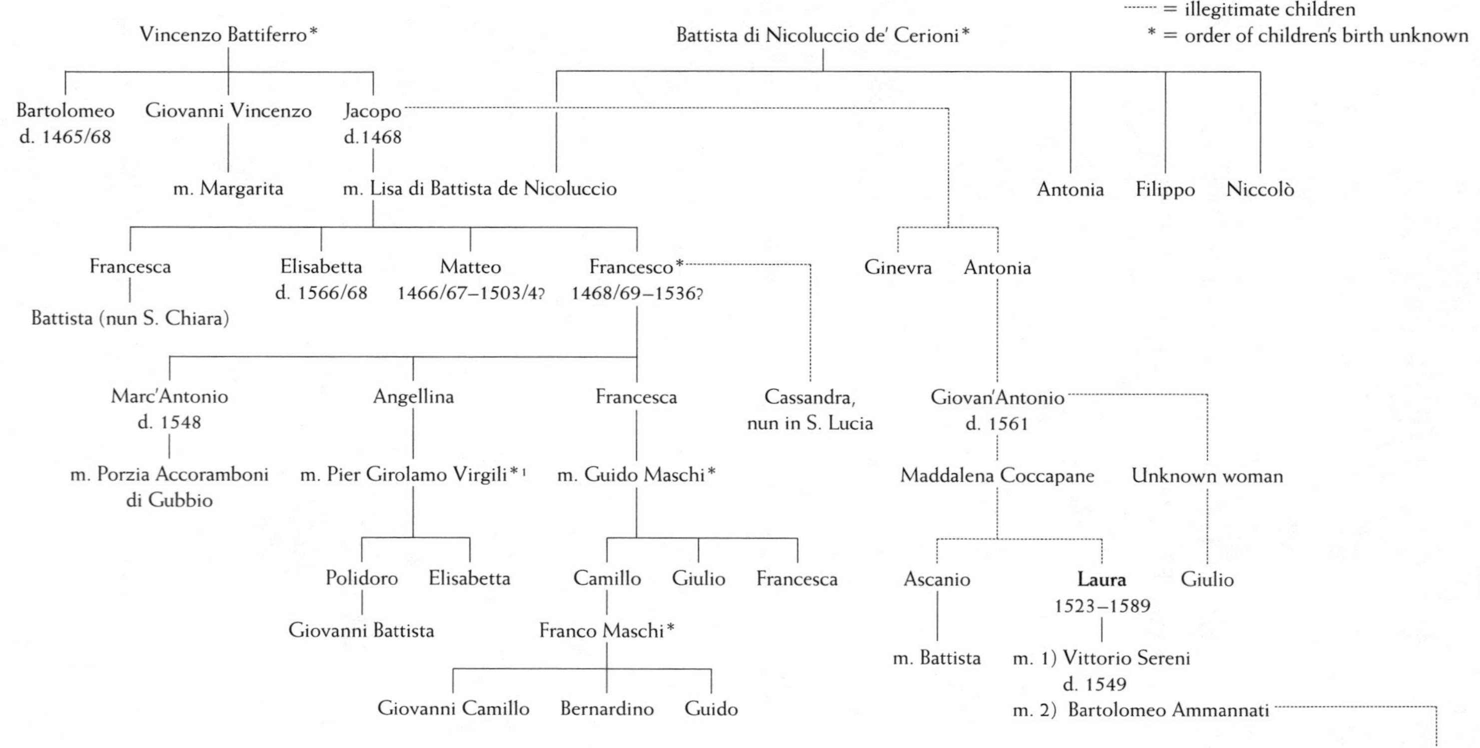

------ = illegitimate children
* = order of children's birth unknown
Vincenzo Battiferro*
Battista di Nicoluccio de' Cerioni*
Bartolomeo
d. 1465/68
Giovanni Vincenzo
Jacopo
d.1468
m. Margarita
m. Lisa di Battista de Nicoluccio
Antonia
Filippo
Niccolò
Francesca
Battista (nun S. Chiara)
Elisabetta
d. 1566/68
Matteo
1466/67–1503/4?
Francesco*
1468/69–1536?
Ginevra
Antonia
Marc'Antonio
d. 1548
m. Porzia Accoramboni
di Gubbio
Angellina
m. Pier Girolamo Virgili*[1]
Francesca
m. Guido Maschi*
Cassandra,
nun in S. Lucia
Giovan'Antonio
d. 1561
Maddalena Coccapane
Unknown woman
Polidoro
Giovanni Battista
Elisabetta
Camillo
Franco Maschi*
Giulio
Francesca
Giovanni Camillo
Bernardino
Guido
Ascanio
m. Battista
Laura
1523–1589
m. 1) Vittorio Sereni
d. 1549
m. 2) Bartolomeo Ammannati
Giulio
Magdalena, the widow Guiducci
Claudio

1. Pier Girolamo was a brother of the famous scholar Polidoro Virgili.

APPENDIX C
GENEALOGICAL CHART OF THE CIBO, DELLA ROVERE, VARANA, AND FARNESE FAMILIES

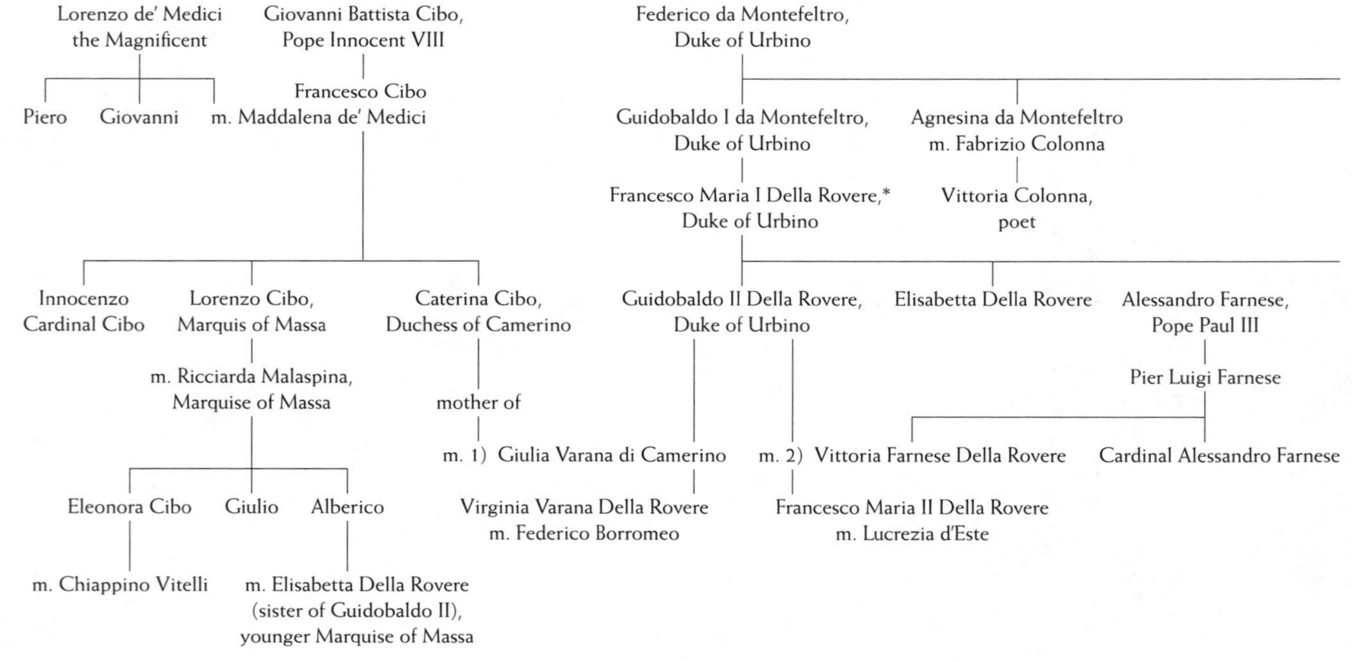
Lorenzo de' Medici
the Magnificent
Giovanni Battista Cibo,
Pope Innocent VIII
Piero
Giovanni
Francesco Cibo
m. Maddalena de' Medici
Federico da Montefeltro,
Duke of Urbino
Guidobaldo I da Montefeltro,
Duke of Urbino
Agnesina da Montefeltro
m. Fabrizio Colonna
Francesco Maria I Della Rovere,*
Duke of Urbino
Vittoria Colonna,
poet
Innocenzo
Cardinal Cibo
Lorenzo Cibo,
Marquis of Massa
Caterina Cibo,
Duchess of Camerino
Guidobaldo II Della Rovere,
Duke of Urbino
Elisabetta Della Rovere
Alessandro Farnese,
Pope Paul III
m. Ricciarda Malaspina,
Marquise of Massa
mother of
Pier Luigi Farnese
m. 1) Giulia Varana di Camerino
m. 2) Vittoria Farnese Della Rovere
Cardinal Alessandro Farnese
Eleonora Cibo
Giulio
Alberico
Virginia Varana Della Rovere
m. Federico Borromeo
Francesco Maria II Della Rovere
m. Lucrezia d'Este
m. Chiappino Vitelli
m. Elisabetta Della Rovere
(sister of Guidobaldo II),
younger Marquise of Massa

*nephew and adoptive son

APPENDIX D
GENEALOGICAL CHART OF THE MEDICI, TOLEDO, COLONNA, AND MONTEFELTRO FAMILIES

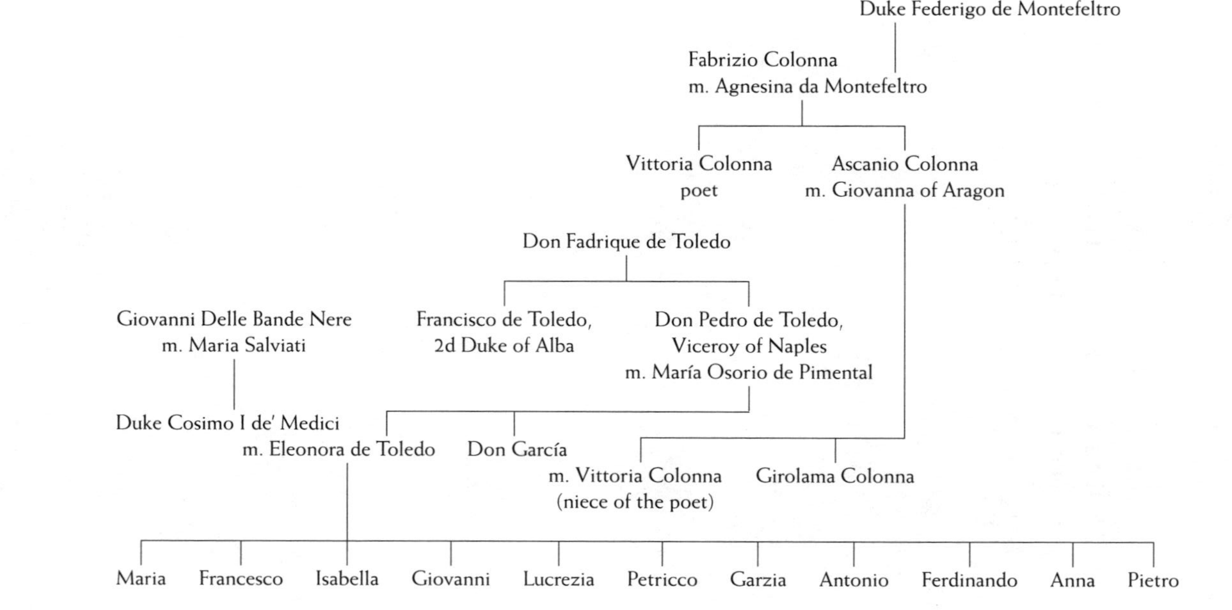

Duke Federigo de Montefeltro
Fabrizio Colonna
m. Agnesina da Montefeltro
Vittoria Colonna
poet
Ascanio Colonna
m. Giovanna of Aragon
Don Fadrique de Toledo
Giovanni Delle Bande Nere
m. Maria Salviati
Francisco de Toledo,
2d Duke of Alba
Don Pedro de Toledo,
Viceroy of Naples
m. María Osorio de Pimental
Duke Cosimo I de' Medici
m. Eleonora de Toledo
Don García
m. Vittoria Colonna
(niece of the poet)
Girolama Colonna
Maria
Francesco
Isabella
Giovanni
Lucrezia
Petricco
Garzia
Antonio
Ferdinando
Anna
Pietro

APPENDIX E
SOURCES OF THE SELECTIONS AND TEXTUAL VARIANTS

For the key to the abbreviations, see appendix F, "List of Manuscripts and Printed Editions." Note that when manuscript R (Rome, MS Casanatense 3229) is bracketed, it contains only the first line of the poem. Where there is more than one source, an asterisk (*) indicates the text on which a selection is based. Abbreviations have been expanded; original spellings of proper names have been retained; capitalization has been modernized for consistency.

CHAPTER 1

Rime di M. Laura Battiferra degli Ammannati

Epistola dell'Illustrissimo Signor Pietro Vettorio
All'Illustrissimo Signor Mario Colonna: R 2r–5v.

I. Di Messer Gherardo Spini a Madonna LAURA Battiferra: *1564, Fv recto; [R 5v, unnumbered sonnet].

II. Del Reverendo Signor Don Silvano Razzi, Monaco nel Munistero degli Angeli in Firenze / Alla Medesima: *1564, Fv verso; [R 5v, unnumbered sonnet].

III. Del Padre Frate Agostino de' Copeti Alla medesima: *R 5v–6r, unnumbered sonnet; F6 435r.

1. Alla Duchess di Fiorenza, e di Siena: F 1r: line 11 n'andrei volando in piu lontana parte; *1560, 9; [R 7r].

2. Al Duca di Fiorenza, e di Siena: F 1v; *1560, 9; [R 7r].

3. Al Prencipe di Fiorenza, e di Siena: F 2v; *1560, 10; [R 7r].

4. Al Signor Paolo Giordano, Orsino: F 3r; *1560, 10; [R 7r].

5. Al Re Filippo: F 5r; *1560, 11; F14 271r; [R 7r].

6. Alla Reina Maria: F 5v; *1560, 11; F14 271v; [R 7r].

7. Al Duca d'Urbino: F 6v; *1560, 12; [R 7r].

8. Alla Duchessa d'Urbino: F 7r; *1560, 13; [R 7r].

9. Al Prencipe d'Urbino: F 7v; *1560, 13; [R 7r].

10. A Donna Verginia Varana della Rovere: F 8r; *1560, 14; [R 7r].

11. Nelle Nozze del Signor Federigo Buonromeo e della Signora Donna Virginia della Rovere: 1560, 49: line 12, FEDERICO; [R 7r].

12. Alla Medesima: 1560, 50; [R 7r].

13. Alla Medesima: 1560, 50; [R 7r].

14. Alla Medesima: 1560, 51; [R 7v].

15. Al Cardinal de' Medici: 1560, 121: line 4, allegar; [R 7v].

16. Al Duca di Fiorenza, e di Siena: 1560, 121; [R 7v].

17. Alla Duchess di Fiorenza, e di Siena: 1560, 122; [R 7v].

18. Per Madama Lucretia da Este Principessa d'Urbino: R 8r.

19. Per la Medesima: R 8r.

20. A Papa Paolo Terzo Farnese: R 8v.

21. Ad Instanza dell'Illustissima Signora Donna Isabella de' Medici: R 8v–9r.

22. Per la Medesima: R 9r.

23. Per la Medesima: R 9r–9v.

24. R 9v.

25. R 10r.

26. R 10r.

27. Per la Signora Donna Hieronima Colonna: Sammarco 1568, 94r: Lines 12–13, "Tacciasi or chi morendo accrebbe tanto / vera onestà" [Be silent whoever so increased true honesty by dying]. The second tercet in the earlier *Il tempio* contains an allusion too vague for clear identification, whereas the variant in Battiferra's late unpublished *Rime* must call to mind Lucretia; *R 10v; N fol. 85v [=86v].

28. Al Signor Chiappino Vitelli: F 8v; *1560, 14; [R 10v].

29. Al Medesimo: F 9r; *1560, 15; [R 10v].

30. Alla Signora Leonora Cibo de' Vitelli: F 10r; *1560, 16; [R 10v]; Bergalli 1726, 189.

31. Alla Medesima: F 10v; *1560, 16; [R 10v].

32. Alla Medesima: F 11r; *1560, 17; [R 10v].

33. Alla Signora Hersilia Cortesi, de' Monti: F 12r; *1560, 18; [R 11r].

34. Per la Signora Livia Colonna: F 12v; *1560, 18; [R 11r].

35. Alla Signora Hortensia Colonna: F 31r; *1560, 20; [R 11r]; F12 142r: The word "stampato" [printed] is written beside the sonnet; Guidi 2000: line 1, mi.

36. Nelle Nozze del Signor Vespasiano Piccolhuomini e della Signora Lucrezia Soderina: F 32v; *1560, 22; [R 11r].

37. Per la Marchesa di Massa: F 33v: lines 13–14, Leggiadra donna, anzi sovrano honore / d'UMBRIA e di MASSA, ad inchinarla volte; *1560, 23; [R 11r]; Guidi 2000: line 1, Appennin.

38. Al Signor Don Grazia di Toledo: Pe 213r: line 1, Poiche del proprio et generoso fianco; line 2, devoto; line 11, securo; line 12, qual corona; line 13, fiero artiglio; line 14, salvaste; *R 11v.

39. Al Signor Chiappino Vitelli: Pe 213v: line 7, Come fu già nel ciel; line 13, ch'abbia in fuga; *R 12r.

40. Al Signor Alessandro de' Medici: R 12v.

41. R 13v.

42. Alla Signora Eufemia: F 34v; *1560, 24; [R 13v]; Bergalli 1726, 190 [=191].

43. A Messer Giovan Battista Strozzi: F 40r; *1560, 29: line 10, è 'ndimion tuo solo; *[R 13v]; De Blasi 1930, 210; Guidi 2000: line 7, sovra Olimpo ed Atlante; line 10, e'ndimion tuo solo.

44. A Madonna Laudomia Rucellai: R 14r.

45. A Messer Vincentio Grotti: F 17r; *1560, 39; [R 14r].

46. F 18v; *1560, 41; [R 14v]; F12 76v: The word "stampato" [printed] is written beside the sonnet. Line 4, carche di fior, di frutti ambe le sponde; line 11, lidi.

47. F 19r; *1560, 41; [R 14v]; F12 142v: The word "stampato" [printed] is written beside the sonnet.

48. F 20r–21r; *1560, 42–43; [R 14v]; F12 188v–189r: The word "stampato" [printed] is written beside the sonnet; F14 278r–279r: line 7, orrido mare; line 19, Deh, volgi ora in porto questa nave; line 26, e senza vento o sarte ricca nave; line 27, e dura l'aura, e molli, e fiori scogli; line 27, che si celi da me l'alta mia luce; line 28, che tante alge [sic] non ha fiume ne mare; line 36, senza assalti temer d'alpestri scogli; line 37, lungi da scogli; line 38, luci il vago.

49. F 37r; *1560, 26; [R 14v]; F14 279r; Bergalli 1726, 191; De Blasi 1930, 209.

50. F 37v; *1560, 26; [R 14v].

51. F 38r; *1560, 27; [R 14v]; De Blasi 1930, 209.

52. A Messer Francesco Monte Varchi: F 44r; *1560, 34; [R 14v].

53. F 44v; *1560, 34; [R 14v]; De Blasi 1930, 210; Flora 1962, 160; Baldacci 1975, 175.

54. F 45v; *1560, 35; [R 14v]; F14 268v: line 7, aggiunte; Bergalli 1726, 194: line 9, duri campi.

55. F 46r; *1560, 36; [R 14v]; Bergalli 1726, 194: line 9, soavi accenti.

56. F 46v; *1560, 37; [R 14v]; Gobbi 1709, 2: 97; Bergalli 1726, 195; Poetesse 1787, 242; Fiori 1846, 23: the one poem that represents Battiferra; Gianni 1997, 59: the one poem that represents Battiferra; Ponchiroli 1958, 399.

57. F 15v; *1560, 38; [R 15r]; F14 270v.

58. F 16v: v. 5 is missing; *1560, 39; [R 15r]; Bergalli 1726, 196; Baldacci 1975, 276. In R three consecutive poems are numbered 97.

59. A Messer Luca Martini: 1560, 120; [R 15v].

60. Per Messer Luigi Alamanni: R 16r.

61. A Messer Bartolomeo Strada fisico: R 16v.

62. Al Padre Claudio Acquaviva Generale della Compagnia di Giesu: an autograph correction, apparently the hand of Ammannati, modifies the original title, inserting the name "Claudio Acquaviva" to give it greater relief on the page. R 17v.

63. A Don Silvano RAZZI: Calzolari 1561, A iiiv: A Don silvano Razzi, Monaco Camaldolese: line 2, vi sie; *R 17v: vi fie; T 35r.

64. R 18r.

65. Alla Signora Bianca Cappella: R 18v.

66. A Messer Hannibal Caro: F 27v; *1560, 52; [R 19v]; Fo: unnumbered folio preceding Caro's "Laura, sì voi mi sete e lauro e Clio"; Caro 1572, 34; Ronna 97.

67. Risposta: F 28r; *1560, 52; Atanagi 1565, 6r: line 13, fregio; [R 19v]: line 1, Laura, se voi mi sete; Fo: unnumbered folio following Laura's "Caro, se 'l basso stile e 'l gran desio": line 1, Laura, se voi mi sete; Caro 1572, 34.

68. Al Medesimo: F 28v; *1560, 53; [R 19v]; Guidi 2000: line 5, delizia.

69. A Messer Benedetto Varchi: F 29v; *1560, 54; [R 19v].

70. Al Capitan Pietro Buonaventura: F 51v; *1560, 59; [R 20v].

71. Risposta: F 52r; *1560, 59; [R 20v].

72. A Don Gabriello Fiamma: F 50v; *1560, 60; F 7 62v; F14 292v.

73. Risposta: F 51r; *1560, 60; F 7 56r; F14 309v.

74. Di Messer Antonio Gallo: F 57v; *1560, 66; Pml 136v.

75. Risposta: F 58r; *1560, 66; Pml 137r.

76. Del Bronzino Pittore: F4 119v; F 60v; *1560, 69: line 11, vede.

77. Risposta: F4 120r; F 61r; *1560, 69.

78. Di Messer Girolamo Razzi: *F 65v; 1560, 74: line 1, Ben tu puo.

79. Risposta: F 66r; *1560, 74.

80. Di Messer Benvenuto Scultore: F 66v; *1560, 75: chetosi.

81. Risposta: F 67r; *1560, 75.

82. Di Messer Federigo Lanti: F 67v: line 2, s'infondo; *1560, 76; Bulifon, 1694: line 2, s'infonde; Guidi, 2000: line 2, s'infonde.

83. Risposta: F 68r: line 11, lodarvi; line 14, alto; *1560, 76.

84. Di Messer Girolamo Bargagli Material Intronato: F 68v; *1560, 77.

85. Risposta: F 69r; *1560, 77.

86. Del Lasca: 1560, 81.

87. Risposta: 1560, 81.

88. Del Bronzino Pittore: 1560, 82; F4 184v; F14 316v.

89. Risposta: 1560, 82; F4 185r.

90. De Messer Lucio Oradini a Messer Bartolomeo Ammannati: F 72v; *1560, 86 [= 89]; F14 308v.

91. Risposta: F 73r; *1560, 86 [= 89]: line 10 reads "vosta," clearly a printer's error; F14 309r.

92. Di Messer Lelio Bonsi a Messer Bartolomeo Ammannati: F 76r; *1560, 88 [= 91]: Di Messer Lucio Oradini a Messer Bartolomeo Ammannati; F14 281v: line 5, non fossero e i bei carmi, e; v. 14 ends with a question mark.

93. Risposta IV: F 78r; *1560, 93.

94. A Madonna Alessandra de' Corsi: R 23r.

95. Risposta: R 23r.

96. In Morte di Messer Benedetto Varchi: *R 26r–26v; Stufa-Varchi 1566, F ii verso: line 10, or ch'io ti piango.

97. Di Messer Antonio Allegretti: R 29v.

98. In Morte di Donna Maria de' Medici: F 78v; *1560, 91 [=94]: 12 non tra; [R 30r]; F1 90v–91r; F6 301r: line 6, scielse di lei.

99. In Morte di Messer Lelio Capilupi: F 83v; *1560, 99.

100. In Morte di Madonna Hirene: F 85v; *1560, 101; Atanagi 1561, 117.

101. Nella Malattia del Cavallier Fra Paolo del Rosso: *R 30r; Pm1 42r: line 2, al bel permesso.

102. A Messer Giovan Battista Cini, in morte di madonna Maria Berardi sua consorte: *R 31v; F1 26v–27r; F6 419r.

103. In morte del Gran duca di Toscana: *R 31v–32r; F15 106r–107r: the order of the stanzas differs and runs 1, 3, 4, 2; line 24, ognor si posa; line 25, l'alma del tuo servo, che pur dianzi.

104. In Morte della Serenissima Giovanna d'Austria Gran Duchessa di Toscana: *R 33r; F8 50r: line 1, Spargete gigli e fiori; line 7, or e fatta e degna. The same madrigal appears with slight spelling variations in this ms. on fol. 170r; F9 61r: line 10, ne deggia.

105. Per la Medesima: R 33v.

106. R 33v: line 8, che t'inspoglia.

107. R 34r.

108. R 34r.

109. R 34v.

110. R 34v.

111. R 35r.

112. R 35r.

113. R 35v.

114. R 35v.

115. R 36v.

116. R 36v.

117. In morte di Francesco Bennucci figlio dolcissimo: *R 37v; F7a 170v: Ne la morte del figlio Francesco.

118. R 37v: Il medesimo Francesco alla Madre; F7a 171r: "Il medesimo Francesco a la madre sua madonna Dorotea Tancredi de' Benuccij."

119. In morte di Papa Gregorio xiij: R 38r.

120. Egloga Terza: R 38v–42r.

SECONDA PARTE delle rime spirituali di madonna Laura Battiferra de gli Ammannati all'Illustrissima et Eccellentissima Signora padrona mia sempre osservandissima la Signora Vittoria Farnese dalla Rovera Duchessa D'Urbino Laura Battiferra de gl'Ammannati, etc. Sonetti spirituali della medesima autrice

1. *1564, F iii recto; [R 43r]. The rubric and the letter to the Duchess of Urbino are numbered 1 and 2 in the Casanatense manuscript.

2. *R 43r: line 8, e d'altri a cantar.

3. I sette salmi Penitenziali del santissimo David Profeta tradotti in lingua Fiorentina da Madonna Laura Battiferri degli Ammannati. Con gl'argomenti sopra ciascuno di essi composti dalla medesima. Argomento del Salmo Primo alla Reverenda et Illustirssima signora suor xxx [sic]. Salmo sesto, e primo de' Penitentiali: *1564, 7–8; [R 43v].

4. *1564, F iii verso; [R 46v]; Bergalli 1726, 200–201; Rigamonti 66.

5. *1564, F iv verso; [R 46v]; Gobbi 1709, 2: 96; Bergalli 201–202; Ronna 96; Ponchiroli, 400.

6. *1560, 28; [R 46v]; Flora 1962, 159; Baldacci 1975, 275.

7. *1560, 44; [R 46v].

8. Della Compagnia di Giesu: *R 47r–47v; R1 41v.

9. R 48v.

10. R 48v.

11. R 49v: line 12, adre.

12. *R 50r; F2 5r: line 6, l'altro del sommo sole alto soggiorno; R1 41r: line 1, Se gli occhi innalzo a rimirar talhora; line 6, l'altro del sommo sole almo soggiorno; line 9, O quanto son di voi stelle; line 11, che si giran; Ponchiroli 1958, 400.

13. R 51v.

14. R 51v: line 3 aspri.

15. Alla Compagnia di Giesu: R 52v: line 4, pure.

16. R 53r.

17. F 22r; *1560, 44; [R 53v]; F14 314r.

18. R 55r.

19. R 56v.

20. R 58r.

21. F 39v; *1560, 28; F10 167r; R 59v: line 6, ville.

22. R 59v–60r.

23. Sopra la tavola dell'inventione della Croce: R 60v.

24. Pistola di Lentulo Re, al senato tradotta in versi: R 63r–64r.

25. Stanze della fede, et obedienza di Abramo, et amore verso Dio nell'offerire il suo fgliuolo: R 64r–67r (*sic*). The stanzas are not numbered. There is some confusion in the manuscript at this point. Folio 65 contains 4 terzine: Ascende in Ciel, siede alla destra parte [repeated from top of folio 63r].

26. R 67v–70r.

The remaining folios in the manuscript are blank.

CHAPTER 2

1. Offredi, 259: Di Madonna Laura Battiferro.

2. *F4 132v: A Madonna Laura Battiferra delli Ammannati; F10 165r: A madonna Laura Battiferra delli Ammannati il Bronzino pittore; FB14 129v: il Bronzino pittore; Bronzino 1823, 19: A madonna Laura Battiferra delli Ammannati In morte di messer Luca Martini.

3. *F4 133r: Di Madonna Laura in Risposta; FB14 130r: Laura Battiferra degli Ammannati; Bronzino 1823, 19: Di madonna Laura in Risposta.

4. F3 28r: A Madonna Laura Battiferra degl'Ammannati.

5. F3 65r: Sonetto di Madonna Laura Battiferra in Risposta di quello di Messer Benedetto Varchi, che incomincia Questa nostra caduca e fragil vita.

6. F3 40r: A Messer Bartolommeo Ammannati.

7. *F6 377r: Di Messer Gherardo Spini nella Morte del Padre di Madonna Laura Battiferri; F1 136r: Sonetto di messere Gherardo Spini nella morte del padre di Madonna Laura Battiferri. Line 4, si veggon; line 5, mi giovi; line 7, poscia le preci; line 11, n'incontra; F1 137r: Two verses are missing.

8. *F6 377v: Risposta di Madonna Laura; F1 136v: Risposta di madonna Laura. Line 2, fin ch'el; line 4, non destino; line 10, aggio uno sol ch'ancor; line 12, SPINA.

9. *F4 149r: A Madonna Laura Battiferra degl'Ammannati. A rubric on fol. 148r precedes this sequence: Sonetti in Morte di messer [blank space] Padre di madonna Laura Battiferra delli Ammannati; Bronzino 1823, 32: Alla medesima in morte di suo padre.

10. *F4 149v: A Messer Benedetto Varchi; Bronzino 1823, 31.

11. Domenichi 1563, 54: Gherardo Spini All'Eccellente Messer Bartolomeo Amannati, in materia del Palazzo de' Pitti, per la Morte della signora Duchessa.

12. *Ferrara 1563, B iij verso; Per la morte del Cardinal de' Medici, Laura Battiferra. Line 8, dolce, ne caro; Domenichi 1563, 66 [= p. 59]: In morte di Don Grazia (*sic*) Di madonna Laura Battiferra. Line 8, dolce, ne caro; line 9, Or che nel sommo sol; line 10, vivono eterni.

13. *Ferrara, 1563, C recto; In Morte della Duchessa / Laura Battiferra; Domenichi 1563, 67: line 13, qui non mi sei.

14. *Ferrara, 1563, C verso; In Morte di Don Grazia Laura Battiferra; Domenichi 1563, 67: Unattributed. The order of the poems differs from that in the Ferrara edition; here the cardinal is first, then Garzia and then duchess: line 9, non perciò.

15. *Pm2 1: 18v: A Madonna Laura Battiferra; 2: 7v: A madonna Laura Battiferra 1560; 3: 9r; Bo 61r.

16. Pm1 37r: Di Madonna Laura Battiferra. Verso: Sonetti per la venuta di monsignore in Toscana.

17. Gonzaga, *Rime* 44b, in Quondam 1997.

18 F5 19r: Risposta di Madonna LAURA Battiferra in Risposta di quello del Varchi che incomincia Prima dopo la mia primiera fronde.

19. *Michelangelo 1564, C2v–C3r: Nella Morte di Michelagnolo Buonarroti. Laura Battiferra degli Ammannati; Wittkower 1964, 86–87.

20. *Michelangelo 1564, F1r–F2v: Canzone nella morte di Michelagnolo Buonarroti. di M. Laura Battiferra degli Ammannati; Wittkower 1964, 126–31.

21. Gamucci, 1585, 6r–6v: Di Madonna Laura Battiferra de gli Ammannati.

22. F13 134r: La Compagnia della Scala la vigilia di San Giovanni 1577 cantò questo madrigale sopra un carro dove Dio padre coronava la Vergine.

23. Sanleolino, 113v: De Laura Batiferria Ammannata.

24. Cellini, *Opere*, ed. Ferrero, 905–906.

25. *F4 56r: Del Lasca sopra il ritratto di Madonna Laura Battiferra al Bronzino; Kirkham 1998, 73–74; Plazzotta 1998, 261.

26. *F4 56v: Risposta; Kirkham 1998, 75–76; Plazzotta 1998, 261.

27. *F4 58r: A Madonna Laura Battiferra delli Ammannati; Kirkham 1998, 122; Plazzotta 1998, 261.

28. *F4 58v: Di Madonna Laura Battiferra a Bronzino; Kirkham 1998, 77; Plazzotta 1998, 261.

29. F4 73r; Bronzino 1960, 100.

30. F4 183r; Bronzino 1960, 102.

31. F12 63v: A Messer Bartolomeo Ammannati scultore.

32. F11 64r: Di Madonna Laura Battiferra.

33. F11 65r: Di Madonna Laura Battiferra.

34. Chi 169v: Madonna Laura Battiferra.

35. Colonna 1589, 50: Alla Medesima [A Madonna Laura Battiferra].

36. Colonna 1589, 50: Risposta di Madonna Laura.

37. F16 79v–80r: Alla Signora Laura Battiferra degli Amannati, Laura Terracina.

38. F16 80r–80v: Alla signora Laura Terracina degli Incogniti Laura Battifferra risposta.

39. F1 91r: Sonetto di Madonna Laura Battiferri de gl'Ammannati. Line 1, exalando; line 4, la tomba del tuo aspetto; line 7, l'armi l'alto; line 10, cangia; *F6 310v: Laura Battiferra degli Ammannati.

40. F2a 61r: Risposta di Madonna Laura Battiferra al sonnetto che incomincia Quando io penso tra me, che 'l penso ogn'ora.

CHAPTER 3

M 137r–141v: Oratione sopra il Natale di Nostro Signore di madonna signora Laura Battiferra de gli Ammannati.

CHAPTER 4

1. FV, No. 1.18; Gargiolli, 14–15.

2. ASF. Urbino. Cl. I, Div. G, CCXXXVI, terza parte, fols. 1172r–v.

3. ASF, Conventi Soppressi da Leopoldo, *filza* 238, fol. 32r.

4. FV, No. 1.27; Gargiolli, 42–44.

5. *Il primo libro dell'opere toscane di Madonna Laura Battiferra degli Ammannati* (Florence: Giunti, 1560), Aii recto–verso.

6. FV, No. 1.28; Gargiolli, 45–46.

7. Varchi, *Opere*, 2: 822–23.

8. Pe 160r–162v. I thank Enrico Maria Guidi for informing me of this letter and sending a photocopy.

APPENDIX F
LIST OF MANUSCRIPTS AND PRINTED EDITIONS

POETRY

Manuscripts

Bologna

Biblioteca Comunale dell'Archiginnasio

Bo MS B 233. *Vita di monsignor Lodovico Beccadelli . . . poesie del Beccadelli e rime di altri.* 18th c. Albano Sorbelli, *Bologna Biblioteca Comunale dell'Archiginnasio,* in Giuseppe Mazzatinti, ed., *Inventari dei manoscritti delle biblioteche d'Italia,* vol. 69 (Florence: Olschki, 1939), 69: 35–41.

Chicago

Chi Newberry Library. Strozzi MS Case 6A 11. *Canzonette e miscellanee diverse.* 16th–17th c. Maria Xenia Wells, *Italian Post-1600 Manuscripts and Family Archives in North American Libraries* (Ravenna: Longo, 1992), 68.

Florence

Biblioteca Nazionale

F1 MS Magl. 2.4.233. Miscellany, 16th c. Giuseppe Mazzatinti, *Inventari dei manoscritti delle biblioteche d'Italia* (Forlì: Luigi Bordandini, 1890–), 10: 156–61.

F2 MS Magl. 2.8.38. Miscellany, 16th–17th c. Mazzatinti, *Inventari dei manoscritti* (1901), 11: 235–37.

F2a MS Magl. 2.8.137. Benedetto Varchi, *Sonetti contra gl'Ugonotti.* 16th c. Mazzatinti, *Inventari dei manoscritti,* 11: 249.

F3 MS Magl. 2.8.140. Benedetto Varchi, ed., *Cento sonetti sopra la morte di Luca Martini* (d. 1561). Mazzatinti, *Inventari dei manoscritti,* 11: 249.

F4 MS Magl. 2.9.10. Bronzino, *Rime.* Mazzatinti, *Inventari dei manoscritti,* 11: 257.

F5 MS Magl. 7.341. Sonnets by Benedetto Varchi "sopra il dolorosissimo e pericolosissimo accidente dell'illustrissimo et eccellentissimo Duca," 1564. Mazzatinti, *Inventari dei manoscritti,* 13: 341.

F6 MS Magl. 7.346. Miscellany, 16th–17th c. Mazzatinti, *Inventari dei manoscritti* (1905–1906) 13: 65.

F7 MS Magl. 7.380. Miscellany, 16th c. and later. Mazzatinti, *Inventari dei manoscritti,* 13: 87.

F MS Magl. 7.778. Holograph of *Primo libro,* before 1560. [= Guidi RB]. Mazzatinti, *Inventari dei manoscritti,* 13: 170.

F7a MS Magl. 7.779. *Rime,* Lattanzio Benucci. Mazzatinti, *Inventari dei manoscritti,* 13: 170.

F8 MS Magl. 7.874. Miscellany, 16th and early 17th c. Mazzatinti, *Inventari dei manoscritti,* 13: 183.

F9 MS Magl. 7.1024 (Strozzi 981). Miscellany, 16th–17th c. *Strozziana Classi I–XX,* 1: [n.p.]; Paul Oskar Kristeller, *Iter italicum. Accedunt alia itinera: A Finding List of Uncatalogued or Incompletely Catalogued Humanistic Manuscripts of the Renaissance in Italian and Other Libraries* (London: Warburg Institute, 1977), 2: 511–12.

F10 MS Magl. 7.1030 (Strozzi 1163). Miscellany, 16th c. *Strozziana classi I–XX,* 1: [n.p.].

F11 MS Magl. 7.1185 (Strozzi 763). *Poesie toscane di diversi autori.* Miscellany. *Strozziana classi I–XX.*1 [n.p.].

F12 MS Magl. 7.1206 (Strozzi 841). Miscellany. Collected poetry, all in same hand, after 1560. *Strozziana classi I–XX.*1 [n.p.].

F13 MS Magl. 7.1293. Miscellany, 16th c. Kristeller, *Iter italicum,* 2: 510.

F14 MS Magl. 7.1388. Miscellany, 16th–17th c. Kristeller, *Iter italicum,* 2: 511.

F15 MS Magl. 27.104. *Varie Orazioni e rime fatte in Morte del Serenis. Cosimo de' Medici Granduca di Toscana. Et alcune in morte del Rev.mo Monsig.r Antonio Altoviti Arcivescovo di Firenze. Messe insieme e scritte da NR l'anno 1575 in Pisa. Strozziana classi XXVII–XXX,* 9: [n.p.].

F16 MS Palat. 229. *Rime spirituali morte di Principj, et di signori titulati, et non titulatj, con altri sonetti a particulari gentil'homini et Donne. Conposti per la signora Laura Terracina.* Libro Nono. Luigi Gentile, *I codici palatini della R. Biblioteca Nazionale Centrale di Firenze.* In *Cataloghi dei manoscritti della Real: Biblioteca Nazionale Centrale di Firenze compilati sotto la direzione del Prof. Adolfo Bartoli.* Vol. 1, fasc. 1 (Rome: Presso i Principali Librai, 1885), 319–27.

Biblioteca Moreniana at the Riccardiana

FM Biblioteca Moreniana, MS Fondo Bigazzi 210, inserto 3, Miscellany, 16th–18th c. *I manoscritti della Biblioteca Moreniana* (Florence: Tipografia Nazionale, 1976–79), vol. 3, fasc. 1–9: 275.

Casa Buonarroti (Biblioteca Medicea-Laurenziana)

FB14 Florence, Casa Buonarroti, MS Buonarroti 14 (on microfilm at Biblioteca Laurenziana, Archivio Buonarroti, 14). Copies of poems. Kristeller, *Iter italicum,* 2: 507.

Foligno

Fo Biblioteca Lodovico Jacovilli del Seminario Vescovile, MS B V 8. Miscellany, 16th c. Kristeller, *Iter italicum,* 5: 629.

Naples

N Biblioteca Governativa dei Gerolamini, MS cart. 188. *Il tempio della divina Signora Geronima Colonna d'Aragona,* 16th c. Kristeller, *Iter italicum,* 1: 397.

Parma

Pm1 Biblioteca Palatina, MS 557. Miscellany of poems sent to Ludovico Beccadelli, 16th c. Kristeller, *Iter italicum,* 2: 37.

Pm2 Biblioteca Palatina, MS 972. Ludovico Beccadelli, *Rime.* Kristeller, *Iter italicum,* 6: 133.

Perugia

Pe Biblioteca Augusta. MS G 63. *Lettere di mons. Ercolani Vescovo di Perugia (Epistolario di Timoteo Bottonio),* 16th c. Mazzatinti (1895), 5: 134.

Rome

R1 Biblioteca Angelica, MS 1882. *Quinquaginta fere auctorum et praesertim academicorum Intronatorum Senensium carmina italica.* 16th c. Albano Sorbelli, *Roma. R. Biblioteca Angelica.* In Mazzatinti (1934), 5: 62–73.

R Biblioteca Casanatense, MS 3229 [Guidi RB 1]. *Rime di Laura Battiferra degli Ammannati.* Before April 1592. Brackets [ ] indicate that the ms. contains only the first line of the poem. Kristeller, *Iter italicum,* 2: 96.

Todi

T Biblioteca Comunale, MS 238. *Collection of Rime,* 16th c. Kristeller 6: 233.

Poetry by Laura Battiferra degli Ammannat

1560 *Il primo libro dell'opere toscane di m. Laura Battiferra degli Ammannati* (Florence: Giunti, 1560).

1564 *I sette salmi penitentiali del santissimo profeta Dauit. Tradotti in lingua Toscana da madonna Laura Battiferra degli Ammannati. Con gli argomenti sopra ciascuno di essi, composti dalla medesima; insieme con alcuni suoi Sonetti spiritali* (Florence: Giunti, 1564).

1566 *I sette salmi penitentiali del santissimo profeta Dauit. Tradotti in lingua Toscana da madonna Laura Battiferra degli Ammannati. Con gli argomenti sopra ciascuno di essi, composti dalla medesima; insieme con alcuni suoi Sonetti spirituali* (Florence: Giunti, 1566).

1570 *I sette salmi penitentiali del santissimo profeta Dauit tradotti in lingua toscana, da madonna Laura Battiferra degli Ammannati. Con gli argomenti sopra ciascuno di essi composti dalla medesima; insieme con alcuni suoi Sonetti spirituali* (Filippo Giunta & Fratelli, 1570).

1694 *Rime della sig. Laura Battiferra nuovamente date in luce da Antonio Bulifon* (Naples: Antonio Bulifon, 1694).

2000 *Il primo libro delle opere toscane,* ed. Enrico Maria Guidi (Urbino: Accademia Raffaello, 2000).

2005 *I sette salmi penitentiali di David con alcuni sonetti spirituali,* ed. Enrico Maria Guidi (Urbino: Accademia Raffaello, 2005).

Poetry by and to Battiferra in anthologies by other editors

Offredi 1560 Giovanni Offredi, ed., *Rime di diversi autori eccellentissimi* (Cremona: Vincenzo Conti).

Atanagi 1561 Dionigi Atanagi, ed., *Rime di diversi . . . in morte della Signora Irene delle Signore di Spilimbergo* (Venice: Domenico and Giovanni Battista Guerera Fratelli).

Calzolari 1561 Pietro Calzolai [Calzolari], *Historia monastica di D. Pietro Calzolai, da Buggiano di Toscana, Monaco della Badia di Firenze, della congregatione di Monte Casino, Distinta in cinque giornate, nella quale, brevemente si raccontano tutti i Sommi Pontefici, e quelli, che hanno predicata la fede Christiana a i Gentili. Gl'imperadori, i Re, Duchi, Principi, e Conti. L'Imperatrici, e Reine, et altre Donne Illustri, e Sante. Huomini dotti, che hanno scritto qualche opera. E Santi, i quali sono stati dell'ordine Monastico* (Florence: Lorenzo Torrentino; reprint Rome: Vincenzio Accolti, 1575).

Fiordiano 1562 Malatesta Fiordiano da Rimini, *La bellezza delle donne* (Rimini: Giovanni di Nicola da Modona).

Domenichi 1563 — Lodovico Domenichi, ed., *Poesie toscane, et latine di diversi eccel. ingegni, nella morte del S. D. Giovanni Cardinale, del Sig. Don Grazia de Medici, et della S. Donna Leonora di Toledo de Medici Duchessa di Fiorenza et di Siena* (Florence: L. Torrentino Impressor Ducale).

Ferrara 1563 — *Rime di diversi eccellentissimi autori fatte nella morte dell'Illustriss. et Eccell. Duchessa di Fiorenza et Siena, et degli Illustriss. Signori suoi figliuoli* (Ferrara: Valente Panizza Mantovano).

Mantua 1564 — *Rime di diversi aggiunte a quelle degli Accademici Invaghiti in morte del Card. Ercole Gonzaga* (Mantua: Jacopo Ruffinelli). See Gonzaga, Curtio, *Rime dell'illustrissimo Curtio Gonzaga* (Vicenza: Nella Stamperia Nova, 1585).

Massolo 1564 — Pietro Massolo [Don Lorenzo monaco cassinese], *Primo, et secondo volume delle rime morali* (Florence: Appresso i figliuoli di M. Lorenzo Torrentino, et Bernardo Fabroni compagni; reprint *Rime morali,* Venice: Gio. Antonio Rampazetto, 1583).

Michelangelo 1564 — *Esequie del divino Michelagnolo Buonarroti celebrate in Firenze dall'Accademia de' Pittori, Scultori, et Architettori nella Chiesa di S. Lorenzo il di 28 Giugno MDLXIIII* (Florence: I Giunti), in *The Divine Michelangelo. A Facsimile Edition of Esequie del Divino Michelagnolo Buonarroti,* ed. Rudolf and Margot Wittkower (London: Phaidon, 1964).

Atanagi 1565 — *De le rime di diversi nobili poeti toscani, raccolte da M. Dionigi Atanagi, libro primo. Con una tavola del medesimo ne la quale, oltre a molte altre cose degne di notitia, talvolta si dichiarano alcune cose pertinenti a la lingua Toscana, et a l'arte del poetare* (Venice: Lodovico Avanzo, 1565).

Gamucci 1565 — Bernardino Gamucci da San Gimignano, *Le antichità di Roma* (Venice: G. Varisco; reprint 1569, 1580, 1585, 1588).

Stufa-Varchi 1566 — Piero Stufa, ed., *Componimenti Latini, e Toscani da diversi suoi amici composti nella morte di M. Benedetto Varchi* (Florence: Lorenzo Torrentino e Carlo Pettinari Compagni).

Sammarco 1568 — Ottavio Sammarco, ed., *Il Tempio della divina signora donna Geronima Colonna D'Aragona* (Padua: Lorenzo Pasquati).

Turchi 1568 — *Salmi penitentiali, di diuersi eccellenti autori con alcune rime spirituali di diuersi illust. cardinali, di Reuerendissimi uescoui, et d'altre persone Ecclesiastiche. Scelti dal reuerendo P. Francesco da Triuigi Carmelitano [Francesco Turchi]* (Venice: Gabriel Giolito de'

	Ferrari; reprint 1569, 1570, 1572, 1749 [contains Batti-ferra's *Sette salmi penitentiali*]).
Caro 1572	Annibal Caro, *Rime del Commendatore Annibal Caro* (Venice: Aldo Manuzio, 1569; reprint 1572; Venice: Bernardo Giunti, 1584; Venice: G. Novelli, 1757).
Tasso 1573	Faustino Tasso. *Il primo e secondo libro delle rime toscane. Raccolte da diversi luoghi et date in luce da Girolamo Campeggio* (Turin: Francesco Dolce e Compagni).
Varchi 1573	Benedetto Varchi, *Sonetti spirituali* (Florence: Filippo e Jacopo Giunti).
Sanleolino 1578	Sanleolino, Sebastiano. *Serenissimi Cosmi Medycis primi Heturiae Magniducis Actiones Sebastiano Sanleolino I. C. Florentino Auctore* (Florence: Typis Georgij Marescoti).
Massolo 1583	*Rime morali di M. Pietro Massolo Gentilhuomo Vinitiano, Hora Don Lorenzo Monaco Cassinese Divise in Quattro Libri; Col Commento di M. Francesco Sansovino. Et con quattro Tavole cosi de i sonetti, come anco delle materie d'esso Commento, et dei personaggi alle quali sono scritti dal Poeta diversi soggetti* (Venice: Gio. Antonio Rampazetto).
Gonzaga 1585	Curzio Gonzaga, *Rime del Illustrissimo Signor Curtio Gonzaga* (Vincenza: Stamperia Nuova). Cited from Quondam 1997.
Bobali 1589	Savino Bobali [Sabo Mišetic Bobaljevic], *Rime amorose, e pastorali, et satire del Mag. Savino de Bobali Sordo, Gentil'huomo Raguseo* (Venice: Aldo Manuzio).
Colonna 1589	Mario Colonna, *Poesie toscane dell'illustris. sign. Mario Colonna, et di M. Pietro Angelio con l'Edipo Tiranno Tragedia di Sofocle Tradotta dal medesimo Angelio,* ed. Bernardo Medici (Florence: Bartolomeo Sermartelli).
Gobbi 1709–11	Agostino Gobbi, ed., *Scelta di sonetti e canzoni de' più eccellenti rimatori d'ogni secolo* (Bologna: Costantino Pisarri; reprint 1718, 1727, 1739).
Carmina 1720	*Carmina illustrium poetarum italorum* (Florence: Typis Regiae Celsitudinis, apud Joannem Cajetanum Tartinium, et Sanctem Franchium).
Bergalli 1726	Luisa Bergalli, ed., *Componimenti poetici delle più illustri rimatrici d'ogni secolo* (Venice: A. Mora).
Crescimbeni 1730	Giovan Maria Crescimbeni, *Dell'istoria della volgar poesia scritta da Giovan Mario Crescimbene,* 6 vols. (Venice: Lorenzo Basegio) 4: 96.

Grazzini 1741–42	Antonfrancesco Grazzini, detto il Lasca, *Rime*, 2 vols. (Florence: Francesco Moücke).
Mazzoleni 1750	*Rime oneste de' migliori poeti antichi e moderni scelte ad uso delle scuole dal signor abate Angelo Mazzoleni* (Bergamo: P. Lancellotto; reprint Venezia: Stamperia Remondini, 1761; Bassano: Remondini, 1777, 1791, 1801, 1816, 1821).
Rigamonti 1765	*Rime di pentimento spirituale tratte da' canzonieri de' più celebri autori antichi e moderni*, ed. Giuseppe Rigamonti (Bergamo: Francesco Locatelli; reprint Bologna, 1815; Milan, 1821, 1855).
Poetesse 1787	*Costanzo, Torquato, Bernardo Tasso, e poetesse del secolo XVI.* Parnaso Italiano, vol. 30. (Venice: Antonio Zatta e figli; reprint 1816).
Bronzino 1823	*Sonetti di Angiolo Allori detto il Bronzino ed altre rime inedite di più insigni poeti*, ed. Domenico Moreni (Florence: Magheri).
Ronna 1843	A. Ronna, ed., *Gemme o rime di poetesse italiane antiche e moderne* (Paris: Baudry, Libraria Europea).
Fiori 1846	*Fiori di rimatrici italiane dal secolo XIV al XVIII* (Venice: Alvisopoli).
Varchi, 1859	Benedetto Varchi, *Opere*, vol. 2. (Trieste: Lloyd Adriatico).
Croce 1930	Benedetto Croce, *Poesia popolare e poesia d'arte. Studi sulla poesia italiana dal tre al cinquecento* (Naples: Bibliopolis; reprint ed. Piero Cudini, 1991).
De Blasi 1930	Iolanda De Blasi, ed., *Le scrittrici italiane dalle origini al 1800* (Florence: Casa Editrice "Nemi").
Bronzino 1960	Andrea Emiliani, ed., *Bronzino* (Busto Arsizio: Bramante). With *Antologia poetica*, ed. Giorgio Cerboni Baiardi.
Flora 1962	Francesco Flora, ed. *Gaspara Stampa e altre poetesse del '500* (Milan: Nuova Accademia).
Baldacci 1957	*Lirici del cinquecento*, ed. Luigi Baldacci (Florence: Salani; 2d ed. Milan: Longanesti, 1975).
Ponchiroli 1958	*Lirici del cinquecento*, ed. Daniele Ponchiroli (Turin: Unione Tipografico-Editrice Torinese).
Wittkower 1964	See Michelangelo 1564.
Gianni 1997	Gianni, Angelo, *Anch'esse "quasi simili a Dio": Le donne nella storia della letteratura italiana, in gran parte ignote o misconosciute dalle Origini alla fine dell'Ottocento* (Lucca: Mauro Baroni).
Quondam 1997	*Archivio della tradizione lirica*, ed. Amedeo Quondam. Archivio Italiano CD-ROM (Rome: Lexis).

PROSE

Manuscripts

Florence

Archivio di Stato

Conventi Soppressi da Leopoldo *filza* 238.

Urbino. Cl. I, Div. G, CCXXXVI, terza parte.

Biblioteca Nazionale

FV MS Aut. Pal. 1, 18–33. Letters from Laura Battiferra to Benedetto Varchi. Autograph, January, 1556 [=1557 modern style]–March, 1563. Kristeller, *Iter italicum,* 1: 147.

Casa di Michelangelo (Biblioteca Medicea-Laurenziana)

FB6 Florence, Casa Buonarotti, MS Buonarroti 6 (on microfilm at Biblioteca Laurenziana, Archivio Buonarroti, 6). Letters from Ammannati and others to Michelangelo. Kristeller, *Iter italicum,* 2: 507.

Macerata

Biblioteca Comunale Mozzi-Borgetti

M MS 137 (formerly 5 II E 12, then 5 I B 10). *Oratione sopra il natale di Nostro Signore.* Aldo Adversi, *Inventari dei manoscritti delle biblioteche d'Italia,* vol. 100, pt. 1 Macerata (Florence: Olschki, 1981), 23–25.

Perugia

Biblioteca Augusta

Pe MS G 63. 16th c. Mazzatinti 5: 134.

Editions (for letters)

1560 *Il primo libro dell'opere toscane di m. Laura Battiferra degli Ammannati* (Florence: Giunti). Dedicatory letter to Eleonora di Toledo.

1564 *I sette salmi penitentiali del santissimo profeta Dauit. Tradotti in lingua Toscana da madonna Laura Battiferra degli Ammannati. Con gli argomenti sopra ciascuno di essi, composti dalla medesima; insieme con alcuni suoi Sonetti spiritali* (Florence: Giunti). Dedicatory letter to Vittoria Farnese Della Rovere.

Gargiolli 1879 *Lettere di Laura Battiferri a Benedetto Varchi,* ed. Carlo Gargiolli (Bologna: Romagnoli; reprint 1968).

NOTES

CHAPTER 1

1. This letter, in an unattributed Tuscan translation of the Latin original, prefaces Battiferra's *Rime* as they are preserved in the manuscript that she hoped to publish as her third book (Rome, Biblioteca Casanatense, MS 3229). Piero Vettori, the sender, recalls the recent funeral of Benedetto Varchi, which gives him an occasion to praise Battiferra, present for the ceremony but forced to observe it from the confines of a matroneum. Vettori (1499–1585) was one of the most erudite Florentine humanists of the sixteenth century and Renaissance Italy's last great scholar of Greek. A professor at the universities of Pisa and Florence, he published editions of ancient classics as well has his own Latin epistles, and he orated famously at funerals of state, including those of both Eleonora de Toledo and Duke Cosimo. Battiferra refers to him with respectful excitement, describing their first encounter in one of her letters to Varchi, sent from Florence on July 26, 1561: "Yesterday, which was Sunday, Messer Pier Vettorio and the humanist from Pisa came here to the house, escorted by Messer Baccio Valori, to whom I am much obliged because he did me a great favor since I wanted so much to see those two great men, whom I hadn't known before." Mario Colonna was the son of the soldier Stefano Colonna di Palestrina, who moved his family from Rome to Florence after he was named Duke Cosimo de' Medici's lieutenant general in 1541. From 1562 Mario was in the service of the duke, and in 1564 he traveled as an ambassador to the new emperor Maximilian II. He wrote poetry both in Latin and Italian, much of the latter in *ottava rima* after Boccaccio for the lady he loved, Fiammetta Soderini, herself a poetess and a friend of Battiferra. In 1568 he published twenty-three Latin poems, including epitaphs for Michelangelo and Varchi. His *Rime toscane,* dedicated to Piero Vettori and containing sonnets exchanged with Battiferra, were published posthumously by his friend Bernardo Medici at Florence in 1589.

2. good arts (buone arti): Arts here and elsewhere in the letter mean field of study, branch of learning, or discipline, as in the Liberal Arts.

3. Bartolomeo (Baccio) Valori (1535–1606), a judge who served as grand ducal high commissioner of Pisa, was a wealthy patron of the arts.

4. Lionardo Salviati (1540–89), born into one of the great Florentine patrician families and a cousin of Cosimo de' Medici (whose mother was Maria Salviati), studied

with Piero Vettori and became a protégé of Benedetto Varchi. As a budding humanist he distinguished himself in 1562 with a three-hour virtuoso Latin funeral oration for Garzia de' Medici, published with a dedication to Cosimo's son-in-law Paolo Giordano Orsini in 1564. When Michelangelo died in 1564, Salviati was among the eulogists with an offering characterized as "bellissima" by Vasari. His collected orations, much admired in their time, were eventually published by his friend Don Silvano Razzi in 1573. Although later criticized for a bowdlerized edition of the *Decameron,* he became an arbitor of grammar with his *Avvertimenti della lingua sopra 'l Decameron* (1584–86) and a founding member of the Accademia della Crusca.

5. Benedetto Varchi (1504–December 18, 1565), scion of an old Florentine family, was a personage whose amazing intellectual energies carried him into many branches of contemporary culture—lyrical, pastoral, and spiritual poetry, dramatic writing, Dante studies, history, philosophy, linguistic theory, esthetics, even alchemy and Pythagorean numerology. Titian painted his portrait (fig. 13). He corresponded with countless contemporaries and mentored younger writers, among them Tullia d'Aragona and Laura Battiferra. Ordained a priest late in life, he orated at Michelangelo's funeral in 1564 and was present, just two days before his death, when Giovanna d'Austria, daughter of Charles V, made her formal entry into Florence as the bride of Francesco I de' Medici on December 16, 1565. His funeral was celebrated in the church of Santa Maria degli Angeli, and Salviati's oration was published immediately afterward. Poems were collected for a commemorative anthology and published by Piero Stufa, a canon of Santa Maria del Fiore, in a volume entitled *Componimenti Latini, e Toscani da diversi suoi amici composti nella morte di M. Benedetto Varchi* (1566). Battiferra, whose letters reveal what a dear friend Varchi became to her, participated in that effort, both as an author and a silent coeditor. Her activity in obtaining contributions to the volume is attested by surviving correspondence from Bernardo Tasso and Annibal Caro.

6. *a man:* Duke Cosimo I de' Medici, for whom Varchi wrote his compendious *Storia Fiorentina* and gave new impetus to Cosimo's Accademia Fiorentina. More than 1,000 sonnets by Varchi survive.

7. *our city:* Florence. Vettori alludes to the burst of genius at the origins of Italian letters in the fourteenth century with Dante, Petrarch, and Boccaccio—the Three Crowns of Florence.

8. Vettori says that this woman at the funeral should have been granted the same privilege as Plato was when he was exempted from the harsh law of Aegina, ruled by the tyrant Dionysius. It required any Athenian who set foot on their island to be put to death, but Plato was judged instead as a philosopher and so was spared.

9. Maximus of Tyre (Cassius Maximus Tyrius): a rhetorician and philosopher, 2d c. C.E., precursor of the Neoplatonists. The women poets of the sixteenth century were often compared to Sappho.

10. Laura Battiferra degli Ammannati, a native of Urbino who moved from Rome to Florence with her husband in 1555. Gregorio Farulli, *Istoria cronologica del nobile ed antico Monastero degli Angioli di Firenze, del Sacro Ordine camaldolese* (Chronological History of the noble and ancient Monastery of Santa Maria degli Angeli at Florence, of the Holy Camaldolite Order) (Lucca: Pellegrino Frediani, 1710), confirms that Battiferra

had to watch the funeral from "a narrow window in the little women's oratory." In poetry by Battiferra and their friends, her husband the sculptor and architect Bartolomeo Ammannati is affectionately called a new "Phidias" after the famed Athenian sculptor of the 5th c. B.C.E. Sappho was reputed to be a Lesbian. Battiferra, a faithful wife and devout Catholic, was considered a paragon of virtue.

11. This and the following two sonnets, which form an introductory trio to Laura Battiferra's *Rime,* bear greetings from men who were her friends. The Casanatense manuscript does not assign them numbers; I have identified them with large Roman numerals I, II, III. The first two, by Spini and Razzi, originally appeared with her penitential psalms of 1564, hence their allusions to King David. The third, by Agostino de' Copeti, may not have been written until after 1574, when he became theologian to the Medici Grand Duke.

12. 1.I. Gherardo Spini (sometimes also Spina), a friend of both Ammannati, was a man of letters and a lover of architecture who served as secretary to Cardinal Ferdinando de' Medici in the late 1560s. See Susan Butters, "Ammannati et la villa Médicis," in *La Villa Médicis,* ed. André Chastel and Philippe Morel (Rome: Académie de France à Rome, 1991), 2: 257–316; and Zygmunt Waźbiński, *L'accademia medicea del disegno a Firenze nel Cinquecento,* 2 vols. (Florence: Olschki, 1987). Absent from Battiferra's *Primo libro* of 1560, he sent her a sonnet of consolation on the death of her father (1561), to which she replied (2.7–8). He appears in *I salmi penitentiali* with this sonnet. Lodovico Domenichi featured him in the witty anecdotes of his *Historia varia* (1564). In 1564, Spini published an edition of Giovanni Della Casa's *Rime et prose di M. Giovanni della Casa* [Rhymes and Prose Writings], ed. Gherardo Spino (Florence: Giunti, 1564), to which the Florentine publisher Filippo Giunti attached a *Rimario* (concordance of the rhyme words) dedicated to Laura Battiferra (see below, note 134). In October of that year, Spini sent her a remarkable letter from Prague, describing the beauty and social power of its women (4.8), and the following year he contributed to the funeral volume that Battiferra helped Piero della Stufa compile for Varchi *Componimenti latini e toscani* (1566).

13. Line 2, King David. Lines 5–8, this new Laura, a sun like her Petrarchan ancestress, dwells on the Arno, tames her readers, and teaches them the way to God with her beauty (the "rays" of her eyes) and with her poetry ("stile"). Cf. Vittoria Colonna, *Rime amorose,* ed. Alan Bullock (Bari: Laterza, 1982), consulted in Amadeo Quondam, ed. *Rime, Archivio della tradizione,* CD-ROM, 1997, 89.67: "'l mio vivo sol" (my living sun). Spini's *vago stil* plays on Petrarch's *vario stile* (varied style), *RS* 1.5. Lines 10–14, Laura has deprived Tiber of honor by moving to Florence, and she has diminished Jordan's glory by recasting David's Psalms in her voice. Line 13, Spini makes a Petrarchan pun on Laura and "l'aura" (breeze). The "Hebrews' holy man" is David.

14. 1.II. Girolamo Razzi (in religion, Don Silvano Razzi) was a literary man who became a Camaldolite monk around 1561. He lived and served as abbot in the Florentine monastery of Santa Maria degli Angeli. Battiferra mentions him in two of her letters to Varchi: "I received from Messer Girolamo Razzi the apples and chestnuts that Your Lordship sent me; they were dear to me and sweet, and I thank you" (November 9, 1557); "Late yesterday evening I received your letter with the sonnet by Razzi along with your answer; they appear to me very fair and fine" (December 11, 1557). While still Girolamo, he contributed two sonnets to the *Primo libro* (1560). As Don

Silvano, he is the recipient of a sonnet from Battiferra in Calzolari's *Historia monastica* (1561), and he appears in Battiferra's *Salmi penitentiali,* with the poem here reproduced. He mentions "Madonna Laura Battiferra degl'Ammannati" as one of the distinguished people who often went up to Fiesole to visit Varchi at his villa, the setting for Girolamo Razzi's dialogue on the active vs. the contemplative life, *Della economia christiana* [On Christian and Civil Economy . . . In Which a Noble Gathering of Ladies and Men Discuss Household Care and Management according to Christian and Civil Law] (Florence: Bartolomeo Sermartelli, 1568).

15. Line 1, *nuova fronde* (new frond): cf. *RS* 34.7, "sacra fronde" (holy frond). Razzi defines Laura as the new offshoot of the laurel tree, recalling Petrarch's appropriation of the Apollo and Daphne myth: Ovid, *Metamorphoses,* trans. Frank Justus Miller, 2 vols. (Cambridge, Mass.: Harvard University Press, reprint 1966–68), 1.452–565. Line 2, *gloria e onor del secol nostro* (glory and honor of our century): see 1.4. Lines 7–8, David, the "contrite" king who composed the Psalms. Lines 9–14, In hyperbolic language Razzi praises Laura for her many already recognized virtues. Now they are heightened by the project of translating the Psalms, which will win her a place in heaven and laurels on earth. Line 14, *tempi* (temples): metaphorically, perhaps a "temple" of poetry—a collective tribute like those made for Giovanna d'Aragona and Girolama Colonna (1.27).

16. 1.III. This little known poet is identified only as a monk ("Fra") in the manuscripts that contain his single sonnet to Battiferra. His name seems to be a Tuscanized form of Agostino de' Cupiti da Evoli [Eboli], a Franciscan Minorite who published in 1592 a collection of spiritual rhymes on such subjects as the life of the Virgin, Saint Catherine, the Magdalene, the Crucifixion, and the Eucharist. Agostino's dedicatory letter to his patron, the Spanish Viceroy of Naples, praises poetry for its moral capacity and reports that he has time to write, inspired by Dante and Petrarch (but not the presumably "unchaste" Boccaccio), now that he is "released from my former ordinary chores of reading theological lessons in our Order's schools and serving as Theologian and Preacher to Francesco of blessed memory, Grand Duke of Tuscany, who resided in Florence." Battiferra would have known Friar Agostino when he served Cosimo's successor, Francesco de' Medici, who assumed partial responsibilities from 1564 and then ruled officially after his father's death as grand duke from 1574 to 1587. Perhaps because she lacked parallel replies to Spini and Razzi, Battiferra did not include her response to Copeti in the *Rime,* which another manuscript preserves (F6 435v): "Che 'l mio nome sia scritto in ciel fra loro" (That my name be written in heaven among those). Repeating Copeti's rhyme scheme, she asks him to pray for her.

17. Lines 1–4. *stil* [style]: a Petrarchan pun on the "stylus" (or pen) as instrument of writing and "style" of writing. Agostino alludes to Orpheus, perhaps with another pun in mind on the Italian "Orfeo" and "oro," meaning "gold" and probably with reference to Pietro Bembo's *Asolani* (Turin: Unione Tipografico-Editrice Torinese, 1996), 12: "Orfeo, che le vaghe fiere de' lor boschi e gli alti alberi dalle lor selve e da' lor monti le sode pietre e i precipitanti fiumi de' lor corsi ritoglieva" (Orpheus, who pulled lovesome beasts from their woods and tall trees from their forests and solid rocks from their mountains and rushing rivers from their courses). The sense is that heaven has endowed Battiferra's poetry with magical qualities: it can transmute base metal into gold or make flowing waters stand still. Lines 6–8, *colui* (the man): Or-

pheus. After the Maenads tore him to pieces, his head and lyre floated cradled in the river Hebrus out to the salty seashore (Ovid, *Met.* 11.1–66). Lines 9–11, Laura is the new Orpheus.

18. *Prima parte.* Here, after three unnumbered male-authored prefatory sonnets, begin Battiferra's own poems in the *Rime.* They are headed by a rubric in the manuscript that reads only "First part, etc." (fol. 7r). It must stand for one of the titles Battiferra herself had proposed for the *Primo libro* in her letter to Varchi of November 25, 1560: *Prima parte delle rime e de' versi di Laura* or *Prima parte dell'opere toscane.* I have expanded the abbreviation with the second option since it retains key elements of the title that was, in fact, chosen for the first edition. (See 4.5 for the dedicatory letter to the duchess Eleonora.)

19. 1.1. Eleonora de Toledo (1519–62), to whom Battiferra dedicated her *Primo libro,* was the daughter of Don Pedro de Alvarez de Toledo, the Spanish Viceroy of Naples, and Doña María Osorio Pimentel. She married Cosimo de' Medici, Duke of Florence, in 1539 and between 1540 and 1554 gave him eight children who reached adulthood (app. D). In this sonnet, elegantly constructed on inversions of the lyric tradition, Eleonora is praised as "honor of the century" and "a sun," taking on the attributes of Petrarch's Laura. She will bring fame to the poetess, who dares to equate herself with Petrarch. At the same time, Battiferra is also a new Laura who, among her fellow poets in the fantasy world of art, carries the name Dafne, while the duchess, in her likeness to the sun, slips into the role of Apollo, mythological Daphne's lover. From Ovid's tale, an archetype mediated by Petrarch, Battiferra here creates a new couple in which the lady unexpectedly addresses the object of her affection as Laura-Daphne and asks for the love (patronage) of the Apollonian female sovereign.

20. Line 1, *donna real* (royal lady): Tullia d'Aragona, *Rime della signora Tullia di Aragona; et di diverse a lei* (Venice: Gabriel Giolito de' Ferrari, 1547), 12.1 and 13.2 (both also to Eleonora); Varchi, *Rime,* in *Opere,* 2 vols. (Trieste: Lloyd Adriatico, 1858–59), also consulted in Quondam, 3.67.1 (to Eleonora's daughter, Isabella Orsini). The duchess Eleonora de Toledo is addressed as if she were a queen, flattery in tune with Cosimo's hopes for elevation to the title of King of Tuscany. Lines 1–2, cf. Chiara Matraini, *Rime e lettere,* ed. Giovanna Rabitti (Bologna: Commissione per i Testi di Lingua, 1989), consulted also in Quondam, 4.1–2: "A voi consacro il mio debole ingegno, / alma real, che senz'essempio sete" (To you, royal soul, who are without equal, I consecrate my weak mind). Line 4, *saraggio* (will be): Battiferra worried about using this alternate future form instead of the regular "sarò" because it was not in Petrarch, as she wrote Varchi with a wry allusion to the slavish Petrarchismo of Lodovico Castelvetro, probably not long before her book was published (the letter is undated): "I would not want to fall under Castelvetro's censure because I say in a verse of the first sonnet to the Duchess *saraggio;* since neither Petrarch nor anyone else I can remember said it, I'm asking for Your Lordship to get back to me with your opinion, because if I make it say *sarò,* it seems to me that the verse doesn't suffer for that: 'And if ever I was or will be or am anything.'" Line 7, cf. *RS* 344.5: "Quella che fu del secol nostro onore" (she who was the honor of our century). Line 9, Laura aspires to parity with Petrarch, who sang of Laura near Vaucluse, along the banks of the Sorgue River. Line 11, cf. *RS* 307.9–11: "Mai non porria volar penna d'ingegno, / non che stil grave o lingua, ove Natura / volò tessendo il mio dolce ritegno" (Never could any pinion of

wit, let alone a heavy style or tongue, fly so high as Nature did when she made my sweet impediment). Lines 12–13, cf. *RS* 248.3–4: "un sol, non pur a li occhi mei / ma al mondo cieco" (a sun, not merely for my eyes, but for the blind world).

21. 1.2. Cosimo I de' Medici (1519–74), Duke of Florence from 1537, added Siena to his title after he had conquered that city in the war of 1553–55 and been granted it as a fief by Philip II of Spain in 1557. While Eleanor was "honor of our age" in the preceding sonnet, now that epithet attaches echoically to the happy day of Cosimo's birth, when an ideal celestial conjunction prophesied military triumph. Cosimo attached serious importance to astrology, and the symbols of his natal horoscope frequently appear in art he commissioned.

22. Line 1, *quel largo cerchio* (that wide ring): the Empyrean, which encircles the Primum Mobile (the ninth sphere) in the Dantean cosmos. Lines 3–4, the eighth sphere or Zodiac, which contains the fixed stars, i.e., the constellations. Line 5, the heavens were optimally configured the day Cosimo was born, June 12, 1519. Line 8, *nel più bel soggiorno* (in the fairest abode): the heavens. Line 9, *arabi odori* (odors of Araby): cf. Petrarch's sonnet on his gilded phoenix, *RS* 185.12–13: "Fama ne l'odorato et ricco grembo / d'arabi monti lei ripone et cela" (Fame puts her away and hides her in the fragrant rich bosom of the Arabian mountains). From this descend many variants: Anton Francesco Raineri, *Cento sonetti,* ed. Guglielmo Gorni, Tesi di Laura, Università di Pavia, in Quondam, 15.3: "spargete arabi odori" (spread odors of Araby); Giovanni Guidiccioni, *Rime,* ed. Carlo Minutoli, 2 vols. (Florence: Barberà, 1867), also consulted in Quondam, 59.1, "arabi odori / spargete"; Bernardo Cappello, *Rime* (Venice: Domencio e Gio. Battista Guerra Fratelli, 1560), also consulted in Quondam, 203.1–4: "Apra . . . il grembo a l'erbe, a' fiori / che 'l ciel di preziosi arabi odori / spargan" (May [earth] open her bosom to grasses, to flowers, that spread heaven with precious odors of Araby). Cf. Luigi Alamanni, *Rime,* ed. P Raffaelli (Florence: Le Monnier, 1859), in Quondam, 1.77.436, "Arabi odorati." Line 10, *l'aura soave* (the soft air): *RS* 109.9–10: "L'aura soave che dal chiaro viso / move" (the soft breeze that moves from her bright face). Line 12, with the renewed greening of the laurels, Battiferra alludes to the idea of a return to the golden age that Florence had known in the Quattrocento under Lorenzo il Magnifico. Lorenzo was poetically and emblematically "Lauro" (laurel tree), and the *broncone* or laurel stump with a new sprout was a Medici family device (Janet Cox-Rearick, *Bronzino's Chapel of Eleonora in the Palazzo Vecchio* [Berkeley: University of California Press, 1993], 268). Line 13, Mars, god of war, was powerful in Cosimo's natal horoscope, a sign of his military victories to come, especially the conquest of Siena. Line 14, *il buon Cosmo invitto* (good Cosimo unvanquished): the epithets, classical in flavor, imply a benign, just, and victorious ruler, as had been predicted in a horoscope offered to him before the battle of Montemurlo (1537), decisive in establishing his power as duke (Raffaella Castagnola, "Un oroscopo per Cosimo I," *Rinascimento* 29 [1989]: 125–89).

23. The prince is Francesco de' Medici (1541–87), second child and heir to the duchy as eldest son of Cosimo and Eleonora. Cosimo yielded power to him in 1564, and he succeeded his father as Grand Duke of Tuscany on the latter's death in 1574. In 1565, when Francesco wed Giovanna d'Austria, her *entrata* into the city was an occasion for elaborate decorations by all the leading artists, including Ammannati's *Neptune Fountain* in Piazza della Signoria (1.39). After Giovanna's death, which Battiferra

mourned in several sonnets, Francesco married his mistress, the Venetian Bianca Cappello, to whom the poetess also paid tribute (1.65).

24. Lines 1–3, Cosimo and Eleonora's first child had been a daughter, Maria, but the first son is the "first hope" of his father, "best leader." Line 3, the sun. Lines 5–6, *in sì giovenil core / sì canuti pensieri* (such hoary thoughts . . . in so youthful a heart). Cf. Petrarch, *Triumph of Chastity,* 88: "penser canuti in giovanile etate" (hoary thoughts in youthful age). The poet uses the *puer senex* topos to suggest the young man's precocious maturity. Lines 9–14, invoking a classic topos, Battiferra imagines that his accession will transform the present "dark ages" into a luminescent era with hints of a golden age. The verses resonate with memory of Virgil's *Fourth Eclogue* via Dante, *The Divine Comedy,* ed. and trans. Charles S. Singleton, 6 vols. (Princeton: Princeton University Press, 1970–75), *Purg.* 22.70–72. The sonnet closes with an image of Francesco's apotheosis.

25. 1.4. Paolo Giordano Orsini (1539–85), Duke of Bracciano and head of the most powerful family in Rome, became the husband of Cosimo and Eleonora's third child, Isabella de' Medici (1542–76). Betrothed in 1555, they wed on September 3, 1558, when Isabella was sixteen. A tragic union with adultery on both sides, it ended in uxoricide, the murder of Orsini's second wife Vittoria Accoramboni, and his own ruin (Fabrizio Winspear, *Isabella Orsini e la corte medicea del suo tempo* [Florence: Olschki, 1961]). This sonnet doubtless celebrates Orsini's entry into the Medici family after the nuptials, when Cosimo required his new son-in-law to spend six months of every year living with Isabella in the Medici Palace in Florence (Kirkham, "Laura Battiferra's 'First Book' of Poetry," 363–65). In the hyperbolic flattery of the sonnet, Orsini is imagined as a new Romulus, greater than the most powerful emperors. In reality, Orsini was an irresponsibly lavish spender, a man of arms more physical than intellectual whose favored pastime was hunting, and an unfaithful husband to Isabella, a lover of culture and poetry for whom Battiferra composed mournful, romantic verses (1.21–26).

26. Quirinus: Romulus. Cf. Virgil, *Eclogues, Georgics, Aeneid,* trans. H. Rushton Fairclough, 2 vols. (Cambridge Mass.: Harvard University Press, 1974), *Aen.* 1.292 with its reference to "Quirinus with his brother Remus"; also 6.859; *Geor.* 3.27; Ovid, *Fasti,* trans. Sir James George Frazer, 2d ed. rev. G. P. Goold (Cambridge, Mass.: Harvard University Press, 1989), 4.910. From the name derives an adjectival form, "Quirinale."

27. 1.5. King Philip II of Spain (1527–98) was the son of Charles V and ruler of the first empire in history to encircle the globe, stretching from Florida to Tierra del Fuego and across the Pacific to the Philippines. Duke Cosimo I and Philip maintained a delicate diplomatic alliance in which a key link was Eleonora de Toledo, whose uncle was the powerful Duke of Alba. On July 3, 1557, Philip granted Cosimo as a fief Siena, a city that had been allied with Spain's traditional enemy France. On December 11 of that year, Battiferra writes to Varchi that some of her sonnets have reached Philip's court in Spain and been admired there: "This week I had a letter from Messer Bernardino Bazino from the court of King Philip, and he informs me about certain sonnets of mine, which made their way to that land, I know not how; and he says that they have been praised, and he begs me to write something in praise of that king or queen. I, who doubt whether I am able or know how to loosen my tongue for

such a high subject, much less sing, answer him with this sonnet that I now send you, and afterwards, I know not how, I wrote these two as you can see."

28. Line 1, *Invitto rege* (Unvanquished king): cf. Varchi, *Rime* 1.514.7: "invitto / Anglico rege" [unvanquished Anglican king]. Line 2, *dal nostro al Antartico Polo* (from our pole to the Antarctic): Varchi, *Rime* 2.44a.3, to Francesco Bolognetti, whose voice will be heard pole to pole. Lines 3–4, God, all-powerful above, gave Phillip the whole world to rule. Battiferra interweaves the verses with oppositions: heaven vs. earth, singular vs. universal. Line 6, *gallico stuolo* (Gallic herd): perhaps with reference to Philip's recent defeat of the French at Saint-Quentin and certainly an allusion to the conquest of Siena, which had been allied with France. Cf. Cappello, *Rime* 263.9: "gallico stuol." Lines 9–10, *nemico di Gesù* (Jesus' enemy): the Turks. Cf. Varchi, *Rime* 1.286.1–2 , to Don Pietro de Toledo, who will lead a fleet against them: "Or che l'iniquo ed orgoglioso, ed empio / Nemico nostro e di Gesù" (Now that the iniquitous and proud and wicked enemy of ours and of Jesus). Ruled by Suleiman the Magnificent, the Turks had attacked Spain's North African bases with a powerful fleet in 1551, beginning two decades of wars. Their presence in the Mediterranean continued to menace Europe until a truce was signed after the battle of Lepanto (1571). The struggle against the Turks, here mentioned for the first time in the *Rime,* is a motif that often returns in Battiferra's poetry, even more insistently in pieces dating from after the publication of her *Primo libro.* Line 12, presumably a reference to the New World. Lines 13–14, the "scepter" is that of the Spanish monarch, the "law" that of the Church of Rome.

29. 1.6. Mary Tudor (1516–58), second of King Philip's four wives, was the daughter of King Henry VIII of England and Catherine of Aragon. The Catholic queen of England known as "Bloody Mary" for her ruthless suppression of the Protestants, she was tutored as a child by the Spanish humanist Juan Luis Vives, who wrote for her *The Education of a Christian Woman.* After securing the throne (1553), she wed Philip, eleven years her junior, at the urging of his father (and her cousin), the emperor Charles V, the aim being to bring England back into the Catholic fold. Their marriage, during which Philip was mostly absent, took place on July 25, 1554 and ended when she died at age 42 in November 1558, producing no issue. Maria is here a vehicle for praise of Spain's imperial might and the necessary second half of a couple in whose union happiness seems historically to have played little part. This sonnet presents an anachronism since by the time the *Primo libro* appeared, Mary Tudor had died and Philip had married, in January of 1560, the fourteen-year-old Elizabeth Valois, eldest daughter of Henry II of France and Catherine de' Medici.

30. Line 1, *Sacra reina* (Holy queen): the epithet would be more predictable with reference to Maria, Queen of Heaven, and it is so used by Giovanni Muzzarelli, *Rime,* ed. G. Hannüss Palazzini (Mantua: Arcari Editore, 1983), in Quondam, 35.121. Line 4, as secular leader of the Catholic Church, Philip fought the Turks, and he aggressively pressed the religious wars against Protestants in the Low Countries with occupying forces captained by the Duke of Alba, whom Chiappino Vitelli served as field marshal (1.28–29, 1.39). Lines 6–7, *ritornar nell'antico oro il ferro nostro* (restore our iron to ancient gold): cf. Pietro Bembo, *Rime,* in *Prose della volgar lingua. Gli Asolani. Rime,* ed. Carlo Dionisotti (Turin: Unione Tipografico-Editrice Torinese, 1966), also consulted in Quondam, 84.12–13 (to an unknown *condottiero*): "del nostro ferro vile / far

secol d'oro" (make a golden age of our base iron); Varchi, *Rime* 1.467.12–13: "nostro vil ferro al pare / Del antico oro" (our base iron a peer of ancient gold). Mary's wish is to restore golden age peace to the present, "iron" being a synecdoche for the sword and other weapons of war. Lines 12–14, the chosen, happy couple reigns without opposition, not just over a kingdom, but over the entire world. This angel from heaven recalls the *dolce stil novo* as filtered through Petrarch, but here amorous praise is adapted to the lady-ruler of an empire on which the sun never sets.

31. 1.7. As a native of Urbino, Battiferra was a subject of Guidobaldo II Della Rovere (1514–74), who became the duke in 1538. Her sonnet to him, which might seem merely routine praise of a Renaissance prince, is surely an occasional poem that refers to her long legal battle to recover the dowry from her first marriage (see also her petitions to the duke, 4.2–3). This poem appeals to Guidobaldo as a Solomonic figure in a vocabulary that recalls technical definitions formulated by Aristotle and Saint Thomas Aquinas. They distinguish between distributive justice, which assures everyone his just dues, and commutative justice, which rewards and punishes as circumstances warrant. Battiferra hopes the duke, who both "metes out honors" (distributive justice) and "gives punishment" (commutative justice), can at last put an end to her "sorrows"—continuing bureaucratic frustrations and financial need.

32. Line 1, *Saggio signor* (Wise lord): Varchi, *Rime* 1.342.1 (to Duke Cosimo), in identical position at the sonnet's incipit, probably suggested by Bembo, *Prose della volgar lingua, Rime* 21.1 (to Ercole I, Duke of Ferrara): "Grave, saggio, cortese, alto signore" (Solemn, wise, courteous, lofty lord). Line 6, cf. *RS* 36.9: "Tempo ben fora omai" (It would be time by now); 316.1: "Tempo era omai da trovar pace o tregua" (It was by then time to find peace or truce); 358.9: "et non tardar, ch'egli è ben tempo omai" (and do not delay, for it is surely time by now). Line 11, *caonia pianta* (Chaonian plant): the oak, emblem of the Della Rovere family (*rovere* = "oak"). Ovid had used the adjective "Chaonian" to refer to the grove of Chaonia at Dodona in the country of Epirus, where Jupiter had an oracle (Ovid, *Met.* 7.623 and 10.90; and cf. Virgil, *Aen.* 3.334ff; *Georg.* 1.8). See also Piperno, *L'immagine del duca,* 70. Since the oak was sacred to Jupiter, by invoking the Ovidian epithet Battiferra likens Guidobaldo to the king of the gods. Lines 12–14, cf. *RS* 9.9: "onde tal frutto e simile si colga" (that one may pick such fruit and others like it). The Della Rovere dynasty will accomplish such great deeds that it will restore—indeed, already has—the golden age, when life was sustained solely by nature's bounty with food like acorns and honey.

33. 1.8. Vittoria Farnese Della Rovere (1521–1602), a granddaughter of Alessandro Farnese (Pope Paul III), became the second wife of the widowed Guidobaldo II Della Rovere on June 29, 1547. This may be the sonnet referred to by Annibal Caro in a letter from Rome of 1552 to his friend Claudio Tolomei in Pesaro, administrative headquarters of the Urbino court:

> I ask you as a favor, use the enclosed sonnet to take care of the errand with the Most Excellent Signora Duchess that the woman who writes in it about her deserves by virtue of intelligence and social position, she being Madonna Laura Battiferri, her Urbino subject, wife of Ammannati, the Florentine sculptor. It seems to me that for a woman, she has conducted herself extremely well and deserves from Her Excellency some praise and sign that her virtue and devotion are well received. Her husband tells me that she will soon come there to finish

> some business concerning her dowry, and she desires this favor. Kindly use this to clear the way before their Excellencies. And when she is there, please show her that favor and kindness that your courtesy dictates toward everyone, and more besides, as is owed women, especially a witty one like this.

Battiferra later would dedicate to this duchess her *Sette salmi penitentiali* of 1564.

34. Lines 1–2, cf. Bembo, *Rime* 22.10: "là dove bagna il bel Metauro." The Metauro flows through the valley beneath Urbino. Lines 7–8, Jove by his largesse showers the duchess with such grace that he promises more honor to his ancient, beloved boughs (the oak, hence the Della Rovere family) than Apollo to his tree, the laurel. Lines 9–11, Laura wishes that she could make the whole world, from its easternmost horizon to the far west, where the sun slips away from our sight, reverberate with Vittoria Della Rovere's name. Line 11, cf. Gaspara Stampa, *Rime,* ed. Rodolfo Ceriello, 3d ed. (Milan: Rizzoli, 1994), also consulted in Quondam, 2.276.2: "fin dove il sole a noi nasce e diparte" (as far as where the sun is born to us and departs). Line 14, Battiferra reverses Petrarch's penitential tone to pay courtly flattery. Cf. *RS* 365.1–2: "I' vo piangendo i miei passati tempi / i quai posi in amar cosa mortale" (I go weeping my past time, which I spent in loving a mortal thing).

35. 1.9. Francesco Maria II Della Rovere (1549–1631), son of Giudobaldo II and Vittoria Farnese Della Rovere, was the last Duke of Urbino, ruling from 1574 until his death. Although Battiferra addresses a boy who must have been less than ten years old, she adopts a grandiloquent style signaled by anaphora and rhetorical questions. Her strategy is in keeping with the high hopes pinned on Guidobaldo's only masculine heir, not born until his second marriage and long awaited in the duchy. This dynastic sonnet climaxes with a vision of the prince victorious over the Turks. Battiferra imagines him grown to a great *condottiero* like the grandfather whose name he bore, Francesco Maria I Della Rovere, painted by Titian (1538) in splendid armor surrounded by his batons of military command.

36. Line 1, Battiferra imagines that the oak's branches shade not only the Duchy of Urbino, but cover the whole world, a sign of the global fame she attributes to the family. She adapts her image of the oak branch from Bembo's sonnet on the Della Rovere pope, Julius II (*Rime* 26, "De la gran quercia, che 'l bel Tebro adombra" [From the great oak that shades the Tiber]). For the anaphora "Non è questo" (Is not this), cf. Petrarch's canzone "Italia mia," *RS* 128; Jacopo Sannazzaro, *Rime e canzoni,* ed. A. Mauro, in *Opere volgari* (Bari: Laterza, 1961), in Quondam, 82. Lines 1–2, cf. Cappello, *Rime,* 330.1–2: "Un de' rami più cari / de l'alma pianta che 'l Metauro adombra" (One of the dearest branches of the bountiful plant that shades the Metauro). Line 4, *piaggia aprica* (open slope): cf. *RS* 303.6: "Valli chiuse, alti colli e piagge apriche" (Closed valleys, high hills, and open slopes); L. Alamanni, *Rime* 1.102.1: "Liete rive, alti colli e piaggia aprica" (also in rhyme with "antica") (Happy shores, high hills, and open slope). Line 6, Francesco Maria I Della Rovere adopted as a device the palm tree bent down and crushed under a block of marble with the motto, "Inclinata resurgit" (Bent it resurges). In the ducal palace built in the 1550s by Girolamo Genga on the Pesaro city square, oaks and palms decorated the doors and mantelpieces (Dennistoun, *Memoirs of the Dukes of Urbino,* 3: 108). Line 6, the Tiber's tribute may be an allusion to the title Prefect of Rome, a masculine military honor that the dukes of Urbino enjoyed as a hereditary right. Line 11, *grandi avoli* (great forebears): Battiferra

emphasizes the child's identity in his family's dynastic succession. Line 12, *fiero scita* (fierce Scythian): for the epithet, cf. V. Colonna, *Rime epistolari* 26.11; Guidiccioni, *Rime* 110.9; Luigi Tansillo, *Il canzoniere,* ed. Erasmo Pèrcopo, 2 vols. (Naples, 1926, [reprint 1996]), also consulted in Quondam, 6, sonnet 196.3; Varchi, *Rime* 1.333.8. The Scythians, an ancient tribe of warriors from northeastern Europe, signify the Turks, fierce invaders that swept into Europe from the Orient.

37. 1.10. Virginia Varana Della Rovere was the daughter of Duke Guidobaldo II by his first wife, Giulia Varana of Camerino. Guidobaldo's father, Francesco Maria I Della Rovere, arranged the marriage to consolidate his power over Camerino, a small state in the March of Ancona long fiercely contested among lords of the Varano family, the dukes of Urbino, and the papacy. Virginia's hereditary right to Camerino through her mother gave Guidobaldo hopes of blocking the nepotistic designs of Pope Paul III on that territory. Honored here as a member of Urbino's ruling family, Virginia Varana also has a connection to the poet's network through her maternal grandmother, Caterina Cibo, who was Duchess of Camerino (1.45) and the aunt of Battiferra's friend Leonora Cibo de' Vitelli (1.30–32; app. C). The five poems Battiferra sends to this princess of Urbino and Camerino elevate her to high status in the *Primo libro.* In the first, Virginia is a "virgin" heroine who will bring freedom to her long oppressed people; the other four recreate scenes from her magnificent state wedding, celebrated from Pesaro to Rome.

38. Lines 1–4, the Roman virgin Virginia, daughter of Aulus Virginius, was raped by the mad decemvir Appius Claudius, who accused her of being a fugitive slave. To save her honor, her father killed her publicly; after the sacrifice the decemvirs were forced to resign and restore liberty to the people. Battiferra knew the story from a long tradition (Livy, *History of Rome,* trans. B. O. Foster et al, 14 vols. [Cambridge, Mass.: Harvard University Press, 1919–57), 3.44–50; Valerius Maximus, *Memorable Doings and Sayings,* trans. D. R. Shackleton Bailey, 2 vols. [Cambridge, Mass.: Harvard University Press, 2000], 6.1.2; Giovanni Boccaccio, *Famous Women,* trans. Virginia Brown [Cambridge, Mass.: Harvard University Press, 2001], chap. 58. Line 8, *lieta . . . sicura* (joyful . . . secure): cf. *Par.* 15. 67. The modern Virginia will have a happier destiny than that of her ancient namesake because she will survive to become the sovereign of Camerino, which thus will serve her. Lines 9–11, the souls looking down from heaven are her ancestors, the Varano, exiled or unjustly deprived of power, who see in her the family's hope for restoration. Lines 12–14, her father, Guidobaldo, will live long enough to realize his political ambitions, as Camerino will pass from the Farnese to the duchy. *mortal velo* (mortal veil): Petrarchan metaphor for the body. Cf. *RS* 302.11, 319.14, 362.4.

39. 1.11. The Borromeo name had variant spellings. Cf. Giovanni Andrea Gilio, *Due dialogi di M. Giovanni Andrea Gilio da Fabriano* (Camerino: Antonio Gioioso, 1564), 8: "Bonromeo."

40. Of enormous political importance, this wedding was celebrated in Pesaro on May 9, 1560, after which the couple made a triumphal progression into Rome. Federico Borromeo ("Buonromeo") of Milan (1535–62) was the favorite nephew of Giovanni Angelo de' Medici, no relation to Cosimo, but noteworthy as the Milanese prelate who ascended the throne of Saint Peter's as Pius IV on December 25, 1559. Cosimo enjoyed optimal relations with this pope, who bore the same surname as he

did, and he cultivated Federico as a vehicle for influencing the pontiff to promote him to the rank of King of Tuscany. Before the Duke of Florence could achieve his goal, however, young Borromeo fell ill with fever and died.

41. Line 8, *la rozza musa mia* (my coarse muse): cf. Bernardo Tasso, *I tre libri de gli amori* (Venice: Gabriel Giolito de' Ferrari, et fratelli, 1555), also consulted in Quondam, 2.114.16: "la rozza mia Musa." Line 9, *sacra quercia antica* (the ancient sacred oak): Bernardo Tasso, *Amori*, in *Rime*, ed. D. Chiodo and V. Martignone (Turin: RES, 1995), 5.24.1 (in Quondam) (to Girolamo da la Rovere), "O gentil ramo de la Quercia antica" (O noble branch of the ancient Oak). Jove's tree, the Chaonian oak, emblem of the Della Rovere family. See above, 7.11. Line 12, the graphics of the Casanatense transcription, which "marry" the couple through the typographic proximity of their names, embedded in block capitals, further suggest a nuptial pun on "Federico," literally "rich in faith," in other words, a man who will be true to his wife. Line 14, *RS* 43.11: "in più di mille carte"(on more than a thousand pages); *RS* 103.14: "mille et mille anni" (a thousand and a thousand years).

42. 1.12. Battiferra now garbs in graceful mythological imagery the couple's departure from Urbino (1.12), their anticipated arrival in Rome, where in December 1560, they made a formal *ingresso* (1.13), and the future birth of their children (1.14). The poet's classical allusions must echo decorations made both in Urbino and Rome for the public marriage festivities.

43. Line 1, the horn of plenty from which tumble forth riches watered by Metauro. Line 2, *fior . . . frutti* (flowers . . . fruits): Petrarchan binomial (*RS* 337.3; *Triumph of Fame* 3.20) that becomes a favorite formula in Battiferra's poetry, typically with reference to the lush vegetation a river brings to its shores (1.13, 1.42, 1.44). Line 6, *valore e cortesia* [valor and courtesy]: cf. Dante, *Inf.* 16.67, "Cortesia e valor dì se dimora" [tell me if courtesy and valor dwell] and *Dec.* 1.8 (Victoria Kirkham, "The Tale of Guiglielmo Borsiere (I.8)," in *The Decameron: First Day in Perspective*, ed. Elissa Weaver, 179–206 [Toronto: University of Toronto Press, 2004]); Bembo, *Rime* 22.11: "valor e cortesia"; Aragona, *Rime* 19.1: "valore e cortesia." Line 10, Federico, nephew of Pope Pius IV. Line 11, Virginia, daughter of the Duke of Urbino, who is Battiferra's "duce" because Laura is his subject. The epithet "just" returns from the sonnet to Guidobaldo (1.7).

44. 1.13. The sonnet turns on a final revelation: it is the Tiber who speaks, proud that like Metauro he can offer an abundance of gifts as he welcomes the nymph-bride.

45. 1.14. Now the metrical form shifts to a madrigal, signaling the end of the Borromeo-Varana nuptial sequence. The principal deities of love, marriage, and fertility are convoked to assure a dynastic union that will be blessed with children.

46. Line 1, Venus, goddess of love, dwells as a planet in the third heaven of the Aristotelian-Ptolemaic universe. Cf. Dante, *Par.* 8–9. Lines 3–4, Juno, wife of Jupiter and goddess of marriage. Line 5, Hymen, god of marriage. Line 8, the Isauro is a small tributary of the Metauro, near Urbino. See above, 1.8. Line 12, *feconda prole* (fertile offspring): L.Alamanni, *Rime*, 2.11.13 (for Francis I).

47. 1.15. Giovanni de' Medici (1543–62), the second son of Cosimo and Eleonora, was destined from childhood to an ecclesiastical career with the papacy as its goal.

At the instigation of Cosimo, the Medici pope Pius IV made him a cardinal when he was only sixteen, with the hope that he would duplicate the career of another Giovanni de' Medici, that son of Lorenzo il Magnifico who became Pope Leo X (1513–21). Battiferra asserts the connection by citing conspicuously from a canzone to Leo X by his grateful courtier Giovanni Muzzarelli, a young poet whom Bembo had helped obtain from that pontiff a well salaried position as Prior of the Rocca of Mondaino, near Urbino. News of Cosimo's son's appointment, made in March 1560, officially reached Florence in August, carried by the new Papal Nuncio (Kirkham, "Laura Battiferra's 'First Book' of Poetry"). Battiferra greets the new Leo-lion ("Leone"), a *Giov*anni with likeness to Jove ("Giove"), son of Cosimo (Saturn) and Eleonora-Ops (Berecynthia). This mythological role-playing duplicates the code in a program of frescoes designed by Cosimo Bartoli and executed by Vasari in Palazzo Vecchio (Victoria Kirkham, "Creative Partners").

48. Line 1, *Terrestre Giove* (Terrestrial Jove): cf. Muzzarelli, *Rime* 35.1–3, a canzone to Pope Leo X (Giovanni de' Medici): "Terreno Giove, a cui l'alto governo / ha posto in mano il Re de l'universo / e commesso del cielo ambo le chiavi" (Earthly Jove, to whom the King of the universe has put in your hand the lofty command and committed both keys of heaven). Lines 1–2, *le chiavi e 'l freno / del ciel ne' più verdi anni e della terra* (in your budding years . . . the keys and rein of heaven and earth): cf. Varchi's sonnet to Alessandro Farnese, *Rime* 1.315. Line 3, *alto motor* (lofty mover): the Prime Mover, God. Lines 5–6, *seno . . . senno* (bosom . . . wisdom): Leo X was made a cardinal at the age of thirteen. Cosimo's son, not much older, is a good candidate for the *puer-senex* topos, a boy with the wisdom of a grown man. Lines 9–11, Jove was the son of Saturn, who here stands for Cosimo. Giovanni should obey and honor his father with filial piety. The adjective "pio" recalls Virgil's "pius Aeneas." Line 12, *Berecynthia:* another name for Cybele, queen of Frigia (where Mount Berecynthus is located). She is the *Magna Mater* of Jove and the gods, a great goddess of fertility. Here she stands for Eleanora, the fertile wife of Cosimo-Saturn and mother of Giovanni-Jove. Cybele's attribute, significantly, is the lion. Both Virgil (*Aen.* 3.111) and Ovid (*Met.* 10.704) mention the goddess in her lion-pulled cart. On Berecynthia, see Ovid, *Fasti* 4.179–359 and cf. *Aen.* 9.79–92. Line 12, *a paro a paro* (measure for measure): cf. Dante, *Purg.* 24.93 and Petrarch, *Triumphi*, ed. Marco Ariani (Milan: Mursia, 1988), *Triumph of Love* 4.25.

49. 1.16. Battiferra celebrates the expansion of the ducal territories in Tuscany ("Etruria") with the addition of Siena, to which she alludes by naming the river Arbia. For Battiferra, Cosimo's conquest heralds his dominion over all Italy, rising power that she translates into a vision of his apotheosis. On October 28, 1560, Cosimo made with his family a formal entry to claim the conquered city. The "statues, colossi, arches, and trophies" are the public decorations constructed along the stages of the triumphal route by Ammannati in the months preceding, precisely the period when this sonnet would have been composed (Kirkham, "Dante's Fantom, Petrarch's Specter" and "Creative Partners").

50. Line 2, *Etruria:* the Latin name from which the adjective Etruscan derives, whence "Tuscany." Cf. Virgil, *Aen.* 8.494; 12.232. Battiferra's vocabulary reflects a political choice, dictated by Medici propaganda that promoted the idea of direct, uninterrupted connection between the ancient Etruscans and the contemporary Tus-

cans, Cosimo's subjects. Sprung from a collateral line of the Medici as a new prince who had seized power from Republican leaders, Cosimo needed instant legitimacy to strengthen his power and ennoble his line, and he pursued it by appropriating "roots" in a distant past (Giovanni Cipriani, *Il mito etrusco nel rinascimento fiorentino* [Florence: Olschki, 1980]). Line 9, *Arbia:* the river as synecdoche for Siena has precedent in Dante, *Inf.* 10.86. Cf. Aragona, *Rime* 5, addressed to Duke Cosimo, whose "virtues" have drawn Tullia from Siena to Florence: "da l'Arbia . . . mi trasser d'Arno a le felici sponde" (from the Arbia . . . they drew me to the happy shores of Arno). Battiferra's sonnet reverses the actors and direction of events; it is Cosimo, not Tullia, who will travel, and he will leave Florence for Siena. Line 10, cf. Raineri, *Cento sonetti* 1.14: "colossi, archi, trofei, trionfi e marmi" (colossi, arches, trophies, triumphs, and marbles); Cappello, *Rime* 124.3: "statue, colossi e archi trionfali" (statues, colossi, and triumphal arches); Varchi, *Rime* 1.340.3: "terme, templi, colossi, archi e trofei" (baths, temples, colossi, arches, and trophies). Lines 10–12, contemporary descriptions (Anton Francesco Cirni, *La reale entrata dell'ecc.mo signor duca et duchessa di Fiorenza, in Siena, con la significatione delle Latine inscrittioni, e con alcuni Sonetti, scritta per Anton Francesco Cirni Corso* (Rome: Antonio Blado Stampator Camerale, 1560; Antonio Martellini, *La solenna entrata dello illustrissimo, et eccellentiss. sig. il sig. duca di Fiorenza et Siena* [Florence: Laurentius Torrentinus, 1560]) make reference to the decorations. The singing swans are all the poets who celebrate the event.

51. 1.17. The two rivers Arno and Arbia, personifications of Florence and Siena, bow before the duchess, who accompanied Cosimo on his triumphal Sienese *ingresso.* With these words of farewell to her patron (the sonnet is the last poem in the *Primo libro*), Battiferra raises Elenora to the honorific rank of "queen." It is both an affirmation of humble obedience and a way of elegantly promoting Cosimo himself to king.

52. Line 2, *Arno . . . Arbia:* Battiferra finds occasion to use this homophonic couple several times in her *canzoniere,* reminding readers of the twin jewels in Cosimo's crown. Cf. Aragona, *Rime* 5.7–8; Varchi, *Rime* 2.43a. 13–14. Line 5, *una* (a woman): Laura Battiferra, who in good ceremonial form protests her terrible inadequacy. Lines 12–14, *il gran Giove* (the great Jove): God. The verses recall the end of the *Divine Comedy, Par.* 33.145: "L'amor che move il sole e l'altre stelle" (the love that moves the sun and the other stars). Perhaps Cosimo too is implied, the suggestion being that he had already accepted some of the author's verse. In a letter of December 11, 1557, she had written Varchi, "I had letters from Signor Chiappino and from Messer Sforza (Almeno), who say my sonnet much pleased the court."

53. 1.18. Lucrezia d'Este (d. 1598), sister of Alfonso I, Duke of Ferrara, was contracted in marriage to Francesco Maria II Della Rovere, son of Guidobaldo II, in December 1569, and she made her formal entry into Pesaro as his wife on January 9, 1571 (Piperno, *L'immagine del duca,* 96–102). She brought a thundering dowry of 150,000 scudi, but the marriage produced no heir and failed, owing in part to her advanced age (nearly forty and thirteen years older than her husband) and in part to her husband's affectional preference for his uncle. She returned afterwards to Ferrara, where she lived many years, a benefactress to Torquato Tasso among others (Dennistoun, *Memoires of the Dukes of Urbino,* 3: 135–38). Since Battiferra addresses her as "Princess" and not "Duchess," this sonnet and its twin predate Francesco Maria's rise to power on the death of his father in 1574. They are occasional poems inspired by

news of the wedding in Urbino. Battiferra imitates Petrarch, who had compared his Laura to the phoenix, the mythic bird only one of which at a time lives in the world (*RS* 210). This Lucrezia is the same unique creature. In the upper reaches of her high flight, symbolizing aristocratic rank, fame, and moral purity, she encounters Jove, who tells her to make her nest in the tree sacred to him, that is, in the oak ("rovere"), emblem of the Urbino ducal family. The nest, a maternal image apt for a bridal sonnet, distantly recalls the female bird that keeps watch over her young in Dante's beautiful simile at the beginning of *Par.* 23.

54. Line 2, *fenice aurata* (golden phoenix): *RS* 185.1: "Questa fenice de l'aurata piuma" (This phoenix with the gilded feathers); 321.1–2: "'l nido in che la mia fenice / mise l'aurate et le purpuree penne" (the nest where my phoenix put on her gold and purple feathers). Line 6, *fronda amata* (beloved branch): cf. Dante, *Par.* 23.1 "Come l'augello intro l'amate fronde" (as the small bird amongst beloved branches); *RS* 188.1–2: "Almo sol, quella fronde ch'io sola amo / tu prima amasti" (Bountiful sun, the one branch that I love you first loved).

55. 1.19. The Metauro River of Urbino should not envy the Tiber for ancient Lucretia, who to preserve her honor committed suicide ("made night for herself at midday"). Now a new Lucrezia will restore Urbino to a golden age. The rivers are personified as old men who pour forth their waters from vases and offer abundance from horns of plenty (cf. 1.12).

56. Line 4, the reference is to Roman Lucretia (Livy 1.57–60; Valerius Maximus 1.6.1), the wife of Porsenna, who cut her own life short by committing suicide after being raped by Tarquinius Superbus. See also below, 1.27. Cf. for the conceit Giovan Battista Strozzi (The Elder), *Madrigali inediti,* ed. M. Ariani (Strassburg: Biblioteca Romanica, 1909), 97.1–4, in Quondam: "Morte, sì dura vista, / ombra, anzi notte nel bel viso adorno, / Morte pentita e trista / del bel sol da lei spento a mezzo 'l giorno" (Death, such a hard sight, shadow, nay, night in the fair adorned face, Death repentant and wretched for the fair sun it snuffed out in the middle of the day); B.Tasso, *Amori* 5.152.1–2, on the premature death of his lady: "Sparve il mio sole a mezzo il giorno, e scura / misero portò notte agli occhi miei" (My sun disappeared in the middle of the day and, miserable, brought night to my eyes). Line 7, Metauro's circle of "triumphal honor" is no less than Tiber's. That is, triumphal plants like the laurel abound on his banks too. Cf. *RS* 263: "Arbor vittoriosa triunfale" (Victorious triumphal tree). Line 9, "Lucrezia" is the modern Italian spelling of the name that in Battiferra's day was still typically spelled in the Latinate form "Lucretia," a homonym that tightens the parallel between Francesco Maria's bride and the Roman heroine. Lines 13–14, the poet is thinking of the great mythic heroes of antiquity with successors in a new golden age under the continuation of the Della Rovere dynasty. Francesco Maria, who in fact failed to produce a male heir, was the last Duke of Urbino.

57. 1.20. The long pontificate of Alessandro Farnese, Pope Paul III (1534–49), marks the start of the Catholic Reformation with the first sessions of the Council of Trent, which he convened in 1545. Battiferra's father Giovan Antonio, an apostolic scriptor at the Vatican, was privileged as a "familiar" of Paul III, who in 1543 legitimized his three children. One of her earliest known poems, this sonnet reveals Battiferra's mastery of the Bible and anticipates her later project on the Penitential Psalms. It is a "get-well card" that may relate specifically to the pontiff's last illness,

between November 2 and 10, when he passed on to his reward at the ripe old age of eighty-two. Some ten years later, as she was shaping her *Primo libro,* Battiferra excluded it, less because Paul was now dead than because of his anti-Medicean politics. The sonnet becomes suitable for her *Rime,* no longer dominated by hopes of Medici patronage, but more spiritual in their overall orientation.

58. Line 4, *trema il tenebroso chiostro* (the tenebrous cloister trembles): hell, perhaps an allusion to the Harrowing of Hell, with which the story of Hezekiah (see below, lines 12–14) was associated in the liturgy at Tuesday Lauds and at Lauds in the Office of the Dead. I thank Ronald Martinez for this suggestion. Battiferra reverses Dante's description of heaven as "beato chiostro" (blessed cloister) in *Par.* 25.127. Cf. *Par.* 7.48. Lines 4–5, *chiostro . . . inchiostro* (cloister . . . ink): Petrarch pairs these words in rhyme (*Triumph of Love* 3.116–18), inaugurating a long tradition. Cf. Varchi, *Rime* 2.33a and 2.83b. Lines 9–11, Lachesis was the Fate who spun the thread of life. Peter healed the sick with his shadow as he walked past them (Acts 5:14–15). The "great king" is Hezekiah, whose life God prolonged by turning back time ("the shadow" on a sundial). Cf. Tansillo, *Canzoniere* I, sonnet 98.6 Lines 12–14, as a parallel to the New Testament allusion, with Peter's name in block capitals to underline his connection to the current pope, Battiferra adds an Old Testament episode. After the prophet Isaiah told King Hezekiah to put his house in order because his time was fast approaching, the ruler prayed for a reprieve and God granted his faithful servant an additional fifteen years of life (2 Kgs 20:8–11; Is. 38:1–8). This passage was to gain prominence in debates concerning the Copernican theory of the universe; like the story of Joshua who commanded the sun to stand still, it was cited by those who clung to the old Aristotelian-Ptolemaic model of the cosmos.

59. 1.21. The gifted Isabella de' Medici (1542–76), third daughter of Cosimo and Eleonora, is said to have begun composing lyrics that she set to music for lute and recorder and even to have arranged a ballet at the precocious age of ten. Knowledgeable in Latin, Spanish, and French, she grew up to become the admired mistress of a sparkling salon in Florence. Her dynastic marriage to Paolo Giordano Orsini, intended to unite the Medici with one of Rome's most powerful clans, proved an unhappy match. Long separations, when her soldier husband sojourned in Rome or was absent hunting, led her to take as a lover his cousin and her chamberlain, Troilo Orsini. As the story goes, one day Paolo Giordano arrived unannounced from Rome and without explanation summoned her to their villa, Cerreto Guidi near Empoli. After they had dined, as he pretended to kiss her, he strangled her with a noose suspended from the floor above through a hole in the ceiling, which his four accomplices then withdrew. Afterwards, her husband gave it out that she had died of stroke while washing her hair. Isabella's body, its face disfigured, was buried unmarked in the church of San Lorenzo beside other members of the Medici family.

Unique in Battiferra's corpus, this sequence of six poems is the longest dedicated to another woman (Virginia Varana Della Rovere receives five; Leonora Cibo de' Vitelli, a three-sonnet set). It closely resembles Giovan Battista Strozzi's much longer series of madrigals, headed by a rubric that helps explain the circumstances of Battiferra's offering: "This and the thirty following were made at the request of Signora Isabella de' Medici when her consort Signor Paolo was in Rome and she was in Florence." Strozzi's third madrigal for Isabella gives an idea of the similarities:

Deh, se pur la mia vita
or sì lungi e sì presso mi dà morte,
che farà poscia al fin di nostra vita?
Che farà poscia morte?
Ahi più che morte dispietata vita,
tu non sei più, no, vita, anzi pur vita
e morte, anzi sol vita:
peggio io non so che vita.

[Pray, if my life [Paolo]
even so far and so near gives me death,
what will happen then at the end of our life?
What will death then do?
Ah, life pitiless more than death,
you are no longer life, no, rather both life
and death, rather only life,
worse than I know not what life.]

An important model for both Strozzi and Battiferra is the verse Bembo scripts for Perottino, his spokesman for unhappy love in book 1 of the *Asolani.*

In the Casanatense manuscript, the only source to preserve the verse Isabella requested from Battiferra, the title has been scratched out and a vertical line runs alongside all six poems. Beside the first, Battiferra's note instructs the printer: "these sonnets are not to be printed." In spite of obliterating pen strokes, however, the words "At the request of" remain visible in the rubric and the addressee's name can just barely be deciphered. An explanation for the disappearance of Isabella's name from the *Rime* (but not the poetry written for her) lies in the appalling circumstances of her death, plotted by her own husband, who wanted to marry his mistress, Vittoria Accoramboni. After the treacherous pair had spent several stormy years together, Accoramboni was herself murdered by vengeful relatives of her victims and the renegade Orsini came to a miserable end. Chroniclers, poets, and playwrights seized on the tragedy, some accounts of which report that he too was assassinated.

Battiferra's six poems for Isabella are a creative confluence of two highly cultured women. They rectify, as it were, the artificial situation of medieval Italian love lyrics, particularly the powerful Petrarchan and Dantean models, where ladies speak through male cross-voicing. In the sixteenth century, Vittoria Colonna and Veronica Gambara had established precedent for a mournful female voice, and here Battiferra transfers that voice to another woman, writing in her stead. These verses, which lack distinguishing detail, are graceful in their flow, with moments of mournful simplicity that recall the style of popular balladry. Perhaps this set of lyrics was meant to be sung to the accompaniment of a lute, and if so, Isabella would have been the performer. In the first poem, which turns on the opposition of life and death, we hear Isabella's lament for her departed lover. The last verse encloses the two poles in the tension of the Petrarchan oxymoron, "I live dying always." In form it is a *canzonetta* or an ode with a rhyme scheme *aBaBbCcdd, efeggFFbb.* Similar stanzas can be found in Bernardo Tasso's *Amori* of 1555. Here the divisions of the traditional *canzone* stanza are still in evidence: vv. 1–4 = *frons* or *fronte* ("front"); vv. 5 = *verso chiave* or *verso di volta* ("key verse," "turning point"); vv. 6–9 = *sirima* ("coda", "tail").

60. Line 6, *duro privilegio degli amanti* (harsh privilege of lovers): *RS* 15.13: "questo è privilegio degli amanti" (this is the privilege of lovers).

61. 1.22. The hope that her lover will return is a sweet thought that keeps Isabella company in her solitude. Again the form is that of a *Canzonetta* or ode. Its stanzas are concatenated through the repetition of the b rhyme: AbBaCacC, DbDdbEeFf. The rhyming couplet of the final verses repeats the first rhyme of the second stanza (*e*) in the poem above.

62. Line 1, *giorno . . . ora* (day . . . hour): she keeps time as Petrarch did. Cf. *RS* 12.11: "gli anni, e i giorni, et l'ore" (the years, the days, and the hours); 295.5: "l'ultimo giorno et l'ore estreme" (the last day and the final hours). Line 3, *RS* 37.31: "poco m'avanza del conforto usato" (little is left me of my familiar comfort). Line 5, *mi pasci di speranza* (feed me on hope): *RS* 331.6: "di speme il cor pascendo" (feeding my heart on hope).

63. 1.23. Love should not boast about his victory over Isabella, a defenseless woman who for many years has suffered bitter torment in his ranks. The only reward for serving Love is death.

64. Line 2, *sotto l'insegna tua* (beneath your ensign): the sonnet opens on an image of war, but Isabella is unarmed on the battlefield of love. So too was Petrarch when struck by Cupid (*RS* 2). Line 4, *RS* 21.1: "Mille fiate, o dolce mia guerrera" (A thousand times, O my sweet warrior); 103.14: "mille et mille anni" (a thousand and a thousand years).

65. 1.24. All things are subject to Love's rule; not even Death can offer escape since cruelty blocks that release. The sonnet, like its companions, reprises Petrarchan rhetoric in figures of oxymoron ("vere frodi"), antithesis ("finte . . . vere"), gemination ("aggrada e piace"), and fragmented body parts in polysyndeton ("collo . . . piedi . . . braccia"). Sonnets 23–26 are linked by *concatenatio,* recalling the Provençal technique of *coblas capfinidas,* in which the last verse of one stanza is repeated in the first verse of the stanza that follows.

66. Line 2, *empio signor* (wicked lord): Amore. *RS* 360.1: "Quel antiquo mio dolce empio signore." Line 8, *catene adamantine* (adamantine chains): Battiferra reverses Bembo (*Rime* 2.11), defiantly unrepentant for his love of a lady who has bound him in identical chains. Line 14, pitilessness makes her abode at love's side.

67. 1.25. So great is love's suffering that it is better to close one's eyes than look upon a handsome face or listen to well-spoken words. Battiferra reverses the message of sonnets like Dante's in praise of Beatrice in the *Vita nuova.*

68. Line 1, pitilessness makes her abode at death's side. Line 3, cf. Dante's inscription over the gate of Hell, *Inf.* 3.3: "per me si va tra la perduta gente" (through me you enter among the lost). Line 5, *Voi che mirate* (you who gaze): *Inf.* 9.61–62: "O voi che'avete li 'ntelletti sani, / mirate la dottrina (O you who have sound understanding, / mark the doctrine). Lines 11–13, The rhyme "laccio-impaccio" occurs in *RS* 134. Line 14, *mortal lingua o stile* (mortal tongue or style): for the coupling "language and style" see Petrarch, *Triumph of Time* 35, perhaps suggested by *Par.* 6.65 "lingua né penna." The "mortal" style of the lover bound for death reverses Bembo, *Rime* 1, where he asks the Muses to make his style "live."

69. 1.26. Not even the planetary gods above the circle of the moon, where all is supposed to be immutable and eternal, are immune to the effects of love, a poisonous serpent. Isabella, as any reasonable person can see, is severely weakened by his besiegement.

70. Line 5, *angue* (asp): this serpent is also present in *RS* 323.69, but in an allusion to the myth of Orpheus and Eurydice. Cf. Petrarch, *Triumph of Love* 3.157. Battiferra's reptile, which responds to the charm of music, has antecedents in the bestiaries. To avoid being enticed from its cavern by the music of an enchanter, the asp was reputed to push one ear against the ground and cover the other with its tail. Lines 12–14, the final tercet recalls Petrarch's sense of public guilt. Cf. *RS* 1: "favola fui gran tempo" (for a long time I was the talk of the crowd). Line 13, *petto e panni:* literally, "breast and clothing." The alliterative word chunk comes from *Triumph of Love* 1.57. Line 12, *chiaro esempio* (plain example). Contrast Bembo, *Rime* 1.12, "duro exempio" (hard example).

71. 1.27. Girolama Colonna united the blood lines of two illustrious families as the daughter of Ascanio Colonna, Constable of Naples, and Giovanna of Aragon, granddaughter of King Ferdinand I of Naples. This poem first appeared in Ottavio Sammarco's *Il Tempio della divina signora donna Geronima Colonna D'Aragona* (Padua: Lorenzo Pasquati, 1568), an uninspired imitation of Girolamo Ruscelli's major compilation of poems dedicated to her mother, *Del Tempio alla Divina signora donna Giovanna d'Aragona, fabricato da tutti i più gentili Spiriti, et in tutte le lingue principali del mondo* (Venice: Plinio Pietrasanta, 1555). Sammarco's smaller project assembles authors of ninety rhymes in Italian and sixty in Latin or Greek (98, 45, and 8 folios, respectively, in the volume). Among the vernacular poets are seven women: Celia Romana, Cornelia Cotta, Emilia Brembata Solza, Isotta Brembata Grumella, Laura Battiferra, Leonora Maltraversa, and Olimpia Malipiero. This sonnet, not one of the poet's most original, finds a logical place in Battiferra's *Rime,* assimilated by gender to the preceding sequence of six for Isabella de' Medici. Geographically, it closes a longer sequence that belongs to the Roman sphere, beginning with the poem to Paul III.

72. Line 2, *Apollo:* the god of poetry who dwells with the Muses on Mount Parnassus. Line 4, *sacro monte* (sacred mount): Parnassus, where the "sacred" laurel grows. Cf. *RS* 34.7: "sacra fronde" (sacred leaves). Line 10, COLONNESE: of the Colonna family. The manuscript has it in block capitals, as was the convention of the times, to emphasize the embedded name of the dedicatee. Line 11, *Tevere, Vaticano:* All Rome, secular (the Tiber) and sacred (the Vatican), admires Giovanna. Line 12, Roman Lucretia, the matron who chose death over dishonor and whose suicide ended the tyranny of the Tarquinii, marking the beginning of the republic (Livy, 1.57–60). Lucretia in death became a universal paragon of female virtue, but Geronima, still living, outshines her. Cf. above, 1.18–19 for Lucrezia d'Este. Line 13, *stil sovrano* (sovereign style): a Petrarchan pun on "style" and "stylus" or "pen." In other words, all the best poets praise Girolama in the *Temple* raised to honor her.

73. 1.28. Giovan Luigi ("Chiappino") Vitelli, born of a powerful Umbrian family in Città di Castello, had a long career as a cavalry officer (1519–75), early distinguishing himself in skirmishes with the Turks. Here he is the hero of the Sienese campaign, 1553–55. He continued in Cosimo's service as an officer in the field, as a fortification engineer, and as an ambassador to the court of Phillip II of Spain and

Ferrara, until called by the latter to fight in the Low Countries in 1567. To reward his loyalty, Cosimo honored him with the title Duke of Cetona (near Siena) and in 1562 named him as the first knight in his new Order of Saint Stephen. In sharp dissent from Battiferra's fulsome praise, history has painted an ugly picture of this man, so grotesquely obese that he was forced to support his stomach in a sling around his neck; cruel and bloodthirsty from youth, when he is said to have murdered his father's killer. Vitelli died despised in Flanders, violently as he had lived, when he fell (or was pushed) into a ditch from a sedan chair on a dike (Carlo Promis, *Biografie di ingegneri militari italiani dal secolo XIV alla metà del XVIII*, in *Miscellanea di storia patria* [Turin: Fratelli Bocca Librai di S.M., 1874], 14: 428–46).

Battiferra undertook a set of poems for Chiappino Vitelli and his wife, Leonora Cibo de' Vitelli (married in 1549), at the latter's request. So we learn from her letter to Varchi of November 9, 1557:

> Signora Leonora, wife of Signor Chiappino, sent word to me that she would like me to do a sonnet for her husband; and because I wanted to serve her, I did this one for him, notwithstanding that my muses have a mind of their own and don't want to do anything except what strikes their fancy. I send it to you as extremely needy of your help.

She then adds in a postscript: "I also did this other sonnet to Signora Leonora. I had thought that I wouldn't want to bother you so much all at once and to send it another time, but look them over when it is convenient for you." It seems plausible to assign to the same period the other poems that were added to create a microsequence for this married couple, three for the husband followed by three for the wife. All appear in the *Primo libro,* and all are sonnets except the last, a madrigal, a metrical change that signals the end of the series. All told, in Battiferra's corpus the Vitelli receive eleven poems, indicating their importance to the Ammannati as patrons, mediators with the Medici, and probably also as friends.

74. Lines 1–4, Homer and Virgil in the *Iliad* and *Aeneid.* For the lexical cluster here ("ornar le carte . . . valorosi cavallieri . . . Marte"), cf. Bernardo Tasso, *Salmi,* ed. D. Chiodo and V. Martignone (Turin: RES, 1995), 2.55.1–10, in Quondam. Line 9, *Alcide:* Hercules, the giant of Greek myth who accomplished twelve superhuman labors. Line 10, *Ettore:* the noble Greek hero who killed Achilles, Priam's chief warrior at Troy; *Ulisse:* the wily Greek leader who created the Trojan horse to plant his men secretly inside the besieged enemy city. Line 11, *Africano:* Scipio Africanus, the hero who conquered Carthage and Hannibal in the Second Punic War, sung by Petrarch, following Livy, in his epic *Africa.*

75. 1.29. In one of her favorite formulas of praise, Battiferra credits Chiappino with transforming the dull uncivilized present "iron age" into a new golden age.

76. Line 1, *purgato inchiostro* (refined ink): cf. Bembo's influential sonnet of 1525, "Molza, che fa la tua donna" (Molza, what is your lady doing) to Francesco Maria Molza, a poet adept in both Latin and Italian (*Rime* 104.12–13): "Che scrivi tu, del cui purgato inchiostro / già l'uno e l'altro stil molto s'avanza?" (What are you writing, whose refined ink / already much advances one style and the other?). Following Bembo, the phrase spreads like wildfire. Cf. Vittoria Colonna, *Rime amorose disperse,* in *Rime,* 33.5; Aragona, *Rime* 55 (from Lattanzio De' Bennucci); Matraini, *Rime* 24; Isabella Morra, *Rime* (ed. Maria Antonietta Grignani (Rome: Salerno Editrice, 2000),

5.3; Stampa, 2.31.1 (from Baldassare Stampa), etc. Line 2, Petrarch had coupled the two poets in *RS* 186.1: "Se Virgilio et Omero avessino visto." Line 8, cf. 1.6. Line 9–10, *Phidias*: fourth century B.C.E., the preeminent sculptor of classical Greece (ancient counterpart of Ammannati, nicknamed "Fidia"). *Pyrgoteles, Apelles*: Vitelli becomes implicitly a twin of the mightiest Greek conqueror, Alexander the Great. Battiferra's immediate source for clustering Pyrgoteles and Apelles is Petrarch, who alludes to Alexander in *RS* 232: "ché li val se Pirgotile et Lisippo / l'intagliar solo et Apelle il depinse?" (What does it help him that only Pyrgoteles and Lysippus / engraved and only Apelles painted him?). Petrarch in turn was remembering his Pliny, according to whom Alexander granted sole privileges, respectively, to Pyrgoteles for carving his image in marble, to Lysippus for casting it in bronze, and to Apelles for painting it (Pliny, *Natural History*, trans. H. Rackham et al, 10 vols. [Cambridge, Mass.: Harvard University Press, 1938–62], 7.37). Battiferra retains the Petrarchan series of artistic materials, but eliminates the name of Lysippus in order to bring Phidias into the trio. See below, 1.39, in which she announces that Ammannati plans to sculpt Chiappino in the guise of Hercules.

77. 1.30. With this sonnet, the first of three for Chiappino's wife, Battiferra initiates a sixteen-unit "chapter" in the *Rime* set apart for women, carried over from *Il primo libro*. The three to Leonora form their own logical narrative unit: if Leonora inspires Laura to heavenly flights (1.30), she is herself of heavenly origins (1.31), and a little catalog of her supramundane qualities leads to the conclusion that heaven is diminished by her existence on earth (1.32).

78. Leonora (Eleonora) Cibo de' Vitelli (1523–94), widow of a Genoese nobleman, was the niece of Cardinal Innocenzo Cibo, himself a nephew of Pope Innocent VIII. After the death of her second husband Chiappino in 1575, Leonora withdrew to the Florentine convent of Le Murate, where she had spent her childhood. She brought with her an imposing dowry of 3,000 scudi plus an additional 960 scudi to purchase cloth for new habits for all the nuns (Judith C. Brown, "Everyday Life, Longevity, and Nuns in Early Modern Florence," in *Renaissance Culture and the Everyday*, ed. Patricia Fumerton and Simon Hunt (Philadelphia: University of Pennsylvania Press, 1998). There she was buried beside her aunt, Caterina Cibo, the Duchess of Camerino (1.45). Educated by Caterina, Leonora knew Latin, Greek, and perhaps also Hebrew. Giuseppe Betussi praised her in his dialogue *La Leonora* (Lucca, 1557), and the prolific Lodovico Domenichi dedicated to her an Italian translation of Augustine's treatise *Del libero arbitrio* (Florence, 1563). She is counted among the poetesses of Italy, thanks to a single surviving sonnet, preserved in the *Rime toscane* published by Faustino Tasso (Turin, 1573). Battiferra's madrigal below (1.32) suggests that she may also have been a talented musical performer.

79. Line 1, *casta bellezza* (chaste beauty): *RS* 228.10. Lines 5–6, *verno . . . maggio* (winter . . . spring): a variation on the formula of changing iron to gold, transforming the dull present to a new golden age. Cf. B. Tasso, *Amori* 1.36.6. Line 8, cf. *Vita nuova* 19: "E quando trova alcun che degno sia / di veder lei . . . / sì l'umilia, ch'ogni offesa oblia" (and when she finds a man worthy / of seeing her . . . / she so humbles him that he forgets every offense). Line 10, *ali del pensier* (wings of thought): cf. *RS* 362.1. Line 11, *bianco augel* (white bird): cf. Raineri, *Cento sonetti* 55.12: "augel canoro e bianco" (bird singing and white).

80. 1.31. Battiferra implies of Leonora what Dante had said of Beatrice (*Vita nuova* 26): "she seems to be a thing come from heaven to earth to display a miracle." The Dantesque ring of the language here can also recall lessons in *Paradiso* from Beatrice, a literary ancestress of this lady who teaches us how to go to heaven.

81. Line 1, *alma dea* (bountiful goddess): Venus, who dwells in the third heaven (1.14). From Roman times and Latin poetic usage, the epithet was traditional. See, e.g., L. Alamanni, *Della coltivazione* 1 (Florence: Appresso Bernardo Giunti, 1549), also consulted in Quondam: "Primavera," 268: "alma Ciprigna dea" (bountiful Cypriot goddess); Aragona, *Rime, Eclogue* 4.158 (by Girolamo Muzio): "l'alma dea di Cipri" (the bountiful goddess from Cyprus). Line 3, *colei ch'eguale a Dio ne rende* (she who makes us the equal of God): wisdom. Line 7, *Colui che sol se stesso intende* (He who alone understands Himself): God; cf. *Purg.* 28.91: "Lo sommo ben, che solo esso a sè piace" (The highest Good, who Himself alone does please Himself). Dante several times uses the formula "sommo ben," e.g., *Par.* 3.90, 7.80, 14.47. Battiferra's Latinate usage (cf. "summum bonum") recalls the Scholastic language of Aristotle and Aquinas.

82. 1.32. The sequence dedicated to the Vitelli ends with this madrigal, following five sonnets, a metrical shift that marks closure. Body and soul, Leonora is a creation of the heavens. The last two verses neatly wrap up the list of her divine virtues with the finishing touch of her "veil," in the Petrarchan code, her body, which deprives heaven to adorn earth. Others before had exploited the idea of an earthly being perfected by contributions from various parts of the heavens. Compare, for example, Bernardo Cappello's praise of a subject named Settimia, *Rime* 179: "Tutti sette i pianeti a prova intenti" (All seven planets intent on the effort); or Gaspara Stampa's recital of how her lover was made, *Rime* 1.4: "Quando fu prima il mio signor concetto" (When my lord was first conceived).

83. Line 1, *alma gentile* (noble soul): cf. Bembo's famous *canzone* of mourning (142.1), which begins with a similar formula, "Alma cortese" (Courteous soul). Line 2, *spiriti celesti* (heavenly spirits): the angels; cf. *RS* 335.4. Line 5, *mother of Love:* Venus. Line 7, *Phoebus and his sister:* Apollo, the sun, and Diana, the moon. Line 8, *rubella* (rebel): cf. *RS* 29.18: "rubella di mercé" (rebel against mercy). Line 9, *bel velo* (fair veil): cf. *RS* 302.11. In the Petrarchan lexicon, "veil" often refers to the body, the veil of the soul. The rhyme "velo . . . cielo" (veil . . . heaven) also appears in Cappello's sonnet no. 179.

84. 1.33. With this sonnet for Ersilia Cortese de' Monti (1529–after 1587), the sequence for women in the *Rime* shifts to Rome. Born into a prominent Modenese family, she was the niece of Cardinal Gregorio Cortese. Legitimized like Battiferra by Paul III, Ersilia was given in marriage to Giovanbattista Del Monte, a nephew of Cardinal Giovanni Maria Ciocchi Del Monte (d. 1555), who received the tiara as Julius III on February 7, 1550, two months before Battiferra remarried. This sonnet must date from the years of his papacy, when Ammannati enjoyed the pope's patronage and Ersilia was the most powerful matron in Rome. She was the recipient of sonnets from prominent *literati* including Annibal Caro. Pietro Aretino was one of her correspondents, Sperone Speroni speaks of her with admiration, Bernardo Tasso names her among illustrious ladies in his *Amadigi* of 1560, and Girolamo Ruscelli devised for her an *impresa* that alludes to the reversals of fortune she endured in widowhood. Some of her own poetry appears in Muzio Manfredi's collection, *Per donne romane* (1575). In her later years, she edited the writings by her uncle, Cardinal Gre-

gorio Cortesi, dedicating them to Pope Gregory XIII. Virtually unknown today, she is a literary personality who merits further study. In this delightful sonnet, Battiferra plays on her subject's maiden and married names, literally "courteous mountain." Since she addresses a "Monte" (mountain), the sonnet becomes a smiling little inventory of famous peaks. Ersilia, naturally, towers over all of them.

85. Line 1, Olympus, home of the gods, is a mountain in Thessaly with a peak that rises above the clouds. When Perseus uncovered the head of Medusa before the giant Atlas, the latter was changed into an enormous mountain of the same name, so high that it is always snow-covered and seems to hold up the sky (*Met.* 4.631–62). The Atlas Mountains are in north Africa. *Olympus . . . Atlas:* Petrarch connects them as part of a longer series of geographical allusions in *RS* 146.11; Matraini isolates them as a couple, *Rime e lettere* C.72.2, but a more resonant source is the sonnet from Battiferra's Urbino compatriot Antonio Gallo (cf. 1.73) to Bernardo Tasso in the latter's *Amori* 5.16a.1–4: "Or s'erga l'Appennino infino al Cielo, / Di cui gli ceda Atlante il grave peso / Gli inchini Olimpo il capo non offeso / Da nube o pioggia, né da vento o gielo" (Let now Apennine surge upward to the Heaven, whose heavy weight let Atlas yield to him, and may Olympus bow to him his head, unharmed by cloud or rain, or by wind or frost). Lines 5–6, the olive is sacred to Minerva and a symbol of wisdom. Lines 7–8, Ersilia's poetry ("nectar") carries her fame not only up the moon and Mercury, but to the heaven at the outer limits of the universe, the Primum Mobile. Battiferra's perspective on the skies recalls the language of Dante's *Paradiso.* Lines 9–10, Ersilia outstrips the god of poetry Apollo, to whom the laurel belongs, and the nine Muses, dwellers on Mount Parnassus. Line 12, the other "Mount" is the lady named "Monte," who wins her own laurels ("other boughs") on the Tiber ("other shores"). Line 13, "cortese" (courteous) is the same as Ersilia's maiden name.

86. 1.34. Livia Colonna, belonging to one of Rome's most distinguished families, was married to Marzio Colonna in 1538 and murdered by her brother-in-law in 1554. In 1555, Francesco Christiani published an encomiastic volume of poetry for her, *Rime di diversi eccellenti autori, in vita, e in morte dell'illustrissima Livia Colonna* (Rome: Antonio Barrè for M. Francesco Christiani, 1555). Annibal Caro and Dionigi Atanagi are among the contributors, but not Battiferra, who instead commemorates Livia in her own *Primo libro* with three successive sonnets. In this, the first, the poet displays her virtuosity with two sets of identical rhymes built on paronomasia. Livia, who flashes like a bolt of lightning into the mental night of her contemporaries, transcends even the most famous ladies of Italian poetry, Petrarch's Laura and Dante's Beatrice.

87. Lines 1–2, Livia's radiant virtue makes her outshine Phoebus, the real sun. Line 3, the "shadow" that has snuffed out present "lights" (living beings) is death. Line 6, *ogni nebbia sgombra* (dispels all fog): *RS* 270.36. The verb "sgombrare," here rendered as "to dispel," is the focus of Varchi's letter to Battiferra (4.7). Line 10, *Laura . . . Bice:* Bice is a diminutive of Beatrice. The formula, copied in such poets of Battiferra's as Cappello, Tansillo, and B. Tasso, seems to have originated in a sonnet by Varchi to Luigi Alamanni, probably written during the latter's visit to Florence in 1539 (1.60), in L. Alamanni, *Rime* 2.101b.13.

88. 1.35. Ortensia Colonna was Livia's sister (Guidi, *Il primo libro,* 50). The recipient of four sonnets in the *Primo libro,* she must have been important in Battiferra's life. The

first compares Ortensia, like Livia (and Petrarch's Laura before her), to a sun who warms cold hearts with desire wherever she turns with her light. The last two, about the joys and pains of love, must have been written at Ortensia's request, like those Battiferra composed for Isabella de' Medici. This poem, the second in the sequence, seems to have been written soon after the Ammannati moved from Rome to Florence (summer 1555). Notwithstanding the "cultured intellects" and other poets in her new surroundings, Laura misses her Roman friend Ortensia. Nevertheless, she continues to compose poetry, now in a vein of sadness. Battiferra's nostalgia for this lady recalls her other expressions of regret at leaving the Tiber city (1.50).

89. Line 1, in Florence. Line 6, these men of culture would have included such figures as Benedetto Varchi, Bronzino, and other members of the Accademia Fiorentina. Line 8, the distinction between "raccontare" (recount) and "scrivere" (write) suggests narrative vs. lyric activity. Those authors whose subject was love could include either past masters (Dante, Boccaccio, Petrarch) or contemporaries (e.g., il Lasca, Bronzino). Lines 10–14, in Rome she wrote happy verses, now her words weep. The adjective "diversi" could imply both the originality of her poetic inventions and their variety. Line 13, *mesto e turbato* (downcast and troubled): L. Alamanni, *Rime* 2.51.199.

90. 1.36. Lucrezia was the daughter of the poet Fiammetta Soderini (Guidi, *Il primo libro*, 53) Battiferra speaks affectionately of a Soderini woman in a letter to Varchi of December 30, 1556: "Be so kind as to review the sonnet to Soderina, whom I love as Dafni does Tirinto." She sends four poems to Lucrezia in the *Primo libro*, two that must predate her marriage and two for her wedding, which united two of Tuscany's most prominent families—the Piccolomini of Siena and the Soderini of Florence, one branch of which resided in Rome. The festivities, commemorated here, involved one of Rome's most remarkable gardens, built on the mausoleum of the emperor Augustus by Cardinal Francesco Soderini, who had purchased that monument on the banks of the Tiber in the aristocratic Campo Marzio neighborhood in 1549 and turned it into an outdoor museum for his collection of ancient sculpture. The circular garden, visited by contemporary travelers as a marvel, was eighty-nine meters in diameter with beds in two concentric zones surrounded on the inside of the circling wall by trees and statues (David R. Coffin, *Gardens and Gardening in Papal Rome* [Princeton: Princeton University Press, 1991], 66, fig. 50). The wedding poems for Lucrezia Soderini call attention to the union of Florence ("Arno") and Siena ("Arbia") under the rule of Cosimo, who fashioned himself as a new Augustus (Kurt W. Forster, "Metaphors of Rule: Political Ideology and History in the Portraits of Cosimo I de' Medici," *Mitteilungen des kunsthistorischen Institutes in Florenz* 15 (1971): 65–104; Janet Cox-Rearick, *Bronzino's Chapel of Eleonora in the Palazzo Vecchio* [Berkeley: University of California Press, 1993], 302–3). Since Francesco Soderini had helped Bartolomeo Ammannati in 1558 obtain overdue payment for a tomb he had begun for Francesco del Nero in Santa Maria sopra Minerva, the Florentine church in Rome (Charles Davis, "Ammannati, Michelangelo, and the Tomb of Francesco del Nero," *Burlington Magazine* 118.880 (July 1976): 472–84), this pair of wedding poems may constitute a gesture of thanks to the cardinal. Francesco's sister was Fiammetta Soderini, a friend of Battiferra's, as we know from the anecdote recorded by Lodovico Domenichi in one of his 1565 collection of witty sayings (see volume editor's introduction).

91. Line 1, Juno is the goddess of marriage. Line 5, Hymen, whose attribute is the nuptial torch, is also a tutelary deity of matrimony. Line 7, the mother of Love is

Venus. Lines 10–11, one of B. Tasso's funeral sonnets for Orazio Farnese (d. 1553) alludes to the mausoleum of Augustus, *Amori* 4.34.

92. 1.37. This sonnet must refer not to Ricciarda Malaspina (1497–1553), wife of the Marquis of Massa Lorenzo Cibo, but to the wife of Ricciarda's son Alberico, who inherited the marquisate in 1553, the year his mother died. This younger marquise of Massa was Elisabetta Della Rovere (1529–61), the ninth of eleven children born to Duke Guidobaldo I, hence a younger sister of Duke Guidobaldo II (app. C). Battiferra imagines her returning "another time" to her native place, where all the surroundings rejoice. Battiferra also wrote a sonnet on Elisabetta's death with wording that sparked a literary debate involving Bronzino and Varchi (see 4.6–7).

93. Line 1, Urbino is perched on a peak in the Appenine mountain range (see 1.8). The idea of nature entering a hyperbolic state to celebrate a political event earlier occurs in Bembo's sonnet on the birth of an heir to Duke Francesco Maria Della Rovere of Urbino in 1511 (the child did not survive), *Rime* 39, "Verdeggi a l'Appennin la fronte e 'l petto"; cf. also Raineri, *Cento sonetti* 59. Line 2, the third heaven belongs to Venus. Lines 3–4, Parnassus, sacred to poets, is the home of Apollo and the Muses. Cynthus is the mountain on Delos from which the goddess Diana takes her epithet Cynthia (Ovid, *Met.* 6.204). Lines 7–8, *Metauro:* Urbino's river, imagined personified as a male figure with a cornucopia (cf. 1.8, 1.9, et seq.). His Petrarchan bounty, "frondi e frutti," suggests fertile land around the river. Lines 9–11, Jove's tree is the oak, emblem of Urbino's ducal family, Della Rovere (1.7). If Battiferra is recalling her Dante, the sun would rise at Ganges and set at Gibraltar. In a post-Columbian era, it is not clear where she would envision the western limits. The idea, however, remains unchanged: the oak of Urbino should fill the whole world.

94. 1.38. Don García of Toledo (b. 1514), who became viceroy of Naples and Sicily, was a brother of the duchess Eleonora and the husband of Vittoria Colonna, a niece of the homonymous poet (app. D). Battiferra celebrates him as a military hero of the Siege of Malta, where on September 8, 1565, the forces of Phillip II, aided by Don García, won a clamorous victory over the superior Turkish enemy, blocked their advance toward Italy, and freed from a crushing siege the Knights of the Order of Saint John of Jerusalem. Criticized for waiting so long to send help, Phillip II afterward made García his scapegoat and removed him from command (Bryan Blouet, *A Short History of Malta* [New York: Frederick A. Praeger, 1967]; cf. 1.39). Battiferra's bombastic rhetoric blows García up into a huge invincible shield between the Christians and the Turks, as if he alone were responsible for protecting all Europe. Lively language describes the enemy, imagined with diabolical features that recall the rebel angels of *Par.* 3.38. Their sharp claws are typical of devils in popular imagination, as in Dante's Malebolge (*Inf.* 22.137) and church art of the Last Judgment. This and the sonnet following, to Chiappino Vitelli, were sent by Rinaldo Corso in a letter of October 19, 1565, to Timoteo Bottonio in Perugia. Since Corso was then in Rome in the service of Cardinal Girolamo da Correggio (son of the poet and ruler Veronica Gambara), Battiferra's sonnets on the Siege of Malta, broken by Christian forces on September 8, date from immediately after the battle and traveled rapidly from Florence. I thank Enrico Maria Guidi for information about the Perugia manuscript MS G 63, *Epistolario di Timoteo Bottoni.*

95. Line 2, *popol di Gesù divoto* (people devoted to Jesus): the formula adapts Petrarch's "popol di Marte" (people of Mars) from the political canzone, "Spirto gentil" (Noble

spirit); *RS* 53.26. Lines 5–8, the wandering and firm stars are the planets and signs of the zodiac, respectively (cf. 1.48), invoked in a figure of adynaton. Lines 9–14, *him* (*"quei"*): García. If now you win laurels of victory on earth, can we imagine how much greater your heavenly reward will be?

96. 1.39. This sonnet announces a monument to Vitelli (1.28–29) for his service at the Siege of Malta (Kirkham, "Creative Partners"). It will be a Hercules, a new colossus like those of antiquity and like the *Neptune* by Battiferra's husband Bartolomeo Ammannati ("Fidia"). Ammannati early established his reputation as a sculptor of colossi, beginning with his *Hercules* for the Paduan jurist Marco Mantua Benavides. His most famous is the *Fountain of Neptune,* first displayed for the entry into Florence in December 1565 of Giovanna of Austria, with an iconographic program that exalts Cosimo's navy. The duke's new galleys were outfitted and sent to sail with the fleet that saved the Knights of Malta in September 1565, a campaign in which Chiappino participated with Don García, hence the successive order of these poems in the *Rime.* Battiferra here defends her husband's *Neptune,* which people derisively labeled "il Biancone" (Big Whitey) and mocked in a jingle for its cramped standing pose: "Ammannato, Ammannato, / che bel marmo hai sciupato" (Ammannati, Ammannati, / what a fine marble you have spoiled!) In the playful poetic code language of Battiferra and her circle, Ammannati is always Fidia, a nickname that equates him with Phidias, the most famous sculptor of Greek antiquity. Since this sonnet postdates the *Neptune,* announced as already existing, perhaps Battiferra refers to a piece that was planned but never realized. A little more than a year after the Siege of Malta, Philip II asked Cosimo to release Chiappino for the Spanish wars in Flanders, where he died.

97. Line 1, *valor invitto* (valor invincible): cf. V. Colonna, *Amorose* 5.6; *Rime epistolari* 2.7, both in *Rime.* Lines 2–3, the Turk. Line 8, *nel ciel . . . prescritto* (forewritten in heaven): cf. Giovanni Della Casa, *Rime,* ed. Roberto Fedi [Milan: Biblioteca Universale Rizzoli, 2000], 46.73: "nel ciel forse è prescritto" (in heaven it is perhaps forewritten). Lines 9–11, Ammannati's *Neptune* in Piazza della Signoria. His "adversaries" are the winds, referring to the dramatic scene in *Aeneid* 1, where the god of the sea quiets the winds and saves Aeneas from drowning in the tempest. Line 13, Hercules, a descendent of Alceus. Cf., e.g., Ovid, *Heroides, Amores,* trans. Grant Showerman, rev. G. P. Goold (Cambridge, Mass.: Harvard University Press, 1977), *Heroides* 9.

98. 1.40. This Alessandro (d. 1606) is the son of Bernardetto, whose father was an old Medici loyalist, Ottaviano de' Medici. Bernardetto in 1559 married Giulia, natural daughter of the tyrant Alessandro de' Medici, murdered in 1534 and succeeded by Duke Cosimo I. Battiferra's poem must predate 1567, when Bernardetto transferred to Naples. Bernardetto's brother, the uncle and protector of this child, was another Alessandro de' Medici, a saintly man who became archbishop of Florence in 1574, and on April 1, 1605, at the age of seventy was elevated to the papacy as Leo XI, only to die after twenty-seven days. In form, the poem is a *canzonetta,* composed of seven- and eleven-syllable lines. Charming in its simplicity, the artistry reflects the taste of a period that in paintings loved scenes with clouds of Amorini.

99. Line 1, in heaven. Lines 2–3, *mensa . . . dispensa* (board . . . dispenses): the rhyme is Dante's, *Par.* 5.35–37. Cf. Tansillo, *Canzoniere* 5, Ode 1.69–70. Line 6, *mother:* Venus. Line 11, the tree sacred to Apollo is the laurel, as Ovid tells in *Met.* 1.452–

565. Line 12, Arno, as typically in Battiferra, appears personified as an ancient river god. Line 13, *palme . . . trofei* (palms . . . trophies): classical emblems of military victory. Cf. Raineri, *Cento sonetti* 2.6; Varchi, *Rime* 1.342.10. Lines 17–19, the laurel. *Felice ramuscel* (Happy branchlet): cf. Raineri, *Cento sonetti* 102a.5 (to Annibal Caro): "ramoscel felice." For the laurel as a symbol of Medici family renewal, see above, 1.2.12 and note.

100. 1.41. Battiferra pays tribute to the Christian army of King Philip II at Malta. Their victory is achieved with delaying tactics, which wear down the Infidel as hostilities continue into the short days of autumn, when the stormy east wind blows. Battiferra alludes to the delayed arrival of the imperial fleet at the Siege of Malta in September 1565, a tactical error that she attributes to clever planning (1.38). Her statement is an antiphonal to Bembo's sonnet on the Turkish advances in Europe, dedicated to Clement VII (*Rime* 110), which ends with the poet's hope that the "clement" pope will halt the enemy, "e direnti Clemente e forte e saggio" (and we shall call you Clement and strong and wise).

101. Line 6, *tarditate* (delay): the subtext here is Petrarch's *Triumph of Fame* in an early redaction (1a.35–36), where "tarditate" appears as a *hapax* with reference to the long-lived Roman hero Quintus Fabius Maximus, "the Temporizer," who used stalling tactics to defeat Hannibal at the Battle of the Metauro: "il vecchio ch'Aniballe / frenò con tarditate e con consiglio" (the old man who braked Hannibal with delay and with counsel). Line 11, *Eurus:* the cold, wintry east wind, opposite of Zephyr. It is one of the unleashed blasts that brings the tempest at the beginning of Virgil's epic (*Aen.* 1.85), a locus that Battiferra and her husband must have often discussed since it was the textual source for his *Neptune.* Line 13, cf. Bembo, *Rime* 109.14.

102. 1.42. The musician "Madonna Eufemia" "drew in her train all Rome, where she stayed for a long time" (Francesco Saverio Quadrio, *Della storia e della ragione d'ogni poesia,* 4 vols. [Bologna: Ferdinando Pisarri, 1739], 2: 2, 342). Battiferra, who must have heard Eufemia perform there, elegantly appropriates language of the *Dolce stil nuovo* to create an image of the angelic lady. Like Dante's Beatrice, Eufemia has come down from heaven, whose very spheres, not to mention all earthly life, cease in their movement to hear her. Graphic layout in the *Primo libro* capitalizes two centrally placed nouns, "Augelli" and "Angeli." The case shift and positioning of these words, one just below the other in a vertical coupling, focus the eye on wordplay pivotal in Battiferra's conceit of angels as birdlike creatures and a woman who sings like an angel.

103. Line 1, *coro eterno . . . eterne genti:* chiasmus that immediately connects Eufemia with the eternal. Lines 5–6, Petrarchan polysyndeton built on a trio of internal pairings. Eufemia is like Orpheus in her effects. Line 9, Sebeto (now called Maddalona) is the name of a stream in Naples, for which it functions as a synecdoche. Eufemia is the pride of Naples. Cf. Statius, *Silvae,* in *Silvae, Thebaid,* ed. J. H. Mozley, 2 vols. (Cambridge, Mass.: Harvard University Press, 1928; rpt. 1967), 1.2.263. Lines 9–10, *Sebeto . . . Tebro* (Sebeto . . . Tiber): for the coupling, cf. Raineri, *Cento sonetti* 121.8. Line 11, *dall'Indo al Mauro* (from the Indian to the Moorish Sea): the eastern and western limits of the world, respectively. *RS* 269.4: "dal mar Indo al Mauro." Line 12, *frutti . . . fiori* (fruit . . . flowers): Petrarchan binomial. Cf. nos. 12, 13, 44. Lines 12–14, the river god preens himself, displaying full regalia as it were, to show his pride in this lady who enriches the city.

104. 1.43. Giovan Battista Strozzi (1505–71), whose chosen form was the madrigal, created verse memorable for its charming landscapes. Although not published until after his death, this poetry circulated widely in manuscript and was highly admired, as is evident from Battiferra's letter to Varchi of December 11, 1557: "I couldn't resist sending you a madrigal by Messer Giovan Battista Strozzi, which makes all Florence marvel at its beauties, and lucky the man who praises it most, as you can see." Battiferra honors him by composing a pair of madrigals in his style. The *Rime* restore his name as dedicatee, suppressed in the 1560 edition because, even though Giovan Battista had made his peace with the Medici regime and resided in the splendid Florentine family palace, the powerful Strozzi clan under his kinsman Filippo's leadership had been bitter republican enemies of Cosimo, exiles tightly allied with the French in the war between Florence and Siena.

105. Lines 1–4, Minerva's plant is the olive. There are several places in Tuscany named Monte Oliveto. This madrigal may commemorate Battiferra's visit with her husband to the most famous of them, the great Benedictine Abbey of Monte Oliveto Maggiore south of Siena, decorated with major pictorial cycles by Signorelli and Sodoma. Line 7, *Olimpo ed Atlante* (Olympus and Atlas): see 1.33. Line 10, *Cinthia* (Cynthia): an epithet for Diana, from Mount Cynthus on Delos, where she was born. See Ovid, *Met.*, 2,465. *'ndimion:* Endymion, Diana's lover (in an unusual syncopated form to keep within the requisite number of syllables for this tightly packed hendecasyllable). Battiferra contemplates the moon over the mountain in a nocturnal scene.

106. 1.44. This sonnet, the first of two for Laodomia in the *Rime,* is probably connected with Ammannati's work for the jewel merchant, Orazio Ruccellai (1521–1605), a man so fabulously wealthy he gambled with the king of France. Ammannati, who became his friend, did work for him both in Rome (Palazzo Ruspoli, on the Corso, begun on 1556) and in Florence (the trapezoidal structure at the Canto Tornaquinci, where Via della Vigna Nuova and Via della Spada merge, ca. 1578). Baglione mentions the Roman house (Susan Butters, "Ammannati et la villa Médicis," 2: 257–316), which would have been virtually next door to the Battiferri residence at the Arco di Portogallo. "Laud-worthy" Laodomia, who could have been Orazio's daughter, bears out the medieval axiom "Names are the consequence of things" in Battiferra's word play. She has joined the "daughters of Jove," that is, the Muses, and become a poet under the tutelage of Apollo, setting an example for Battiferra's writing.

107. Line 1, cf. Guido Guinizelli, *Rime,* in *Poeti del dolce stil nuovo,* ed. M. Marti (Florence: Le Monnier, 1969), 12.1–2, in Quondam: "Gentil donzella, di pregio nomata, / degna di laude e di tutto onore" (Noble damsel, famous for merit, worthy of praise and all honor). Line 3, *figlie di Giove* (Jove's daughters): the Muses. The same formula appears in the proemial sonnet of Della Casa's *canzoniere, Rime* 1.12. If a Christian key is intended, the "virgin" Laodomia could be a nun. Line 6, cf. Cappello's sonnet to Della Casa, *Rime* 134, "Casa che 'n versi od in sermone sciolto / ne l'antico idioma e nel moderno / quei pareggiate" (Casa, who in verses or in unrhymed speech, in the antique idiom and in the modern, equal those). Line 8, Apollo, god of poetry. Perhaps Laodomia had sent Laura a poem. Line 10, *Eurotas:* a river of ancient Greece, in Laconia. Ovid refers to it (*Met.* 2.247 and 10.169), but context suggests that the reference Battiferra had in mind was Virgil, *Ecl.* 6.82–84: Phoebus once sang on the banks of Eurotas, who listened and bid the laurel trees to learn from him. Cf. also

Aeneid 1.498, with the reference to the virgin goddess Diana's haunts along the Eurotas. *Parnaso . . . Eurota:* coupled by Sannazzaro, *Arcadia* (in Quondam), chap. 10, 188. Line 13, a mountain in Thessaly and a seat of the Muses. Cf. Virgil, *Ecl.* 10.11. Raineri, *Cento sonetti* 102a, imagines that Caro has been crowned with laurel plucked on Mount Pindus or along the shores of Eurotas. Line 14, *man . . . stil:* cf. *RS* 78.2; Della Casa, *Rime* 1.1–2.

108. 1.45. This noblewoman who provides "food" for Christian thought is Caterina Cibo (1501–57), a granddaughter of Giovanni Battista Cibo (Pope Innocent VIII) through her father and of Lorenzo the Magnificent through her mother; a sister of Cardinal Innocenzo Cibo and by marriage the Duchess of Camerino (see 1.10; app. C). Said to have known Latin, Greek, and perhaps Hebrew, Caterina was the recipient of a spiritual sonnet from Varchi and Agnolo Firenzuola's *Ragionamenti d'amore* of 1525. She is one of the interlocutors in *Dialogi sette* of 1539 by the preacher Bernardino Ochino, whom she knew through Vittoria Colonna in a connection that hints at sympathies with the religious reformer Valdés (B. Feliciangeli, *Notizie e documenti sulla vita di Caterina Cibo-Varano Duchessa di Camerino* [Camerino: Tipografia Savini, 1891]; Franca Petrucci, "Caterina Cibo," *Dizionario biografico degli Italiani,* 25: 237–41). Battiferra, linked to her through her friend Leonora Cibo de' Vitelli, the niece whom Caterina is credited with educating, longs to join her "troop," which assembles under the loggia of a country villa to converse on sacred subjects that nourish the soul with "manna."

109. Line 1, Battiferra addressed Vincenzo Grotti, otherwise unidentified, with a sonnet of mourning when Caterina Cibo died (*Primo libro,* 92 [=95]). Guidi (*Il primo libro,* 71) suggests that he is the "gentleman" to whom she addresses a sonnet while he was visiting the Duchess of Camerino, mentioned in her letter to Varchi of December 12, 1556. Line 7, *sgombrare il cor de' van pensier gelati* (disencumbering my heart of vain frozen thoughts): *RS* 23.24; Muzzarelli, *Rime* 47.71 (to Bembo): "di gelati pensier gli ingombra il petto" (encumbers his heart with frozen thoughts). For the verb, see 4.7. Line 10, *onorata . . . schiera* (honored troop): cf. *Triumph of Fame* 2.159: "onorata schiera"; Della Casa, *Rime* 47.79: "onorata schiera." Line 13, *manna vera* (true manna): cf. *Par.* 12.84: "verace manna."

110. 1.46. The terrible Arno flood of September 13, 1557, destroyed Ponte Santa Trinita, damaged Ponte alla Carraia, and left much of Florence buried in tons of mud. Bartolomeo Ammannati, as the duke's engineer, designed a plan to clear the mess by moving the river's deposit into earthen bulwarks. He reconnected the city, divided by the loss of two central bridges, with repairs to Ponte alla Carraia that were begun on October 6, 1558, and completed on November 1, 1559. Battiferra's neatly constructed sonnet is at once praise for Ammannati's civic contribution and a plea for Nature to withhold the devastating forces that can send Father Arno over his banks. Addressing Arno, she wishes it "clear waters" in her first verse and sets up a double meaning that emerges in the final tercet, when the adjective "chiaro" returns, but now in the sense of "bright" or "renowned." Underlying the hortatory grammar are all the contrasting things the river has recently been: muddied, angry, storm driven, its banks black with slime.

111. Line 2, *le ninfe e i pastor* (nymphs and shepherds): Battiferra poeples the Arno with pastoral beings. Cf. Aragona, *Rime, Ecl.* 2.139 (by Girolamo Muzio). Line 3,

verdeggin . . . ambe le sponde (may both your shores green): Raineri, *Cento sonetti* 59.1–3: "Verdeggi . . . al felice Metauro ambe le sponde" (May both shores of the happy Metauro green). Line 5, The "honored bough" is the Petrarchan laurel. Line 6, *umido crine* (moist locks): Raineri, *Cento sonetti* 59.6: "umido crin." The adjective, which Petrarch had used, but with reference to the eyes, becomes standard in poetic descriptions of river gods. Cf. Aragona, *Rime* 64.10 (by Nicolò Martelli); B. Tasso, *Amori* 3.25.103. Line 7, *Acheloo:* the first watery body in Battiferra's catalog of six is appropriately Acheloüs. Ovid describes the terrible flooding caused by that river god in a myth that also explains how these deities came to be associated with the cornucopia (*Met.* 8.549–610 and 9.1–88). Lines 9–10, waters from the four corners of the globe—and even the father of waters, Oceanus—bow before the Arno and pay tribute to Ammannati: the Nile to the south in Egypt, the Ister (Danube) in northern Europe, the Indus in the east, and the Tyrrhenian in the west. Line 14, *Fidia:* Ammannati (see 1.29 and 1.39).

112. 1.47. Ammannati has fallen ill. Battiferra begs Apollo, god of medicine, to heal him, "who holds [her] better part." In letters to Varchi of December 14, 1556, and June 9, 1557, she refers to her husband's health problems. Other sources also mention his chronic eye trouble, perhaps a result of his lifelong work as a sculptor.

113. Line 1, Apollo, who loved the nymph Daphne (Ovid, *Met.* 1.452–567). Within that tale (1.521), he refers to himself as the god of medicine: "The art of medicine is my discovery." Line 4, Mount Cynthus is on the Greek island of Delos, where Apollo was born and had a cult. *Cinto e Delo:* cf. Raineri, *Cento sonetti* 57.1–2. Line 5, *mortal suo velo* (her mortal veil): in Petrarchan code, the body. To win the god's favor, Battiferra makes a wish that Daphne might return to life and love Apollo. Lines 9–10, Bembo, *Rime* 111.1–2: "Pon Febo mano a la tua nobil arte, / ai sughi, a l'erbe," (Put your hand, Phoebus, to your noble art, / to the potions, to the herbs), written for an illness of the lady he loved. Lines 12–13, Ammannati sculpted an Apollo for Sanazzaro's tomb (ca. 1538), another that stands in one of the niches on the *Triumphal Arch* he built for Marco Mantua Benavides in Padua (1546), and in Rome he made a fountain for Julius III with an Apollo (before 1555, now lost) from whose head water flowed into a granite basin (Luigi Biagi, "Di Bartolommeo Ammannati e di alcune sue opere," *L'Arte* 26 [1923]: 49–66).

114. 1.48. This is Battiferra's one effort in the very difficult form of the *sestina*. The form has an illustrious history in the Romance vernaculars. Its invention is attributed to the twelfth-century Provençal troubadour, Arnaut Daniel. Dante experimented with it brilliantly in his *Rime petrose* (Stony Rhymes), and Petrarch's several examples brought it to dazzling perfection. To display one's ability in this most difficult of set pieces was thus *de rigueur* for an ambitious Petrarchist. Battiferra's *sestina*, mediated by Bembo's virtuoso double *sestina* in the *Asolani* (1.24), repeats rhyme words used by both Dante and Petrarch. She reverses their precedent, however, by using the form not to describe a situation in which the poet is desperately out of tune with the universe, but rather to suggest a stormy journey on seas of love that ends safely, thanks to a higher protective light, seemingly divine in its origin. The *sestina* has six stanzas of six verses each with six different rhyme words, plus an envoy of three verses that repeat all six rhyme words. The rhyme words follow a rigid scheme of retrograde cruciform movment: ABCDEF, FABCDE, EFABCD, etc. That is, the last rhyme word of each stanza becomes the first of the following stanza.

115. Line 1, cf. V. Colonna, *Rime* 89.1–3: "Mentre la nave mia, lungi dal porto / priva del suo nocchier che vive in Cielo / fugge l'onde turbate in questo scoglio" (While my ship, far from port, deprived of its helmsman who lives in heaven, flees the turbulent waves on this shoal). Line 5, *travagliata nave* (troubled ship): cf. Bembo, *Rime rifiutate,* in *Rime,* 5.5. Line 24, *m'intrica* (be entangled): the verb is unusual, but it has antecedents in Petrarch. Cf. *RS* 139.3 and 360.49. Lines 25–27, a series of adynata, the topos of the world upside-down. Cf. *RS* 22.37–39; *sgombra dal mio petto il gelo* (disencumber my breast of the frost): for the verb, see 4.7. Lines 28–30, "my light" is the subject of "thoughts." Line 38, *vago cielo* (lovesome heaven): the third heaven, of Venus.

116. The next three lyrics form an autobiographical sequence that marks the difficult turning point between Battiferra's Roman and Florentine periods. Pope Julius III, for whom Ammannati had been working, died on March 23, 1555. When Duke Cosimo I de' Medici offered her husband patronage, Battiferra had no choice but to follow him to Florence. These poems are at once a farewell to the land of the Tiber and a prelude to Florence, the next chapter in her life and the focus of her Medici volume. Here Rome's seven hills bloom like an earthly paradise in perpetual spring thanks to the Tiber. As elsewhere in her *Primo libro* (1.14, 1.32), Battiferra uses the madrigal to signal a shift in subject matter. In this case, it initiates the sequence that describes her feelings about being forced to abandon Rome.

117. Line 9, *verde chioma* (green tresses): the trees on your banks. Cf. Bembo, *Canzoni degli Asolani* 15.87, with the same hortatory syntax, referred to a beech tree: "Così mai chioma verde / Non manchi a la tua pianta" (Thus let never your plant lack green tresses); Della Casa, *Rime* 63.5, speaks of a forest with "verde chioma ombrosa" (green shady tresses).

118. 1.50. Here for the first time in her *Primo libro* Battiferra speaks under her pastoral alias, Dafne. This development, significantly placed at the center of an autobiographical sequence, connects her to another Laura-Dafne who was Petrarch's elusive mistress, and before her, to Ovid's nymph Daphne who fled Apollo and was saved when her father, the river god Peneus, transformed her into a laurel. The modern-day Dafne sits dejected beside the Tiber, fearing a dire threat to her happiness. What it might be, she does not say, but context suggests a dreaded, even deathly severance from her beloved Rome.

119. Line 4, Apennine Urbino, Battiferra's native city. Compare her "sacro colle" of v. 4 with Bembo, *Rime* 22.1: "sacro monte, / ch'Italia tutta imperïoso parti" (sacred mount, who imperious divide all Italy). Cf. *RS* 146.13–14: "il bel paese / ch'Appennin parte e 'l mar circonda et l'Alpe" (the lovely country that the Apennines divide and the sea and the Alps surround). Line 3, *terrene membra* (earthly members): cf. *RS* 8.2. Line 11, the text reads "arra" (pledge), unattested in Petrarch and apparently a typographical error. Dante had used the adjective "atra" (black) to modify the word "death." See *Par.* 6.78: "la morte . . . subitana e atra" (sudden and black death). Cf. also Petrarch's famous double *sestina, RS* 332.66: "anzi che Morte / . . . a me fesse atre notti" (before Death made . . . for me black nights). Since it carries a connotation of blacker black than the Italian "nero," I have translated it as "inky black." Line 13, *dolorosa e mesta* (mournful and downcast): Cappello, *Rime* 407.190. Line 14, *giuste querele* (just complaints): *RS* 360.23.

120. 1.51. The next poem confirms the reason for Dafne's tears. Now the moment has come when she must leave Rome. By comparison, Florence looms as an uncivi-

lized, unenlightened place ("blind wilderness") and metaphorically the tomb that will receive her body. The poetess asks the spirits of the blest, whirling above in a vision reminiscent of Dante but calqued linguistically on Petrarch, to intercede on her behalf and keep her spirit alive in Rome. May my name be remembered, she wishes, there among you monuments who have survived through time, along with those of the great people ("treasures") who over the centuries have given Rome its glory.

121. Line 1, cf. Morra, *Rime* 7.1–4: "Ecco ch'una altra volta, o valle inferna / . . . / udrete il pianto e la mia doglia eterna"(Behold, another time, oh infernal valley, . . . you shall hear my weepings and my eternal sorrow). Lines 1–4, cf. *RS* 53.29–35: "L'antiche mura . . . e tutto quel ch' una ruina involve" (The ancient walls . . . and everything which this one ruin enfolds). Lines 5–8, cf. *RS* 53.43–44: "E se cosa di qua nel ciel si cura, / l'anime che lassù son cittadine" (And, if there is any care in Heaven for earthly things, the souls who are citizens up there). Line 10, *orrore:* in modern Italian the word "horror" has the same meaning as in English, but as a Petrarchan form it is associated with isolated, wild spots in nature. Cf. *RS* 176.12: "solitario orrore" (solitary chill); 276.3 "tenebroso orrore" (dark horror); Bembo, *Rime* 4.9: "fido orrore" (trusty retreat). Battiferra here contrasts Rome's ancient urban civilization with the wilds of the countryside around the Arno.

122. 1.52. Battiferra writes in gratitude to a "new Aesculapius" who has saved her life. Benvenuto Cellini recalls in his *Vita* how Luca Martini brought Francesco Montevarchi (Francesco Catani) to treat him medically in Florence after his supposed "death," and in his *Ercolano* Benedetto Varchi praises this prominent physician, who was also a great lover of art (cf. Giorgio Vasari, *Le vite dei più eccellenti pittori,* 4: 349). In a letter to Varchi of February 10, 1555 [=1556 modern style], Battiferra reports,

> Signora the Duchess of Camerino [Caterina Cibo] is still alive, a thing more miraculous and divine than human, and God knows how long she will last. Our Messer Francesco Monte Varchi is constantly there. If only God had wanted him to be called at the beginning, because perhaps her infirmity would have been so well understood that she would not be in such a dangerous state as she is.

As Laura's "earthly sun," Francesco is here likened to Phoebus-Apollo, the mythic god of medicine (cf. 1.47 and 1.61 to the physician Strada). This thank-you sonnet from a woman whose poetic name is Dafne, spins a variant on Petrarch's Apollo-Daphne motif.

123. Line 1, *Nuovo Esculapio* (New Aesculapius): Varchi uses the identical epithet in his sonnet to the same doctor, *Rime* 1.295.7. Line 10, *lei* (her): Death, who is afraid of Francesco's medications, as much as most people fear Death's "bites", that is, mortal illnesses. *l'erbe e i sughi* (herbs and potions): cf. Bembo, *Rime* 111.2.

124. 1.53. A favorite of the anthologists, this lovely pastoral sonnet represents the kind of poetry for which Battiferra is best remembered today. She and her husband had a country house in Maiano, to the northeast of Florence. From Maiano, which here makes its first appearance in her *canzoniere,* she wrote several of her surviving letters to Benedetto Varchi. Battiferra often expresses her love of that quiet retreat near the Mensola stream, canonized as a bucolic site by Boccaccio in his *Ninfale fiesolano.* This sonnet exploits the basic premise of pastoral life, that poor country pleasures are preferable to all the wealth any city can offer, but the sentiment is real. Writing Varchi from Florence on August 6, 1557, she looks forward to escaping the heat: "I'm

thinking once these dog days of summer ("dì di sol leone") are over to return to my Maiano, where in fact I feel better in body and also in mind than I do in Florence."

125. Line 1, *piagge apriche*: *RS* 303.6; *orrori*: see 51.10. Line 3, *soletaria villa* (solitary villa): Petrarch, *Triumph of Chastity* 169. Line 4, Battiferra seems to have had in mind Varchi's sonnet to the Mensola stream (with clear allusion to Boccaccio's *Ninfale fiesolano*) about his walks in the surrounding countryside, *Rime* 1.39.7: "lieto comparto i passi e l'ore" (happily I apportion my steps and hours). Lines 6–7, *sfavilla . . . squilla* (sparkles . . . peal): the same rhyme words, but with different sense, appear in Giovanni Della Casa, *Rime* 1; they reappear in 45.66–70, a context Battiferra clearly recalls: "al primo suon di squilla" (at the first sound of the bell peal). Line 7, *amorosa squilla*: the early morning church bells, perhaps at prime. Line 11, *Mensola*: a nearby stream that in Boccaccio's *Ninfale fiesolano* takes its name from the nymph Mensola, punished by Diana and turned into that rivulet.

126. 1.54. Here the poet addresses all the protagonists of her pastoral landscape as winter yields to spring—Monte Cecero, the Mensola river, and Maiano—each one festively animated because Benedetto Varchi delights in them. This could mean simply that he came to visit, or the occasion might be related to Battiferra's efforts to find a house in the Fiesolan hills. She speaks hopefully of one property in her letter to Varchi of December 11, 1557: "I believe you would be happy with it both for the beautiful view that it has and because it isn't either too near or too far from here. Before springtime, we shan't fail to arrange for a house in a place that we like." In his late years, Varchi lived at Fiesole in the Villa Topaia, made available to him by Duke Cosimo. The idea and syntax expand a sonnet by Varchi to the poet and playwright Lodovico Martelli (d. 1539), in which the writer imagines seeing verses carved on a rock over a stream at the base of the Alps, *Rime* 1.94.4–8: "Corri, gorgo felice, e lieto arriva / Con rene al mar più che l'usato bionde: / e sopra il frate tuo superbo, l'onde / Alza, poi ch'hai di te chi sì alto scriva" (Rush, happy whirlpool, and arrive blithely at the sea with sands blonder than your wont, and raise your waves over your haughty brother [Tiber], since you have one who writes of you so loftily.

127. Line 4, *smalto* (enamel): a word richly resonant in the tradition inherited from Dante (cf. the first of his *Rime petrose*, in Robert M. Durling and Ronald L. Martinez, *Time and the Crystal: Studies in Dante's* Rime petrose (Berkeley: University of California Press, 1990), "Io son venuto al punto de la rota" (I have come to the point on the wheel, *Rime* 43.59) and Petrarch (e.g., *RS* 23.25). Here it refers to the hard, frozen crust of the earth that now will thaw. Line 7, *sposo* (groom): Affrico, who loved Mensola but never won her as a wife in Boccaccio's *Ninfale fiesolano*, which tells how each was turned into the eponymous stream. Lines 12–13, cf. above, 1.46: "e spirin l'aure al corso tuo seconde" (and may favorable breezes blow your currents).

128. 1.55. Continuing the pastoral sequence in a madrigal, Battiferra addresses the landscape that inspires her to compose poetry. The "lofty shepherd" could be Varchi.

129. 1.56. Lines 8–9, *RS* 1.1.

130. 1.56. Calling on Apollo to descend with inspiration, Battiferra hopes for a long enough life to write many more poems about the comforting pastoral landscape she holds so dear—the very setting in which Cellini thinks of her when he writes to Varchi (2.24). This autobiographical poem has appealed to editors across the centuries.

131. Line 4, time. Lines 9–10, if death or destiny does not interfere with her work.

132. 1.57. In her new Tuscan setting, after moving from Rome, the lonely poet addresses her surroundings, a landscape that holds the same essential props as formed the backdrop for Petrarch's strolls far from human concourse. Like Petrarch, Battiferra yearns for a woman, revealed in the final tercet as Rome personified. A beautiful symmetry governs this sonnet in its movement through memory from the hills of Tuscany to those of Rome and Urbino, from outward sights to inward thoughts, from adulthood to childhood, from a difficult present to a sweeter past. This could be the sonnet she mentions with humorous self-irony as a Petrarchist in her letter to Varchi of June 9, 1557: "these mountains and these slopes, where I walk and often think, since there is no one else to whom I can say what I feel, if only they knew, perhaps they wouldn't stay as mute as they do."

133. Line, 1 *Alto monte, ima valle* (Tall mountain, sunken valley): cf. *RS* 145.10: "alto poggio . . . valle ima" (tall hill . . . sunken valley); B. Tasso, *Salmi* 2.34.34: "in alto poggio o 'n ima valle." The reference is to Mount Cecero, in the Fiesolan hills near the village of Maiano. Varchi, too, speaks affectionately of "Cecero" in his *Rime* 1.30.11, 1.32.1, 1.176.4, 1.444.4, and *Ecl.* 2.227. Lines 1–3, *RS* 303.5–6: "fior, frondi, erbe, ombre, antri, onde, aure soavi, / valli chiuse, alti colli, et piagge apriche" (flowers, leaves, grass, shadows, caves, waves, gentle breezes, closed valleys, high hills, and open slopes). Lines 3–4, the invulnerable, evergreen laurel, loved by the sun god Apollo first as Daphne, then as his tree. Julius Caesar and the god Janus refer, respectively, to the months of July and January. Cf. *RS* 41.6. Line 6, *RS* 145.8: "a la matura etate od a l'acerba" (in ripe age or raw). Line 10, *RS* 349.3: "così dentro et di for mi vo cangiando" (thus within and without I go changing). Line 12, cf. *RS* 53.106: "da tutti i sette colli" (from all seven hills). Lines 12–14, the "seven hills" refer to Rome; her native land is Apennine Urbino.

134. 1.58. Battiferra performs a variation on one of Della Casa's most famous sonnets, *Rime* 54: "O sonno, o de la queta, umida, ombrosa / notte placido figlio" (O sleep, placid son of the quiet, damp, shadowy night). Her fame as his follower wins recognition from Gherardo Spini and the publisher Filippo Giunti, who attached to their 1564 edition of the *Rime, et prose di M. Giovanni della Casa* a *rimario* prefaced by a dedicatory letter to Laura Battiferra. Addressing her, the publisher Giunti writes:

> Since I know your rare virtue—for not knowing it, truly in the guise of those who don't see the sun, I could call myself completely blind—I wanted to give the world further testimony of this knowledge of mine and the reverence I bring to your singular worth. But since I judge nothing of what is within my power worthy of coming before you, I have arranged, with the favor and means of your worthy and virtuous friends, to give you a certain gift that should please you and be deserving of your most excellent discernment. What it is, then, is a Rhyming Dictionary, drawn from the poems of Monsignor Della Casa, which all judicious intellects so praise and hold in esteem that they should be nothing if not most welcome to you, who in that profession are not only unique among the women of our age, but are held in esteem among the rare men.

Battiferra's homage to Della Casa actually resulted in a double variation on his theme. See 2.1, "O sonno, o de l'amena ombra fugace," this sonnet's twin—and a more elegant poem. Here she imitates Della Casa's characteristic features of periodicity (vv. 1–8) and enjambement (vv. 9–10).

135. Line 5, "heart" is understood. Lines 9–10, sleep dwells in a cave in the distant land of the Cimmerians (Ovid, *Met.* 11.592–615). Line 12, in Ovid's description, the river Lethe flows from the black depths of Sleep's cavern (*Met.* 11.603). Line 14, *archi e trofei* (arches and trophies): the binomial appears in B. Tasso, *Amori* 4.63.11: "sacra tutta Europa archi e trofei" (all Europa consecrates arches and trophies). Battiferra appropriates it more than once. Cf. 1.16: "statue, colossi, archi e trofei" (statues, colossi, arches, and trophies) with reference to triumphal arches for Duke Cosimo's entry into Siena.

136. 1.59. Luca Martini (d. 1561), a prominent figure and major patron of art in Cosimo's court, was the Medici administrator (*provveditore*) in Pisa from 1547 until his death. In his portrait by Bronzino, this highly cultured gentleman displays a map of the Pisan territory that he helped drain as the duke's hydraulic engineer (Jonathon Nelson, "Creative Patronage: Luca Martini and the Renaissance Portrait," *Mitteilungen des Kunsthistorischen Institutes in Florenz* 39.2/3 (1995): 282–305). A member of the Academia Fiorentina, he was an important Dante scholar, and he delighted his elite circle with jocose verse in the manner of Francesco Berni. Vasari (*Le vite dei più eccellenti pittori, scultori e architetti,* 3: 728 and 4: 680) reports on sculpture he commissioned from Pierino da Vinci and Stoldo di Lorenzo that he gave to the duchess Eleonora; she sent the pieces to her brother Don García de Toledo, who in turn shipped them to Naples for the garden of his villa at Chiaia. Battiferra's flattery of Martini here, as in her "Third Eclogue" (1.120), was probably a bid for patronage for Ammannati. In the *Primo libro,* this somewhat awkward sonnet was a late addition (Kirkham, "Laura Battiferra's 'First Book' of Poetry"). Battiferra invites Martini to leave Pisa and return to Florence, which has long awaited him, adapting a formula developed by Bembo (*Rime* 21) and ultimately descended from Petrarch (*RS* 10).

137. Line 1, *sol:* Duke Cosimo de' Medici. Line 10, *Flora:* Florence. Line 14, *Arbia . . . Arno:* for the pairing, see above, 1.17. Arbia is a river of Siena, hence by metonymy Siena itself, recently conquered by Cosimo.

138. 1.60. Luigi Alamanni (1495–1556) was a Florentine Republican who spent much of his life in political exile, serving the French kings François I and Henri II. During an Italian trip of 1539 in the entourage of Cardinal d'Este, he was in contact with such *literati* as Benedetto Varchi, Pietro Bembo, and Vittoria Colonna. Of his abundant production as poet and translator, Battiferra might have especially admired his *Opere toscane,* first published at Lyon in 1522–33 and several times reprinted in France and Italy; his *Elegie,* which included a volume of spiritual verse; and his *Salmi penitentiali.* He was one of the first to write in *versi sciolti* (free verse), which she adopted as the meter of her own *Salmi penitentiali.* She seems also to have been familiar with his verse treatise on agriculture, *Della coltivazione,* in the tradition of Virgil's *Georgics* with practical advice in farm management. Here Battiferra addresses Alamanni after his death to praise him for his famous poetry, to say what comfort he must take in his two sons, and to acknowledge him as a writer from whom she takes inspiration. The sonnet, which reverses expectations by not consoling the aggrieved sons but rather congratulating the dead father for his surviving children, would have been inappropriate for the *Primo libro* because of Alamanni's anti-Medicean politics, but it finds a place in the poet's late *Rime.*

139. Line 1, *Arbor gentil* (Noble tree): cf. *RS* 60.1; Malipiero, *Petrarca spirtuale* 46.1: "Arbor gentil, che forte amai molt'anni" (Noble tree, that I strongly loved many years).

Alamanni, a poet, is metaphorically the Petrarchan laurel. For the deceased as a great tree in contrast to her own dessicated trunk, see Battiferra's sonnets on the death of her father (2.8) and Luca Martini (2.3). Line 3, *Cinthia e Flora,* ladies for whom Alamanni wrote poetry. The lady he called "Cinthia" appears in his verse of 1524; he sings of "Flora" (Chiara Ferini) before his first exile from Florence in 1522. In a topographical sense, Flora is Florence, while Cinthia refers to France. Lines 5–6, *mondo . . . mendico* (world . . . barren): cf. L. Alamanni, *Rime* 1.148.11; Della Casa, *Rime* 58.1–3. Line 7, *ciel più bello* (fairest heaven): the Empyrean, home of the blest. Line 9, probably Alamanni's sons Battista and Niccolò by his first wife, Alessandra Serristori.

140. 1.61. Battiferra offers a sequence of three poems to Strada in her *Rime.* The first, a sonnet, puns on his surname ("street") by describing him as a road to long life; the third, in the form of a *canzonetta,* announces that Laura will no longer pray to Apollo, god of medicine, but will now praise a "new sun" on earth, who wants her to follow another "strada" and write about him—the suggestion being that he would rather be paid in poetry than in money. The second is this clever madrigal, a single sentence with the rapid movement of a fugue, in which Battiferra mixes Ovid and Petrarch to thank the doctor as a grateful patient. She called out weakly from her sickbed for Apollo, the god of medicine, who did not respond because he was angered that another shepherdess should have the same name as his beloved. Then her prayers for help were answered another "way" ("Strada"). This is the second doctor she thanks in her poetry (cf. 1.52 to Francesco Montevarchi).

141. Lines 5–6, Daphne (Laura Battiferra). The river god Peneus was the father of the nymph Daphne, who fled Apollo along his banks and was changed by him into a laurel (Ovid, *Met.* 1.452–565).

142. 1.62. Contacts between the Ammannati and the Jesuits had begun at least as early as 1572, when they offered assistance for the Jesuit *collegio* and church in Florence, San Giovannino. A letter from Claudio Acquaviva (1543–1615) to Ammannati of July 28, 1581, makes it possible to date this sonnet, written to congratulate the prelate on his election as the fifth General of the Society of Jesus on February 19 of that year. In closing, Acquaviva writes:

> I desire that Your Lordship greet on my behalf Madonna Laura, your consort, from whom insofar as I had in the past few days a fine sonnet in witness of her devotion toward the Society, I trust she will lend me all those spiritual aids that can make me the worthy soldier of Christ she wishes me to be in her sonnet (ASF, Comp. Soppr. da Pietro Leopoldo, filza 239, fols. 2r–2v).

Inflamed by the same zeal that motivates these teaching fathers, Battiferra sees them as a wise militia, who under the command of their "general" cover the entire earth to combat the world, the flesh, and the devil and to bring all peoples into the papal sheepfold. The Petrarchist technique of punning on proper names here appropriates Gospel language to make Acquaviva a Christological "fountain of living waters." Many sonnets inspired by the Jesuits will follow in Battiferra's *Rime* (cf. 1, pt. 2.8). Appropriately, the first to mention the Order is her tribute to its General.

143. Line 3, the world, the flesh, and the devil. Line 6, *Indo . . . Mauro: RS* 269.4: "dal mar Indo al Mauro" (from the Indian to the Moorish sea). A set formula (cf. 1.42) to indicate the eastern and western limits of the world respectively. Line 7–8, the pope,

in 1581, Gregory XIII; *ambe le porte* (both the gates): the pope's two gates must be the portals to hell and heaven, damnation or salvation. The formula recalls Dante's "ambo le chiavi" (*Inf.* 13.58). Cf. *Inf.* 27.104 and poem 1.119 below. Lines 9–11, in the Gospel of John, Christ slakes spiritual thirst with living waters. Cf. John 4:14: "acqua, quam ego dabo ei, fiet in eo fons acque salientis in vitam aeternam" (the water that I will give him shall become in him a fountain of water, springing up unto life everlasting). Line 10, *acqua viva* (living water): cf. V. Colonna's sonnet to Bembo, *Rime spirituali* 137.1. Line 14, *infiammarei* (I would inflame): cf. V. Colonna, *Rime amorose disperse* 19.11; Matraini, *Rime e lettere* A 79.53.

144. 1.63. This poem, together with a sonnet by Varchi, heads Don Pietro (Piero) Calzolari's *Historia monastica* of 1561, a five-day dialogue among pious men and women who gather like the storytellers in Boccaccio's *Decameron* and the conversationalists in Castiglione's *Book of the Courtier.* Their purpose is to recall "popes, preachers, emperors, kings, dukes, princes, and counts, empresses and queens, and other illustrious and holy women, learned men . . . and saints." Five sonnets in her *Rime* connect Battiferra to Razzi, honored as one of the men whose sonnets introduce the volume (1.II). He appears three times in the *Primo libro* as Girolamo Razzi; this poem celebrates his decision to become a monk and addresses him by his new religious name, Silvano.

145. Lines 3–4, *mondana . . . schiera* (worldly troop): cf. *Inf.* 105, where Beatrice comes to the aid of Dante, who because of her left "the vulgar troop" ("uscì per te de la volgare schiera"). Lines 5–8, Battiferra refers to Calzolari and his new book of religious history. Lines 10–12, Saint Benedict of Nursia (5th c.), founder of the Benedictine order. Benedetto in Italian means literally "blessed." All Benedictines should join Battiferra and Don Silvano in praising Piero, who was a Benedictine in the Florentine Badia.

146. 1.64. Writing in pastoral code, Battiferra sends "Damon" (Varchi) a poem to accompany wine she has casked for him and an apple from her orchard. Although gift giving is a classic motif of bucolic poetry (Victoria Kirkham, "Cosimo and Eleonora in Shepherdland," 149–75), her sonnet may convey real offerings and an invitation to "come down" for a poetic conversation to Maiano from Fiesole. Varchi, for his part, also sent gifts to her. See, for example, Battiferra's letter to him of November 9, 1557: "I had from Messer Girolamo Razzi the apples and chestnuts that Your Lordship sent to me, which were dear and sweet to me, and I thank you for them."

147. Line 1, Bacchus was the god of wine. Line 3, *da te poco lontano*: they were neighbors in their country dwellings, in Fiesole and Maiano. Line 5, *Etruria*: see 1.16.2 and note. Lines 7–8, Varchi's poetry has the same civilizing effect as that of Orpheus. Line 10, cf. *Inf.* 34.108: "vermo reo" (referred to Lucifer). Line 13, "The garland" could be a new poem that Battiferra has "woven" in her rustic setting.

148. 1.65. Linked scandalously for fifteen years with Francesco de' Medici, who is said to have murdered her husband, the Venetian Bianca Capello became the grand duke's wife immediately following the death on April 11, 1578, of Giovanna d'Austria, his first consort (see 1.104–105). The lovers were married privately that June and again in a public ceremony with official festivities on October 12, 1579. Battiferra's sonnet, the first of a trio composed to trumpet Bianca's "thousand and thousand virtues" (no. 113 in the *Rime*), doubtless celebrates the latter occasion, when

Giovanna was crowned grand duchess. Although the poet here pretends that Bianca had before kept herself hidden ("se stessa palesar già non voleva") and only now reveals her true splendor, the fact is that Bianca interacted quite publicly with the court and was a subject of malicious gossip throughout Europe (G. De Caro, "Bianca Capello," *Dizionario biografico degli Italiani,* [Rome: Istituto dell'Enciclopedia Italiana, 1960–], 10: 15–16). This is not Battiferra at her best, either on moral or esthetic grounds, but if she bows so deeply, it must have been to remain in the good graces of the court in the interest of continuing patronage.

149. 1.66. Annibal Caro (1507–66) was Battiferra's chief literary advisor in Rome and a friend of her Florentine mentor, Benedetto Varchi. From 1548 to 1563, he served as secretary to Cardinal Alessandro Farnese, the powerful grandson of Paul III (Clare Robertson, *Il gran cardinale: Alessandro Farnese, Patron of the Arts* [New Haven: Yale University Press, 1992]). Translator of the *Aeneid* and author of comic plays, Caro published in 1558 a satirical *Apologia* against Lodovico Castelvetro in the Petrarchist debate on literary imitation. Today he is best remembered for his collected letters, addressed to a vast network of personages, including five to Battiferra. Although nothing of their correspondence survives from Battiferra's side, his humorous reply in 1552 to a request that he review one of her sonnets gives a sense of their affectionate relationship:

> As for the sonnet, aside from my praise, there is nothing to reproach about it. Nevertheless, your Master [Caro], figuring he's good for exercising his prerogative with you, has decided to bend it a bit in a few places. Take your revenge on his response, which is such that it would have been ashamed to come before you if it weren't a greater shame not to respond. Or else, maybe it can be excused because in these times and with the shouting that goes on, it couldn't get the Muses either very friendly or very relaxed. If your Muses in all that quiet, under your native sky [Urbino], dictate to you anything else, I pray you share it with me, though I would rather hear them sing close by (Annibal Caro, *Lettere,* ed. Aulo Greco, 3 vols. [Florence: Le Monnier, 1957–61], 2: 119–20).

Battiferra's sonnet to Caro and his response are probably these poems in her *Primo libro,* which initiate her exchanges with male correspondents, all to be reprinted in the *Rime.* She addresses him with mythological allusions neatly suited to a classicist—Lethe, Phoebus, Phaethon, and Icarus. She couples the last two, much as Dante had connected them in *Inf.* 17.105–11, where he describes his terror during the descent to lower Hell on the back of the monster Geryon. In the *Comedy,* they are emblems of pride, the sin at the root of trespass, which literally means "to go beyond a limit." It implies presumption, also the idea in Battiferra's poem, but in an esthetic rather than a moral sense.

150. Line 1, *Caro:* Battiferra puns on Annibal's last name and the Italian word for "dear" (caro); *basso stile* (lowly style): cf. *RS* 332.24: "alto soggetto a le mie basse rime" (high subject of my low rhymes); Matraini, *Rime e lettere* B 5.6–7: "parlar di cosa tanto alta e gentile / in così basso stile" (speak of a thing so lofty and noble / in such lowly style); B. Tasso, *Amori* 5.41.2 (to the Duchess of Urbino): "Forse, Donna reale, avete a sdegno / Che di voi canti basso stile o scriva" (Perhaps, royal lady, you disdain / a lowly style that sings or writes of you). Line 4, Lethe is the river of oblivion. Cf. Virgil, *Aen.* 6.705–15; Dante, *Purg.* 26.108 and 33.94–99. Cf. 1.58. Line 6, Phoebus

Apollo, the god of poetry. Line 9, *figlio di Apollo* (Apollo's son): Phaethon, who in his hubris lost control of the chariot of the sun and was cast down by Jupiter into the Po River. See Ovid, *Met.* 2: 1–328. Line 10, *Icaro:* the inventor Daedalus fashioned wings of feathers and wax for himself and his son, Icarus. Heedless of his father's warnings, the boy flew too near the sun, which melted the wax and caused Icarus to fall to his death in the sea. See Ovid, *Met.* 8.183–235. Lines 9–10, (*Fetonte*) . . . *Icaro:* cf. Stampa, *Rime* 1.166.12; Matraini, *Rime e lettere* A 21.13.

151. 1.67. Caro replies, punning on Laura's name as the laurel tree and his own as "dear." The capitalization pattern, in chiastic symmetry, links typographically the two partners in this sonnet exchange. Dionigi Atanagi, curiously, excludes from his anthology of Tuscan lyrics the sonnet by Battiferra that Caro's answers. In the index, under "Annibal Caro," Atanagi notes, "He answers a sonnet by Madonna Laura Battiferro of Urbino, whom he praises highly for her intelligence and her ability in Tuscan poetry, as truly this new Sappho of our times deserves." Atanagi's important anthology generally pays slight notice to women. Only three are represented: Veronica Gambara (nine poems), Giulia Cavalcanti, and Giulia Premarini.

152. Line 1, *Clio:* the Muse of history. Ovid claimed he did not have the benefit of "Clio and her sisters" when he wrote *The Art of Love* (1.27). Lines 5–6, if ever a laurel crown sit upon my hair. Line 8, in Ovid's account, Apollo was unable to catch Daphne as she fled.

153. 1.68. The teenage poet and musical prodigy Silvio Antoniano (1540–1603), early patronized by Annibal Caro in Rome and then by Duke Ercole II d'Este at the court of Ferrara, visited Florence around 1556. On that occasion, which seems to be the subject of this sonnet, Varchi called the amazing young man "a phenomenon and miracle of nature" (Paolo Prodi, "Silvio Antoniano," *Dizionario biografico degli Italiani,* 3: 511–15). Antoniano subsequently returned to Rome, where he was active in the Academy of the Vatican Nights and became vice-rector of the new La Sapienza University. Eventually, he donned the habit of a monk, wrote a still-remembered book on the Christian education of children, and rose to a cardinalate. Caro and Varchi, friends from the 1530s, are linked in the embedded capitals of this poem, which creates a sense of the literary community Cosimo fostered.

154. Line 1, *Caro:* see above, 1.66.1; *verga:* in the sense of secondary branch or offshoot of a tree, a fitting reference to a young man still in his teens. Line 4, Ferrara lies on the Po River. Line 9, Cosimo, who cultivated an image of himself as Caesar Augustus. Line 11, the new Virgil Maro is Silvio Antoniano, who composed elegantly in Latin. Lines 12–14, the duke takes pleasure in watching the men he patronizes, the "new Maro" and Varchi. Varchi must have been at work writing his history of Florence, commissioned by Cosimo (see above, Vettori's prefatory letter, n. 6). Line 14, the lofty deeds are Cosimo's.

155. 1.69. Battiferra again recalls Icarus (cf. 1.66) to express her own feelings of artistic inadequacy before the older, more masterful poet, a guiding sun in her life. Nevertheless, her art contradicts her modesty. With this, the first poem of her *Primo libro* directly addressed to Varchi, she echoes the sonnets sent him by Bembo (no. 131) and Della Casa (no. 53), connecting herself in a memory chain to distinguished male antedecents: Bembo > Della Casa > Varchi > Battiferra.

156. Line 1 *Varchi:* the poet puns on the name of her addressee, playing on the noun "pass," "opening," "passage" (varco, pl. varchi). Line 2, the poet as swan is a topos. Cf. 1.16.12. Line 4, Apollo, the sun. Line 7, *presenti . . . passate: RS* 272.3: "et le cose presenti et le passate" (and present and past things). Line 11, *augel palustre* (swamp bird): the lowliest of poets. Petrarch used the word *palustre* once to describe marshy lowlands in *RS* 145.10: "in ima valle et palustre" (in a deep and swampy valley). For the combination "swamp bird" see Della Casa's sonnet to Varchi on the death of the "swan" Bembo, *Rime* 53.1–5: "Varchi, Ippocrene il nobil cigno alberga / . . . / Ma io palustre augel" (Varchi, Hippocrene shelters the noble swan . . . but I, a swamp bird).

157. 1.70. Pietro Bonaventura of Urbino (d. 1565) belonged to an old and honorable family unswervingly loyal to the Della Rovere dukes. In 1554 he was a rector of Urbino's charity hospital, Santa Maria della Misericordia, and he was elected as *gonfaloniere* of the city in 1558. In February 1562, he joined a group of young men from Urbino who accepted a challenge from their cohorts in Pesaro to compose and stage a comedy for the duke (Raffaella Michelangeli, *I Bonaventura: Una famiglia del patriziato urbinate* [Urbino: Arti Grafiche Stibu, 1999], 34–35). In the summer of 1565 he assisted Guidobaldo in finding employment for a young organist (Piperno, *L'immagine del duca,* 90), and in the fall of that year he commanded three hundred infantry representing the duke at the siege of Malta (Cirni, *Comentarii d'Antonfrancesco Cirni corso, ne quali si descrive la guerra ultima di Francia, la celebratione del Concilio Tridentino, il soccorso d'Orano, l'impresa del Pignone, e l'Historia dell'assedio di Malta diligentissimamente raccolta insieme con altre cose notabili* [Rome: Giulio Accolto, 1567], 104v), where he received a fatal injury. Battiferra's sonnet to him recognizes his political allegiance and his participation in the literary life of Urbino. Bernardo Tasso, whom he befriended, dedicated to him in gratitude his discourse on poetry. Caro, too, was in his network and advised him on his response to this poem (1.71).

158. Line 1, Claudius Nero Gaius was a Roman general who defeated Hasdrubal at the Battle of the Metauro in 207 B.C.E. Cf. *Triumph of Fame* 1.6–8: "di Claudio dico, che notturno e piano, / come il Metauro vide, a purgar venne / di ria semenza il buon campo romano" (of Claudius I speak, who nocturnal and softly, when he saw the Metauro, came to purge the good Roman field of evil seed). Line 3, *Apollo e Marte:* Bonaventura is favored both by the god of poetry and the god of war. Lines 12–14, cf. 1.13, where the Tiber speaks in similar fashion of Virginia Della Rovere. Line 14, *invitto:* the epithet assimilates Pietro to Caesar "invictus."

159. 1.71. Bonaventura sought advice for his response to Battiferra's sonnet from Annibal Caro, and the latter wrote to him in Urbino from Firmignano (near Pesaro) on August 16, 1559: "Finally, give your own [sonnet] to Madonna Laura, for it can stand perfectly well, and she herself will help you ascend that mountain" (Caro, *Lettere,* no. 567). Battiferra, who often depicts herself as far the lesser poet in her sonnet exchanges with male contemporaries, here in a reversal is the stronger of the two, as it becomes Pietro's turn to compose flattering verse and ask her to help him climb Mount Parnassus. She has already arrived.

160. Lines 1–2, the Hippocrene spring on Mount Parnassus. Line 10, Lethe is the river of oblivion. Cf. 1.58, 1.66, 2.1. Line 14, *per segno . . . per duce* (as sign or guide): cf. Sannazzaro, *Sonetti e canzoni* 83.52.

161. 1.72. After the first verse of this sonnet there follows a note to the printer in the Casanatense manuscript: "Qui seguitasi nel libro stampato da questo numero di sonetti 131, fino al 200 a carta 93" (Here follow in the printed book from this sonnet numbered 131 up to 200, on p. 93). In other words, the printer was to reproduce unchanged all the remaining sonnet exchanges between Battiferra and her male correspondents from the *Primo libro* (represented here below by nos. 72–93 inclusive).

162. Of the Venetian patriciate, the churchman Gabriello Fiamma (d. 1585) held appointments as a canon regular in the Lateran, abbot of the Carità in Venice, and from 1584, Bishop of Chioggia. Famous in his day, he was said to be a Demosthenes in eloquence, an Aristotle in philosophy, and an Ambrose in theology. He distinguished himself as a Petrarchist by converting that lyric tradition to the service of piety. In addition to sermons and other sacred writings, he published his *Rime spirituali* framed by a rich commentary of his own devising (1570, 1575). Its preface deplores mothers and fathers who put Petrarch into the hands of their children, because while he can teach adults Platonic love, young people reading him learn lascivious love. Varchi addressed one of his spiritual sonnets to Fiamma, and Battiferra highlights him with three exchanges in the *Primo libro.* She puns on his name, as he himself did from the opening sonnet of his book with a gloss that explains how the Old Testament Hebrew priests every morning rekindled the temple altar fire, a foreshadowing of the New Testament love of God, which burns in our hearts, the fire "Fiamma" wants to nourish with his verse.

163. Line 1, *Fiamma del ciel* (Flame of heaven): the formula reverses Petrarch's curse on the whore of Avignon (the Papacy) in *RS* 136.1: "Fiamma dal ciel su le tue treccie piova" (May fire from heaven rain down on your tresses). Perhaps she suggests that Fiamma's fiery sermons "rain down" a purifying influence on earth. Battiferra's sonnet is closely related to Strozzi, *Madrigali inediti* 41.1, also dedicated to Gabriello Fiamma and probably her source, "Fiamma in terra del ciel, quasi un ardente / fulmine" (Flame on earth of heaven, almost a burning lightning bolt). V. Colonna, *Rime spirituali* in *Rime,* 109.2, uses the same formula "fiamma del ciel" of the Virgin. Line 2, *quality:* the word is used in its scientific sense from the Aristotelian and Scholastic tradition, meaning the nature of a thing, its essence. Lines 10–11, Battiferra praises Fiamma as an eloquent preacher. For *tromba di Dio* (trumpet of God), cf. Morra, *Rime,* "tromba celeste" (celestial trumpet), 13.45.

164. 1.73. Fiamma responds in a lyric tour de force, with identical rhyme words in a sonnet structured on clever Petrarchan antithesis and mannerist word play.

165. 1.74. Born in Urbino around 1510, the soldier and poet Antonio Gallo (Galli) was much favored by Duke Guidobaldo, who sent him on diplomatic missions and entrusted him with the education of his son, Francesco Maria II (together with whom the young Torquato Tasso sat for instruction). Battiferra could have met Gallo either in her native city or in Rome, when he served as an emissary from the court of Urbino to Pope Julius III. Perhaps she knew his translations of the Psalms, preserved in a manuscript at the Vatican. His unseasonable death in 1561 deprived Urbino of a gentleman fondly remembered for eloquence, philosophical learning, and exquisite courtesy. Whether because he died so young or for reasons of modesty, little he wrote made its way into print, but contemporaries, including Ariosto, Bernardo

Tasso, Varchi, Aretino, and Caro, praised him for Italian as well as Latin verse; he was involved in comic play production at Guidobaldo's court (Piperno, *L'immagine del duca*), and he is credited with inventing the pastoral fable some years before Torquato Tasso's *Aminta.* Gallo and his friends seem to have been influential in Battiferra's invitation to join the Accademia degli Intronati (Guido Zaccagnini, "Lirici urbinati del secolo XVI"). Both his daughter Vittoria and his son Federigo were also poets (Filippo Ugolini, *Storia dei conti e duchi d'Urbino* [Florence: Grazzini e Giannini, 1859], 2: 343; Filippo Vecchietti, *Biblioteca Picena o sia Notizie istoriche delle opere e degli scrittori piceni,* 5 vols. [Osimo: Domenicantonio Quercetti, 1790–96], 4: 260–63). The latter, who fought at the Battle of Malta beside Pietro Bonaventura, was a founding member of Urbino's *Accademia degli Assorditi,* to which Battiferra is said to have belonged. She must have had a special affection for this older compatriot, whom she honors with three sonnet exchanges in the *Primo libro.* His poems to her, of high literary quality, begin with a sonnet that praises her as the "prize and honor" of Parnassus. He must follow her at a distance, gathering the "lilies and flowers" that spring in her footsteps—that is, reading her poems. The following two sonnets close their six-part correspondence.

166. Line 1, "L'aura" blows breezes of inspiration; her inspiration is her poetry. Line 8, the gods defeated the giants, who had tried to scale Olympus, by hurling thunderbolts at them on the plain of Phlegra (Ovid, *Met.* 10.151). Line 9, *Eolo:* Aeolus rules the winds, which he can contain or unleash. Cf. Virgil, *Aen.* 1.52–54. Line 10, Pyrrha and her husband Deucalion were the only two humans to survive a primordial flood that devastated the world (Ovid, *Met.* 1.283–355). *Proteo:* a sea god charged in Homer's *Odyssey* (4.365, 4.385) with herding Poseidon's marine flock (Guidi, *Il primo libro*). The source with a watery context that Gallo and Battiferra had in mind, however, is probably Virgil's account of Proteus in the *Georgics* (4.387–452).

167. 1.75. Gallo is an inspiring model for Battiferra. She laments their separation, which has left her soul in a torpor with no one to rouse and guide it. Dante's episodes of Casella and Belacqua (*Purg.* 2; 4) hover in the background of the language here.

168. Lines 1–2, Gallo's inspiration carries him up into the heavenly spheres of light. Line 4, *pigro sonno* (lazy slumber): *RS* 53.15. Line 5, *la mia* (mine): my soul. Lines 12–14, Battiferra hopes she is not unworthy of continuing to exchange poetry with Gallo (to hear his "song"). The object of "raise" is "unworthiness."

169. 1.76. Bronzino (Agnolo di Cosimo di Mariano, 1503–1572), was the greatest painter-poet of the Italian Renaissance after Michelangelo. A brilliant mannerist, he produced many portraits of the Medici and private individuals, including a stunning profile image of Battiferra that today hangs in Florence at the Palazzo Vecchio (Kirkham, "Dante's Fantom, Petrarch's Specter"). Together with Varchi, Luca Martini, and Pontormo, he was a supporter of the Catholic Reform movement, in sympathy with Valdesian ideas. (Guidi, *Il primo libro,* 108). In addition to racy burlesque verse, he compiled a major anthology of Petrarchan lyrics. Polyvocal in the style that had become fashionable, like Battiferra's *Primo libro,* its participants are his circle of friends, such men as Varchi, il Lasca, Caro, Cellini—and one woman, Battiferra herself (Deborah Parker, *Bronzino: Renaissance Painter as Poet*). Here, in the first of four sonnet exchanges with Bronzino that Battiferra published in her *Primo libro,* he sorely mourns the death of Pontormo (1494–1557), the master teacher whom he had loved as a father (Elizabeth Pilliod, *Pontormo, Bronzino, Allori: A Genealogy of Florentine Art* [New Ha-

ven: Yale University Press, 2001]). Bronzino and Battiferra had other exchanges about the death of Luca Martini, the death of her father, and the portrait he painted of her (2.2–3, 2.9, 2.27–28).

170. Lines 3–4, Pontormo has died. Lines 4–8, Laura is imagined as a gentle breeze ("aura"); the light ("ray") from her eyes ("living gems" in the Petrarchan code) makes him open his eyes. Lines 9–14, the wording is obscure but the sense is that her powers are not sufficient to overcome the sorrow to which destiny has condemned him.

171. 1.77. Battiferra responds "per rime," connecting her first verse to his last through repetition of the Petrarchan kernel "fermo destino."

172. Lines 1–4, Bronzino's soul weeps for Pontormo's, although the latter is happily in heaven and sorry only that Bronzino grieves. *RS* 362.12: "Egli è ben fermo il tuo destino" (Your destiny is certain). Cellini reprises the formula in his sonnet on the death of Luca Martini (1561), *Poesie* 89.5: "Ora non sapete ch'è fermo il destino" (Now do you not know that it is certain destiny). Lines 3–4, Pontormo's soul. Line 11, the one who can show Bronzino how to stand apart from the mob is probably Varchi. Line 13, *alta chiostra* (lofty cloister): Varchi, *Rime,* 3.143.4

173. 1.78. In the fluvial code favored by Battiferra, Razzi (1.II) announces that now the Arno has a new source of pride. Beyond his friend Varchi, on whose name he puns with reference to the verb *varcare,* meaning "to cross over," there is Battiferra, whom he links with her husband ("Fidia"). She wins his praise for moral purity and a classical style that makes her the equal of contemporary poets.

174. Line 2, the "king of rivers" is the Po. Cf. *RS* 180.9; *Orlando furioso* 35.6.1. Line 4, *varca . . . vero* (he who crosses over to the first truth): Benedetto Varchi, on whose name Razzi makes the obvious pun. Cf., e.g., Benvenuto Cellini's sonnet to Varchi that puns on both his first and last names: "Benedetto quel dì che l'alma varchi / lasciando omai la spoglia di lei sazia" (Blessed the day that the soul crosses over, leaving sated at last its mortal remains). The verb "varcare" (to cross over) and its noun "varco" (crossing, passage) resonate strongly of Dante's *Comedy,* where they refer to many "crossings," all related to the great crossing over, from time to eternity, from life on earth to salvation in heaven. Cf. for *primo vero* (first truth), *Par.* 3.96. Line 8, *Metro:* the Metauro, Urbino's river. Arno belongs to a "flowered" realm because it flows through Firenze, the name of which was thought to derive from the verb "fiorire" (to flower).

175. 1.79. Battiferra asserts her determination to follow in the footsteps of her "demigods," the poets who walked before her, but she protests that her light is tiny and uncertain compared with theirs. She takes inspiration from Varchi, a sun in Razzi's circle at Santa Maria degli Angeli. His monastery, where painters and poets gather, is a *cenacolo* likened to Parnassus. With Varchi to light her way, she dares to aspire to artistic heights together with her husband, "Fidia."

176. Line 2, *quasi numi* (demigods): the writers of the past, who in the context of this exchange can be understood as Battiferra's favored Latin poets, especially Virgil and Ovid, as well as the Italian vernacular classical authors. Lines 3–4, poets pursue enduring values, unlike the vulgar mob, bound to worldly vanities as ephemeral as a shadow or puff of smoke. Line 5, Battiferra protests that she is not worthy of being considered the equal of the classical writers. Line 6, for the rhyme *numi . . . dumi,* see

Varchi, *Rime* 1.99.3. Line 9, the "sun" is probably Razzi's friend, Varchi, who in the sonnet above "crosses over to the first truth." Line 10, *Ritondo:* Razzi served as abbot of Santa Maria degli Angeli, a Camaldolite monastary founded late in the thirteenth century and suppressed in the nineteenth. Rich in cultural history, its distinctive architectural feature was a Rotunda, begun in 1434 by Filippo Brunelleschi. Guidi (*Il primo libro,* 115) attributes the cloister design to Ammannati, but cites no source. According to an undocumented tradition, Ammannati was responsible for the first and second crossings in the church of the Angeli. (Michael Kiene, *Bartolomeo Ammannati* [Milan: Electa, 1995], 243). Line 12, Fidia, the modern Phidias, is Ammannati. Cf. 1.39 and 1.120.

177. 1.80. Like Michelangelo and Bronzino, Benvenuto Cellini (1500–1571) was both an artist and a writer. In addition to his *Vita* and a treatise on sculpture, he wrote bawdy verses as well as refined Petrarchan lyric poetry (Margaret Gallucci, *Benvenuto Cellini* [New York: Palgrave Macmillan, 2003]). Cellini composed several sonnets to Battiferra or about her (2.24). This exchange must date from before 1559–60, when he and Ammannati were rivals in the competition for the commission to carve the *Neptune Fountain* in Piazza della Signoria. Furious at losing, Cellini insulted Ammannati in his *Vita* by sneering that Battiferra had been cuckolding him, an accusation utterly at odds with her reputation. Here, by contrast, Battiferra incarnates the *Dolce stil nuovo* motif of the angelic lady, and she is like Orpheus. Whereas Orpheus only visited hell, however—and in a mission that failed—she has risen to heaven on Petrarchan wings as Simone Martini did to take inspiration for his portrait of Petrarch's Laura (*RS* 77).

178. Line 1, *dolce legno* (sweet lyre): the instrument to which Orpheus sang his enchanting poetry. Line 2, the Greek poet Orpheus told his sad tale in so sweet a song to the rulers of the underworld that he persuaded them to let him take back his new wife Eurydice, who had died of a snake bite. Orpheus, however, violated Pluto's condition that he not look back on the way out of the Valley of Avernus, and Eurydice was lost to him forever. See Ovid, *Met.* 10.17–77. Line 3, Cerberus, the three-headed dog who guards the entrance to hell. Cf. Virgil, *Aen.* 6. 417–25; Dante, *Inf.* 6.22–27. Tartarus is the underworld (see, e.g., *Aen.* 6.543). For the adjectival form, cf. *RS* 358.6: *tartaree porte* (Tartarean gates). Line 5, *pegno* (pledge): Eurydice. Line 8, *scendere:* with the meaning "ascendere" (to climb).

179. 1.81. Battiferra responds with compliments that outdo her correspondent's, all the while protesting her inadequacy, perhaps as an echo of Petrarch's regrets about the silence of Simone's portrait (*RS* 78). Benvenuto had flattered her as the new Petrarch; now she announces that he reincarnates the great talent of antiquity—and in double measure, through two sculptors. Since Benevenuto not only incorporates the best of Pyrgoteles and Lysippus, but is one of Apollo's dearest friends, she admires him as much for his poetry as his sculpture.

180. Line 10, *Pirgotele e Lisippo: RS* 232: "ché li val se Pirgotile et Lisippo / l'intagliar solo et Apelle il depinse"? (What does it avail him that only Pyrgoteles and Lysippus engraved and only Apelles painted him?). Petrarch's source was Pliny, *Natural History* (book 7, chap. 37), according to whom Alexander granted sole privileges to Apelles for painting his portrait, to Pyrgoteles for carving his image in marble, and to Lysippus for casting it in bronze. Battiferra retains only the two who represent the arts in

which Cellini excelled. Lines 13–14, wryly hidden in the sonnet's final punch line is the suggestion that Battiferra too is one of the "most perfect" for her art.

181. 1.82. Federico Lanti (Lante), of an important Urbino family, served as the city's *gonfaloniere* in 1567 and dictated his will in 1572. A handful of his sonnets survives in published anthologies by Battiferra and others: Varchi's *Sonetti* (1555–57), Dionigi Atanagi's *Rime di diversi* (1565), and Manfredi Muzio's *Per donne romane* (1575). Lanti here celebrates Battiferra's induction into the Accademia degli Intronati, so named because the members conceived it as a retreat from the noisiness of the world, which left them "intronati" (dazed). A venerable organization that still exists today in Siena, they prided themselves on being the first academy with a symbolic name, an allegorical emblem, and pseudonyms for the members (Michele Maylender, *Storia delle accademie d'Italia,* 5 vols. [Bologna: Licinio Cappelli Editore, 1926–30], 3: 356). We know something about how Battiferra became a member from a letter that Bartolomeo Ammannati wrote from Siena on November 3, 1559, to Cosimo's secretary Bartolomeo Concini with a report on the decorations he was making for the duke's triumphal entry (it took place on October 28, 1560). At the end he added, "My wife Laura Battiferri from Urbino, a woman adorned with poetry, has come here much visited and carressed by these Academics, and they want her to be in one of their academies, whichever one most contents her of the three, that is, the Intronati, the Rozzi (Clods), and the Desiosi (Wishful). I think she'll choose the Intronati, and some fine minds have already made some good sonnets" (Adolfo Venturi, "Bartolomeo Ammannati," 349). Battiferra, who became the first female to be "Dazed," seems to have taken the name "la Sgratiata" (Guido Zaccagnini, "Lirici urbinati del secolo XVI," 99), its meaning "graceless" chosen by humorous antithesis.

182. Line 5, *Aura:* Lanti, like many of her correspondents, puns on her name Laura. She is Apollo's beloved, hence filled with inspiration from the god of poets, as well as a source of inspiration to others like Lanti, whom her breath ("aura") transforms from dead charcoal to a bright torch. I have retained from the 1560 edition capitalization, by which Lanti, in a technique of concrete poetry, conjoins Laura ("L'Aura") to the city of the Intronati. Line 6, *schiera Intronata* (troop of the Dazed): see Bargagli's poem below and Battiferra's reply, written for the same occasion. For discussion of *schiera,* see the volume editor's introduction to this volume. Lines 9–11, Lanti imagines that Battiferra is a goddess adored in all the cities that know her, now not just Florence on the Arno, Rome on the Tiber, and Urbino on the Metauro, but also Siena, city of the Arbia. Defining the city by its river is a favorite Petrarchan routine (cf. 1.8, 1.9, etc.).

183. 1.83. Whereas in other sonnets Battiferra asserts her inadequacy by likening herself to a "croaking bird," here she mixes metaphors (not very gracefully) to insist on her weakness in comparison with Lanti's poetic strength.

184. Lines 4–5, *bassa . . . canna* (lowly reed): instrument of the pastoral poet. Cf. Varchi, *Rime* 2.144a.9; *Ecl.* 2.373. Line 9, *spenta facella* (spent torch): *RS* 135.63. Line 10, *struggo e scarno* (I am consumed and grow thin): *RS* 308.4; L. Alamanni, *Rime,* 1.114.117; Varchi, *Rime,* 1.44.4, 1.428.4, 1.523.7, etc., 109.187. Line 13, she is only a very small laurel tree. Line 14, *pinge e colora* (paints and colors): cf. Cappello, *Rime,* 152.7: "pinge ed indora" (paints and gilds).

185. 1.84. One of the most illustrious members of the Accademia of the Intronati, where his nickname was "Material," the Sienese nobleman Girolamo Bargagli (d.

1586) read civil law for many years in his native city and later was called to visiting appointments as a jurist in Florence and in Genoa. He composed a *Dialogo de' giuochi che nelle vegghie sanesi si usano di fare* (Dialogue of Games It Is the Custom to Play in Sienese Gatherings) as well as a comedy, *La Pellegrina Commedia* (The Female Pilgrim), performed in Florence in 1589 for the wedding of the Grand Duke Ferdinando de' Medici with Cristina di Lorena and published by his brother Scipione. His poetry survives in several anthologies, including Battiferra's *Primo libro,* which preserves two sonnet exchanges with him. The occasion for this sonnet is Battiferra's induction into the Intronati in 1560. Battiferra's *Rime,* fol. 24r, preserve another exchange with the Count of Monte d'Oglio, called "lo Sdegnoso" (Disdainful), which seems to have been prompted by the same event.

186. Lines 1–2, Athena, or Minerva, the goddess of wisdom. Lines 3–4, Venus, whose home is Cyprus. Line 5, *più celeste diva* (a more celestial divinity): Battiferra. Lines 6–8, the greater deity is perhaps Apollo. With Battiferra as a member, the Intronati will be the best academy in Italy. Lines 9–10, the Penates were the Roman household gods. Pumpkins, hollowed out and dried, were used to store salt and are-associated with the salt of wit. The Intronati chose the pumpkin as their emblem with the motto "Meliora latent" (The best things are hidden). Lines 13–14, in the classical and mythological key of the sonnet, the wishes of the academy members to honor Battiferra, a "divinity," become metaphorically votive offerings like those placed on altars in antiquity.

187. 1.85. Battiferra thanks her lucky star and the Intronati for the honor of joining their group, although her skills as a poet are inadequate to praise so illustrious a company.

188. Line 1, *amica stella* (friendly star): see 1.87.4. The epithet is frequent among Battiferra's contemporaries. Lines 1–4, the day Battiferra was inducted into the Accademia degli Intronati. Line 5, *schiera* (troop). See 1.82 and volume editor's introduction. Lines 5–8, she need no longer fear passing time because now as a member of the Intronati, thanks to the efforts of others and her own hard work ("sweat"), she will be immortal. Line 6, *vigilie . . . sudore* (vigils . . . sweat): the second noun is Dantesque (and very un-Petrarchan) and is uncharacteristic of Battiferra's polished style, but it was not unknown to the sonneteers. Cf. Cellini's complaint that Cosimo has neglected him, *Rime* 58.8: "E' questo il premio del mio gran sudore" (This is the reward for all my sweat.)

189. 1.86. The Florentine Antonfrancesco Grazzini (1503–1584) composed *novelle,* comic plays, and poetry in both the burlesque and Petrarchist modes. An independent spirit committed to the vernacular language, he was a founder in 1540 of the Accademia degli Umidi, whose members believed "all the good which comes to man has its source in dampness" (Robert J. Rodini, *Antonfrancesco Grazzini: Poet, Dramatist, and Novelliere, 1503–1584* [Madison: University of Wisconsin Press, 1970]. 8), hence their acquatic nicknames. Grazzini retained his, "il Lasca" (the roach fish), even after they reorganized as the Accademia Fiorentina in 1542. His wide cultural circle included Benedetto Varchi, Tullia d'Aragona, Antonfrancesco Doni, Luca Martini, Lionardo Salviati, Benvenuto Cellini, and Agnolo Bronzino, with whom he exchanged sonnets on the portrait of Battiferra (2.25–26). Late in his life, he helped create the Accademia della Crusca.

190. Line 2, *Flora:* Florence.

191. 1.87. Battiferra, responding with identical rhyme words, credits il Lasca with reanimating her poetic style by his example.

192. Line 4, the sun enters the constellation of Taurus on April 21. Line 5, *antica madre* (ancient mother): Earth, who gives birth to all manner of life. Lines 9–11, *vago aprile* (winsome April): cf. B. Tasso, *Amori* 2.39.20: "Tu un vago e lieto aprile / teco portasti" (You brought a winsome and joyful April with you).

193. 1.88. Laura, whose name links her with the laurel as a symbol of her talent, wins high praise from Bronzino for verse of moral probity. He says, in effect, that she is his favorite poet. Not only is she more worthy than Petrarch's Laura and Dante's Beatrice, she may even be superior to the men who wrote about them for the sweetness of the lyrics she composes.

194. Lines 1–2, *viva fronde* (living bough): the laurel. Battiferra was christened Laura at the baptismal font, but Bronzino could also be thinking of the fountain of the Muses on Parnassus. Lines 3–4, Apollo. Lines 5–7, *tal* (such a one): Laura, a woman admirable for her chaste lyrics. Lines 9–11, *Oretta e Bice:* variations on the names of Petrarch's Laura (Lauretta) and Dante's Beatrice, whose fame rests not just on their worth, but on the "senno" (sense, wise thoughts) and efforts of the poets who wrote about them.

195. 1.89. This sonnet, complex in its syntax and allusions, answers Bronzino *per rime* and point by point, following his articulation of content through the four parts of the poem. Battiferra says that if her natal stars had been as friendly as Bronzino's—that is, if she had been born with as much talent as he, who is both a poet and a painter—it would be right for him to praise her so highly, to an extent that only he deserves for his own rhymes. As she enters the sestet, repeating his qualifying "perhaps," she admits that she might, too, be as happy as Laura and Beatrice if he were really telling the truth about her. Instead, although motivated by true fondness for her, he has exaggerated the facts and thus veiled his remarks with untruth. In the end, she asks for "double life" from him since he alone of their contemporaries is entitled to give that. If the idea is that he can bring people to life both in his portraits and poems, then it would seem to be an invitation to him to paint her portrait, which he did, apparently after the *Primo libro* had been published. But *doppia vita* should also be understood by implied antithesis to *doppia morte,* the "double death" of body and soul. In other words, Bronzino with his art can make people live twice, once in this world and still longer, after death in eternity.

196. Line 4, Apollo is the god of poetry; Apelles was the most famous painter of antiquity. *Apelle, Apollo:* the binomial alludes to Bronzino's double identity as poet and painter. Cf. Varchi's sonnet to Bronzino, *Rime,* 3.89.9–10: "voi che sete / sì grande Apelle e non minore Apollo" (you who are so great an Apelles and no less an Apollo). For discussion, see Parker *Bronzino,* 15, 60–61, which also quotes from a sonnet by Sellori in Bronzino's *Rime* that addresses the recipient as "un nuovo Apollo, un nuovo Apelle" (a new Apollo, a new Apelles). Lines 9–10, the two women who stand above all others beside their lovers eternally in heaven are Laura and Beatrice, to whom Bronzino had compared Battiferra in the corresponding tercet of his sonnet. Line 13, *doppia vita* (double life): Celio Magno, *Rime,* ed. Francesco Erspamer, in Quondam,

136.12–14: "O cieca dunque e lagrimabil sorte / di chi gioir potendo in doppia vita / elegge anzi perir di doppia morte" (O blind and tearful fate then of the man who can rejoice in double life and chooses instead to perish in double death).

197. 1.90. A literary man from Perugia, Lucio Oradini left his mark as a cultivated member of the Accademia Fiorentina, where he gave readings on two poems by Petrarch, published by the Torrentino press in 1550; one on "Delle misure de' cieli, della terra, e de' pianeti," and another on "Quali fossero più nobili le leggi, o le armi." Varchi, who esteemed him highly enough to put him in his dialogue on language *Ercolano,* addressed sonnets to him, and Oradini's verse appears in several other lyric anthologies of his era (Giovan Battista Vermiglioli, *Biografia degli scrittori perugini e notizie delle opere loro,* 2 vols. [Perugia: Vincenzio Bartelli e Giovanni Costantini, 1829], 2: 157–58). His connection to Bartolomeo Ammannati may have arisen through their mutual interest in taking the measurements of distant objects (a portion of Ammannati's autograph notebook in the Riccardiana Library deals with such questions of engineering and surveying). Oradini's modesty here belies his skill. He has produced a tightly packaged single-sentence sonnet embellished with *rima equivoca,* the paradoxical sense of which is, if I could write a poem that adequately praised your art, it would be the best ever written.

198. 1.91. Battiferra protests that compared with Oradini's Apollonian sunburst of poetic talent, she is only a weak light. He inspires her and does her honor with his verse, which will also bring fame to her husband Ammannati, who already robs death and time with his enduring art in marble and bronze.

199. Line 2, Apollo doubles as sun and god of poetry. Line 4, *sgombrate:* the verb ("disencumber," "carry away," etc.) discussed in Varchi's letter to Battiferra (4.7). Lines 7–8, Her husband, Ammannati. Line 11, *pregiato alloro* (prized laurel): Raineri, *Cento sonetti* 102a.2; B. Tasso, *Amori* 1.2.3; 5.187.113; *Salmi* 2.31.61. Line 12, Ammannati, both a sculptor and a metal caster. For *marmi . . . bronzi:* cf. Cellini's sonnet to Michelangelo, *Poesie* 65.6 in Benvenuto Cellini, *Opere,* ed. Giuseppe Guido Ferrero (Turin: Unione Tipografico-Editrice Torinese, 1971); Varchi's sonnets to Cellini 3.87.11; and to Ammannati, 2.6.3; and below, no. 92.3, Bonsi's sonnet to Ammannati. Line 14, cf. *RS* 269.4, and above, 1.42.

200. Although a printer's error obscures her intention, Varchi's protégé Bonsi was meant to have a privileged place in Battiferra's *Primo libro.* He appears once, properly credited, near the end of the exchanges initiated by male poets ("Quando, da lungo e grave sonno desta": [When awakened from a long and heavy sleep]). Then, after Oradini's exchange with Battiferra (1.90, 1.91), he returns as the voice featured at an internal finale, the eight-sonnet sequence dedicated to Ammannati that closes the *in vita* portion of her *canzoniere.* Linked by the old Provençal technique of *rimas capfinidas* (in which the closing words of one stanza or poem are echoed in the opening verse of the next), the first four are by Bonsi (misattributed in the printed edition to Oradini); the last four are Battiferra's replies. Immediately following comes the funeral procession of death sonnets, beginning with a poem of mourning for Maria de' Medici. Bonsi himself corroborates the mix-up in a letter of February 8, 1561, to Timoteo Bottonio, a Dominican friar from Perugia: "Now having come to Florence and found the rhymes of Madonna Laura Battiferra in print, I acquired a volume and send it to you with this letter, cautioning you that the printers made a lot of mistakes, and

among others, I found this one: the four sonnets near the end of the book, which are immediately under one by Messer Lucio Oradini addressed to Madonna Laura, are mine and not Messer Lucio's as is printed." Guidi, who publishes this excerpt in the original Italian (*Il primo libro,* 135), speculates that Bonsi's sonnets to Ammannati celebrate his *Fountain of Juno.*

201. 1.92. Several references to Lelio Bonsi (b. 1532) appear in Battiferra's correspondence with Varchi, whose letters to Battiferra this mutual friend sometimes delivered. In her letter of November 14, 1556, she reports that she has received a sonnet Lelio sent her and intends to reply. In another of August 9, 1557, she writes that her husband Bartolomeo sends his greetings both to Varchi and to Bonsi, who can look into matters in Bologna (presumably Battiferra's legal battle to recover her dowry). A volume collecting *Cinque lezzioni* that Bonsi had read to the Accademia Fiorentina, of which he served as an officer in the early 1550s, along with his treatise on comets and a Holy Thursday sermon on the Eucharist, were published by Giunti in Florence in 1560. He is among the poets, including Varchi and Bronzino, whose verse was anthologized at the end of Cellini's *Two Treatises* on the art of the goldsmith and sculptor (Florence, 1568).

202. Line 3, *chiari marmi e vivi bronzi:* see above, 1.91.12. Lines 5–8, the harmony of Battiferra's spiritually uplifting verse raises the soul to heaven. The subject of "opens" is "harmony." Line 11, Cosimo and the duchy of Florence and Siena. Line 12, *Flora:* Florence, whose adornment is Cosimo (cf. "cosmetic"). His name will be eternal, thanks to both Ammannati, unparalleled in their arts.

203. 1.93. Battiferra's previous sonnet had praised to the skies Cosimo, whom Ammannati plans to celebrate with a work of art, perhaps his *Neptune Fountain.* Its ending becomes the first verse of the sonnet below. The final tercet of the sonnet preceding reads,

> Ed anco il nuovo Fidia mio disia
> or con marmo, or con bronzo, opera fare,
> che del tuo gran valor minor non sia.
>
> (And my Fidia too desires,
> now with marble, now with bronze, to make
> a work that not be less than your great worth.)

She continues her paean to Cosimo, here in his role as sponsor of the arts, while at the same time she compliments her husband and another poet, surely Varchi. If Ammannati is a new Lysippus and Varchi a new Virgil, then their patron Cosimo is both a new Alexander and a new Augustus. The symbolic center of this cultural activity, with implied laurels as thick as those on Mount Pindus, is the "Ritondo" of Santa Maria degli Angeli, which sheltered an important *cenacolo* (see above, 1.79). When Varchi died, it was the scene of his funeral, described in the letter by Piero Vettori, that heads Battiferra's *Rime.*

204. Lines 1–8, the sense is "your lofty mind discerns a thousand pathways, not just one, that will be as greatly worthy as you are." Lines 1–4, Cosimo of great worth, personifies the ideal ruler: kind to his good subjects and bellicose to his enemies. Cf. *Aen.* 6.853: "parcere subiectis et debellare superbos" (to spare the humbled and tame the proud in war). He deserves to rule the whole world. Line 6, *occhio cervero* (lynx-

like eye): the borrowing is contextually targeted to *RS* 238.2: "occhio cerviero," from a catalog of praise for an unidentified ruler. It appealed to Varchi, e.g., *Rime* 2.41a.1: "occhio cerviero / non fu mai come 'l vostro acuto e presto (lynx-like eye was never as keen and quick as yours). Line 9, the sculptor Bartolomeo Ammannati. Line 10, the "pen" must be Varchi's. Line 11, *Ritondo:* Santa Maria degli Angeli, a Camaldolite monastary. See 1.79.10 where it figures in a similar context and is compared to Parnassus: "Ritondo il bel Parnaso." The Rotunda "makes shade" because it is symbolically a place of poetic activity, associated with laurel groves. Lines 13–14, *Lisippo:* according to Pliny (*Nat. Hist.* 7.37), Alexander the Great granted the sculptor Lysippus the privilege of casting his portrait in bronze. *Maro:* Virgil. Cosimo cultivated an image as the new Augustus.

205. 1.94. Punning on her subject's name, Battiferra speaks of a chaste young beauty, wise in years, for whom the sparks of friendship had long lain dormant but now blaze again. Describing his own works, Vasari mentions a Simon Corsi, with whom he was "very friendly" and who commissioned art (*Le vite dei più eccellenti pittori, scultori e architetti,* 4: 724).

206. Lines 12–14, the verses are obscure, perhaps a reference to Ammannati.

207. 1.95. This poem by Alessandra Corsi is the only one by another woman in all of Battiferra's *Rime.* Alessandra does her best to summon the necessary formulas, but her affirmation of friendship is cliched.

208. Line 6, *dritta via* (straight way): Alessandra recalls Dante's *Inf.* 1.3.

209. 1.96. Varchi died on December 18, 1565. Battiferra echoes the sonnet by Petrarch on the death of his friend the poet Sennuccio del Bene (d. 1349), whom he imagines has gone to the heaven of Venus and joined the spirits of all the others who wrote of love:

> Ma ben ti prego che 'n la terza spera
> Guitton saluti, et messer Cino, et Dante,
> Franceschin nostro et tutta quella schiera.
>
> (But I beg you to salute all in the third sphere:
> Guittone and messer Cino and Dante,
> our Franceschino, and all that troop) (*RS* 287).

Petrarch's verse became an important model not only for the death of a poet, but also for the ideal of poetic community (see volume editor's introduction). Whereas a member of the Medici family leads off the funeral procession in Battiferra's *Primo libro* (Cosimo's young daughter Maria), in her *Rime* the poet gives a personal structure to the order of the death sonnets, which begin by commemorating a lady named Lucrezia de' Piccinini of Ravenna and continue with twelve sonnets for Varchi. The longest microsequence in the *Rime,* this is verse that Battiferra wrote or helped collect behind the scenes for the funeral anthology edited by Piero Stufa, *Componimenti Latini, e Toscani da diversi suoi amici composti nella morte di M. Benedetto Varchi* (Latin and Tuscan Compositions by Diverse of His Friends Composed on the Death of Messer Benedetto Varchi).

210. Line 1, *su nel terzo giro* (up in the third circle): cf. *RS* 287.9: "'n la terza spera" (in the third sphere). See below, 2.3.11 and commentary. Cf. Giovanni Boccaccio, *Rime,*

ed. Vittore Branca, in Giovanni Boccaccio, *Tutte le opere,* vol. 5, pt. 1 (Milan: Mondadori, 1992), 126. Line 3, *lucido speglio* (lucid mirror): Battiferra recalls the noun from Dante's *Paradiso,* where Adam speaks it in a memorable passage (26.106). The clarity of this looking glass recalls Saint Paul's promise, "For now we see as through a glass darkly, but then face to face" (1 Cor 13:12). For the combination "lucido speglio," see B. Tasso, *Salmi,* app. 3.28; Varchi, *Rime* 1.492.10. Line 5, *meco di me talor m'adiro: RS* 1.11. Line 14, *dura condizion* (harsh condition).

211. 1.97. The Florentine Antonio Allegretti (d. 1566) lived in Rome in the household of Monsignor Giovanni Gaddi, who was, like Battiferra's father, a cleric in the Apostolic Chamber whom Annibal Caro served as secretary. Cellini mentions in his *Vita* Allegretti's ten-year friendship with Caro. Some of Allegretti's poetry was published by Dionigi Atanagi in his anthology *De le rime di diversi nobili poeti toscani* (Rhymes of Diverse Noble Tuscan Poets) (1565). This follows two sonnets by Battiferra in her *Primo libro* and her *Rime* on the death of Caro (1566), about which Allegretti now condoles with her from Rome. She replied with a sonnet beginning, "Aura mortal ch'a poco a poco priva" (Mortal aura little by little deprived) (R 29r).

212. Line 1, a pun on Laura's name and the Italian "l'aura" (breeze, aura) to suggest how her spirations fan the flames of virtuous love. Line 5, *l'arbor Caro* (the Caro tree): literally, the "dear" tree. The image of the dear departed as a tree that has died is Petrarchan. Cf. Battiferra's poem on the death of her father, also a tree struck down (2.8).

213. 1.98. Maria, the first child of Cosimo and Eleonora (1540–57) and the first to die after surviving childhood, perished of malaria at the family palace in Livorno, a loss that is said to have deeply saddened her father. This Medici tribute initiates the funeral cortege in the *Primo libro.*

214. Line 1, Duke Cosimo, her father. For *terreno . . . frale* (earthly . . . frail): Celio Magno, *Rime* (in Quondam), 360, 2.90; B. Tasso, *Amori* 3.39 (also a sonnet of mourning, hence a likely point of reference). Line 5, *biondo crin fatale* (fatal blond lock): B. Tasso, *Amori* 2.114.59. King Nisus of Megara had a purple lock of hair that made him invincible, but his daughter Scylla cut it off while he slept, ending her father's life and sacrificing his realm to King Minos, with whom she was in love. Ovid, *Met.* 8.6–151. Line 10, the Virgin Mary, queen of heaven. *RS* 366.1–2: "Vergine bella, che di sol vestita / coronata di stelle" (Beautiful Virgin who, clothed with the sun and crowned with stars).

215. 1.99. Lelio Capilupi (1497–1560) came of a Mantuan family of poets. In this sonnet, the second of two Battiferra dedicates to his death, she links him with his illustrious compatriot and inspiration, Virgil. Like his father, who was a secretary to Isabella d'Este, he served the Gonzaga and was in contact from Rome and Mantua with Isabella's daughter, Eleonora Gonzaga, after she became the Duchess of Urbino. A Petrarchist follower of Bembo, he had a long friendship with Bernardo Tasso, whose interest he shared in imitating the Latin classics. Although Ariosto praised him in the *Orlando furioso* (45.12), most of his poetry was only published posthumously. A good chunk of his vernacular verse appeared in the volume compiled by Dionigi Atanagi, *De le rime di diversi nobili poeti toscani* (Rhymes by Diverse Noble Tuscan Poets) (1565). What he and his brothers had written appeared as *Rime del S. Lelio, e fratelli de Capilupi* (Mantua, 1585), and his Virgilian centos on the monastic life were

printed in 1590. He is doubtless of interest to Battiferra politically for his Urbino connection, and she places him poetically with the most elite—Virgil, Dante, Petrarch, and Bembo.

216. Line 4, *terzo ciel* (third heaven): See 1.96 and 2.2. Line 10, Pietro Bembo (1470–1547), whose influential edition of Petrarch's lyric poetry was published by the Aldine Press in Venice in 1501 and whose own much imitated *Rime* appeared in three authorial editions (1530, 1535, 1548). Line 14, *opre elette* (elect deeds): Cappello, *Rime* 413.4; Muzzarelli, *Rime* 35.11.

217. 1.100. Marking the end of the fifteen-sonnet funeral procession in Battiferra's *Primo libro,* this was written for Atanagi's *Rime di diversi nobilissimi et eccellentissimi autori in morte della signora Irene delle signore di Spilimbergo, alle quali si sono aggiunti versi latini di diversi egregij poeti in morte della medesima signora* (Rhymes by Diverse Most Noble and Most Excellent Authors on the Death of the Lady Irene of the Ladies of Spilimbergo, to Which Are Added Latin Verses by Diverse Distinguished Poets on the Death of the Same Lady) (Venice, 1561). One hundred forty-three named contributors gather here to celebrate Irene (1538–59), a young woman of such astonishing talents that she was said to have learned the art of painting from Titian in just six weeks (Anne Jacobson Schutte, "Irene di Spilimbergo: The Image of a Creative Woman in Late Renaissance Italy," *Renaissance Quarterly* 44 [1991]: 42–61). Atanagi, from the town of Cagli in the Urbino territory, after spending some years at the Roman court, served Duke Guidobaldo II and was a friend of Bernardo Tasso, whom he assisted in bringing to publication in 1560 the latter's long chivalric poem *Amadigi* (Corsaro, "Dionigi Atanagi e la silloge per Irene di Spilimbergo").

218. Line 1, *doglie e pianti* (sorrows and tears): cf. Matraini, *Rime* A 26.9; B. Tasso, *Amori* 2.22.6. Line 2, *ingorda morte acerba* (greedy, bitter death): cf. V. Colonna, *Rime Epistolari* 8.3, "l'empia Morte, ingorda e avara" (wicked death, greedy and grasping): Tansillo, *Il canzoniere* 6, sonnet 262.10.

219. 1.101. Of eclectic interests, the gentleman Paolo del Rosso from Parma was a Knight of Jerusalem whose anti-Medici politics resulted in his imprisonment. In spite of Battiferra's get-well wishes, he apparently did not recover from the illness that was the occasion for this poem, since the next two sonnets in her *Rime* mourn his death (1569). He is a noble "vaso eletto" (chosen vessel), like the apostle Paul whose name he bore. In addition to composing lyric poetry, he translated from Latin into Italian the *Lives of the Caesars* by Suetonius (1554) and the statutes of the Knights of Malta; wrote a commentary on Guido Cavalcanti's famous *canzone,* "Donna mi prega" (A Lady Prays Me), published in Florence in 1568; and wrote a didactic poem in *terza rima* entitled *The Physics* (Paris, 1578). He receives sonnets from Varchi and Cellini (to whom he sent a sonnet in praise of his *Crucifixion*), and he appears among the poets whose verse is collected in Tarsia's commemorative volume on Michelangelo's death. Battiferra takes inspiration from a sonnet by Bembo for Gaspare Pallavicino, one of the participants in Castiglione's *Book of the Courtier* and the victim of a long illness (that would cause his early death).

220. Line 2, Pheobus Apollo, who killed the snake (Ovid, *Met.* 1.438–51), in mythological code language the Savior, who healed the wound of Original Sin caused by the serpent's evil doing in Eden. Battiferra is praying to Christ. Line 9, Rossi comes under Apollo's tutelage, both as a poet and a man with medical interests.

221. 1.102. Giovan Battista Cini (1528–86) engaged vigorously with the Medici cultural scene. A member of the Accademia Fiorentina, he authored *intermezzi* for the 1565 production of Francesco d'Ambra's play *La cofanaria* (The Boxmaker), which was performed in the grand salon of Palazzo Vecchio for the wedding of the prince Francesco and Giovanna of Austria; a comedy called *La vedova* (The Widow) (1569); carnival songs; a description of the festivities on the arrival of the Archduke Charles of Austria in 1569; letters; and a history of Duke Cosimo's life (Michel Angelo Feo, "Giovan Battista Cini," in *Dizionario biografico degli Italiani* [Rome: Istituto dell'Enciclopedia Italiana, 1960–], 25: 609–12). He probably commissioned for the family chapel in Santo Spirito Alessandro Allori's finest painting, *Christ and the Woman Taken in Adultery* (1577), and he is perhaps represented playing the cithar in the panel he ordered a year later from the same artist for his sister in Palermo, an *Adoration of the Shepherds* (Simona Lecchini-Giovannoni, *Alessandro Allori* [Turin: Umberto Allemandi & Co., 1991], 240, 244). His country villa "The Roses" seems to be the setting for Battiferra's "Third Eclogue" (1.120). Perhaps that is the place to which she refers as his retreat in grief. This sonnet is the first of two in her *Rime* for the widower Cini.

222. Line 14, the verb "trastulla" (to entertain, amuse, beguile) is often used to describe how a mother keeps happy a child on her lap. It is as if Madonna Berarda were holding her husband like a baby in a maternal embrace. Cf. Bembo, *Canzoni degli Asolani* 9: "dentro mi trastulla / l'anima" (it beguiles my soul within).

223. 1.103. Duke Cosimo I de' Medici died in 1574, having been elevated from duke to the grand ducal title in 1569 by Pope Pius IV. In form a *canzonetta,* this poem plays on court iconography that connected the name "Cosmo" with "cosmos," which in its Greek derivation denotes "beauty," "adornment."

224. Lines 1–2, cf. Cappello's sonnet to Cosimo, *Rime* 244.1: "O Cosmo in ornamento al mondo dato" (O Cosmo, given to the world as an ornament). Lines 7–10, perhaps a reference to Lazarus.

225. 1.104. The *Rime* preserve five poems mourning the death of the grand duchess Giovanna of Austria (d. 1578). She died in childbirth, as Battiferra says in *Rime* 301, "allor che 'n maggior copia a noi porgea / gl'amati frutti" (just when she was bearing us beloved fruits in greatest abundance)—that is, when she had finally produced a male heir after a disappointing run of females. This infant, Filippo, was sickly and also died not long after his baptism (see 2.22). Except for Eleonora de Toledo, no other Medici received so many death poems from Battiferra. Aside from the poet's wishes to remain in Medici favor, she must have admired Giovanna's pious nature, which prompted the latter often to visit convents (Elissa Weaver, *Convent Theater in Early Modern Italy: Spiritual Fun and Learning for Women* [Cambridge: Cambridge University Press, 2002]). Her fate of death from too many childbirths clearly moved the poet, whose own marriages had remained barren. This poem plays on the well-known etymology of Giove (Jove) as "adjuvant," or "one who avails," punning on the grand duchess's name "Giovanna" and the verb "giovare."

226. Line 1, *rose e fiori* (roses and flowers): Tullia d'Aragona, *Rime* 1.1. Lines 5–6, *giovar* (to avail): cf. Bembo, *Rime* 118.1: "Signor, che per giovar sei Giove detto" (Lord, who are called Jove from avail).

227. 1.105. In a favorite device of mourning poetry, the mother's dead child now speaks with a promise of reunion and a golden crown. See below (1.117–18) for another such dialogue between the poet Lattanzio Bennucci and a boy he lost.

228. 1.106. Following her funerary offerings for Cosimo and Giovanna of Austria, Battiferra places a sequence of nine sonnets she wrote to mourn the death of her first husband, Vittorio Sereni of Bologna (1.106–14). A musician who served Guidobaldo II Della Rovere, as organist, he dictated his will in a final illness on January 25, 1549. These very private and early poems do not appear in her books, published after her marriage to Bartolomeo Ammannati. Although the first sonnet is too general for certain identification of the deceased, whom she does not name until the fifth, its object can be deduced from context and from Battiferra's most prominant source (after Petrarch), Vittoria Colonna (1492–1547). Significantly, Battiferra's first mourning sonnet connects with the initial poem in Colonna's *Rime:*

> Scrivo sol per sfogar l'interna doglia
> ch'al cor mandar le luci al mondo sole,
> e non per giunger lume al mio bel sole,
> al chiaro spirto e a l'onorata spoglia.

> (I write only to vent inner sorrow,
> sent to my heart by the sole lights of the world,
> and not to bring light to my fair sun, to the bright
> spirit and honored remains.)

Colonna, whose soldier husband was fatally wounded at the Battle of Pavia (1525), became an archetype for the devout female voice in sorrow. Her collected poetry first appeared unauthorized in 1538 and was many times republished. It was natural that Battiferra in her widowhood should turn for a model to the marquise of Pescara.

229. Line 3, *giunger . . . lume* (add . . . brightness): cf. V. Colonna, *Rime* 1.3: "giunger lume." Line 4, *sfrenata voglia* (unbridled will): *RS* 29.11. Lines 5–8, *invoglia . . . inspoglia* (makes me want . . . despoil): the rhymes are cognate with Colonna's and in the same positions: "doglia," "spoglia," "invoglia." Line 14, the double meaning implies that she will still have her husband "Vittorio."

230. 1.107. Battiferra addresses her husband in heaven, now a friendly spirit. If she cannot die as well, she takes comfort in the belief that all God's souls glow alike with charity.

231. Lines 1–2, cf. *RS* 153.3: "se prego mortale al ciel s'intende" (if mortal prayer is heard in heaven); Cappello, *Rime* 318.12 (a poem of mourning): "se giusto uman prego in ciel si stende" (if just human prayer reaches heaven). Line 3, *disacerbi . . . dolore* (make less bitter my . . . sorrow): cf. *RS* 23.4: "cantando il duol si disacerba" (singing, pain becomes less bitter). Line 4, *tronchi il debil stame* (cut the weak thread): cf. V. Colonna, *Rime* 2.9: "quel colpo che troncò lo stame" (that blow that cut the thread); *squarci il velo* (rend the veil): cf. Dante, *Purg.* 32.71; *RS* 28.62 and 362.4. Allusions to the thread of life, which the Fate Clothos cuts, and the veil of the body, torn away from the soul at death. Line 13, *gli eletti suoi* (his elect): cf. Gambara, *Le rime,* 57.2, a sonnet on her deceased husband that expresses her Reformist ideas on election.

232. Although premature, Sereni's death seems to have been peaceful, but Battiferra grieves at the brevity of her marriage—not even a few years. Here she imagines herself surrounded by female mourners of myth and poetry—the Fates, the Graces, and the Virtues. Her lament recalls Luigi Alamanni's pastoral dialogue between Dameta and Dafni, "The Death of Adonis," *Rime* 1.20.

233. Line 1, *luci* (lights): eyes. Lines 3–4, *crudel Parche* (cruel Fates): the Fates, Clothos, Lachesis, and Atropos spin, weave, and cut the thread of life. Cf. Bembo, *Rime* (on the death of his Morosina) 160.5. Line 5, torch-bearing Hymen is the god of marriage.

234. 1.109. Joining a long tradition descended from Petrarch, Laura addresses her eyes, tired from weeping, and reminds herself that her sorrow can only trouble the soul of her departed husband, now in the heavenly kingdom.

235. Line 1, *occhi miei lassi* (tired eyes of mine): *RS* 14.1; Cappello, *Rime* 373.13; Matraini, *Rime e lettere* A 87.5; Stampa, *Rime* 1.164. Line 3, *posto la terrena salma* (laid . . . earthly remains): cf. Tansillo, *L'egloga e i poemetti, Ecl.* 859; *Stanze* 463. Lines 12–14, the soul of her husband is understood.

236. 1.110. Battiferra names the husband she mourns, Vittorio, with a pun on his winning appearance. It is perhaps not coincidental that his naming occurs only once, and in this poem, central in the sequence of nine.

237. Line 1, *Discolorato è il viso* (Drained of color is the face): *RS* 283.1: "Discolorato ai, Morte, il più bel volto" (You have discolored, Death, the most beautiful face). Line 4, *empia Morte . . . prima i miglior fura* (wicked Death . . . steals first the best): cf. V. Colonna, *Rime, Epistolari* 8.3–4: "l'empia Morte, ingorda e avara, / ch'i più cari tesor più presto sgombra" (wicked Death, hungry and greedy, who sweeps away soonest the treasures that are dearest). Lines 7–8, the pain of grief comes after and lingers long.

238. Line 1, *gran pianeta ardente* (great burning planet): the sun. V. Colonna, *Rime* 86.1: "Come il calor del gran pianeta ardente" (As the heat of the great burning planet). Line 4, *nudrir e crear* (nurture and create): the hysteron proteron combining these two verbs appears in Petrarch, but in a negative context. *RS* 138.6: "il mal si nutre et cria" (evil is created and nourished). Line 11, *sol ch'avent'il strale* (if only it loose its arrow): the verb "aventare" usually refers to Love as the arrow shooter. Cf. *RS* 86.2. Line 14, the subject is "my friend thought."

239. 1.112. Battiferra describes herself dressed in black mourning clothes, repeatedly striking a chord in which the dignity of funerary rituals resonates. The poem, which must date from the year of Vittorio Sereni's death (1549), imitates closely a sonnet by Bernardo Cappello on the death of the Duchess of Urbino, Guidobaldo II Della Rovere's first wife, Giulia Varana (d. 1547), the mother of Virginia Varana Della Rovere (1.10). Cappello consoles the duke, alluding to a god-like man with a remedy, Pope Paul III, whose granddaughter Vittoria Farnese becomes Guidobaldo's second wife and produces an heir to the duchy, Francesco Maria II Della Rovere. Although Cappello did not publish his *Rime* until 1560, the same year as Battiferra's *Primo libro,* his sonnet on the duke's bereavement, two years before Vittorio Sereni's death, evidently circulated in manuscript, which is how Battiferra would have seen it:

Signor, cui negra e lagrimosa vesta
copre gli omeri e 'l petto, e doglia il core,
poiché di questa vita uscita è fore
la bella e saggia vostra sposa onesta: 4
degno è l'abito vostro, e degna è questa
voglia di pietà colma e di dolore;
e degno l'alto suo funebre onore,
e la memoria in noi che di lei resta. 8
Ma dignissimo è ancora che gli occhi vostri
si volgano a mirar qual vi prepara
di ciò, chi Dio ne sembra, ampio ristoro; 11
e di beltà vedrete, e di tesoro
adorna, e di virtù donna sì rara,
che farà voi felice, e i tempi nostri. (*Rime* 1560, 155) 14

(Signor, whose black and tearful dress
covers your shoulders and breast, and sorrow your heart,
since your fair spouse, wise and true,
has gone forth from this life, 4
worthy is your clothing, and worthy is this
full wish for pity and sorrow,
and worthy her lofty funeral honor,
and the memory in us that remains of her. 8
But most worthy it is, too, that your eyes
turn to behold what ample remedy for it
someone who seems to us God is preparing for you, 11
and you will see a woman so rare,
adorned with beauty and treasure and virtue,
that she will bring happiness to you and our times.) 14

240. Line 1, *negra vesta* (black dress): cf. *Triumph of Death* 1.31: "una donna involta in vesta negra" (a woman wrapped in black dress); Della Casa, *Rime* 37 (on the death of Bembo in 1547), lines 1–2: "Or piagni in negra vesta, orba e dolente / Venezia" (Now weep in black dress, bereaved and mournful Venice).

241. 1.113. While still connected to the mourning sequence by their references to a tearful style, the next two sonnets in the *Rime* introduce an important new theme, Battiferra's emergence as a poet. Here, alluding to her first name, she claims a place as "third" laurel in an illustrious line of succession from Apollo's Daphne to Petrarch's Laura. Like Vittoria Colonna, this young widow defines herself as a plaintive voice, a woman used to weeping. She assimilates her real sorrow to a ready and recent antecedent in the literary tradition, Colonna's poetry, which had gone into some ten editions between 1538 and 1548, the year before Vittorio Sereni passed away. A young laurel, Battiferra casts metaphorically less shadow and scent than her famous predecessors, meaning that she is still unpracticed; not many people have heard of her or felt her influence because her circle is not yet wide.

242. Line 1, Daphne, loved by Apollo and turned into a laurel tree. Ovid, *Met.* 1.452–567. Line 3, *candida aurora* (bright dawn): Raineri, *Cento sonetti* 15.1: "Ecco l'alma dal ciel candida aurora" (Behold from heaven the bountiful bright dawn). Lines

5–6, the second "laurel," often sighted along the Sorgue River in southern France, is Laura, the lady sung by the Tuscan poet Petrarch. *Toscan* (Tuscan): cf. L. Alamanni, 2.84.94.2: "gran Toscan," referring to Petrarch.

243. 1.114. The unknown person here addressed has praised Battiferra in verse, and she wittily demurs, claiming to have been nourished only on tears and to have nothing of the laurel but its name.

244. Line 1 *Frate* (brother): the greeting repeats Virgil's words to a fellow poet, Statius, when the latter tries to embrace him on Dante's Mount Purgatory (*Purg.* 21.131). Line 4, the first laurel, going by the sonnet above, was Apollo's Daphne. Line 5, Apollo made her immortal by making her his tree. Line 6, the Italian *canto* can mean both "song" and "corner." Battiferra puns, saying that the first laurel deserves praise in all poetry in every corner of the world. Line 7, the tears refer to Laura's widowhood. Line 8, Daphne and Apollo were shot by Cupid's arrows; Battiferra has been wounded by the arrow of death—the hurtful loss of her husband.

245. 1.115. The manuscript does not name the person for whom Battiferra composed this poem, which lacks the confident grace of her most mature compositions. It falls in the section of the *Rime* that moves from sonnets of mourning for Vittorio Sereni to Battiferra's emergence as a poet and her arrival on the Roman scene. Context and tone, more solemn than in the sonnet above, suggest the "divine" Michelangelo, from whom Bartolomeo Ammannati had received an important career boost in the form of a papal commission. The younger sculptor continued to collaborate with Michelangelo after entering Duke Cosimo de' Medici's service in Florence, and his wife assisted him in writing letters to Michelangelo that express the deepest respect (chap. 4, introduction). Both Ammannati would contribute to his funeral in 1564, Laura by composing commemorative verse (2.19–20). Assuming Michelangelo was the intended recipient, this piece dates from the early years of her second marriage, ca. 1550–55 (see Kirkham, "Creative Partners").

246. Line 2, Michelangelo excelled in all three arts of sculpture, painting, and poetry. Cf. Varchi, *Rime* 1.179, to Michelagnolo Buonarroti, "non sol per opra d'incude e martello / . . . ma coi colori e col pennello" (not only by deed of anvil and hammer . . . but with colors and with brush). For the same trinity, cf. Raineri, *Cento sonetti* 32.10–11: "inchiostri . . . metalli . . . marmi" (inks . . . metals . . . marbles). Line 9, *cosa divina* (divine thing): *Triumph of Fame* 1a.22: "Ella a veder parea cosa divina" (she seemed a divine thing to see). The "Divine Michelangelo" acquired his famous epithet from the angelic connection suggested by his name, but his genius reinforced his identity as a man above mere mortals. Lines 9–13, for the rhyme "divina" and "pellegrina," cf. *RS* 213, 270.

247. 1.116. As the daughter of a churchman headquartered for decades at the Vatican, Battiferra loved the Eternal City, awesome for the ancient pagan monuments and Christian relics that preserve memory of its past glory. This sonnet must date, like the one above, from the early years of Battiferra's second marriage. Her final plea, that peace prevail, implies a time within collective memory of the terrible wars between pope and emperor that in 1527 unleashed on Rome the sacking armies of Charles V. The poet here reverses the sentiment in a sonnet by Giovanni Guidiccioni (d. 1541), who laments Rome's decline:

. . . Che 'l nome sol di Roma ancor tenete,
Ahi che reliquie miserande avete
Di tante anime eccelse e pellegrine!
Colossi, archi, teatri, opre divine,
Trïonfal pompe, glorïose e liete,
In poca cener pur converse siete,
E fatte al vulgo vil favola al fine.

(. . . Proud hills, and you sacred ruins, which have nothing anymore but the name of Rome, ah, what pitiable relics you have of so many surpassing and rare souls;
Colossi, arches, theaters, works divine,
triumphal pomps, glorious and happy,
still you are turned into a handful of ashes
and made in the end the base talk of the vulgar mob.) (Guidiccioni, Giovanni, *Opere*, Carlo Minutoli, ed., 2 vols. [Florence: G. Barbèra, 1867], 1: 71)

Guidiccioni was a Tuscan churchman who had spent time in Rome in the service of Pope Paul III and a literary friend of men whom Battiferra knew—Bernardo Tasso, Annibal Caro, Benedetto Varchi.

248. Line 1, *superbi monti* (proud hills): Tansillo, *Canzoniere* 4.240.10; *memorie antiche* (memories of antiquity): *Triumph of Fame* 3.15. Lines 1–8, for similar catalogs of the things in Rome, cf. Cappello, *Rime* 124 (for Pope Paul III) and 170; Muzzarelli, *Rime* 37; Raineri, *Cento sonetti* 1 and 118; Varchi, *Rime* 1.340.

249. 1.117. Four poems in Battiferra's collections leave traces of a friendship with Lattanzio Benucci (1521–98). She accords him an honored place in her *Primo libro,* where he leads the sequence of sonnet exchanges initiated by Laura's interlocutors: he praises her as a literary inspiration, and she responds with regret in the sestet of her sonnet that he is leaving for the distant Venetian shore:

voi su l'Adria d'amor cantando andrete,
che 'l mondo regge con sì dolce verga
pellegrin cigno in voce alta e canora;
ed io su l'Arno quasi augello in rete
garrirò mesta, o pur non si disperga
la voce mia, mentre si lagna e plora

(you will go singing of love to the Adriatic,
which rules the world with such a sweet baton,
a rare swan in lofty and canorous voice;
and I on the Arno, like a bird in a net
shall downcast chirp, else let not my voice be dispersed,
for as long as it is moans and weeps.)

Two more poems, probably written after 1560 and preserved in the Casanatense manuscript, mourn one of Benucci's sons, a boy named Francesco. The identical poems appear in Bennucci's autograph *canzoniere* (Florence, Bib. Naz., MS Magl. 7.779, fol. 170r). There the rubric reads, "Ne la morte del Figlio Francesco. Parla in questo sonetto Francesco al glorioso San Francesco del quale vestì l'abito per devozione de' suoi genitori" (On the death of his Son Francesco. In this sonnet Francesco speaks to the glorious Saint Francis whose habit he wore because of his parents' devotion). It is not clear whether this death sonnet and its mate are by Benucci or Battiferra. He commemorated the loss of other children with notes in his manuscript. Beneath a sonnet for his daughter Beatrice, he noted "vixit dies xlvij" (she lived forty-seven days); beneath another on the death of his son Mario, "vixit dies xxxj" (he lived thirty-one days).

Benucci, the son of a Sienese nobleman and poet-mother, began composing verse in childhood. A student of law, he made his career as a diplomat and judge, traveling extensively as far as Spain and spending long periods in Florence. There he came into contact with Tullia d'Aragona, who enlisted him as an interlocutor in her *Dialogue on the Infinity of Love* (1547). She also published verse to and by him in her *Rime*. Lodovico Domenichi featured him in several anecdotes of his *Facetie, motti, et burle, di diversi signori et persone private* (Humor, Witticisms, and Jokes of Diverse Gentlefolk and Private Persons) (1565), one of which captures his wit and religious sentiment: a gentleman in Rome complained of having fallen on such hard times that he had commended his soul to God; when Benucci noticed the big grease spot on his velvet jacket, worn as smooth and shiny as satin, he said, "and received extreme unction, too" (441–42). Apart from commentaries on the *Divine Comedy* and the Psalms (the latter lost), he left a a rich personal collection of his verse (autograph, Florence, Bib. Naz., MS 7.779) and sonnets scattered in manuscript miscellanies (Florence, Bib. Naz., MS Magl. 7.346, fol. 403r, "Sonnet to Say before Communion"; MS Magl. 7.1185, "To the Mensola River"). Only a handful found their way into print, including three in Christiani's 1555 death anthology for Livia Colonna (see above, 1.34) and the one in Battiferra's *Primo libro*.

250. Line 2, *glorioso Francesco* (glorious Francis): the adjective means that Francis is "in glory," that is, in heaven among the blest. Cf. the incipit of Dante's *Vita nuova*. The same formula appears repeatedly in the secular contexts of Luigi Alamanni's poetry, referred to his patron, the living King Francis I of France. Line 4, *doglia e pianto* (grief and tears): *RS* 332.5. A binomial widely diffused among the Petrarchists. Line 5–7, Francesco lived less than two years. Line 12, *gravose some* (heavy burdens): L. Alamanni, *Rime* 1.144.195 (an anti-Lutheran context). Cf. *RS* 37.2: "gravosa mia vita" (my heavy life).

251. 1.118. Like Giovanna d'Austria's dead child (1.105), Francesco now speaks to reassure his mother.

252. Line 5, *carcer terreno* (earthly prison): cf. *RS* 306.4: "carcer terrestro" (earthly prison). The variant appears twice in Michelangelo Buonarroti's *Rime*, ed., E. N. Girardi (Bari: Laterza, 1960), in Quondam (e.g., 264.5), but closer contexts with the verb "uscire" are in Cappello, *Rime* 118.119 (on the death of Bembo) and Muzzarelli, *Rime* 27.37 (with the identical construction "uscire fora"). Line 13, *lagrimosa e mesta* (tearful and downcast): *RS* 102.7; Matraini, *Rime e lettere* A 87.3.

253. 1.119. Pope Gregory XIII (Ugo Buoncompagno, 1572–85) founded the Roman College of the Jesuits and sent his nephew, Cardinal Filippo Buoncompagno, to lay the foundation stone of the new Florentine church of San Giovannino, patronized by both Ammannati. Early in his papacy he had commissioned Bartolomeo Ammannati to sculpt figures in the Camposanto at Pisa for a tomb for another nephew, the jurist Giovanni Buoncompagno. Ammannati's creation, with Christ standing be-

tween Justice and Peace, so pleased the pontiff that he awarded a bonus to the artist, who reports in his *Letter to the Academy of Design* of August 22, 1582, what moral satisfaction he drew from the undertaking. When news of Gregory's death reached Florence, Battiferra eulogized him with a sonnet in which the departed pontiff speaks, giving an account of his accomplishments.

254. Line 1, *ambe le chiave* (both the keys): following Petrarch, most occurrences describe keys to the heart: *RS* 91.5; Aragona, *Rime* 16.9; Bembo, *Rime* 12.8 (but in 139.9 they are keys of the "celestial kingdom"). Christ promised Peter, the first pope, the keys of the kingdom of heaven (Mt 17:16–19). Cf. *Inf.* 13.58 and 27.104 and above, 1.62.8. Line 11, *Indiana greggia* (Indian flock): a reference to missionary activity of the Jesuits in the New World.

255. 1.120. Battiferra's corpus, mostly sonnets, includes three Italian eclogues. "Europa" is attached to the final section of her *Primo libro.* Her second eclogue, "Dafne," has disappeared except for the tantalizing traces of its title and first verse, recorded in the manuscript of the *Rime* from the lost Beta manuscript. The *Rime* preserves the full text of the third. Here she imagines an inner court circle of five people gathered on a Medici holiday at a beautiful site called "The Roses," situated in the vicinity of the rivers Arno and Greve. This place just south of Florence may correspond to a village called Le Rose, near the Sanctuary of the Madonna of Impruneta; more specifically, it may refer to Villa Le Rose, acquired in 1551 by Giovan Battista Cini (Feo, "Giovan Battista Cini"; 1.102). If it is Cini's villa, the two chief guests of honor in the eclogue, "Alfeo" and "Galatea," are probably Cini, a native of Pisa, and his wife. The other three are Laura ("Dafne"), her husband ("Fidia"), and Cosimo's ducal administrator in Pisa, Luca Martini ("Tirsi"). Battiferra writes in the style of Cini himself, who composed elegant court *intermezzi.* Her charming tableau of an ephemeral entertainment carries hints of maneuvering for patronage as it praises the Medici at an apex of their political history (Kirkham, "Cosimo and Eleonora in Shepherdland"). Laura's eclogue mentions prayers to Mars for peace, which could date it to after the end of war with Siena (1555). It must in any event predate the death of Martini (1561), a Medici loyalist of many accomplishments—amateur Dantista, patron of the arts, Cosimo's ducal administrator (*provveditore*) in Pisa, and the hydraulic engineer who drained swamps in the surrounding territory, represented on the map he holds in Bronzino's portrait of him.

256. Lines 1–5. Kirkham, "Cosimo and Eleonora in Shepherdland," proposed Fiesole as the setting, but that should undoubtedly be corrected to a place south of Florence, which would be consistent with the location of the village called Le Rose and the allusion to the River Greve in lines 201–204. Line 9, *Flora:* Florence. Line 10, *gradito albergo* (welcome hostel): Nannini, *Epistole d'Ovidio* 2.188. Line 12, since the setting is "Le Rose," a more likely candidate than Cosimo as initially suggested by Kirkham in the article above would seem to be that villa's owner, Giovan Battista Cini, born in Pisa, where relatives of his continued to live. The name Alfeo implies Pisan connections (Kirkham, "Cosimo and Eleonora in Shepherdland"). *toschi campi* (Tuscan fields): cf. L. Alamanni, *Rime* 1.174.101 (the last verse of the poem, which describes a pastoral contest). Line 16, *Galatea:* if Alfeo is Cini, Galatea is probably note the duchess, Eleonora de Toledo but one of Cini's two wives, Maria Berardi or Alessandra di Luigi d'Alberto Altoviti (Feo,"Giovan Battista Cini"). Line 23, the "king of the months" is August, named for Augustus Caesar. Cosimo declared August 2 a

holiday to commemorate his battle victory over the rebel republican faction at Montemurlo in 1537, the year he acceded to power. Line 27, *venia* (pardon): Sannazzaro, *Arcadia*, Dedic. 23. Line 34, *Tirsi:* Luca Martini, Cosimo's ducal administrator in Pisa. See above, 1.59 and n. 136 and below, 2.2–6. Line 40, *Fidia:* Bartolomeo Ammannati. Line 41, *pastorella incolta* (unlearned shepherdess): his wife, Laura Battiferra. Line 46, she is a poet who follows in the footsteps of Apollo, the god of poetry. Line 48, her pseudonym is Dafne. Line 50, *fiorito e verde* (flowery and green): *RS* 125.74 and 243.1. Line 60, perhaps Santa Maria dell'Impruneta, founded in 1160, sanctuary and pilgrimage site for its miracle-working Madonna. Line 81, Dafne's song. Line 87, Apollo. Line 90, *di Minerva insegna* (ensign of Minerva): the olive. Line 100, the pine tree is sacred to Venus. Line 106, her sons are the Amorini, Cupids. Line 119, Jove's daughters are the Muses. Line 126, Apollo, who pursued Daphne in Thessaly. Line 130, Apollo's branch is the laurel. Line 152, Alfeo's song, which resembles that of Orpheus. Line 171, Tirsi's song (Luca Martini sings). Line 172, the song is perhaps related to a court entertainment, or "mascherata." Line 204, sunset.

257. Battiferra chose the Duchess of Urbino, Vittoria Farnese Della Rovere (1519–1602), as recipient of her *Sette salmi penitentiali* published in 1564. The dedicatory letter from that volume was to reappear at the beginning of the "Seconda Parte" of the *Rime*, where it introduces the *Rime spirituali* and forms a symmetrical counterpart to the prefatory epistle from Piero Vettori of January 31, 1566. To justify her project, Laura boldly places herself in the same family of poets as King David. A successor in translating to Saint Jerome, the church father responsible for the "authorized" Latin Bible, she appropriates the language of Saint Paul to make a declaration of her militant Christian mission. Many of the faithful in those years immediately following the Council of Trent must have profited from her translation, which was reprinted separately in 1566 and again in 1568, 1570, and 1572 as part of a small pocket anthology edited by Francesco Turchi, *Salmi penitenziali, di diversi eccellenti autori* (Penitential Psalms by Diverse Excellent Authors). Granddaughter of Pope Paul III, Vittoria was the second wife of Duke Guidobaldo II Della Rovere (see 1.8).

258. *Human letters* ("umane lettere"): secular literature, as opposed to holy scripture.

259. The Seven Penitential Psalms (6, 31, 37, 50, 101, 129, and 142 in the Vulgate numbering) express the penitent's awareness of sin and hope for pardon. Defined as a canon in the sixth century by Cassiodorus, they were from the time of Pope Innocent III (1198–1216) required in Lenten devotions, and they became one of the sequences in the prayer structure of the Book of Hours. Following the Council of Trent, Pius V (1566–72) assigned these seven Psalms to the Friday ferial Office of Lent. Petrarch, whom Battiferra quotes in the first of the sonnets that follow the Psalms in her 1564 volume, provides an unacknowledged antecedent for her translation since he composed his own Latin prose version of the Penitential Psalms—actually prayers—early in the 1340s. Battiferra would have had closer antecedents for translations of the Psalms by Luigi Alamanni, Antonio Gallo, and Bernardo Tasso. In 1586, perhaps influenced by Battiferra's example, Chiara Matraini of Lucca published her *Considerazioni sui sette salmi penitenziali* (Considerations on the Seven Penitential Psalms).

260. Saint Jerome, who had translated the Bible from Greek into Latin, creating the Vulgate, which would have been the version known to Battiferra.

261. King David.

262. The reference is to Homer's *Iliad.*

263. The reference is to Virgil's *Aeneid.*

264. Laura adopts the language of Saint Paul in Eph 6:13–17: "Therefore take up the armor of God . . . the shield of faith . . . the helmet of salvation and the sword of the spirit, that is the word of God."

265. March 25, the feast of the Incarnation, marked the beginning of the new year in the old Florentine calendar.

266. 1, pt. 2.1. This is the first sonnet from the sequence that followed Battiferra's translations of the Psalms in the 1564 edition. (The Casanatense manuscript numbers the title and dedication rubrics as nos. 1 and 2.) In the *Rime* she makes it precede the Psalms, investing it with the honor of introducing the second half of her *canzoniere.* Laura describes an inner conversion modeled on the experience that Petrarch reported in the first poem of his *Rime sparse,* to which she connects by quoting verbatim its final verse as her final line. The Renaissance sonneteers who ordered their poems into narratives often so linked themselves with the master. Gaspara Stampa, for example, had repeated his first verse ("Voi ch'ascoltate in rime sparse il suono" [You who listen in scattered rhymes to the sound]) with a striking variant in her first sonnet that sets the tone for her lyric self-presentation, "Voi ch'ascoltate queste meste rime" (You who listen to these downcast rhymes).

267. Line 14, *RS* 1.14: "che quanto piace al mondo è breve sogno" (whatever pleases in the world is a brief dream).

268. 1, pt. 2.2. When the Apostles were gathered at Jerusalem on Pentecost, the Holy Ghost descended in flamelets upon their heads and endowed them with the gift of tongues so they could preach the Gospel to all peoples (Acts 2:1–4). Recalling this miracle, which marked the founding of the universal pentecostal church, Battiferra invokes inspiration from the Holy Spirit for her own proselytizing, citing the words of the Psalmist 50:17, "O Lord, open thou my lips."

269. Lines 9–11, Dante, *Purg.,* 23.11: "Ed ecco piangere e cantar s'udìe / *'Labïa mëa, Domine'* per modo / tal, che diletto e doglia parturìe" (lo in tears and song was heard: *"Labïa mëa, Domine,"* in such manner that it gave birth to joy and to grief). Lines 11–14, The nurturing bride is the church, whose members ("children") recite the Psalms in prayers throughout the liturgical day from their Book of Hours or from a breviary.

270. 1, pt. 2.3. Here in the *Rime* follows the seven Penitential Psalms with their "argomenti," or subject matter laid out in individual letters of dedication. The women to whom Battiferra addresses the Psalms are all ladies of prominent families living as cloistered nuns in the great houses of Florence (Faustina Vitelli in the Murate, Vincenzia Bardi da Vernio in the Murate, Lucia Stati in the Chiarito, Vincenzina Bilotti in Santa Marta, Guilia Franchi in Santa Marta) and of Urbino (Angela de' Vergili and Violante de' Maschi in Santa Chiara, Cassandra de' Battiferri and Anna Vannuzia in Santa Lucia). Cassandra de' Battiferri was raised by an uncle of Laura's father, Francesco Battiferri, "as if she were his own." She may have been his natural daughter, making her Laura's aunt. The Faustina Vitelli here addressed, probably a young woman not yet married, was a natural legitimized daughter of Chiappino Vitelli, whose husband Vincenzo Vitelli (a first cousin once removed) was a Roman noble and *condot-*

tiero in the service of the church and was appointed governor of the Borgo (district of the Vatican) in 1565. Each dedication begins with a prose description of the Psalm's contents and closes with a request that the nun pray for Laura. The translations are remarkable for the simplicity of their lexical register and their experimental metrical range. The first consists of eleven stanzas, corresponding to the structure of the Psalm, each one of four verses with rhyming couplets of seven and eleven syllables. Its compact forms and rhyme scheme would have made it an easy text to recite from memory.

271. 1, pt. 2.4. After the Penitential Psalms in the *Rime,* Battiferra returns to the spiritual sonnet sequence that followed them in the 1564 edition. Here she translates Ovid into a Christian register. The poet's Apollo, smitten with love for Daphne when Cupid's arrow pierced his heart, becomes "true" as Christ, wounded by the lance of Longinus. Amorous pursuit becomes the metaphor for Christ's efforts to melt the resistance in this Dafne's icy heart and capture the "errant" lady, that is, win her to a Christian way of life and save her soul. Laura must have venerated the relic of Longinus's lance in the Vatican, at the Chapel of Innocent VIII, to which her father held an appointment as chaplain. The chapel is dominated by the famous, monumental funerary statue that Innocent VIII commissioned of Pollaiuolo to commemorate the gift of that relic to him from the Turk Bajazet (Sultan Beyazid II) in 1492.

272. Lines 1–2, *RS.* 197.2: "Amor ferì nel fianco Apollo" (Love smote Apollo in the side); Vittoria Colonna, *Spir. disp.* 3.6: "il vero Apollo" (the true Apollo). Line 7, *errant Dafne:* pun on "wandering, roaming" and "in error, sinful." Line 8, *RS* 165.14: "son fatto un augel notturno al sole" (I have become a nocturnal bird in the sun).

273. 1, pt. 2.5. The poet compares herself to a man who has narrowly escaped death in a storm at sea, a frequent image of the soul in travail. Dante had compared himself to the survivor of a shipwreck in the first extended simile of the *Comedy* (*Inf.* 1.22–27), and Petrarch often recurs to the metaphor (*RS* 272, 277, 366), a Renaissance commonplace. Recall Michalengelo's famous sonnet, "Giunto è già 'l corso della vita mia, / con tempestoso mar, per fragile barca, / al comun porto" (The course of my life, / with a stormy sea in a fragile boat, has already reached / our common port).

274. Line 3, *RS* 366.67: "tempestoso mar" (stormy sea). The same unit appears in L. Alamanni, *Rime* 1.182.25 (but with reference to Florence); Aragona, *Rime:* 43.9 and *Ecl.* 4.4; and Michelangelo, *Rime* 285.2. It appears repeatedly in B. Tasso, *Amori* 1.132.27, 2.62.2, and 5.24.8: "io son quasi fragile navicella / Che tempestoso mar scuote" (I am as a fragile little boat that a stormy sea shakes); *Salmi* 1.30.15: "Padre pietoso, a quell'anime belle che 'n questo tempestoso mar ti furono ancelle" (Compassionate Father, to those souls who in this stormy sea were your handmaidens); 2.2.27: "il tempestoso mare / di questo mondo indegno" (the stormy sea of this unworthy world).

275. 1, pt. 2.6. Petrarch's anniversary poems, typically spells of guilt-ridden self-examination before the specter of approaching death, become paradigms for three birthday poems in the *Primo libro* (see below, 7 and 17). In this lovely sonnet, the earliest by Battiferra to which a date can be attached (1548), she takes stock of her life as she completes her twenty-fifth year. Her hastening step in a pastoral landscape at the beautiful moment of moonrise signals a heightened awareness of passing time as, metaphorically, she prepares her thoughts for the homeward path to God.

276. Lines 1–6, *RS* 50.29–31: "Quando vede 'l pastor calare i raggi / del gran pianeta al nido ov' egli alberga / e 'mbrunir le contrade d'oriente" (When the shepherd sees the rays of the great planet falling toward the nest where it dwells, and the eastern countryside becoming dark). Lines 10–11, *i lustri . . . dal quinto* (the lustrums . . . from the fifth): a lustrum is a five-year period. Cf. Petrarch, *Triumph of Time* 103.

277. 1, pt. 2.7. In the second of her three anniversary poems, entering her thirtieth year, Battiferra announces her penitential rejection of worldly goals as she addresses a forgiving Christ, contemplated on the cross. The poem engages Petrarch's description of the eleventh anniversary of his Good Friday enamorment (*RS* 62), turning it into an intense personal meditation literally connected to an image of the crucified Lord. This sonnet, datable to 1552, follows Battiferra's *sestina* (1.48 above) in the *Primo libro*. For the *Rime,* she advanced it into the "Second Part," among her spiritual rhymes.

278. Line 1, *RS* 62.9: "Or volge, Signor mio, l'undecimo anno" (Now turns, my Lord, the eleventh year). B. Tasso declares his liberation from earthly bonds in a poem that marks entry into his thirty-third year, a Christological point of arrival. See his *Amori* 1.108: "Ben posso omai con le man giunte al Cielo / Signor erger la voce e l'intelletto" (Well can I raise to heaven with hands joined, Lord, my voice and intellect). Line 11, *fida scorta* (trusted guide): cf. *Inf.* 12.100: "scorta fida"; B. Tasso, *Amori* 3.36.11 (to Pope Paul III): "fida scorta." Line 14, *RS* 62.14: "oggi fusti in croce" (today you were on the cross). Matraini wrote penitential poems referring to God's "gran clemenza" (*Rime* C 63, 86).

279. 1, pt. 2.8. Returning to the imagery that describes the Jesuits as a militant force led by Claudio Acquaviva (see above, 1.62), Battiferra now envisions their Society as an army soldiering under the banners of Christ on the battlefied of life, inspirited by the three theological virtues of faith, hope, and charity. The appearance of this sonnet among the three by Battiferra anthologized in the Intronati manuscript at the Biblioteca Angelica in Rome (see also below, 1, pt. 2.12) indicates that even if the *Rime* did not circulate as a collection, excerpts of her Jesuit poetry did.

280. Line 12, The two wars, one hidden and one open, refer to the private spiritual struggle of each Jesuit and to their missionary activity around the world.

281. 1, pt. 2.9. Lines 1–8, *"fiamma . . . mamma . . . dramma."* Cf. Petrarch, *Triumph of Chastity,* 68–70, 72, where the same rhyme words occur in a context that describes the Amazon maiden Camilla, who goes into battle with only her "left breast" ("sinistra mamma") intact. Line 5, the lance of Longinus (see 1, pt. 2.4). For *ferro* ("iron"), see Vittoria Colonna, *Spirituali,* 122,129, 136.

282. 1, pt. 2.10. The poet, in rapt in visionary joy, imagines that she enters the wound of Christ, where she finds her own spiritual healing.

283. 1, pt. 2.11. Battiferra addresses a cloistered nun, a wise virgin whom she asks to pray for her. Other poems in her collected lyrics also address such virgin sisters, and women in nunneries (including Battiferra's own aunt) are recipients of her seven penitential psalms.

284. Lines 3–4, *Re del sommo Regno . . . umile ancella* (King of the highest kingdom . . . humble handmaiden): cf. B. Tasso, *Amori* 5.27.3–5 ("to the Most Christian Queen"): "umile ancella . . . Moglie del maggior Re di tutti i Regi" (humble handmaiden . . . wife of the greatest King of all Kingdoms).

285. 1, pt. 2.12. This sonnet evidently enjoyed private circulation. The fact that it appears in a manuscript with poems by "The Dazed," *Quinquaginta fere auctorum et praesertim academicorum intronatorum senensium carmina italica* (Italian Poems by Nearly Fifty Authors, Chiefly Members of the Sienese Academy of the Intronati) suggests that Battiferra may have chosen it as one of the work samples she presented when she was inducted into that august body. Other authors in the Florentine miscellany that contains a copy of this sonnet are Bembo, Michelangelo, Della Casa, Grazzini, Guarini, and Isabella Andreini (verses on the death of her husband). Here the poet loses herself in contemplation of the immensity and beauty of the universe, feeling a sense of exaltation that seems to anticipate Leopardi's poem of immersion in the natural world, "The Infinite."

286. 1, pt. 2.13. This sonnet gives a remarkable insight into an inner conflict between Battiferra's conscience, which tells her to retreat into prayerful isolation, and another part of her, which cannot give up the worldly gatherings of "the troop" that is the "honor of Parnassus." She struggles to break away from her fellow poets, but long habit gets the better of her, and she keeps returning to their circle.

287. 1, pt. 2.14. In the intensity of her mystical ardor, the poet wants to duplicate Christ's passion. Concentrated in the culminating torments of the Crucifixion, her thought ends on the hope for resurrection into the blessed life. Vittoria Colonna, too, meditates on the crucified Christ (*Rime spirituali* 77), "Veggio in croce il Signor nudo e disteso" (I see on the cross the Lord nude and stretched out), but with much greater calm and detachment.

288. Line 8, the lance of Longinus. Cf. above, 1, pt. 2.4 and 2.9.

289. 1, pt. 2.15. Christ as husbandman, speaking from heaven, summons the Jesuits to enlarge the vineyard he planted, metaphorically a beloved woman and hence the body of the church. A heavenly reward awaits their efforts, which will bring back pristine perfection to the world. The poem smoothly blends biblical language (the vineyard of the bride in Song of Songs, the vineyard of the Lord in Isaiah, the parable of the vineyard in the Gospels), the Petrarchan code ("fruit and flower"), and memories of classical antiquity (the allusion to the golden age, the tradition of Virgil's *Georgics*).

290. Lines 1–2, *eletta vigna* (elect vineyard): cf. L. Alamanni, *Della coltivazione,* 785: "eletta vigna." Line 3, *sangue . . . sudore* (blood . . . sweat): V. Colonna, *Rime spirituali* 87.5: "con la croce, col sangue e col sudore" (with the cross, blood, and sweat). Line 14, *paghi . . . contenti* (well-pleased and happy): gemination suggested by V. Colonna, *Rime spirituali* 100.4, where the light of the "true sun" kept "paghi e contenti" the Virgin's eyes while she lived; 143.4, where the poet addresses Christ, "li spiriti avete in lei (in an image of divine love) paghi e contenti" (in it your spirits are satisfied and content).

291. 1, pt. 2.16. In a dramatic monologue, the poet speaks in the voice of the penitent Mary Magdalene, who laments over the bloodied feet of the dead Christ, amazed and humbled that he has sacrificed himself for love of one like her. The Magdalene, in an act of supreme contrition for her former life as a courtesan, had washed Christ's feet with her tears and hair and anointed them with oil at the home of the Pharisee (Lk 7:36–50).

292. 1, pt. 2.17. The third and last of Battiferra's anniversary poems (see also 1, pt. 2.6 and 2.7), this is the source that identifies the feast of Saint Andrew, November 30,

as the day of her birth (Zaccagnini, "Lirici urbinati del secolo XVI"). She has now reached "one year less than the sixth lustrum," in other words, her twenty-ninth birthday. The sonnet would thus seem to have been written at the same time as "Oggi, Signor, che nel trentesimo anno" (1, pt. 2.7 above), where she prays before an image of the crucified Lord. Here, in parallel, she prays before an image of Saint Andrew, martyred on the x-shaped structure that carries his name, the Saint Andrew's cross. *Mutatis mutandis,* the poet connects her petition for Andrew's intercession to Petrarch's Good Friday. His earthly love was born when Christ gave up the ghost; Laura's physical birth coincides with the death of a spiritual intercessor who, like Christ, was crucified.

293. Line 1, *servo fedel* (faithful servant): the apostle Andrew. V. Colonna addressed no. 177 of her *Rime spirituali* to Saint Andrew. The sonnet recalls also Malipiero, *Petrarca spirituale,* 135.1–3: "Amor mi manda al cor dolce pensero / di farmi fedel servo a quel ch'in due / nature in croce per me affisso fue" (Love sends to my heart the sweet thought of making myself faithful servant to him who in two natures was affixed to the cross for me). Line 12, *Andrea:* cf. V. Colonna, *Rime spirituali* 117.1: "Quante dolcezze, Andrea, Dio ti scoverse" (How many sweetnesses, Andrea, God disclosed to you).

294. 1, pt. 2.18. The poet describes the Massacre of the Innocents. After King Herod learned from the Magi that a boy was born in Bethlehem who would become king of the Jews, he ordered all the male children under two years of age to be slaughtered there. Warned by an angel in a dream, Joseph fled with Mary and the Babe into Egypt (Mt 2:1–18). Christ was spared on earth, and the Innocents became Christian martyrs.

295. Line 1, *un re* (a king): Herod. Line 9, *pargoletti* (babes): cf. V. Colonna, *Rime spirituali* 25.13 (on the Massacre of the Innocents): "cari e pargoletti amori" (dear and cherubic babes). Line 10, *Campi Elisei* (Elysian Fields): the abode of the blessed in Virgil's *Aen.* 6.

296. 1, pt. 2.19. Line 1, *RS* 366.1: "Vergine bella, che di sol vestita" (Beautiful Virgin who, clothed with the sun). Line 9, the devil. Line 14, the Virgin has the power to protect God's victory and reassert Satan's defeat.

297. 1, pt. 2.20. The Bible (Daniel 13 in the Vulgate) tells the story of Susannah, a beautiful and virtuous wife unjustly accused of adultery by two elders who lusted after her as she bathed in her enclosed garden. When she refused to lie with them, these wicked judges testified that she had dismissed her servant women so as to admit a young lover. Battiferra dramatizes the crucial moment when Susannah, being led to death, cries out to the Lord for help. In answer to her plea, young Daniel steps forward; by interrogating the elders separately, he cleverly proves they were lying. Susannah and the elders was a frequent theme in the visual arts, represented in illuminated Books of Hours and by such Italian artists as Lorenzo Lotto, Titian, Artemesia Gentileschi, and Tintoretto. It was probably some such painted version of the story that inspired Battiferra's sonnet, which also reflects her interest in the book of Daniel, her source for the epic she was writing (below, 1, pt. 2.26). A biblical counterpart to Lucretia—but luckier in outcome—Susannah is a model of female chastity and faith in God.

298. Lines 12–14, God's compassion restored her good reputation and life; his justice condemned the wicked elders.

299. 1, pt. 2.21. Christmas must have held a moving fascination for Battiferra because it is a theme that keeps returning to her art. After she and her husband had moved from Rome to Florence in 1555, Laura speaks of it to Benedetto Varchi in a letter of December 30, 1556, when she sends her new friend, influential in the circle of the Accademia Fiorentina, a sampling of three poems, requesting his judgment as a more expert writer. There are two sonnets and a madrigal, "just a few things," she modestly says, adding "I did the madrigal on Christmas night." This madrigal, which appeared in her *Primo libro,* is pure Petrarchism in its incipit, but it contains expressive formulas (e.g., "sun of justice") identical to those in her late prose meditation, "Orison on the Nativity of Our Lord."

300. Line 1, cf. *RS* 126.1: "Chiare, fresche et dolci acque" (Clear, fresh, sweet waters).

301. 1, pt. 2.22. Vibrant with awe in the great Christian mysteries of the Incarnation and the Resurrection, these verses are a metrical tour de force. A single pair of rhyme words, semantic opposites, structures the entire sonnet. Each pair occurs once in each verse, in alternating order (terra-cielo; cielo-terra . . .) and in alternating in rhyme position (cielo-terra-cielo-terra . . .), except for the last, where "Heaven" is framed at the center by two occurrences of "Earth." The effect of this keyword interweaving is a tremendous concentration of cosmic tension and salvific energy within the tiny confines of the sonnet—a miniature form tightly pressed into the space of fourteen lines and 154 syllables. Declaring a mighty, awesome compenetration of heaven's glory and our humble clay, it resonates with the same passionate spirituality as Battiferra's "Orison on the Nativity of Our Lord" (chap. 3).

302. 1, pt. 2.23. After Constantine the Great decreed Christianity an official religion of the Roman Empire in 313, his mother Helena traveled to the Holy Land to propagate the faith. There, according to legend, she forced a Jew called Judas to reveal the whereabouts of the cross on which Jesus had been crucified and recovered it as a holy relic. The most famous representation of the story in the visual arts is the fifteenth-century fresco cycle at Arezzo by Piero della Francesca. Since Battiferra's title refers to a panel painting ("tavola"), she is evidently citing some other version.

303. 1, pt. 2.24. Publius Lentulus was believed to have been a Roman governor of Judea who wrote a letter to the Roman senate describing the appearance of Christ, his contemporary, said to be the most handsome of men. No such governor ever existed, and the apocryphal letter attributed to him was probably the work of a fifteenth-century Latin humanist working from Greek sources. The text, which still today circulates among the devout, may be found together with a note on its history in *The Catholic Encyclopedia* (http://www.newadvent.org/cathen/09154a.htm). How Battiferra knew it is uncertain, but she must have believed in its authenticity. With its enumeration of Christ's physical features, the "Letter" lends itself to stylistic incursions from the repetoire of Petrarchism (e.g., "white hand"). The metrical form of the *ternario* (a poem in *terza rima*), sanctioned by Dante's *Comedy* and Petrarch's *Triumphs,* is unusual for Battiferra. It had served her for "The Orison of Jeremiah the Prophet Translated into *Terza Rima,*" among the last poems of the *Primo libro,* and for the poem preceding this "Epistle" in the *Rime* on "The Mysteries of the Life of Christ," a list that reflects her study of Ignatius Loyola's *Spiritual Exercises.* See Florence, MS Magl. 7.380, fol. 5r, a miscellany that contains poetry by Battiferra, for a possible prose source of this epistle. The prose version, to which Battiferra is very close in de-

tails, differs in its designation of Lentulus, not calling him a king. The heading of the prose letter reads "Lentolo Romano presidente di Giudea scrive a Tiberio in questo tenore" (Lentulus, the Roman president of Judea, writes to Tiberius in this tenor).

304. Lines 7–8, death. This mannerist repetition of the verbs with a rhetorical figure of chiasmus is a technique the poet employs in her "Orison on the Nativity of Our Lord." Lines 10–11, illnesses associated with these organs are understood. Line 21, zephyr: the south wind, which blows in spring. The mythological allusion belongs to the armory of Petrarchism (cf. *RS* 310.1). Line 29–30, the body part so ready to criticize is the mouth.

305. 1, pt. 2.25. Battiferra here puts her hand to the traditional Italian narrative verse form, *ottava rima,* to tell the story of the sacrifice of Isaac (Gn 22 : 1–19). In style this is a marked departure from her elegant sonnets, steeped in Petrarchist classicism. Here she attempts to reproduce the simple, ingenuous narrative voice of the *cantastorie,* minstrel-poets who performed in the piazza, reciting popular tales called *cantari* in eight-verse stanzas closed by a final rhyming couplet. Their subject matter was often based on the Carolingian and Arthurian legends. Her purpose is to teach a lesson in faith, which emerges as the message at the structural center of the composition and dominates its second half. Whoever wishes to be saved should, like Abraham, take "living faith as a faithful friend." One senses the female author in the special attention she brings to the reunion afterward with Sarah, a scene that does not figure in the biblical account. Battiferrra, who did not become a mother, must have been moved by the story of this late-born only son. In the briefest of vignettes, she imagines Sarah's maternal love for Isaac and her great joy at his return.

306. The last entry in the *Rime,* this untitled fragment breaks off abruptly after only eighteen stanzas of *ottava rima.* That Battiferra intended it as the beginning of an epic is clear from the elevated language and mythological invocations of the opening stanzas as well as the metrical form, *ottava rima.* Rhyming octaves had become standard for the genre from the time Boccaccio adopted it for his *Teseida* (ca. 1340), the first heroic poem in the Italian vernacular and the ancestor of the Renaissance chivalric epics. Enough survives to reveal Battiferra's source as the biblical account of the birth of Samuel, whose father had two wives. Peninnah ("Fenenna") mothered many children, but Hannah ("Anna"), who suffered the taunts of her rival, was barren until she prayed to the Lord in the temple of Shiloh and He opened her womb (1 Sm 1 : 1–13). The story resembles other scriptural narratives of wives who conceive through divine favor—Sarah, Rebecca, Rachel, and Elizabeth. Perhaps the motif also had personal resonance for the poet, who in Hannah's impassioned plea for a child (stanza 15), could be expressing her own disappointment as a wife. Although twice married, she bore no children—at least none that lived, nor did she have any known pregnancies, although Ammannati fathered by another woman an illegitimate son named Claudio (Kirkham, "Creative Partners").

307. 1, pt. 2.26. Stanza 1, cf. *Aen.* 1.1: "Arma virumque cano" (I sing of arms and the man).

308. Stanza 2, *Verace Apollo:* God. Battiferra's allusions function on both a mythological and biblical level of meaning. See her *Rime spirituali* above, 1, pt. 2.4. Dante had invoked Apollo at the opening of the *Paradiso.*

309. Stanzas 2–3, Battiferra invokes twin authorities, male and female. Minerva is the goddess of wisdom. According to the Bible, God created Wisdom even before making the world.

310. Stanza 4, the "eternal graces" are the Muses, who dwell on Mount Parnassus, site of the Pierean Spring. The mount to which Battiferra aspires recalls also Dante's Mount Purgatory with its cleansing waters, a place that corrects past error.

311. Stanza 7, Cynthia is an epithet of Diana; Lucina is goddess of childbirth. Since Cytharea (Venus) would be more expected here, Laura must have in mind not Diana simply as chastity, but the goddess whom Boccaccio calls "tepid," that is, she who tempers the flames of Venus to assure fidelity in matrimony. Cf. *Par.* 11.84.

312. Stanza 9, The biblical source in Samuel does not specify the sacrificial animal, but Battiferra probably imagines a lamb. Such offerings, which often figure in the Old Testament (cf. the stories of Cain and Abel, Abraham and Isaac) are consistent as well with rituals of classical epic.

313. Stanza 12, *Ecco la serva tua* (behold your . . . servant): cf. Lk 1:38: "Ecce ancilla Domini."

314. Stanza 14, Battiferra quotes verbatim the first verse of the first *sestina* of Petrarch's *Rime sparse* (22.1) in the first verse of this stanza.

315. Stanza 17, the priest is obviously inspired by Dante's Cato (*Purg.* 1.31–39), with some interference from the noble pagans of the Limbus. His eyes, described in the stanza below, recall *Inf.* 4.112: "Genti v'eran con occhi tardi e gravi" (there were people with grave and slow-moving eyes). The first clause in the stanza lacks a main verb.

316. Stanza 18, the marble lady recalls Dante's *Rime petrose* as well as Petrarch's Laura (*RS* 171.11).

CHAPTER 2

1. 2.1. This carefully worked sonnet appeared in the *Rime di diversi autori eccellentissimi* published by Giovanni Offredi at Cremona in 1560. The first of her poems to be anthologized in print by another editor, it resembles closely in composition and rhyme scheme another that appears in her *Primo libro dell'opere toscane* (1.58). Both take inspiration from Giovanni Della Casa's famous sonnet to sleep. For its limpid diction, flowing syntax, and mythological allusions, the sonnet is distinctly classical in style.

2. Lines 1–3, cf. Sannazzaro, *Sonetti e canzoni,* 62.1: "O sonno, o requie e triegua degli affanni" (O sleep, O peace and truce of our struggles); Della Casa, *Rime* 54: "O sonno, o de la queta, umida, ombrosa" (O sleep, you of the quiet, damp, shadowy night). Line 4, the daughter of Latona is Diana, the moon. Cf. Dante, *Par.* 10.67. Lines 9–10, Homer describes the Valley of the Cimmerians (*Odyssey* 11), but Battiferra's more immediate source was certainly Ovid's description of the House of Sleep, an inky cave through which flows the stream of Lethe (*Met.* 11.592–615). Line 11, she corrects "my eyes" to "yours" because she has given over her eyes to sleep. Line 12, Lethe is the river of oblivion. Cf. Virgil, *Aen.* 6.705; Dante, *Purg.* 28.130 and 30.143. Line

14, the sonnet ends on a note that preserves its classical key. In the epic tradition, ancient warriors dedicated conquered objects such as enemy shields ("trophies") to the gods who had answered their prayers ("vows") and protected them in battle.

3. 2.2. This and the four sonnets following on the death of Luca Martini appear in Bronzino's *Delle rime*. Bronzino here addresses Battiferra. Martini (d. January 1561), whose image survives in a handsome portrait by Bronzino (Florence, Pitti Palace), was a much admired court gentleman—a patron of the arts, poet, Dantist, hydraulic engineer, and the chief Medici administrator in Pisa. Ammannati seems to have hoped for support from him, either in the form of direct patronage or court lobbying for a Medici commission. Battiferra flattered him with one sonnet in her *Primo libro* (1.59), and she gave him a privileged place under his pastoral nickname "Tirsi" in her "Third Eclogue" (Kirkham, "Cosimo and Eleonora in Shepherdland"; 1.120). Several sonnets in Bronzino's *canzoniere* mourn Martini's passing, including this exchange (2.2–2.3), a copy of which survives among Michelangelo's papers.

4. Line 2, *cultor* (cultivator): Bronzino's poetry à clef is often difficult to decode. Parker, *Bronzino*, 64–65, seems to understand a double allusion in the unnamed man who "cultivates" Battiferra—both Bronzino himself and Luca Martini. The reference is, however, singular, and Martini is dead. Going by the final tercet of the sonnet, a third person seems to be understood; he could plausibly be Varchi. Cf. B. Tasso, *Amori*, 5.55.9: "O gran cultor del sempre verde alloro" (O great cultivator of the evergreen laurel), a reference to Apollo, whose tree was the laurel. Line 5, cf. *RS* 109.9–10: "L'aura soave che dal chiaro viso / move" (The gentle breeze that moves from her bright face). Line 11, *RS* 287.11: "tutta quella schiera" (all that troop). Bronzino borrows a keyword from Petrarch, placing it in exactly the same position in his own sonnet. On the importance of this coterie in Bronzino's *canzoniere*, see the volume editor's introduction and Parker, *Bronzino*, chap. 2. Lines 12–14, the idea is that before long, Varchi and Bronzino will join Luca Martini in heaven, the former through his just desserts and the latter through faith that he will be saved.

5. 2.3. Battiferra counters the salutation in Bronzino's sonnet, presenting a desolate self-image as a "sterile tree." The icon is conditioned, of course, by her Christian name "Laura," which makes her a laurel in the language of Petrarchism. The barren tree is a symbol of death, as in Petrarch's sonnet of double mourning (*RS* 269) for Giovanni Colonna and Laura, "Rotta è l'alta colonna e 'l verde lauro" (Broken are the high column and the green laurel), and in Battiferra's sonnet on the loss of her father (2.8). Here that icon is transferred from the deceased to the mourner, who feels her life at a low ebb, her "breeze" nearly stilled. The "sterility" probably does not refer to her childlessness, as one critic has suggested, but rather her poetic inspiration, stifled by grief.

6. Line 2, her husbandman ("cultor") is probably Varchi. Line 11, Battiferra acknowledges that she is aware of Bronzino's Petrarchan allusion, which she now draws out more explicitly. Petrarch had addressed the recently departed poet Sennuccio del Bene in heaven, where he imagines that his friend has rejoined all the other love poets—followers of Venus, goddess of the third planetary sphere: "Ma ben ti prego che 'n la terza spera / Guitton saluti, et messer Cino, et Dante, / Franceschin nostro et tutta quella schiera" (But I beg you to greet all in the third sphere: Guittone and messer Cino and Dante, our Franceschino, and all that troop). Cf. Boccaccio, *Rime*

256, "Or sei salito, car signor mio" (Now you have arisen, dear my lord), to Petrarch now in the third heaven, with Laura, Fiammetta, Sennuccio, Cino, and Dante. Line 12, it is significant that *chino* (bowed down) appears only once in Petrarch's *Rime sparse,* in the famous poem of mourning for Giovanni Colonna and Laura (269).

7. 2.4. The death of Luca Martini, who was buried in San Marco on January 11, 1561, prompted Benedetto Varchi to compile one hundred sonnets for a commemorative volume linking fifty-six friends in choral grief (Florence, Biblioteca Nazionale, MS Magl. 2.8.140). While other participants receive only one sonnet from him, and not all of them send a reply, Battiferra is represented in four exchanges with Varchi, who also addressed a sonnet of condolences to her husband.

8. Lines 1–4, *bino languir* (twin despondency): why there are two causes for mourning is made clear in the sonnet following, Battiferra's reply. Varchi liked to "count" his friends in poetry: Laura is his second "laurel," and she is his third friend. His first "laurel" was Lorenzo Lenzi, the Italian name for "Lawrence" being the male counterpart to "Laura," a name alluding to the laurel (Lorenzo de' Medici, poetically, had been "Laur"). See, e.g., Varchi's sonnet to Battiferra in his book *Sopra il dolorosissimo e pericolosissimo accidente [del] Duca* (On the Most Grievous and Dangerous Misfortune of the . . . Duke), Florence, MS Magl. 7.341, fol. 15r: "Prima dopo la mia primiera fronde, / e terzo prezioso mio ritegno" (First after my first frond, and third precious support of mine); and see below, 2.18, for Battiferra's reply. His second friend was Giulio della Stufa, whose pastoral alias was Carino (Kirkham, "Cosimo and Eleonora in Shepherdland"). For Carino's rank as "second," see the sonnet from Lucio Oradini to Varchi, "Varchi gentil, che tra i più chiari lustri" (Noble Varchi, who among the brightest lights). Varchi, says Oradini, is a "bright swan," as his laurel tree knows (i.e., Lorenzo Lenzi), "E non pure ei di ciò testimon fia; / Ma 'l bel Carin, ch'al gran foco di pria [i.e., Varchi] / Giungne seconda fiamma alta e giulìa" (and not only is he witness to that, but fair Carino, who comes to the fire above a second flame lofty and joyful) (Varchi, *Opere,* 2: 956; Guido Manacorda, *Benedetto Varchi: l'uomo, il poeta, il critico* [Pisa: Tipografia Succ. Fratelli Nistri, 1903], 76–77). Line 8, paradoxically, the woman from whom Varchi hopes for life is death, for she frees the soul from the body, allowing it to live everlastingly in heaven. Line 11, the body has cheated the soul of heaven.

9. 2.5. Battiferra, replying in rhyme, laments not only Martini, but a fellow poet from her native Urbino, Antonio Gallo (1510–February 12, 1561). A favorite of Duke Guidobaldo Della Rovere, whom he served as soldier, ambassador, and palace tutor, Gallo came of a local patrician family and died when he was only fifty-one. Battiferra had dedicated three sonnet exchanges to him in her *Primo libro* (1.74).

10. Line 2, death. Line 6, *Flora*: Florence. For the binomial see L. Alamanni, *Rime* 2.85.5: "La bella Italia . . . / col viso umido e chino" (Beautiful Italy, . . . with her face damp and bowed). Lines 10–11, no entertainment or pleasure can distract these mourners from their grief. Lines 12–14, may we break free of the body. The wordplay suggests that the divine will is going to thwart whatever willpower they muster to seek an immediate death. The striking verb *squarciare* (to rend), reaches Battiferra from Dante (*Inf*. 33.27; *Purg*. 32.71–72) via Michelangelo, whose *Rime* 87.9: "Squarcia il vel tu, Signore" (Do thou rend the veil—i.e., of the body—Lord), couples the verb with an object close in meaning to Battiferra's "spoglia" (remains).

11. 2.6. In addition to the eight sonnets Battiferra and Varchi exchanged in his anthology *Cento sonetti sopra la morte di Luca Martini* (F3) mourning Luca Martini, Varchi sent this poem there to Ammannati. His art and Battiferra's writing together will console Varchi.

12. Line 6, *prose . . . carmi*: a Petrarchan gemination. Cf. *RS* 239.20: "come si legge in prose e 'n versi" (as one reads in prose and in verses). Actually, her production was overwhelmingly in verse, and she wrote in Italian, not Latin, as "carmi" might suggest. Line 12, *sbigottito e smorto*: cf. Battiferra above, 1, pt. 2.3.

13. 2.7. The following two-sonnet exchange appears in two manuscript miscellanies of the sixteenth century. See app. E, nos. 7–8. For Gherardo Spini, see 1.I. Giovan'Antonio Battiferri dictated his last will and testament on his deathbed in Rome on August 3, 1561, and died five days later.

14. Line 2, the Euxine Sea is the Greek name for the Black Sea. Cf. B. Tasso, *Amori* 5.185.14: "Legno sembr'io nel tempestoso Egeo / Qualor Austro combatte e Aquilone" (I seem a ship in the stormy Aegean sea when Auster fights Aquilo); *Salmi* 2.24.1: "Freme talora il tempestoso Egeo" (the stormy Aegean at times shudders). Line 3, *pietose* (daughterly): the adjective alludes to filial piety (cf. "pius Aeneas"). Line 6, in Spini's hyperbole, Battiferra's weeping is a cataclysm that brings stormy weather to the whole western half of the Italian peninsula. Line 9, tearing one's hair was a conventional gesture of grief. Line 13, Battiferra is successor to Petrarch, who sang of the Sorgue River at Vaucluse.

15. 2.8. Spini argued that Battiferra should console herself in the knowledge that she has become heir to Petrarch in a succession of poetic generations, just as politically in the *translatio imperii* Rome superseded Carthage. She replies, again in hyperbolic measure, that she will continue weeping until the day she dies but shifts the semantic field to genealogical generations. Although the image of the stricken tree is not unusual in a poem of mourning, it is significant that Battiferra steps into the place of the male heir, making herself the branch that represents the father's progeny.

16. Line 2, the fateful day: Death. Lines 4–8, the tree is her father, who taught her the Christian values that lead to salvation. He seems to have died at an advanced age. For *dritto cammino* (straight path), cf. Dante, *Inf.* 1.3. Line 8, *squallido*: B. Tasso, mourning the lady who was the light of his life (his wife), laments that death has uprooted a flower and left him behind, "squallido e veglio / tronco" (*Amori*, 5.152.9). Lines 9–11, time conquers all, but hope does not die with the body; it springs eternal. Lines 12–14, she thanks Spini for writing poetry that will keep the family name alive.

17. 2.9. Bronzino's *canzoniere, Delle rime,* contains a sequence of five sonnets exchanged among Battiferra's friends on the death of her father, whose name he evidently did not know because the space for it is left blank in the manuscript of his lyric poems. It begins with this, which contrasts the eternal spring of heaven with the wintry prison of earth. For Bronzino and his sonnets in the *Primo libro,* see 1.76–77 and 1.88–89.

18. Lines 1–4, Battiferra should not mourn because her father has entered the realm of eternal life. Line 9, the veil in this context signifies the body (cf. 1.103.26). Line 10, Giovan'Antonio Battiferri was prominent in his own right, and he shared in Battiferra's fame. Lines 12–14, not entirely clear, but evidently, Battiferra saw to it that her father passed from this life with all that filial piety could do for him, and now she continues to pray for his soul. Perhaps whence Battiferra "departed" is heaven.

19. 2.10. Bronzino, in the second poem, asks Varchi ("Damon") to rush to Battiferra and rescue her from life-threatening sorrow. The sequence will then continue with Varchi's reply to "Crisero" (Bronzino): Battiferra and her husband have lost all happiness, but, he asks, how can he console them when he himself is weeping more than all the souls in the Valley of Hell? Next Bronzino addresses a sonnet to "Alcon" (Piero della Stufa), in which he wonders how they can go on living after the sight of Battiferra's tearful eyes. Those very eyes that inspired them both to such high deeds now make Bronzino feel he is freezing and turning to stone in sympathy with her torment. The sequence ends with this sonnet.

20. Line 1, Damon is Varchi's pastoral name. In other poetry, Varchi refers to Battiferra as his "third flame" after the first two, in other words, his third best friend (cf. above, 2.4). Line 4, Auster is the south wind that blows the cutting scirocco. Virgil, *Aen.* 1.51; *RS* 269.4. Lines 4–8, she can hardly restrain her tears.

21. 2.11. Late in 1562, tragedy struck the house of Medici when Eleonora, Giovanni, and Garzia died of malarial fever during a hunting expedition in the swampy Tuscan Maremma. This shocking loss was mourned in two nearly identical anthologies of poetry: *Rime di diversi eccellentissimi autori fatte nella morte dell'Illustrissima et Eccellentissima Duchessa di Fiorenza et Siena, et degli Illustrissimi Signori suoi figliuoli,* published by Valente Panizza Mantovano (Ferrara, 1563); and *Poesie toscane, et latine di diversi eccel. ingegni, nella morte del S. D. Giovanni Cardinale, del sig. Don Grazia de Medici, et della S. Donna Leonora di Toledo de Medici Duchessa di Fiorenza et di Siena,* edited by Lodovico Domenichi (Florence, 1563), who seems to have plagiarized the Ferrara edition. Battiferra first appears in these volumes as the recipient of a sonnet from Benedetto Varchi, which she answers. As when Luca Martini and Giovan'Antonio Battiferri died, her husband is also remembered in consolatory verses, this time by Gherardo Spini in the Domenichi volume (1.I; 2.7). In 1560, Bartolomeo Ammannati won a major commission to take charge of expanding the Pitti Palace, which the Duchess Eleonora de Toledo had purchased for her family. Her death (December 18, 1562) must have thrown into question the future of the project, already well underway.

22. Lines 1–2, the "nest" is the Pitti Palace, being remodeled in a classical style that will rival the greatest structures of antiquity. Line 3, Luni is the Italian region near Carrara; Paros is an Aegean island in the Cyclades famous for its marbles. Lines 5–8, Eleonora is the "sun" whose eyes will no longer light up the palace. Now she is in heaven with the sun, Apollo. The Delphic Oracle was said to be located at the earth's umbilical; Eleonora had made Florence the center of the world. Line 10, Scopas was a famous ancient Greek sculptor of Paros (4th c. B.C.E.). Leone Leoni (1509–1590), Ammannati's close contemporary, acquired great wealth as a medalist and sculptor for a stellar array of patrons, including Emperor Charles V, Phillip II, the Duke of Alba, the Duke of Mantua Cesare Gonzaga, and Pope Pius IV. Vasari writes of him with unstinting admiration. Line 11, her eyes ("rays") perfected Ammannati's works in marble.

23. 2.12. Thanks to Cosimo's influence, Giovanni de' Medici (1543–November 20, 1562) was created a cardinal in the spring of 1560 at the age of sixteen (1.15). His premature death dashed hopes that he would follow in the footsteps of an earlier Giovanni de' Medici, that son of Lorenzo the Magnificent who had been a cardinal at fourteen and who later wore the tiara as Leo X. Battiferra, here cited from the Ferrara anthology, elegantly bathes Giovanni in light: Giovanni's short life is a mere

lightning flash; in life he was a "splendor"; in death he can gaze straight into the sun with his *lumi* ("eyes," but literally, "lights"); as a soul he is now *luce* (a "light") unequalled by any other.

24. Lines 9–11, I have preferred the Ferrara reading "intenti" to Domenichi's "eterni" because of antecedents for the former in Dante's *Paradiso,* where Beatrice can look straight at the sun and so, too, do the poet's eyes acquire that power as he approaches the final vision. The word *lumi* as a metonym for eyes in v. 10 (literally, "lights") appears in Petrarch (e.g., *RS* 156.5: "e vidi lagrimar que' duo bei lumi" (And I saw those two beautiful lights weeping); for Dante the eyes of Beatrice can be "luci" (e.g., *Par.* 18.55.)

25. 2.13. There can be no doubt that both Ammannati must have been severely shaken by the news that Eleonora had succumbed to malarial fever (December 18, 1562). These verses corrorborate the duchess's personal role in sending prime commissions like the *Neptune Fountain* Ammannati's way, and they recall what Battiferra had written to Eleonora in the dedicatory letter of her *Primo libro* (4.5). Here she recalls her "lowly rhymes" for Eleonora in that anthology, published just two years before, associating the event with a major turning point in her life, when she put aside womanly tasks like sewing and abandoned her female dress ("skirt") to become, as it were, a man when she embarked on a career as a published poet after many years of only circulating her work privately.

26. Lines 4–8, the sculptor, as if turned to stone himself from paralyzing grief, sheds tears of marble. Line 10, *Amphrysus:* a river in Thessaly; *Aeas:* a river in Epirus. Battiferra borrows the binomial from Ovid, *Met.* 1.580: "lenisque Amphrysos et Aeas." Ovid names these rivers in a passage that belongs, significantly, to the closing verses of his Apollo-Daphne story. They are among the waters that flow from Peneus, the river god who was the nymph Daphne's father. What Battiferra says, in other words, is that she "became" Daphne, changing from a woman into a poet.

27. 2.14. In the 1563 funerary anthology from Ferrara, the order of Battiferra's poems for the deceased members of the Medici family follows a hierarchy: first the cardinal, who was the older of the two boys and held an elevated ecclesiastical rank; then his mother the duchess; and last, the younger boy Garzia, who died at only seventeen (1547–December 12, 1562). One could also think of it as a portrait, with the mother flanked by her sons.

28. Line 2, the halcyon was a legendary bird resembling the kingfisher that supposedly had the power to calm the sea in the depth of winter. Line 5, *appio:* from the Latin *apium,* umbrelliferous plant liked by bees. One marsh variety, *apium graveolens* (water parsley), was used in antiquity to make garlands. See Virgil, *Ecl.* 6.68, probably the source for the suggestion here: "apio crinis ornatus amaro" (locks crowned with bitter parsley). The word is hapax in Battiferra's oeuvre. Lines 7–8, Neptune and Thetis are king and queen of the seas. Battiferra knew the winds from the storm at sea in Virgil, *Aen.* 1. Notus is the south wind; Aquilo, the north wind. Cf. Battiferra's poem on the *Neptune Fountain,* 1.39. Lines 9–14, Jason and the Argonauts left the Greek city of Colchis to sail in search of the Golden Fleece (Ovid, *Met.* 7.1 ff.). Perhaps Battiferra alludes to the fact that Garzia's father, Cosimo, had received the Order of the Golden Fleece, but Garzia died too young to be so honored. Nevertheless, he will be remembered in the four corners of the earth—north (Boreas), south (Auster), west, and east.

29. 2.15. Eight sonnets by Battiferra appear among papers now in Parma that belonged to the Bolognese prelate who became archbishop of Ragusa (Dubrovnik), Lodovico Beccadelli (1502–1572). A churchman with humanistic values who wrote biographies of Petrarch, Bembo, and the English cardinal Reginald Pole—but an advocate of the Index of Prohibited Books at the Council of Trent—he loved the vernacular poetry descended from the Provençals, composed lyrics of his own, and participated as a corresponding member of the Florentine Academy. His piece for Battiferra is preserved on a folio facing his sonnet for Christopher Columbus in a manuscript made of poems he addressed to other illustrious personages, including the Emperor Charles V, Titian (who painted his portrait), Michelangelo, Bembo, Vittoria Colonna, and Della Casa. The date, recorded in a rough draft copy as 1560, confirms that it celebrates the publication of her *Primo libro*.

30. Line 2, *Castalia:* fountain on Parnassus sacred to Apollo and the Muses. Line 13, *Euterpe:* the muse of music.

31. 2.16. Three years later, when Beccadelli visited Florence, Battiferra composed this sonnet, preserved autograph in Parma with a notation in her hand on the verso of the folio she sent to Beccadelli: "sonnets for Monsignor's coming to Tuscany 1563."

32. Line 1, Arno is personified as a river God. Line 2, the silver and amber could refer to reflected lights on the surface of the river at different times of day and night. Line 6, Peneus is the river in Thessaly who was father of the nymph Daphne. The little "Reno" is the river of Bologna, where the Beccadelli were a prominent family, as opposed to the large "Reno" (Rhein) in northern Europe. Line 9, *Felsina:* Bologna; *Flora:* Florence. Line 10, *Illyria:* ancient region on the eastern shores of the Adriatic Sea, the Dalmatian coast, where Beccadelli was archbishop in Dubrovnik, formerly Ragusa; *Epidaurus:* a city of ancient Greece. Line 13, Tuscany and "King" Cosimo.

33. 2.17. The young Mantuan poet Curzio Gonzaga (1536–99) sent Battiferra a sonnet inviting her to eulogize his relative Cardinal Ercole Gonzaga (d. March 3, 1563). A man of the highest intellectual and moral standards, the cardinal had authored a treatise on Christian life, served as ambassador to popes and kings, brought order to the Duchy of Mantua as regent, performed great works of charity, and distinguished himself as presiding legate at the Council of Trent from 1561, where he died attended by the Jesuit Lainez. Battiferra, who would have admired his activity as a religious reformer and as a benefactor of the Jesuit College in Mantua, answered with this sonnet, which elicited in turn another sonnet "replica" from Curzio. Hers is a display piece with verse that works like a jeweler's mount to encase a burst of learned allusions, all enclosed within the syntax of a single complex sentence constructed on clauses in apposition and subordination.

34. Line 1, Curzio Gonzaga's *Rime,* in which the triple exchange to which this sonnet belongs appeared, were published at Vicenza in 1585. Line 4, the one who "pricked" Aglauros was the venomous hag Envy, whom Minerva sent to punish the maiden for having violated her order not to open a basket containing Apollo's son Erichthonius (Ovid, *Met.* 2.542–61 and 2.737–832). Curzio, in other words, is beyond envy, whom he sends back into her cave. Lines 4–8, Mount *Catria* (1,700 meters) lies near Cagli, in territory that belonged to the Duchy of Urbino, where the river Metauro flows. Thanks to Curzio, little Catria takes on laurels that allow it to rival in stature giant Mount Olympus; the cultural enrichment Curzio brings makes

the Metauro flow metaphorically with gold. The soothsayer Manto, daughter of Tiresias, who left Greece and wandered in Italy, eventually founded the city of Mantua. Mount Catria is an area of Italy associated with Sybilline activity. Line 11, *Busirus*: a king of Egypt who shed travelers' blood in his temples and was slain by Hercules as one of his labors (Ovid, *Met.* 9.182–83). The Hydra who dwelt in the swamp of Lerna had a hundred heads, and even though two grew back for every one of them that Hercules cut off, he managed to slay the monster (*Met.* 9.69–74). Ercole Gonzaga, a devout Catholic, worked like his mythical namesake to slay the monsters of his times—infidels and heretics. Lines 13–14, by praising the cardinal, Battiferra imitates Curzio, who had composed his own sonnet on that theme (*Rime,* 5.24).

35. 2.18. This sonnet appears at the end of a small manuscript *Sonetti di Benedetto Varchi sopra il dolorosissimo e pericolosissimo accidente dell'illustrissimo et eccellentissimo duca,* dated Saint Simon's day, 1563 (January 5, 1564, modern style). His booklet celebrates Cosimo's return to health after the loss of his wife and sons with sonnets addressed to the duke, his other surviving children, and fellow poets including Battiferra, who is one of three recipients to send Varchi a reply. Her classical nautical image, which reverses *RS* 189, conveys a flattering political message: the Florentine ship of state, captained by Cosimo, nearly sank during his desperate mourning, but now he is back at the helm, and the populace rejoices to see government on course again.

36. Line 2, the "sign" is the pole star by which sailors navigate. Metaphorically, Duke Cosimo is the Florentine's "tramontane," or guiding star (v. 11). Line 6, God sent Noah a rainbow after the flood as a sign of hope (Gn 9.13). Line 10, cf. *RS* 359.42: "librar con giusta lancia" (to weigh with an accurate balance). The image, which asserts Cosimo's fairness as a just ruler, is of a set of scales, calibrated so that the hand ("lancia") points always to the number that gives accurate weight.

37. 2.19. Duke Cosimo appointed Ammannati, Cellini, Vasari, and Bronzino, founding members of the recently established Academy of Design, to organize Michelangelo's funeral, held at San Lorenzo on June 28, 1564. At the center of the church stood the great catafalque, to which mourners attached poems, which were published the same year in *Esequie del Divino Michelangelo Buonarroti*. Battiferra is represented by this sonnet and the *canzone* following (2.20). Michelangelo helped Ammannati professionally in Rome in the early 1550s (cf. 1.115), and the two corresponded after Laura and Bartolomeo moved to Florence. In a letter of April 5, 1561, from Florence Ammannati enclosed some spiritual poems by his wife, and two of her sonnets can be found among Michelangelo's notebooks. Here Battiferra remembers Michelangelo first as a sculptor, then a painter, an architect, and finally—in the culminating position of the poem—as a rare, distinctly individual lyric voice.

38. Line 1, *Ragion è ben* (Well right it is): *RS* 70.11; G. Muzio, *Rime* 2:34.1; Tullia d'Aragona, *Rime* 13.9. Line 2, cf. above, 1.115.12. Line 12, *Aganippe*: a spring on Mount Helicon, sacred to the Muses, its "chorus." Raineri, *Cento sonetti* 102a.6 (to Annibal Caro): "d'Aganippe il coro." Line 14, in Battiferra's moving tribute, the man known as the divine Michelangelo (literally, "Michael, the angel" or "angelic Michael") is now, in fact, an angel.

39. 2.20. This is one of only two known *canzoni* by Battiferra (excluding her sestina, 1.48). The other appears in her *Primo libro*. Her clear preference was for the shorter forms, sonnet and madrigal.

40. Lines 11–13, death has snuffed out Michelangelo.

41. This refers to Michelangelo's dramatic foreshortening techniques. Lines 14–18, death has shot him with her bow and arrow. Line 25, *scorci* (angles): (Rudolf Wittkower and Margot Wittkower, *The Divine Michelangelo: The Florentine Academy's Homage on His Death in 1564. A Facsimile Edition of Esequie del Divino Michelangnolo Buonarroti Firenze 1564* [London: Phaidon Press, 1964]).

42. Line 29, *Angel divino* (divine Angel): a pun on Michelangelo (literally, Michael the angel).

43. Line 40, the Muses.

44. Line 63, *'l BUON spirto, a' miglior spirti ARROTO*: a pun on Michelangelo's surname, Buonarroto (Buonarroti): "buon" (good) + "arroto" (cf. "arrotare," meaning "to sharpen," as a knife on a whetstone). This stanza seems to be missing a verse.

45. Lines 65–66, Ammannati. Line 67, the "king" of the nest is Cosimo. Lines 69–73, Michelangelo praised Ammannati to Cosimo. A good candidate for the envious "spirits" from whom Michelangelo's words shielded Ammannati would be Cellini, whose jealousy is transparent in his *Vita*.

46. Lines 78–80, the *congedo* or envoy depicts the collective grief that has made Florence as "pale" as the dead Michelangelo. Daedalus, Apollo, Apelles, and Phidias, representing the different arts, could refer to the committee that organized the funeral. Ammannati's nickname was Fidia (Kirkham, "Creative Partners"); in poetic exchanges Bronzino was called "Apelles and Apollo." Perhaps Daedalus alludes to Cellini and his cunning inventions as goldsmith.

47. 2.21. Bernardo Gamucci, of distinguished family, was a scholar of antiquities and an architect from the Tuscan hilltop town of San Gimignano. His *Antichità della città di Roma,* published at Venice in 1565, enjoyed four reprints in the sixteenth century. Belonging to a popular family of guidebooks to Rome, it describes in topographical order the city's principal monuments, illustrated with many woodcuts. Gamucci dedicated his book to the Medici prince, Francesco, whose father he praises for the Pitti Palace project. Later, when describing a portal in one of the Roman acqueducts, he explains, "That order has been imitated by Bartolomeo Ammannati, no less excellent as a sculptor than as an architect, in the beautiful construction sponsored by the great Cosimo de' Medici at the Pitti in the city of Florence, in which by universal judgment, this rare and expert architect has demonstrated how much knowledge needs to be spent on a major city building" (1565, 95). Varchi, Battiferra, and Spini, in that order, each contributed a dedicatory sonnet, printed at the beginning of Gamucci's book.

48. Line 7, the children of Mars are the Romans. Line 12, the Elsa river flows in Tuscany, near San Gimignano. Hence Gamucci's book on Rome makes his native Tuscany famous, but no matter how much Romans or Tuscans may praise him, it is still "frugal" compared to what the young author deserves.

49. 2.22. These verses are preserved, signed and in the poet's own hand, in a sixteenth-century manuscript miscellany with the following notation: "The Company of the Scala on the eve of San Giovanni, 1577, sang this madrigal on a float where God the Father was crowning the Virgin." San Giovanni is the patron saint of Florence, whose feast day falls on June 24. The "Company" responsible for making the

float was the prestigious Confraternity of the Archangel Raphael, lay worshippers long headquartered at the Ospedale della Scala (Konrad Eisenbichler, *The Boys of the Arcangel Raphael: A Youth Confraternity in Florence, 1411–1785* [Toronto: University of Toronto Press, 1998]). Always the focus of major celebrations, Saint John's day was especially memorable in 1577 because on May 20 of that year a new prince had been born to Francesco de' Medici and Giovanna d'Austria. Their first son following six daughters, he was named Filippino, "Little Phillip," after Phillip II of Spain. To celebrate the heir's long-awaited arrival, money and bread were thrown from the palace, free wine flowed, and there were lavish fireworks and public festivities like the procession for which this madrigal was composed. Ammannati directed the artists who constructed decorations for the baptistry of San Giovanni, where the child was solemnly christened on September 29 (Eve Borsook, "Art and Politics at the Medici Court II: The Baptism of Filippo de' Medici," *Mitteilungen des Kunsthistorischen Institutes in Florenz* 13.1–2 [December 1967]: 95–114). The floats in the parade typically recapitulate salvation history from the Fall of Lucifer to the Assumption of Our Lady, the culminating scene for which Battiferra wrote.

50. Lines 5–6, the child was sickly and would survive only a little more than a year. Line 7, for "Etruria" as Tuscany, see above, 1.16. Line 8, Battiferra expresses a hope that the Medici dynasty may long endure and that its rulers may join the blest in the afterlife as souls made beautiful by their heavenly status.

51. 2.23. Sebastiano Sanleolino's *Serenissimi Cosmi Medycis primi Hetruriae Magniducis Actiones,* published at Florence in 1578, is a collection of Latin encomia to the ruler who had died four years earlier. Beginning with Cosimo's ascension, it lists his many admirable accomplishments—his military conquests of the Turks in Tuscan territory, aided by his soldiers Stefano Colonna and Chiappino Vitelli, and the defeat of Siena, which conjoined the "wolf" and the "lion," symbols, respectively, of the Arbia and Arno cities. A catalog of Cosimo's great urban improvements, including the Pitti Palace and Boboli Gardens, praises Ammannati for rebuilding Ponte Santa Trinita and as the "Phidias" and "Myron" who created the *Neptune Fountain*. The last part of this compilation contains "various" poems by Sanleolino, among them this distich on Battiferra, in which Clio, muse of history, expresses wonderment at Battiferra's talent. Annibal Caro had called Laura his "laurel and Clio" in a poem for her *Primo libro* (1.67).

52. 2.24. This poem, which records a snatch of conversation among established men of letters about the new woman poet who has appeared on their scene, complements the pastoral sonnets Battiferra composed from Maiano after 1555, when she and her husband moved to Florence. Cellini, who joins in a flattering sonnet exchange for the *Primo libro,* here refers to a new young laurel plant (Laura) shooting up in Varchi's vicinity, at Maiano, with song that will make him and Florence famous. This sonnet could date from ca. 1557, the first year of Battiferra's surviving letters to Varchi. Battiferra's own poetry celebrates Maiano (1.53–54), the country that Varchi loved too. Cf. also 1.80 for the sonnet from Messer Benvenuto that Battiferra placed in her *Primo libro*.

53. Line 1, *acerba* (unripe): she is still young. Born in 1523, Battiferra would have been in her early thirties. Line 8, she is improving as a poet. Lines 12–14, she is writing pastoral and political poetry.

54. 2.25. Anton Francesco Grazzini (1503–1584) was known as il Lasca ("the roach fish") from the name he took for the Accademia degli Umidi ("Academy of the Damp"), renamed the Accademia Fiorentina in 1542. He authored comic plays, novellas, and verse, but he was also adept in the high Petrarchan register. In that mode he exchanged sonnets with Battiferra, who includes him in her *Primo libro*. Like the following three sonnets, this one, preserved in Bronzino's *Delle rime*, presumably discusses the painter-poet's portrait of Battiferra that today hangs in Palazzo Vecchio.

55. Line 1, il Lasca puns on Bronzino's first name, Agnolo, a Tuscan form of *angelo* ("angel"). Lines 12–14, cf. *RS* 77.5–8: "Ma certo il mio Simon fu in Paradiso / onde questa gentil donna si parte; / ivi la vide, et la ritrasse in carte / per far fede qua giù del suo bel viso" (But certainly my Simon was in Paradise, whence comes this noble lady; there he saw her and portrayed her on paper, to attest down here to her lovely face).

56. 2.26. Bronzino responds *per rime* to il Lasca, whom he thinks overgenerous in praise, with a sonnet that attributes all his talent to God.

57. Line 2, cf. *RS* 78.1–2: "Quando giunse a Simon l'alto concetto / ch' a mio nome gli pose in man lo stile" (When Simon received the high idea which, for my sake, put his hand to his stylus).

58. 2.27. This puzzling sonnet evidently refers to another picture of Battiferra, perhaps an imaginary one that belongs to their pastoral literary games. We could envision Bronzino's Laura dressed as a shepherdess, holding or leaning on a richly ornamented crook—hence the "gorbia" (shaft, staff, pole) ringed by a golden "ghiera" (a metal circlet used to encase the end of such objects as umbrella shafts).

59. Line 4, perhaps the "highest honors" go to Varchi, but the allusion is unclear.

60. 2.28. Battiferra thanks Bronzino for her "new image." In Bronzino's *canzoniere*, this sonnet directly follows his puzzling verses to Laura as shepherdess, but little apart from placement suggests a connection with the poem just before. No rubric identifies it as a "risposta," nor does it echo the rhymes of the preceding sonnet, as would be customary in a reply. Perhaps then this is a poem of thanks for Bronzino's known portrait of her, the same one praised by il Lasca. Here Battiferra and Bronzino, who pose as lovers in their poetic correspondence, reenact the parts of Laura and Petrarch, whose mythological ancestors were Daphne and Apollo, but with two new twists: both are poets, and their sentiments are reciprocal. Although his fame towers over hers, fragile because it is still young, through him she can aspire to an enduring reputation now that with twin homage of pen and brush he has boosted her visibility.

61. Line 2, *Crisero*: Bronzino's pastoral name, literally "the golden one," may be a learned Hellenic equivalent to the Tuscan "Bronzino," the reference being to his reddish blond or coppery colored hair. The nickname could also suggest the "golden" quality of his words (cf. Saint John Chrysostom, or "Golden mouth"). Lines 9–11, Bronzino, a rival to the god of poetry Apollo, can expect his laurels to reach the heavens. Lines 12–14, his painting and poetry will strengthen twice over the trunk ("stelo") of her own cherished laurel, making it resistant to the winds of time.

62. 2.29. The same manuscript of Bronzino's poetry that contains the above series of poems on his portrait of Laura includes a number of other sonnets explicitly ad-

dressed to her, as well as many that clearly refer to her, but lack a dedicatory title. This one, highly mannered in its style, creatively turns the name of the Isauro river into a feminine adjective rhyming with "Laura" in a catalog of homonyms that culminates with the lady's name. Such clever punning turns on the poet's "double" ardor for a lady whose split identity connects her with two cities, Florence on the Arno and Urbino on the Isauro. Wherever she is, near or far, her effects are consequentially twofold: she at once makes him burn, and she cools him with her refreshing "aura"; she inspires "double" hope; while he bows humbly before her, she raises him up in understanding.

63. Lines 1–4, whether it is dawn or noon, whether she is in the east (Urbino) or "here" in Florence, her effects on the poet are the same. Lines 5–8, Battiferra is a laurel (Laura) whose "odor," (poetry) is making her famous. Line 14, Bronzino desires both Lauras.

64. 2.30. In the poetic dialogue between Bronzino and Battiferra from *Delle rime,* as recalcitrant mistress she combines features of Petrarch's Laura-Daphne and Dante's Petra, the cold lady of the *Rime petrose*. No longer as hard-hearted as a rock, she is still an unattainable love object, composed of iron encased with ice. Here the conceit of the "iron lady" reiterates the idea in Bronzino's portrait of her that she is inflexible and refuses "to bend" to his wishes (Kirkham, "Dante's Fantom, Petrarch's Specter").

65. Lines 1–8, Bronzino asks Love if he is not tired of wearing himself out with the poet, all for a Laura-Dafne whom even the god Apollo could not catch. Line 10, *'l ferro onde ha radice* (the iron in which she has her roots): the Battiferri family name, literally, "iron pounder" (blacksmith). Line 11, Daphne, the daughter of the river god Peneus, turned into a laurel but remained visible in that form; Bronzino fears that his Laura might disappear altogether, even as a "laurel." Lines 12–14, the questions are addressed to Love.

66. 2.31. Unattributed, this is the sole copy of a sonnet preserved in a manuscript all neatly copied in the same hand. Its frontispiece reads Madrigals by G. B. Strozzi the Elder, but there are poems by others as well, among them Michelangelo, il Lasca, and Varchi, the last of whom may have composed this joint tribute to Ammannati and his wife.

67. Lines 1–4, Ammannati's lifelike sculptures make their subjects live eternally and bring him fame everlasting. Line 13, Scopas of Paros (5th c. B.C.E.), Praxiteles of Athens (4th c. B.C.E.), and Phidias of Athens (4th c. B.C.E.) were the three most famous sculptors of Greek antiquity. Ammannati, of course, was affectionately nicknamed "Fidia."

68. 2.32. A single manuscript miscellany preserves these octaves, evidently written for a pageant in Florence. According to the Gospel (Mt 25), the wise virgins had supplied oil for their lamps and could arise in the night to meet the bridegroom when he arrived unexpectedly; the foolish ones, their lamps empty, were unprepared for his coming and could not join the wedding feast. The story teaches that we should always be ready to receive Christ, the bridegroom, for we know neither the day nor the hour of his coming. Here it serves as an allegory of Florence.

69. Lines 1–3, Cosimo's wisdom is greater than that of any other mortal; it is superhuman. Lines 4–8, perhaps it is a personification of Wisdom who speaks (see below,

1.33). Line 14, Florence lives righteously under Medici rule, a city morally prepared for the Second Coming.

70. 2.33. These lines follow the octaves on the wise and foolish virgins in the manuscript and are also attributed to Battiferra. Perhaps Battiferra composed them for the same occasion.

71. Lines 1–2 the goddess could be a personification of Wisdom.

72. 2.34. These verses belong to an anthology of lyric poetry by various authors, copied in the hand of Giovan Battista Strozzi the Younger (1551–1634) in the Strozzi Collection manuscripts at the Newberry Library (1: fols. 169r–171r). They are part of a sequence, clearly composed for a Medici pageant and probably all by Battiferra, although her name only appears in the manuscript with this one, the second. The other speakers are Lady Tuscany and her personified rivers—Arno, Ombrone, and Arbia. The presence of Arbia, who makes reference to peace following discord, suggests that the occasion celebrated was Cosimo's conquest of Siena.

73. Line 3, Tiber comes with the other rivers to pay tribute to the duke. Lines 7–9, perhaps a reference to Cosimo's hopes for papal support in obtaining a crown as king of Tuscany.

74. 2.35. Mario Colonna (fl. 1560), recipient of the letter from Piero Vettori that prefaces Battiferra's *Rhymes,* composed verse not published until 1589, after his death. His *Tuscan Poetry* includes a sequence with one sonnet from him to Battiferra that lacks her reply plus three complete sonnet exchanges. (Battiferra's *Rhymes* preserve only one of their sonnet exchanges; its first poem is the same as in Colonna's *canzoniere,* and its second part restores the reply of hers that had been missing from his lyrics.) From the compliments they trade, it is clear that Battiferra is the older poet. Her fame is bright, "even where the great Danube freezes over," writes Colonna, who had been sent by Duke Cosimo as an ambassador to congratulate Maximilian II on his succesion to the throne in 1564. Cf. Spini's letter to Battiferra, 4.8. In his second sonnet to Battiferra, Colonna laments the death of three people ("three blows"), perhaps Eleonora de Toledo and the two Medici princes. The third poem, here reproduced, could refer to the same general time of mourning. Colonna urges her to rejoin her intellectual circle of friends in town ("the unsullied troop true to Arno"), perhaps from her country retreat at Maiano.

75. Lines 3–4, her devotees miss her company. Line 5, *mirti . . . amaranti* (myrtles . . . amarynths): Amaranthus is a pastoral flower. It has the epithet "immortal" in Sannazzaro's *Arcadia* (10.340). Lines 10–11, *candida schiera* (troop): cf. 2.2 and the volume editor's introduction. Metaphorically swans, the troop of poets is also "white" because of its pure moral values. Her friends in Florence are weeping; their tears raise the level of the Arno. Line 12, Jove is Cosimo. Line 13, *cigni* (swans): poets. Colonna protests his inadequacy.

76. 2.36. Laura "hides" in the blackest caves she can find—perhaps a metaphor for her mourning. If the occasion was the death of the duchess, Giovanni, and Garzia de' Medici, these poems exchanged in manuscript did not pass into print until more than thirty years after they were written.

77. Lines 5–9, the blackest caves are like those of Cimmeria (see 2.1). She is too downcast to be in poetic voice ("accents") worthy of her literary circle ("swans"). Line

5, *giusto sdegno* (just disdain): Dante, *Inf.* 13.70–72. Line 8, *cigni sì canori* (such canorous swans): cf. A. F. Raineri, *Cento sonetti* 15.9: "Dite, o canori cigni" (Speak, O canorous swans).

78. 2.37. This exchange seems to have taken place soon after the death of Eleonora de Toledo (1562), a loss to which Battiferra alludes in the reply she sent to Terracina. Eleonora, a daughter of the Spanish viceroy of Naples, had spent her teen years at that southern Italian court, where Terracina was active as poet. The verse missive that Terracina sent to Battiferra, of interest because it connects two famous literary women, is indicative of the culture that flowed between Florence and Naples, political allies in the empire of Philip II. Laura Terracina (1519–after 1577), writing from Naples, sends her highest compliments to Battiferra in Florence. Although another "laurel," she only produces ugly, worthless rhymes—"weeds" and "stones" instead of healthy Petrarchan "fruits and flowers." In a witty game of contrasts, she poses as a poet bereft of talent to magnify her recipient's literary wealth, a miraculous gift that makes her a repository of all the ability bestowed cumulatively on the world's poets. The sonnet is preserved in the last of Terracina's nine books of poetry, the only one left in manuscript at her death. The first eight were published between 1548 and 1561 (Nancy Dersofi, "Laura Terracina (1519–c. 1577)," in *Italian Women Writers: A Bio-Bibliographical Sourcebook,* ed. Rinaldina Russell [Westport, Conn.: Greenwood Press, 1994], 423–30; Luigi Montella, *Una poetessa del Rinascimento: Laura Terracina con le Le None Rime inedite* [Salerno: Edisud, 1993]).

79. Line 3, the olive is a symbol of wisdom. Line 6, Mergellina: a seafront section of Naples where Virgil's tomb is located.

80. 2.38. Battiferra replies in the same spirit, addressing Terracina with reference to the Neapolitan academy of which the latter was a member. She vindicates Terracina's right to dwell among the Muses, but claims with self-demeaning tactics to be out of favor with them and Apollo, so much so that whatever she writes makes her blench with embarrassment. The second half of the sonnet reveals the cause for her inability to write: she has lost the woman honored by Arno and Iberia, a personage who can only be Eleonora de Toledo (cf. 2.13).

81. Line 1, the Muses. Mount Helicon and the fountain Aganippe, where the Muses dwell, belong to the Aonian Mountains in Boeotia. Lines 6–7, Apollo and the muses have turned against her; she lacks poetic inspiration.

82. 2.39. Absent from her *Rhymes,* this poem appears attributed to Battiferra immediately following her sonnet on the death of Maria de' Medici (1.98) in two manuscript miscellanies in gatherings that were copied one (Florence, MS Magl. 2.4.233) from the other (Florence, MS Magl. 7.346). MS 7.346 is the sort of collection one could imagine would have been in Laura's library, with sonnets by il Lasca, Luigi Alamanni, Benedetto Varchi, Annibal Caro, Mario Colonna, and Benvenuto Cellini. It includes verse of Urbino interest (to the duchess Vittoria Farnese della Rovere, to the duke on taking the baton of power), which probably accounts for the inclusion of poems by Battiferra. Here Laura addresses Christ, alluding to the moment of his death on the cross. The sonnet is typical of her late writing.

83. Lines 1–4, as Christ gave up the ghost, the earth quaked, rocks were rent, and tombs opened (Mt 27.46–52). Even his power, however, cannot break the hardness

of her heart. The stony motif recalls Dante's *Rime petrose* and Medusa's threat at the gates of Hell (*Inf.* 9).

84. 2.40. Benedetto Varchi's *Sonetti contro gl' ugonotti* preserved in an unpublished manuscript at the Biblioteca Nazionale in Florence (Magl. 2.8.137) contains two exchanges with Battiferra, hitherto unnoted in her biographical tradition. The volume, offered to Paolo Giordano Orsini (1.4), is undated. References in its dedicatory letter to the "sudden and dangerous movements and tumults of the Huguenots," countered by Fabrizio Serbelloni and Lorenzo Lenzi, whom Varchi praises as heroes in the poems, suggest a dating of ca. 1562, when the religious wars broke out in France. Late in 1561, Pope Pius IV sent Serbelloni with 2,000 cavalry and infantry to Avignon. He named Lenzi, who was the bishop of Fermo, Varchi's longtime protégé, and the chief object of his affection (his "first laurel"—see above, 2.4), as Vicelegate of that city, at the geographic epicenter of the first disturbances (Paolo Sarpi, *Istoria del Concilio Tridentino,* ed. Corrado Vivanti. 2 vols. [Turin: Einaudi, 1974], 733; Umberto Pirotti, *Benedetto Varchi e la cultura del suo tempo* [Florence: Olschki, 1971], 49). In this sonnet, responding to Varchi's expression of fear that his "lord," presumably Lenzi, will die in the violence, Battiferra reassures him that the Church of Rome will triumph.

85. Line 1–8, the Church of Rome, personified as Christ's bride, from her dwelling beside the Tiber, is sad to see the heretical Huguenots and glad that her armies are slaughtering them. Line 8, *cammin dritto* (straight path): cf. Dante, *Inf.* 1.3 "diritta via" (straight way). Lines 12–14, Lenzi will return to Italy decked with honors.

SERIES EDITORS' BIBLIOGRAPHY

PRIMARY SOURCES

Alberti, Leon Battista (1404–72). *The Family in Renaissance Florence.* Translated by Renée Neu Watkins. Columbia: University of South Carolina Press, 1969.

Arenal, Electa and Stacey Schlau, eds. *Untold Sisters: Hispanic Nuns in Their Own Works.* Translated by Amanda Powell. Albuquerque: University of New Mexico Press, 1989.

Astell, Mary (1666–1731). *The First English Feminist: Reflections on Marriage and Other Writings.* Edited and introduction by Bridget Hill. New York: St. Martin's Press, 1986.

Atherton, Margaret, ed. *Women Philosophers of the Early Modern Period.* Indianapolis, IN: Hackett, 1994.

Aughterson, Kate, ed. *Renaissance Woman: Constructions of Femininity in England: A Source Book.* London: Routledge, 1995.

Barbaro, Francesco (1390–1454). *On Wifely Duties* (preface and book 2). Translated by Benjamin Kohl in Kohl and R. G. Witt, eds., *The Earthly Republic.* Philadelphia: University of Pennsylvania Press, 1978, 179–228.

Behn, Aphra. *The Works of Aphra Behn.* 7 vols. Edited by Janet Todd. Columbus: Ohio State University Press, 1992–96.

Boccaccio, Giovanni (1313–75). *Famous Women.* Edited and translated by Virginia Brown. The I Tatti Renaissance Library. Cambridge, MA: Harvard University Press, 2001.

———. *Corbaccio or the Labyrinth of Love.* Translated by Anthony K. Cassell. 2nd rev. ed. Binghamton, NY: Medieval and Renaissance Texts and Studies, 1993.

Brown, Sylvia. *Women's Writing in Stuart England: The Mother's Legacies of Dorothy Leigh, Elizabeth Joscelin and Elizabeth Richardson.* Thrupp, Stroud, Gloucestershire: Sutton, 1999.

Bruni, Leonardo (1370–1444). "On the Study of Literature (1405) to Lady Battista Malatesta of Moltefeltro." In *The Humanism of Leonardo Bruni: Selected Texts.* Translated and introduction by Gordon Griffiths, James Hankins, and David Thompson. Binghamton, NY: Medieval and Renaissance Studies and Texts, 1987, 240–51.

Castiglione, Baldassare (1478–1529). *The Book of the Courtier.* Translated by George Bull. New York: Penguin, 1967. *The Book of the Courtier.* Edited by Daniel Javitch. New York: W. W. Norton, 2002.

Christine de Pizan (1365–1431). *The Book of the City of Ladies.* Translated by Earl Jeffrey Richards. Foreword by Marina Warner. New York: Persea, 1982.

———. *The Treasure of the City of Ladies.* Translated by Sarah Lawson. New York: Viking Penguin, 1985. Also translated and introduction by Charity Cannon Willard. Edited and introduction by Madeleine P. Cosman. New York: Persea, 1989.

Clarke, Danielle, ed. *Isabella Whitney, Mary Sidney and Aemilia Lanyer: Renaissance Women Poets.* New York: Penguin, 2000.

Crawford, Patricia, and Laura Gowing, eds. *Women's Worlds in Seventeenth-Century England: A Source Book.* London: Routledge, 2000.

Daybell, James, ed. *Early Modern Women's Letter Writing, 1450–1700.* Houndmills, England:: Palgrave, 2001.

Elizabeth I: Collected Works. Edited by Leah S. Marcus, Janel Mueller, and Mary Beth Rose. Chicago: University of Chicago Press, 2000.

Elyot, Thomas (1490–1546). *Defence of Good Women: The Feminist Controversy of the Renaissance.* Facsimile Reproductions. Edited by Diane Bornstein. New York: Delmar, 1980.

Erasmus, Desiderius (1467–1536). *Erasmus on Women.* Edited by Erika Rummel. Toronto: University of Toronto Press, 1996.

Female and Male Voices in Early Modern England: An Anthology of Renaissance Writing. Edited by Betty S. Travitsky and Anne Lake Prescott. New York: Columbia University Press, 2000.

Ferguson, Moira, ed. *First Feminists: British Women Writers 1578–1799.* Bloomington: Indiana University Press, 1985.

Galilei, Maria Celeste. *Sister Maria Celeste's Letters to Her Father, Galileo.* Edited by and Translated by Rinaldina Russell. Lincoln, NE: Writers Club Press of Universe.com, 2000. Also published as *To Father: The Letters of Sister Maria Celeste to Galileo, 1623–1633.* Translated by Dava Sobel. London: Fourth Estate, 2001.

Gethner, Perry, ed. *The Lunatic Lover and Other Plays by French Women of the 17th and 18th Centuries.* Portsmouth, NH: Heinemann, 1994.

Glückel of Hameln (1646–1724). *The Memoirs of Glückel of Hameln.* Translated by Marvin Lowenthal. New introduction by Robert Rosen. New York: Schocken Books, 1977.

Henderson, Katherine Usher, and Barbara F. McManus, eds. *Half Humankind: Contexts and Texts of the Controversy about Women in England, 1540–1640.* Urbana: Illinois University Press, 1985.

Hoby, Margaret. *The Private Life of an Elizabethan Lady: The Diary of Lady Margaret Hoby 1599–1605.* Thrupp, Stroud, Gloucestershire: Sutton, 1998.

Humanist Educational Treatises. Edited and translated by Craig W. Kallendorf. The I Tatti Renaissance Library. Cambridge, MA: Harvard University Press, 2002.

Joscelin, Elizabeth. *The Mothers Legacy to Her Unborn Childe.* Edited by Jean leDrew Metcalfe. Toronto: University of Toronto Press, 2000.

Kaminsky, Amy Katz, ed. *Water Lilies, Flores del agua: An Anthology of Spanish Women Writers from the Fifteenth Through the Nineteenth Century.* Minneapolis: University of Minnesota Press, 1996.

Kempe, Margery (1373–1439). *The Book of Margery Kempe.* Translated by and edited by Lynn Staley. A Norton Critical Edition. New York: W. W. Norton, 2001.

King, Margaret L., and Albert Rabil, Jr., eds. *Her Immaculate Hand: Selected Works by and about the Women Humanists of Quattrocento Italy.* Binghamton, NY: Medieval and Renaissance Texts and Studies, 1983; second revised paperback edition, 1991.

Klein, Joan Larsen, ed. *Daughters, Wives, and Widows: Writings by Men about Women and Marriage in England, 1500–1640.* Urbana: University of Illinois Press, 1992.

Knox, John (1505–72). *The Political Writings of John Knox: The First Blast of the Trumpet against the Monstrous Regiment of Women and Other Selected Works.* Edited by Marvin A. Breslow. Washington, DC: Folger Shakespeare Library, 1985.

Kors, Alan C., and Edward Peters, eds. *Witchcraft in Europe, 400–1700: A Documentary History.* Philadelphia: University of Pennsylvania Press, 2000.

Krämer, Heinrich, and Jacob Sprenger. *Malleus Maleficarum* (ca. 1487). Translated by Montague Summers. London: Pushkin Press, 1928. Reprint, New York: Dover, 1971.

Larsen, Anne R., and Colette H. Winn, eds. *Writings by Pre-Revolutionary French Women: From Marie de France to Elizabeth Vigée-Le Brun.* New York: Garland, 2000.

de Lorris, William, and Jean de Meun. *The Romance of the Rose.* Translated by Charles Dahlbert. Princeton, NJ: Princeton University Press, 1971. Reprint, University Press of New England, 1983.

Marguerite d'Angoulême, Queen of Navarre (1492–1549). *The Heptameron.* Translated by P. A. Chilton. New York: Viking Penguin, 1984.

Mary of Agreda. *The Divine Life of the Most Holy Virgin.* Abridgment of *The Mystical City of God.* Abridged by Fr. Bonaventure Amedeo de Caesarea, M.C. Translated from the French by Abbé Joseph A. Boullan. Rockford, IL: Tan Books, 1997.

Myers, Kathleen A., and Amanda Powell, eds. *A Wild Country Out in the Garden: The Spiritual Journals of a Colonial Mexican Nun.* Bloomington: Indiana University Press, 1999.

Russell, Rinaldina, ed. *Sister Maria Celeste's Letters to Her Father, Galileo.* San Jose: Writers Club Press, 2000.

Teresa of Avila, Saint (1515–82). *The Life of Saint Teresa of Avila by Herself.* Translated by J. M. Cohen. New York: Viking Penguin, 1957.

Weyer, Johann (1515–88). *Witches, Devils, and Doctors in the Renaissance: Johann Weyer, De praestigiis daemonum.* Edited by George Mora with Benjamin G. Kohl, Erik Midelfort, and Helen Bacon. Translated by John Shea. Binghamton, NY: Medieval and Renaissance Texts and Studies, 1991.

Wilson, Katharina M., ed. *Medieval Women Writers.* Athens: University of Georgia Press, 1984.

———, ed. *Women Writers of the Renaissance and Reformation.* Athens: University of Georgia Press, 1987.

Wilson, Katharina M., and Frank J. Warnke, eds. *Women Writers of the Seventeenth Century.* Athens: University of Georgia Press, 1989.

Wollstonecraft, Mary. *A Vindication of the Rights of Men and a Vindication of the Rights of Women.* Edited by Sylvana Tomaselli. Cambridge: Cambridge University Press, 1995. Also *The Vindications of the Rights of Men, The Rights of Women.* Edited by D. L. Macdonald and Kathleen Scherf. Peterborough, Ontario, Canada: Broadview Press, 1997.

Women Critics 1660–1820: An Anthology. Edited by the Folger Collective on Early Women Critics. Bloomington: Indiana University Press, 1995.

Women Writers in English, 1350–1850. 15 vols. published through 1999 (projected 30-volume series suspended). Oxford University Press.

Wroth, Lady Mary. *The Countess of Montgomery's Urania.* 2 parts. Edited by Josephine A. Roberts. Tempe, AZ: MRTS, 1995, 1999.

———. *Lady Mary Wroth's "Love's Victory": The Penshurst Manuscript.* Edited by Michael G. Brennan. London: The Roxburghe Club, 1988.

———. *The Poems of Lady Mary Wroth.* Edited by Josephine A. Roberts. Baton Rouge: Louisiana State University Press, 1983.

de Zayas, Maria. *The Disenchantments of Love.* Translated by H. Patsy Boyer. Albany: State University of New York Press, 1997.

———. *The Enchantments of Love: Amorous and Exemplary Novels.* Translated by H. Patsy Boyer. Berkeley and Los Angeles: University of California Press, 1990.

SECONDARY SOURCES

Ahlgren, Gillian. *Teresa of Avila and the Politics of Sanctity.* Ithaca, NY: Cornell University Press, 1996.

Akkerman, Tjitske, and Siep Sturman, eds. *Feminist Thought in European History, 1400–2000.* London: Routledge, 1997.

Allen, Sister Prudence, R.S.M. *The Concept of Woman: The Aristotelian Revolution, 750 B.C. – A.D. 1250.* Grand Rapids, MI: William B. Eerdmans, 1997.

———. *The Concept of Woman.* Vol. 2, *The Early Humanist Reformation, 1250–1500.* Grand Rapids, MI: William B. Eerdmans, 2002.

Andreadis, Harriette. *Sappho in Early Modern England: Female Same-Sex Literary Erotics 1550–1714.* Chicago: University of Chicago Press, 2001.

Armon, Shifra. *Picking Wedlock: Women and the Courtship Novel in Spain.* New York: Rowman & Littlefield Publishers, Inc., 2002.

Backer, Anne Liot Backer. *Precious Women.* New York: Basic Books, 1974.

Ballaster, Ros. *Seductive Forms.* New York: Oxford University Press, 1992.

Barash, Carol. *English Women's Poetry, 1649–1714: Politics, Community, and Linguistic Authority.* New York: Oxford University Press, 1996.

Battigelli, Anna. *Margaret Cavendish and the Exiles of the Mind.* Lexington, KY: University of Kentucky Press, 1998.

Beasley, Faith. *Revising Memory: Women's Fiction and Memoirs in Seventeenth-Century France.* New Brunswick: Rutgers University Press, 1990.

Beilin, Elaine V. *Redeeming Eve: Women Writers of the English Renaissance.* Princeton, NJ: Princeton University Press, 1987.

Benson, Pamela Joseph. *The Invention of Renaissance Woman: The Challenge of Female Independence in the Literature and Thought of Italy and England.* University Park, PA: Pennsylvania State University Press, 1992.

Benson, Pamela Joseph, and Victoria Kirkham, eds. *Strong Voices, Weak History? Medieval and Renaissance Women in their Literary Canons: England, France, Italy.* Ann Arbor: University of Michigan Press, 2003.

Bilinkoff, Jodi. *The Avila of Saint Teresa: Religious Reform in a Sixteenth-Century City.* Ithaca: Cornell University Press, 1989.

Bissell, R. Ward. *Artemisia Gentileschi and the Authority of Art.* University Park: Pennsylvania State University Press, 2000.

Blain, Virginia, Isobel Grundy, AND Patricia Clements, eds. *The Feminist Companion to*

Literature in English: Women Writers from the Middle Ages to the Present. New Haven, CT: Yale University Press, 1990.

Bloch, R. Howard. *Medieval Misogyny and the Invention of Western Romantic Love.* Chicago: University of Chicago Press, 1991.

Bornstein, Daniel and Roberto Rusconi, eds. *Women and Religion in Medieval and Renaissance Italy.* Translated by Margery J. Schneider. Chicago: University of Chicago Press, 1996.

Brant, Clare, and Diane Purkiss, eds. *Women, Texts and Histories, 1575–1760.* London: Routledge, 1992.

Briggs, Robin. *Witches and Neighbours: The Social and Cultural Context of European Witchcraft.* New York: HarperCollins, 1995; Viking Penguin, 1996.

Brink, Jean R., ed. *Female Scholars: A Tradition of Learned Women before 1800.* Montréal: Eden Press Women's Publications, 1980.

Broude, Norma, and Mary D. Garrard, eds. *The Expanding Discourse: Feminism and Art History.* New York: HarperCollins, 1992.

Brown, Judith C. *Immodest Acts: The Life of a Lesbian Nun in Renaissance Italy.* New York: Oxford University Press, 1986.

Brown, Judith C. , and Robert C. Davis, eds. *Gender and Society in Renaissance Italy.* London: Addison Wesley Longman, 1998.

Bynum, Carolyn Walker. *Fragmentation and Redemption: Essays on Gender and the Human Body in Medieval Religion.* New York: Zone Books, 1992.

———. *Holy Feast and Holy Fast: The Religious Significance of Food to Medieval Women.* Berkeley: University of California Press, 1987.

Cambridge Guide to Women's Writing in English. Edited by Lorna Sage. Cambridge: University Press, 1999.

Cavanagh, Sheila T. *Cherished Torment: The Emotional Geography of Lady Mary Wroth's* Urania. Pittsburgh: Duquesne University Press, 2001.

Cerasano, S. P. and Marion Wynne-Davies, eds. *Readings in Renaissance Women's Drama: Criticism, History, and Performance 1594–1998.* London: Routledge, 1998.

Cervigni, Dino S., ed. *Women Mystic Writers. Annali d'Italianistica* 13 (1995) (entire issue).

Cervigni, Dino S., and Rebecca West, eds. *Women's Voices in Italian Literature. Annali d'Italianistica* 7 (1989) (entire issue).

Charlton, Kenneth. *Women, Religion and Education in Early Modern England.* London: Routledge, 1999.

Chojnacka, Monica. *Working Women in Early Modern Venice.* Baltimore: Johns Hopkins University Press, 2001.

Chojnacki, Stanley. *Women and Men in Renaissance Venice: Twelve Essays on Patrician Society.* Baltimore: Johns Hopkins University Press, 2000.

Cholakian, Patricia Francis. *Rape and Writing in the "Heptameron" of Marguerite de Navarre.* Carbondale: Southern Illinois University Press, 1991.

———. *Women and the Politics of Self-Representation in Seventeenth-Century France.* Newark: University of Delaware Press, 2000.

Christine de Pizan: A Casebook. Edited by Barbara K. Altmann and Deborah L. McGrady. New York: Routledge, 2003.

Clogan, Paul Maruice, ed. *Medievali et Humanistica: Literacy and the Lay Reader.* Lanham, MD: Rowman & Littlefield, 2000.

Clubb, Louise George (1989). *Italian Drama in Shakespeare's Time.* New Haven, CT: Yale University Press.

Conley, John J., S.J. *The Suspicion of Virtue: Women Philosophers in Neoclassical France.* Ithaca, NY: Cornell University Press, 2002.

Crabb, Ann. *The Strozzi of Florence: Widowhood and Family Solidarity in the Renaissance.* Ann Arbor: University of Michigan Press, 2000.

Cruz, Anne J., and Mary Elizabeth Perry, eds. *Culture and Control in Counter-Reformation Spain.* Minneapolis: University of Minnesota Press, 1992.

Davis, Natalie Zemon. *Society and Culture in Early Modern France.* Stanford: Stanford University Press, 1975. Especially chapters 3 and 5.

———. *Women on the Margins: Three Seventeenth-Century Lives.* Cambridge, MA: Harvard University Press, 1995.

DeJean, Joan. *Ancients Against Moderns: Culture Wars and the Making of a Fin de Siècle.* Chicago: University of Chicago Press, 1997.

———. *Fictions of Sappho, 1546–1937.* Chicago: University of Chicago Press, 1989.

———. *The Reinvention of Obscenity: Sex, Lies, and Tabloids in Early Modern France.* Chicago: University of Chicago Press, 2002.

———. *Tender Geographies: Women and the Origins of the Novel in France.* New York: Columbia University Press, 1991.

Dictionary of Russian Women Writers. Edited by Marina Ledkovsky, Charlotte Rosenthal, and Mary Zirin. Westport, CT: Greenwood Press, 1994.

Dixon, Laurinda S. *Perilous Chastity: Women and Illness in Pre-Enlightenment Art and Medicine.* Ithaca: Cornell Universitiy Press, 1995.

Dolan, Frances, E. *Whores of Babylon: Catholicism, Gender and Seventeenth-Century Print Culture.* Ithaca: Cornell University Press, 1999.

Donovan, Josephine. *Women and the Rise of the Novel, 1405–1726.* New York: St. Martin's Press, 1999.

De Erauso, Catalina. *Lieutenant Nun: Memoir of a Basque Transvestite in the New World.* Translated by Michele Ttepto and Gabriel Stepto; foreword by Marjorie Garber. Boston: Beacon Press, 1995.

Encyclopedia of Continental Women Writers. 2 vols. Edited by Katharina Wilson. New York: Garland, 1991.

Erdmann, Axel. *My Gracious Silence: Women in the Mirror of Sixteenth-Century Printing in Western Europe.* Luzern: Gilhofer and Rauschberg, 1999.

Erickson, Amy Louise. *Women and Property in Early Modern England.* London: Routledge, 1993.

Ezell, Margaret J. M. *The Patriarch's Wife: Literary Evidence and the History of the Family.* Chapel Hill: University of North Carolina Press, 1987.

———. *Social Authorship and the Advent of Print.* Baltimore: Johns Hopkins University Press, 1999.

———. *Writing Women's Literary History.* Baltimore: Johns Hopkins University Press, 1993.

Farrell, Michèle Longino. *Performing Motherhood: The Sévigné Correspondence.* Hanover, NH: University Press of New England, 1991.

The Feminist Companion to Literature in English: Women Writers from the Middle Ages to the Present. Edited by Virginia Blain, Isobel Grundy, and Patricia Clements. New Haven, CT: Yale University Press, 1990.

The Feminist Encyclopedia of German Literature. Edited by Friederike Eigler and Susanne Kord. Westport, CT: Greenwood Press, 1997.

Feminist Encyclopedia of Italian Literature. Edited by Rinaldina Russell. Westport, CT: Greenwood Press, 1997.

Ferguson, Margaret W. *Dido's Daughters: Literacy, Gender, and Empire in Early Modern England and France.* Chicago: University of Chicago Press, 2003.

Ferguson, Margaret W., Maureen Quilligan, and Nancy J. Vickers, eds. *Rewriting the Renaissance: The Discourses of Sexual Difference in Early Modern Europe.* Chicago: University of Chicago Press, 1987.

Ferraro, Joanne M. *Marriage Wars in Late Renaissance Venice.* Oxford: Oxford University Press, 2001.

Fletcher, Anthony. *Gender, Sex and Subordination in England 1500–1800.* New Haven, CT: Yale University Press, 1995.

French Women Writers: A Bio-Bibliographical Source Book. Edited by Eva Martin Sartori and Dorothy Wynne Zimmerman. Westport, CT: Greenwood Press, 1991.

Frye, Susan and Karen Robertson, eds. *Maids and Mistresses, Cousins and Queens: Women's Alliances in Early Modern England.* Oxford: Oxford University Press, 1999.

Gallagher, Catherine. *Nobody's Story: The Vanishing Acts of Women Writers in the Marketplace, 1670–1820.* Berkeley: University of California Press, 1994.

Garrard, Mary D. *Artemisia Gentileschi: The Image of the Female Hero in Italian Baroque Art.* Princeton, NJ: Princeton University Press, 1989.

Gelbart, Nina Rattner. *The King's Midwife: A History and Mystery of Madame du Coudray.* Berkeley: University of California Press, 1998.

Glenn, Cheryl. *Rhetoric Retold: Regendering the Tradition from Antiquity through the Renaissance.* Carbondale: Southern Illinois University Press, 1997.

Goffen, Rona. *Titian's Women.* New Haven, CT: Yale University Press, 1997.

Goldberg, Jonathan. *Desiring Women Writing: English Renaissance Examples.* Stanford: Stanford University Press, 1997.

Goldsmith, Elizabeth C. *Exclusive Conversations: The Art of Interaction in Seventeenth-Century France.* Philadelphia: University of Pennsylvania Press, 1988.

———, ed. *Writing the Female Voice.* Boston: Northeastern University Press, 1989.

Goldsmith, Elizabeth C., and Dena Goodman, eds. *Going Public: Women and Publishing in Early Modern France.* Ithaca: Cornell University Press, 1995.

Grafton, Anthony, and Lisa Jardine. *From Humanism to the Humanities: Education and the Liberal Arts in Fifteenth-and Sixteenth-Century Europe.* London: Duckworth, 1986.

Greer, Margaret Rich. *Maria de Zayas Tells Baroque Tales of Love and the Cruelty of Men.* University Park: Pennsylvania State University Press, 2000.

Hackett, Helen. *Women and Romance Fiction in the English Renaissance.* Cambridge: Cambridge University Press, 2000.

Hall, Kim F. *Things of Darkness: Economies of Race and Gender in Early Modern England.* Ithaca, NY: Cornell University Press, 1995.

Hampton, Timothy. *Literature and the Nation in the Sixteenth Century: Inventing Renaissance France.* Ithaca, NY: Cornell University Press, 2001.

Hannay, Margaret, ed. *Silent But for the Word.* Kent, OH: Kent State University Press, 1985.

Hardwick, Julie. *The Practice of Patriarchy: Gender and the Politics of Household Authority in Early Modern France.* University Park: Pennsylvania State University Press, 1998.

Harris, Barbara J. *English Aristocratic Women, 1450–1550: Marriage and Family, Property and Careers.* New York: Oxford University Press, 2002.

Harth, Erica. *Ideology and Culture in Seventeenth-Century France.* Ithaca: Cornell University Press, 1983.

———. *Cartesian Women: Versions and Subversions of Rational Discourse in the Old Regime.* Ithaca: Cornell University Press, 1992.

Harvey, Elizabeth D. *Ventriloquized Voices: Feminist Theory and English Renaissance Texts.* London: Routledge, 1992.

Haselkorn, Anne M., and Betty Travitsky, eds. *The Renaissance Englishwoman in Print: Counterbalancing the Canon.* Amherst: University of Massachusetts Press, 1990.

Herlihy, David. "Did Women Have a Renaissance? A Reconsideration." *Medievalia et Humanistica,* NS 13 (1985): 1–22.

Hill, Bridget. *The Republican Virago: The Life and Times of Catharine Macaulay, Historian.* New York: Oxford University Press, 1992.

A History of Central European Women's Writing. Edited by Celia Hawkesworth. New York: Palgrave Press, 2001.

A History of Women in the West.

Volume I: *From Ancient Goddesses to Christian Saints.* Edited by Pauline Schmitt Pantel. Cambridge, MA: Harvard University Press, 1992.

Volume 2: *Silences of the Middle Ages.* Edited by Christiane Klapisch-Zuber. Cambridge, MA: Harvard University Press, 1992.

Volume 3: *Renaissance and Enlightenment Paradoxes.* Edited by Natalie Zemon Davis and Arlette Farge. Cambridge, MA: Harvard University Press, 1993.

A History of Women Philosophers. Edited by Mary Ellen Waithe. 3 vols. Dordrecht: Martinus Nijhoff, 1987.

A History of Women's Writing in France. Edited by Sonya Stephens. Cambridge: Cambridge University Press, 2000.

A History of Women's Writing in Germany, Austria and Switzerland. Edited by Jo Catling. Cambridge: Cambridge University Press, 2000.

A History of Women's Writing in Italy. Edited by Letizia Panizza and Sharon Wood. Cambridge: University Press, 2000.

A History of Women's Writing in Russia. Edited by Alele Marie Barker and Jehanne M. Gheith. Cambridge: Cambridge University Press, 2002.

Hobby, Elaine. *Virtue of Necessity: English Women's Writing 1646–1688.* London: Virago Press, 1988.

Horowitz, Maryanne Cline. "Aristotle and Women." *Journal of the History of Biology* 9 (1976): 183–213.

Howell, Martha. *The Marriage Exchange: Property, Social Place, and Gender in Cities of the Low Countries, 1300–1550.* Chicago: University of Chicago Press, 1998.

Hufton, Olwen H. *The Prospect Before Her: A History of Women in Western Europe, 1: 1500–1800.* New York: HarperCollins, 1996.

Hull, Suzanne W. *Chaste, Silent, and Obedient: English Books for Women, 1475–1640.* San Marino, CA: The Huntington Library, 1982.

Hunt, Lynn, ed. *The Invention of Pornography: Obscenity and the Origins of Modernity, 1500–1800.* New York: Zone Books, 1996.

Hutner, Heidi, ed. *Rereading Aphra Behn: History, Theory, and Criticism.* Charlottesville: University Press of Virginia, 1993.

Hutson, Lorna, ed. *Feminism and Renaissance Studies.* New York: Oxford University Press, 1999.

Italian Women Writers: A Bio-Bibliographical Sourcebook. Edited by Rinaldina Russell. Westport, CT: Greenwood Press, 1994.

Jaffe, Irma B., with Gernando Colombardo. *Shining Eyes, Cruel Fortune: The Lives and Loves of Italian Renaissance Women Poets.* New York: Fordham University Press, 2002.

James, Susan E. *Kateryn Parr: The Making of a Queen.* Aldershot: Ashgate, 1999.

Jankowski, Theodora A. *Women in Power in the Early Modern Drama.* Urbana: University of Illinois Press, 1992.

Jansen, Katherine Ludwig. *The Making of the Magdalen: Preaching and Popular Devotion in the Later Middle Ages.* Princeton, NJ: Princeton University Press, 2000.

Jed, Stephanie H. *Chaste Thinking: The Rape of Lucretia and the Birth of Humanism.* Bloomington: Indiana University Press, 1989.

Jordan, Constance. *Renaissance Feminism: Literary Texts and Political Models.* Ithaca: Cornell University Press, 1990.

Kagan, Richard L. *Lucrecia's Dreams: Politics and Prophecy in Sixteenth-Century Spain.* Berkeley: University of California Press, 1990.

Kehler, Dorothea and Laurel Amtower, eds. *The Single Woman in Medieval and Early Modern England: Her Life and Representation.* Tempe, AZ: MRTS, 2002.

Kelly, Joan. "Did Women Have a Renaissance?" In her *Women, History, and Theory.* Chicago: University of Chicago Press, 1984. Also in Renate Bridenthal, Claudia Koonz, and Susan M. Stuard, eds., *Becoming Visible: Women in European History.* 3rd ed. Boston: Houghton Mifflin, 1998.

———. "Early Feminist Theory and the *Querelle des Femmes.*" In *Women, History, and Theory.*

Kelso, Ruth. *Doctrine for the Lady of the Renaissance.* Foreword by Katharine M. Rogers. Urbana: University of Illinois Press, 1956, 1978.

King, Catherine E. *Renaissance Women Patrons: Wives and Widows in Italy, c. 1300–1550.* Manchester: Manchester University Press (distributed in the U.S. by St. Martin's Press), 1998.

King, Margaret L. *Women of the Renaissance.* Foreword by Catharine R. Stimpson. Chicago: University of Chicago Press, 1991.

Krontiris, Tina. *Oppositional Voices: Women as Writers and Translators of Literature in the English Renaissance.* London: Routledge, 1992.

Kuehn, Thomas. *Law, Family, and Women: Toward a Legal Anthropology of Renaissance Italy.* Chicago: University of Chicago Press, 1991.

Kunze, Bonnelyn Young. *Margaret Fell and the Rise of Quakerism.* Stanford: Stanford University Press, 1994.

Labalme, Patricia A., ed. *Beyond Their Sex: Learned Women of the European Past.* New York: New York University Press, 1980.

Laqueur, Thomas. *Making Sex: Body and Gender from the Greeks to Freud.* Cambridge, MA: Harvard University Press, 1990.

Larsen, Anne R. and Colette H. Winn, eds. *Renaissance Women Writers: French Texts/American Contexts.* Detroit, MI: Wayne State University Press, 1994.

Lerner, Gerda. *The Creation of Patriarchy* and *Creation of Feminist Consciousness, 1000–1870.* 2 vols. New York: Oxford University Press, 1986, 1994.

Levin, Carole, and Jeanie Watson, eds. *Ambiguous Realities: Women in the Middle Ages and Renaissance.* Detroit: Wayne State University Press, 1987.

Levin, Carole, et al. *Extraordinary Women of the Medieval and Renaissance World: A Biographical Dictionary.* Westport, CT: Greenwood Press, 2000.

Lewalsky, Barbara Kiefer. *Writing Women in Jacobean England.* Cambridge, MA: Harvard University Press, 1993.

Lewis, Jayne Elizabeth. *Mary Queen of Scots: Romance and Nation.* London: Routledge, 1998.

Lindsey, Karen. *Divorced Beheaded Survived: A Feminist Reinterpretation of the Wives of Henry VIII.* Reading, MA: Addison-Wesley, 1995.

Lochrie, Karma. *Margery Kempe and Translations of the Flesh.* Philadelphia: University of Pennsylvania Press, 1992.

Lougee, Carolyn C. *Le Paradis des Femmes: Women, Salons, and Social Stratification in Seventeenth-Century France.* Princeton, NJ: Princeton University Press, 1976.

Love, Harold. *The Culture and Commerce of Texts: Scribal Publication in Seventeenth-Century England.* Amherst: University of Massachusetts Press, 1993.

MacCarthy, Bridget G. *The Female Pen: Women Writers and Novelists, 1621–1818.* Preface by Janet Todd. New York: New York University Press, 1994. Originally published 1946–47 by Cork University Press.

Maclean, Ian. *Woman Triumphant: Feminism in French Literature, 1610–1652.* Oxford: Clarendon Press, 1977.

———. *The Renaissance Notion of Woman: A Study of the Fortunes of Scholasticism and Medical Science in European Intellectual Life.* Cambridge: Cambridge University Press, 1980.

MacNeil, Anne. *Music and Women of the Commedia dell'Arte in the Late Sixteenth Century.* New York: Oxford University Press, 2003.

Maggi, Armando. *Uttering the Word: The Mystical Performances of Maria Maddalena de' Pazzi, a Renaissance Visionary.* Albany: State University of New York Press, 1998.

Marshall, Sherrin. *Women in Reformation and Counter-Reformation Europe: Public and Private Worlds.* Bloomington: Indiana University Press, 1989.

Masten, Jeffrey. *Textual Intercourse: Collaboration, Authorship, and Sexualities in Renaissance Drama.* Cambridge: Cambridge University Press, 1997.

Matter, E. Ann, and John Coakley, eds. *Creative Women in Medieval and Early Modern Italy.* Philadelphia: University of Pennsylvania Press, 1994. (Sequel to the Monson collection, below.)

McLeod, Glenda. *Virtue and Venom: Catalogs of Women from Antiquity to the Renaissance.* Ann Arbor: University of Michigan Press, 1991.

Medwick, Cathleen. *Teresa of Avila: The Progress of a Soul.* New York: Knopf, 2000.

Meek, Christine, ed. *Women in Renaissance and Early Modern Europe.* Dublin-Portland: Four Courts Press, 2000.

Mendelson, Sara and Patricia Crawford. *Women in Early Modern England, 1550–1720.* Oxford: Clarendon Press, 1998.

Merchant, Carolyn. *The Death of Nature: Women, Ecology, and the Scientific Revolution.* New York: HarperCollins, 1980.

Merrim, Stephanie. *Early Modern Women's Writing and Sor Juana Inés de la Cruz.* Nashville, TN: Vanderbilt University Press, 1999.

Messbarger, Rebecca. *The Century of Women: The Representations of Women in Eighteenth-Century Italian Public Discourse.* Toronto: University of Toronto Press, 2002.

Miller, Nancy K. *The Heroine's Text: Readings in the French and English Novel, 1722–1782.* New York: Columbia University Press, 1980.

Miller, Naomi J. *Changing the Subject: Mary Wroth and Figurations of Gender in Early Modern England.* Lexington: University Press of Kentucky, 1996.

Miller, Naomi J., and Gary Waller, eds. *Reading Mary Wroth: Representing Alternatives in Early Modern England.* Knoxville: University of Tennessee Press, 1991.

Monson, Craig A., ed. *The Crannied Wall: Women, Religion, and the Arts in Early Modern Europe.* Ann Arbor: University of Michigan Press, 1992.

Musacchio, Jacqueline Marie. *The Art and Ritual of Childbirth in Renaissance Italy.* New Haven, CT: Yale University Press, 1999.

Newman, Barbara. *God and the Goddesses: Vision, Poetry, and Belief in the Middle Ages.* Philadelphia: University of Pennsylvania Press, 2003.

Newman, Karen. *Fashioning Femininity and English Renaissance Drama.* Chicago: University of Chicago Press, 1991.

Okin, Susan Moller. *Women in Western Political Thought.* Princeton, NJ: Princeton University Press, 1979.

Ozment, Steven. *The Bürgermeister's Daughter: Scandal in a Sixteenth-Century German Town.* New York: St. Martin's Press, 1995.

Pacheco, Anita, ed. *Early [English] Women Writers: 1600–1720.* New York: Longman, 1998.

Pagels, Elaine. *Adam, Eve, and the Serpent.* New York: HarperCollins, 1988.

Panizza, Letizia, ed. *Women in Italian Renaissance Culture and Society.* Oxford: European Humanities Research Centre, 2000.

Parker, Patricia. *Literary Fat Ladies: Rhetoric, Gender, and Property.* London: Methuen, 1987.

Pernoud, Regine, and Marie-Veronique Clin. *Joan of Arc: Her Story.* Revised and translated by Jeremy DuQuesnay Adams. New York: St. Martin's Press, 1998 (French original, 1986).

Perry, Mary Elizabeth. *Crime and Society in Early Modern Seville.* Hanover, NH: University Press of New England, 1980.

———. *Gender and Disorder in Early Modern Seville.* Princeton, NJ: Princeton University Press, 1990.

Perry, Ruth. *The Celebrated Mary Astell: An Early English Feminist.* Chicago: University of Chicago Press, 1986.

Petroff, Elizabeth Alvilda, ed. *Medieval Women's Visionary Literature.* New York: Oxford University Press, 1986.

Rabil, Albert. *Laura Cereta: Quattrocento Humanist.* Binghamton, NY: MRTS, 1981.

Ranft, Patricia. *Women in Western Intellectual Culture, 600–1500.* New York: Palgrave, 2002.

Rapley, Elizabeth. *A Social History of the Cloister: Daily Life in the Teaching Monasteries of the Old Regime.* Montreal: McGill-Queen's University Press, 2001.

Raven, James, Helen Small, and Naomi Tadmor, eds. *The Practice and Representation of Reading in England.* Cambridge: University Press, 1996.

Reardon, Colleen. *Holy Concord within Sacred Walls: Nuns and Music in Siena, 1575–1700.* Oxford: Oxford University Press, 2001.

Reiss, Sheryl E., and David G. Wilkins, ed. *Beyond Isabella: Secular Women Patrons of Art in Renaissance Italy.* Kirksville, MO: Truman State University Press, 2001.

Rheubottom, David. *Age, Marriage, and Politics in Fifteenth-Century Ragusa.* Oxford: Oxford University Press, 2000.

Richardson, Brian. *Printing, Writers and Readers in Renaissance Italy.* Cambridge: University Press, 1999.

Riddle, John M. *Contraception and Abortion from the Ancient World to the Renaissance.* Cambridge, MA: Harvard University Press, 1992.

———. *Eve's Herbs: A History of Contraception and Abortion in the West.* Cambridge, MA: Harvard University Press, 1997.

Rose, Mary Beth. *The Expense of Spirit: Love and Sexuality in English Renaissance Drama.* Ithaca, NY: Cornell University Press, 1988.

———. *Gender and Heroism in Early Modern English Literature.* Chicago: University of Chicago Press, 2002.

———, ed. *Women in the Middle Ages and the Renaissance: Literary and Historical Perspectives.* Syracuse: Syracuse University Press, 1986.

Rosenthal, Margaret F. *The Honest Courtesan: Veronica Franco, Citizen and Writer in Sixteenth-Century Venice.* Foreword by Catharine R. Stimpson. Chicago: University of Chicago Press, 1992.

Sackville-West, Vita. *Daughter of France: The Life of La Grande Mademoiselle.* Garden City, NY: Doubleday, 1959.

Sánchez, Magdalena S. *The Empress, the Queen, and the Nun: Women and Power at the Court of Philip III of Spain.* Baltimore: Johns Hopkins University Press, 1998.

Schiebinger, Londa. *The Mind Has No Sex? Women in the Origins of Modern Science.* Cambridge, MA: Harvard University Press, 1991.

———. *Nature's Body: Gender in the Making of Modern Science.* Boston: Beacon Press, 1993.

Schutte, Anne Jacobson, Thomas Kuehn, and Silvana Seidel Menchi, eds. *Time, Space, and Women's Lives in Early Modern Europe.* Kirksville, MO: Truman State University Press, 2001.

Schofield, Mary Anne, and Cecilia Macheski, eds. *Fetter'd or Free? British Women Novelists, 1670–1815.* Athens: Ohio University Press, 1986.

Shannon, Laurie. *Sovereign Amity: Figures of Friendship in Shakespearean Contexts.* Chicago: University of Chicago Press, 2002.

Shemek, Deanna. *Ladies Errant: Wayward Women and Social Order in Early Modern Italy.* Durham, NC: Duke University Press, 1998.

Smith, Hilda L. *Reason's Disciples: Seventeenth-Century English Feminists.* Urbana: University of Illinois Press, 1982.

———. *Women Writers and the Early Modern British Political Tradition.* Cambridge: Cambridge University Press, 1998.

Sobel, Dava. *Galileo's Daughter: A Historical Memoir of Science, Faith, and Love.* New York: Penguin, 2000.

Sommerville, Margaret R. *Sex and Subjection: Attitudes to Women in Early-Modern Society.* London: Arnold, 1995.

Soufas, Teresa Scott. *Dramas of Distinction: A Study of Plays by Golden Age Women.* Lexington: The University Press of Kentucky, 1997.

Spencer, Jane. *The Rise of the Woman Novelist: From Aphra Behn to Jane Austen.* Oxford: Basil Blackwell, 1986.

Spender, Dale. *Mothers of the Novel: 100 Good Women Writers Before Jane Austen.* London: Routledge, 1986.

Sperling, Jutta Gisela. *Convents and the Body Politic in Late Renaissance Venice.* Foreword by Catharine R. Stimpson. Chicago: University of Chicago Press, 1999.

Steinbrügge, Lieselotte. *The Moral Sex: Woman's Nature in the French Enlightenment.* Translated by Pamela E. Selwyn. New York: Oxford University Press, 1995.

Stocker, Margarita. *Judith, Sexual Warrior: Women and Power in Western Culture*. New Haven, CT: Yale University Press, 1998.

Stretton, Timothy. *Women Waging Law in Elizabethan England*. Cambridge: Cambridge University Press, 1998.

Stuard, Susan M. "The Dominion of Gender: Women's Fortunes in the High Middle Ages." In*Becoming Visible: Women in European History*, edited by Renate Bridenthal, Claudia Koonz, and Susan M. Stuard. 3rd ed. Boston: Houghton Mifflin, 1998.

Summit, Jennifer. *Lost Property: The Woman Writer and English Literary History, 1380–1589*. Chicago: University of Chicago Press, 2000.

Surtz, Ronald E. *The Guitar of God: Gender, Power, and Authority in the Visionary World of Mother Juana de la Cruz (1481–1534)*. Philadelphia: University of Pennsylvania Press, 1991.

———. *Writing Women in Late Medieval and Early Modern Spain: The Mothers of Saint Teresa of Avila*. Philadelphia: University of Pennsylvania Press, 1995.

Teague, Frances. *Bathsua Makin, Woman of Learning*. Lewisburg, PA: Bucknell University Press, 1999.

Tinagli, Paola. *Women in Italian Renaissance Art: Gender, Representation, Identity*. Manchester: Manchester University Press, 1997.

Todd, Janet. *The Secret Life of Aphra Behn*. London: Pandora, 2000.

———. *The Sign of Angelica: Women, Writing and Fiction, 1660–1800*. New York: Columbia University Press, 1989.

Valenze, Deborah. *The First Industrial Woman*. New York: Oxford University Press, 1995.

Van Dijk, Susan, Lia van Gemert, and Sheila Ottway, eds. *Writing the History of Women's Writing: Toward an International Approach*. Proceedings of the Colloquium, Amsterdam, 9–11 September. Amsterdam: Royal Netherlands Academy of Arts and Sciences, 2001.

Vickery, Amanda. *The Gentleman's Daughter: Women's Lives in Georgian England*. New Haven, CT: Yale University Press, 1998.

Vollendorf, Lisa, ed. *Recovering Spain's Feminist Tradition*. New York: MLA, 2001.

Walker, Claire. *Gender and Politics in Early Modern Europe: English Convents in France and the Low Countries*. New York: Palgrave, 2003.

Wall, Wendy. *The Imprint of Gender: Authorship and Publication in the English Renaissance*. Ithaca, NY: Cornell University Press, 1993.

Walsh, William T. *St. Teresa of Avila: A Biography*. Rockford, IL: TAN, 1987.

Warner, Marina. *Alone of All Her Sex: The Myth and Cult of the Virgin Mary*. New York: Knopf, 1976.

Warnicke, Retha M. *The Marrying of Anne of Cleves: Royal Protocol in Tudor England*. Cambridge: Cambridge University Press, 2000.

Watt, Diane. *Secretaries of God: Women Prophets in Late Medieval and Early Modern England*. Cambridge: D. S. Brewer, 1997.

Weber, Alison. *Teresa of Avila and the Rhetoric of Femininity*. Princeton, NJ: Princeton University Press, 1990.

Welles, Marcia L. *Persephone's Girdle: Narratives of Rape in Seventeenth-Century Spanish Literature*. Nashville: Vanderbilt University Press, 2000.

Whitehead, Barbara J., ed. *Women's Education in Early Modern Europe: A History, 1500–1800*. New York: Garland, 1999.

Wiesner, Merry E. *Women and Gender in Early Modern Europe.* Cambridge: Cambridge University Press, 1993.

———. *Working Women in Renaissance Germany.* New Brunswick, NJ: Rutgers University Press, 1986.

Willard, Charity Cannon. *Christine de Pizan: Her Life and Works.* New York: Persea Books, 1984.

Winn, Colette and Donna Kuizenga, eds. *Women Writers in Pre-Revolutionary France.* New York: Garland, 1997.

Woodbridge, Linda. *Women and the English Renaissance: Literature and the Nature of Womankind, 1540–1620.* Urbana: University of Illinois Press, 1984.

Woods, Susanne. *Lanyer: A Renaissance Woman Poet.* New York: Oxford University Press, 1999.

Woods, Susanne, and Margaret P. Hannay, eds. *Teaching Tudor and Stuart Women Writers.* New York: MLA, 2000.

INDEX OF FIRST LINES

GENERAL INDEX

Italicized page numbers indicate references in the poetry.